Introduction to Forensic and Criminal Psychology
2nd Edition

Introduction to
Forensic and
Criminal Psychology

2nd Edition

Dennis Howitt

Loughborough University

PEARSON
Longman

Harlow, England • London • New York • Boston • San Francisco • Toronto • Sydney • Singapore • Hong Kong
Tokyo • Seoul • Taipei • New Delhi • Cape Town • Madrid • Mexico City • Amsterdam • Munich • Paris • Milan

Pearson Education Limited
Edinburgh Gate
Harlow
Essex CM20 2JE

and Associated Companies throughout the world

Visit us on the World Wide Web at:
www.pearsoneduc.com

First published 2002
Second edition published 2006

ISBN-10 0130-29758-9
ISBN-13 978-0-13-029758-7

British Library Cataloguing-in-Publication Data
A catalogue record for this book is available from the British Library

Library of Congress Cataloging-in-Publication Data
Howitt, Dennis.
    Introduction to forensic and criminal psychology / Dennis Howitt. – 2nd ed.
        p. cm.
    Rev. ed. of: Forensic and cirminal psychology. 2002.
    Includes bibliographical references and indexes.
    ISBN 0-13-016985-4 (pbk.)
    1. Criminal psychology. 2. Forensic psychology. I. Howitt, Dennis. Forensic and
criminal psychology. II. Title.

    HV6080.H69 2005
    364.3—dc22

                                                                    2005053908

10 9 8 7 6 5 4 3 2 1
10 09 08 07 06

Typeset in 10/12pt Sabon by 35
Printed and bound by Ashford Colour Press, Gosport

To the continued memory of Professor Marie Jahoda who died in 2001. I have a big personal debt. Not only did she let me study on the psychology degree course she had set up at Brunel University, but she showed me that some things in life are worth getting angry about.

Contents

Figures

Tables

Boxes

Preface

This second edition of *Introduction to Forensic and Criminal Psychology* builds on the previous edition and updates the material covered to reflect progress and trends in the field since then. The work continues to be a labour of love tinged with frustration. I can be very enthusiastic about forensic and criminal psychology, which has been one of the fastest developing and most popular aspects of psychology in recent years. My first real contact with the criminal justice system was the six months I spent at Wakefield Prison, in Yorkshire, living at the Staff College across the way. My strongest recollection of this period was the emerging realisation that, for the most part, the men there seemed like ordinary men despite the fact that they were incestuous fathers or killers or had committed some other unfathomable crime. Nobody at university, staff or student, shared my interest in the field of crime and I had no idea of how my fumbling research interest could be turned into good psychology. Sex offenders fascinated me and I tried to research incestuous fathers but this was not a serious topic for research in the prevailing ethos of those days. A few years on and the sexual abuse of children became a massive area for research in several disciplines. I perhaps could have been responsible for that but I was not. The boat was missed. Others, a little later, had much better ideas of what were the important things to think about, research and practise.

After many years in some way associated with forensic and criminal psychology, it still perplexes me that a field so full of crucial issues, invigorating theory and skilful practitioners still tends to be delivered in a rather piecemeal way. My original idea for this book was for a relatively compact single volume that helps the reader to become familiar with the range and complexity of forensic and criminal psychology. This second edition has a greater depth of coverage and has introduced two new chapters – ones which should have been in the first edition but simply did not make it. I have attempted to present a comprehensive and contemporary account of the field as it can be found in the research literature and professional writings on the topics. There are plenty of other books that cover a selection of the main topics in the field but comprehensive surveys of the entire field like this one are rare.

Features of the book I feel particularly important include the following:

- The book is modular in structure and comprehensive. Consequently, it can serve as a stand-alone text for a wide variety of modules and programmes in the broad field of forensic and criminal psychology. Of course, many issues potentially cut across different chapters of the book. The reader is helped with extensive cross-referencing, but the indexes should also be consulted when searching for material.

- There are a number of obvious pedagogic features of the book such as summaries and boxes. Nevertheless, there are others which are not so obvious. One of the common faults of books recommended to students is their lack of sufficient detail to allow students to construct their essays or reviews effectively. Too little detail means that students may write inaccurately or vaguely. While it is not possible to provide extensive detail about everything mentioned, students should have a resource that allows them to develop their arguments sure-footedly and with confidence.

- Boxes have been employed to present material that is relevant to but distinct from the main structure of each of the chapters. This should encourage students to 'dip into' the material more as well as provide variety in the book's structure. Various forms of diagrams have been employed to much the same end. Flow diagrams, for example, may provide a quick introduction to a complex topic. The human mind is visual as well as verbal and not all ideas are best presented in the sort of temporal sequence encouraged by the written word.

- The international character of forensic and criminal psychology is highlighted in this book. Researchers and practitioners from all over the world work together and meet together to advance the discipline. Excellent quality research and theory has no national boundaries. Nevertheless, the international character of the discipline does cause problems since criminal justice systems vary between countries and even within countries. It would be impossible to accurately reflect the legal situation in every country where this book is read. Consequently, the strategy is to reflect the diversity of criminal justice systems throughout the world and to prepare the reader for this. Normally, I have mentioned the geographical location in which the research took place. This is important because the particular legal jurisdiction in question has a great bearing on what the findings mean and their relevance elsewhere. Of course, any writer has most knowledge of their own society, so please forgive me for not representing all countries equally.

- The perspective of the book is wide and stretches within psychology to all corners of the discipline. So clinical, developmental, cognitive and biological perspectives have been incorporated in the greatest measure. A great deal can also be learnt from related fields – especially that of criminology. Often it is impossible to see where the dividing line between criminology and psychology lies so I have crossed it regularly to the benefit of the book.

- The book is strongly committed to presenting theory as a means of integrating the research in the field.

- Practitioner issues have been incorporated at all possible stages. At the same time, it was *not* the intention to produce a manual of good practice. Nevertheless, it is important to reflect the maturity of psychology as a discipline so I have opted to use research based on real-life situations as far as possible but this is not always the case.

A book with such a wide agenda as this cannot truly be held to be the work of any one individual. So, although they may not realise it, I have a great debt to many forensic and criminal psychologists whose work I know and admire. These are individuals whose work I greatly respect and trust so I felt free to rely on much of what they have written and said. Although the following is an incomplete list, I feel that the risk of overlooking individuals is less than the disservice of not acknowledging those whose expertise I have mined and whose academic judgement I employed when in doubt:

Peter Ainsworth
Ramon Arce
Deborah Bekerian
Nicola Brace
Chris Brewin
Kevin Browne
Ray Bull
David Canter
David Carson
Julia Cherryman
Brian Clifford
Hans Crombag
Guy Cumberbatch
David Farrington
Charlie Frowd
Graham Davies
Donald Grubin
Gisli Gudjonsson
Lionel Haward
Zoë Henderson
David Hodge
Clive Hollin
Kevin Howells
Saul Kassin

Mark Kebbel
Richard Kemp
Vladimir Konecni
Peter Van Koppen
Sally Lloyd-Bostock
Frederick Losel
James McGuire
Mary McMurran
Amina Memon
Edgar Miller
Rebecca Milne
Joanne Motzkau
Emma Palmer
Steven Penrod
Graham Pike
Lorraine Sheridan
Max Steller
Donald Thompson
Bob Thompson
Aldert Vrij
Wilhelm Wagenaar
Graham Wagstaff
Tony Ward
Wilhelm Winkel

My gratitude also to Sue Becker and Kelly Benneworth of Loughborough University for providing me with materials and ideas that I would otherwise have overlooked.

Finally, anyone wishing to explore the possibility of becoming a forensic and criminal psychologist is advised to use the WWW to search for up-to-date information. The *American Psychology and Law Society* (American Psychological Association) and the *Division of Forensic Psychology* (British Psychological Society) are good starting places for these countries and provide appropriate search terms. Elsewhere search for the national psychological association or governing body.

Acknowledgements

We are grateful to the following for permission to reproduce copyright material:

Figure 3.1 from *Psychology and Crime: Myths and Reality*, Longman (Ainsworth, P.B., 2000); Figure 3.3 from Fear of crime and criminal victimisation in *British Journal of Criminology*, Vol. 38, (3), 473–84, by permission of Oxford University Press (Winkel, F.W., 1998); Figure 8.1 from Multi-factorial model of serial killing in *British Journal of Criminology*, Vol. 34, 1–14, by permission of Oxford University Press (Gresswell, D.M. and Hollin, C.R., 1994); Table 13.1 from *Profiling Violent Crimes: An Investigative Tool*, Sage Publications (Holmes R.M. and Holmes, S.T., 1996); Table 17.1 from Forensic interviews of children in *Handbook of the Psychology of Interviewing*, John Wiley & Sons Ltd (Lamb, M.E., Sternberg, K.J. and Orbach, Y., 1999); Table 22.1 from *Offender Rehabilitation and Treatment: Effective Programmes and Policies to Reduce Re-offending*, John Wiley & Sons Ltd (Redondo, S., Sanchez-Meca, J. and Garrido, V., 2002); Table 23.4 from How to Use Empirical Findings for the Prognosis of Mentally Disordered Offenders, Paper presented at the Tenth European Conference of Psychology and Law, Limassol, Cyprus (Gretenkord, L., 2000).

In some instances we have been unable to trace the owners of copyright material, and we would appreciate any information that would enable us to do so.

Chapter 1

What is forensic and criminal psychology?

Overview

- Forensic psychology is literally psychology applied in law courts. However, the term is used far more widely than this. Criminal psychology is the psychology of criminal behaviour. The term *forensic psychology* can be focused narrowly on the work of the relative small number of psychological practitioners who work directly in law courts. A wider definition is employed in this book, which embraces the activities of all psychologists whose work is related to the criminal justice system such as psychologists working in the prison system. Hence the use of the phrase *forensic and criminal psychology* to encompass the entire field.

- Psychology and the law are very different disciplines although both try to understand human nature. Their ways of understanding are not the same and sometimes they are incompatible. Even when the lawyers and psychologists use identical words, they may have very different meanings.

- There are many practitioner-researchers in forensic and criminal psychology. Practitioners who are both skilled researchers and skilled practitioners can add a great deal to the development of such an applied discipline.

- Crucial changes in the criminal justice system over the centuries have gradually increased the need for psychological expertise within the system. Most forensic and criminal psychology is very recent and mainly confined to the last 25 years or so. Academically, forensic and criminal psychology is nearly as old as modern psychology itself. It was being practised and researched shortly after Wundt set up his psychological laboratory in Leipzig – an event which is often lauded as the start of modern psychology. However, interest in the field was at best spasmodic and minimal until the late twentieth century when it grew rapidly.

- Forensic and criminal psychology has developed differently in different parts of the world. Nevertheless, it now constitutes an important branch of modern psychology which benefits greatly from its international nature. It unites psychology from a variety of fields of psychology.

Defining *forensic and criminal psychology* is not without its difficulties. Forensic psychology literally is psychology to do with courts of law. The terms *forensic* and *forum* have the same Latin origins. A forum is merely a room for public debate, hence the word *forensic*. Criminal psychology is mainly to do with psychological aspects of criminal behaviour and includes issues such as the origins of criminality. The difficulty in defining the field is to do with where precisely boundaries are to be drawn. Modern law deals with an incredible variety of aspects of life and so psychology, when applied to the legal system, is potentially boundless in what it encompasses. Few, if any, aspects of life are unaffected by the law including:

- where we live;
- where we are educated;
- by whom we are educated;
- who may work;
- when we can work;
- what we may do at work;
- how we get to work;
- when we may retire;
- what happens to us when we die.

There is, of course, much more that is covered by legislation. The practice of psychology itself is governed by legislation and many of the vocations into which students trained in psychology move are also conspicuously subject to legislation. A very good example is social work in its many forms, which substantially deals with matters subject to government legislation including children and the family. Other examples include education, mental health, health and advertising, all of which are closely governed by law. Furthermore, all sorts of psychologists may provide expert evidence on virtually any matter to courts of law. So precisely who should be designated a forensic and criminal psychologist? Many psychologists work primarily in the criminal justice system (i.e. police, criminal courts and prisons). Should they all be classified together as forensic psychologists, for example?

Some psychologists have defined the field of forensic psychology in terms of the professional activities of those practitioners working primarily in courts of law. Gudjonsson and Haward (1998) are good examples of proponents of such a viewpoint. They define *forensic psychology* as:

> . . . that branch of applied psychology which is concerned with the collection, examination and presentation of evidence for judicial purposes.
>
> *(p. 1)*

The key words in this definition would seem to be 'evidence' and 'judicial'. While they do not have to mean this, Gudjonsson and Haward seem to be referring to legal evidence for the use of lawyers and judges. This clearly sets limits to the meaning that they wish to apply to judicial purposes also. Definitions exist for a purpose and in this case the purpose is to limit the field of forensic psychology to those working in close collaboration with officials of the court. The following is essentially similar:

> [forensic psychology is] the provision of psychological information for the purpose of facilitating a legal decision.
>
> *(Blackburn, 1996, p. 7)*

What these definitions exclude is equally as important as what is included. They leave out the work of psychologists in settings such as prisons and special hospitals for psychologically disturbed criminals. The activities of psychologists in such settings is clearly relevant to courts of law though such psychologists may only rarely, if ever, work directly in courts.

In contrast, Wrightsman (2001) defines forensic psychology in much broader terms. He regards forensic psychology as:

> . . . any application of psychological knowledge or methods to a task faced by the legal system.
>
> *(p. 2)*

This is a wide definition since he lists some of the psychologists who are included as:

- A clinical psychologist in private practice. This psychologist works as a consultant to police departments.
- A mediator psychologist employed by a law firm to mediate between parties in an attempt to resolve legal disputes.
- A social psychologist dealing with civil cases such as commercial litigation. The psychologist conducted surveys of role-playing 'jurors' in order to assess what might work in a real trial.
- A counselling psychologist who works on the assessment of potentially violent behaviours for the US secret service. For example, threats of violence are often made to the national leaders – which ones are to be taken seriously?
- A correctional psychologist who assesses the competence of prisoners to stand trial and makes suggestions about possible treatments for particular offenders.

Whether by intention or oversight, it is notable that all of the above examples are of *practitioners* rather than researchers. They may do research, but it is not the primary focus of their work. The examples Wrightsman gives seem very unrepresentative of the majority of psychologists who describe themselves as forensic psychologists. The problem is that Wrightsman's broad definition of forensic psychology may be adequate, but his list needs to be extended. In other parts of the world, psychologists working in the prison service, psychologists teaching and working in university departments, psychologists working in the mental health field and others all claim at least some identity with forensic psychology.

Not surprisingly, others have acknowledged that there is a lack of consensus over the definition of forensic psychology (e.g. McGuire, 1997). The use of the term is disorderly – the description 'chaos' has been applied (Stanik, 1992). Nevertheless, one would experience similar problems when attempting to define practically any sub-field of psychology. A key to making progress in defining forensic psychology is to differentiate between defining the *field of forensic psychology* and identifying *who should be entitled to call themselves forensic psychologists?* The first (what is forensic psychology?) is essentially addressed by all of the definitions discussed so far. The question of who is qualified to call themselves a forensic psychologist has been approached in a different way. The issue becomes that of identifying the nature of the skills and knowledge required by anyone working in the field, apart from a basic training in psychology itself. In the United Kingdom, it has been suggested that forensic psychologists (i.e. all chartered forensic psychologists) should possess the following knowledge and skills (DCLP Training Committee, 1994). The list probably would be much the same elsewhere in the world though the precise mix of skills varies with the area of practice within the field:

- Understanding the conceptual basis of their work context in terms of:
  - the psychology relevant to the study of criminal behaviour;
  - the legal framework including the law and structure of the criminal justice system, for example, of the country in which they practise.
- An understanding of the achievements and potential achievements of the application of psychology to:
  - criminal investigation processes;
  - legal processes;
  - custodial processes;
  - treatment processes (for both offenders and victims).
- A sufficiently detailed understanding of the psychology relevant to the following individuals, including adults and children where appropriate:
  - offenders (whether or not mentally disordered);
  - victims;
  - witnesses;
  - investigators.
- An understanding of the practical aspects of forensic psychology in terms of the following:
  - different demands for assessment;
  - processes of investigation, prosecution and defence;
  - decision making in respect of innocence, guilt, sentencing, custody, treatment and rehabilitation;
  - approaches to assessment;
  - professional criteria for report production and giving of testimony.

  This is combined with an additional requirement of having had extensive practical experience in at least one area of forensic psychology (pp. 10–11).

This comprehensive list defines the knowledge and skill base of practitioners in the discipline. It also indicates that no matter the exact specialism of the forensic psychologist, he or she knows more about their working context and relevant research than the minimum needed to function on a day-to-day basis.

Defining *criminal psychology* tends to be less controversial. This is partly because it is not a title that is claimed by any significantly large or influential group of psychologists. Like forensic psychology, criminal psychology may be defined relatively narrowly or somewhat broadly. The narrow definition would merely suggest that it concerns all aspects of the psychology of the criminal. A difficulty with this is that it seems to concentrate solely on the offender. Does it or should it also include psychological aspects of the wider experience of the criminal, for example, in courts of law or prison? Criminality, as we shall see, is not a characteristic of individuals that can be separated meaningfully from the social context of crime and the criminal justice system. Thus the field of criminal psychology must be defined in terms of knowledge and skills which substantially overlap those of the forensic psychologist described above. Indeed, one might suggest that the main difference between the two is that forensic psychology may involve the civil law as well as the criminal law. The use of the phrase 'forensic and criminal psychology' in this book acknowledges problems in the definition of both *forensic and criminal psychology*. There is no intention to suggest that the two things effectively differ substantially. Forensic psychology and criminal psychology are to be regarded as inseparable rather than two separate things combined.

Other terms sometimes used include *psychology and the law* and *legal psychology*. These more clearly hint of an interface between the two disciplines and practices – psychology and the law. Again, there is some merit in a designation of this sort. In particular, it stresses the two disciplines in combination. The implication is that both lawyers and psychologists may be interested in similar issues but from their differing perspectives. Contributions from both lawyers and psychologists are important in the field's development. While the terms suggest that researchers/practitioners should be knowledgeable about both psychology and the law, this is also a weakness. Very few researchers/practitioners are trained in both disciplines. The club has a miniscule membership.

Forensic and criminal psychology may also be understood in terms of the organisational infrastructure that supports it. For example, it is not possible to define the discipline of medicine without reference to the medical associations that support and organise it. Some individuals have 'permission' or a licence to practise medicine, others do not. The institutional basis of forensic and criminal psychology varies from country to country. It is mainly associated with the professional associations of psychologists such as the American Psychological Association and the British Psychological Society.

The relationship between psychology and the law has not always been an easy one. Both psychologists and lawyers may have difficulties when engaging with each other's discipline. Psychology is not a compact discipline united by a single theory or approach. It is a broad church which psychologists themselves often find lacking in coherence. Clifford (1995) suggests that lawyers may be excused for regarding psychology as a 'bewildering confederacy' (p. 26). Eastman (2000) writes of two countries – Legaland and Mentaland. They differ, like countries do, in terms of their culture, language, history and terrain. When the inhabitants of these two lands mix together things are difficult because they have big differences of purpose. Nevertheless, there are times when the people of Legaland need the help of people from

---

Box 1.1

Forensic psychology in action: the expert witness

Given that psychologists are experts in many different aspects of human nature and behaviour, it is not surprising that their knowledge is frequently applicable in court. The extent of their involvement is dependent on a number of factors. According to Groscup *et al.* (2002), a quarter of expert witnesses in American criminal appeal hearings were from the social and behavioural sciences. Different legal jurisdictions have different requirements of expert witnesses and certain expert evidence may not be admissible in all legal systems. An expert witness differs from any other witness in court since they are allowed to express opinions rather than simply report facts. The opinions of forensic and criminal psychologists will normally be supported by scientific evidence and they will be required to establish their scientific credentials. The expert witness should not offer evidence outside the terms of their expertise. These matters are normally determined at the stage

▶

of the *voir dire* (usually described as a trial within a trial but essentially a preliminary review of matters related to the trial such as jurors and evidence) in the Anglo-American system. Different legal jurisdictions vary in terms of how the expert witness is employed. In the Anglo-American system, the adversarial system, this is normally the decision of the prosecution or the defence. Inquisitorial legal systems such as those common in Continental Europe (Stephenson, 1992) are likely use experts employed by the court itself (Nijboer, 1995) and, furthermore, they will be regarded much as any other witness. Guidelines for expert witnesses are available (e.g. British Psychological Society, 1998) as is advice (e.g. Coleman, 1995).

The *Daubert* decision currently influences which 'experts' may be allowed to give evidence in American courts. The Daubert case was about a child, Jason Daubert, who was born with missing fingers and bones. His mother had taken an anti-morningsickness drug and sued the manufacturers. 'Rules' designed to exclude 'junk' science were formulated. What is interesting is that the decision formulated what should be regarded as proper scientific methodology. That is, it should be based on the testing of hypotheses, which are refutable. Furthermore, in assessing the admissibility of the expert evidence, attention should be paid to issues such as whether the research had been subject to review by others working in the field (Ainsworth, 1998). Perry (1997) lists Daubert criteria as including:

- whether the technique or theory is verifiable;
- whether the technique or theory is generally accepted within the scientific community;
- what the likelihood of error in the research study is.

This obviously causes problems for expertise that is not part of this model of science: for example, therapists giving evidence on the false memory syndrome in which there is a fierce debate between practitioners and academics (see Box 12.1).

In England and Wales, the main guidelines according to Nijboer (1995) are as follows:

- Matters that the judge believes are within the capacity of the ordinary person – the juror – in terms of their knowledge and experience are not for comment by the expert witness.
- The expert witness cannot give evidence that 'usurps' the role of the judge and jury and connection with the principal issue with which the trial is concerned.
- Expert opinion is confined to matters that are admissible evidence.

A survey of American lawyers (including judges) investigated how mental health experts were selected to give evidence (Mossman and Kapp, 1998). Their academic writings and national reputation were rarely criteria – nor was the fee that they asked. Apart from knowledge in a specific area, the key criteria for selection were their communicative ability and local reputation. There may be reason to be concerned about the value of some expert testimony since there are many examples of what might be described as pseudo-science. Coles and Veiel (2001) took issue with the willingness of psychological expert witnesses to reduce complex matters to fixed characteristics of the individual. So the idea of fitness to plead is regarded in the thinking of some psychologists as a characteristic of some individuals – that is, it is a characteristic of their personality. But the legal definition of fitness to plead (see Chapter 19) concerns whether an individual has the intellectual resources to contribute effectively to their own defence. Naturally, this means that fitness to plead evaluations need to take into account the complexity of the trial in question. Someone may be perfectly fit to plead where the trial is simple but unfit to plead in a complex trial. Furthermore, they may appear competent in one area but not in another area. An individual may be perfectly capable of communicating with their lawyer but unable to understand the purpose of the trial.

Mentaland. Legaland language is confusing to the people of Mentaland – and *vice versa*. Legaland people are often more powerful and make it extremely clear that the ideas of Mentaland are secondary to those of Legaland. It is the people of Mentaland who need to make it abundantly clear that Mentaland ideas are subservient to those of Legaland and that Mentaland people will have to adjust their language. Mentaland people also sometimes need the people of Legaland to give them the authority for things they do. For example, social and public policy legislation may need to be tested by Legaland, then interpreted for the people of Mentaland. In this way the people of Mentaland obtain extra tools to get on with their job.

Researcher-practitioners

The concept of the 'scientist-practitioner' originated in the late 1940s among clinical psychologists seeking to improve both research and practice. Some argue that the synergy resulting from combining research and practice has not been achieved (Douglas *et al.*, 1999). Traditionally in psychology, researchers and practitioners have been seen as at odds with each other – each side being dismissive of the contribution of the other. Academics criticise practitioners for their lack of knowledge of the pertinent research; practitioners criticise academics for their ignorance of clinical needs and practices. Whatever the truth of this in clinical psychology, the reality of much of forensic and clinical psychology is very different. Increasingly, employers of forensic and criminal psychologists require that practitioners should partake fully in a research-led discipline. Practitioners do not just apply psychological knowledge, they create it. As is appropriate for an applied discipline such as forensic and criminal psychology, the preferred usual term is researcher-practitioners rather than scientist-practitioners. The latter reflects a view of psychology which many practitioners have difficulty relating to. For some, the purpose of psychology is not to develop scientific laws of human behaviour but to ground the discipline in social reality through the effective use of empirical research.

So in forensic and criminal psychology, the division between researcher and practitioner is breached. It is a generally accepted principle that training in both research and practice is crucial to effective practice. Practitioners who understand research methods well are much more likely to be able to employ the findings of other researchers into their therapies, assessments and when giving their professional advice to clients and colleagues. Furthermore, practitioners are usually in a good position to know what sorts of research are needed by them compared to academics whose knowledge of practitioner requirements cannot be so direct. Indeed, academic researchers may have academic and theoretical priorities that are different from those of practitioners. There is nothing wrong with this. Many academic psychologists make important contributions despite lacking the practical experience and training of practitioners. The roles of the academic researcher and the researcher-practitioner are not quite the same and the contributions of both of are equal value.

Figure 1.1 illustrates some of the major components of forensic and criminal psychology. Notice how widely from the field of psychology contributions are drawn. Also note the underlying dimension of applied research/practice and academic. The distinction is not rigid but must be considered as an essential component of the structure of the field.

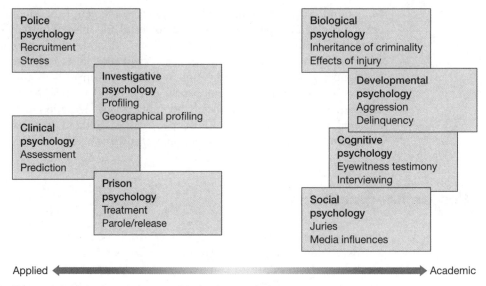

Figure 1.1 Major components of forensic psychology

History of forensic and criminal psychology

Any history depends on the teller since history has to be written from a viewpoint. American and European academics may give somewhat different versions of the history of forensic and criminal psychology – each offering accounts that stress the contribution of their traditions to the discipline. The history as written by a psychiatrist will be different from that of a psychologist since it may ignore the contribution, say, of cognitive psychology. And the history written by a lawyer would be different from both of these. Some key elements in the history of forensic and criminal psychology are shown in Figure 1.2.

Changes in the law

A number of crucial developments in the law that occurred many years before psychology was founded are vital to understanding the development of forensic and criminal psychology. For example:

- Madness was not always a consideration under law. Before the thirteenth century, in English law, the doing of something evil was sufficient to establish the individual liable for that evil. The offender's mental condition was simply irrelevant to sentencing (Eigen, 2004). The first English trial in which the accused was acquitted on the basis of insanity occurred as early as 1505. However, not until the eighteenth century did courts begin to develop criteria to assess insanity. The criterion developed at this time essentially held that insane persons are equivalent to wild beasts – which, of course, are not capable of committing crime. Such a definition was a difficult one to meet but nevertheless required no degree of psychiatric knowledge

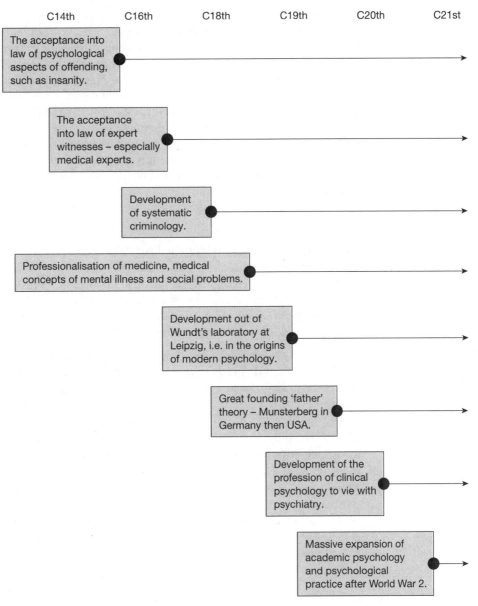

Figure 1.2 Different components in the historical origins of forensic and criminal psychology

to apply – ordinary members of the jury could identify such an extreme case as this. So expert advice from the medical profession, such as it was at this time, was not needed. Insanity became an important issue in the nineteenth century when deluded reasoning became part of the legal test of insanity. Such a definition required the advice of experts much more than the wild beast criterion had. Expert witnesses were required with increasing frequency and, as a consequence, lawyers became more concerned that evidence of experts might replace the jury in deciding the verdict.

- The issue of competence to stand trial (see Chapter 19) is a development originating in eighteenth-century English common law (i.e. law not laid down by statutes but essentially by tradition). The crucial concept was the idea that the defendant must be competent at certain minimal levels in order to have a fair trial (Roesch et al., 1993). Although competence is a legal matter and one to be defined by the courts and not psychologists or psychiatrists, the development of the expert witness encouraged the eventual use of medical and other practitioners to comment on the mental state of the defendant. As might be expected, even these key changes which contributed to a need for expert witnesses had their roots in earlier times. For example, the notion that some individuals were unfit because of their limited intellectual ability had actually entered the legal consideration of cases much earlier in fourteenth-century England.

Links with the parent discipline

It is not possible to separate developments in forensic and criminal psychology from developments in psychology in general. To fully study the history of forensic and criminal psychology one needs to understand the changes that occurred in psychology in general. The following illustrates this:

- The study of memory has been common in psychology since the pioneering work of Ebbinghaus. Obviously, the psychology of memory is very relevant to eyewitness testimony. Not until the 1960s and later did psychologists properly begin to address the important issue of memory for real events. This set the scene for expansion of research into eyewitness testimony beginning in the 1970s.
- The new emphasis in social psychology on group dynamics in the 1960s was associated with a rise in interest in research on the dynamics of decision making in juries.
- Many of the psychological assessment techniques, tests and measurements used, particularly, in assessment of offenders for forensic purposes have their origins in other fields of psychology. Their availability to forensic and criminal psychologists is contingent on developments in academic, educational and clinical psychology in particular.

Social change

Both the law and psychology are responsive to changes in society in general. Here are a few examples that illustrate this:

- Child sexual abuse: while nowadays concern about child sexual abuse (and rape and domestic violence for that matter) is extensive and ingrained, this has not always been the case. The massive social impact of feminism during the 1960s and 1970s brought concern about a number of issues. Among them was child sexual abuse which was found to be more common than had been thought. This interest brought to forensic and criminal psychology a need to understand and deal better with matters such as the effects of child sexual abuse, the treatment of abusers and the ability of children to give evidence in court. The history of the radical change in the way in which professionals regard child sexual abuse victims makes fascinating reading (e.g. Myers *et al.*, 1999). Dominant themes in early writings on sexual abuse contrast markedly with modern thinking. For example, a century or so ago children were regarded as being the instigators of their own victimisation, their mothers were held to blame for the fate of the children and sexual abuse was construed as rare. This does not mean that prosecutions for sexual offences against children were unknown. They, in the United States at least, increased steadily during the twentieth century, although Myers *et al.* describe the rates as modest by modern standards. It is worth noting that other countries may experience apparently different patterns. For example, Sjogren (2000) claims that the rates of child sexual abuse in Sweden were as high in the 1950s and 1960s before concern about sexual abuse rose due to American influences as they were in the 1990s.

- Government policy: the work of forensic and criminal psychologists is materially shaped by government policy on any number of matters. For instance, government policy on the treatment of offenders (say to increase the numbers going to prison and the length of their sentences) is critical. Similarly, the issue of the provision of psychiatric/psychological care (say increasing the numbers managed within the community) profoundly changes the nature of the work of practitioners. Furthermore, changes in research priorities may well be contingent on such developments.

We can now turn from the broad societal and legal framework in which forensic and criminal psychology developed to consider some of the key events in the history of research and theory in forensic and criminal psychology.

Early work in the disciplines of criminology, sociology, and psychiatry

The intellectual origins of forensic and criminal psychology are to be found in related disciplines, especially criminology, sociology and psychology. Indeed, some of the earliest criminological contributions seem unquestionably psychological in nature. There are a number of aspects to consider:

- One could regard the work of the Italian Cesare de Baccaria in the later 1700s as a contender for the first example of forensic and criminal psychology. De Baccaria regarded humans as possessing free will. This was subject to the principles of pleasure and pain. This is an 'economic' model in which we are seen to evaluate the costs and benefits (pleasures and pains) of our actions prior to engaging in them, such as when we decide to commit a crime. He believed that punishment for criminal behaviour was not desirable in itself. It was important, though, to deter people from crime. Thus punishments need to be proportionate or commensurate with the crime – and inflicted as a means of deterrence. It is argued by some that De Baccaria's ideas led directly to the abandonment of barbaric torture of prisoners in a number of European countries (McGuire, 2000).
- The publication of the first official crime statistics was a crucial development that occurred in France in 1827. Statistical data allowed the development of investigations into the geographical distribution or organisation of crime. This continues in criminology today and geographical profiling of crime is important in areas

of forensic and criminal psychology. The Frenchman Andre-Michel Guerry and Belgian Adolphe Quetelet began the tradition of crime statistics. Modern computer applications have refined this approach enormously. It is now possible to study databases specifying the geographical locations down to the household level.

- The idea of the biological roots of crime was an important late nineteenth-century idea in the work of the Italian doctor Cesare Lombroso. He took groups of hardened criminals and carried out what might be called an anthropological study of their features. He compared the criminals' features with those of soldiers on whom he practised his medicine. Lombroso believed that certain structural anomalies of the skull were commoner in the criminal group. He interpreted these abnormalities as indications that criminals represented an earlier stage of evolution of humanity than the rest of society had achieved. According to Lombroso, criminal characteristics include a lack of skull-space for brain tissue, pronounced structural differences between the two sides of the skull, ears that stick out, a bent or flat nose, colour blindness, left-handedness and a lack of muscular strength. His comparisons could get more specific. For example, different characteristics distinguished murderers from sex offenders. Murderers' eyes are bloodshot, cold and glassy, whereas the eyes of sex offenders glint. Lombroso is largely remembered for being wrong and few give his ideas any credence. For example, Lombroso's findings could not be replicated just a few years later in Britain by Charles Goring. Harrower (1998) argues that the observation that some criminals are mentally deficient is indirect support for Lombroso's point of view. Her idea is that in Lombroso's time biological defects including mental deficiency were seen as linked, though Goring's evidence was that criminals had low intelligence, not that they showed the cranial characteristics Lombroso claimed. Just to confirm how wrong the theory was, Lombroso claimed that it could be used even to explain the lack of criminality in women. It was not that women are socially more evolved than men. Quite the reverse. They were so backward in terms of human development that they had not evolved to the stage at which it was possible to be criminal!

European psychology's early contribution to forensic and criminal psychology

One of the earliest concepts related to forensic and criminal psychology was that of *kleptomania*. The term appears in modern dictionaries and has some popular currency today among the general public. Mathey, in 1816, coined the term *klopemania*, which means 'stealing insanity', whereas Marc, in 1840, used the term *kleptomania*, which means exactly the same thing (Fullerton and Punj, 2004). The main characteristics of kleptomania for these early physicians were as follows:

- Impulses to steal things of negligible value.
- Economic necessity was not a reason.
- The theft was accompanied by an elated state of exhilaration together with relief from feelings of tension.
- Kleptomaniacs tend to be women.

Perhaps, not surprisingly, given its emergence at a time of great economic growth in terms of industrialisation and commerce, the concept was popular throughout the nineteenth and twentieth centuries. Its explanation though was difficult since kleptomania was not fuelled by economic necessity and the things stolen were of little economic worth and frequently the thief would not even unwrap the item or use it. The motive was sexual according to some. The psychoanalytical psychiatrist Wilhelm Stekel held it to be a suppressed sexual desire (Stekel, 1911). Women, it was argued, suffered from penis envy (envy at not possessing a penis) so might seek to replace their missing penis through symbolic objects that they stole (Fenichel, 1933). Kleptomania is not an outmoded concept in the sense that it is a diagnostic category in the American Psychiatric Association's current diagnostic and statistical manual (DSM-IV). See Box 18.1.

A little later, the development of modern psychology at the University of Leipzig in the late nineteenth century quickly led to an interest in forensic issues. Generally speaking, it is accepted that the origins of modern psychology lie in the establishment of the psychological laboratory at this university in 1875. This was part of the legacy of Wilhelm Wundt to psychology. It was a number of his students, colleagues and co-workers who took the initial steps in developing forensic and criminal psychology:

- Albert Von Schrenk-Nortzing (circa 1897): in 1896, Von Schrenk-Nortzing appeared at a Leipzig court in a role that some might describe as the first true forensic psychologist. His was early testimony into the effects of the media on matters relevant to the courtroom. He argued that witnesses at a murder trial confused their actual memories of events with the pre-trial publicity given to the event in the media. They were not able to distinguish what they had witnessed and what they had read in the newspapers. Von Schrenk-Nortzing described this memory effect as 'retroactive memory falsification'. Related issues continue to be studied although the researchers do not necessarily concur with Von Schrenk-Nortzing – for example, Roberts and Blades (1995) asked whether children confuse television and real-life events. Their answer was that children as young as 4 years are good at identifying the source of their memories correctly. Significantly, at the lower age studied they can be confused by the way they are questioned into making errors.

- J.M. Cattell (circa 1895): investigated using the techniques of laboratory experiments into human memory on the quality of eyewitness testimony. He was an American who returned to the United States and studied forensic issues after studying in Wundt's laboratory. His research included situational influences on eyewitness accuracy as well as the issue of whether some individuals tend to be resistant to error and outside influences. Binet, the originator of intelligence testing, in France, replicated Cattell's work. He focused particularly on the question of the amenability of testimony to outside suggestion in interrogations. In Germany, at about the same time, William Stern conducted research on similar themes to those of Cattell in relation to both adults and children.

- Sigmund Freud did not write about legal matters although his ideas about human nature so profoundly affected the legal system that he was given an honorary doctorate in law from an American university. Nevertheless, a number of the psychoanalytically influenced followers of the psychodynamic psychology of Sigmund Freud made contributions to the field. For example, in 1929, Theodor Reik wrote about the compulsion to confess, Erich Fromm, in 1931, discussed the psychological diagnosis of fact (Jakob, 1992). Also in Germany, around 1905, C.G. Jung experimented with using word association to test a criminal suspect – that is, the characteristics of the delay of responding to different words with another word. Emotional stimulus words tend to produce greater delay.

- Udo Undeutsch in 1953 presented arguments to a German Psychological Association meeting that moved the issue of testimony to the question of the veracity of a statement rather than the credibility of the witness.

American roots of forensic and criminal psychology

The timescale is short between the German origins of forensic and criminal psychology and it beginning to appear in the United States. This is because a significant number of early American psychologists actually trained at Wundt's laboratory and either returned home or emigrated to the United States as academic positions became available. Thus early work in the United States involved both American researchers as well as European émigrés:

- L.W. Stern (circa 1910) continued the tradition of testimony research in the United States.
- Hugo Munsterberg was the first major and one of the most resolute applied psychologists. He was another of Wundt's students and he developed a lifelong interest in forensic issues. While still in Europe, he worked in support of Flemish weavers who were being sued by a customer. They were accused of supplying material of a different colour shade from that ordered. They disputed this. Munsterberg, with the help of the great physiologist of the visual system, Helmholtz, showed that the apparent difference in colour was a function of the different lighting conditions involved. The shades were *not* different. After migrating to the United States, he found that the adversarial Anglo-American system of law was not so sympathetic to hearing psychological opinion as the European system had been. His interests were wide in the field of applied psychology (Howitt, 1992) and included jury decision making as well as eyewitness testimony in the domain of forensic psychology. One of Munsterberg's students, William Marston, essentially developed the lie detector test (polygraphy) in 1915. His prototype of polygraphy was known as the 'systolic blood pressure deception test' and employed repeated blood pressure measurement during questioning. He claimed that changes in systolic blood pressure are indicative of lying (Grubin and Madsen, 2005/in press).
- Karle Marbe (circa 1911) testified in court that human reaction time latencies were such that an engine driver had no chance of stopping his train in time to prevent a crash. This was possibly the first psychological testimony at a civil rather than criminal trial. Less praiseworthy, Marbe also argued in court that the alleged victims of child sexual abuse made unreliable witnesses against their teacher. Society has changed a great deal since that time in terms of its attitudes to children.

The modern development of forensic and criminal psychology

Forensic and criminal psychology has different historical antecedents in different countries. This is particularly the case in terms of the institutional basis of forensic and criminal psychology internationally. The institutional basis of the discipline is not the same in all countries. For example, although universities may provide the training in the legal area of psychology in Western Europe, the training is more likely to be in non-university settings in other countries. To illustrate how the origins of forensic and criminal psychology may be different in different countries, we can consider the example of Spain. The first textbook on legal psychology (or judicial, which may be preferred by some to the term forensic psychology) was written by a Spanish psychiatrist in 1932 (Royo, 1996). The author left Spain along with many other intellectuals because of the Spanish Civil War. It was not until 1971 when the Barcelona College of Barristers created a Department of Sociology and Legal Psychology that the field was reopened. The first international meeting on Legal Psychology in Spain was held in 1976. While the specific details differ from country to country (see accounts of the development of the discipline in Hungary in Szegedi, 1998; in Portugal in Goncalves, 1998), generally speaking it would be common experience in different countries that forensic and criminal psychology, despite early interest, was in the doldrums until the 1970s (cf. Wrightsman, 2001) certainly in the United States and Western Europe. It should also be noted that the pattern of the steady expansion of forensic and criminal psychology since that time is not characteristic of all nations, especially those in Eastern Europe (Kury, 1998). In recent years, forensic and criminal psychology has developed extensively as a discipline as well as in its institutional base. As with many academic and practical fields, this has involved the establishment of specialist journals in which to publish research and ideas, organisations devoted to psychology (e.g. American Psychology and Law Society and the European Association for Psychology and Law), and national and international conferences devoted to the general field and specialist topics. Royo (1996) suggests that there are four basic ways in which a discipline may be consolidated. These are the formation of associations, the creation of specialised books and journals, the legal institutionalisation of the discipline as part of the process of criminal justice and the creation of university courses devoted to the subject. All of these may be recognised as characteristic of forensic and criminal psychology in many countries. There has been a general interest in integrating lawyers and psychologists in a variety of ways. An obvious example is joint conferences involving legal experts as well as psychologists specialising in the field.

The field of forensic and criminal psychology is not now fixed with its foci, boundaries and future clearly defined. It is an evolving field that will inevitably change:

- Developments in both the law and psychology will ensure that new issues become incorporated into the field. The development of the concept of stalking and its first incorporation into law in California in 1990 (Emerson *et al.*, 1998) led to considerable psychological and psychiatric effort to understand stalking behaviour.
- Increased employment of psychologists as personnel within different components of the criminal justice system will bring their own developments. So too will increases in private practice in the field. For example, a broadening of the role of psychology in police organisations – such as recruitment of officers – will bring a shift of interest in that direction in the field.
- Increasing numbers of students training in the field will ensure a fuller professionalisation of work and practice.

Main points

- The sub-discipline of forensic and criminal psychology deals with aspects of psychology relevant to the criminal justice system though, taken literally, the term *forensic psychology* refers to psychology in the context of law courts. The wider definition of the field underlies the selection of material in this book. As a consequence of the broad definition, the field unites psychologists from a wide variety of academic and practitioner backgrounds.

- Forensic and criminal psychology began to become important in the 1980s and increasingly so afterwards. The history of the field can be taken back many centuries to the times when issues such as diminished responsibility and fitness to stand trial were first developed in the legal system and so the demand for expert help from outside of the court itself. There was a period of interest in the field during the early years of academic psychology around 1900. However, for most of the twentieth century there was very little interest in the field.

- Forensic and criminal psychology has developed an appropriate infrastructure to ensure the continued development of the field. This includes specialist international organizations and journals in which the latest research is published.

Chapter 2

The social context of crime

Overview

- Many sources provide information about crime in society. For example, the mass media devote substantial amounts of space to crime and the criminal justice system. Government crime statistics are frequently presented as news items. For many of us, family, friends and acquaintances are additionally sources of information about the nature and levels of crime. Personal experience as a victim of crime or even a perpetrator can also contribute to our knowledge and beliefs. Nevertheless, misconceptions about crime and criminals are common.

- Crime statistics provide some insight into levels of crime though they have their shortcomings. Crime trends can change rapidly for a number of reasons and so forensic and criminal psychologists should keep up to date. The Internet is a ready and reliable resource for information on the most recent crime trends for many countries such as the United States and the United Kingdom.

- Criminal and crime statistics are based on data collected from a range of different sources. Sometimes information collated by the police will be used but there are also statistics, for example, by surveying the general public. Different types of statistical information may superficially appear incompatible because of the different types of data involved. Each method of data collection has its own advantages and disadvantages that should be taken into account when trying to assess their implications. The various approaches should be regarded as complementary and any differences in what the different approaches indicate should not be regarded as indicative of the uselessness of crime statistics but as part of the challenge of making sense of crime in society.

- Crime statistics have to be interpreted and different researchers will interpret them differently in some cases. Consequently, there are alternative interpretations possible for crime statistics depending on one's viewpoint.

- A great amount of research has demonstrated that criminal behaviour is quite common – sufficiently so that it might be described as normal. Of course, relatively trivial incidents of stealing form the bulk of this criminal activity. Nevertheless, there is evidence that half of males and nearly a third of females admit to committing at least one crime such as burglary, theft, criminal damage, robbery, assault or selling drugs at some stage in their lives.

- International comparisons tend to suggest considerable variation in levels of crime in different nations. Furthermore, international trends in crime statistics do not indicate that levels of crime invariably increase over time. For some crimes (homicide is a good example), the trends are downwards or flattening out in some countries traditionally believed to be violent.

- The great variety of criminal justice systems in the world poses a challenge to forensic and criminal psychology. Justice is administered differently and is based on different principles in different parts of the world. Even where the systems are closely related (e.g. the United Kingdom and the United States) there may be crucial differences in certain respects. So avoid the assumption that the principles of forensic and criminal psychology are universally applicable.

Most people's ideas about the world of crime come from a wide variety of sources. Personal experience clearly must play some part but imagery of crime and the criminal justice system is everywhere. For example, Howitt (1998c) found that the largest proportions of UK media news stories concerned crime and the criminal justice system. Characteristically, almost by definition, the news is about unusual, new or sensational events. As such, it is not intended to be indicative of the mundane reality of most crime. Studies demonstrating a lack of correspondence between the reality of crime and the contents of newspapers go back many years (Croll, 1974; Davies, 1952; Roshier, 1971, 1973). Property crimes such as theft are grossly under-represented in newspapers, yet these are the very crimes that the general public are most likely to experience. Similarly, violent crime including homicide is disproportionately over-reported (Chermak, 1995). The situation is more extreme for movies and television. These are replete with cops and crime. In other words, to the extent that the media determine people's perceptions of crime, the risk is that they receive a rather distorted view.

The extent of crime

Specifying the reality of crime is not simple. There is no single reality to be described. Take, for example, the criminal statistics that are commonly collected by national agencies in many countries. These include the following:

- Surveys of *the general public's experience of crime* in, say, a particular year. These are usually known as victim or victimisation surveys. Basically, members of the public are interviewed about their experience of crime in the previous year. These have their difficulties. They are subject to problems of recall and accuracy over the period in question. Not surprisingly, such surveys tend to produce the highest estimates of the rates of crime and victimisation. Crimes for which the victim is corporate (a big company) or for which there is no obvious victim (such as vandalism in the public park) are likely to be omitted from the data collected. Furthermore, they may include events that may well not lead to a conviction by a court of law.

- Aggregate data of *crimes recorded by/reported to the police*. These are affected by reporting biases. For example, some victims may decide not to go to the police. The police may decide that certain events are best ignored and no attempt made at arrest (e.g. racist chants at a football match). The police may choose to see the events as not being a crime for some reason. How the police classify events as crimes or not crimes and particular types of crime may affect the overall pattern. Crimes recorded by the police are not the same as crimes reported to the police. When a victim reports a crime, the police may decide that it is not appropriate to record it as a crime.

- *Court statistics* that codify the numbers and types of offences being processed in a given year and the outcomes in terms of sentencing of these different cases. The obvious biases here are in terms of the factors that lead to prosecution as opposed to no charge.
- *Prison statistics* provide breakdowns of the numbers in prison at any one time, their offence categories, their sentence and so forth. Biases here may be due to sentencing policies at the time. For example, a concerted clampdown on burglary may lead to an increase in the numbers of burglars in prison.
- *General population offender surveys* have recently been developed in which members of a random sample of households are interviewed about the crimes they have committed ever in their lives and/or recently, say, in the previous year. This is likely to include at least some crimes that would be ignored by the police and other components of the criminal justice system as being too trivial to warrant prosecution. Furthermore, there is probably a bias against the more serious crimes since those who have committed the more serious crimes may well have been arrested, prosecuted and sent to prison so that they are excluded from such surveys.

For obvious reasons, the rates of crime that would be estimated from these different statistics vary. One would rightly expect that surveys of victims produce substantially higher levels of crime in general than any of the other statistical indices. A number of matters warrant consideration:

- None of the statistics is simply wrong. They each provide different perspectives on criminal activity.
- Each of the statistics has its own value and may be more useful for a particular purpose than others. Even though, say, crimes recorded by the police may be just a fraction of crimes committed, they may still be very useful for examining changes in crime rates over time. This is especially true if the biases in reporting crimes to the police remain relatively constant over time. Unfortunately, this is difficult to ascertain. So, for example, if we find more cases of child sexual abuse in the 1990s than in the 1960s, is this due to higher levels of sexual abuse? The data are equally consistent with there being an increased awareness in the danger of abuse which makes people more vigilant and more prepared to report crimes. It may also reflect an increase due to retrospective prosecutions of previously unreported abuse that happened many years earlier.
- Care is always needed in terms of the interpretation of any of these statistics. For example, legal and other changes may result in crimes being classified differently at different points in time. A change in the definition of rape to include, say, male rape may produce an increase in the numbers of rapes. While it is common practice for statisticians to signal changes in the basis on which the statistics are compiled, it is much more difficult to adjust previous years on the basis of such information unless the compilers do so. This is not simply a matter of governments manipulating crime statistics for their own political advantage, it reflects the changing nature of the law and the fact that what is criminal changes over time.

In short, while some will point to the inadequacies of crime statistics as fatal flaws in those statistics, it is better to regard crime statistics as being of limited usefulness in limited circumstances. This makes them very similar to much of the data that psychologists collect. That they are the result of a complex social process makes their understanding all the more important; it is not an excuse for dismissing them as worthless. Often the problem is not the nature of the data but how they should be interpreted. The more familiar one is with a variety of different sorts of crime statistics and just how particular crime statistics are compiled, then the more adequate one's interpretations are likely to be.

Because there are broad changes in crime over time and considerable international variation in its levels, crime statistics go out of date rapidly. Increasingly, extensive information about crime statistics are published on the Internet by governments and other organisations. Obviously, Internet addresses can change overnight, but good search engines readily find suitable sites. Useful search terms are crime statistics and criminal statistics. This material is probably as up to date as any publicly available since it is far quicker to update web material than books or pamphlets. As with any material on the Internet, one should always carefully assess the adequacy of its source and try to anticipate the sort of spin that may be put on what the statistics mean or just what statistics are presented. This applies to all sources of information, it is not simply a consideration when using the Internet as a source.

The term *crime index* is commonly used in relation to criminal statistics. This is merely a composite measure of the number of crimes based, usually, on the more serious types. US sources will be referring to a composite of murder and non-negligent manslaughter, forcible rape, robbery and aggravated assault (these are the contribution of violent crimes) and burglary, larceny theft, motor-vehicle theft and arson (the property offences included). Other countries may have their own variants on this, more appropriate to the major crime categories in those countries. These indices provide a very broad picture of crime trends. The sub-components of the index may actually be showing rather different trends. For example, rape may be increasing but since motor-vehicle theft is decreasing much faster, the overall trend is downward.

The extent of criminality

One of the classic ideas of criminology and sociology is that of white-collar or middle-class crime. This is not just about the extent to which white-collar workers are punished for matters such as fraud and embezzlement, for instance, although the prosecution of these may be difficult. It is also about activities such as 'borrowing' stationery from the office or using the office telephone for private calls. These activities are ones that would be regarded as criminal from other perspectives. Generally, those who engage in them regard these activities as acceptable, if not normal. Tax evasion, for some people, is seen as almost morally justified and hence not truly a crime.

The extent of criminality in the population is remarkably high. Even if we take the stringent criterion of imprisonment, in the United States the chances of a person going to prison during their lifetime is estimated at just over 5% according to the latest available estimates (Bureau of Justice, 2004a). The odds are much worse for some groups, which may reflect biases in the criminal justice system:

- The figure is 11% for men but only 2% for women.
- A black person has a 19% chance compared to 3% for white people.
- The figure for black males is 32% as opposed to 6% for white males. That is, nearly one in three black males will spend time in prison!
- Over 65% of jailed persons were of racial or ethnic minority origin in 2001.

The extent of potential criminality in behaviour can also be seen from studies of youngsters. For example, Wilson (1980) took samples of 10- to 17-year-olds living in deprived housing estates in inner city or suburban settings. Evidence concerning their criminality was obtained directly from police records of convictions and cautions:

- Twenty per cent of the boys had a record of crime. Theft and burglary were the commonest offences.
- This should be contrasted with their self-reported misbehaviours. Crime is much more common in terms of self-reported offences rather than criminal convictions – over 40% had shoplifted, 67% had drawn graffiti in the street and so forth.

The British Crime and Justice Survey (Budd and Sharp, 2005) extends our knowledge of self-reported rates of crime in that a national sample of the general household population in the age range of 10 to 65 years were asked in detail. These offences were burglary, vehicle related thefts, other thefts, criminal damage, robbery, assaults and selling drugs. Over 50% of males had committed at least one of these core crimes in their lives and 30% of females. Given that other types of offences such as sexual ones were omitted from the survey, it is likely that the figure for people who had ever committed a serious offence would be higher. Of course, some of these crimes were not very serious since they involved property of low value or involved assaults that did not lead to injury. About 20% of the population had committed a serious offence at some stage and this usually involved assault with injury. The survey also assessed the numbers who had committed an offence in the last year. These figures are naturally smaller than the equivalent lifetime percentages. Six per cent of people had committed a property crime in the last year and 5% had committed a violent offence. For juvenile offenders the majority of offences were violent in nature though generally these did not involve injury. For people above the age of 25 years, the majority of offences were to do with property. Drug offences were commoner than property offences and much more common than violent offences in the 18- to 25-year-old age group.

There is a further approach that warrants attention in this context: that is, the field experiments into honesty/dishonesty carried out by psychologists. Carefully staged situations, of a variety of sorts, have been contrived in order to investigate dishonesty. The origins of this were in the classic studies of Hartshorne and May (1928) who investigated aspects of dishonesty such as lying, cheating and stealing in pubescent children. Among their measures was the failure or not of children to return a coin they had been given. This and later research is reviewed in Farrington (1979). A range of other ways of assessing stealing has been developed. For example, some researchers have deliberately 'lost' money in the street to see whether the finder attempts to return the cash or merely just keeps it. Farrington and Kidd (1977) lost envelopes in the street containing varying amounts of money:

- With no money enclosed, 95% of the envelopes were returned to the address in the enclosed letter.
- With £1 in cash enclosed, 75% were returned and with £5 in cash enclosed, then 55% were returned.

This is a notably high rate of dishonesty given that, in the United Kingdom, to keep money knowing that one is depriving its rightful owner of it constitutes theft. Many of these studies were carried out to investigate the effects of different environmental circumstances on the rates of honesty. They also indicate the baseline rates of dishonest behaviour in fairly general samples of the population.

Of course, there is an important implication for forensic and criminal psychology in all of this. That is, in many ways the study of criminal behaviour is the study of the behaviour of normal people given that so many have committed some sort of crime in their lives no matter how trivial. That does not imply that there are no abnormal psychological features in any criminal, merely that much crime has to be explained in terms of normal behaviour.

Crime rates compared internationally

The International Crime Victimisation Survey (2001) revealed a great deal about the relative rates of crime in countries in different parts of the world. To survey national populations in such diverse locations is, manifestly, logistically complex. Indeed, sampling in economically developing countries was very much confined to cities as a consequence. The surveys were not all conducted at exactly the same time in the different nations, so it is really only possible to describe the data as being collected in the 1990s. The data for industrialised countries is the most pertinent to forensic and criminal psychologists, as this is where they are almost certain to work. It should be stressed that this was a victimisation survey, not a collation of, for example, crimes known to the police. So the information was obtained directly from the public, thus avoiding the sorts of reporting bias that can affect the numbers of crimes known to the police. Of course, surveys of the public are subject to all of the potential biases of any survey (refusals to take part, for instance). Nevertheless, victim surveys generally indicate greater rates of victimisation than do the number of crimes known to the police. How much the two are truly different is difficult to assess as this particular survey reported prevalence rates as opposed to incidence rates. The meanings of prevalence and incidence are as follows:

- Prevalence rates are simply the percentage of people who report having been a victim of crime or a particular sort of crime in the previous year. If they have been robbed twice, for example, this is not recorded in prevalence figures. The choice is between having been victimised or having not been victimised. They give the probability of being a victim in a given year; multi-crime victims are treated in the same way as single-crime victims.
- Incidence rates reflect the frequency of being victimised and, as such, would be better estimates of the numbers of crimes committed annually. So one could not multiply the prevalence rate by the size of the population to obtain the number of crimes committed in a particular country in a given year.

The international survey included Australia, Austria, Belgium, Canada, England and Wales, Finland, France, Germany (the West prior to reunification), Italy, Malta, Netherlands, New Zealand, Northern Ireland, Norway, Scotland, Spain, Sweden, Switzerland and the United States. The crimes surveyed ranged from property offences against cars, such as theft of the car, damage to the car and theft from the car, on the less serious side, to sexual offences and assault and threat.

Table 2.1 Prevalence rates for England and Wales versus the United States

	England and Wales (%)	United States (%)
Sexual crime	3.0	2.5
Assault and threat	5.0	5.7
Burglary	3.5	2.6

Internationally there is considerable variation in the likelihood of victimisation and, for some countries, noticeable variation over time. Overall, the chances of victimisation were the highest in England and Wales. The prevalence rate was almost 31% for victimisation for any sort of crime. Other countries had rates of 25% or so. For example, the figure for the United States in the 1990s was 24%. In general, Belgium and Northern Ireland had the lowest victimisation rates. Table 2.1 gives a few comparisons between England and Wales and the United States. Despite there being substantial differences between the two countries in terms of perceptions of the relative levels of crime, the victim data suggest little difference. It should also be noted that according to crime report figures, there were major reductions in levels of violent crime in the United States in the 1990s (Bureau of Justice, 2001b).

For certain types of offence, it is not common practice to report the crime to the police. Assault has reporting rates of 38% in England and Wales and 45% in the United States. Sexual offences are less likely to be reported. The figures are 20% for England and Wales and 28% for the United States. There is a lot of international variation in reporting sexual offences. For example, the rate is 5% in Spain and 43% in Northern Ireland. Reporting rates found from victim surveys allow the 'true' rate of crime to be assessed from known numbers of crimes reported to the police. Thus, for example, the true rate of rape in England and Wales should be multiplied by approximately five (i.e. victim surveys suggest that just over 20% of rapes are reported) in order to correct for the low reporting rate.

Rates of reporting are highest for burglary in virtually all countries. The reason is probably the insurer's requirement that the crime is reported to the police if an insurance payment is to be made. Chapter 4 discusses, in part, the psychology of reporting crime.

Figures suggest that, in a lifetime, the vast majority of North Americans become victims of an index crime recorded by the police – 83% will be victimised by violence in this way and 99% by theft. Criminality may be common; victimisation is a virtual certainty (Bureau of Justice, 2001e). The British Crime Survey of 2000 (Home Office, 2001b) found that 17% of the population had been, in the previous year, the victim of a crime reported to the police. Fifty-nine per cent of people had at some time in their life been the victim of a crime reported to the police. In contrast, only 10% had been in court as a person accused of a crime. In other words, in terms of experiences of crime, the victim role is the commonest despite the centrality of the offender in forensic and criminal psychology.

There have been other attempts to compare crime rates internationally. One of the most recent involved a cross-national comparison of eight countries – England and Wales, Scotland, Canada, United States, Australia, Holland, Sweden and Switzerland (Farrington, Langan and Tonry, 2004). As with other studies, there are difficulties involved in making statistical comparisons between different countries. For example, in some European countries burglary and vehicle theft are not distinguished in the legal code from other types of theft. This meant that the rates of burglary and vehicle theft in these countries had to be estimated from general theft data. The period studied was the two decades between 1980 and 2000. One of the startling features of the data is that different countries may show exactly the opposite trend rates of particular crimes. In some countries, the rates of recorded burglary per 1,000 population increased over time (e.g. Australia and Holland), in other countries the rates of recorded burglary decreased over time (United States). Some countries have several times the rate of recorded burglaries of other countries. Australia had the highest rate overall and Switzerland the lowest rate. Rates can change dramatically within a country over time. So the United States had far higher rates of robbery than England and Wales in the 1980s but at the end of the study period, rates in the two countries were virtually identical. Rates in the United States had declined markedly and rates in the United Kingdom had increased markedly.

Statistics may rapidly go out of date as will a psychologist's knowledge of them. Furthermore, what may be true of one type of crime (e.g. homicide) may not be true of other types of violent crime. Blackburn (1995b) was almost certainly correct at the time to point out national differences in terms of violent crimes, especially. He suggested that the United States was a nation especially prone to such crime. The variation is remarkable, as Blackburn suggests, but crime statistics are not necessarily stable even over a relatively short period of time. He argues that different homicide rates may be due to socio-cultural factors: but just what socio-cultural factors could be responsible for rapidly changing homicide rates? Changes in crime policy may produce changes in policing, sentencing and punishment that result in a quick reduction in crime statistics. Governments make claims about the efficacy of their criminal justice policy based on declining rates of certain crimes.

To be precise, for the United States the statistical evidence is that homicide, adjusted for the size of the population, has become less frequent in recent years. By 1999 it was at a low level equivalent to the figures for the latter part of the 1960s – in 1999 the rate was 6 homicides for every 100,000 people in the population. This is substantially less than the rate of 10 homicides per 100,000 in 1980 – the United States's peak homicide year for the latter part of the twentieth century (Fox and Zawitz, 2004). Homicide rates in the United States have been more or less constant since 1999. For the latest year available (2002), the homicide rate in the United States remained at under 6 per 100,000 population (Bureau of Justice, 2004).

According to important international comparative data (Farrington, Langan and Tonry, 2004), homicide has also tended to decline since 1980 in some countries included in the survey. In Australia, the homicide rate is about 2 homicides but has declined slightly; in Canada the rate has dropped from 3 to 2 per 100,000 of population. Holland's homicide rate stayed remarkably constant over the period at 1. The United Kingdom figures have increased slightly over time but still are currently approximately 1.5 per 100,000 in the population. Other data (Barclay, Tavares and Siddique, 2001) shows that the United States's homicide rates, although two or three times the rate for Western European countries, are comparatively low. For example, Finland has a homicide rate of 12, Russia a rate of 21, and South Africa a rate of 56 – nearly ten times the rate in the United States. National rates tend to disguise the fact that some areas within a country may have disproportionately high homicide rates. For example, the rate for Washington DC in the United States was virtually the same as the massive South African one at 51 per 100,000.

It cannot be emphasised too much that, even for a so-called violent society such as the United States, the crimes recorded by the police are overwhelmingly property crimes. In 1999, larceny theft was 60%, burglary 18% and motor-vehicle theft 10% of crimes. Violent crimes appear next in the list with aggravated assault at 8% of crimes, robbery at 3%, rape at less than 1% and murder at one recorded crime in a thousand crimes (Bureau of Justice, 2001b). Furthermore, great care should be taken over whether homicide rates truly reflect the violent nature of different countries. If we compare the rate of assault for England and Wales with that of the United States, it would appear that England and Wales is proportionately more violent. In 1999, the rate of serious assaults per 100,000 population in England and Wales was 1,395 based on victim surveys and 415 based on serious assaults recorded to the police. For the United States, the serious assault rate was 669 according to victim surveys and 336 based on those recorded by the police (Farrington, Langan and Tonry, 2004). These rates paint a different picture of violent crime from that painted by homicide rates.

Conservative and radical interpretations

No matter how carefully obtained, criminal statistics are subject to interpretation. For any set of figures there are several equally viable interpretations. Crime statistics are aggregates of many distinct happenings and, by and large, we have little knowledge of the detail. For example, the US data on felony convictions in state and federal courts for 1994 (Bureau of Justice, 2001c) reveal that drug trafficking accounted for 20% of convictions and drug possession for 12% of convictions. That is, combined, the drugs offences are responsible for nearly a third of convictions. What does one conclude from these figures? One interpretation is that drugs offences are such a major crime problem that more should be done to arrest and punish offenders. This would probably imply a need for greater police activity, which ought to result in even more convictions. An alternative, more radical, view would be to point out that such high figures reflect the failure of policy on drugs to make significant inroads in reducing drug use. The country might be better off decriminalising drugs or some such strategy. The savings to the criminal justice system would be enormous simply in terms of time and money. Naturally, each of these positions can be criticised with further arguments. Nevertheless, the basic point should be clear – crime statistics do not carry with them implicit meanings: interpretation has to be imposed.

Take another example: black people are over-represented in both the homicide perpetrator and victim figures in the United States. In terms of rates standardised by population size, a black person has six times the risk of being a victim compared to a white person, and is eight times more likely to be a perpetrator (Fox and Zawitz, 2004). While some authors (Rushton, 1990) might interpret this as indicative of racial differences in the inheritance of criminal tendencies, for others they reflect the huge social inequalities experienced by black communities and biases in policing (e.g. Howitt and Owusu-Bempah, 1994; Stark, 1993). Of course, some explanations become more and less viable when other statistical information is incorporated. For example, the United States has achieved substantial reductions in violence between intimates (partners, spouses, etc.) which cannot possibly be accounted for by changes in the gene pool (e.g. Bureau of Justice, 2001d).

International variations in justice systems

Whatever the means by which crime rates are assessed, the socio-legal contexts in which forensic and criminal psychologists operate differ in many other respects. The variability in criminal justice systems, broadly defined, is immense. This is not generally problematic as most will work solely within one criminal justice system. Nevertheless, it is important to understand that a given system is just one of many possibilities. Furthermore, each criminal justice system has many components of which practitioners need to be aware. By way of illustration, Table 2.2 gives some information from three criminal justice systems – Japan, France, and England and Wales (other parts of Britain have different systems). The data are taken from an international compendium of information about criminal justice systems around the world (International Crime Victimisation Survey, 2001). Despite the data being supplied by specialist researchers, certain information is unavailable from particular countries. A few areas of comparison have been taken to illustrate the similarities and diversities in countries both near together and far apart. The following points are fairly self-evident and are mostly illustrated in Table 2.2:

Table 2.2 Some international comparisons of criminal justice systems

	Japan	**France**	**England and Wales**
Legal system	Influenced historically by French and German systems but more adversarial in recent times	Inquisitorial system – essentially the judge seeks the facts of the case from a variety of sources	Adversarial system based on cases put forward by prosecution and defence
Jury system	Not in use in fact despite being available	Not used	Jury system for more serious crimes
Age of criminal responsibility	20 years of age	18 years of age	10 years of age but special provision up to 18 years
Crime statistics	Murder: 1,238 cases reported to police in 1990 Rape: 1,548 cases Larceny: 1,444,067	Intentional homicides: 625 in 1990 Rape: 735 Armed robbery: 800	Homicide: 729 in 1994 Rape: 5,039 Offences against property: 5.3 million
Police system	Two-layered structure: (1) the national police and (2) the prefecture police	Four police divisions: (1) General Information (2) City Police – city law enforcement (3) Judiciary Police (4) Territory Surveillance – state security	No national police force but many separate forces at local level. Some smaller forces such as railway police.
Prison	Daily prison population: 44,875, including 37,522 who were convicted	Daily prison population: 137,757	Daily population of sentenced prisoners: 40,000
Civil cases	–	A court can hear both civil and criminal cases	Separate systems for civil and criminal cases

- *The legal system*: France has an inquisitorial legal system in which judges or magistrates seek to obtain the truth about a particular case from various sources. In other words, they have a leading role in determining what evidence and expert advice is needed. In England and Wales (and other countries such as Canada, the United States and Australia, which derive their legal systems from Britain), the adversarial system is adopted: that is, the prosecution and defence are adversaries who battle to convince the judge or jury that theirs is the winning argument. Their success is then judged, often by a jury. The different systems vary in terms of the sorts of evidence that may be admitted as valid and the need to consider the fitness of the accused to stand trial. Japan basically moved from one system to another.

- *Jury system*: some legal systems do not use juries but rely on judges and magistrates to decide issues of guilt. Other systems use juries but there can be substantial differences in the sizes of the jury used or the rules used for determining the verdict of the jury. In some systems, it is possible for the judge to take part with the jury in determining guilt. (See Chapter 20.)

- *The age of criminal responsibility*: this is twice as old in Japan (20 years) as in England and Wales (10 years). Of course, there may be provision for treating young people separately, such as juvenile courts and other institutions, which reduce the apparent huge differences between the various countries. It may be helpful to note that Heilbrun *et al.* (1997) suggest that in most parts of the United States the trend is to allow younger people to be tried in adult courts. They report that in the majority of jurisdictions, 14-year-olds can now be tried in criminal courts. This touches on fundamental beliefs about the nature of crime and how it is dealt with. This is dealt with more fully in Chapter 3.

- *Crime statistics*: while, as we have seen, the figures vary among nations, it is equally important to note that crime classifications in different countries may not be the same. In other words, direct comparisons may be impossible. It is also notable that actual numbers of certain crimes such as murder and rape are probably rather lower than most people believe them to be.

- *Police system*: there are a number of differences among police organisations across nations. One particularly obvious dimension is the extent to which police organisations are national or local. Often there is a mixture of the two, but sometimes, as in the case of England and Wales, there are numerous small forces covering areas of just a few million people. The more small units there are then the greater the communication problems and, consequently, the greater the need for provision to ensure good inter-force communications.

- *Prison*: different nations differ substantially in their prison populations. This may be indicative of different base levels of crime, but it may also reflect profound differences in penal policies.

- *Civil cases*: civil law deals with legal cases that are about private rights rather than the public concern of crime. Criminal penalties (such as prison) do not apply in civil cases where financial payments to the aggrieved party are the means of righting wrongs. In some jurisdictions, they are dealt with by the same courts, whereas in other jurisdictions there is a totally separate civil law court system. Civil courts may sometimes deal with criminal matters (e.g. civil actions have been brought against alleged criminals but these do not result in criminal penalties).

It is a substantial task to become sufficiently familiar with the legal system of any country to practise as a forensic and criminal psychologist. The international nature of research in the field should encourage researchers to develop a knowledge of these different systems of justice. If nothing else, such knowledge will help one to understand why certain sorts of research will be of interest in only some countries. Jury research may be relevant in the United States, Australia, Canada and the United Kingdom, but of much less interest to forensic and criminal psychologists from much of mainland Europe, for example. Some issues such as inquisitorial versus adversarial systems have been fairly extensively researched (e.g. Stephenson, 1992).

Main points

- It is important for forensic and criminal psychologists to be familiar with trends in crime as reported in crime statistics and from surveys of the general population. A degree of sophistication is necessary in their interpretation since each source has its own particular characteristics. Crime rates obtained from victim surveys are different from those obtained by collating the number of crimes recorded by the police. Court statistics and prison statistics give us different sorts of information. It is unwise to regard the characteristics of different statistics as flaws.

- Quite high proportions of the general population are known to have been involved as a victim and a perpetrator of crime at some stage in their lives. Experimental studies have shown that various forms of dishonesty are very common. Of course, the precise figures will depend on quite how crime is defined. Clearly, the number of persistent offenders is a much lower figure.

- International comparisons reveal many differences between the criminal justice systems in different parts of the world. So research that is important in one country may have no bearing on what happens in another country. Similarly, crime statistics vary internationally in important ways. England and Wales seem to have disproportionately high rates of victimisation.

Chapter 3

Crime and the public

Overview

- What is a crime is defined in terms of a complex social process. Each stage of the process requires detailed examination in order that we obtain a full understanding of the nature of crime. Identical events may be classified as crime or otherwise depending on circumstances. The decision to report events to the police as a crime is just one important aspect of this. Other factors are also influential. Government policy on crime is a sensitive political issue that can be sensitive to public opinion, for example, such that certain crimes may be targeted for police attention.

- There is evidence that the public appear to have a tough-minded attitude towards crime. This may influence the way in which criminal justice is administered perhaps by influencing politicians to be more tough minded on crime themselves.

- The public's knowledge about aggregate rates of crime and trends in criminal statistics tends to be poor and generally inaccurate. This is partly the consequence of the difficulty of thinking statistically in terms of percentages and probabilities.

- Moral panics are essentially an overreaction against some event (such as a crime) that has been perceived as a threat or a risk to society's major values. The alarm generated may lead to demands that action should be taken against the source of the threat. The strength of feeling tends to be self-nurturing such that the panic escalates.

- The media and personal experience form the basis of the public's knowledge about crime. The links between the two are far from simple and not apparent in all research. There is often little or no relationship between an individual's risk of victimisation and their level of fear of crime. This may be termed the fear-victimisation paradox. Understanding the psychological processes involved in the fear of crime seems to improve predictions about media influences on the individual and the consequences of victimisation.

- Theories about the origins of the fear of crime suggest that: 1) the distorted image of crime portrayed by the media affects heavy television viewers disproportionately (cultivation theory); 2) any source of information may provide the individual with a particularly vivid but negative impression of a particular crime or a particular sort of crime such that the individual responds to similar situations to the vivid imagery with fear (availability heuristic); and 3) fear of crime is the consequence of the independent influences of beliefs about the negative consequence of being victimised and the subjective risk of being victimised (cognitive theory).

Crime does not just involve the criminals. It is the result of a complex social process, which operates at virtually every conceivable level of social and psychological analysis. The nature of the task facing forensic and criminal psychologists cannot be fully appreciated without understanding the social context of crime. Crime is not simply (or even) the product of the mind of the criminal, it is a social product. Crime can only be understood by knowing:

- what laws apply;
- what the set of circumstances surrounding the events is;
- what the public thinks about crime;
- what the victim thinks about crime;
- what the ethos of the policing system is;
- what the system for dealing with psychiatric cases is;
- who decides whom to prosecute;
- the rules governing court procedure;
- the skills of the lawyer;
- the characteristics of the judge;
- what the jurors have read in the newspapers about the case or any one of a number of other aspects of the crime, the criminal and the criminal justice system. Each is essential and, in some circumstances, any may become crucial.

According to Ainsworth (2000a), the path from the commission of a crime to the punishment of an offender is a long, complex and tortuous one (p. 15). There is a very real sense in which a crime is committed only once a court hearing has determined that one has occurred. The reason is that very much the same events can be seen very differently according to the prevailing circumstances. If a person takes a few coins from a colleague's desk at work to pay for a lunchtime sandwich, fails to tell the colleague that the money has been taken, and then fails to pay it back, has a crime been committed? Was it really the intent to deprive the colleague of the coins? If so, then surely this is a crime? What if the colleague fails to notice that the money is missing? Would this mean a crime had not taken place? What if the colleague realises the money is missing but the boss does not want the police informed? Does this mean that a crime has not taken place? What if the police decide that the sum of money involved is very small anyway and suggest to the owner of the money that perhaps they may have forgotten they had spent it? Does this mean that a crime has not taken place? What if the police (or other body) decide that there is little point in prosecuting in this case because the colleague was taking antidepressant drugs at the time and these were having unfortunate side effects on his memory and behaviour? Does this mean that a crime has not taken place? What if the colleague is prosecuted but the case is discharged because of irregularities in the way in which the police obtained a confession? Does this mean that a crime has not been committed? Finally, the colleague pleads guilty and is convicted by the court of stealing the money, then fined. Does that mean that a crime has been committed?

At each of these stages, a crime may or may not have been committed. The process of defining a crime is not just complex but will have a multiplicity of perspectives. Crime is a category, which is the result of a process involving different individuals, different institutions and different settings. From one perspective a crime may have been committed, from another a crime may not have been committed.

'Will the victim notice the crime?'
e.g. being hit by a supermarket trolley is likely to be an accident but it could be a deliberate assault.
In cases such as vandalism there may not be an obvious victim as the damage may be in a remote location and the ownership is public.

'Will the victim report the crime?'
e.g. a person raped by another may choose not to report the crime because of extra trauma involved in going to the police or, perhaps if the victim is male, he may not know that what happened to him was a crime.
A crime may be reported if there is insurance on the property but the victim of an identical crime may decide that there is little point in reporting if there is no insurance cover.

'Will the police record the "crime" as such?'
e.g. the police may more willingly record racial abuse if there is a political initiative against racism.
The police may be unaware that there are legal sanctions against certain activities, e.g. using a mobile phone in a car dangerously without specific legislation against that practice.

'Will the offender be caught by the police?'
e.g. police clear-up rates may be high for serious crimes where there is an obvious suspect or witnesses capable of identifying the offender.
However, for less serious crimes that would entail massive police work to detect, the clear-up rates may be low.

'Will the perpetrator receive an appropriate sentence?'
e.g. would the victims or their families see the sentence as appropriate?

'Will the offender be prosecuted?'
e.g. police/prosecuting authorities may be reluctant to prosecute if chances of conviction are low or a preliminary court could reject the case. Especially where prosecuting authorities are elected, the decision to prosecute may be influenced by the political climate.

'Will the perpetrator be found guilty?'
e.g. some areas of law – especially rape – have been regarded as biased in favour of the accused.
False convictions occur at rates which some have suggested amount to a few per cent of the number of prosecutions.

Figure 3.1 Stages in the process of crime described by Ainsworth
Source: Ainsworth, P.B. (2000) *Psychology and Crime: Myths and Reality.* © Longman, 2000

All of these things are dependent on the jurisdiction involved since the practice of the law varies. The thief who is so mentally impaired that they do not know that they are committing a crime may be not guilty of theft in the eyes of the court. The driver who inadvertently drives over the speed limit because his speedometer is faulty, in law may well be committing a crime even though he had not intended to, simply because this is a strict (i.e. absolute liability) offence. Once in a while, there may be behaviours that would seem to be criminal but against which there is no law (for example, running a child down while trying to make a mobile telephone call). Legal processes are social in nature and cannot be understood simply through knowledge of what the relevant law is.

Figure 3.1 shows something of the complexity of the processes involved. A number of issues should be considered:

• The figure suggests a relatively closed criminal justice system but this is an incomplete picture. It is a more open system than this implies.

- Legislation is the result of a political process that may involve interest groups pressuring the government, for example. An illustration of this would be the pressure of feminist groups to change the laws and practices concerning domestic violence.

- Furthermore, some actions by the police – such as attempts to control private sexual practices that may be illegal in a technical sense – may bring media and public condemnation.

- The figure would seem to indicate that the criminal law is the recourse for the victim. However, there are other remedies available such as using the civil law to achieve compensation. Private prosecutions of homicide suspects who have been acquitted by the criminal courts are an example of this. Standards of evidence are slightly less exacting in the civil law and the penalties are also less serious – financial costs rather than imprisonment being involved.

- Single arrows operating in just one direction join the elements of the system in Figure 3.1. In reality, each of the elements of the system may interact with other elements. For example, if rape cases appear to the public to be failing to lead to the conviction of the offender in sufficient numbers of cases, there may be an unwillingness of the victim to report the crime to the police.

Attitudes towards crime

Crime is an issue with the public in a multiplicity of ways. It is part of the broader political agenda that attracts many commentators from a wide variety of party affiliations. For that reason, public attitudes may impinge on government policy on crime. For example, research in Canada has shown that the public supports trying youngsters in the same courts as adults (Sprott, 1998). Those believing in this also tend to have a harsher attitude to the punishment of juveniles. These attitudes at least support if not create the situation in which increasingly the separate youth system of justice is being eroded in Canada and the United States. It is not easy to identify the precise influence of public opinion on the criminal justice system. It is clearly present in particularly dramatic cases such as the Moors Murderers (Ian Brady and Myra Hindley) in the United Kingdom. The influence stretches from prosecution and sentencing to the eventual disposal of offenders back into the community. Take, for example, recidivism. If recidivism was infrequent after conviction then the case for keeping prison terms, say, short would be stronger and, perhaps, attitudes towards the rehabilitation of offenders might be more positive. Unfortunately, the public seems to believe that recidivism is rife and almost the norm for many types of offence.

Evidence for this comes from a study of a range of individuals in Spain and Canada who have good educational backgrounds and, mostly, a close interest in criminology (Redondo *et al.*, 1996). The Spanish sample believed that for a first offender the average likelihood of them reoffending for drug trafficking offences was high:

- On average, they thought that the likelihood of reoffending was 61% within five years. The figure reached 100% average prediction of reoffending for multi-recidivists (i.e. individuals having offended and been convicted many times).

- This contrasts with actual rates of 11% and 44% for the two types of offender in Spain. These figures are clearly much lower than the public's expectations.

- Similar findings were obtained for sexual offences. Recidivism estimates ranged from 31% to 54% in both the Canadian and Spanish samples for first offenders, recidivists and multi-recidivists. In reality, recidivism for sex offences tended to be rather low in sex offenders in both countries.

In other words, it would seem that the public strongly tends towards the view that once a criminal always a criminal. Perhaps that is why custodial sentences are regarded by many of the public favourably.

Thus the public's concern about crime needs to be understood since it may impinge on how criminal justice is administered. Of course, in many countries there is no direct link between public opinion and the criminal justice system (few countries have publicly elected officials in the criminal justice system of the sort employed in the United States). Understanding public attitudes, for example, may be very relevant to recommendations about the disposal of sex offenders once their prison sentence has been completed. Public demonstrations against their release into the community have been seen in a number of countries.

Box 3.1

Key concept: moral panics

The concept of moral panic had its origin in Stanley Cohen's study of the phenomenon of youth crime in Britain in the 1960s (Cohen, 1972, 1980). At the time, the two opposing teen gangs – Mods versus Rockers – came to the attention of the media and the public. Clashes between the two, often at seaside towns at weekends and holiday times, was reported in terms that, to Cohen at least, seemed out of proportion to the scale of the actual phenomenon. There was a sense of outrage and distress, fuelled by the media, which led for calls for action against such youth crime. Furthermore, there was a process of escalation in which the media overstated the situation and attributed to Mods and Rockers much more threat than existed in real life but, at the same time, the Mods and Rockers were attracted by the publicity and excitement that it brought. So there was a sort of spiral which fed public opinion.

A little later, Hall *et al.* (1978) applied the concept to an analysis of those street crimes commonly called mugging. Once again, the perceived threat was greater than the evidence of the real-life phenomenon. Nevertheless, the public feeling was that something had to be done about mugging. This encouraged police activity in the community which, again, could not be justified by the more objective evidence.

The term *moral panic* has commonly been used to describe the circumstances in which demands for new legislation or other forms of legal action are intense. So, for example, the term has been used to describe situations in which there is a high level of demand that action is taken against a particular form of crime or criminal: for example, legislation to deal with child sexual abuse protests against paedophiles living in the community and so forth. While it may be true that emotions are intense in such cases, the term *moral panic* is merely descriptive of the events rather than an explanation of why interest was at such levels. Hall *et al.* (1978) suggested that moral panics tend to occur when two ideologies are in conflict. For example, the Mods and Rockers may have been the result of traditional moral values held by adults and emerging youth cultures with different ideas about the freedom and appropriate lifestyle of young people. It is the conflict between these two ideological positions that results in the moral panic.

Knowledge of crime

There is plenty of evidence that the public's perceptions of rates of crime are rather inaccurate no matter how measured. For example, Ainsworth and Moss (2000) surveyed students at a British university. Not only would we expect students to be more knowledgeable than the general population, but the fact that they had enrolled on an undergraduate module on crime and deviance would suggest that these should be among the most sophisticated about the topic. The students were asked a number of questions and provided with a range of answers:

1. How many crimes were recorded by the (England and Wales) police per year in the 1990s?
   3 million
   5 million
   8 million
   12 million

Only about a quarter correctly chose 5 million. There was a tendency to overestimation.

2. What proportion of officially recorded crimes do crimes of violence make up?
   5%   10%   20%   30%   40%   50%

Again, about a quarter chose the correct answer, 10%. About a half said more than the true figure.

3. What percentage of crimes result in someone being convicted and sentenced in court?
   2%   5%   10%   20%   30%   40%

Only one in ten chose the first option of 2% of crimes. In other words, the vast majority failed to appreciate what a low figure it is.

Without going into other examples of the public's imprecise knowledge of crime, it is clear that it is futile, possibly unrealistic, to expect the public to have an accurate perception of the nature and extent of crime. Some researchers suggest that such aggregate, statistical or actuarial estimates are not realistic expectations of the general public's thinking styles (Howitt, 1992, 1998b). To be able to answer such questions accurately would require an awareness that is possibly not easily achieved. After all, criminologists, sociologists and psychologists would have to obtain the answers to the questions from rather 'dry' official statistics on crime. Perhaps more important is the public's general perception of the extent to which society might be becoming increasingly criminal and risky (Docherty, 1990).

The nature of the fear of crime

In 1977, a survey showed that two-thirds of Polish citizens were not afraid of crime in the slightest (Szumski, 1993). Another quarter said that they were rarely afraid of crime. Overwhelmingly there was little fear of crime in Poland at that time. A few years later, in 1988, 60% of Polish people regarded Poland as a safe country.

Interestingly, the crimes regarded as the most dangerous to society were profiteering, bribery and corruption, appropriation of public property and theft of private property, and abuse of power by persons holding executive office. At this time Poland was still a communist state. Violent crime was scarcely referred to as problematic in any way. Although Polish people at the time perceived their country as safe, surveys in Western nations provided evidence that high levels of fear of crime are common. In Poland, the police gathered crime statistics not in terms of offences known to them but as offences confirmed by the police. Thus the discretion of the police to define a notifiable offence was central to the nature of crime statistics. Crime statistics provided propaganda to shape public attitudes in line with the political ideology of the powerful communist elite. A declining threat of crime was held to indicate progress in building a socialist society. If crime increased then the State would claim that criminal activity was causing the deteriorating economic outlook. Similarly, increasing crime figures justified amendment to legislation, resulting in even more repressive social policies. Szumski argues that the figures were essentially manipulated. Eventually, as crime rates increased, detection rates fell dramatically since the numbers of crimes had been held at unrealistically low levels because of the recording process involved. Fear of crime, it would seem, is not an objective response to the reality of crime. Neither is it a totally irrational thing.

Surveys of the public's fear of crime are now regularly conducted. One of the most useful of these is that of the British Crime Survey, which regularly asks a random sample of the public about a range of crime-related matters including their fear of crime (Allen, 2004). Although those who were very worried about crime have tended to decline in number over the years 1998 to 2003, quite sizeable proportions of the population claim to be very worried about certain types of crime. Twenty-one per cent were very worried about violent crime in 2003 and 15% were very worried about burglary. However, to put this in context, very nearly three quarters of the people surveyed did not have a high level of worry about either violent crime or burglary. Some sectors of society are more fearful of crime than others. Women were disproportionately worried about burglary and violent crime than men. Those over 75 years of age tended to be the least worried about these crimes (this is an unusual finding as generally fear of crime studies suggest that older people have greater fear). People who reported that their general health was poorer tended to be more likely to be worried about crime – those with poor health were nearly twice as likely to report being very worried about burglary than those in good health. Professionals were the least likely to be worried about crime and people living in the most deprived areas tended to be the most worried about crime. People who believed that crime rates had increased in the previous two years were more likely to have high levels of worry about crime.

Traditionally, increasing levels of crime have been regarded as a clear sign of the disintegration of society – that people cannot be trusted any more and that neighbours no longer care. There is a belief that once upon a time doors did not have to be locked for fear of burglars. Whether or not there was such a golden age free from crime has little relevance to modern experience. The fear of crime touches people emotionally in all sorts of unexpected ways. There is little that is common sense or predictable in the fear of crime – the research findings tend to be complex and, superficially at least, a little inconsistent. Some things have been established with some certainty. Most important among these is that the fear of crime has no clear and invariant relationship to the statistical risk of being a victim of crime.

There are three main ways in which our levels of fear of crime might be influenced:

- Our direct knowledge about crimes in the immediate community and beyond. This includes personally being victimised, members of our family being victimised, seeing others being victimised and gossip about crimes in the local neighbourhood.
- The mass media contain a lot of crime news. Our beliefs about crime may be affected from these sources. A number of difficulties are involved when considering this possible connection:
  - media crime news is massively selective in favour of the more serious and sensational crimes (Marsh, 1991; Schlesinger *et al.*, 1991);
  - generally speaking, it is difficult to find a correspondence between the newspaper an individual chooses and their perceptions of levels of crime;
  - people tend to read little of the crime news available to them (Graber, 1980) so it is somewhat unpredictable what information they become aware of.
- Aspects of our personality and social characteristics may make us more or less afraid of crime. For example, Bazargan (1994) found that fear of victimisation at home related to factors such as feeling lonely, having poorer educational standards and believing that one lives among neighbours who are not trustworthy and lack vigilance when it comes to crime.

Examples of the mismatch between fear of crime and the objective risk of being victimised are easy to find. Asked about the risk of violence and their personal fear of it, the elderly tend to report the highest levels (Bazargan, 1994). Yet when we look to see who is statistically the most likely to be the victim of violence the victims turn out to be much the same group as their victimisers for the most part: that is, males in their late adolescent and early adult years – the very group who in some surveys claim to be the least bothered by the risk of being victimised. Clark (2004) describes this as the fear-victimisation paradox, which refers to the often unpredictable relationship between reported fear of crime and personal victimisation.

Women seem to have higher levels of fear of crime than males. Feminists have claimed that women are discouraged from being independent through being inculcated with a fear of an unpredictable attack by a stranger (Walter, 1996). Put another way, this is a means of keeping women in their place. Women tend to fear the sorts of crime that could be perpetrated against them by strangers in public places (Stanko, 1995; Voumvakis and Ericson, 1982). The following should be considered:

- Men are actually most at risk of attack in public places and of attack by a person whom they do not know.
- Women are most at risk from the physical violence of people whom they know. There is also a substantial likelihood that they will be sexually attacked by persons who are relatively close. Date and marital rape are neither rare nor trivial matters (Ainsworth, 2000a; US Department of Commerce, Economics and Statistics Information, 1996).
- Finally, even in the area of child abuse, the public's perceptions and the reality differ. If asked 'what is the most dangerous (risky) stage of life in terms of homicide victimisation?' the temptation is to say childhood. This is not correct except for the first year or so of life when the risk is high. Generally, though, the factual reply ought to be adulthood, especially young adulthood (Howitt, 1992).

Farrall and Gadd (2004) query the extent to which fear of crime is a significant feature of most people's lives. It is one thing to suggest that many people have a fear of being a crime victim than to suggest that people frequently have fears about crime – that is, regularly feeling anxious about possible victimisation. So surveys have suggested that as many as 25% of people are very afraid of certain crimes such as burglary and rape. However, just how often do individuals feel very afraid? The researchers asked participants 'In the past year, have you ever felt fearful about the possibility of becoming a victim of crime?' (p. 128) They were also asked the number of times they felt this in the year and how fearful they felt. One third of participants said that they had felt fearful in the previous year. Nearly 50% said that they had felt fearful between one and four times. Fifteen per cent of the entire sample claimed to have experienced quite or very high levels of fear. However, only half of these were individuals who had felt afraid five or more times in the year. This is a relatively small percentage who felt high levels of fear more than once every three months or so. In some ways, this puts fear of crime into perspective.

Just what is meant by 'fear' in the fear of crime? Clark (2004) asks whether the fear of crime is actually a crime phobia, which like other phobias would be a debilitating condition that can severely constrain a person's day-to-day activities. So to what extent is fear of crime as measured in surveys akin to other phobias? Clark's approach was to take Australian survey data which contained both fear of crime items and items related to various types of phobia. The first thing to note is that the three phobias that she studied – social phobia, blood-injury phobia and agoraphobia – tended to coexist. Those who had a social phobia were more likely to have the other two phobias and so forth: that is, some individuals are more inclined to phobias than others. If fear of crime is a phobia like these other phobias then one would expect that those with high levels of phobias in general would tend to have the highest levels of fear of crime. This simply was not the case. If anything, there was a slight negative correlation between fear of crime and the other phobias. That is, fear of crime has a slight tendency to be lower in those with greater levels of other phobias. So Clark's conclusion is that fear of crime is not like other phobias. Fear of crime was measured for personal crime (violence), property crime, and sexually-based crime. The findings for each type of crime followed the general trend. All of this may indicate that fear of crime measures are not pure measures of a basic psychological emotion – fear. According to Clark, there is no evidence available in the vast literature on fear of crime to suggest that fear of crime is dysfunctional or even completely irrational. She suggests that fear serves protective functions and so to reduce the fear may be to encourage the abandonment of protective strategies.

Theories of fear of crime

Whatever measures of the fear of crime actually indicate, concerns about fear of crime need explanation. There are three significant theories that should be considered:

- cultivation theory;
- availability heuristic theory;
- cognitive theory.

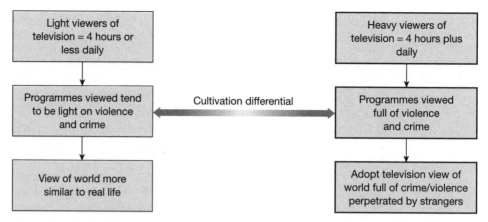

Figure 3.2 Media effects on worldview according to the cultivation analysis model

Cultivation theory

Cultivation theory (Gerbner, 1972) builds on the assumption that the mass media, and television in particular, are means of cultural transmission. The world of television is believed to be full of crime and violence that fails to capture the essence of crime in reality. For example, crime on television is highly biased towards violent acts perpetrated by strangers. A media researcher and theorist, Gerbner carried out numerous immense analyses of the content of American television. The message obtained from the aggregate classifications of the content of programmes is one of a distorted world of crime (Gerbner, 1972; Gerbner *et al.*, 1977; Signorielli and Gerbner, 1988). The viewing diet of heavy viewers of television tends to consist disproportionately of this distorted model. Lighter viewers may prefer to watch, say, news programmes in proportionately greater amounts to the rest of television. Hence, the world that the heavy viewer perceives on television is much more distorted than that experienced by the lighter viewer. In other words, there is a difference or differential between the two groups in terms of the potential of the viewing to distort their view of crime. See Figure 3.2. The basic prediction of the model is that the culture of crime cultivated in the heavy viewer will be more like the television view than that inculcated in the lighter viewer. So since the world of television involves attacks by strangers, then the heavy viewer should believe that he or she is at risk from strangers, for example.

The main things to remember concerning the value of the theory are as follows:

- In Gerbner's analyses, there does seem to be a very weak relationship between heavy viewing and having a distorted perception of crime and violence. This relationship is not due to 'third' variables such as social class which may be related to viewing and perceptions of crime and violence. However, even shortly after Gerbner's studies were first published, other researchers were reanalysing the original data. They concluded that when the influence of variables such as type of neighbourhood and other demographic characteristics of the sample were removed statistically, the relationship between media and fear of crime became negligible or even reversed (Ditton *et al.*, 2004).

- The relationship where it is claimed is very small statistically and dependent on very large samples to achieve statistical significance.

- The relationships may not occur in all communities. For example, the evidence seems to be that the relationship has not been found in the United Kingdom despite a number of studies (e.g. Gunter, 1987). This may reflect a cultural difference, perhaps even a difference in media environments.

Caution must be exercised about these findings. Gerbner's approach is fairly gross in terms of its predictions of effects. Research that predicts subtler relationships between media use and fear of crime may obtain stronger relationships and greater insight into the impact of media coverage on the public. For example, Liska and Baccaglini (1990) examined responses to the questions 'how safe do you feel in your local neighbourhood in the day? at night?' It was possible to predict feeling unsafe in the neighbourhood by reference to the local media coverage. In the communities where people tended to feel unsafe, the local newspapers covered more local crime. The more news about, say, non-local homicides then the less the fear of the neighbourhood.

Availability heuristic theory

Certain sorts of information are more readily available from memory than other sorts of information. This may vary substantially from person to person. Nevertheless, it is important to consider just what happens when approached by a researcher asking about fear of crime in the local neighbourhood. People probably do not spend their days routinely computing risks of being victimised in each location they enter based on statistical knowledge of crime risks. They may feel unsafe in some situations, but this is different. A woman who steps into a car with a man she has only just met at a nightclub may become afraid when she suddenly remembers that a young woman had been found murdered a few miles away having left a nightclub in the same circumstances:

- The *availability heuristic* (Shrum, 1996) suggests that to the extent the media (or any other factor) create a vivid and readily accessible image of crimes in the mind of the individual, this imagery will be rapidly accessed and will partly determine fear of crime.
- Shrum studied the contents of television soap operas over a two-week period. The story lines during this period were reviewed for 'critical portrayals' which are those events that were dominant in the soap episodes. Crime was a major theme and especially rape.
- Consequently, the viewers of the programmes should have rape imagery more readily available. Those who did not watch the programmes might be expected to have less rape imagery available.
- The availability heuristic hypothesis was supported. Viewers were quicker in answering questions such as 'What percentage of women are raped in their lifetime?' This appeared to be a specific effect and not related to the general amounts of television the individual watched.

These findings are supported by other research (Vitelli and Endler, 1993). These researchers used a more general measure of the availability heuristic. They based their index on the number of crimes participants knew of through the media, but other information in addition:

- the number of times they had personally been victimised;
- the information they had obtained from other people.

For men, one study showed that the availability of media imagery went together with a lack of a belief that they could cope with victimisation situations. For women, the media were also important. Additionally, higher levels of fear were also associated with their general levels of anxiety.

Cognitive theory

Winkel (1998) points out that much of the research indicates that there are two distinct components of emotional vulnerability:

- The subjective belief about the likelihood or risk of the event.
- The belief about the seriousness of the consequences of experiencing those events.

He suggests that these are much the same dimensions that emerge in the study of the fear of crime. The first element he calls the *subjective victimisation risk* and the second element is the *perceived negative impact* that would result from victimisation. Thus fear might be seen as reflecting the product of risk and seriousness. The implication of this is that increased fear of crime will follow from events such as being a victim or seeing a news programme about a particular crime – that is, if the following apply:

- The event makes the individual aware of there being a risk of victimisation and of the consequences of victimisation (i.e. the priming effect).
- There is an increase in the subjective victimisation risk or the negative impact or both increase as a consequence (i.e. the change effect).

An example may be helpful. An American in, say, Dallas sees on the television news of a serious bank robbery in Germany. This probably will not prime that person's awareness of his or her own risk of victimisation. The distant events in Germany will not impact on the viewer's fear of crime. On the other hand, take the case of a woman who sees a television programme about rape. She may discover for the first time the extent of the violence and humiliation that may be associated with rape. This may well increase her fear of victimisation.

An important aspect of Winkel's theory is the relative independence of risk and seriousness in the creation of fear. It is possible to imagine events in which the risk perception increases but the seriousness perception decreases. For example, a household has just been burgled. Members of the household rightly discern that the risk of them being a victim is higher than they previously thought. However, in their case the burglar simply took some money and did not foul or ransack the place. The householders also find that they were less bothered and disturbed by the burglary than they had previously imagined. In these circumstances, the seriousness perception may move to regarding the crime as less serious. More generally, downward comparison processes may achieve adaptation or coping: that is, the development of the view that one got off lightly compared with what could happen or what has happened to other people. In this theory, fear is hypothesised to be a product of risk × seriousness. So, in some circumstances, although the perception of risk has increased this may be compensated by the reduction in the perception of seriousness. In other words, there is no change in fear of crime. Figure 3.3 presents this schematically as a model.

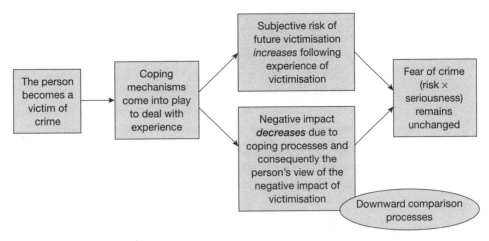

Figure 3.3 Winkel's model of the fear of crime
Source: Winkel, F.W. (1998) Fear of crime and criminal victimisation. *British Journal of Criminology*, **38**, 473–84.
Reproduced by permission of Oxford University Press

Of course, downward comparison processes may not be possible in all crimes. For example, does the rape victim whose rapist is acquitted in court following a court hearing in which her character is besmirched show such processes?

Winkel (1998) reports empirical evidence in support of the model based on research on a variety of crime victims compared with a control group:

- Over a data collection period of about two years, there was evidence that the subjective victimisation risk perceived by victims converged with that of the non-victim control group.
- If anything, in terms of the negative impact of being victimised, the gap between the victims and the controls increased. Victims saw less of a negative impact from further victimisation than did the control group. This is just what the theory suggests would happen.

Nevertheless, we need to understand better the victims for which these compensatory processes do not appear to work. The evidence that some victims are profoundly affected by their victimisation in terms of stress and distress (Miethe, 1995) suggests that we have much to learn about the public's perceptions of and fears about crime. Predicting who is most at risk of the consequences of victimisation is one important task to be faced (Winkel and Vrij, 1998).

Chapter 4 discusses psychological concepts related to victimisation.

Alternatives to the statistical/actuarial models

One advantage of the availability heuristic hypothesis is that it does not assume that everyone will have the same experiences and imagery of crime, even when it is obtained 'second-hand' through the media. Thus the relative failure of the cultivation approach to gain empirical support does not impinge on the availability heuristic theory. This, in itself, does not mean that the media and personal direct experience factors have no impact on the level of fear experienced in different situations by different individuals. Despite what has already been written, the levels of fear of crime and the asymmetry between statistical risk and fear of crime may be overemphasised (Gilchrist *et al.*, 1998). These authors prefer to interpret the evidence as follows:

- Fear of crime is actually at fairly low levels.
- The differences between men and women are not particular startling. For example, the British Crime Survey (Home Office, 2001b) indicates:
  - burglary: 18% of males claim to be very worried compared with 26% of females;
  - mugging: 12% of males being very worried compared with 26% of females.

Thus the idea of people being confined to their homes through fear of crime is more of a stereotype than a reality. Gilchrist *et al.* studied groups of men and women in Glasgow. They compared groups consisting of fearful men, fearful women, fearless men and fearless women:

- Fearful people irrespective of gender give victimisation of others as a source of fear. They also were apprehensive about the possibility of a serious offence following on from a relatively minor one. A fear of a particular type of assault was not mentioned but the possibility that a weapon might be used was given as a reason for fear.
- Fearless people tended, for example, to feel less vulnerable because they took precautions and could cope.
- There were differences between the sexes in terms of how they talked about the fear of crime. These were smaller, though, than the differences between members of the same sex who were high or low on fear of crime.

Main points

- Although crime has an impact on the public, the public also has an impact on crime either directly or indirectly. Victims of crime may or may not decide to report events as a crime and public opinion may influence government and police policy on crime, for example. All aspects of the process of criminal justice may be influenced by the public although perhaps in rather indirect ways.
- Surveys have demonstrated many aspects of the public's attitudes towards crime and there is at least some evidence that relatively tough attitudes are expressed about the ways in which criminals should be dealt with. However, it would appear that the public have a rather poor understanding of such matters as the extent of crime and trends or patterns in criminal activity.
- The fear of crime is both a researcher's and a policy maker's concept. Surveys of the general public's levels of fear of crime are now regularly conducted on behalf of some governments. The fear of crime is not at similar levels throughout all sectors of society. It has proven notoriously difficult to understand the fear of crime as it does not seem to follow commonsensical patterns. There is little relationship between fear of crime and the objective risk of being a victim. Researchers have questioned whether the fear of crime is as central to most people's lives as some surveys suggest.

Chapter 4

Victims of crime

Overview

- Gradually, victims are becoming a priority in criminal justice systems. Changes have been made that work to the benefit of victims in recent years, for example, the increasingly sympathetic treatment of rape victims by many police organisations and sensitivity to the needs of child witnesses. Governments increasingly have an interest in demonstrating their concern. Care has to taken not to reproduce the basic problem of early victimology, which was to directly or indirectly hold the victim partly responsible for their victimisation. An alternative is to concentrate on how psychology can help the victim.

- Restorative justice is justice that concentrates on the harm done by crime to its victims though victims can be widely defined to include the offender and their family. All parties should come out of the process of restorative justice feeling that they have been dealt with fairly. Some criminal justice systems include reparation for the victim although currently in some countries this is confined to cases involving young offenders.

- Post-traumatic stress disorder (PTSD) is a consequence of serious trauma of which some crimes such as rape and extreme violence are examples. There is some argument that repeated but apparently relatively minor events such as criminal victimisations may accumulate to have a similar effect. Flashbacks to the events and nightmares are among the characteristics of the condition. It is a psychiatric condition listed in the *APA Diagnostic and Statistical Manual* since 1980. There is evidence that post-traumatic stress disorder is associated with the consequences of having committed a crime. A substantial minority of homicide offenders show symptoms.

- Psychological help for victims of post-traumatic stress disorder has to recognise that suppression of the memories which leads to their re-emergence in flashbacks is counterproductive. The victim needs to work through the memories repeatedly using methods such as structured trauma writing.

- Victims, whether or not severely affected by the experience, have to make decisions about whether or not to report the crime to the police. Usually it is the nature of the crime which determines whether or not it will be reported. It is common for victims to talk with others before deciding to report the crime or not. Often they receive advice about what to do and act in accordance with that advice.

- The decision to report a crime is dependent on the rewards for reporting and the costs, emotionally arousing crimes tend to be reported more commonly, and the social push from those around the victim to report the crime.

Until relatively recently, victims of crime had few rights within the criminal justice system. Things have gradually begun to change but the needs of victims may still appear to be peripheral to the massive effort and resources put into dealing with offenders. Nevertheless, there has been progress in many areas such as allowing vulnerable child witnesses to give evidence through video links. There is also clear evidence that victims have become a major focus of government policy in many parts of the world. One major stimulus to this was the influence of the feminist movement, which highlighted the plight of victims of domestic violence and rape, for example, and provided support to victims. Governments have begun increasingly to resource organizations dedicated to the needs of victims. In increasing numbers of countries, schemes are being introduced to provide financial compensation to victims. The United Nations Declaration of Basic Principles of Justice for Victims of Crime and Abuse of Power recommends the improvement of access to justice and fair treatment for crime's victims in terms of restitution, compensation and social assistance. The rhetoric used by governments is one of 'balance' in which the rights of the victim are contrasted with those of the perpetrator of the crime (Edwards, 2004). This has enormous popular appeal, of course. Edwards suggests that this shifts responsibility for crime more towards the community and less on government. Furthermore, it allows 'good customer relations' to be the criterion of crime policy success rather than reductions in crime figures. Crime is, of course, a political 'hot potato'.

In criminology, *victimology* developed to describe the interface between the victim and the offender. That is, the characteristics of the offender which are linked to being victimised. This was sometimes criticised as being anti-victim since, in a sense, it could be construed as an exercise in holding the victim responsible for their victimisation. After all, everyday explanations of crimes such as rape include the suggestion that the victim was 'asking for it' by dressing provocatively. The proper study of victims avoids such an implication and, for example, may see victimisation as involving the offender choosing their optimum victims. The term *victimology* is used in a more general sense more recently to denote the study of the victim in all respects. Often in modern usage the term *victim* is replaced by the term *target*. This has the advantage that it emphasises the decision-making processes of the criminal rather than the characteristics of the offender's chosen victim as such. This has resulted in numerous important findings about the experience of being a victim and the patterns of victimisation. Among the important findings concerning property crime, for example, are:

• Trickett *et al.* (1995) were interested in what household characteristics are predictive of property offences, particularly burglary and theft by persons given admittance to the property. Some of their findings are of considerable importance. The group that, in general, was most at risk of being a victim of a property offence was the young professional worker household. Indeed, for all of the locations studied the pattern was consistent: the young were most victimised, followed by the middle-aged, followed by the retired. Professional workers (irrespective of the age of the householder) were more likely to be a victim than non-professionals. It is noteworthy that the area where the research was carried out had a substantial bearing on the findings. Retired, non-professional households that were the least at risk in one area had substantially more risk than a young professional household did in another area: that is, the area influence was massive compared with household lifestyle. Property crime was associated with locations in which there are high proportions of households *not* owning a motor vehicle. Intriguingly, it was not such relatively poor households that were actually the most at risk. Instead, the households of professional individuals living in a detached or semi-detached property in those poor areas were the most at risk. Poor people living in wealthy areas were similarly less likely to be victimised. There was a substantially elevated risk of being victimised if one had just moved home.

- Trickett *et al.* (1992) showed that high-crime areas are not simply areas where many more individuals get victimised. In this study the researchers assessed personal crime – involving coming into contact with the criminal directly. The high-crime areas are those where repeat or multi-victimisation is much more common. These are not modest increases. Victims of crime in these areas suffer three times the number of victimisations that they would if victimisation were randomly distributed throughout the community.

- Further research by Ellingworth *et al.* (1997) provided similar data that confirmed this general finding about risk of victimisation. They studied car theft, burglary, theft from the person and assault. In the cases of car theft, burglary and assault, there was evidence that prior victimisation substantially elevates the risk of those crimes compared with similar households without prior victimisation. Property crime carries a 70% extra risk for those who had been victimised within the previous four years through burglary or assault. More specific relationships include the fact that prior burglary virtually doubles the risk of burglary and prior assault similarly doubles the risk of a member of the household being a victim of criminal damage.

The important message in all of this is that crime victimisation follows patterns. These patterns cannot be understood solely on the basis of psychological characteristics of the victim – indeed, much of this research makes no reference to psychological characteristics but uses geography and knowledge of the everyday activities of offenders in terms of the territory that they inhabit and visit.

Forensic and criminal psychology has yet to focus on the victim as a major issue for research and theory. Nevertheless, there are important issues that are beginning to be addressed. In this chapter we will deal with some psychological issues which are to do with victims. These include the psychological effects of victimisation.

Box 4.1

Key concept: restorative justice

One emerging trend in criminal justice systems around the world involves the concept of restorative justice. This is primarily a practice-led activity and not a theoretical idea originating from psychology. It refers to processes involving some sort of mediation between the offender and the victim. According to Wright (2002), there are a number of characteristics of restorative justice:

- Restorative justice concentrates on the harm caused by crime not the criminal activity in itself.
- Those who are harmed are the focus. Thus crime's victims may even include the offender and the offender's family. Children may be construed as victims of the crime because, say, their father has been sent to prison. Consequently, the child may no longer have the positive benefits of his or her day-to-day parenting. Visits may be infrequent because of transport difficulties to a prison which may be several miles away. Social stigma may affect adversely the children of offenders (Philbrick, 2002). The consequences of crime spread very widely. One can include

▶

police officers in the list of victims, for example, because of the trauma that dealing with distressing crime may cause them.

- Healing and reintegration are the main objectives.
- The ideal outcome from restorative justice includes a satisfied victim and an offender who feels that they have been dealt with fairly. Thus the process of restoration is the focus, not merely financial compensation for the victim.
- The community is involved in the outcome.
- Integration of parts of the system so that victims and offenders, in dialogue with one another, identify the pressures that led to the crime (e.g. social and economic pressures). In this way, the process can inform community crime reduction strategies.

Although restorative justice programmes have been in existence since the 1970s, the term itself was first used in the 1980s. The community benefits from restorative justice as well as the victim. Victims benefit in a variety of ways – the opportunity to express their emotions in the presence of the offender, the opportunity to be forgiving and a possibility of peaceful coexistence of the offender and victim in the community. The process of restorative justice may take quite some time. For example, some victims are not open to the idea immediately after being victimised and will not talk about restorative justice procedures immediately after the offence. It may take them time before they become receptive to the idea. Some victims may never be willing to be involved. Restorative justice is largely administered and organised by mediation services. They work with victims and offenders in order to enable the process to work. This may be difficult because it may be counterproductive to pressurise victims into participating.

Some countries such as Australasia and England and Wales have included reparative procedures into some legislation. However, they have chosen to concentrate on young offenders (under the age of 18 years). The mediation service elicits the victim's proposals for reparation or compensation following an instruction from the court. Wright (2002) suggests that although a criminal act has taken place, the criminal courts may not be the best way of dealing with it especially in those cases which occur from within a relationship and involve a dispute between two or more parties.

Post-traumatic stress disorder and victims

The characteristics of PTSD

One frequently mentioned consequence of victimisation is the risk of post-traumatic stress disorder (PTSD). Being a victim of crimes such as rape and extreme violence is traumatic for many victims and they may have great difficulty dealing with the psychological consequences of the trauma. Although PTSD is an extremely familiar idea, it is important to be clear as to its major characteristics. None of the characteristics alone define the condition but collectively they help establish what post-traumatic stress disorder is. These characteristics include:

- Repeatedly reliving the trauma in the form of being disturbed by intrusive flashbacks of the events during the day. At night, the events may be incorporated in nightmares. Anything that reminds the victim of the distressing incident may be avoided. Things like the anniversary of the trauma can lead to renewed upset. Because of the intensity of some flashbacks, victims can believe that they are experiencing the events once again. Unlike normal autobiographical memory for life events, which is largely verbally coded and stored, flashbacks are overwhelmingly full of vivid sensory detail such as loud sounds or other images though they tend to be of a somewhat fragmentary nature (Brewin and Holmes, 2003). Intriguingly, good working memory capacity (which is an individual's ability to 'hold and manipulate' material which is the focus of attention) is associated with the ability to exclude unwanted ideas from intruding into activities. In this way, the intrusions are prevented from adversely affecting performance on the activity. Since flashbacks are also intrusions into thought, it might be expected that those with good working memory capacity should be less affected by flashbacks. Low intelligence, which may be associated with poorer working memory capacity, is a risk factor for post-traumatic stress disorder (Brewin, Andrews and Valentine, 2000).

- Profound depression and possible thoughts of suicide.
- Sleep disturbances of all sorts. Some may have difficulty sleeping, some may sleep for abnormally long periods.
- Oversensitivity to noise. Such noises cause a startle response since the fight/flight reflex is heightened.
- Paranoia or fear of others: the victim may feel afraid of the reoccurrence of the traumatic event which causes them to be uncomfortable with people who may be their future victimisers (Broken Spirits Network, 2004).

In a forensic setting, post-traumatic stress disorder is more likely to be assessed against the psychiatric features of the condition. The diagnostic category of post-traumatic stress disorder was first introduced into the *Diagnostic and Statistical Manual of the American Psychiatric Association* with the release of DSM-III in 1980. The current version of the *Diagnostic and Statistical Manual* (DSM-IV) requires that the following criteria are met in order to apply a diagnosis of post-traumatic stress disorder. In many respects, these are more stringent and precise requirements than those we have just described:

- There needs to be a clearly defined traumatic event in which a person experiences or witnesses a death or its threat or a threat to the bodily integrity of themselves or others. The response at the time should involve helplessness and/or horror and/or intense fear.
- The symptoms should be present for at least a month.
- There is clinically significant distress or significant impairment in important areas of the individual's functioning socially, at work, or other aspects of life (Grey, 2002).

It is the presence of certain memory phenomena (flashbacks/dissociation) that distinguishes post-traumatic stress disorder from other conditions such as depression and anxiety (which may occur in PTSD).

PTSD among offenders

Of course, there is nothing in the nature of PTSD which in itself implies that only victims can suffer. Pollock (1999) raises the superficially paradoxical question of whether perpetrators of crime also suffer PTSD. There are two main possibilities why there might be a link between offending and PTSD: (1) that a person suffering post-traumatic stress disorder has a heightened propensity to act violently. Hence the association is that PTSD leads to violence. For example, battlefield trauma leading to PTSD has been implicated in later antisocial behaviour according to Pollock; (2) that the person who commits an horrific violent act cannot cope with the act and develops post-traumatic stress disorder. In this case, we have the reverse association that violent experiences lead to PTSD. Both may be true, of course. However, Pollock notes research which identified 2% of criminals as having PTSD before committing their crime but 15% showed the symptoms after committing the crime (Collins and Bailey, 1990). This would be consistent with both of the above sequences. Pollock argues that the key thing about a homicide which may lead to post-traumatic stress disorder in the offender are circumstances when an individual's beliefs about themselves are undermined by the event. If the violence were unplanned, for example, then the risk of trauma is heightened because that violence is not seen by the offender as part of their personality or character. A sample of homicide offenders was studied by Pollock of which 42% exhibited the criteria for a post-traumatic stress disorder diagnosis. It was found that reactive violence tended to be associated with PTSD – that is, non-goal directed, unplanned, angry aroused violence typically directed at a known victim considered by the participant to have contributed to the offence by provocation (p. 193). Typically it was controlled and inhibited offenders who show PTSD and not psychopaths.

Cognitive and other factors in PTSD

Quite a lot is known about the sorts of factors associated with the trauma or the victim which may lead to post-traumatic stress disorder:

- Intense levels of feelings of helplessness, fear, or horror at the time of the traumatic event are associated with the likelihood of PTSD six months after the traumatic event. However, post-traumatic stress disorder may occur without such high levels of emotion at the time. According to Brewin, Andrews and Rose (2000), 89% of people who went on to have PTSD following a traumatic happening reported such intense responses. However, 44% of those reporting intense levels of these emotions failed to manifest PTSD later. Thus there would appear to be about 11% of individuals who experienced traumatic events who did not experience intense levels of helplessness, fear or horror, who nevertheless did develop PTSD. However, it is worth noting that the 11% who did not manifest these emotions actually reported high levels of anger or shame.
- PTSD is associated with negative beliefs about the world (including the self and others) following trauma. Victims tend to believe that the trauma has caused a permanent negative change in the individual and their ability to achieve life goals (Brewin and Holmes, 2003). These negative feelings are not necessary at the time of the trauma but may be a consequence of later appraisal processes.
- The onset of PTSD is more likely in those who demonstrate 'dissociation' during traumatic events (although not those who show dissociation later). Dissociation is when the sense of possessing a single identity which links our life stages together is temporarily disrupted (Brewin and Holmes, 2003).

Situations that threaten an individual's life have a high likelihood of promoting PTSD. Nevertheless, subjective beliefs about the threat to life can be even more influential than size of the actual threat. Understanding the cognitive processes involved is important to understanding PTSD (Brewin and Holmes, 2003). One important explanation is that the trauma actually destroys core attitudes, beliefs and assumptions about the nature of their world and the victim's ability to cope with it. For example, the belief that other people are benevolent and well-intentioned may be shattered by the traumatic event. Someone who is subject to a malicious attack may find this difficult to reconcile with a sense of community conducive to positive social relationships. Of course, people will naturally try to cope with PTSD themselves. However, research suggests that simply attempting to avoid the disturbing thoughts is counterproductive since it may delay recovery. Social support is important in recovery though the presence of negativity in the support network is worse than having little or no social support (Brewin and Holmes, 2003).

Theoretical accounts of post-traumatic stress disorder clearly have a variety of aspects of memory to explain as much as anything else since PTSD refers to memory phenomena. Among the main theories explaining the condition according to the important review by Brewin and Holmes (2003) are the following:

- Stress response theory (Horowitz, 1986): The traumatic event fundamentally disturbs the victims's beliefs about the world, the future and themselves. The new view and the old view are very different. Prior to victimisation, the individual may feel competent and in control of their lives and the situations they face. Following the trauma, the victim may see themselves as vulnerable and driven by external events rather than being personally driven. Traumatic events produce a complex psychological situation in which the victim needs to avoid memories of the traumatic event since those intrusions are distressing but, in order to deal with the traumatic events, the victim also needs to relive the traumatic events through memory. Flashbacks, intrusions and nightmares provide an opportunity to process the old cognitions of the world alongside those brought about by the trauma. So there is a defensive mechanism (avoiding memories of the trauma) and the healing mechanism (working with the memories) which are fundamentally in opposition to each other.

- Conditioning theory: Keane, Zimering and Caddell (1985) suggested that PTSD involved a two-state process along the lines of Mowrer's (1960) two-factor learning theory. The traumatic events naturally produce a fear response such as when an individual's life is at risk in a hostage situation. At the same time, aspects of the traumatic situation which, in themselves, do not have fear evoking properties actually are conditioned to be fear arousing by association with the fear response. For example, if the hostage is threatened with death by a man wearing a red cap then a red cap may become capable of evoking fear. Avoiding memories of the event by blocking or suppression merely ensures that the normal processes of deconditioning cannot operate – that is, normally, thinking of red caps would gradually cease to evoke fear. However, avoidance of red caps is rewarding in that it is associated with reductions in fear levels. So avoidance is conditioned. The consequence of this is that the PTSD is maintained and healing cannot take place. Brewin and Holmes (2003) suggests that one of the weaknesses of the theory is that it deals ineffectively with the types of cognitions that are associated with PTSD since it concentrates merely on a simple conditioning process.

- Dual representation theory (e.g. Brewin *et al.*, 1996): This suggests that ordinary memories and traumatic memories are fundamentally different processes. Trauma memories are problematic when they are dissociated from ordinary memories. Recovery from PTSD is partly dependent on transforming the trauma memories into ordinary memories (so-called narrative memory). This alternative memory system is known as 'perceptual memory' and it consists of information that has had little or no conscious processing. Perceptual memories are not verbally coded whereas narrative memories are. There is research which suggests that people fail to actively perceive things in their field of vision that are not expected. This is known as inattentional bias. Despite being unaware of these things they may nevertheless affect the individual. Brewin points out that some trauma victims claim that they have not noticed, say, shots fired at the scene of the trauma. Perceptual memories for highly emotional and important things may be long lasting. Therapeutic improvement will occur when the elements of the traumatic situation are substantially encoded into the narrative memory. Until this stage, stimuli like the red cap will trigger the intense perceptual memory. Once the red cap is more likely to trigger the more reasoned and processed cognitive narrative memory, then the power of the intrusive memories of the trauma is disabled.

Trivial crime and PTSD

So far we have discussed PTSD in terms of the traumatic consequences of very serious criminal acts. However, despite this, is the assumption of seriousness crucial to the development of PTSD necessary? What of the plight of people who suffer repeated but trivial criminal victimisation? We can readily apply the concept of PTSD to serious criminal acts such as rape or some other serious sexually violent incidents. Shaw and Pease (2002) argue that the police, for example, are not able to deal with the multiple trivial incidents that profoundly impact their victim in the same way as they can deal with the clearly traumatic incident such as rape. Some provisions for the support of rape victims are sophisticated multi-agency initiatives employing carefully trained personnel. There is another reason why the neglect of seemingly trivial incidents is unsatisfactory. It fails to acknowledge that early trivial incidents may well lead to something much more serious. Shaw and Pease give details of an interview with a woman victim who had noted that children and drunkards were often to be seen hanging out around a hostel for the homeless which was close to her home:

> [they] use the wall outside as a toilet . . . the drunks sit at the bottom of the stairs and I'm scared of them throwing bottles through – this is what happened before. I wish someone would move them on. The police know but the CCTV doesn't cover that bit – the station and the alleyway on the back of the shops behind the building. About eight drunks loiter there most nights to drink because there's an old carpet they can sit on. I'd come down the next day and the windows would end up being put through again.
>
> *(p. 43)*

Her complaint was largely about what might happen to her and the sources of her concern were trivial. Despite this, it eventually culminated in a situation in which the victim and her property were attacked. According to Shaw and Pease, successive minor incidents may make it increasingly difficult for the victim to cope. Furthermore, if other stress is occurring in the individual's life perhaps, say, as the result of a bereavement then the effect of the repeated trivial victimisations may be worse.

Psychological help for victims

It is inevitable at the moment that the front line psychological support for victims comes largely from friends, family, police officers and others largely untrained in psychology. Even in the medium term, psychological support is often provided by people less than fully trained in psychology such as volunteers and police officers (Winkel and Blaauw, 2001). It is difficult to assess the value of such support. Winkel and Blaauw argue that one common error made by such personnel is to assume that victims compare themselves with someone better off than themselves by deciding that 'I am worse off than . . .'. This is termed an *upward comparison process*. However, victims are much more likely to employ a *downward comparison process* in which they compare themselves with someone who is worse off than themselves.

As already mentioned, one approach to dealing with memories of trauma is through the use of structured trauma writing. This may employ homework exercises as well as one-to-one interactions with support workers. Structured trauma writing provides the victim with the possibility of self-confrontation, self-disclosure and emotional disinhibition, and something called narrativation. By employing self-confrontation the traumatic events are effectively relived and so the intensive traumatic response to those events may become extinguished. Describing the traumatic events in words in a form of self-disclosure is therapeutic. Pennebaker (1995) provided a number of exercises based on the fundamental assumption that when stressful/traumatic experiences are articulated into words, physical and mental health are improved. Thus he claimed that talk about traumatic events may lead to fewer medical problems, better work performance and even better immune functions. In this context, narrativation is the construction of a story or narrative about the distressing and traumatic events.

Winkel and Blaauw (2001) asked a group of people to ventilate their deepest fears and emotions about a traumatic event; another group (downward comparison) was encouraged to write about the ways in which they were doing well in comparison to other groups; and the third group engaged in a rather trivial writing process (about, for example, their plans for the next day). The downward comparison condition was much more effective than the emotional expression condition in terms of clinically significant improvements in terms of intrusion symptoms. Examples of intrusions would include having difficulty sleeping because ideas and thoughts about the traumatic events keep occurring and thinking about the events when one did not mean to. On the other hand, avoidance symptoms were better improved by emotional expression writing. Avoidance symptoms include avoiding letting oneself get upset by thoughts of the events and trying not to talk or think about the events. Stone *et al.* (2000) explored possible therapeutic processes which are involved in the use of structured trauma writing. There was no evidence that improvement was the result of lowered levels of perceived stress, improvement in the quality of sleep, changes in affect or changes in the use of medications.

Victim decision making

Victims are the major gatekeepers in the process that brings a crime into the ambit of the criminal justice system. Three fifths of crimes in the United States are reported to the police by the victims (Greenberg and Beach, 2001). Other important groups of people responsible for reporting crimes include the police themselves and bystanders who have witnessed a crime. Whether or not a crime gets reported is largely determined by the nature of the offence. The characteristics of the victim are rather less important. Although the seriousness of the crime has an influence on reporting, the perception that there is a benefit to be gained from reporting the crime to the police is more important. Thus the theft of a motor vehicle is highly likely to be reported because it is necessary to do so in order to make an insurance claim. Furthermore, crimes involving violence, especially if they result in injury, have a high likelihood of being reported.

Although there is plenty of evidence from social psychological research, for example, that bystanders may be influenced by the social situation not to intervene, there is limited evidence to suggest that bystanders may influence the process by which a victim decides to report a crime. Experimental research has been carried out in which a bogus crime occurred and a bystander attempts to influence the victim to report the crime. The bystander was influential on the actions of the victim especially when the victim was the sole victim – that is, there was no co-victim (Greenberg and Beach, 2001). Field research indicates further the extent to which victims of crime talk with other people about their victimisation. The precise figures vary somewhat according to the type of crime involved. The majority (78%) of victims of sexual assault at a rape crisis centre talked to others about the crime and of these 76% received advice and of these 84% followed the advice. A similar pattern occurred for a sample of burglary, theft and robbery victims who had reported the crime to the police. Sixty-two per cent talked to others before reporting the crime, 58% of these received advice and 95% of these followed the advice. Of course, these are victims who made the decision eventually to report the crime. It is difficult to generalise from this to victims in general, many of whom decide not to report the crime.

To understand both reporting and non-reporting of crime better, Greenberg and Beach (2001) contacted a sample from the community at random by telephone. Anyone agreeing to take part was asked whether they had been a victim of a crime in the previous 12 months. Those over 18 years of age who had been victims of burglary or theft and were personally responsible for the decision of whether or not to report the crime to the police were interviewed in greater depth. About half had reported the crime to the police. Again, a majority (three-fifths) discussed the crime with others before making the decision of whether or not to report the crime to the police. Family members (60%) and friends (24%) were the major categories of people with whom the events were discussed. Mostly (i.e. in 61% of cases) this social contact was actually present when the crime was discovered. Forty-seven per cent of those who talked about the crime before making the reporting decision had also received advice from that other person. The researchers then studied the relative influence of a number of predictors of reporting or not using logistic regression (see, for example, Howitt and Cramer (2005) for a readable account of this complex statistical procedure). The most powerful factor in the decision to report the crime to the police (once demographic variables such as age, sex and race had been taken into account) was the type of advice given by those around the victim. So, if the advice was to call the police then this was extremely influential in the sense that the victim would call the police in a high proportion of instances. The type of crime was important since burglaries were much more likely to be reported than theft. The financial loss had a significant but small influence on the willingness to report as did generalised arousal which is a sort of measure of the emotional response the victim had to the crime.

However, it would be wrong to think that this is simply the consequence of social influence. This would be to assume that the victim had no independent view of whether or not to report the crime since the other person may simply agree with what the victim had decided in the first place.

Greenberg and Beach (2004) studied how victims of property crime decide to report the crime to the police. They tested the idea that the decision-making process includes three broad mechanisms:

1. Reward/costs driven – basically are the gains of going through the reporting process and possibly court appearances as a witness sufficiently warranted by the monetary value of their loss. If the value of the loss is small then victims will be less likely to report the crime to the police. In the study, this was measured on the basis of the amount stolen in dollars.

2. Affect driven – the arousal of emotion on being victimised may influence reporting in a number of ways. The more emotionally arousing it is then the more their attention will continue to be focused on the crime and the more likely they are to report. Alternatively, a crime that raises fear or anger may arouse patterns of behaviour which involve seeking the protection of the legal system by reporting the matter. Emotional arousal was assessed by asking how they felt immediately after becoming aware of the crime – such as how angry, afraid and upset.

3. Socially driven – the decision to report the crime is taken under the influence of significant social others who advise or inform the victim about what to do. If the victim had been advised to call the police immediately after the crime had been discovered then the report was classified as socially driven.

A sample of victims of burglary and theft was obtained using random telephone contact methods. Eligible participants had to be 18 years of age, had been a victim of ONE of a burglary or theft but no other crime, and was the person who took the decision to report the crime to the police or not to do so. It was found that ALL of the above three explanations for reporting the crime to the police were influential in the reporting process. However, they worked independently in that the effect of each type of variable had a distinct influence from other types. There was no inter-action between the predictors in the sense that, say, those who were very angry and who had received advice to call the police were not disproportionately more likely to report the crime to the police. The victims of burglary were more than three times more likely to report the crime irrespective of the dollar value involved than the victims of theft were. Maybe burglary was seen as a more personally invasive crime than theft.

Main points

- The victims of crime have increasingly been regarded sympathetically as a consequence of a number of changes. The feminist movement, for example, pushed for public awareness of the plight of the victims of crimes such as domestic violence and sexual abuse. It was argued that often the victim was revictimised by the police investigation and the subsequent trial. While elements of this remain, the concept of restorative justice changes the focus of the criminal justice system onto the needs of the victims of crime rather than simply the disposal of the offender through the criminal justice system. It also allows for victims to express their emotions towards their victimiser. A court may seek a victim's proposals for reparation.

- There are many consequences of crime some of which have been dealt with elsewhere such as cycles of abuse. Post-traumatic stress disorder is a psychological state in which the victim is unable to effectively deal with their memory of the traumatic events which the criminal subjected them to. By trying to suppress the distressing memories the psychological processes of healing cannot take place. Nevertheless, the memories are still there and burst through into consciousness in the form of nightmares and flashbacks, for example. Treatment involves working through the memories safely. These memories tend to be sensory motor ones rather than narrative ones. Trauma memories are converted to ordinary narrative memories and so can be dealt with by the victim through a normal healing process which was previously unavailable.

- Victims of crime are also the major source of information to the police. The process by which they choose to report the crime or not is therefore of great importance in the criminal justice system. It is clear that this is a social activity since a large proportion of victims of crime talk the crime over with friends, relatives and others and solicit their advice. The decision to report a crime is influenced by a range of factors including the emotional significance of the crime and the benefits/costs ratio involved in the decision to report the crime.

Chapter 5

Theories of crime

Overview

- There are many general theories relevant to the study of crime, only a portion of which can be classified as psychology. However, it is important to appreciate that crime can be understood from a variety of perspectives and forensic and criminal psychologists can benefit from insights from other disciplines. Theories dealing with more specific aspects of crime are dealt with as appropriate in other chapters.

- Levels of explanation of crime range from the biological/genetic through to the social and economic. Psychological theories tend to be more limited but nevertheless cover much of that range between the biological and the social. The theories described in this chapter are fairly general theories trying to address the broad range of crime. Any reasonably complete understanding of crime should consider every different level of explanation. Few theories operate at more than one level of analysis.

- Theories of crime may be divided into: 1) societal or macro-level theories; 2) community or locality level theories; 3) group and socialisation influence theories, and 4) individual level theories. Most psychological theories of crime would be classified in the last two categories.

- Few, if any, of the theories compete in the sense that they make different predictions about crime and criminal activity. In other words, it is unlikely that one can reject a theory simply because another theory makes better predictions. Few of the theories have been falsified. Rather, they should be seen as complementing or supplementing each other.

- Among theories described and eveluated are: 1) physiological; 2) genetic; 3) intellectual deficits; 4) psychoanalytic; 5) addiction; 6) biosocial; 7) social learning, and 8) social constructionist approaches.

Theories of crime come in a variety of styles, types and shapes. Crime is of concern to a number of disciplines and it is possible to find economic, geographical, sociological, psychiatric, psychological and biological theories – and ones from other disciplines such as social work may have their own distinctive features. Indeed, it might be fair to suggest that forensic and criminal psychology has contributed less theory than some other disciplines. While there is little space here to explore theories from all of these disciplines, they are very relevant to understanding crime from a wide perspective. Indeed, they are almost essential to anyone working in the field of forensic and criminal psychology wishing a broad perspective on crime. Figure 5.1 illustrates the various levels of theories of crime from the societal through the psychological to the biological. (McGuire (2000) adopts a similar sort of scheme and some of the ideas are borrowed from him.) These are not theories in the sense that research can establish which is the best theory empirically. They are alternative perspectives, sometimes on the same matters to do with crime and criminality but, more often, reflecting different aspects.

- *Societal or macro-level theories*: the broadest level of analysis, according to Figure 5.1, comprises the societal or macro-level theories which basically suggest that crime is a consequence of social structure rather than, say, genetic tendencies or psychiatric problems. Marxist conflict theory regards the criminal justice system as a means by which the dominant or privileged classes retain their dominance and privilege. Possibly this is most clearly seen in the way land has become owned whereas once it belonged to nature. More immediately linked to psychology is the feminist analysis that fundamentally assumes that power is gendered in society and that male power is reflected in laws that, for example, have regarded females as the possessions of their fathers and husbands. Another example of a theory that links psychological process to macro-societal changes is the idea that there is a connection between hate crime (e.g. lynchings of black people in post-depression United States) and prevailing economic conditions such as unemployment. Although early evidence claimed a link, the connection is less than clear or consistent (Green *et al.*, 1998a, b).

- *Community or locality theories*: crime is not randomly distributed geographically and neither is criminality. Some parts of cities tend to suffer more crime and others (perhaps the same areas) tend to be home to more than their fair share of criminals. If crime is geographically organised, why is this so? The answers vary somewhat but basically the theories suggest that there is either something different about those areas or that different areas provide different opportunities for criminality. In general, crime tends to be committed fairly close to the offender's home base but, often, with a sort of buffer zone just around home where they do not offend. Within that zone they may not offend because the risk of recognition is high. One suggestion is that the social problems of migrants into these 'twilight' areas are particularly great. They are economically deprived, for example, thus heightening the risk that youngsters, in particular, offend.

- *Group and socialisation influence theories*: these are more about direct social influences on criminal behaviour. In a sense they are about the influence of the group (including the family) on criminality. They vary widely but basically they assume that associates may determine whether or not the youngster gets involved in delinquent activities. These approaches are particularly important if they are regarded as a contrast with the purely individual theories that assume that the roots of criminality lie in the individual.

Societal or macro-level theories

Marxist conflict theory holds that society has evolved in a state of conflict between competing groups in society over material resources and institutionalised power. The dominant class uses laws to control other groups and maintain its command or hegemony.

Robert Merton's strain theory recognises that society's goals (prosperity, achievement, etc.) are only available to a limited few. The rest can achieve the goals only through deviant means. Some of these deviant forms of adaptation are innovative, as in some gang property crime. Others adapt to the strain by retreating into alcoholism, drug addiction, suicide and vagrancy.

Feminist theory holds that criminality is associated with males. Males seek to maintain power in the gendered social system through the deployment of violence against women and, by extension, children. Male control is through their access to power over social institutions such as the law, though relatively powerless men are inclined to the cruder expressions of power which lead to their imprisonment.

Community or locality theories

The *Chicago School* of the 1920s held that there are transitional zones of cities that harbour the greatest levels of crime. These were essentially twilight zones that had been deserted by the middle classes which gravitated to the suburbs. Migrants of all sorts would settle in the transitional zones and experience numerous social pathologies. As their affluence grew, these migrant groups would move to the suburbs and cease to be a crime problem.

Differential opportunity theory explains the patterns of crime likely to be exhibited by individuals in terms of the range of crime opportunities close to home. Different individuals display different modes of adjustment or adaptation to their particular social strains.

Group and socialisation influence theories

Subcultural delinquency theories: youngsters with problems especially to do with the home and school tend to associate with gangs and other groupings in which they can achieve some status. Through criminal activity, delinquent groups may provide an opportunity to achieve a sense of self-esteem.

Differential association theory: Edwin Sutherland viewed criminal behaviour as learned. The circumstances of an individual's upbringing determine their exposure to crime and pressure to commit crime. This theory claims to apply at different strata of society. The process of learning to be a criminal in middle-class communities may encourage exposure to fraud, tax evasion and similar, more middle-class, crimes.

Lifestyle and routine activities: most crime is trivial and impulsive with an element of opportunism. A mix of motivated offenders inadequately supervised by the community plus the availability of suitable targets for crime are the basic requirements of this theory, formulated by Cohen and Felson (1979).

Individual

Personality theories of crimes: Hans Eysenck's biosocial theory is a prime example of this. It emphasises the link between biological factors, personality and crime. Nevertheless, many others have attempted to find the particular patterns of personality associated with either specific crime or crime in general.

Biological theory: Many attempts have been made to identify the particular biological characteristics of offenders – their genetic make-up, brain activity irregularities and hormonal imbalances being typical examples. Evolutionary theories are related to genetic theories but concentrate on just how evolutionary factors lead to the selection of certain genes, including those associated with gender, to be passed on to the next generation (Quinsey, 2002).

Figure 5.1 Levels of explanation of crime

- *Individual approaches*: while no psychologists seriously believe that criminality can be divorced from the social and societal context, some stress the importance of biological and psychological differences as a root cause of criminality. However, distinguishing between the influences of the individual characteristics and more social influences is not very easy at all. Generally speaking, it is not possible to identify personality characteristics that are associated with criminality very precisely. Investigations using traditional psychometric measures of personality to try to understand the characteristics of particular offender groups (for example, paedophiles) have not, in general, produced very convincing findings. There are some aspects of personality types that are associated with criminality. Psychopathy and the somewhat similar antisocial personality disorder are among the exceptions.

Concentrating on psychological theories still leaves us with a considerable range of different approaches to deal with. The theories to be outlined are illustrative of psychological approaches. They also constitute a useful body of theory for any forensic and criminal psychologist since they reflect the range of levels of theory from the biological to the social. Since the theories may be associated with more than one level of psychological theorising, Table 5.1 lists the theories and the types of psychology they reflect. The classifications, on occasion, may be disputed, but it can be seen that as we move down the table the analysis tends to be more social. At the start of the table, the theories are much more biological in nature. Also, it should be clear that some theories are practically confined to a particular type of psychology (e.g. the biological only for the first two) but others such as Eysenck's theory, especially, involves several different types of psychology.

One should appreciate that many of the colleagues that a psychologist works with will have been trained in fields which differ quite significantly from that of psychology. The better able a psychologist is to understand the theoretical orientations of these other disciplines, the better will he or she be able to relate effectively with colleagues such as medics, psychiatrists, social workers and the like. The perspective of psychiatrists is much more medicine-based than the typical psychologist's. Social workers probably will have been trained to eschew genetic explanations of criminal behaviour in favour of societal explanations which depend on social structures such as social class.

Table 5.1 Some theories of crime and the types of psychology they involve

Theory	Biological	Psychoanalytic	Cognitive	Individual differences	Learning	Social
Neuropsychology	✓	✗	✗	✗	✗	✗
XYY	✓	✗	✗	✗	✗	✗
Intelligence	✓	✗	✓	✓	✗	✗
Bowlby's attachment	✓	✓	✗	✗	✗	✓
Addiction model	✗	✗	✓	✓	✗	✗
Eysenck's biosocial	✓	✗	✗	✓	✓	✓
Learning theory	✗	✗	✗	✗	✓	✓
Social constructionism	✗	✗	✗	✗	✗	✓

Neuropsychology of offending

Miller (1999a) argues that biological explanations of crime tend not to be popular among forensic psychologists and criminologists. This is for the obvious reason that there is a vast amount of evidence to suggest important social and psychological causes of crime. There have been numerous attempts to find physiological, anatomical, genetic and similar defects in criminal subgroups such as rapists, child molesters, etc. From time to time biological differences are detected, or so it is claimed, but technical problems make their interpretation difficult. For example, if participants are tested who have lived in a psychiatric or penal institution for a long time, their physiological characteristics may be the result of this long-term institutionalisation rather than the cause of their criminality. A good example of this is the enzyme *serum creatine kinase*, which has been found in higher levels in psychotic patients. Hillbrand *et al.* (1998) studied this in a forensic psychiatric population. It was found that involvement in aggressive incidents was associated with higher levels of the enzyme. Importantly, this was only true of patients on antipsychotic medicine. Those not on such medication showed no such trend. In other words, here is a biochemical difference that is predictive of aggression but only in limited circumstances. So, while it is of interest, this difference does not readily explain aggressive crime in general. Another example is Stalenheim's (1997) study of the extent of psychopathy in a Swedish forensic psychiatric population. He found that the enzyme platelet monoamine oxidase was to be found at lower levels in psychopaths but the levels of the enzyme were not correlated with the amount of criminal behaviour exhibited. A further point should be considered. Even if an anomaly is found that is related to crime, there remains the question of why this anomaly should cause crime.

Head injuries can occur in a number of circumstances: road accidents are a significant cause, especially in young males, but Miller (1999a, also see Miller, 1999b) lists assault, falls, sports injuries and injuries at work. Head injuries can be divided into:

- *penetrative head injuries* in which an object penetrates the skull and enters the brain; and
- *closed head injuries* which may involve fractures of the skull. The damage is actually caused by the force of momentum, say, on the head as an accident occurs and its sudden deceleration. Closed head injuries may cause generalised damage to important parts of the brain. The frontal, temporal and occipital lobes seem especially vulnerable.

Head injury may involve unconsciousness lasting for just a few seconds to a much longer term. Memory and attention are among the cognitive functions that suffer long-term impairment. Furthermore, there are personality changes such as loss of ability to plan and to see the likely consequences of one's actions. Lack of tact is another consequence. The effects of brain injury very broadly are predictable from knowledge of the site in the brain where injury has occurred. This is the consequence of the specialisation of different parts of the brain to serve different functions. An apathetic personality may result from damage to the frontal lobe of the brain. Such injuries also cause a tendency to persist with inappropriate courses of action, a degree of irritability and unrealistic/grandiose thoughts. Such individuals show *disinhibition* – a lack of response to the social niceties that makes behaviour acceptable in most people.

Some fairly well-established, pertinent findings include the following, according to Miller:

- Electro-encephalogram readings (EEG) tend to show higher rates of abnormal electrical activity in the brains of aggressive/violent offenders than other offenders and non-offender controls. Abnormal EEG activity is especially likely in the left temporal lobe.

- Positron emission tomography (PET scan) uses radioactive markers injected into the bloodstream to detect differences in blood flow through different areas of the brain. There is some evidence that metabolism of a chemical based on glucose is lower in parts of the brain for some criminals.

- Offender groups seem to have greater rates of head injury in their medical histories. Frequent loss of consciousness is commoner among them – and this can be a sign of brain injury.

- Difficulties around the time of being born and evidence of early brain damage are associated with violent crime. They are known as perinatal complications.

- There are studies of the effects of brain injury on rates of offending after the injury compared with before. When statistical adjustments are made for the decline of offending with age, there is evidence that there is on average a small but consistent increase in offending rates, certainly of less than 5% of the sample.

Methodological difficulties abound in this sort of research:

- Violent people are likely to get into fights and consequently suffer brain damage. So their violence caused the brain damage rather than vice versa. Perinatal studies, for example, somewhat negate this possibility.

- Some of the samples used may be non-representative. Thus murderers on death row might be disproportionately black, poor and of low intelligence and may well suffer from other disadvantages. In essence, they may be on death row because of these handicaps rather than simply because of their crime.

- Pre-injury/post-injury comparison studies tend to use participants who have been on intensive rehabilitation programmes – that is, the most seriously injured – so a misleading picture may emerge.

- The appropriate comparison figures are difficult. Offender groups tend to be working class – the group most likely to suffer head injury. So without carefully matching on social class, the findings may be misleading.

The biological approach is fascinating in its potential but less practical than at first appears. For example, Evans and Claycomb (1998) found an abnormal EEG pattern in violent criminals with a history of violence who denied that they had been involved in a particular act of violence or claimed to have been guided by external forces such as Satan. They demonstrated extremely strong alpha-type brain wave patterns in the frontal part of their brains. While this is clearly of great interest, whether or not such patterns could be used to distinguish genuine cases of 'hearing voices' from those in which the offender feigns psychiatric problems requires much work.

Evaluation of the theory

Pros:

- Knowledge of a biologically based cause of criminality would contribute to better-targeted treatments. Medical treatments rather than psychological therapy might be considered for appropriate cases. Unfortunately, it is very difficult to establish such a relationship for individual cases except where changes have followed accidents, etc.
- The evidence to date suggests that biological factors have some influence on criminality although they are probably restricted to a small proportion of cases. This possibly applies to the notion of the genetic transmission of criminality though evidence on this is virtually always interpretable in terms of environmental influences also.

Cons:

- We seem to be a long way from fully understanding any biological basis to criminality let alone the mechanism by which this possible influence might operate.
- For most forensic and criminal psychologists, whatever the biological basis of crime, biological approaches at the moment do not deal with the immediate task of helping treat criminals through therapy or with the problems of making assessments about individuals and their future behaviours.

Intelligence and crime

It has been a traditional theme that offenders tend to be lacking in intelligence and, consequently, are somewhat under-equipped to cope with their social and work environments. Countless early criminological discussions of offenders would describe them as typically being feeble-minded. Superficially, the idea that low intelligence leads to criminality is compelling. Low intelligence being indicative of poor learning skills might mean that the individual takes senseless risks, lacks the resources to avoid detection, is unlikely to have good earning power in the workplace and so forth. Some of the factors that are known to be associated with criminality are potentially associated with low intelligence. These factors would include school failure, unemployment and similar characteristics. Nevertheless, few criminal and forensic psychologists seem to regard intelligence as a particularly important factor in crime. There are, of course, some offenders of low intelligence but, in general, these appear to be seen as a special case, not the norm.

Relatively recently the argument that poor intelligence is associated in a causal way to any number of social ills has reappeared – poverty, for example, being seen as a result of low intelligence, genetically determined, rather than social factors. More important to the work of forensic and criminal psychologists is the claim that low intelligence is associated with crime. Herrnstein and Murray (1994) essentially argued that cognitively limited individuals are almost invariably likely to experience and to be involved in social ills. Many psychologists reject this point of view on the grounds that intelligence, as measured by IQ (intelligence quotient) tests, is little determined by hereditary factors relative to environmental ones and that it is virtually impossible to separate the inherited from the environmental influence (Kamin, 1977). Is IQ a fixed characteristic largely determined by poor genetic potential? Is it, on the other hand, more or less affected by the quality of life experienced by the individual perhaps from before birth, but certainly in interaction with parents and others in the fastest stages of development in early childhood? This is an argument that became increasingly common in psychology from the 1970s onwards, especially in connection with the view that a person's race is associated with intelligence, so social disadvantage is an almost inevitable consequence of race rather than racism and discrimination. A wide range of authorities has dismissed such a view (Howitt and Owusu-Bempah, 1994). Some would regard positions such as Herrnstein and Murray's as being part of a right-wing political agenda critical of liberal welfare and other service provisions. If social position is fixed biologically through intelligence, then it is a waste of money to try to change things. Of course, forensic and criminal psychology is subject to political influence in many respects (crime is a political issue) so the political implications of the theory in themselves are not a reason for its rejection.

Cullen *et al.* (1997), going beyond general criticisms of the theory, have systematic-ally integrated the research on intelligence and criminality. They reach the conclusion that IQ is only weakly or modestly related to criminality. More importantly, they regard criminality as being largely influenced by identifiable factors other than intel-ligence. These influential factors are largely amenable to change. If Herrnstein and Murray were right, social welfare policy is misdirected and tougher crime control policies would be a better strategy, Cullen *et al.* suggest. On the other hand, if crime can be affected by welfare provision, then tougher crime control policies are unnecessary and probably counterproductive:

- Cullen *et al.* (1997) reanalysed data crucial to Herrnstein and Murray's point of view. This concerns the relationship between the AFQT (Armed Forces Qualification Test) and various measures of criminality. These measures of criminality included: a) being in the top 10% on a self-reported crime scale, and b) having been interviewed in a correctional facility. The relationships are only modest at their highest. The correlation would be approximately 0.3 between IQ and ever having been interviewed in a correctional facility. However, this correlation is the one obtained if no attempts are made to adjust for the influence of social class which tends to be associated with both of these variables. If socio-economic status is removed from the correlation, then the correlations become much smaller – at best about 0.15. In contrast, in further analyses, it turns out that criminality is more strongly but inversely related to measures such as being religious, expectations of future work and academic aspirations. These relation-ships are not supportive of the theory as they suggest environmental influences are stronger. Furthermore, living in urban environments and low social class are implicated in criminality in precisely the ways that those who believe in environ-mental causes of crime would predict.

- A number of meta-analyses of studies of the relationship between IQ and crim-inality exist. A meta-analysis is a sort of secondary analysis of several similar stud-ies into a particular topic. So it provides us with understanding of the general trends in the research on related themes (see Box 5.1). At best, adult criminality correlates only 0.1 with IQ although it is closer to 0.2 for juveniles. In com-parison, other risk factors correlate with criminality at up to approximately 0.5.

In other words, overall, research reveals the importance of environmental influences more than hereditary ones. This is simply because the other risk factors for crime have a much stronger influence than IQ: for example, criminogenic needs such as attitudes, values, beliefs and behaviours like associating with other delinquents.

Quite clearly, intelligence is a relatively minor aspect of criminality compared to many more social variables. The failure of the Herrnstein and Murray thesis to be sustained by the research evidence should be taken by psychologists as indicating the potential for social and psychological interventions to affect criminality.

Box 5.1

Key concept: meta-analysis

Meta-analysis is based on statistical techniques. The purpose is to combine and summarise the findings of studies on a particular topic. The quality of the studies on which the meta-analysis is based is obviously important. In terms of the effectiveness of, say, cognitive behavioural programmes for the treatment of offenders, a researcher would search every possible database for empirical studies of the effectiveness of the treatment in the penal setting. Unpublished research, which may show different trends, is as important as the published research. The researcher needs to define the domain of interest for the analysis. For example, she may confine herself to studies that use a control group and that measure recidivism in terms of its incidence (whether or not there is any reoffending) versus its prevalence (how often reoffending is done).

The meta-analyst then computes a measure of effect size – this is merely an index of how much effect the cognitive behavioural treatment has on recidivism compared with the untreated control group. Although the original researchers may have expressed this as a difference in means, percentages or any of a range of appropriate indexes, these are converted using simple formulae to a standard effect size index. Although there are a number of effect size indices, the commonest are Cohen's d and the Pearson correlation coefficient. There is a simple relationship between these two and one can easily be converted to the other. Howitt and Cramer (2005) provide a table for doing this. They also recommend the correlation coefficient as the best measure since it is familiar to most psychologists. So the effect size of cognitive behaviour therapy would simply be the correlation between the treatment variable (treated or not treated) and the outcome variable (reoffends within a given time of release versus does not reoffend). If treated is coded 1 and not treated coded 2, and then reoffends is coded 1 and does not reoffend is coded 2, the Pearson correlation between the two variables is the effect size expressed as a correlation coefficient. Some will refer to this as the phi-coefficient.

It is relatively easy to compute a (weighted) average of these effect sizes in order to assess the effects over a range of studies.

Another useful feature of meta-analysis is that it allows the researcher to refine the analysis by examining trends in selected aspects of the data. For example, it would be possible to compare the effect size of cognitive behavioural programmes carried out in the community with those in prison. Any type of difference between studies – the type of sample, the size of sample and so forth – may also correlate with the effect sizes obtained by the researcher.

Evaluation of the theory

Pros:

- If we tease out the biological issue from the ability issue, knowledge that crime is associated to some extent with low ability, low educational achievement and low measured intelligence is useful to psychologists. It suggests that action to alleviate such factors may have a positive contribution to make. This is generally recognised as penal systems frequently offer educational and vocational courses to help remedy such deficits (see Chapter 22). Any assessment of offenders needs to include ability and intelligence testing as this suggests appropriate courses of action.
- We know that crime and criminality are not equally distributed through different levels of social structure. As such, it is attractive to seek simple explanations that justify the status quo. Unfortunately, this quickly turns to a con when it is realised that the case against the theory is strong.

Cons:

- The biological (genetic) approach to social policy generally receives little support from psychologists wherever it appears, though such notions have been disseminated through books and other media to the general public. The idea that social problems are basically intractable offers little for professionals dedicated to reducing criminality. Indeed, it is a good reason for not developing psychological services aimed at offenders as such.
- Even if the theory is regarded as true, it is of little practical value when working with offenders.

Psychoanalysis and crime

Psychoanalysis, especially that closest to Sigmund Freud's original writings, has little to say directly about crime (Valier, 1998). Freud carried out no analyses of criminals and lacked apparent interest in them. He regarded them as manifesting disturbances of the ego that resulted in their incapacity to be honest. Nevertheless Freud had some impact on legal thinking. In 1909 Freud was given an honorary doctorate in law from Clark University, Worcester, MA, United States. This recognised his impact on legal thinking through ideas of unconscious motivation and the like. A number of Freud's followers dealt with crime issues directly. However, other psychoanalysts such as Bion and Bowlby did attempt to treat criminality (Valier, 1998).

John Bowlby is probably the most famous of the 'neo-psychoanalysts' to modern psychologists. This is largely because of his ideas about early separation of a child from its mother. These were enormously influential in terms of justifying social policy about the employment of mothers in the workforce, which was relatively uncommon at the time. Mothers, he indicated, should not work. The reason was that the separation of the ties between mother and baby destroyed the emotional bond between the two that was essential for the effective social development of the child. It was Bowlby's belief that there is a human predisposition to form attachment to others. The primary care givers – usually the parents – are a sort of bedrock for future relationships (Bowlby, 1944, 1951, 1973, 1980). Positive, intimate attachments are required for attachment to be satisfactory, otherwise long-term problems may ensue.

Once the bonds are broken, the child develops in ways indicative of an inability to form functional social relationships.

One of Bowlby's cases (he was a psychiatrist) was the child he called Derek who had been hospitalised for nearly a year starting before he was one. When he returned to the family he addressed his mother as 'nurse' and lacked affection for any members of the family. The period of separation, in Bowlby's terms, resulted in Derek's inability to form social relationships. Indeed, in his study 'Forty-four juvenile thieves', Bowlby showed the role of maternal separation in the aetiology of a number of delinquents. To stress, this was in terms of the 14 delinquents out of the 44 whom he classified as affectionless characters. Maternal separation was rather rarer in the other delinquents he studied. Valier (1998) writes of the notion of latchkey kid being a popularisation of Bowlby's ideas – for latchkey kid simply read potential delinquent.

Another Freudian influence was the way that psychology until the last third of the twentieth century regarded homosexuality as a clinical deviation rather than a chosen sexuality. Where homosexuality resulted in individuals being in trouble with the law their homosexuality could be treated – that is, they could be diverted back to heterosexuality. This is an idea that appears to be singularly old-fashioned in the light of current ideas about homosexuality. Valier quotes East and Huber (1939, p. 93) as saying of a homosexual, 'In treatment every effort was made to release as far as possible his heterosexual drives . . . with treatment, stands an excellent chance of developing his heterosexual possibilities.'

Evaluation of the theory

Pros:

- Some of the ideas, especially those of Bowlby, have been highly influential in directing the attention of researchers from many disciplines towards the impact of early life experiences, especially parenting, on later delinquency and criminality (see Chapter 6).

Cons:

- Few modern psychologists make direct use of Freudian concepts. This is because it is generally considered that when subjected to research, the concepts fail to gain the support of researchers.
- Similarly, the evidence is that, in terms of efficiency and effectiveness, psychoanalytic therapies are not simply extremely time consuming but apparently ineffective.

Addiction to crime

One of the mysteries of criminal behaviour is its persistence in some individuals despite its serious negative consequences. This basic observation has led some (Hodge *et al.*, 1997) to propose that crime can have many similarities to behaviours that are classified addiction. At first, it would seem unlikely that a simple biological explanation of addiction could account for crime – after all, there is no substance that is being introduced to the body, no changes in metabolism or brain activity that have been identified. However, few psychologists specialising in the field of addiction hold resolutely to a purely biological model of addiction. There are a number of socio-psychological explanations to explain at least some aspects of addiction. From this wider viewpoint, addiction is a product of the interaction of personal and environmental factors of which stereotypical biological addiction is merely a part. One consequence of this is that concepts such as addiction to sex or addiction to gambling began to be seen in a different light. Reasons for considering some crime as an addiction include the following:

- Addiction, substance abuse and alcohol abuse all co-occur frequently in criminal populations. The co-occurrence of addictions may imply that addiction prone personalities exist or a predisposition explanation of a similar sort. Co-occurrence does not happen with all types of offence. Take, for instance, sex offending. For such crimes, the evidence for co-occurrence is mixed, at best, and fairly weak overall (McGregor and Howells, 1997). However, there is evidence that the risk factors or antecedents or predictors of addictive behaviour are much the same as those for criminality (e.g. school problems, conduct difficulties in childhood, association with delinquent peers).

- Persistence and escalation: despite the well-known tendency for criminal activity to decline with age – to be a product of youth – this is not so for all offenders. For a minority, antisocial behaviour appears more like a lifelong career (see Chapter 6).

- The process of change: successful treatments are much the same for a variety of crimes and a variety of addictions. They tend to adopt a cognitive behavioural model (see Chapter 22). Furthermore, the processes of change in therapy are not dissimilar for substance abuse and crime (McMurran *et al.*, 1997).

The disease model of addiction is a familiar concept in terms of alcohol and drugs. It assumes a genetic or biological predisposition for addiction. Problem drinkers, as in the Alcoholics Anonymous formulation, cannot be 'cured' but must always abstain. Use is followed by increased tolerance and more use. Withdrawal leads, in this account, to profound distress and craving. There is a disease that is out of control (e.g. McGregor and Howells, 1997). The model usually includes a component of 'predisposition' as well as increased consumption as a consequence of consumption. The consequences of withdrawal in the disease model are seen as severe but eventually the wanting and craving will decline as the disease disappears.

In contrast, the cognitive behavioural model of addiction concentrates on social-psychological influences that are distinct from biological vulnerability of individuals to drugs (McGregor and Howells, 1997). Learning processes are involved and the expectation of rewards from drug taking is powerful. Indeed, the learnt expectations may be more powerful than the biological properties of the substance. Drug taking is seen as adaptive since it is the individual's way of coping with stresses. It is not assumed in the cognitive behavioural model that sooner or later the 'disease' (the addiction) will become out of control. The notion of craving is replaced by the idea that withdrawal effects must be understood in terms of the user's expectations of the consequences of withdrawal.

Kilpatrick (1997) argued that the characteristics of addiction could be found in persistent car joyriders in Ireland. She studied a sample of juvenile offenders incarcerated in a special centre for a variety of car-related offences including taking and driving away, allowing oneself to be carried in a stolen car, careless driving, reckless driving, theft of goods from a car and so forth. Six common characteristics of addiction can be evaluated using the data collected from the joyriders:

- Tolerance: the need for more to produce the same effect. Multiple thefts were the norm, ranging from 50 to indeterminate numbers in the hundreds. Faster and more secure cars were particular targets. Universally, the offenders talked of stealing on demand or when they needed the money.
- Salience: the increasing importance of the addition in the lifestyle. The car joyriders frequently seemed to have abandoned their previous interests in things such as boxing, snooker and video games. Car thefts tended to be episodic – that is, following a drinking session or glue-sniffing episode, the youngsters would steal cars over two or three days, exhaust themselves and take a break to get a decent sleep.
- Conflict: increasing awareness of negative consequences. While all of the youngsters were aware of the negative consequences, whether or not this is increasing was difficult to assess. Certainly, over half of them were trying to stop.
- Withdrawal: distress after a period of non-engagement. Some had absconded from the school to joyride, and absconding is a very common feature of joyriders at other institutions.
- Craving: distress associated with desire to re-engage. Some, but by no means all, had daydreams around the theme of joyriding.
- Relapse: reinstatement after decision to stop or reduce. There was some evidence of difficulty in those who were trying to stop but again this was not universal.

Shoplifting and addiction are related. As many as a third of heroin addicts may finance their use through shoplifting. (See Chapter 7 which includes a more detailed discussion of the relationship between drugs and crime.) Among other evidence, McGuire (1997) describes three case studies that he examined for the components of 'addiction'. He found evidence for the following characteristics of addiction in shoplifting:

- Salience: the dominance of the addictive behaviour in thoughts, feelings and behaviour.
- Arousal: depressed state may precede shoplifting and there is excitement at the prospect or actuality of shoplifting.
- Tolerance: the need for increasing amounts to achieve desired effect.
- Withdrawal: there are aversive states of feeling on discontinuation.
- Relief: this occurs for aversive feelings when activity is recommenced.
- Cessation: leads to a repetition of the activity with complete reinstallation even after a long period of cessation.
- The fit of the data to the above cognitive behavioural model to shoplifting of this sort was generally good.

Like other new theories, it may take considerable time before research indicates just how adequate the concepts are.

Evaluation of the theory

Pros:

- The main appeal of the concept of addiction to crime is that it could explain the continued involvement in criminality of those who are otherwise regularly punished for it.

- Criminals tend to be involved in a wide variety of crimes and relatively few are total specialists. Addiction to crime can be applied widely to the offending patterns of criminals.

Cons:

- Without a good deal of research, it is difficult to know whether the concept of addiction to crime explains anything that cannot be explained using other theories. There is a possibility that the theory merely describes features of some deviant behaviour without explaining why the individual is deviant in the first place.

Eysenck's biosocial theory of crime

Hans Eysenck's contribution to understanding crime was largely an extension of his general psychological ideas. His theory might best be described as biosocial since he believed that genetic factors contributed enormously to human behaviour but they have their effects under the influence of environmental or social factors. Genetic variations substantially influence the psychological differences between people that lead to different propensities to crime (and other sorts of behaviour). During his lifetime, Eysenck was a controversial figure who, seemingly, pushed his theory to the limits. He was well known to the general public for his books on self-measurement of intelligence (Eysenck, 1990), smoking and disease (Eysenck, 1980), pornography (Eysenck and Nias, 1978) and racial differences in intelligence (Eysenck, 1973). His views on crime tended to antagonise academic and practitioner colleagues who found his theorising not to follow from the research findings quite so closely as he suggested. Further, his tendency to relate complex social phenomena to fairly gross differences between people was unacceptable to many.

Genetics

Perhaps the most familiar cautionary tale in this connection is to be found in the difficulties of the *XYY chromosome hypothesis*. The basic genetics of sex is that women have two X chromosomes and men have an X and a Y chromosome in the pair that determines sex. Occasionally, some men are born with two Y chromosomes – that is, XYY rather than XY. This is known as Klinefelter's syndrome. Since the Y chromosome is what makes males male rather than female, then, speculatively, one might suggest that the XYY male is extra masculine. Masculinity is associated with aggression, so the XYY male might be more aggressive – they are hyper-masculine after all. So the idea developed that offenders in places such as prison or hospital may well include a big proportion of XYY men (Price *et al.*, 1966). Later research found that they were rare in the general population of men but more common in men involved in crime. The difficulty for the XYY theory was that these men were not particularly involved in violent crime, but only in non-violent crime (Epps, 1995; Witkin *et al.*, 1976). It is reputed that an American serial killer of at least 13 women, Arthur Shawcross, had this chromosomal pattern. Nevertheless, we can be reasonably confident that, since this pattern has not been shown in other cases, irrespective of what caused Shawcross to kill, the XYY theory does not help us to understand other similar offenders (Coleman and Norris, 2000). Epps (1995) describes a case of an adolescent boy with a very rare XXYY pattern. He was sexually abusive of children. XYY theory is now defunct in the research literature and is discredited among forensic and criminal psychology though one still finds reference to it (but not its failings) in many psychology textbooks.

Some psychologists accept a possible minor influence of genetics on crime. However, this may have little relevance to the day-to-day activities of forensic and criminal psychologists. For example, just how does genetics help psychologists, say, in therapy with sex offenders? In contrast, genetics is an essential feature of Eysenck's theories. In relation to crime, he was convinced that evidence from the study of twins brought up together and separately supported the hypothesis that there is a substantial inherited component to crime. Twins identical in their genetic make-up (monozygotic twins) tend to be much more similar in terms of whether they grow up to be criminal or not than twins who share only half of their genetic make-up (dizygotic twins) just as any siblings. Thus he cites Cloninger *et al.*'s (1978) finding that there is a correlation of 0.7 between monozygotic twins in terms of their criminality versus non-criminality. This correlation reduces to the much lower figure of 0.4 for dizygotic twins. If everything else were equal, then this suggests that genetics makes a substantial contribution to the criminality of individuals. Unfortunately for Eysenck's argument, as several authors have shown (e.g. Guthrie, 1998; Kamin, 1977), all other things are not equal. Monozygotic twins may be treated much more similarly because they are identical, which might enhance their similarity in terms of eventual criminality. He also placed importance on 'adoption' studies. For example, one study involved over 14,000 adopted individuals (Mednick *et al.*, 1994). There was no relationship between the number of criminal convictions the adoptee had and the number of criminal convictions of the adopting parents. However, there was a correlation between the criminal convictions of the adoptee and those of their natural parent. This finding was only true for property crimes such as theft; it was not true for violent crime.

Constitutional factors

Moving beyond the genetic factors, Eysenck, again provocatively, argued that there are physical differences between criminals and non-criminals. The idea that there are morphological characteristics of criminal types was the view advocated by Lombroso (1911). While Eysenck accepted that Lombroso was wrong, he nevertheless was interested in the body types proposed by Sheldon (1940, 1942). Basically, Sheldon's idea was that there are three somatypes or body types:

- *Endomorph*: people who most characteristically lay on fat especially around the abdomen.
- *Ectomorphs*: people who have an overabundance of sense organs and the nervous system and brain compared to their body mass.
- *Mesomorphs*: people with a preponderance of bones, muscles, connective tissue and heart/blood vessels.

Research by Sheldon (1949) suggested that delinquents compared with college students were very endomorphic and certainly not ectomorphic. Other studies, according to

Eysenck, gave similar findings. Crucially, according to Sheldon, the three body types correspond fairly closely to three different personality types:

- *Endomorphs*: relaxed, love of physical comfort, love of eating, sociable, amiable, tolerant and communicate feelings easily (this was called *viscerotonia*).
- *Ectomorphs*: assertive, adventurous, like power and dominance, enjoy risk and taking chances, and ruthlessness (*somatonia*).
- *Mesomorphs*: like privacy and need solitude, are not sociable, are very sensitive to pain and are physiologically over-reactive (*cerebrotonia*).

In other words, body type is related to personality, which itself is related to criminality.

Personality

Eysenck believed that there are three major, largely unrelated, components of personality – *extraversion*, *neuroticism* and *psychoticism*. These dimensions were obtained by the analysis of numerous measures of personality that he developed based on the work of others and his own ideas. The following indicates the characteristics of each of these personality dimensions:

- *Extraversion*: active, assertive, creative, carefree, dominant, lively, sensation seeking and venturesome.
- *Psychoticism*: aggressive, antisocial, cold, creative, egocentric, impersonal, impulsive, tough-minded and lacking empathy.
- *Neuroticism*: anxious, depressed, emotional, guilt feelings, irrational, low self-esteem, moody, shy and tense.

Which are characteristic of criminals? According to Eysenck, all of them. Criminals should show higher levels of extraversion, psychoticism and neuroticism. He has some evidence to support this.

Environmental influences

Nothing described, so far, explains why genetics may be associated with criminality. Eysenck's argument is that criminal behaviour (and other forms of antisocial behaviour) results from a failure of socialisation to stop immature tendencies in some individuals. These immature tendencies include being concerned solely for oneself and wanting immediate gratification for one's own needs. The process of socialisation is responsible for making individuals more social and thus less criminal:

- Antisocial behaviour of all sorts is punished by significant others in the life of the child such as parents, siblings, teachers and peers. The process, according to Eysenck, is through classical Pavlovian conditioning – punishment of all sorts acts as an unconditioned stimulus whereas the planning or execution of the behaviour is the conditioned stimulus.
- So socialisation leads to a situation in which even the thought of acting anti-socially leads to the unpleasant pain or anxiety of the unconditioned stimulus. To avoid this pain or anxiety, the individual avoids thinking of or engaging in antisocial behaviour.

This argument requires one further step in order to explain criminality. Those low on extraversion (i.e. introverts) tend to learn quickly through conditioning whereas those high on extraversion (extraverts) condition much more slowly. (Conditioning is the process by which associations are learnt between our actions and the consequences of our actions.) There is evidence to support the idea of the slower conditioning of extraverts according to Eysenck. Slow conditioning leads to poorer socialisation and hence to greater criminality. Such an argument also explains why crime is characteristically the activity of younger people – they have not had time to become completely socialised.

So why the association of crime with psychoticism? Eysenck explains this by pointing to the wider evidence that psychosis (i.e. severe mental derangement which may involve a poor grasp of reality or delusions) is associated with crime. Furthermore, the characteristics of psychoticism are patently associated with non-conforming and antisocial activities. And why neuroticism? One thing that may explain their criminality is that their emotionality may make them rather difficult to socialise and condition. Hence, the conditioning process fails for a different reason than is employed for extraversion. The other possibility is that being emotional, volatile or hyper-reactive implies that one may well overreact to aversive situations (such as those that are stressful or emotional). If their basic repertoire of responses to situations is antisocial or criminal, then these responses are much more likely in the neurotic individual than the more stable individual.

From the point of view of forensic and criminal psychology, the question of the scientific adequacy of Eysenck's theory is perhaps not the key issue. Its practicality is much more important, although Eysenck believed that appropriate therapy for offenders is dependent on understanding their personality in relation to the socialisation or conditioning process. For example, younger offenders seem more amenable to treatment than older ones. Things to bear in mind include the following:

- Even if Eysenck is right about the socialisation process, a great deal of research has indicated that problematic childhoods are associated with long-term criminality. Understanding the failures of parenting and so forth may be a more practical way of dealing with criminality.
- Very few of the concerns of forensic psychology are addressed by Eysenck's theory of crime. Why, for example, do some men rape and others abuse children? Knowing that rapists and child molesters are extravert, neurotic and psychotic does not help us understand their crimes in helpful ways.

In the final analysis, Eysenck's theory was conceived to be part of a grand conception of human behaviour which became reduced to just a few key variables. However, it bred research and hostility in roughly equal proportions. For most of us, we probably gain very little which is of benefit to our understanding of forensic and criminal psychology through exploring Eysenck's theory in depth. It does warrant some appreciation in so far as it tries to integrate the social with the psychological with the biological. Whether that is a futile exercise compared with the more pressing and immediate tasks of forensic work is another matter. Some issues are still current, such as the relationship between accidents and criminality, which were part of Eysenck's theory since they were both seen as having a similar genesis (Junger, 1994; Junger et al., 1995; Junger and Wiegersma, 1995). Furthermore, the impulsivity of delinquents continues to be actively researched (Ruchkin et al., 1998a). However, researchers seem to prefer a leisure activity/lifestyle explanation of the relationship (Junger, 1994; Junger and Wiegersma, 1995).

Evaluation of the theory

Pros:

- Eysenck's theory was remarkable in its scope. Like some other theories, it was an account of general criminality although he believed that some patterns of personality might be commoner in different sorts of offender. His evidence on this, though, was fairly limited.
- The theory brings together several different levels of theorising.

Cons:

- While other theories described in this chapter lack complete support from research findings, Eysenck's theory has tended to be seen by many psychologists as based on flawed data.
- Although the theory is impressive in that it operates at both the biological and the social levels, in fact the social input is little more than a matter of rewards and punishments. Sociological approaches, for example, have little place in the scheme of things.

Social learning theory

It is widely accepted that children and adults may learn effectively from the actions of another person through a process of imitation. 'Modelling' effects have been a central aspect of social psychological theorising since the early work of Miller and Dollard (1941). They regarded imitation as a form of *vicarious* learning. They extended the notion of learning through conditioning acting directly on the individual to include observing the experiences of other people being rewarded or punished. In other words, Miller and Dollard saw the process of learning being mediated, in part, by the consequences of actions for other people. Much more crucial nowadays is the work of Albert Bandura (Bandura, 1973, 1983). This began in the 1950s and eventually led to his social learning theory. This became a relatively complex theory in its eventual form. His early studies demonstrated that young children imitate the actions of adults, modelling behaviours such as hitting an inflatable clown-doll with a hammer (Bandura and Huston, 1961; Bandura *et al.*, 1963). This is taken as evidence that learning can occur in just a single experience of that behaviour (that is, it is not slowly built up through a process of conditioning).

That learning through modelling can take place is not controversial. What is more of a problem is the usefulness of the theory in explaining the acquisition of antisocial behaviours such as crime and the circumstances in which this behaviour will be reproduced. To suggest that people learn their violent and criminal actions from others is a weak argument. Unless violence and crime are entirely genetically transmitted then inevitably they must be learnt socially in some way. Quite clearly, any explanation of violence and crime in terms of learning is not particularly helpful unless the conditions under which it is learnt can be specified. Violence and crime are not the exclusive means by which goals are achieved. A variety of tactics are involved in achieving goals – working rather than stealing to get a television set being a simple example. As work is a major form of modelled behaviour, how can we explain why there is any crime at all if it is simply through social learning?

Bandura (1977), along with others including, most importantly, Miller and Dollard (1941), recognised that rewards and punishments are involved in the reproduction of modelled behaviour. If a model were rewarded for theft then we would expect that the observer would be more likely to reproduce that behaviour, whereas if the model is punished, for example sent to prison, then we might expect the observer to be less likely to exhibit that behaviour. Bandura developed this aspect of his theory poorly in his later writings according to Bjorkqvist (1997). While this suggests that factors other than observing crime are needed to explain the involvement of individuals in crime, from the point of view of the forensic and criminal psychologist even this does not take us very far. For example, it suggests that criminal behaviour is essentially goal-directed. This clearly contrasts with some sociological theories of crime, which emphasise the circumstantial/opportunity features of crime.

Evaluation of the theory

Pros:

- The importance of social learning theory lies in that it deals with the learning of complex forms of behaviour holistically rather than as a process of slow conditioning.
- Social learning theory stresses the importance of normal processes in the acquisition of behaviour. Hence there is no need to assume some sort of pathology in those who become criminal.

Cons:

- The theory's weak ability to explain under what circumstances criminal behaviour will or will not be learnt means that it has limited explanatory power.

The social construction of crime

It is too easy to regard crime as an immutable thing and to understand the task of forensic and criminal psychologists as being merely to understand what leads some individuals to crime. Crime simply is not a static, universal thing that needs no explanation in itself. There is a very real sense in which crime is made not done. As McGuire (2000) points out, there are no acts that can be called crime – crime is not a distinct type of behaviour. It is not always a crime to take something that does not belong to one against the owner's wishes (bailiffs, for example, may quite legally take away the goods of debtors in many countries). To kill another person is not always a crime. It may be an accident or that person may have seriously threatened one's life. To take a particular drug may be a crime in one country but not so in another. Even history changes what crimes are. In the United Kingdom and some other countries, for example, until recently men could not be raped. That is not to say that previously men had not been penetrated anally by other men but it had not been defined. Stalkers could not be readily prosecuted until stalking was made an offence in some jurisdictions. Furthermore, since in many jurisdictions a crime has not been committed unless there is criminal intent, then the situation is even more complex.

Social constructionism can be banal as an explanation and as such is weak in terms of explanatory power. It is not helpful to speak of knowledge being socially constructed without knowing by whom it was constructed and what ends it served. Such a weak version of social constructionism largely serves to reaffirm that we live in a social world and this profoundly affects all we think and do. Social constructionism is sometimes offered as an 'antidote' to the positivist view that there are natural and largely immutable laws or principles of human behaviour that psychological research should strive to discover. Anyone entering forensic and criminal psychology with such a view will rapidly be frustrated to find how situationally specific and, sometimes, unreplicable findings in the field can be. Examples of the difficulties caused by this, for example, for expert psychological witnesses, are given in a number of later chapters.

A more powerful version of social constructionism is elite social constructionism (Howitt, 1992). This assumes that knowledge does not just happen in society but effective knowledge is that which is produced, disseminated and advocated by social groups of some status, standing or power. Much of this knowledge can be seen as partisan or in the interests of the group promoting that knowledge. This has profoundly affected the law, of course, and has implications for the study of forensic and criminal psychology. For example, the medical profession, especially during the nineteenth and early twentieth centuries, had an immense influence on the way in which many social issues were construed and dealt with (Haller and Haller, 1974). Characteristically, the medical model for studying social problems such as crime is based on the idea that a disease (or pathological condition) is the cause – hence the search for biological characteristics peculiar to criminals. Thinking about drugs is a good example since users are assumed to be seen as 'flawed' psychologically and physically susceptible to the substances in question (Howitt, 1991a, b).

Even more directly relevant to forensic and criminal psychology is the case of serial killers. This concept has its origins in the work of the FBI training establishment at Quantico in Virginia. According to Jenkins (1994), promoting the idea of serial killers was in the interest of the Behavioural Science Unit since they benefited as an organisation from public interest and fear. Indeed, there is some suggestion that rates of serial killing were defined in ways that made it seem more prevalent than it probably was. For example, statistics on serial killing have been manufactured that include all cases in which someone was murdered but apparently by someone unknown to them. This inevitably results in spuriously high estimates of the amount of serial killing. Other examples of the effective social construction of issues to do with crime include child abuse, domestic violence, sexual abuse, date-rape, marital rape and other issues which have been particular projects of feminist groups. That the way in which we regard crime and criminals is socially constructed does not mean that there are not serious problems such as child abuse to be tackled. In relation to child abuse, the development of public awareness of the problem does not mean that the problem has got worse, merely that the public nowadays regards violence against children in a different light. The involvement of feminists in these issues was essential to create a shift in ideological foundations of the way they are regarded nowadays. However, one should be aware that the domination of such issues by ideas of male power might create a particular focus of interest and cause the neglect of others. For example, physical and sexual abuse by female perpetrators would be minimised by such a feminist viewpoint (e.g. Straus, 1992).

Evaluation of the theory

Pros:

- The theory encourages awareness of the societal processes that change our ideas of crime and criminals.
- Agencies in the criminal justice system may have their own viewpoints and priorities about the ways in which issues are understood.
- The theory should encourage one to explore the origins of new ways of thinking about crime. For example, the idea of a 'war' on drugs powerfully structures the way in which the policing of drugs may operate.

Cons:

- Social constructionism does not explain crime but it does help us to understand why conceptualisations of crime are what they are.
- Its relevance to the day-to-day activities of forensic and criminal psychologists may be a little remote.

Main points

- Crime can be understood at a number of different levels of analysis ranging from biological factors such as genes through to broad sociological and economic theories. Often they can be conceived as alternative conceptualisations of aspects of crime. Theories at all levels should be part of our understanding of forensic and criminal psychology since they all contribute to a full and rounded conceptual base for the advancement of the discipline.
- Many of the theories probably have very little day-to-day utility in the work of forensic and criminal psychologists. For this reason, the later chapters of this book rarely refer back to these theories but tend to employ much more specific and focused theories instead. Understanding something of the various levels of theory will help facilitate the forensic and criminal psychologist's interactions with other professional colleagues such as social workers and psychiatrists who were trained differently from most forensic and criminal psychologists.
- Most forensic and criminal psychologists will move between theoretical perspectives depending on the matter under consideration. This flexibility can only contribute to the value of the discipline of forensic and criminal psychology.

Chapter 6

Juvenile offenders and beyond

Overview

- Childhood is the starting point of criminality for many offenders whereas, of course, some criminal careers begin in adulthood. While delinquent behaviour occurs throughout society, children from some types of family and environment are more at risk of long-term criminality and involvement with the criminal justice system. Childhood conduct disorder, which is a psychiatric condition, seems to share much the same aetiology as delinquency.

- While the risk factors associated with later delinquency and adulthood criminality are well understood, it is a much more formidable task to say precisely what child-hood factors actually cause the deviancy.

- Risk factors for delinquency include problematic parenting behaviour such as inconsistency in discipline and harsh and abusive parenting styles, low intelligence in the child and living in violent or disorganised areas.

- Strong evidence is available that early social interventions can have a substantial effect on children who are at risk. Educational programmes provided to very young children at kindergarten or some other form of pre-school are a good example of interventions that have demonstrated positive benefits.

- A high proportion of sex offenders are young people in their late teenage years or earlier. For example, about a third of the rapists of adult women are under the age of 18 years.

- Delinquents tend to justify their actions using less mature levels of moral reasoning than comparable non-delinquent youngsters. It should not, however, be concluded that young offenders are necessarily incapable of moral reasoning.

- Parents who use violent methods of dealing with situations tend to pass the propensity to violence to their children. These cycles of abuse are among the ways in which children are brought up to be delinquent. A number of mechanisms that may underlie cycles of abuse have been proposed including Bowlby's attachment theory which would propose that the child subjected to violent parenting develops an insecure attachment style which leads to violent methods of dealing with important relationships.

- It is difficult to research the different patterns of criminal careers despite the potential importance of the field. For example, some individuals will offend only during their adolescence, many are spasmodic offenders who offend from time to time more or less throughout their life though they do little offending in adolescence, and some begin their offending career with any regularity quite late on in life.

For many offenders, the roots of their criminality are manifested in childhood. Important differences between the childhood of criminals and that of others may exist even at birth – perinatal factors may be involved in future criminality. Criminality can result from poor parenting, can be learnt from parents and others, can be encouraged by some types of community and can be affected by the greater opportunities for crime available in some types of community. It is more likely to result from all of these things and more. Although many of us do things at some time in our lives that could potentially lead to criminal convictions, a large proportion of convictions accrue to a small number of individuals. Their criminal activity often begins young and continues for much of their lifetime, as we shall see.

Crime runs in families, to a degree. It is concentrated in a small number of families. Over a third of United Kingdom prisoners claimed that they had a family member also in prison (Walmsley *et al.*, 1992). The trend is even higher for juvenile offenders. Farrington *et al.* (1996) assessed the prevalence of convictions among males with family members who had been convicted of an offence compared with those with family members who had not been convicted. Fifty-three per cent of those with a convicted family member had a conviction themselves; 24% of those without a convicted family member had a conviction themselves. Most family relationships showed this trend – father, mother, older brother, younger brother and older sister. Only the criminality of the younger sister was not predictive. Genetic factors in the inheritance of criminality or adverse family circumstances may be the reason for these intrafamily trends. In truth, it is impossible to disentangle genetic and environmental factors in these data. Indeed, the strongest relationship between family and own criminality is not explicable on either of these bases. Eighty-three per cent of males had a conviction if their wife had a conviction. Only 35% of men whose wife did not have a conviction herself had a conviction. Wives share neither genetics nor parents with their husband. Thus factors such as early environment and heredity are irrelevant to explaining this finding. The concentration of convictions in certain families is such that 1% of the families were responsible for nearly 20% of the convictions. Half of all convictions were the responsibility of just 6% of families.

Most young offenders in custody (in the United Kingdom) are convicted for a number of offences. Rarely are young offenders imprisoned for a single offence (Skett and Dalkin, 1999). Young offenders have a varied repertoire of offending behaviour and recidivism rates are high. Seventy-five per cent reoffend within two years of leaving prison. This is important. It suggests not only a broad criminal repertoire for incarcerated young offenders but that they are highly likely to be quickly reconvicted. Research suggests that for 8–25-year-old males, most offending occurs at about 16–17 years (Farrington, 1990). After this, offending rates tail off to a plateau. Those convicted earliest tend to become the most persistent offenders. Those convicted six or more times are likely to have future convictions in adulthood. Put another way, Farrington (1987) reported that, in London, children rated most troublesome at 8–10 years of age by their peers and teachers amounted to about a fifth of the age cohort. They made up over two-thirds of future chronic/repeated offenders. To illustrate this, Tracy *et al.* (1990) found that boys with five and more contacts with the criminal justice system made up only 7.5% of the age group. Nevertheless, they were responsible for three-fifths of all recorded offences including homicides, rapes and aggravated assaults.

The data seem to indicate that young offenders may be broadly classified into two groups:

- those with a career of delinquency by the time they become adolescent, which is likely to continue into adult crime, and
- those whose delinquency is temporary and confined to their adolescence.

Criminogenic factors in childhood

Understanding just how some families are more vulnerable to rearing delinquent children is not the simplest of matters. Although one can find a number of studies that demonstrate an association between family characteristics and delinquency, convincing evidence that these are causal relationships is harder to come by. Johnson *et al.* (2004) argue that problematic parenting is an important mediating variable in the intergenerational transmission of aggressive and antisocial behaviour. That is to say, parents who have manifested aggressive and antisocial behaviour have offspring who manifest the same characteristics because these are the consequence of problematic parenting. They studied data from New York State mothers who had been interviewed in 1975 when their children were between the ages of 1 and 10 years. The sample was reinterviewed (obviously with some attrition of sample size). Data collected at various stages could be used to assess the important aspects of parenting behaviour and antisocial and violent behaviour. Official investigation records of arrests and charges during an individual's lifetime provided the key information on the dependent variable of criminal activity. Problematic parenting behaviour had been assessed during interviews at various stages. The sort of behaviours in question were inconsistent enforcement of rules by the mother, use of guilt to control the child's behaviour, arguments between the parents in front of the child, problems in controlling anger with the child and so forth.

Even after controlling variables such as parental education, parental income, offspring age and offspring gender, problematic parental behaviours were found to be commoner in parents who had a history of antisocial behaviour. The next stage was to identify whether problematic parental behaviour was related to the antisocial behaviour and aggressive behaviour of the offspring. The researchers found that these were related just as expected. Statistical analysis revealed that problematic parenting was responsible since the relationship between parental antisocial behaviour was related to offspring aggressive behaviour before but not after poor parenting behaviour was controlled. This means that poor parenting behaviour is the mediating factor in the process. There is plenty of evidence from other countries of the relationship between inadequate patterns of interacting in families and delinquent behaviour. In Spain, Arce *et al.* (2004) found that a measure which asssessed inconsistent, harsh or abusive parenting, parental rejection and coldness, inadequate supervision of the child by its parents, little parental involvement with the child, and lack of affection in the family was associated with greater levels of deviant and antisocial behaviour as well as delinquency.

The major childhood factors associated with future criminality are well known. Some researchers may dispute whether these factors actually *cause* delinquency and adult crime. All researchers accept the utility of these correlates in identifying the sorts of children at most risk of becoming criminal. Several authors have reviewed aspects of this research. Haapasalo and Pokelo (1999) concentrated on the longitudinal research (that is, studies involving the assessment of children at different stages of childhood) into the effects of aspects of parenting. These studies go back to the earliest and seminal studies of Glueck and Glueck (1962, 1968) whose work began in the 1950s. The evidence strongly supports the view that the following are antecedents of antisocial and criminal behaviour:

- punitive child-rearing practices and attitudes (including corporal punishment, strict discipline, authoritarian attitudes);
- lack of love or rejection;
- laxness (poor monitoring, lack of supervision);
- family disruption (separations, divorce, instability, marital conflict);
- deviant parental characteristics (criminality, substance abuse, mental problems).

Of course, parenting style is only one aspect of childhood. Many factors are associated with both delinquency and adult crime (Yoshikawa, 1995), suggesting that the two have similar origins. While the important factors are fairly well agreed by researchers, they vary in nature and are extensive. So delinquency, Yoshikawa argues, is the product of the interaction of a multiplicity of factors occurring in a number of settings. These settings include school, home and the community. The *risk* factors she believes to be involved include:

- neurological and biological factors;
- the child has low cognitive ability as measured by low IQ or poor educational achievement;
- the child has a history of antisocial behaviour;
- parental substance abuse;
- violent or socially disorganised neighbourhoods;
- media violence.

The above are single factors which act independently of each other. There are instances of complex interactions where the presence of two or more factors makes the risk of delinquency much worse than the sum of the separate effects. This 'multiplicative' tendency is illustrated by her next five factors:

- perinatal difficulties (i.e. around the time of birth) were associated with low socio-economic status and the presence of family adversity;
- lone parenthood, though probably to do with cases of poor parenting or low socio-economic status;
- insecure attachment of the child to parent made worse by poor parenting, unplanned birth, life stress and low social support;
- parental criminality made worse by early family conflict;
- poor or harsh parenting made worse by marital discord.

There are also instances of buffering effects of second variables which reduce the risk:

- poor or harsh parenting effects are reduced by emotional and community support;
- low socio-economic status effects are reduced by good parenting and age-appropriate verbal ability.

A few factors on the list, such as the effects of media violence, are rather more controversial than she implies (see Chapter 8 for a detailed discussion of media effects on violent crime). Nevertheless, give or take the occasional quibble, the thrust of the evidence is agreed by most researchers.

Of course, some might argue that the predictive factors are so intertwined that it is impossible to say exactly which factors cause later criminality. For example, conflict between parents and the self-confidence of the mother may be interrelated. If they both tend to occur together, it is difficult to know which is the most important. Furthermore, there are some criticisms of some studies as they are dependent on how offenders remember their early family environment. Such recollections may be inaccurate or self-justificatory. However, there would seem to be enough evidence from studies that do not use such *retrospective* procedures to negate this view. For example, McCord (1979) used information from a study of parenting behaviours obtained from counsellors who had visited families. Thirty years later she collected data on their children's criminal behaviour in the ensuing years. She found that characteristics (as measured between 5 and about 13 years of age) such as the following predicted the child's criminality:

- little or casual supervision of the child;
- mother's lack of affection for the child;
- conflict between the parents.

Statistically, such parenting variables in combination actually identified as serious adult criminals about two thirds of men who had no record of offending as juveniles. Furthermore, if one considers those with juvenile criminal records, the parenting variables indicate which go on to have an adult criminal record reasonably well.

Similar trends seem to emerge in countries culturally and geographically very removed from the Western location of the majority of studies. For example, research findings in northern Russia support those from elsewhere quite well. Ruchkin *et al.* (1998b) studied a group of delinquents of 15 to 18 years of age. These were compared with a similar group of non-offenders. Their delinquency was fairly serious but consisted of repeated thefts in the main. A few were more serious cases such as rape and murder:

- Some types of aggression in the delinquents were best predicted by the father's rejection of the boy.
- In contrast, for the control, non-delinquent group, rejection by the boy's mother was associated with aggression.
- According to information obtained from self-reports, delinquents scored higher than controls on rejection and overprotection by both mother and father (Ruchkin *et al.*, 1998c).
- Delinquents also claimed to have problems such as bodily complaints, feeling anxious/depression, difficulty in paying attention, feeling withdrawn and a number of others. It is not clear that these problems are the result of parenting styles since there was little relationship between bodily complaints and parenting styles.

It is not only natural families that can cause problems. The consequences of fostering and institutional placements on children should not be neglected. While these children are clearly ones most likely to have difficulties, the problems are sometimes worsened by such alternative arrangements. Foster placements as well as institutional care can exacerbate, and sometimes cause, problem behaviour. This, of course, may be one way in which long-term criminal careers are maintained during childhood.

D. Browne (1999, 2000), as have others, showed that there is a strong relationship between problem behaviours (such as running away and destructive tantrums) as reported by foster parents and breakdown of the placement. The consequence may well be multiple-foster placements for a child with worsening problems.

Continuity of childhood and adult antisocial behaviour

Let us summarise some of the factors associated with youthful and adult criminality (according to Farrington, 1995; Skett and Dalkin, 1999; and West, 1982):

- large family size;
- low family income;
- poor accommodation;
- criminal parent or siblings;
- poor parenting such as disinterest and inconsistent discipline.

This list is very similar to the factors associated with the aetiology of psychiatric disorders. Not surprisingly, then, researchers have examined more directly the relationship between psychiatric disorder and criminality in childhood. *Childhood conduct disorder* is defined in the *Diagnostic and Statistical Manual of the American Psychiatric Association* (APA, 1987) as disturbed behaviour in childhood which persists for more than six months (see Box 18.1). The behaviours taken to indicate this disorder are at best antisocial and, in some cases, may be regarded as criminal. Table 6.1 lists some of these criteria. In order for the diagnosis of childhood conduct disorder to be applied, a child must exhibit three or more of the types of behaviour listed in the table. In other words, if not showing a range of criminal activities, they

Table 6.1 Diagnostic criteria for childhood conduct disorder and antisocial personality disorder

Childhood conduct disorder: three or more of the following	Antisocial personality disorder: four or more of the following
Animal cruelty	Debts repeatedly defaulted on
Broken into buildings or cars	Drives recklessly or when drunk
Cruelty to people	Employment history unstable
Destroyed property	Impulsive
Destruction of other people's property	Lacks remorse
Fire-setting deliberately	Lies repeatedly
Lies often	Neglects children
Runs away from home overnight more than once	No monogamous 1 year plus relationships
Stolen more than once	Physically fights repeatedly
Truants frequently (the list includes other things)	Steals and vandalises repeatedly

are demonstrating strong antisocial tendencies. Table 6.1 also lists some of the criteria which can be used to identify an individual as suffering from *antisocial personality disorder* (ASPD). Antisocial personality disorder is discussed in Chapter 19. Basically, it is evidenced by an individual showing a range of criminal and other antisocial characteristics which are grossly at variance with social norms. This adult condition is not completely identical with that for childhood conduct disorder, but there are considerable similarities. Indeed, the individual must have exhibited conduct disorder as a child to be classifiable as having ASPD as an adult. There has been considerable research into the factors associated with childhood conduct disorder and ASPD. The research ranges widely from large-scale demographic studies to investigations of a small number of factors. Nevertheless, there is a degree of consistency in the research findings concerning the two conditions. This led Farrington (1996) to argue that childhood conduct disorder and ASPD share much the same aetiological precursors. These precursors, according to Farrington, include:

- low family income;
- poor housing;
- large family size;
- convicted parent;
- harsh or erratic parental discipline;
- low intelligence;
- early school leaving.

These are factors similar to those that predicted delinquency.

Data from several stages of the *Cambridge Study of Delinquent Development* support the sequential progression of antisocial behaviour. This study was begun in the 1960s by the famous criminologist Donald West, though the psychologist David Farrington became associated with the long-term project a few years later. It was (and is continuing) longitudinal research in which the same group of boys is studied intensively at different points in their lives. Data have been collected, as part of the study, on a large number and variety of factors and characteristics that may be associated with criminal offending. Care has to be taken not to assume that these factors are proven causes of delinquency and adult crime. They may be, but proof in this area is notoriously difficult. While the measures taken in the Cambridge study do not overlap precisely with those in the *Diagnostic Manual*, composite measures from the study are available on variables which strongly reflect childhood conduct disorder and ASPD. Antisocial personality as assessed from data collected at ages 10, 14, 18 and 32 years was explored in terms of possible predictors from the rest of the data. Table 6.2 gives the best predictors out of the vast range of different precursor variables for the variable antisocial personality.

Although it contains merely part of the findings, Table 6.2 reveals important things. Crucially, there is a very strong relationship between having characteristics of antisocial personality at one stage and demonstrating antisocial behaviour at later stages. These later stages include adulthood. Of interest, but less important, is that having fewer friends at age 8 years is negatively related to antisocial personality behaviours: that is, youngsters with few friends tend not to become criminal. Nevertheless, apart from their lack of crimes, Farrington points out that such individuals are somewhat dysfunctional as adults – misfits. Having few friends, though, may protect them from peer group pressure which otherwise might have encouraged them to commit offences.

Table 6.2 Major predictors of antisocial personality at different ages

Age group	Best predictors of antisocial personality
10-year-olds	Poor parental supervision Low school attainment at age 10 Poor child-rearing by parents at age 8 High neuroticism
14-year-olds	Antisocial personality score at age 10 Separated from parent at age 10 Low non-verbal IQ at age 8–10 years Many friends at age 8
18-year-olds	Antisocial personality score at age 14 years Convicted parent at age 10 Father not involved at age 12 Father unemployed when child was 14 years
32-year-olds	Antisocial personality score at age 18 years Convicted parent at age 10 years Did not stay at school Hospitalised for illness at age 18 years

Convincing as this may be, the Cambridge study covers the later stages of child-hood into adulthood. There is good reason to think that problems develop at an even younger age than that. Haapasalo and Tremblay (1994), using kindergarten classes containing children of low socio-economic class in a French school board in Montreal, explored antisocial behaviour especially aggression. The main features of their study were as follows:

- Kindergarten teachers rated the behaviour of each boy in the study – over 1,000 remained in the longitudinal follow-up. This included aggression such as fights other children, kicks, bites, hits other children, bullies or intimidates other children.
- The children were grouped by fighting patterns:
  - stable high fighters were high fighters in kindergarten and continued to be in at least two subsequent years;
  - high fighters with late onset were not fighters in kindergarten but became so in subsequent years;
  - desisting high fighters: high fighters in kindergarten but declined in next two or three years;
  - variable high fighters: some years were high fighters, other years were not;
  - non-fighters at any time.
- They were assessed on an index of family adversity based on parents' ages at birth of their first-born child, amount of schooling parents had and occupational status.
- The children provided information about the parents' parenting behaviour: Do your parents know your whereabouts when you go out? Do your parents know with whom you are spending your time when you go out?

- The measure of punishment was based on questions like: Do your parents punish you by slapping or hitting you? Do your parents punish you by not letting you do things you would like to do?
- Parents' use of rules was assessed by such questions as: is there a rule at home about the time to come home in the evenings?, is there a rule at home about how much time you can spend in front of the TV? and so forth.

Stable fighters – those who remained aggressive at each stage of the study – differed from the other groups in terms of background. They came from the more socially disadvantaged home environments according to the index of family adversity. The boys who were classified as non-fighters tended to be the most carefully supervised by their parents and they received the least punishment of all of the groups. Perhaps the most important finding in the present context was that delinquency scores at early adolescence (ages 11 to 14 years) were higher for the groups who fought most in early childhood than the other groups. That is, the consistently violent boys in early childhood were especially prone to delinquency.

Similar continuities between childhood behaviours and later criminality have been found in very different cultures. Viemero (1996) reports longitudinal data from Finland. Again, there was evidence that later criminal behaviour was commoner among youngsters who were identified as more aggressive in childhood and by higher levels of violence in their favourite television programmes.

Social interventions to reduce delinquency

Is it possible to reduce criminality and future criminality in youngsters through social interventions? Does, for example, providing parents with support to improve their parenting compensate for the effects of a poor home background? Early childhood is not too young for initiatives to be effective ways of reducing delinquency. Yoshikawa (1995) argues that to wait until the children have grown into delinquent adolescents before intervening is a mistake. Not to intervene much younger overlooks the findings from decades of criminological, sociological and psychological research. Yoshikawa analysed the outcome of the 40 existing evaluation studies that met certain criteria. These requirements were as follows:

- The intervention should involve the groups of children most at risk of delinquency/ antisocial behaviour. Children with low birth weight and those living in low-income families are examples of this category.
- The intervention should take place between the prenatal stage (i.e. prior to birth) and primary school entry.
- The researchers should study the effects of intervention on juvenile delinquency or the risk factors for long-term juvenile delinquency.

Included were two main sorts of intervention aimed at a variety of factors believed to affect the risk of criminality. These are described below together with the broad trends in the outcomes of these interventions:

- *Educational programmes* focusing on the children involved such provisions as part-time kindergarten or pre-school of one sort or another. Although not all studies evaluated all possible outcomes, there was consistent evidence that children receiving the educational intervention were cognitively (intellectually) more advanced than those who did not.

- *Parent-focused family support programmes* involved matters such as regular home visits from a professional in childcare. The results of these studies seem a little more varied and with mixed success. Some find improvements in the intellectual functioning of children whose parent receives the intervention but others show little difference. Parenting skills also showed mixed outcomes and there were few differences, if any, between the children in terms of antisocial behaviour.
- *Combined family support and early education.* This group of studies showed the most promising outcomes of all. Cognitive abilities of the children and parenting abilities were all improved. Most significantly in this context, antisocial behaviour (aggressive and delinquent behaviour in the long term) was reduced by this mixed intervention.

To be sure, such interventions were costly but not so costly as delay would be. An economic analysis compared costs of interventions with the cost to society dealing with delinquent children in the criminal justice system. Early intervention programmes were more cost effective in these terms.

Despite this, it is remarkable that there are very few evaluation studies of interventions with children who currently offend or who are at high risk of offending in the near future (Nee and Ellis, 2005). It is clearly not very practical to try to research the effects of interventions on future delinquent offending because of the long timescale involved. So, instead, Nee and Ellis studied the influence of intervention on the recipient's scores on a powerful risk and needs assessment tool known as the LSI-R. This stands for the Level of Service Inventory – Revised (Andrews and Bonta, 1995). It measures many of the risk factors which we know are associated with offending. Consequently, it forms a convenient indicator of the success of any treatment programme. About half of the young people were in the age range of 7–12 years of age. Data on police charges were also available. This may be less useful as the police may avoid criminalising such young people if at all possible. The youngsters were overwhelmingly male and they had largely committed offences against property although a small number had supposedly committed sex offences. In some cases, they had referred themselves for help but more usually they had been referred by social workers, their parents and so forth. The programme (The Persistent Young Offender Project) included a range of practices:

- one-to-one mentoring in order to help the youngster reintegrate into the school;
- group work addressing life problem-solving, anger management, victim awareness, interpersonal skills, substance misuse, appropriate sexual behaviour and health;
- self-esteem and social skills building activities such as music, art and drama.

Compared to a similar group with little experience of the programme, the number of police charges for members of the treatment group declined during their time on the programme. Furthermore, risk as assessed by the LSI-R also declined in the treated group. Thus interventions to deal with delinquent behaviour can be effective even with those who are actively delinquent.

Young sex offenders

For whatever reason, many researchers have ignored juvenile sexual offences. This is a surprise given the intense research activity into child victims of sexual abuse. Young offenders, international statistics show, form a moderate proportion of sex offenders (Langstrom, 1999). His figures for Sweden suggest that, compared with their high levels of offending in general, the sex offending of young persons of 15–20 years is low. Nevertheless, over 10% of rape, sexual harassment, child molestation and sexual harassment offences can be attributed to this age group. Children under the age of 15 cannot be criminally prosecuted in Sweden or be subjected to the standard forensic psychiatric evaluation of sanity.

The corresponding figures for other countries, especially the United States and the United Kingdom, seem higher. Note, though, that the age ranges reported are not identical to those used in Sweden. Based on UK Official Criminal Statistics (crimes recorded by the police), sexual offences by offenders under the age of 18 years may include as many as 30% of the rapes of adult women and perhaps up to a half of all sexual offences against children (Langstrom, 1999). British surveys of victims (in which the general public are questioned directly about their experiences of various crimes) suggest that youngsters of less than 18 years carry out over a third of sex crimes against children. Data from the United States indicate that about half of sexual offences against boys and a quarter of sexual offences against girls are committed by young people.

Are the characteristics of childhood that predict general delinquency the same as those that predict sexual delinquency? Langstrom's (1999) sample was all 15- to 20-year-olds that had been subject to the *Forensic Psychiatric Examination* over the period 1988–95. These young sexual offenders had extensive previous histories of sexually abusing others. For example, young sexual offenders brought to the attention of the authorities for the first time already had an average of seven victims. Over a quarter of sexual offenders of 12 or more years of age had a previous history of sexually abusive acts. The predictors of sexual offending included:

- early onset of sexually abusive behaviour;
- male victims;
- multiple victims;
- poor social skills.

These are rather different from the factors predictive of non-sexual delinquency discussed earlier. Not surprisingly, then, in Langstrom's study when we exclude sexual recidivism, general reoffending is predicted by some of the factors we are already familiar with:

- previous criminality;
- early onset (childhood) conduct disorder (DSM-IV);
- psychopathy (PCL-R);
- the use of death threats/weapons at the time of the index offence (the offence which led to the offender being included in the researcher's sample).

Thus the childhood origins of sex offending may be specific ones to that type of offence.

Box 6.1

Key concept: protective factors from delinquency

Farrington (1998) suggests that there are four major methods of crime prevention:

- Situational prevention which involves targeting the physical environment in which crime takes place so as to make it difficult to commit a crime but at the same time making sure that the risks of getting caught, for example, are maximised.

- The traditional criminal justice approach involving deterrents, incapacitation and rehabilitation. For example, the prison service in the United Kingdom uses a variety of accredited offending behaviour programmes. One targeted specifically at young offenders, given their typical varied offence history, concentrates on factors such as criminal thinking and pro-social interpersonal skills. Activities would include enhancing socio-moral reasoning, attempting impulsivity reduction, challenging pro-offending cognitions and helping tackle substance use. Given the aggressiveness common to this age group, anger management courses appear effective at reducing angry events as measured from staff checklists by about a third or more (Ireland, 1999).

- The community prevention interventions which are designed to change social conditions and institutions (e.g. families and parenting as we saw earlier).

- The final category of crime reduction strategy Farrington calls developmental prevention. This involves tackling the risk factors involved in youthful criminality.

In addition, he mentions protective factors. Just what is a protective factor?

One might imagine that if, say, poor parenting is a factor that puts an individual at risk then good parenting is a protective factor for antisocial behaviour in childhood. This would equate protective factors with un-risk factors – that is, the opposite pole of the risk factor. We need to go one stage further. There may be many children whose parents are inadequate and unskilled in various ways. Some of these children will become antisocial, as we know from the research evidence. On the other hand, there will be a proportion of children who grow up in similar circumstances who do not become criminal. This is obvious and a fairly commonsensical notion. Not everyone who smokes gets cancer but smoking is a strong risk factor for cancer. Other factors may protect the individual and make it less likely that they will become ill. Just the same sort of argument may apply to crime. There may be factors which if they co-occur with risk factors will reduce the impact of those risk factors. For example, poor parenting may be a risk factor for antisocial behaviour but some at-risk children may have grandparents close by who take a great interest in the child. Grandparents in these circumstances can be described as a protective factor. This is a made-up illustration, so how can we go about identifying risk factors?

One way of looking at the risk-factor approach is to conceive of it as a deficit model – that is, something is missing in childhood which pushes the young person towards crime. They are, for example, deficient in social skills because of the poor parenting they received. There is a more positive approach that tries to see what it is about some youngsters who are faced with the most unpromising start in life which leaves them capable of resisting the impact of a raft of grave life stressors that turn some youngsters criminal. One exemplary approach is to be found in Bender *et al.*'s (1996) study of adolescents in a residential institution. As one might expect, the backgrounds of many of these had much to be desired. The researchers chose to consult with the teams caring for the youngsters in the institutional setting:

▶

- Protected youngsters: the carers were asked to identify examples of youngsters whose backgrounds were inadequate, who seemed to be at risk of developing serious problems, and who, in fact, had turned out to be pretty decent young people who were not problems.
- The risk-succumbing group: a comparison group was formed from nominations of children who manifested high levels of the risk factors but also exhibited serious behavioural disorders.

These two groups were loaded down with similar risk factors (deaths, divorces and separations, parental unemployment and financial problems, marital conflict and drug and alcohol abuse within the family). Nevertheless, the outcomes in their lives were different. What was it about the resilient youngsters that helped prevent them succumbing to the effects of the risk factors? Things that distinguished the resilient youngsters from the rest (the protective factors) included the following:

- *Personal resources*: resilient youngsters had better technical/spatial intelligence, had flexible temperaments, were approach-oriented, had more positive self-esteem and had active coping styles.
- *Social resources*: the resilient youngsters were more satisfied with social support and experienced the climate of their residential institution as socio-emotionally oriented (openness, autonomy and low conflict).

Bliesener and Losel (1992), using a similar sample of resilients and deviants suffering similar levels of risk factors, found an association between intelligence (especially that involving problem solving) and resilience. The resilients seemed to actively 'face-up-to-problems' rather than simply respond passively – they did not see themselves as in some way fatalistically helpless.

Given the involvement of forensic psychology in the aftermath of parental separation and the ensuing divorce, the work of Czerederecka and Jaskiewicz-Obydzinska (1996) is important. While not specifically concerned with criminal behaviour, the research investigated Polish children involved in divorces for signs of emotional or social problems. Children classified as having no disorder were found to have stayed with their mother as the custodial parent but they also had a 'clearly defined' relationship with their father. By this is meant either having regular contact with their father or *no* contact. They also found that the amount of conflict between the parents did not necessarily lead to problems for the child. It was when the child was put into a position in which they were expected to take sides that the problems arose. A child passively observing parental conflict did not appear to be so affected. In other words, despite our expectations about divorce, these effects can be essentially neutralised in some cases by other factors. A good psychological relationship with both parents seems to be the neutralising agent.

In another study, Losel *et al.* (1999) took the issue of protective factors further. There is a rather well-established physiological fact about children and adolescents who manifest strong antisocial behavioural characteristics: their heart rate tends to be slower when they are at rest or relaxing. Fewer heartbeats when inactive in antisocial youngsters may have a number of explanations. Similar effects are found for cardiovascular, skin electrical activity and cortical responses. According to Losel *et al.*, in excess of 20 studies have found this resting heart rate phenomenon. Only one study has failed to replicate it. Possibly one could describe having a higher resting heart rate as a protective factor – criminal involvement in adults is inversely related to resting heart rate in childhood. One could speak of the protective effect of higher resting heart rate against criminality in adults, as it is a long-term predictor of lack of involvement. This 'protection' seems to be strongest in non-institutionalised, younger samples from relatively normal family backgrounds. In other words, there is a possibility that the factors responsible for antisocial behaviour in families experiencing deprivation and other strain (i.e. social stress) factors are different from those that lead to antisocial behaviour in more normal families.

Losel *et al.* (1999), therefore, chose to study a sample of 16-year-old male students in Nuremberg and Erlangen in Germany. Distinct groups were identified on the basis of a number of measures. These groups were: (1) a group of bullies; (2) a group of victims; (3) a group of normal students, and (4) a group of highly socially competent students. Pulse rate was measured at different times – lying down for short periods of relaxation, after an interactive game, after different stages of a role-play of social conflicts. At every occasion at which resting heart rate was measured, the bullies had the lowest heart rate levels and victims of bullying had the highest. The researchers then re-examined their data in an attempt to see for which boys low heart rate was a particular risk factor. It appeared that the difference between bullies and victims was greater for boys from non-stressed family backgrounds. When boys from stressed family backgrounds were considered, heart rate was not particularly predictive of bullying or victimisation.

Specific explanations of antisocial behaviour in childhood

While the broad childhood factors related to delinquent and adult crime are reasonably well established, there are a number of explanations that warrant description.

Moral reasoning

Moral reasoning changes and develops during childhood. This is the basis of Kohlberg's theory of moral reasoning (Kohlberg, 1963, 1984). This theory extended Piaget's theory of cognitive stages in thinking (Piaget, 1970). Kohlberg argued that moral reasoning develops in similar, relatively discrete stages. The stages differ – not in terms of what the moral decision is but the reasons for that decision whatever the decision is. The earliest stage of moral development is known as the 'preconventional level'. It is driven by external rewards and punishment and subdivided into two stages. These follow together with the remaining four stages:

- *Stage 1* at which the moral task simply involves rule following and avoidance of punishment.
- *Stage 2* involves reward gaining and exercising one's own self-interest. The second stage is known as the 'conventional level'. The expectations of significant social groups and the values of others basically govern this moral stage.
- *Stage 3* is about obtaining social approval and good relations with other people.
- *Stage 4* involves demonstrating respect for authority and doing one's duty. The third level is known as the 'postconventional level' as morality is governed not from the outside but by thought-out values and beliefs.
- *Stage 5* is based on social contracts that provide the principles on which communities can flourish.
- *Stage 6* involves much more abstract principles.

Numerous studies have demonstrated that delinquents tend to reason at lower levels than non-delinquents do. Nelson *et al.* (1990) carried out a meta-analysis (Box 5.1) of 15 studies. Overall, these studies clearly showed that delinquents operate at a lower stage of moral reasoning than appropriate comparison groups.

This seems to make intuitive sense. It suggests poorer moral reasoning may be responsible for some delinquency. There are difficulties that should be considered. For example, by virtually any criterion one wishes to mention, boys are substantially more delinquent than girls. This would suggest that girls, generally, ought to be more morally advanced year on year than boys. Remarkably, some research suggests that girls are actually less likely than boys to achieve the highest stages of moral development! One possible reason for this may be a bias in the theory which places factors that appear to be female at a lower stage (Gilligan, 1982): that is, Stage 3 reasoning seems more female. These findings of a sex difference are actually exceptional. A study by Gregg *et al.* (1994) showed that when age and verbal IQ were controlled for or equated, girls, whether or not delinquent, were at a morally more advanced stage than boys. Others have argued that Kohlberg's theory is biased against any group that is collectivist (community) rather than individualist in social orientation (Owusu-Bempah and Howitt, 2000), which implies that immigrant groups into individualistic Western cultures might be regarded as at a lower stage of moral reasoning if Kohlberg's criteria apply.

Moral reasoning differences between delinquents and non-delinquents are greatest for issues that are especially relevant to criminal behaviour (Palmer and Hollin, 1998). A survey was conducted of young non-offenders (13–22 years) and convicted male offenders (13 and 21 years) in the United Kingdom:

- Self-reported delinquency in the young male offenders was substantially higher than for the non-delinquents (when age and socio-economic status were statistically controlled). Interestingly, there were no differences between male and female non-offenders.
- There were also differences in terms of socio-moral reasoning. Offenders were typically at Kohlberg's preconventional level whereas the non-offenders tended to operate at the level of conventional reasoning. The scale to measure moral reasoning included questions tapping five distinct norms:
  - contract and truth;
  - affiliation;
  - life;
  - property and law;
  - legal justice.
- For each of these areas, male delinquents were at a lower stage of moral development than other males. Interestingly, non-offending boys tended to be at a lower level of moral reasoning than the non-offender females. Delinquent males tended to score at a lower level of development than other males in the following areas:
  - keeping a promise to a friend;
  - keeping a promise to a stranger;
  - keeping a promise to a child;
  - telling the truth;
  - helping your parents;
  - saving the life of a friend;
  - lying even if you do not want to;
  - not taking things that belong to others;
  - obeying the law;
  - sending criminals to jail.

Only on saving the life of a stranger were delinquent males and other males similar. When the moral issue was related to crime, the differential suggesting poorer moral development in delinquents was greatest.

Kerby and Rae (1998), though, show that moral reasoning is quite subtly articulated in young offenders. This is especially the case when the issue of their own personal moral identity is under consideration such as when discussing whether they are good or bad as a person. Young offenders can and do reason morally about a range of issues.

Cycles of abuse

The idea of cycles of violence has been part of professional thinking for quite some time. The violence-breeds-violence hypothesis originates in the work of Curtis (1963) who considered that violent social environments create violent youngsters and adults. Figure 6.1 gives an overview of the range of factors that appear to be involved in the development of aggressiveness (Haapasalo and Tremblay, 1994). This illustrates something of the magnitude of the task facing researchers trying to develop integrated approaches to the development of aggressiveness. The links between violence and

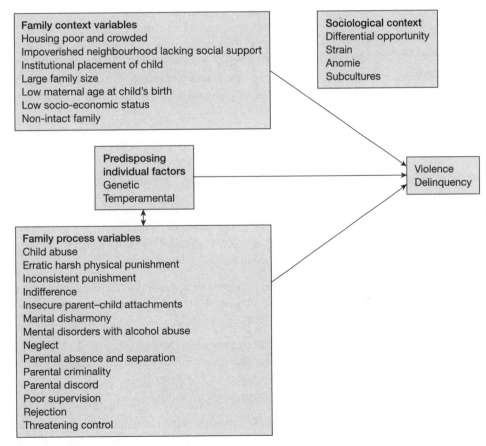

Figure 6.1 Widely established psychological model of aggression according to Haapasalo and Tremblay (1994)

future violence need separating in order to clarify precisely what researchers have shown. It is abundantly clear that there is some sort of relationship between the two, but it depends on what is meant by a cycle of violence. There are several meanings of the term 'cycle of violence' or 'cycle of abuse':

- The process by which women physically abused by their partners are persuaded back by the man with promises of love and that the episode will not be repeated. Events then build up to another episode of violence. She may leave but returns because she 'loves' her abuser or 'for the sake of the children'. Events then lead to more abuse and greater levels of abuse. While these violent acts are frequently severe and warrant criminal prosecution, this is a meaning of cycle of abuse which is not intended in the context of this chapter on the childhood development of crime.
- The effects of early experience on later behaviour. Put simply, does the child who is subjected to physical abuse grow up to be a violent teenager and adult?
- Does a child who is physically abused by its parents grow up to be a parent who abuses their own children?

There are a number of methodological issues involved in assessing cycles of violence:

- Research tends not to involve the direct observation of abuse. Instead, there may be difficulties with information obtained retrospectively in interviews. For example, parents believed to have abused their children may be asked whether they themselves were physically abused as children. This approach risks self-justificatory replies: that is, 'my excuse for abusing my child is that my parents did it to me.'
- The retrospective nature of many studies means that memory processes may affect recollections.
- There is no standard definition of physical abuse common to all or most studies. As a consequence, it is difficult to know what sorts and degrees of violence are necessary to produce what levels of effects.
- Child abuse is associated with a wide range of family characteristics that may be also harmful to children. It may be impossible to tell whether a particular outcome is directly the consequence of abuse or whether other family characteristics associated with abuse are responsible. This is mainly a problem for those wishing to understand the effects of abuse. For practitioners concerned with problem families, it is something of an irrelevance.

Cycles of abuse involve processes that, generally, are somewhat unclear or speculative. Figure 6.2 gives some proposed plausible mechanisms and Figure 6.3 indicates a range of possible models:

- Model 1 (based on social learning theory) suggests that the experience of aggression may result in its incorporation in one's repertoire of behaviours. Direct and vicarious experience are both effective.
- Model 2 is much as proposed by John Bowlby.

Both of these are discussed in some detail in Chapter 5. It is possible that more than one of the processes may be involved: that is, they are alternative processes rather than competing theories. Figure 6.2 brings to our attention the contrast between generalised effects of abuse and specific isomorphic ones. While violence may lead

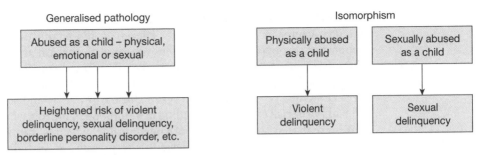

Figure 6.2 Isomorphism versus generalised pathology as a consequence of abuse

Figure 6.3 Psychological models of the cycle of violence

to violence, some researchers believe that the effects of violence are more generally pathogenic than that.

Widom (1989) studied records of a county court in the United Kingdom to find children of 11 years of age or younger who had been subject to child abuse. She then investigated the adult criminal records of these youngsters:

- Twenty-nine per cent of these had later criminal records compared with 21% of controls who had been matched with the research group on variables such as age, class, sex, race and so forth. The findings, using refined statistical techniques, were that there was 1.7 times the risk of getting an adult record if one had been abused as a child. But these are, of course, the extremes of abuse and many offences do not lead to conviction.

- The *isomorphism hypothesis* argues that there is a close relationship between the characteristics of abuse and its effects on the victim (see Chapter 10). In support of this hypothesis, in this study victims of physical abuse had the highest rate of violence offences (16% of sample). This trend was not great. Victims of neglect (at 13%) had similar levels of violent crime. Physical abuse together with neglect victims (7%), sexual and other abuse cases (7%) and sexual abuse (6%) all had lower risk of violent offending in adulthood. Controls who, obviously, had not been abused had a 7% risk of violent crime, which is the same for the latter types of abuse victim. Care is needed in interpreting any such data. Nevertheless, as far as can be seen, physical abuse in childhood does seem to increase the risk of violent offending somewhat compared with the controls. Sexual abuse, for example, is not implicated in violent crime despite the vast range of behaviour problems that have been associated with it in the research literature (Rudo and Powell, 1996).

Lifespan development and criminal careers

Childhood experiences are important in the development of criminality. However, not all criminals reveal their criminality early in life. To be sure, delinquency is reasonably predictable early in some children's lives. Similarly, antisocial behaviour in the form of juvenile delinquency is predictive of adult crime. Some of the research discussed earlier is still continuing over 40 years after its initial stages. It is unrealistic, nevertheless, to expect rapid progress in understanding the development of criminal careers given the timescale of such studies. Especially difficult for such studies is the question of whether criminality that develops late in life can be traced back to childhood. Some criminals do not appear to begin to offend until their 30s or even later.

The Berlin Crime Study (Dahle, 1999) took a sample of male adult offenders admitted into the Berlin prison system in early 1976. Not only were detailed histories taken, but also the offenders were followed up for nearly 25 more years through their prison, legal and health records. Property offences and fraud accounted for nearly 60% of the sentences. Robbery and bodily harm accounted for nearly 10% each, whereas sexual offences and homicide were relatively rare. Inexplicably, nearly 17% of the sample died in the study period. The commonest age of death was between 30 and 45 years of age. Something like 30 times as many of the men died then as would be expected from the relevant national statistics. A number of variables were entered into a statistical analysis (cluster analysis). These included age at first offence, age at most recent offence, the number of offences in each four-year period since the age of 14 and the amount of time spent in prison during each of these periods. There appear to be at least five different types of offending career:

- *Adolescence limited offenders*: this group had reached maximum offending by their early 20s. From then on seriousness and rate of crimes decreased slowly. Early offending was largely associated with peer groups. After this, there is evidence that offending is individual, trivial and drug related. Their childhood featured multiple problems such as unemployment, drinking in parents and so forth. As they got older, despite the peer influence in their early offending, they seemed rather isolated. This group made up about one in six of the sample.

- *Limited serious offenders*: this group was about one in nine of the offenders. They started delinquency and crime escalated in seriousness and violence in their 20s. They dropped out of criminality at about age 30. This group was particularly associated with bio-psycho-social risk factors such as pre- and perinatal complications. Although they had good intelligence and concentration, they were school failures when relatively young. Suicide attempts were quite common among them.

- *Persistent serious offenders*: this group was about one in seven of the sample. They had spent a lot of time in prison and very few of them had succeeded in abandoning crime. They reoffended (recidivated) very quickly. Serious violent crime was common among them. Members of this group had accumulated risk factors across the spectrum of risk factors in childhood. They were also social loners in childhood.

- *Occasional offenders*: this group made up nearly half of the sample. They showed a low level of delinquency during their life though they had little or no adolescent involvement in crime. They were specialists in that they carried out a limited repertoire of crimes. Risk factors in childhood were relatively absent. Nevertheless, in the period leading to their offending, they experienced critical life events such as adultery, debt, bankruptcy and so forth.

- *Late-starting offenders*: these were similar to the occasional offenders and amounted to about one in eight of the sample. They too had a preference for crime specialisation and the crime tended to be fraud or burglary. One suggestion is that they defined themselves as professional criminals and they began offending not because of stressful life events but on the basis of a rational decision to do so.

The origins of criminal behaviour in childhood are a complex matter. Different patterns exist of offending during the lifespan. For the forensic psychologist, it is useful to know that different risk factors are associated with different patterns of offending. Research into this is at such an early stage that caution is appropriate when drawing conclusions. It seems evident, though, that early problem behaviour should not be neglected for two reasons – it is predictive of later, more serious, problems and, if it is acted on, then even simple interventions may be effective at reducing future delinquency.

Main points

- The study of juvenile offending is one of the most thoroughly researched areas of crime. A great deal is known about delinquency, its antecedents and consequences. Not surprisingly, various sorts of deficiencies in the functioning of families have been found to be associated with later delinquency. So deficiencies in parenting (e.g. abusive behaviour leading to cycles of abuse) are closely associated with delinquent and other forms of problematic behaviour in children. Nevertheless, it would be wrong to suggest that all delinquent children are the result of such family inadequacies. Delinquency is the result of many different influences, not all of which are directly to do with the family. Peer pressure to engage in delinquent activity is an obvious example.

- There is very good reason to believe that social interventions in early childhood intended to counteract some of the deficiencies of families known to be associated with delinquency can be very effective. Certain interventions with older children, maybe after they have become delinquent, can also be effective. Especially effective are those programmes which combine early childhood education with direct support for the parents of high-risk children.

▶

- Despite knowing a great deal about the development of delinquent behaviour, there is a gulf between what we know about the risk factors for delinquency and the causes of delinquency. There is strong evidence that violence is transmitted generationally through cycles of abuse but we are less clear about how, say, moral development affects delinquent behaviour. A great deal more needs to be known about the different patterns of criminal careers some of which begin only in adulthood and others are over by adulthood. The implications of these different patterns are difficult to research (as it is such a long-term project to do so) but it is vital to reject the idea that there is a single, simple pathway from problem home backgrounds to delinquency to adult criminality. Sometimes that is the route but equally there are alternatives.

Chapter 7

Theft and other crimes against property

Overview

- Property crime is the most common sort of crime but has been largely neglected in forensic and criminal psychology perhaps because it is so common that it is, in a sense, normal hence needing no special explanation. Two in every five males admit committing a property crime such as theft, burglary and criminal damage at some time in their lives. Mostly the crimes were thefts.

- One of the earliest psychological explanations of crime was actually the concept of kleptomania. It is an impulse to steal without there being a need for the property or money and is said to be associated with some form of positive emotion when committing the offence. However, researchers have failed to find evidence of kleptomania in shoplifters. For example, substantial numbers of shoplifting offences involve pairs or groups of individuals working together. These could not be explained on the basis of kleptomania.

- Shoplifters tend to give different reasons for shoplifting than non-shoplifters use to explain the crime. Non-shoplifters might suggest that shoplifters cannot afford to pay for the goods whereas shoplifters actually are more likely to say that they do not want to pay. It has been suggested that cultural factors may be involved in shoplifting.

- Burglary has a strong connection with drug use. There is a range of explanations of these links such as drug users may associate with criminals so are more likely to get involved in crime. However, the need for finance seems to be an important motive. There is evidence that property offences are more common when supplies of drugs are scarce and they are more expensive as a consequence. There is also evidence that being on methadone support therapy, which helps heroin addicts come off of the drug, actually is associated with a reduction in property crime.

- Rational choice theory regards burglars as decision makers and encourages the study of their decision-making processes. In a sense, this makes the study of burglars the study of normal behaviour rather than some sort of psychological abnormality. There is no absolute process that burglars employ since a suitable target household to burgle will be assessed using different criteria in different circumstances. For example, security measures may deter a burglar even though in other respects the house seems to be a better target than the house that is finally targeted.

- Arson is largely committed by youngsters perhaps for reasons of boredom or thrill seeking. There is a psychiatric disorder, pyromania, which is a deep seated urge to set fires. Not many arsons are committed by pyromaniacs and the figure may be as low as 1% of arsonists are also pyromaniacs. Less than one in five arsonists suffer from a mental disorder.

Forensic and criminal psychology has tended to ignore property crime and one will not find extensive research on all aspects of this topic from a psychological perspective. Nevertheless, the property crime theft is so common that it swamps all other forms of crime in terms of incidence but also in terms of its range of victims. Perhaps because of the mundane nature of most property crime, it has not been the focus of concern in the same way that sexual and violent crime have been. McGuire (2004) puts it this way:

> The role of psychological factors in such offences [property crimes], more than any other type of crime, may appear marginal, even irrelevant. On the other hand, if 'crime is normal', then most of psychology, which is about people generally considered 'normal', is potentially relevant to an understanding of it!
>
> (p. 76)

Actually, the situation is more remarkable even than McGuire suggests since the field of forensic and criminal psychology is replete with examples of the successful application of concepts, ideas and theories developed in relation to the psychology of 'normal people'. Good examples of this include work on eyewitness memory which employs normal memory process, work on the jury which emphasises group dynamics familiar from social psychology, and forensic interviewing which emphasises normal cognitive processes. However, McGuire is correct in that the psychology of criminal behaviour has largely stressed clinical aspects rather than, say, social psychological explanations. This is, of course, partly because clinical approaches to psychology are based on the psychology of abnormal behaviour rather than the psychology of normal behaviour. Nevertheless, if one wishes to consider the profiling approach of the social psychologist David Canter with the more clinical approach of the FBI profilers (see Chapter 13) then the advantages of the non-clinical research epistemology are almost self-evident.

Most of us have been victims of theft. Most of us have probably taken something that did not belong to us at sometime in our lives – keeping change, not going back to the shop when undercharged, taking paper or paper clips from the office to use at home and so forth. Many of us would regard these things as so trivial that we do not see them as criminal in any sense. The normality of property crime is underlined by a survey of households in England and Wales in 2003 (Budd, Sharp and Mayhew, 2005). Participants were asked about their own offending behaviour. A high proportion of the general population reported committing some sort of property offences (theft, vehicle-related theft, burglary and criminal damage, and robbery):

- Forty per cent of males and 22% of females reported committing a property crime at some time in their lives.
- Overwhelmingly, the property crimes involved were relatively minor ones involving theft (e.g. theft from a person, work, school or a shop). Thirty-five per cent of males and 21% of females reported committing a theft. Eleven per cent of males reported vehicle-related thefts (e.g. theft of a motor vehicle or theft from a motor vehicle) though the corresponding figure for females was only 2%.

- Four per cent of males reported committing burglary in their lifetime but only 1% of females. However, the major category was commercial burglary and not domestic burglary. Only 1% of males reported domestic burglary and a fifth of this number of females did so. However, the major categories of theft were those from work, school and shops.
- Thefts from an individual (as opposed to thefts from work, school or shops) were actually very uncommon. Less than 1% of males and half that percentage of females reported ever committing the crime of theft from a person.

The above figures are rates ever in one's lifetime. The researchers also collected information of the numbers of people reporting committing a crime in the previous year. These figures are naturally lower. So, in the year before the survey, 8% of males and 4% of females had committed some sort of property offence. As might be expected, some of the sample committed very few offences and others committed many offences. It was found that 82% of the total number of offences reported to the researchers were actually committed by just 2% of the sample (Budd and Sharp, 2005)!

The variety of property crimes make its explanation difficult. The crimes range from the very serious to the trivial. Furthermore, some property crimes have a component of violence actual or implied – robbery is an example of this. The neglect of property crime in forensic and criminal psychology is all the more surprising given that the concept of kleptomania is about two hundred years old, thus predating many other psychological explanations of crime by many years.

Box 7.1

Key concept: arson and pyromania

In 2001, according to England and Wales fire service figures, 14,800 out of 69,000 fires in dwellings were malicious; 19,700 out of 43,000 fires in other buildings were malicious; and 79,100 out of 102,100 vehicle fires were malicious. However, many of these would not be recorded by the police as arson since the legal definition of arson involves that the fire-setter acted deliberately and/or recklessly.

The UK government's Crime Reduction Toolkit (Home Office, 2005a) for arson identifies the major categories of motivation for arson and indicates the proportion of arsons that are in each category:

- Youth disorder and nuisance: boredom and thrill seeking may be associated with this – 80% of arsons.
- Malicious: revenge and racism are among the motivations for this – 5% of total.
- Psychological: triggered by a mental illness or suicide attempts – 5% of total.
- Criminal: concealment of another crime is the reason for these or where the perpetrator may profit financially from the fire as in the case of insurance frauds – 4% of total.

Given these figures, it is not surprising to find that males under the age of 18 years are about half of the total of individuals either found guilty in court or cautioned by the police for an arson offence. The proportion of females involved is less than 15%. About 10% suffer a mental illness. Similarly, it is perhaps also not surprising to find that only one arson in six is prosecuted as a danger to life. So, in many ways, the explanations of arson should lean more to explaining delinquent behaviour than the deep psychological motivations of arsonists.

▶

One popular view about such fires is that they are caused by individuals who get pleasure out of setting fire to property (Doley, 2003). They might be regarded as pyromaniacs who are driven by deep-seated urges to light fires. So it is believed that flames have an irresistible attraction for them and that they even get sexual satisfaction from their activities. As a consequence, they begin to carry out more and more arson attacks of increasing seriousness purely for reasons of self-gratification. But, of course, pyromania is a psychiatric disorder which is defined in the *Diagnostic and Statistical Manual* of the American Psychiatric Association (see Box 18.1) in terms of:

- A deliberate, purposeful starting of a fire on two or more occasions.
- There is a state of emotional arousal or an experience of tension before the fire is started.
- The individual has an attraction to, 'a fascination in, or a curiosity about fire and the situational contexts of fire (they might be interested in the consequences of fire or with artifacts used in connection with fires).'
- The individual will feel 'pleasure, gratification, or relief' when starting fires or in connection with the aftermaths of fires.
- A number of motives are contra-indicative of pyromania – monetary gain, political ideology, concealment of crime and acts of vengeance are excluded. Furthermore, impairments of judgement such as when intoxicated, having limited intellectual ability and suffering dementia are also contra-indicative.
- There should not be a better way of accounting for the fire starting such as indications of conduct disorder, antisocial personality disorder or a manic episode.

Actually, pyromania seems rare among arsonists (Doley, 2003). It is difficult to say precisely what proportion of them are pyromaniacs as the reported figures vary somewhat though the bulk of studies reviewed. Doley found 0 and 1% of arsonists meet the study's criteria for pyromania. However, some studies find much higher percentages. Indeed, mental disorders are uncommon among arsonists as only 17% of those arrested manifest a mental disorder (Almond *et al.*, 2005). Furthermore, the idea that arson or even pyromania is motivated by sexual urges has little force. Lewis and Yarnell (1951) found that out of more than 1,100 arsonists only 3% reported sexual arousal in association with their crime.

Almond *et al.* (2005) investigated Shye's (1985) action system model in relation to arson. Four different 'modes' of arson emerge in the analysis and there is empirical evidence in support stemming from a study of arsonists in a British psychiatric prison.

- *Adaptive mode*: an external event is exploited for some sort of gain. Setting fire to a crime scene to hide evidence of a crime is an example of this. Because of the links of this mode with criminal activity, it includes variables such as more than one offender involved, business, vehicle, force and theft.
- *Expressive mode*: internal psychological factors are expressed against external targets. The choice of the target for the arson would have a symbolic or emotional significance for the arsonist. Variables associated with this include school and civic buildings.
- *Integrative mode*: internal psychological factors are dealt with by using arson as a means of seeking attention. Variables associated with this include self, own home, and hospital.
- *Conservative mode*: an external source of frustration has an effect on the individual who responds by setting a fire which restores their sense of well-being. Using fire to extract revenge on another person is an aspect of this.

Variables associated with this include victim known, prior threats of violence or arson, arguments and planning.

Shoplifting and kleptomania

It is easy to neglect the extent to which businesses are the victims of property crime compared to individuals. Perhaps the view that it is worse to steal from a person than a wealthy business is responsible for this. Nevertheless, proportionately, crime against business is more common than crime against individuals. For example, 80% of retailers and 63% of manufacturers in the United Kingdom had experienced crime whereas the corresponding figure for the general population was about 30% in 1999 (Hopkins, 2002). Theft by customers was the most common (47% of retailers reported this), then burglary (24%), then theft from vehicles (23%) and then vandalism (22%). Certain sorts of businesses are more likely to be victims of crime – alcoholic drinks shops and DIY stores were the most likely to be burgled.

Kleptomania

Psychology's neglect of property crime is surprising since one of the earliest 'psychological' (psychiatric) explanations of crime concerned theft. This concept, *kleptomania*, has a two-hundred-year history (see Chapter 1) and remains a psychiatric category in the current edition of the American Psychiatric Association's *Diagnostic and Statistical Manual* (2000). It is listed as part of the broader category of impulse control disorders. The APA *Diagnostic and Statistical Manual* describes kleptomania as:

> the recurrent failure to resist impulses to steal items even though the items are not needed for personal use or for their monetary value. The individual experiences a rising subjective sense of tension before the theft, and feels pleasure, gratification or relief when committing the theft.
>
> *(p. 667)*

Since kleptomaniacs are aware that the thefts they commit are both wrong and 'senseless' then the condition is not a psychotic one.

There is some modern research into the question of whether kleptomania is a characteristic feature of shoplifting behaviour. Indeed, there are questions about whether kleptomania explains much theft at all. Sarasalo, Bergman and Toth (1997) conducted a study of shoplifters who, literally, had just been apprehended by store security staff. Those who agreed to take part in the study were interviewed in the short period prior to the arrival of the police. The researchers assessed each shoplifter for the presence of four of the main criteria used in the APA *Diagnostic and Statistical Manual* for identifying kleptomania. Kleptomania cannot be diagnosed simply on the basis of a single characteristics but requires the presence of a number of different ones:

- Criterion A is the 'recurrent failure to resist impulses to steal items even though the items are not needed for personal use or for their monetary value' (American Psychiatric Association). A lot of shoplifters (78%) mentioned needing the stolen object; 90% said that the stealing was a sudden impulse, and 56% mentioned that they had had similar impulses in the past.

- Criterion B is 'a subjective sense of tension before the theft'. Over 84% mentioned a sense of thrill before their offence.

- Criterion C is the 'pleasure, gratification, or relief' experienced on carrying out the theft. Only 40% of shoplifters mentioned that they had experienced a feeling of relief or gratification during their offence.

- Criterion D is that the offence is not due to anger or vengeance and is not the consequence of a delusion/hallucination. On average, only 14% of shoplifters agreed that their offence was the consequence of anger or a need for revenge.

According to Sarasalo *et al.*, in order for an individual to be classified as a kleptomaniac, they should meet the above criteria and more. For example, they argue that 34% of the sample were stealing with the assistance of other people so it is difficult to classify them as suffering from kleptomania since kleptomania is a psychological condition of individuals. Of course, it is possible that the co-offenders were also kleptomaniacs but this is not a realistic possibility since very few of the offenders met Criteria A to D above anyway. Of those who acted alone, only a very few (8%) mentioned an inability to resist impulses to steal unneeded items (Criterion A). However, half of this 8% did not experience the rising sense of thrill before committing the crime and the others did not meet Criterion C since they did not feel pleasure, gratification or relief when they committed the theft. In other words, although a number of shoplifters met certain of the criteria, when more than one criterion is used then there is no evidence of kleptomania in the sample. The commonest reason for taking the thing in question was to use it personally (64%) and 12% intended to sell it and 6% intended to give it away or discard it.

Virtually none of the criminals in this sample were in full-time employment. Some were students and others were unemployed. Another remarkable finding was that about a third reported a history of chronic bodily illness (the mean age of the sample was actually quite low). Furthermore, two thirds of the offenders reported a history of psychiatric disorder.

Culture as an explanation

Kleptomania is a psychiatric classification which strongly hints that offences such as shoplifting are driven by internal psychological states. It is possible to find almost diametrically opposite explanations of shoplifting. One of these identifies cultural variations as a possible influence on patterns of shoplifting. While it is patently obvious that rates of crime vary across cultures, there are questions about how cultural influences impact on the criminal behaviour of individuals. Following many others, Sweeney (2004) argued that key variables identified by cross-cultural psychologists have been shown to be associated with criminal behaviour. She notes that, for example, crime in general and specifically homicide, child abuse, domestic violence against females and rape together with juvenile delinquency all seem to be more common in the individualistic cultures that characterise Western countries. They are less of a feature of the collectivist cultures that characterise other parts of the world. Individualism 'is a multi-faceted outlook on life that emphasises, among other things, independence and self-reliance' (p. 62). Whereas collectivism 'focuses on duty and obedience' (p. 62). Triandis (1995) claimed another dimension of culture has to be taken into account – he suggests that there is a horizontal/vertical dimension. Consequently, when these two dimensions are used, it is possible to identify cultures that manifest one of four different patterns. These are: 1) horizontal individualism; 2) vertical individualism; 3) horizontal collectivism, and 4) vertical collectivism. Horizontal individualists operate largely as individuals doing 'their own thing' as do vertical individualists – however, vertical individualists are competitive with others whereas horizontal individualists do not have this competitive streak and do not constantly need to be better than others. Horizontal collectivists focus their activities around their group/family but do not feel subordinate to that group whereas vertical collectivists are willing to defer their personal needs and wishes in favour of the group's needs and wishes.

Sweeney carried out research into shoplifting based on this cross-cultural perspective on a sample of American university students. Three different groups of shoplifters were distinguished: early shoplifters and later shoplifters. These were compared with a group who had never shoplifted:

- Early shoplifters began offending at the age of about 11 or 12 years or even earlier but never shoplifted after this time.
- Later shoplifters included anyone who shoplifted at over 12 years of age.

Shoplifting had peaked in frequency among this sample at the age of about 13 or 14 years. The explanations they gave for shoplifting were monetary (41%), thrill seeking (21%), peer pressure (18%) and immaturity (14%). Shoplifters were compared with non-shoplifters and actually gave similar reasons why they thought people shoplift. However, there were some differences. Shoplifters, when giving financial reasons for shoplifting, would include words like 'I wanted something and I did not want to pay for it' (p. 64), whereas non-shoplifters would suggest that the shoplifter could not afford to pay. It was uncommon for shoplifters to claim inability to pay rather than not wanting to pay as their financial reason.

The SVS (Schwartz Value Survey) was used to measure individualism-collectivism among the members of the sample. This scale measures a number of pertinent values such as power, achievement, hedonism, stimulation, self-direction, benevolence, tradition, conformity and security. The pattern of values identifying collectivist culture would include conformity, tradition and benevolence. Individualism would be identified by such values as achievement, hedonism and stimulation. There were differences in their values as measured by the SVS. Later shoplifters scored more highly on the power and hedonism values but lower on benevolence and conformity compared to non-shoplifters. Sweeney emphasises that the power value is correlated with vertical individualism, benevolence with horizontal collectivism, and conformity with vertical collectivism. However, care should be taken because this pattern is not simply that vertical individualists are much more likely to shoplift. That is, not all values that are associated with vertical individualism demonstrated a relationship to shoplifting.

One should not assume that shoplifting is necessarily a casual form of criminal activity. Schneider (2005) studied the methods by which persistent offenders who burgle and carry out other forms of theft operate. They were asked about how they disposed of the goods they stole. Thirty-eight per cent gave selling to a handler/fence as their preferred mode of disposal and 24% said sell it friends. Sixteen per cent had as their first choice using the property themselves. This implies the organised nature of some shoplifting.

Burglary

Burglary–drugs connection

Explanations of burglary are varied. One which has been raised frequently is the possibility that drug use is a stimulus to crime of all sorts and property crime in particular. It is not uncommon for researchers to note that there is a relationship between the use of drugs such as heroin and acquisitive crime. Of course, what such an association means is debatable since there are at least three major possibilities:

- Some researchers argue that users of drugs simply associate with people who are more likely to be criminal anyway and this is the reason for the association.
- Others argue that illegal drugs are expensive to buy in the quantities needed by some users and as a consequence the user finds it difficult to finance their drug use. Illegitimate means of obtaining finance may be resorted to. This could include theft and robbery or perhaps sex work (i.e. prostitution).
- The relationship between drug use and property crime is the consequence of a third factor which is a common influence on both. For example, it is possible that inadequate parenting in childhood leads separately to criminality and drug use. Thus the association between criminality and drug use is the consequence of this third factor.

It should be obvious that all three above pathways are feasible and that they are not mutually exclusive.

The association between drug use and property crime has been demonstrated frequently. In Australia, for example, it has been found that 70% of heroin users admit committing acquisitive crimes. However, this begs the question of just what created this trend. One obvious argument is that the cost of drugs determines the need to resort to property crime, which implies that fluctuations in the cost of drugs may be associated with fluctuations in the levels of property crime. Degenhardt *et al.* (2005) took advantage of a sudden change in the availability of heroin in Australia to assess its impact on acquisitive crime among other things. In a market economy, the cost of products (including illegal drugs) is partly determined by the scarcity of the product. So the significance of the 'shortage' of heroin is that one would expect its price to increase as a consequence. Thus, if heroin use causes acquisitive crime because of financial pressures, one would expect that users would need to engage in acquisitive crime more frequently when drugs were in scarce supply. Using a variety of data sources to confirm trends in availability and cost, the researchers were able to show that during the period of scarcity of heroin there were substantial rises in the numbers of property crimes. The crimes that increased included robbery without a weapon, robbery with a weapon other than a firearm, and breaking and entering homes. This seems to indicate the role of financial motives related to the purchase of heroin in property crimes. Certainly, in this study, when supplies began to return to normal, property crime also tended to return to its previous levels.

In this context, it is worthwhile noting Parker and Kirby's (1996) study of the impact of a methadone support programme on crime rates in a community which they suggest had been going through a heroin epidemic with consequent elevated levels of property crime. Methadone is a synthetic drug with properties like those of morphine. It is used in programmes that attempt to help people who are withdrawing from heroin, which itself is a semi-synthetic derivative of morphine. Methadone helps the user to deal with heroin withdrawal symptoms like fever, insomnia and vomiting. It is a dangerous drug in its own right but is used as a means of dealing with the worse evil of heroin addiction. A large sample of addicts undergoing the methadone support programme was compared with a large control group. Self-report questions as well as in-depth interviews were employed. During the period of the study, which reflected a fairly massive methadone support programme, the acquisitive crimes of burglary from a dwelling and theft from a motor vehicle declined 'dramatically'. The vast majority of those on the programme reported reductions in their illicit drug usage as a consequence of being on the programme. About a fifth claimed to have not used illicit drugs at all as a consequence of being on the programme. As a consequence, the treatment sample spent only a fifth of the amount on illicit drugs which the non-treated community sample did. The implications of this for the need for property crime are obvious. Those on the support programme claimed to be involved in less crime in keeping with this.

A study in Australia into the effectiveness of methadone maintenance treatment found similar evidence of its impact on the amount of property crime (Lind *et al.*, 2005). The researchers used a reoffending database to track the offending of drug users during the periods when they were undergoing methadone treatment compared with those when they were not. They also had a separate database that provided information about periods when the drug users were in custody, which could be used to adjust for the time that the user could potentially commit a crime. In terms of theft offences (defined mainly as robbery, theft and related, burglary and breaking and entering, and fraud and forgery), there seemed to be impact on the rates of criminal charges. The extent of the impact depended on gender and age group. Expressing the reductions as numbers of charges per 100 drug users:

- Males under 30 years of age: a reduction of eight theft charges.
- Females under 30 years of age: a reduction of 20 theft charges.
- Males 30 years and over: a reduction of 11 theft charges.
- Females 30 years and over: a reduction of 20 theft charges.

So the methadone maintenance treatment seems to be more effective with females than males.

Of course, methadone is a chemical treatment and not a psychological treatment for drug use. Its importance in this context is that there is clear evidence that making users less dependent on illicit market drugs has the important consequence of crime reduction. The implication is that any treatment which makes individuals less dependent on illicit drugs may result in reductions in crimes against property. A study in the United Kingdom by Gossop *et al.* (2003) partly answers this question. They studied drug users on a variety of drug treatment programmes. These included methadone support programmes of the sort described above but they also included drug dependency units in which drug users, as residents, would undergo some psychiatry-based support programme. Drug dependency units are often housed within psychiatric hospitals and the sort of treatment that would be available would involve multi-disciplinary teams mostly of psychiatrists and nursing staff. The in-patient treatment would last between 2 to 12 weeks. The treatment offered would be some form of detoxification together with psychosocial rehabilitation work. The findings generally confirmed that treatment resulted in lower levels of drug use of various sorts. Furthermore, it was confirmed that there was a substantial drop in reported crime following the commencement of treatment. Acquisitive crime dropped substantially to just about a quarter of the pre-treatment levels in both the methadone community treated group and the residential drug dependency units. Unfortunately, it is not possible to fully disaggregate the effects of detoxification from the effects of the psychosocial work.

Burglar decision making

Many studies of burglary are presented as if they were studies of their victims. However, who and whose property is targeted by burglars is more than just a study of the victim, it tells us a lot about the decision-making processes of burglars. Furthermore, these decisions are actually the result of a complex interplay between the burglar and the burgled. For example, a householder who fits burglar alarms has an influence on the burglar's decision to target or not that householder's property. The burglar also influences the householder to fit the alarm since other burglaries in the area might motivate the purchase of the burglar alarm. So, in a sense, burglary is an interaction between the burglar and the householder though this interaction may be very indirect. As a consequence, it is equally possible to argue that studies of who is victimised are equally studies of the decisions made by offenders about where to burgle.

One of the recurrent themes in research on crime is that offenders are in some way driven to crime by some sort of propensity to criminality. This encourages researchers to try to find the distinctive psychological features of offenders such as burglars. In other words, one needs to seek to find the ways in which burglars differ from the rest of the population. One important theory, rational choice theory (Cornish and Clarke, 1986), is built on a different set of assumptions. The theory sees offenders as decision makers who seek to gain advantage for themselves in ways which are rational within the constraints of the information available, the offender's ability to reason, and the amount of time available to make the decision. Decisions that have to be made instantly may not be optimally rational. Although the theory deals with the decision to become criminal in the first place, its most significant contributions have considered the rationality of the decisions made in relation to particular opportunities for crime. The focus is on the crime event, as a consequence, and not on the personality of the offender, for example. However, the theory does accept the role of background factors such as low intelligence or poor upbringing and the role of situational factors such as being drunk, having a row with one's partner, pressure from friends and so forth. Pease (2001) suggests that rational choice theory freed researchers from trying to find the explanation of crime in the pathological character of the offender. The theory pushes researchers more in the direction of questioning offenders about the methods they employ and the precautions they take in the course of their offending. So, in a sense, the big advantage of the theory is that it pushes researchers in a streetwise direction of listening to offenders.

Sometimes it is suggested that rational choice theory works better for property crime than for expressive crime. Certainly, some of the more profitable research has explored the rationality of burglary. According to Nee (2004), interview research with burglars has led to the view that they are far less opportunistic than was once believed. They plan rather than make impulsive choices as to targets. This does not mean that all burglars plan but merely that only a minority work completely haphazardly. Furthermore, burglars largely search out targets. The motivation for burglary was to obtain cash to finance a relatively lavish lifestyle. Nee (2004) carried out a study in Ireland of the motivation and decision making of burglars. Intriguingly, she included a comparison group who were not burglars, which allowed her to investigate whether the decision making of burglars was truly distinctive or simply what anyone would decide in similar circumstances. Rather than have burglars survey actual properties with the researcher, it was decided to simulate vulnerable residential areas by the use of photographs on slides. The participants were shown numerous pictures of five houses. Rather than single factors being decisive in the decision that a particular household would be a good one to burgle, the burglars had patterns of factors which led to the decision to burgle or not. The same combination of cues to decision making would not apply in every circumstance. For example, the least popular target for burglars would have been somewhat easy to enter because it had timber doors and sash windows. However, it had a scruffy and 'downmarket' appearance and was exposed in that it could easily be observed by people in the street. The burglars, however, may well have seen this house as a better target if it had been next to cheaper housing. The burglars preferred target house had a mature appearance and looked like it would be easy to get inside. The house next to it looked as if it might yield more profits, provided a lot of cover for the burglar and was easy to break in at the rear of the property. Despite this, the burglars were deterred by it because it had a number of security measures installed – things like double glazing, a visible burglar alarm box and mortice locks on the doors.

In contrast, when householders assessed the same houses in terms of how desirable they would be to a burglar as a target they seemed to lack an appropriate strategy or plan for making their decision. They did not choose the same target houses as the burglars did. Furthermore, the householders took rather more time over reaching a decision than the burglars did since they explored a greater number of photographs of the properties before selecting what for them appeared to be the best target. They lacked the experience and expertise that burglars possessed.

There are a number of fairly closely related theories that can be applied to burglary. One is routine activity theory. Again, like rational choice theory, this counteracts the idea that research should identify the distinct social and psychological characteristics of criminals which leads to their offending. In routine activity theory the emphasis is on the day-to-day activities of some individuals and the way their daily lives are structured that provides them with opportunities to commit crime. So, to illustrate this, it is useful to note that studies show that low income households as well as inner city ones have the greatest risk of burglary. This is simply because they are the ones most likely to be in close proximity to where the burglar lives – that is, are encompassed within the routine ambit of the burglar. Felson (1996) identified three different factors which contributed to property crime:

- motivated offenders need to be around (i.e. proximity to potential offenders);
- there needs to be suitable property available at which to commit crime (target attractiveness);
- there needs to be an absence of guardians of the property capable of protecting the property. The guardians may simply be members of the household or neighbours whose presence is noted. Johnson and Bowers (2004) mention guardianship which includes things like household composition, house occupancy and having neighbours who watch the dwelling when it is unoccupied. A high proportion of burglars avoid occupied dwellings. That is social guardianship, physical guardianship is things such as burglar alarms. Suitable targets for burglary are characterised by: 1) greater value as judged by the burglar (target attractiveness), and 2) absence of physical aspects of the target household which reduce its suitability – these include the visibility of the property (the more obscured from public view then the greater risk of being targeted) and the accessibility of the target.

One attempt to test routine activity theory as applied to property crime studied burglary victimisation across three countries (Tseloni *et al.*, 2004). The areas involved were the Netherlands, United States, and England and Wales. They took the major precepts of routine activity theory and tested whether the predictions of the theory worked in such a wide variety of settings. Tseloni *et al.* coded many variables from crime survey data relating to routine activity theory. These were then correlated with known risks of burglary victimisation. It is important to note that the researchers found that their variables measuring aspects of routine activity theory left a great deal unexplained in burglary rates. That is, a great deal is yet to be found out about why certain households are more likely to be burgled than others. Among the general findings:

- The social guardianship variable lone parent (there are fewer adult social guardians) increased the risk of burglary to a similar extent in all three countries.

- Households that had preventative measures against burglary were actually more likely to be burgled than those that did not. This is contrary to expectations. The researchers suggest that the precautions against burglary may have been a consequence of being burgled and that in some of the cases the preventative measures were token efforts which would not deter burglars. The finding should be not taken as indicating that burglars are attracted to houses that take preventative measures.

- Living in inner city or urbanised areas increased the risk of burglary perhaps due to living closer to where offenders live.

With the above exceptions, it should be stressed, though, that there was a degree of inconsistency as to the factors which related to burglary rates in the different countries. So, taken overall, there is evidence in support of routine activity theory but it is also true to say that the fit of the theory to the data on burglary was far from complete.

In terms of the geography of burglary, there are certain areas that tend to have a high concentration of burglaries and so may attract greater police attention as a consequence. Johnson and Bowers (2004) suggest that a perspective from behavioural ecology, optimal foraging theory, may be of help in understanding burglars' thought processes which lead to such hot spots. The theory suggests that animals when seeking food (and so burglars when seeking money) adopt strategies that keep the rate of rewards to a maximum while at the same time keeping to a minimum the amount of time spent foraging and the risk of being caught by other animals (and so the police in terms of burglary). Thus the strategy of at least some offenders is to keep the rewards of their criminal activity at a high level while minimising the time spent committing the offence (which reduces the risk of being caught). This suggests to Johnson and Bowers (2004) that the burglar would burgle one property then continue to target ones close by if they are unlikely to be observed/overlooked, if there are ready escape routes, and if there is a likelihood of stealing valuable goods. This strategy would eventually be recognised by members of the targeted community or by the police. At this stage, the wise burglar would move on from that area. Put another way, there should be a spate of burglaries in a particular area which is contained within a limited period of time. That is, there will be a hot spot for burglary which lasts for just a short time. This is what Johnson and Bower's (2004) research showed – hot spots for burglary move dynamically. Hot spots involve potentially lucrative households in an area but the burglars' strategy is to move on to another location when the yields are poor and/or the risk of arrest is high. This may have important practical policing implications. It may be an ineffective strategy for the police to target those areas which have been shown to have high burglary rates one month since the hot spot is likely to have moved. The chances are, however, that the hot spot moves to a nearby area. Hot spots are likely to be found in the most affluent areas, which are not necessarily the areas where burglary is the most frequent. This is not the consequences of certain households being repeatedly targeted since the researchers excluded such repeat victimisations.

Main points

- Property crime is commonplace and it is probably impossible to find anyone who has not committed some sort of trivial theft at some time in their lives. Perhaps as a consequence, psychologists have not devoted much activity to researching property crime as a specific topic. Relatively large proportions of the general population admit to committing some sort of property crime at some time in their lives. Mainly these are thefts and the proportions reporting having crimes like burglary or robbery are much smaller. There is clearly a need to develop psychological approaches to the understanding of property crime much further.

- Psychiatric classifications such as kleptomania and pyromania seem to have little to do with the vast majority of property crimes or fire-setting offences against property. Their lack of importance to the majority of crimes contrasts somewhat with the familiarity of these terms among the general public. Some forms of theft such as shoplifting, just like fire-setting, are offences overwhelmingly carried out by youngsters. As such they are probably best considered as crimes of delinquency (Chapter 6).

- It is not surprising that financial motives underlie a great proportion of thefts of all sorts. One of the most disturbing property crimes is burglary. There seems to be clear evidence that this sort of crime is partly carried out in relation to the need to finance drug usage. Research has shown that times when heroin becomes expensive because of supply shortages are associated with increases in property crimes such as burglary. Furthermore, methadone treatment (a replacement for heroin to help users come off of heroin) is associated with a decrease in the amount of crime carried out by heroin users.

Chapter 8

Violent offenders

Overview

- Despite the public's belief that violent crime continues to rise, trends in violent crime indicate that the rate may be relatively modest even assessed over the period since records began a hundred years ago. The most serious violent crime, homicide, has shown quite a small increase over a hundred years of about 300%, which is tiny compared to the growth of reported violent crime against the person.

- Violent crime is economically very costly just as is property crime. In addition, it has many direct psychological consequences on the victim (see Chapter 4).

- The effects of media violence on violent crime have rarely been seriously considered by forensic and criminal psychologists. Nevertheless, it is a major area of psychological research relevant to criminology. However, few studies concentrate on media influences on actual criminal violence compared to the voluminous literature on media effects in general. Generally speaking, despite laboratory evidence to the contrary, field research is less indicative of an adverse influence of the media on violence.

- Explanations of violent crime, including homicide, may be at various levels of analysis – the sociological, the psychological and the biological, for example. Of course, societal trends in violent crime (e.g. gender differences) need explanation and cannot be effectively dealt with at the level of individual psychology. Most forensic and criminal psychologists would accept that extreme acts of violence are multiply determined. These may be grouped under headings such as predisposing, maintenance and situational/triggering factors.

- Care must be taken to guard against the assumption that there are many extremely violent individuals who will act violently in many situations and against any target of their violence.

- Violence between intimates in the form of domestic violence and stalking is a significant part of violent crime especially as far as gender relationships are concerned. There are many complex forensic issues surrounding both of these types of violence and they make an important case study in the understanding of how crime is gendered.

Statistically speaking, the vast majority of crime consists of relatively trivial property offences (Chapters 2 and 7). Nevertheless, violent offences occur frequently according to crime statistics. Violent crime appears to be among the most salient factors in the public's perceptions of crime in general and its levels an indicator of society's malaise. Official crime statistics for the last few decades have generally shown increases in all sorts of crime. Violent crime is no exception to this long-term trend although it has reversed in some countries in recent years as has that of other crimes. There is no doubt that the long-term trend has been upwards. In the United Kingdom, for example, crime in general increased 66-fold during a hundred-year period ending in the year 2000/1. The figures for violent crime reflect a high growth rate of 315 times between the start and the end of the twentieth century. These are recorded crime rates. It is generally held that homicide is one of the most accurately recorded crimes. So changes in homicide rates may be an indicator of the true underlying trend. Other forms of violence may be partially the consequence of the increasing unacceptability of violence which lead to greater levels of reporting. Domestic violence is an example of a violent crime that is likely to have gone unreported to the police or ignored by them in the past. Nevertheless, it is particularly striking to note the way in which crime statistics escalated markedly in the second half of the twentieth century (Table 8.1).

Care is needed over the interpretation of these increases. According to the Home Office (2005b) figures, in England and Wales the trend for homicide is actually quite modest in comparison. For example, in 1900 there were 312 homicides in total, in 1950 there were 346, in 1975 there were 515 and in 2000/1 there were 850. This is an extremely slow growth rate of less than three times over the century compared with the figures for violence against the person. Remember that adjustment is also needed for population growth to obtain a reasonable comparison. So the growth in homicide is less than it appears to be from these figures owing to the increase in population size. Improved medical services saving more lives might have affected the trend somewhat also but this would decrease the levels of apparent violence. Taking all of these things into account, as an indicator of violence, homicide seems not to show the pattern that is generally expected.

Statisticians normally distinguish between violent crime and property crime. However, the costs of violent crime are not simply in those of pain and suffering.

Table 8.1 The growth of violent and other crime in the twentieth century

Year	Notifiable crimes recorded by police	Total violence against the person	Homicide recorded crimes
1900	78,000	1,908	312
1925	114,000	1,495	318
1950	479,000	6,249	346
1975	2,106,000	71,002	515
1980	2,688,000	97,246	620
1985	3,612,000	121,731	616
1990	4,544,000	184,665	669
1995	5,100,000	212,588	745
2000/1	5,171,000	600,922	850
2002/3	5,899,000	835,101	1,048

Violent crime has enormous economic costs. The estimate of these costs needs to include factors such as costs of prosecution, imprisonment, lost earning potential and so forth (Brand and Price, 2001):

- The average cost of a case of violence against the person is £19,000 ($27,000).
- Sexual offences are also £19,000 per case.
- Robberies/muggings are £4,700 per case.
- Burglary is £2,300 per case.
- Common assault is £540 per case.
- Murder costs a colossal £1,100,000 on average.

When reported as total amounts, the figures become even more alarming. Each year, the cost of burglary is £2.7 billion (a billion = 1,000 millions), robbery/mugging £2 billion, common assault £1.7 billion, homicide £1.2 billion, sexual offences £2.5 billion and violence against the person the phenomenal total of £16.8 billion.

Nevertheless, forensic and criminal psychology concentrates rather more on homicide and violent crimes (including rape and other sexual offences). Comparatively little attention has traditionally been paid to the more frequent property offences. Trivial offences cost nations dearly – even minor violence costs more than extreme acts of violence in total.

The heading of violent offences includes an array of rather different crimes which need disaggregation. Can a bar brawl be explained in the same terms as a serial killing? Intuitively we would say that they are very different. Yet there are a number of matters to consider. One very obvious thing uniting violent crimes (and all forms of crime) is the profound gender difference in terms of involvement with the criminal justice system. Males make up the majority of violent criminals in categories ranging from simple assault to serial killing. Age is an important factor in violent crime. Violent offenders tend to be young. These things need to be taken into account when studying violent crime. Several of the chapters in this book are very relevant to explanations of violent crime:

- The development of violent crime through childhood was discussed in Chapter 6.
- The role of mental illness in the aetiology of violent crime is discussed in Chapter 18.
- Serial killers are a special focus of Chapter 13 on offender profiling.
- Risk assessment is dealt with in Chapter 23.

Before we move on to examine explanations of violent crime further, it is important to note that much violence is easily explained superficially. The deep and complex psychological motives characteristic of violent offenders as portrayed in the media often give way to more obvious causes. In the United States, substantial numbers of offences are known to be associated with alcohol. Out of the 5 million offenders under various correction agencies, over a third had been drinking alcohol at the time of the offence. The trend is especially clear for violent offences where approximately 40% of those on probation, in local jails and in state prisons had consumed alcohol at the time of the crime. The figure reduces to 20% for those in federal prison for violent crimes.

While there may be a clear association between alcohol and crime in these US figures, this may be somewhat misleading in that it implies that the offenders were drunk rather than that they had merely consumed some alcohol. They may have been drunk, but it is not certain. Figures from a study of arrestees arriving at police stations in London seem to suggest fairly low levels of drunkenness in arrestees (Robertson *et al.*, 1995). Even serious violent offences tended to involve drunkenness relatively infrequently. Nevertheless, only 69% of grievous bodily harm cases were free from signs of drunkenness when they arrived. It is known from the British Crime Survey that 44% of victims of violence believed that their assailant was under the influence of alcohol (Smith and Allen, 2004).

Media influences

Forensic and criminal psychologists have traditionally ignored the role of the media in the genesis of crime. One exception is Blackburn (1993). He reviewed the research evidence on media violence and concluded that the violent content of the media was influential on the violence exhibited by the audience. Harrower (1998), again unusually for the field, devoted considerable space to the topic, though her conclusions are largely rhetorical rather than research-based. If one relied solely on general psychology textbooks rather than on forensic texts, there would be no other conclusion but to accept that media violence has a significant effect on societal violence (e.g. Passer and Smith, 2001). However, there have been a number of reviewers who dispute the media violence causes societal violence notion (e.g. Cumberbatch and Howitt, 1989; Fowles, 1999) though this is far from a universal view (K. Browne, 1999; Pennell and Browne, 1998a). This is not to argue that the media have had no impact on society – that would be patently an absurd suggestion. Nevertheless, apart from laboratory experiments, a range of research employing a variety of methods seems to indicate little or no influence of the media on real-life violence (e.g. Howitt, 1998b). The neglect of media influences by criminologists was noted quite a few years ago (Cumberbatch and Howitt, 1989; Howitt and Cumberbatch, 1975). There are a number of reasons why criminologists have tended to ignore the media as a cause of crime:

- Much of the research on media violence effects is based on laboratory experiments that are of little interest to many researchers.
- Explanations of media violence effects have largely been in terms of social influences rather than the clinical perspectives frequently favoured by some forensic and criminal psychologists.
- Research findings in the field appear somewhat chaotic at first with some studies suggesting effects and others suggesting no effects. Consequently, the complexity of the research is difficult for non-specialists in media research to comprehend.
- Few media researchers have much knowledge of crime. Indeed, the media violence research very rarely involves acts that are likely to be illegal since the 'victim' has agreed to the aggression or it is directed against an inanimate object or it may be verbal aggression.

Research strategies

What is the case for believing that media violence causes violence in society? This can be broken down into several broad research strategies:

Laboratory experiments

There have been numerous laboratory studies of the effects of media violence. This style of research is still current, for example, in relation to videogames (e.g. Ballard and Wiest, 1996). Essentially, and usually, the researchers show one group of participants a violent film/video snippet and another a non-violent snippet. Then their aggression levels as measured by an electric shock machine in the fashion of the classic Milgram experiment on obedience (Milgram, 1974) are compared. Alternatively, as in the case of the Bandura studies of modelling, the extent to which modelling of knocking over and otherwise maltreating a blow-up plastic clown regarded as analogous to other forms of violence (Howitt, 1998b) is assessed:

- It is clear from meta-analysis (Box 5.1) that overwhelmingly the findings of laboratory experiments suggest the strongest effects of media violence of any studies (Hearold, 1986; Paik and Comstock, 1994; Wood *et al.*, 1991).

- However, a number of studies have failed to reproduce findings using different methods and, in some cases, the effects are so specific that they are likely to apply only in the laboratory setting. For example, in Berkowitz's famous studies (Berkowitz and Rawlings, 1963; Berkowitz *et al.*, 1963) the aggression effects claimed were very short lived and applied only to the person who had deliberately insulted participants.

- Howitt (1998b) calls for the criminological relevance of research to be the basis for deciding whether research on media violence should be taken seriously by forensic and criminal psychologists. Research on 4-year-olds imitating the modelled, seemingly play aggression against a squeaky blow-up plastic clown that cannot be knocked over without it bouncing back up, is hardly the sort of activity that warrants the description criminal (Howitt, 1998b). Ultimately, the concern with media violence is its influence on the development of serious violence in the audience.

Studies of the development of aggression during childhood

We saw in Chapter 6 that there are quite a few studies of the development of delinquency. Rarely in these studies is media violence included in the research. Of course, this may be oversight or deliberate. The exception to this is the work of Leonard Eron. In the early 1960s he published a study into factors associated with aggression in a large sample of youngsters of about 8 years of age (Eron, 1963). Peer and teacher ratings of aggression were obtained as well as a range of other measures. The number of hours of television watched each week was one such measure. In addition, the violence level contained in the child's favourite television programmes was assessed. This was based on the nominations *each child's mother* made about their child's favourite television programmes. The amount of television watched did not correlate positively with the aggression exhibited by the youngsters. Indeed, for boys, the less television watched then the more aggressive they were – the reverse of the media causes violence hypothesis. Although, maybe, this ought to have been the end of the story, it was not. The reason was that the *mothers' nominations of the boys' favourite television programmes* were more often violent programmes than were those of the non-aggressive boys. Remember that it was not even the claims of the boys themselves. No such relationship was found for girls. This seems, overall, rather weak evidence that television is responsible for violence.

A few years later, with a number of collaborators, finance was obtained to study the youngsters when they had reached their late teens (Eron *et al.*, 1972). This new stage is probably the most famous. It was that the violent television variable at age 8 years predicted aggression at age 18 years . . . apparently. One major problem was that this measure at age 18 years was actually retrospective. Peers were rating each other as they were quite a few years earlier. In other words, these were ratings of aggression going back close to the time of the original phase of the study. It is hardly surprising that media use at age 8 predicted aggression at age 18 years since aggression at age 18 years was simply not what it appeared to be. There were more follow-ups. The final stage studied the same group when they had reached adulthood. It was possible to check the actual crimes and motor traffic offences they had committed. Remarkably, it looked like adult criminality could be predicted from those ratings of favourite television programmes decades earlier. One interpretation of this is that it is an effect of liking violent television that persists into adult behaviour and results in criminal and other antisocial behaviour (e.g. Newson, 1994a, b). There are other possibilities. For example, we saw in Chapter 6 the continuities between childhood antisocial behaviour and adult antisocial behaviour. Perhaps the mothers when they nominated their son's television viewing favourites were conscious that sometimes their son was a little wayward in his behaviour. Thus when they answered about television programmes they nominated a violent programme because this fitted with their son's personality – the boy was not asked. Consequently, this adult behaviour was merely a continuation of the difficulties that some mothers recognised in their son's behaviour and nothing to do with television at all. If it were television that caused their behaviour, would we not expect the problems to be associated with watching more television, not with watching less?

- Milavsky *et al.* (1982), in a major replication in the style of the above study, found little to support the Eron *et al.* data (Eron *et al.*, 1972; Huesman and Malamuth, 1986; Lefkowitz *et al.*, 1977).
- A later American study by Huesmann and Eron (1986) failed to detect similar effects for boys. This time, quite unlike the original study, some evidence was found that girls' viewing was associated with aggression.
- International studies of the development of aggression supervised by Eron and his co-workers (Wiegman *et al.*, 1992) found, at best, extremely varied results with very little support other than North American research. There were many zero relationships between television viewing indexes and violence in viewers. Indeed, the relationships were very inconsistent even within countries.

Studies of the criminal statistics

While crime statistics can be difficult to interpret (see Chapter 2), they have been used in two ways to study media effects on societal violence:

- Messner (1986) took the crime statistics of different states of the United States and related them to the public's viewing of media violence obtained from surveys of media use. The areas with the greatest amount of public consumption of media violence then should have the greatest levels of societal violence – according to the media cause violence hypothesis. Of course, it is essential in such a study to control/adjust for demographic characteristics when making the comparisons. After that was done thoroughly, Messner (1986) found that the *more* television violence watched the *less* the violence in the community. This is the reverse of expectations if the media violence causes violence hypothesis were true.

- Centerwall (1989, 1993) took a different approach. He studied changes in violent crime rates in the United States for the period before the introduction of television to many years after its introduction. Previous research had found no immediate impact of the introduction of television on US violent crime rates (Hennigan *et al.*, 1982). Nevertheless, Centerwall argues that one would not expect effects until several years later when children have grown into adolescents – the time when they are most likely to demonstrate violence. This is a reasonable idea although many other researchers had studied the immediate effects of witnessing media violence and found effects in the laboratory. At first sight, the crime data appear to support this thesis – a rapid rise in societal violence occurred several years after the introduction of television in the United States. In comparison, in South Africa, where television was not introduced until many years later, there was no such rapid rise at that time. Howitt (1998b) applied Centerwall's idea to Great Britain where television was introduced as a mass medium during the 1950s. He found that there was a steady growth in violent crime during the period researched by Centerwall but no rapid rise at the time predicted by Centerwall's argument. In other words, there is no general effect of television violence on violent crime statistics, which casts considerable doubt on Centerwall's interpretation of the US data.

Studies of delinquent offenders

There has been a small number of studies of the media use of delinquent offenders (Hagell and Newburn, 1994; Halloran *et al.*, 1970; Kruttschnitt *et al.*, 1986). They have generally failed to produce evidence of the influence of media violence on offenders. One study found an association between serious delinquency and television (Browne and Pennell, 1998; Pennell and Browne, 1998b). They took a sample of violent teenage boys in a young offenders' institute for violent offending. The young offenders were compared with appropriate control groups – including a similar group of incarcerated young offenders but *not* convicted of violence and community controls of the same age range, sex and so forth:

- There were differences in the media use of the incarcerated groups and the community groups, such as the offenders tended to prefer violent videos though they also seemed to like soap operas more.
- There were psychological differences such as the lower level of moral reasoning in offender groups which might have contributed to their offending (see Chapter 6).
- Physical abuse by parents was far commoner in the childhood of the violent sample.
- When experience of childhood abuse was taken into account, any differences between the groups in terms of liking violent videos disappeared. Thus their violence is the result of their abusive childhood and their interest in violent video is a consequence of and not a cause of their violence. Abuse creates violent youngsters who then use media violence more frequently than non-abused youngsters.

Does media violence make violent crime?

The answer to the question of whether media violence causes societal violence must concentrate on the criminologically relevant aspects of aggression – criminal violence. This means that much of the voluminous literature on media violence effects is irrelevant as it does not deal with criminal acts. One should also bear in mind that we know a lot about the development of criminality and criminal violence in particular from longitudinal studies of development from childhood into adulthood (see Chapter 6). It is clear that early experience, especially experience of inadequate parenting broadly defined, leads to problem children, problem teenagers and problem adults. With these matters in consideration, the following seems to be a reasonable assessment of the media violence issue as far as it affects criminal violent acts:

- Virtually no developmental evidence exists concerning the influence of the media on criminality. The studies that deal with the media tend to be associated almost exclusively with the work of Leonard Eron and his co-workers. Despite being frequently cited in the debate on media violence effects, the original findings are inconsistent and apply to boys and only in terms of their mothers' assessments of their favourite television programmes. When the amount of television viewed is considered, the evidence suggests that the more television watched, the less impact it has on aggressive behaviour! Later studies fail to reproduce these findings, or find similar outcomes but for girls and not boys which is the reverse of the original findings, or produce inconsistent outcomes for different parts of the world. In short, there is less than convincing evidence of the effects of media violence.

- Crime statistics do not show a relationship with the levels of violence viewed in communities – the reverse trend exists in fact. Crime statistics in the United States have been interpreted as demonstrating a delayed effect of the introduction of violent media but this claim has not been substantiated for the United Kingdom.

- Violent delinquents do seem to have a preference for certain sorts of programme including violent video. Despite this, the biggest factor in their violence is their abuse by their parents in childhood. Once this is taken into account, then their media consumption can be regarded as no different from non-violent controls.

In summary, a forensic and criminal psychologist should exercise great caution before assuming a role of the media in generating violent criminality. Although there have been claims that offenders have been influenced by movies, no court in the United States has accepted such arguments (Lande, 1993). Nevertheless, there have been accusations that movies such as *Child's Play 3* (directed by Jack Bender in 1991) and *Natural Born Killers* (directed by Oliver Stone in 1994) influenced youngsters to kill, the latter in very substantial numbers. However, the evidence in support is weak. For example, whether the culprits actually saw the movie in question is doubtful in some cases and that an accused person attempts to excuse their acts by blaming a movie might be expected. It is not the sort of rigorous evidence that forensic and criminal psychologists normally seek. The inhibition of aggression is socialised from early in childhood, long before the child is capable of giving much attention to television programmes. Failures of parenting at an early age have clearly been shown to be associated with later criminality and violence.

Another, totally independent review of the evidence (Felson, 1996) makes a number of related points. They are worth mentioning as they reinforce some of the comments made above:

- Violent offenders tend to be versatile offenders – they do not confine their activities to violent crime but commit all types of crime. This is somewhat incompatible with the idea that violent offenders have a problem caused by their violence socialisation – either via the media or any other source.

- The contents of the media concerning violence do not appear to give a radically different message about violence than any other source of socialisation. The media give much the same message about when it is appropriate to use violence and when it is not appropriate. The one area where Felson makes an exception is illegitimate violence that is by definition unacceptable. The media show this sort of violence being punished more so than does any other source of socialisation.

Theories of homicide

Societal level theory

There is a tendency to assume that violence can be explained only in terms of the psychology of individuals. Most of us do not murder so there must be something 'odd' about murderers. For most homicides, there is little to implicate psychiatric factors (see also Chapter 18), which indicates that other factors need to be taken into account. This is not to suggest that researchers can ignore psychiatric and other individual factors in violent crime. The evidence that homicide rates tend to increase during a war and show different characteristics from those perpetrated previously is evidence that broad societal events may significantly affect the criminal acts of individuals (Pozgain *et al.*, 1998). Nevertheless, psychiatric factors simply cannot be discounted. For example, Steck (1998) found that spouse murderers in a German sample characteristically had a history more likely to feature a psychologically deviant development especially involving psychiatric disorder and if they are disengaged socially. Nevertheless, this does not mean that other levels of explanation of extreme violent crime are wrong.

One of the more interesting societal level suggestions is Leyton's (1986) view that multiple murders (i.e. those in which the killer kills more than one individual) may be explained in terms of social structure. A problem in understanding multiple killing (including serial killing) is that the targets of such crimes tend not to be a random sample of potential victims. Instead, victims tend to have particular characteristics. Leyton's key insight was that he realised that multiple killing is not merely a recent phenomenon but one with roots in history. He identified three major periods in which multiple killing was common. Then he realised that these three periods varied markedly in terms of the social characteristics of the killers and the victims. The historical epochs in question are the *pre-industrial period*, the *industrial period* and the *modern period*. The typical killer during these times and the typical victim are given in Table 8.2.

Table 8.2 Multiple killers and their victims in different historical periods

Epoch	Social class of killers	Victims
Modern epoch (i.e. 1945 onwards)	Lower/lower middle class	Middle classes
Industrial epoch c. 1800–1945	Middle classes	Lower working class/underclass
Pre-industrial epoch (pre-1800)	Upper classes (aristocracy)	Lower classes (peasants)

What appears to be happening, very broadly, is that the killers have been of decreasing social class since the pre-industrial period. In contrast, their victims have become of higher social class. In the pre-industrial period the typical multiple murderer was Gilles de Rais, a French nobleman who killed peasant children by the hundred. The typical multiple killer of the industrial period was a middle-class individual who killed housemaids or prostitutes. Finally, in the modern period the multiple killer is largely of a lower social status than the victim. If this is true, then the question is why do these changes occur? Basically, Leyton argued that multiple killings are indicative of *homicidal protest*. This is essentially that at different times in history a (social) class becomes under threat from another social class. The general dissatisfaction, concern and anxiety felt by the threatened class becomes expressed by a few of the discontented class through multiple murders of the threatening class. In other words, the murders are symbolic of structural discontent. The epochs differ in the focus of this discontent:

- In the *pre-industrial period* there was challenge to the social order by the peasant classes as well as merchant classes. Revolts and the like illustrate the challenge.
- In the *industrial period*, the middle classes held their position through a 'moral' superiority over the working class. Consequently, the threat to their social position came largely from those in society who most threatened that moral order. Prostitution was a threat by its nature to the family and the patriarchal social organisation of the family. Women who engaged in sexual activity willingly outside marriage would threaten the moral basis of family life. Housemaids, of course, were the lowest level of employment and also single women whose sexuality was a threat. They were also in the sector of employment that somewhat morally disgraced young women could be encouraged to enter if their chances of marriage had been sullied. Killing such women symbolically reinforced the moral superiority of the middle class. Jack the Ripper would appear to represent this type of killer – if he were a member of the middle class rather than royalty, of course, in the light of some claims about the Ripper's identity.
- In the *modern period*, according to Leyton, the challenge to the social order comes from the changed social order in which rigid class structures have loosened and upward mobility is seen as a realistic ambition of the lower social classes. It is when those who expect to progress feel thwarted that *homicidal protest* comes into play. Hence students may be victims of such protest since they have the privileges that the disaffected feel should have been theirs.

There are a number of problems with this theory. The historical record concerning crime, especially in the pre-industrial period, may be inadequate. Can the findings concerning the modern period be replicated away from the North American context? Grover and Soothill (1999) took Leyton's ideas and attempted to apply them to serial killing in recent British criminal history. A total of 17 serial killers (three or more victims) were found for the period beginning 1960. According to Grover and Soothill, it was clear that the victims were simply not the middle classes that the theory predicts that they should be. They were in fact typical of the weak and powerless groups in society – gay men, women, children, young adults and pensioners. The serial killers included Ian Brady, Myra Hindley and Beverly Allitt who killed children, and Dennis Nilsen, Colin Ireland and Peter Moore who killed gay men. While at least a substantial number of the killers could be described as working class, the data do not support the idea of a class-based homicidal protest. Grover and

Soothill suggest that the idea of homicidal protest may be useful if the idea of its basis in social class conflicts is abandoned. It should be replaced by consideration of broader social relations which make certain groups vulnerable.

Psychological disposition theories

There is no easy way of explaining homicide. While it is tempting to regard murderers as exceptionally violent personalities suffering from extremes of psychopathology, this is to ignore the large number of killers who are non-aggressive and not suffering from an identifiable psychopathology. Murderers have been divided into various typologies. After studying murderers in a psychiatric prison hospital, Blackburn (1971) suggested that there are four types of murder:

- paranoid-aggressive;
- depressive;
- psychopathic;
- over-controlled repressors (of aggression).

This pattern has been found in a non-psychiatric group of offenders so it is not merely the result of the extreme psychiatric difficulties of a selected group of offenders.

Biro *et al.* (1992) carried out a standardised interview with Yugoslavian men convicted of homicide offences. As in the above research, the MMPI (Minnesota Multiphasic Personality Inventory) scores of the men were an important aspect of the categorisation. Four categories were identified:

- Normal profiles (28%).
- Hypersensitive-aggressive (49%): this group consists of people with the characteristics of being easily offended, prone to impulsive aggressive outbursts and intolerant of frustration. They are very rigid, uncooperative and permanently dissatisfied with things.
- Psychopathic (17%): these tend to score highly on emotional instability, impulsivity and immaturity. They tend to have poor control of their aggression.
- Psychotic (5%): these seem to be 'mistakes of the system' since they are individuals who show extreme psychiatric signs and would normally have been confined to a special psychiatric unit. Their crimes appear to be bizarre such as the man who cooked his own child in a pot. These offenders had not been psychiatrically evaluated before being sentenced.

The percentages in each category seem to indicate that only in a large minority of the cases is the issue primarily to do with aggression. A quarter plus show normal profiles overall. The normal personality category seems to act aggressively out of a situational pressure, not because its basic personality structure leads to aggression.

Socio-biological theory

At the opposite pole, there are biologically based ideas about murder, which on the surface would appear to be as different as possible from the societal approaches such as that just described. While it is tempting to believe that there may be some biological factor (e.g. brain dysfunction) in extreme violence such as serial killing, the research evidence in its favour is best described as minimal (Coleman and Norris, 2000). There are two important issues here:

- Research on the biological basis of criminality, and criminal violence in particular, is somewhat rare and patchy in scope. There is a lack of a coherent body of knowledge as a consequence. This situation is no help to forensic and criminal psychologists.
- Biological factors are generally beyond the scope of psychologists to change materially.

The typical biological approach seeks to find the biological 'defects' which result in criminal behaviours.

When one considers the topic of violence, it is tempting to point to the statistics that show that violent crime is an overwhelmingly male activity. This, surely, must be irrefutable evidence of a firm biological basis to violent crime. A little care is needed. Bjorqkvist (1994) argued males and females do not differ in their aggressiveness. What is different is the way in which it is expressed. Bjorqkvist goes so far as to indicate that the claim that males are the more aggressive is nonsensical. Aggression is largely seen from a male perspective that equates aggression with physical aggression. It is this male perspective that has dominated research on human aggression. If men are the most aggressive, then the fact that same-sex aggression (female vs. female, male vs. male) seems to be more common than cross-sex (male vs. female) is difficult to explain. Bjorqkvist argues that the physically weaker sex, women, is likely to learn different aggressive strategies from those used by the physically stronger sex, men (Bjorkqvist and Niemela, 1992; Bjorkqvist et al., 1992). It is inappropriate then to extrapolate from animal studies to human aggression since animal aggression is mostly physical. For adults, the reasonable assumption is that physical aggression is the least common form of aggression.

The putative link between testosterone and aggression is very much a dubious proposition for humans. According to Bjorkqvist, the closer an animal species is to humankind the less is the link between testosterone level and aggressiveness. Injecting testosterone experimentally, which should if the theory is correct lead to higher aggression levels, does not have clear-cut results. Sometimes such experiments seem to suggest no link between the testosterone and aggression. Edwards (1969) and Edwards and Herndon (1970) found that female mice given the male hormone androgen at birth grew up to be more aggressive as adults compared with non-treated mice. While this appears to support the view that maleness = aggression, perhaps this is not the case. Similar female mice given the female hormone oestrogen at birth also tended to fight rather more than non-treated mice as adults. Bjorkqvist proposed an effect/danger ratio theory for human aggression. This is based on the notion that there is a subjective estimation of the ratio between the effect of the intended strategy (such as physical aggression) divided by the danger involved of such a strategy. This operates in such a way that risk is minimised while the effect of the strategy is maximised. Hence, women have a greater risk if they engage in physical aggression than men so they may prefer other strategies. There is some evidence that aggression in males is expressed directly (perhaps in the form of fighting) whereas aggression in females is expressed indirectly (perhaps in the form of maliciously telling a teacher something).

Bjorkqvist and Niemela (1992) had peers rate Finnish 7-year-olds, indicating what each child did when angry. Direct means were kicks/strikes, swearing, chasing the other child and pushes/shoves. Indirect responses included gossiping, becoming friendly with another child in revenge, suggestions that the other child should be shunned in some way. The study was essentially repeated with a similar sample of 11-year-old and 15-year-old adolescents. At the younger age, it was clear that boys used direct forms of aggression more than did girls. There was no difference in terms of indirect aggression. But during adolescence girls were still using direct aggression less than did boys whereas they used more indirect forms of aggression. The girls seem to manipulate their friendship networks as a means of effecting some of this indirect aggression. Similar findings were found concerning indirect aggression in females cross-culturally (Osterman *et al.*, 1998). Others have found that relational victimisation of this sort (telling lies about another person so they will be disliked or leaving another person out of social activities when one is angry with them) is more characteristic of girls (Crick and Bigbee, 1998) even at the pre-school age level (Crick *et al.*, 1997). There is evidence that girls see social aggression as little or no different from physical aggression in terms of its hurtfulness (Galen and Underwood, 1997). Thus if aggression is seen as the intention to hurt or harm another then the use of indirect aggression by females relates more closely to physical aggression. It might be argued that it is physical aggression that is sanctioned in law, not the indirect forms of aggression. This is to ignore, for example, libel and slander laws which are clearly about controlling what might be described as verbal social attacks on individuals. Lindeman *et al.* (1997) had Finnish adolescents self-rate themselves in terms of their strategies in conflict situations. In this context, in late adolescence, the preferred mode for male adolescents was to join in with any verbal aggression. In contrast, girls said that they would adopt a strategy of withdrawal from the situation or used a more social model of response such as 'I would clearly tell the backbiters that their behavior is mean and I would ask them to stop' (p. 343). Of course, some have argued that direct forms of physical aggression are becoming more characteristic of females. Much of the physical aggression between girls concerns their relationships with males and threats to those relationships (Artz, 1998). As such, the aggression is regarded as the right thing to do.

It is worthwhile noting Crick's (1997) findings concerning social-psychological adjustment as assessed through self-ratings and teacher ratings. Gender normative aggression was associated with good adjustment ratings. Boys who engaged in aggression through relationships and girls who were overtly aggressive tended to be less well adjusted. In other words, there is evidence of the deeply-seated nature of these gender differences in aggression.

There is a substantially different perspective concerning gender differences in aggression. Daly and Wilson (1988) put forward a socio-biological explanation of homicide. They worked primarily on the basis of the following established socio-biological principles:

- The process of natural selection shaped human nature: that is, random genetic variation produces diversity of offspring and those best fitted to survive tend to pass on their genetic material. While the ideas are essentially those of Charles Darwin, Herbert Spencer's phrase 'survival of the fittest' is the most familiar way to describe it. In this context, survival is survival of the genes or species rather than a particular individual. Fitness really refers to those who are able to transmit their genes – individuals who do not win out in mating may live to an old age, but they have not passed on their genes so they were not fit in terms of the species.

- Daly and Wilson use the term 'adaptively constructed' to describe the way we are – that is, we are what we are because that is what allowed the species to survive. There is a competition in mating whereby the fittest (best genes) tend to be transmitted to the next generation.
- People (as well as other creatures) have evolved such that they spend much of their efforts on the posterity of their genes: that is, sex is not some sort of secondary motivation that comes into play when hunger and thirst, for example, have been satiated. It is much more to the forefront than that.
- Homicide, like any other field of human activity, should show characteristics that reflect in some way the characteristics of how we have been adaptively constructed.
- Daly and Wilson accept that there is cultural variation over and above socio-biological influences on homicide. Some cultures seem to exhibit higher levels of killings than others. Nevertheless, part of the pattern of homicides is socio-biologically determined.

These basic ideas, in themselves, did not take Daly and Wilson far. Something else needs to be considered. They recognised that much of the available statistical evidence was incapable of answering crucial questions about homicide. Furthermore, the available database needed reanalysis to provide helpful answers. To illustrate, in the context of the family, socio-biological thinking would suggest that both parents should have an interest in ensuring that their offspring (their genes) survive. At the same time, Daly and Wilson argue that we are often encouraged to believe that the family is a dangerously violent place in which the offspring are at considerable risk. In other words, rather than preserve their genes, parents may kill their offspring, thus destroying the future potential of their genes. This is certainly the impression created by the research literature on family violence. There is a problem with this. When homicide of children is subdivided into killing by natural biological parents and by step-parents, interesting findings emerge. Put another way, natural parents kill their offspring rather rarely in comparison to step-parents who kill the children of the family relatively frequently. Step-parents are not destroying their own distinctive genes by killing, say, a child fathered by the woman's previous partner.

Another example is their argument concerning intra-sexual homicide – that is, men killing men, women killing women. The genes of males, they argue, are best helped to survive by fertilising as many women as possible. Hence other men are a handicap to genetic survival since they monopolise women. Females help their genes survive best by protecting and nurturing their offspring. Thus Daly and Wilson argue that males should kill males much more frequently than females kill females. The data on homicide suggest that this is the case. Indeed, young males are much more in competition for mating than older males – and crime statistics suggest that young men kill each other much more frequently. There are a number of matters to bear in mind:

- The socio-biological approach, since it attempts to explain society from the point of view of biology, competes with social explanations of the same phenomena. For example, step-parents may murder children of the family more often simply because the stresses in step-parent families are likely to be greater. Furthermore, bonds between step-parents and step-children may have had less opportunity to develop. It is difficult to decide which is the better explanation. Socio-biological approaches tend not to have any verifiable genetic evidence: both they and societal explanations rely on observations of the same social processes.

- Socio-biological approaches to a variety of social phenomena tend to be a little unhelpful because of the assumption that what is genetically fixed becomes incorporated into social structure. Forensic and criminal psychologists are more interested in changing individuals rather than in regarding their criminality, for example, as a built-in feature.
- Whatever the long-term value of Daly and Wilson's approach in helping us to understand homicide, it teaches a valuable lesson about crime statistics: that is, statistical compilations of data may sometimes hide important relationships simply because very different things are classified together in published tables.

The multi-factorial approach

Generally speaking, most forensic and criminal psychologists would take the view that extreme acts of violence, including homicide, have multiple causation. Rarely is a single factor seen as sufficient to explain violent crime. Since extreme violence, such as serial killing, is such a rare phenomenon, it is unlikely that a single factor could be identified which is only associated with serial killing. Extremely violent behaviour may, then, best be understood by the application of the sort of multi-factorial framework suggested by Gresswell and Hollin (1994, 1997). This is illustrated in Figure 8.1. Basically it involves three levels of factor – *predisposing factors*, *maintenance factors* and *situational/triggering factors*. These three types should be considered as part of

Predisposing factors

- A failure of normal bonding with parents or other primary care-givers, leading to a lack of similar feelings towards others.
- Traumatic experiences are not dealt with properly, as a consequence.
- Fantasies about the traumatic experience may develop and dominate.
- Through fantasy, feelings of power, which are lacking through poor interpersonal skills and so forth, can be experienced and so the fantasy becomes increasingly rewarding.

↓

Maintenance factors

- Cognitive inhibitory factors: most children gradually learn not to act aggressively through normal socialisation processes. A child with unsatisfactory bonding and social relationships may fail to learn.
- Cognitive facilitative processes: the tendency towards fantasy may allow the use of violent fantasy to deal with situations.
- Operant processes: the feeling of power experienced through fantasy is rewarding, encouraging further fantasy. It also serves to isolate the individual from the bad aspects of life.

↓

Situational/triggering factors

- These are the factors that encourage the acting out of the fantasy against a real person.
- Particularly influential may be stressful situations such as financial problems, employment problems and relationship problems.

Figure 8.1 Multi-factorial model of serial killing
Source: Gresswell, D.M. and Hollin, C.R. (1994) Multi-factorial model of serial killing. *British Journal of Criminology*, **34**, 1–14. Reproduced by permission of Oxford University Press

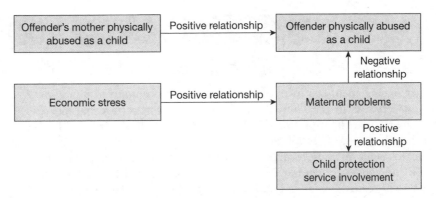

Figure 8.2 The relationship between cycles of abuse and economic stress

the explanation of a homicide. No particular specific factor is assumed to be essential to homicide. Nevertheless, the accumulating pattern of factors when applied to a particular case may help understand that case. It is clear from Figure 8.1 that serial killing is rare because the contributing factors in themselves may not be common and the presence of several of them together may be a rare situation.

Equally, when considering the many frequent minor assaults that pervade the criminal statistics concerning violence, we might look for commonly occurring factors. However, the likely influence of factors acting separately may not be the same as factors acting in combination. For example, Haapasalo (1999) examined inter-generational cycles of physical abuse by taking a Finnish offender sample. He collected a variety of information about physical abuse as well as other matters such as marital conflict and involvement with the child protection services. In a sense, studies such as this are particularly important for forensic and criminal psychologists since they are about their main clientele. Studies involving the general population are less relevant to their work and may show less strong or even dissimilar trends. Following a complex statistical analysis (Lisrel), it became clear that the paths leading to the sons being physically abused in childhood can have unexpected twists. As shown in Figure 8.2, there was clear evidence that the variable *mother physically abused in childhood* leads fairly directly to her son being *physically abused in childhood*. This is probably very much what one might expect on the basis of the assumption that aggression is, in part, socially learnt.

What of the influence of another variable *economic stress* (financial and related difficulties)? We would expect, surely, that the more stress on the mother the more likely she would be to physically abuse her children since stress makes her irritable and moody among other things. Take a look again at Figure 8.2. Starting with the factor *economic stress*, we can see that it leads to a higher level of *maternal problems*. But the most likely route from there is involvement of the child protection services for some reason. This might include, for example, some sort of respite help for the mother. The path from *maternal problems* to the son being *physically abused in childhood* is the reverse of expectations: that is, the greater the maternal problems the *less* the likelihood that her son would be physically abused in childhood. Whether the mothers regard economic stress as a warning sign that they are not coping cannot be addressed simply from these data. Nevertheless, this is feasible, which may make them more inclined to seek the help of social services. This completely unexpected finding tells us to avoid making simplistic assumptions about how social and psychological factors influence violent behaviour.

Box 8.1

Forensic psychology in action: anger management

Anger management is a form of treatment which is employed in a variety of contexts including prison services. In the United Kingdom, the prison service has developed a National Anger Management Package (Towl, 1995) which is used with prisoners with temper control difficulties. It is based on group-work with two facilitators present and a group of six to eight prisoners over, typically, eight sessions. Its main aims are to heighten awareness of the process of becoming angry in the individual, to increase awareness of self-monitoring of one's own behaviour, to learn the benefits of controlling anger, and to enhance their knowledge and skill at managing their anger (Keen, 2000). The following sessions are included:

- Session 1 Introduction: to learn the aims of the course, to keep an anger diary to monitor their feelings, to understand the bad side of losing one's temper and to learn the rules of conduct for the group.
- Session 2 Changing behaviour: recognition of bodily signs of anger and why non-aggressive body language is preferable.
- Session 3 Changing thoughts: the relationship between thoughts and behaviour and the use of self-calming statements during anger.
- Session 4 Controlling arousal: what happens to the body during anger and ways of dealing with the arousal of anger (e.g. relaxation techniques).
- Session 5 Assertiveness: the difference between passivity, anger and assertiveness.
- Session 6 Handling criticisms and insults: the difference between criticisms and insults. Being aware of and dealing with group pressure.

The final two sessions are devoted to overview and review.

Theoretically (Howells *et al.*, 1997), the emphasis of such programmes is on cognitive components of anger and, in particular, the process of appraisal. The event is appraised and an emotional response is the consequence:

Event → appraisal → emotion

For anger to emerge, the individual must be displeased about the related undesirable event and disapprove of someone's blameworthy action. So, if we hit our finger with a hammer we are unlikely to feel anger. On the other hand, if we hit our finger with a hammer at the time that someone starts talking to us we may well get angry. There is thus an aversive event and a blameable individual. Of course, anger is an inappropriate emotion in these circumstances since the other person almost certainly did not wish to cause harm to you.

The difficulty is the lack of consistency in the causes of violence in violent individuals. Some may be psychopaths who act violently *not* out of anger but dispassionately in order to achieve their particular goals – perhaps to obtain money. Others may lack self-esteem and be vulnerable to taunts by others. In the first case, a general package of anger-reduction may be of no advantage and perhaps even counterproductive since efforts to get such a person to control their temper misperceive the origins of the violence. It is a mistake to assume that violence in the context of a theft, say, cannot be helped with anger management. The reasons for the violence need to be understood first.

Domestic violence: forensic issues

Much of this chapter has dealt with explanations of extreme acts of violence. It is important for a forensic and criminal psychologist to understand the range of theoretical approaches that can be brought to the discipline. At the same time, forensic and criminal psychology is not merely a branch of psychological research and theory, it is also a practical discipline that seeks to help deal with otherwise tricky questions for the criminal justice system. Let us take a particularly difficult issue – that of domestic violence within a family. There are a number of aspects to this. One is that this is the sort of situation with which social workers, the police and sometimes psychologists may have to deal. So what can we say if we know that a man at 25 Beeches Road has split up with his partner? There are children in the household and social workers insist that he lives at another address. He attempts to obtain visitation rights to have the children at his new home at the weekend. The mother objects. Her reason is that he has been violent to her on numerous occasions and that every time there has been a meeting in the past, the children have become distressed. Called in to give advice or even evidence to court, just what practical suggestions might a psychologist make?

Common notions suggest that violence is a trait in some people, and that such people act aggressively in a wide variety of situations. The suggestion is sometimes heard that a particular person has a short fuse, for example: that is, the person is readily provoked to be aggressive. Unfortunately, one cannot rely on folklore as a definitive treatise on human behaviour. Put more formally, the issue is one of the co-occurrence of spousal abuse and physical child abuse – if the one is present, how likely is it that the other is also present? This has been sporadically an issue for research since the 1970s when it was first suggested that if there was spousal abuse in the family the risk of that child being abused was increased. It was not until the 1990s that it became recognised that child abuse and spousal abuse were simply different aspects of family violence (Appel and Holden, 1998). This has clear implications for forensic issues such as whether spouses who batter their partners are fit to be the custodial parent on divorce or separation. According to Appel and Holden, what at first appears to be a relatively simple question becomes a complex one when the research literature is addressed. Issues include the following:

- The criteria employed to decide whether spouse abuse and child abuse had occurred. The mother's report, the father's report, the child's report and professional assessment may all be expected to produce different findings.
- The sorts of act classified as abuse may profoundly influence rates of co-occurrence. For example, if a gentle slap of a child were to be regarded as physical child abuse, then since a gentle slap is a very frequent form of discipline in families it is extremely likely that a man who has abused his partner will also have abused the child.
- What period of time was covered by the retrospective reports? The greater the time period the greater co-occurrence.

Appel and Holden reviewed studies of different types of sample: community (or non-clinical) samples, samples of battered women and samples of maltreated children. Self-reports, agency records, hospital records and clinical impressions were included. The detail of the outcomes of the studies differed quite widely although it is fair to suggest that, generally, co-occurrence does take place but the magnitude of this varies:

- Most of the work on community samples (i.e. general population samples) has been carried out by Gelles (e.g. Gelles, 1979; Gelles and Cornell, 1985). They use the *Conflict Tactics Scale*, which consists of a list of ways in which conflict between family members has been resolved during the year. Figures on violent means of conflict resolution give a 6% occurrence figure for spousal and child abuse. This increases substantially when the period under consideration is extended. If violent methods of conflict resolution are considered for any time during the relationship (i.e. if violence ever occurred), then the figures increase: 11 to 21% overlap depending on the study in question (Silvern *et al.*, 1995).
- Studies using data from battered women showed bigger variation. Overlap between spousal and child abuse varied from 10% to 100%. The studies using the Conflict Tactics Scale tended to suggest 51% to 72% overlap between spousal and child abuse. Of course, battered women as a group might be expected to produce more extreme tendencies than those in the general public. For example, the battered women may go to the shelters not for their own safety but for the safety of their child.
- Reported child abuse to the authorities gave figures of co-occurrence varying between 26% and 59%.

In other words, just basing one's assessment of risk to the child on the fact that the spouse claims to have been beaten seems unsatisfactory. The increase of risk is very difficult to know with any precision. Furthermore, we have already seen that the risk of violence by step-parents is greater than the risk from natural parents: that is, there is more to put into the equation than the act of spousal abuse alone.

There are still further considerations. Appel and Holden argue that the structure of violence within families falls into a variety of types which are, at least, theoretically feasible:

- Single perpetrator model: the man beats the woman and the child.
- Sequential perpetrator model: the man beats the woman who then beats the child.
- Dual perpetrator model: the man beats the woman and the woman also beats the child.
- Marital violence model: the woman and man beat each other and both beat the child.
- Family dysfunction model: all three family members beat each other – including the child who beats the adult perpetrators.

There is at least some evidence in favour of each model. Each of them may apply at least in a proportion of cases. So, if we do not understand the family dynamics in more detail, we may make unfounded assumptions. The child may be at risk from the mother as well in some types of family.

Quite clearly, simplistic common sense assumptions about violence may prove woefully inadequate in the setting of professional forensic and criminal psychology work. Confirmation of this comes from US data on homicide of partners. Estimates suggest that, annually, a minimum of 2.5 million women are battered by their partner/spouse. Twelve hundred are killed annually by their partners/spouses. Thus domestic violence is quite a poor predictor of murderous outcomes given the ratio of abuse to deaths, statistically stated: there is a 2,100 to 1 chance of a death compared with the numbers of battering households. What makes this an even more formidable statistic is that about half of such homicides were not preceded by violence/battering at any stage (Walker and Meloy, 1998). While it is clear that domestic violence is predictive of homicide, at least weakly, just about half of the spousal murders are not associated with abuse. See Chapter 23 on risk assessment for more details.

Domestic violence by women against men

Radical changes in the ways police forces around the world deal with domestic violence have occurred in the past 20 or so years. The police attitude has moved from that of regarding violence within the household as a domestic matter and not normally one for police involvement to one where they are pro-active about the issue. This is partly the result of the massive changes in gender relations brought about by feminist activists in the 1970s and 1980s especially. It would seem obvious that most domestic violence is the actions of men against women. Certainly the public seem to believe so. In a study in the United States, Stalans (1996) found that the public estimated the two-thirds of the victims of domestic violence where the police are called out were the woman, 17% thought that the victim was the man and another 17% saw the injuries as being to both. The message is clear from this. Women are overwhelmingly the injured victims of domestic violence.

However, one researcher in particular, Murray Straus, seems to take a different view. Straus was one of the first researchers to carry out major studies into the extent of domestic violence. His work with Gelles (e.g. Gelles and Straus, 1979) was profoundly influential partly because it exposed the extent of the problem. Few would doubt the impact of this work. The method used by these authors was the Conflict Tactics Scale which has been extensively used by researchers in the field of family violence (Straus *et al.*, 1996). As we have already seen, the scale does not directly ask about the extent of violence but, instead, how conflicts are resolved within the family. Various means of dealing with conflict are considered ranging from verbal conflict resolution techniques (e.g. 'discussed issues calmly', or 'got someone to help settle things') to minor physical aggression (e.g. threw something, pushed or slapped), to severe physical aggression (e.g. burned, used a knife, or fired a gun).

Straus (1992) argued that one of the aspects of his work which has been neglected was the extent and seriousness of the violence of women against men. Numerous US family violence surveys, he argues, have demonstrated the extent to which violence by women against men is almost as common as violence by men against women. The concept of 'husband-battering' (Steinmetz, 1977), he suggests, has been ridiculed and not taken seriously. Some have taken issue with Straus on the basis of what the Conflict Tactics Scale measures. For example, the measure may be so general that it fails to effectively differentiate between a woman slapping a man once and a man beating a woman on several occasions. In addition, based simply on the 'act' it is not possible to know the motivation for the violence. For example, if a person slaps another, one cannot assume that it was done as part of an unprovoked attack or in retaliation. However, there have been claims that violence by women is treated more seriously in the legal system than that by men. For example, it has been suggested that homicides of the female partners of men are relatively leniently treated compared to where a woman kills her male partner (Roberts, 1995).

The issues can be regarded as boiling down to the question of whether or not female domestic violence against males is symmetrical or assymetrical (Dobash and Dobash, 2004). By this is meant the extent to which violence against men by women has the same damaging consequences as that by men against women. Even if women are as likely to resort to violence as men, does it, for example, lead to the same level of serious injuries? Straus's view, therefore, is an example of the symetrical argument. Dobash and Dobash, in an attempt to shed light on what they regard as a puzzling issue, studied the reports of men and women involved in court cases involving domestic violence – the men had all been convicted of an assault on their female partner. As one might expect, there was a difference between the reports of men and women concerning issues of domestic violence, so it is difficult to summarise some of the trends exactly. A number of things were clear in terms of violence against partners:

- Women were less likely to have acted violently against their partner in the previous year.
- Men were more likely to have carried out a series of violent acts than were the women.
- Men were much more likely to punch, scratch, slap, kick the body, use objects as a weapon and so forth. In the extreme example, men were about 50 times more likely to choke their partner. There was no category of violent act in which the rates by females exceeded those by males.
- The injuries sustained by women were much more common – bruises, black eyes, cuts, scratches, split lips, fractured teeth or bones, and black-out unconcious.
- Ratings of seriousness of the violence were on average higher for men's violence than for women's violence. Somewhere between a quarter and a half of the ratings for men's violence were in the serious or very serious category whereas only about one in twenty of the acts perpetrated by women were placed in these extreme categories.

Although this is rather convincing evidence of the dangerousness of men's domestic violence, it does not mean that we can totally disregard those cases were women are initiating extremely serious acts of violence against their partner. And the issue does not stop there. We can turn to stalking, which frequently follows the break-up of a relationship.

Stalking: what sort of crime?

Stalking may be motivated by a number of different factors and may be of a number of different types. What is important to realise is the extent to which it arises out of intimate relationships and involves people previously close to the victim. The origins of anti-stalking legislation in some ways belie its true nature. Initially, it was the stalking of the famous which provided impetus for legislation. Among the famous victims of stalking are the British television presenter Jill Dando, actress Brooke Shields who was stalked for 15 years, the actress Jodie Foster – who was stalked by John Hinckley who shot President Ronald Reagan in the belief that this would gain her attention – David Letterman, Madonna, and Rebecca Schaeffer who was killed by her stalker in 1989. Some of these could be described as cases of *erotomania* which is obsessive, excessive, unwanted or delusional love according to Fitzgerald and Seeman (2002). So in these instances, it would seem an appropriate description since the offender suffered from a delusional belief that the celebrity in question was in love with them – examples of this would include the Madonna, David Letterman and the Rebecca Schaeffer examples. Erotomania is defined as a delusional disorder in the *Diagnostic and Statistical Manual* (American Psychiatric Association, 2000). Part of the diagnosis is that there is little or no prior contact between the erotomaniac and their target. While these high profile examples have been important in developing anti-stalking legislation, they do not define the typical stalking offence or offender. Stalking had not really been established as criminal behaviour until after the Rebecca Schaeffer killing.

Stalking is a form of predatory behaviour that is characterised by repeated patterns of harassment of a particular individual to a degree which may frighten the victim or worse (Sheridan and Davies, 2001). Among the examples of stalking/harassment behaviours that have been described in a number of studies are annoying telephoning, letters, visiting the victim at home, following the victim, verbally threatening violence, physical assaults, gift-giving, visiting the place where the victim works, face-to-face contacts, aggressive letters and property damage.

A number of surveys have demonstrated the extensiveness of stalking behaviour. The precise figures obtained depend somewhat on the style of the survey and the sources of information. One of the better studies is Tjaden and Thoennes' (1998) national violence against women survey. This was basically a telephone survey of a sample of the general population in the United States. It did not only include female victims and both males and females were surveyed. For the purposes of this survey, three key characteristics were used to define stalking behaviour:

- The victim is spied on, sent unsolicited letters or receives unwanted telephone calls, finds that someone is standing outside their home and other behaviours of this sort.
- These behaviours had to be carried out by the same person on at least two occasions.
- These incidents had to make the victim either 'very frightened' or fear that they would be the victim of violence.

Of the people in the survey reporting that they had been stalked, 78% of them were women and 22% were men. For the women, overwhelmingly it was men who stalked them – 94% of stalkers of women were men. Most significantly, 48% of the stalkers were intimates of the women in the sense of being a past husband or partner or having had a brief sexual relationship with the stalker. The average stalking continued for 1.8 years. Approximately 1.3 million American women would be stalked annually if we extrapolate from the base rate figures collected in this survey (Tjaden and Thoennes, 2000). The fear of violence is not unrealistic. Meloy (2002) reports a number of studies of interpersonal violence among obsessional followers, stalkers and criminal harassers. The figures vary, of course, but most studies report rates between 30% and 50%. Furthermore, some studies where the victimiser is a former 'intimate' of the victim yield figures of around the 60 to 90% level.

Different legal jurisdictions have very different approaches to stalking according to Sheridan and Davies (2002) and none of the legal or research definitions effectively distinguishes between the dangerous, predatory stalker and what they term 'the over-attentive suitor'. In the United States' legislation, the fear of physical injury or death is a requirement whereas in the United Kingdom the requirement is merely a minimum of two acts of harassment. Australian legislation includes the word 'intends' into aspects of the definition such as intending to cause serious physical harm or intending to cause fear (Sheridan and Davies, 2002). Quite clearly these are very different and give very different powers to the police to intervene at an early stage.

Sheridan and Davies (2001) had participants in a study rate a number of vignettes in terms of stalking. Different participants were given different instructions about the criteria to employ. Three groups had either US, British, or Australian legal definitions to work with and another group just based their assessment on their own opinions. Some transcripts seem to exemplify the different penal codes more effectively than others. For example, the following was more likely to be judged stalking according to the US principles:

> After our divorce, whenever I saw my ex-husband he would use obscene and threatening language towards me when such was entirely inappropirate (i.e. not during an argument situation). He also threatened to kill me. I also received an obscene threatening telephone call from his girlfriend.
>
> *(p. 11)*

The following is perhaps even more illustrative since it was regarded as the most like the UK legal definition of stalking but least in keeping with the US definition of stalking:

> A chap in the recent past kept turning up at my house uninvited and just walking in. He was sometimes difficult to get rid of. The relationship was flirtatious at first but his behaviour I considered inappropriate and I therefore cooled off a bit in friendliness towards him. He failed to acknowledge or accept this and chose to write weird poetry and one particularly worrying letter to me which was menacing and full of 'magical thinking' abstract type stuff. This behaviour stopped after a few weeks.
>
> *(p. 11)*

This is another reminder that jurisdictions differ and what is true in one may not apply elsewhere.

Box 8.2

Forensic psychology in action: violent offender programmes

Special therapeutic programmes for violent offenders are uncommon compared with those for sex offenders. However, this will probably change as special therapeutic programmes for violent offenders are gradually evolving and being introduced into the penal services. The British prison service has piloted the Cognitive Self-Change Programme which is aimed at reducing the risk of reoffending in men with a record for violent offending. The idea is that cognitive factors including thoughts, feelings, attitudes and beliefs support violence. The programme assumes that violence is usually intended so that offenders need to do various things to change that behaviour. They need to take control of their lives and become motivated to become skilful at controlling their thoughts and feelings.

According to Attrill (1999), three findings about violent offenders are at the root of treatment:

- Violence is learned behaviour that is adopted as a way of coping with difficult life experiences. Violence, then, works effectively and reliably for them and serves to reinforce their sense of their own power and self-efficiency.
- Patterns of criminal behaviour include a diversity of criminal acts and are rarely confined to violent behaviour. Studies suggest that reoffending by, say, those convicted of crimes against property may well be because of violence rather than another property crime.
- Patterns of violent and criminal behaviour are entwined within ways of thinking that support those acts.

Offenders show a sort of antisocial logic, which makes violence seem acceptable and normal, necessary, justified. Attrill indicates that if an offender sees himself as one of society's victims he may regard this as sufficient justification to behave just as he wants. Anyone who interferes with this is being unfair and further victimising the offender. So a prison sentence would be seen as justifying further offending because it was unfair. On the other hand, the offender believes that he is entitled to do what he pleases and should not be told what to do by others. Consequently, if his violent acts in support of these beliefs go unpunished they further reinforce his feelings of entitlement.

The programme is divided into six blocks, each of which consists of sessions totalling 100 hours or so:

- Skills are taught which allow offenders to observe and report their thoughts, feelings, attitudes and beliefs.
- Identification of the thinking patterns which have and will result in their offending and violent behaviour in general.
- Offenders try to identify new ways of thinking and ways of stopping these thought patterns.
- A relapse prevention plan is prepared and the strategies are practised.
- The offenders practise the relapse prevention plan in prison.
- The final block has the offender back in the community with structured support and supervision.

Main points

- As violent crimes range from the most trivial of assaults to the most disgusting of serial killings, a range of theoretical perspectives are needed in order to begin to explain such crimes. Similarly, given that violent crime has traditionally been found to be commonest among young men, we should not expect to find a single psychological explanation to be sufficient. Nevertheless, there is a great deal to suggest that violence is socially learnt. It has often been claimed that media violence is part of the cause of violence in the young though this has not been a major theme in forensic and criminal psychology or criminology for that matter. Evidence in support of the media causing violence is strongest from laboratory studies and much less a feature of field studies asking the same question. There is virtually no evidence concerning the media and actual acts of criminal violence.

- Homicide might seem to be largely determined by psychological factors but evidence of psychiatric abnormalities in such crimes is generally fairly exceptional. Furthermore, it has been shown that broad societal factors (e.g. periods of wartime) may affect levels of homicide. Leyton (1986) claimed that homicide is related to social structure (social class). Others have provided socio-biological explanations of such phenomena as the different rates of killing of step-children and biological children by their parents.

- There are a number of particularly forensic issues. Psychologists now have methods of helping individuals with their aggression in the form of anger management treatment and, in the prison service, violent offender programmes. Part of the challenge, however, is to identify the future most violent individuals. This is difficult because violence, say in the form of domestic violence, is commonplace. Related to this is stalking, which often is the aftermath of the break-up of an intimate relationship.

Chapter 9

Sexual offenders 1: rapists

Overview

- Nowadays, rape tends to be defined in terms of unwanted penetration of the vagina, anus, or mouth of another person. Statutory rape is penile penetration of any child below the age of consent to sexual intercourse. The law in some countries has changed markedly under the influence of feminist arguments about the nature of the crime since rape is frequently regarded as a crime of power and control rather than sexual gratification.

- The frequency of rape is difficult to assess and is surrounded by controversy. It is widely accepted that reported rape does not reflect the true levels of rape and reporting rape to the police may be declining in some countries. In a British survey, approximately 5% of woman claimed to have been raped at some point in their lives. The treatment of rape victims has changed to some extent but it remains a crime for which conviction is relatively low despite efforts to redefine its nature and to extend its scope into date-rape and marital rape, for example.

- Various researchers have claimed that there are several different patterns of rape. Groth *et al.* (1977) identified power-assurance rape, power-assertive rape, anger-retaliatory rape and anger-excitement rape. This typology is based on the psychological motive of the offender. Hostility, control, theft and involvement have been identified as the four major characteristic patterns in behaviour at the rape scene.

- Ideas conducive to rape are common in Western cultures. Rape myths are beliefs about women and their sexuality which place the blame on the woman rather than the rapist. However, there is no convincing balance of evidence which demonstrates that sex offenders are more extreme in their acceptance of rape myths.

- Offenders use pornography but developmental studies tend not to hold pornography responsible for creating their deviance. Furthermore, research on sexual fantasy tends to indicate that fantasy has a potentially complex relationship with offending.

- Phallometry or plethysmography is a technique for measuring the volume or circumference of a penis as an index of sexual 'arousal' in a man. There are doubts that it is sufficiently precise to identify men likely to offend and there is reason to believe that it is somewhat outmoded as alternative, simpler ways of achieving the same end are available.

There are a number of definitions of rape. The legal definition is just one of many but is the most important in this context. There is no universal legal definition of rape and its precise meaning varies from jurisdiction to jurisdiction and changes over time. Although it is important to differentiate legal definitions from other definitions of rape, this is not so easily done while reading psychological and social scientific writings on rape. Feminists, in particular, tend to extend the definition far beyond its typical legal meaning to include all forms of sexual act that women may not wish (e.g. Kelly, 1988, 1989). For example, some writers may well include salacious comments to a woman about her breasts in the definition. Legal definitions refer almost exclusively to penetration by a penis. Traditionally, penetrative vaginal sex has been a crucial criterion. Increasingly, it is accepted that this is too limited a conception and the anal penetration of either sex may be rape in some jurisdictions as can oral penetration. A conviction for rape requires that the victim has not given consent to the sexual act. In some jurisdictions, intercourse with youngsters regarded as too young to give their consent is classified as rape – *statutory rape.*

Rape, along with domestic violence and sexual and physical abuse of children was increasingly seen as a matter of social concern under the influence of feminists and others from the 1970s onwards. There are many accounts of the reasons why rape is a political issue for feminists. To take just one example, Los (1990) explained how rape laws have tended to reinforce the position of the powerful male over the less powerful female. From her Canadian perspective, although much the same may be said of other jurisdictions, Canadian law served interests of men at the expense of those of women in the following ways, among others:

- by giving the husband the unrestricted right to sexual access to his wife;
- by defining rape as heterosexual penetration and defining other forms of penetration as less serious, thus putting the risk of the wife being made pregnant by another man equivalent to the most serious offence;
- by protecting women from men who seduce them with the false promise of marriage – such as in breach of promise legislation – which essentially implies the weakness of women;
- by requiring that women report their rape immediately otherwise invalidating their case – the delay, putatively, would give them time to make up the story;
- by indicating that women's credibility in court rests on their sexual reputations whereas men's does not.

The current Canadian Assault Law of 1983 adopted a gender-neutral definition of rape. In part, this was an accommodation to a great deal of feminist lobbying. Other changes in conceptions of rape are obvious in issues such as marital rape, which previously in some jurisdictions was not a possibility or extremely difficult to prosecute, and the development of the idea of date-rape (Lees, 1995).

Frequency of rape

Not surprisingly, the frequency of rape is very difficult to assess with certainty. The answer, like the answers to all such statistical questions, clearly depends on the source of information and the definition employed (Chapter 2). Sexual crimes are likely to be under-reported to the police for a variety of reasons. These include the possible (but misplaced) shame and embarrassment of the victim, fear of a particularly hostile treatment by the police or lawyers, a wish to avoid more distress, ignorance that an offence has been committed (e.g. as in the case of rape by a sexual partner) and so forth. Conviction rates and police crime reports are unsatisfactory as indicators for other reasons. For example, they partly depend on police or other officials' decisions about which crimes to prosecute and the police finding someone to prosecute. Lack of consent to sexual activity is very difficult to prove for rape on dates. Victim surveys, while possibly being the best indicators of actual frequency of rape, have their own biases since the lack of consent may be clearer to the victim than it might be, say, to police officers. Rapes in England and Wales reached only 500 cases recorded by the police per annum in 1959. By the late 1990s, the figure had reached 5,000 cases annually. Male rape began to be recorded as such in 1995 onwards. The numbers are less than 350 per annum – much the same as the figures for rape of females prior to 1950s. These are *numbers* and not rates. The 2003 figure for recorded rapes is 14,000 (http://www.truthaboutrape.co.uk/index2.html)

The rates from the United States of America for rapes reported in the Unified Crime Statistics (FBI, 2001) for 1999 were just over 79,000 forcible (as opposed to statutory) rapes if attempts at rape are omitted. This corresponds to a rate of about 29 rapes per 100,000 of the population. The US National Crime Victimisation Survey, as might be expected, gave a higher figure of reported victimisation by rape for the same year. The figure is 90 per 100,000 of the population (Bureau of Justice, 2001d). The definition of rape given the participants was 'forced sexual intercourse including both psychological coercion as well as physical force. Forced sexual intercourse means penetration by the offender(s). Includes attempted rapes, male as well as female victims and both heterosexual and homosexual rape. Attempted rape includes verbal threats of rape.' Given the differences in definition, the disparity is not so great as sometimes claimed between crimes known to the police and victim survey statistics – about a third of rapes being reported to the police, it would seem.

Perhaps of most interest, the US crime victimisation survey reveals a startling trend in rape as reported by its victims – the rates had declined to just over a third of the 1973 figure by 1999. The rate in 1973 was 250 per 100,000 of population, in 1983 210, in 1993 160 and in 1999 just 90 per 100,000. And this is not the only evidence of downward trends in sex offending. Egg (1999) provides evidence that sex offences in Germany show no long-term increasing trend. The pattern is somewhat unstable with decrease being discernible over time. Offences of sexual child abuse decreased from 30 per 100,000 inhabitants to 20 over the period 1960 to 1985. Since then it has been stable. What is different is that more offenders have been convicted in the 1990s – the figures are up by 60%. Given that the input of suspects has been steady over these years, it suggests more charges and convictions being made.

The British Crime Survey is a random survey of households which attempts to assess the rates of crime including those not reported to the police. Participants can use a Computer Assisted Self-Interviewing procedure, which is operated using a lap-top computer and which may reduce interviewer influences significantly. The women in the study were asked questions that identified them as having been through some form of sexual victimisation. Other questions followed if they had. This enabled the researchers to classify whether an offence was a rape or not. The researchers defined rape as the woman being forced to have sexual intercourse (vaginal or anal penetration) though they did not require penile penetration in their definition. A sexual assault was anything identified as sexual which did not meet the requirements of rape:

- Four women in a thousand described incidents that could be classified as rape in the previous year.
- Forty-nine women in a thousand women claimed to have been raped since the age of 16 years.
- Nine women in a thousand claimed to have suffered some form of sexual assault victimisation in the previous year.
- Ninety-seven women in a thousand had suffered some form of sexual assault since the age of 16.

Overwhelmingly, victims of rape know the rapist: 45% of rapists were the woman's current partner, 16% were acquaintances, 11% were ex-partners, 11% were dates and 10% were other intimates. In this study, only 8% of rapes were committed by men not known to the victim. However, women who were raped by a stranger were more likely to report it to the police – 36% of them did whereas only 8% of women raped by a date reported this to the police.

However, the woman's belief that her experience was rape was not always correct as far as the researchers could ascertain. Nevertheless, the women and the researchers agreed that the events were rape in 60% of the cases.

Youthful sex offenders

We saw in Chapter 6 that it is a general trend for sex offending to begin in the early life of an offender. This sort of crime tends to follow the same sort of pattern associated with violence. Violent crime is most commonly a youthful offence that declines sharply in middle age and beyond. This suggests that rape is best conceived as a crime of violence rather than sexual lust. Certainly there is good reason to believe that rape is associated with anger in many offenders. Childhood abuse is also commoner in sex offenders:

- Worling (1995) carried out a study of adolescent sex offenders – one group had offended in a 'hands-on' fashion against peers and older women. The other group had offended against younger children. A range of measurements was taken including acceptance of rape myths (see pp. 129–31) and experience of physical punishment and sexual abuse. Those offending against a woman rather than a peer had experienced greater levels of physical punishment. Interestingly, sexual abuse by men tended to lead to abuse against younger children by the victims. In contrast, victims of sexual abuse by females tended to become the offenders against peers and older women.
- Haapasalo and Kankkonen (1997) studied the self-reported experiences of childhood abuse in men whose victims were women above 18 years. These were compared with violent offenders with no record of sexual offences. The two groups were matched according to a number of family problems – including matters such as being in care in childhood, having experienced parental divorce in childhood, having parents who were substance abusers and a number of other factors. Sex offenders claimed to have experienced more psychological (verbal) abuse (such as yelling, threatening, ridiculing) than the violent offenders. Furthermore, psychological rejection and isolation were commoner in sex offenders' childhood. For example, their parents were more openly hostile and negative towards them as children, they tended to be ignored, other siblings were better favoured and they

were locked up in closed environments more frequently and isolated from other people. There were further differences:

- father threatened to hurt me;
- father belittled me;
- father did not want me near him;
- mother threatened to hurt me;
- mother belittled me;
- mother did not want me near her;
- father made me do shameful things.

It is easy to understand the origins of the hostility that some rapists feel. A number of researchers have commented on the role of this. For example, Hall and Hirschman (1991) suggest that there are a numbers of precursors to rape which may motivate the crime:

- Sexual arousal: deviant sexual arousal.
- Cognitive motivation: rape myths (see later).
- Developmental problems.
- Emotional (e.g. anger towards women).

While anger as a component of rape appears to be common, very little is known about precisely how it contributes to offending. It is generally accepted that some rapes are driven by sadistic fantasies which eventually are acted out in behaviour (e.g. MacCulloch *et al.*, 1983). Moreover, anger has been more directly associated with sex offending than this indirect route implies. For example, 94% of rapists report that anger is associated with the offence, a figure that is not much lower in other types of sex offender (Pithers *et al.*, 1988).

There is a general assumption that rape is a crime committed by younger offenders and a number of surveys have demonstrated this. However, the type of rape can make a significant impact on these age trends. Muir and Macleod (2003) showed that rapes in an unspecified UK metropolitan area were generally committed by offenders under the age of 40 years. Only 22% of rapes were committed by older persons. However, in the case of rape by strangers, 61% of offenders were under 30 years of age whereas the rape of intimates involved only 24% of offenders who were under 30 years of age. Rape by acquaintances was more commonly associated with men under 30. Acquaintance rape was committed by men under this age in 61% of occasions. In the light of this, it is not surprising that younger women tend to feature more strongly in rape statistics. Only 8% of rapes were committed against victims of 40 years or older. 75% were committed against women of under 25 years of age and 30% are against 14-year-olds and under. Probably a high proportion of the latter are statutory rapes. The 15- to 24-years-old age group was the most at risk but this was largely of stranger and acquaintance rape.

Patterns in rape

Gradually, forensic and criminal psychologists are beginning to explore the nature of rape. One important step in this process is attempts to identify patterns in rape offences in order to assess whether there are different types of rape. This is a form of analysis of crimes related to profiling (Chapter 13). Hakkanen, Lindlof, and Santtila (2004) studied data to be found on the police database for rapes by strangers in Finland. Case files included various records: witness statements, medical statements, forensic evidence, the interview with the victim and the interview with the suspect. A long list of possible characteristics of the rape was compiled and each case record coded in terms of the presence or absence of each of these characteristics. A complex statistical technique, multi-dimensional scaling, was used to identify what sorts of behaviours tended to be associated with each other. For example, in some of the rapes the offender had apologised to the victim. In others, the offender had bit the victim. Do these characteristics tend to coexist or does the presence of one, an apology, tend not to be associated with biting?

Some behaviours were virtually universal in the rapes. Vaginal penetration from the front was achieved or attempted in 89% of the rapes. In contrast, vaginal penetration from the rear or an attempt at this was relatively uncommon (7% of rapes). The rapist revealed information, true or false, about themselves in 40% of cases. In 23% of rapes, the offender carried out multiple acts of violence against the victim – these were not simply attempts to control the victim. Among the rare characteristics were penetration achieved more than once (6%), the offender had taken a weapon to the scene of the crime (6%) and the offender implied knowing the victim before the attack (5%).

Three separate patterns were identified in rape:

- Theft: the offender had stolen identifiable items such as credit cards from the victim; the offender rummaged or searched through the victim's property; a condom was used; the offender stole things like money which cannot be identified.

- Involvement: the offender tried to reassure the victim though this might include reassurance that he did not intend to carry out the act; the offender complimented the victim; the victim was drugged by the offender; the rapist implied that he knew the victim; the offender attempted an intrusion into the victim's home.

- Hostility: the offender carried out vaginal penetration from the rear; the offender bit the victim; the offender carried out a single act of violence but not to control the victim; the offender penetrated the victim's vagina digitally; the weapon had been taken from the scene of the crime.

An earlier study using British data by Canter *et al.* (2003) had generated a similar classification of rape based on the transcripts of statements made verbatim by rape victims. This supplied a number of characteristics of rapes which could be analysed statistically for patterns in stranger rape. The terminology is much the same though the rape characteristics used to define each pattern were not the same in every case. The control pattern did not emerge in the Finnish study though theft, involvement and hostility are similar despite the characteristics not being exactly the same:

- Control: the victim was bound or gagged, use of mask or blindfold and using a weapon were characteristic of this. About a tenth of rapes were in this category.

- Theft: goods would be demanded from the victim, the personal property of the victim would be stolen, identifiable goods were stolen and stealing unidentifiable goods. About a twentieth of rapes were in this category.

- Involvement: the victim may be complimented about her appearance: for example, the offender would make sexual comments in the course of the offence, the victim is kissed, and the offender implies that he knows the victim. About a third of rapes were in this category.

- Hostility: the offender removed the victim's clothing in a violent manner, there was an attempt to penetrate the victim anally, the victim was threatened at some time in the offence, and demeaning or insulting the victim such as by the use of verbal insult. This amounted to about a quarter of rapes.

Some rapes showed mixed patterns.

Canter *et al.* (2003) argue from these crime activity typologies that rapists are best distinguished in terms of the sorts of interpersonal behaviours which occur as part of the rape. It is less important and profitable to study the types of sexual behaviours involved.

The nature of rapists

So, it is clearly too simplistic to regard rape as the result of an uncontrolled, intense sexual lust. There are many reasons to be dubious about this formulation. For example, there is some evidence that sexual deprivation is not an essential component of rape (Howitt, 1991a). Rape commonly involves physical violence, of course. This, in some cases, goes substantially beyond the levels required to force the victim to participate in sex. Lloyd and Walmsley (1989) found that rapes in the United Kingdom typically were accompanied by violence. Around 25% contained no violence. About one in eight resulted in the victim being hospitalised owing to the level of the violence. Whatever the explanation of rape, its explanation cannot rest on erotic needs alone or necessarily in part.

Rape may manifest itself in a variety of forms. Hazelwood (1987), an offender profiler, suggests that the following types of rapist should be considered (following Groth *et al.*, 1977).

The power-assurance rapist:

- This describes the commonest type of rapist.
- The rape is concerned with dealing with their insecurities about their masculinity.
- As the offence may not help with the insecurities and because the insecurities are deep, there may be only a short interval before he needs to offend again.
- Force is not great and threats may be involved. Weapons are not common in this form of rape.
- Usually the rape is planned – there may be prior surveillance of the victim.
- If the victim is sufficiently passive to allow this, sexual fantasies may be expressed during the course of the rape.
- 'Trophies' such as clothing or some other article may be taken. These may be used, for example, in future masturbation.

The power-assertive rapist:

- This type of offender is sexually confident.
- Rape expresses his virility and sexuality, and power over women.
- Victims may be found in social locations such as discos, pubs or parties.
- Initially his manner may be friendly but may quickly change.

- Violence is extreme especially in the later stages. He does not appear to be the stereotypical rapist as he is socially skilled.
- Offences may be scattered and irregular in terms of frequency of occurrence.
- This pattern may be common in date-rape.

The anger-retaliatory rapist:

- The offender has extremely high levels of anger towards women such that, for example, degrading activities may be involved in the rape.
- It involves short intense attacks (blitz).
- Characteristically, there is a similarity between the victim and the woman he has a grudge against.
- Attacks may be fairly regular as a consequence of the build-up of anger.

The anger-excitement rapist:

- This is the least common type of rapist.
- The rapist gains pleasure and sexual excitement from viewing the distress of his victim.
- Thus the infliction of pain is common and violence is at such high levels that the victim may be killed. Torture is common.
- There is careful, methodological planning.
- He will bring such items as blindfolds, gags and ropes to the rape.
- Victims are usually total strangers to the offender.
- Photo and video recordings may be taken.
- Usually attacks are irregular, in part determined by the time at which his careful planning is complete.

It is quite clear from this typology that rape takes a variety of forms in terms of the motives and behaviours of the rapist. Understanding the different types of rapist may be helpful in deciphering the different crime scenes.

Box 9.1

Forensic psychology in action: phallometry (also known as plethysmography)

The phallometer is a device that measures the size of a penis as an indicator of sexual arousal. There are two types:

- *Volume phallometry* measures the volume of the penis. Essentially, a man's penis is put inside a glass tube. Changes in the size of his penis will cause changes in the pressure inside the tube. These changes may be measured through a meter or recorded on a electrical, moving pen device (much like a lie-detector machine – see Chapter 16).
- *Circumference phallometry* measures the circumference of the penis with a flexible 'tube'. Changes in circumference lead to changes in the electrical signals that are fed to the recording device.

▶

The underlying theory is obvious – the size of a man's penis is an indicator of his level of sexual arousal. Thus, if a man is shown a pornographic video of a rape, then the potential rapists should show greater increase in penis size than so-called normal men. There are a number of practical difficulties that need consideration:

- Penises vary in size both between men and over time. One consequence of this is that the measures used tend to be expressed in relative terms: that is, rather than the change in penis volume or circumference being used, the *percentage increase* in volume or circumference would be the measure of arousal. Alternatively, the man may be encouraged to masturbate to full erection and his response to the sexual stimuli assessed as a percentage of this maximum.
- Phallometry is undertaken in circumstances that are not conducive to sexual arousal for all men. These investigations are relatively public, cold, clinical and intrusive: for example, being connected up to the apparatus by a clinician, being sat in a chair in a small room or cubicle in a corner of a hospital or clinic, and being shown pornography which might be alien to one's sexuality. These factors mean that for some men, at least, the assessment process is ineffective as little or no sexual response is produced.
- It is possible to fake responses in a number of ways. Secret masturbation may allow the offender to show apparent arousal to 'normal stimuli'. Fantasising to alternative arousing imagery and tensing muscles in the area of the anus/scrotum may allow the same control on arousal. Disinterest in certain stimuli may be faked by fantasising about non-arousing themes while the clinician is showing otherwise arousing material to the man. For example, the man may be carrying out mental arithmetic while the arousing material is being shown. Alternatively, by pressing heavily on a nail or splinter in the chair he may cause an unpleasant and distracting sensation.

Attempts may be made to detect or prevent faking. One way of doing this is to ensure that the participants are concentrating on the video material by setting them a task such as answering questions about what they have seen or, for example, to signal when a light flashes in the video.

There are a number of techniques using phallometry which assess sexual arousal to different types of 'sexual' stimulus and possibly, then, the different types of victim. For example, Abel *et al.* (1977) developed the *rape index*. This compares a man's responses to various types of erotic material including that with force and coercion. Men highest on response to the latter type of material are regarded as those with the greatest rape potential. Similarly, Avery-Clark and Laws (1984) put forward a *dangerous child molester* index which identifies the men with the greatest response to coerced sex with children.

As ever, a crucial question is that of the extent to which the different types of offender can be differentiated using phallometry: that is, if one is trying to identify paedophiles, just how many of them would be correctly identified as such and just how many of them would not be identified? Furthermore, how many normal men would be classified as paedophiles and how many would be identified as normal by the test in question? The evidence seems to be that circumference measures are fairly poor at correct identifications (Baxter *et al.*, 1984, 1986; Murphy *et al.*, 1986). Volume phallometry is better (McConaghy, 1991). Unfortunately, all that can be said currently is that if one has two groups of men, one group normals and the other group paedophiles, phallometry will help you correctly choose the group of normals and the group of paedophiles. It is rather less good at deciding for any group of men who is a paedophile and who is not.

The important question, to the clinician, is whether phallometry can identify rapists and paedophiles from the rest of the population. If high proportions of normal men are wrongly classified as paedophiles or rapists, and offenders are often misclassified as normal, then it is an ineffective test. For example, Quinsey *et al.* (1975) found that normal men showed erections to pictures of pubescent and young girls that were 70% and 50% of their responses to erotic pictures of adult females. In a study by Wormith (1986), the classification accuracy based on circumference phallometry was 64% for groups of paedophiles, rapists and non-sex offenders. Only 50% of paedophiles were correctly classified as such, and 42% were classified as normal.

Perhaps more importantly, Hall *et al.* (1993) carried out a meta-analysis (Box 5.1) of a number of published studies. These studies compared penile responses when shown sexually aggressive materials in men known to be sexually violent with appropriate control participants. These studies only used audiotaped materials, which included both consenting sexual activity and sexual violence (rape). Using tables in Howitt and Cramer (2000), the correlation (effect size) obtained over the varied studies was about 0.14. This is a rather small correlation despite showing a relationship between responses to rape stimuli and being a rapist: that is, many men would be misclassified.

Using the rape index (Abel *et al.*, 1977), the correlation was much higher at the equivalent of 0.33. This proved to be a rather inconsistent finding since some studies obtained large relationships and others small relationships. According to Hall *et al.*, the studies finding large effects were those comparing rapists with non-sexually violent men. Smaller differences were found for the studies in which rapists were compared with paedophiles, for example.

Other worries include the simplistic equation that links erections to sexual offending. This assumes that sexual motives underlie rape and other forms of sexual offending whereas there is considerable evidence that offenders may suffer sexual dysfunction in that they cannot achieve penetration and that there are non-sexual motives involved in some of the crimes.

Some recommend confronting suspected sex offenders with phallometric evidence in order to elicit a confession (Travin *et al.*, 1985). This has its own risks such as false confession. While phallometry may be effective enough for research purposes, it appears to be rather risky for clinical assessment purposes. Indeed, there is some evidence that self-reports may be at least as effective as phallometry in detecting offenders (e.g. Howitt, 1995a). Furthermore, the results appear to be better for cooperative (admitting) offenders than uncooperative (non-admitting) offenders. This again lessens their attractiveness as an objective assessment technique.

Penile plethysmography is problematic in a number of obvious ways. It involves relatively expensive instrumentation which needs time and appropriate space to administer. Furthermore, there is no universal standard way of administering the phallometry which is applied consistently from one clinical setting to another. Laws and Gress (2004), among a number of researchers, have increasingly regarded viewing time of 'erotic' imagery as an alternative to phallometry since it involves no equipment attached to a man's genitals and is equally suitable for assessing females. Viewing time measures are simply the amount of time that, say, a sex offender spends looking at particular types of erotic stimuli. It is now possible to administer viewing time procedures using computers, which can also be used to generate standard imagery without having to recourse to pictures of real people.

Rape myths

Cognitive factors conducive to rape increasingly became a focus for researchers following Burt's (1980) work on the cultural myths concerning rape. She developed the *Rape-Myth Acceptance Scale* based on the observation that Western culture had essentially blamed the victims of rape for the attacks on them. Such victim-blaming strategies have been identified as characteristic of the criminal justice system. In a male-dominated culture, ideas develop that, by essentially blaming the victim, either encourage men to rape or provide them with an excuse for their sexually aggressive acts against women. Women, it is held, deserve to be or want to be raped. Men, according to the myths, are almost justified in raping. This is best illustrated by considering a number of items taken from the *Rape-Myth Acceptance Scale*:

If a girl engages in necking or petting and she lets things get out of hand, it is her own fault if her partner forces sex on her.

If a woman gets drunk at a party and has intercourse with a man she's just met there, she should be considered 'fair game' for other males at the party who want to have sex with her too, whether she wants to or not.

A woman who is stuck-up and thinks she is too good to talk to guys on the street deserves to be taught a lesson.

The final item above also illustrates the idea that rape is part of male domination/ control of women. There are other measures, which reflect similar ideas such as the Mosher Scale *Sexually Callous Attitudes Towards Women* (Mosher and Anderson, 1986). This appears to measure somewhat tough, unsympathetic and heartless attitudes on the part of men towards sex with females and female sexuality:

You don't ask girls to screw, you tell them to screw.

You never know when you are going to meet a strange woman who will want to get laid.

There is evidence that this sort of measure of the cognitive aspects of rape is associated with at least expressed views about willingness to offend. The most controversial of these measures is Malamuth's *Self-Reported Likelihood to Rape* measure (Malamuth and Ceniti, 1986). This is also known as the proclivity to rape. It is basically a single item measure:

How likely do you think you would be to commit rape if you can be assured of not being caught?

This is a controversial measure because of the inherent difficulty in knowing quite what men mean if they agree with this statement. Does it mean that they are likely to rape even if they might get caught? Does it mean that they are unsure of why they do not rape so feel that they might rape in some circumstances? Or what do the answers mean? A number of researchers have shown that there is a small or modest relationship between acceptance of the rape myths and proclivity to rape. For example, Tieger (1981) found that the men who score higher on the *Likelihood to Rape* measure also tend to see rape as an enjoyable seduction for the victim and hold the victim to blame for her victimisation. Men who report regarding rape as a serious crime and who are not overtly stereotyped in their thinking about sex roles tend to score lower on the *Likelihood to Rape* measure. Some researchers stress these cognitive components and, for an extreme version of this viewpoint, Russell's (1988, 1992) model warrants attention in so far as she draws together much of the work in this area to make the case for the cognitive basis of rape.

The acid test of this cognitive model has to be whether these cognitive factors help us differentiate between rapists and non-rapists. Here the theory seems to fail. There is some evidence suggesting that such cognitive factors do not differentiate rape offenders from others. For example, Overholser and Beck (1988) found no evidence that rapists differed from non-rape offenders and non-offenders on a number of attitude scales including acceptance of rape myths as well as attitudes to sex and attitudes to the use of violence. Stermac and Quinsey (1986) found no evidence that rapists were different from other groups in terms of their attitudes to women. The finding that adolescent sexual assaulters against women did not differ from the less overtly aggressive offenders against younger children supports this. Perhaps this is no surprise given what we know about the offending and reoffending patterns of rapists. They tend to have been previously imprisoned for non-sexual offences and their reoffending is likely not to be sexual (Lloyd and Walmsley, 1989).

It is not easy to make the case that rape myths are a crucial factor in rape because of such evidence. Nevertheless, work on the cognitive aspects of sex offending, including the factors discussed in this section, is extremely common in the psychological treatment of sex offenders (see Chapter 22). There is no distinct evidence of the effectiveness of therapy on rape myths on recidivism separate from the total effects of the treatment programme. Any improvement in the social functioning that might enable an offender to establish a non-offending lifestyle is welcome irrespective of what aspect of the therapy is responsible.

Socio-cultural factors and sexual violence

Hall and Barongan (1997) argue that socio-cultural factors may be involved in rape. By this they mean that certain sorts of cultural organisation may encourage males to rape and others may reduce the risk of rape. One dimension on which cultures differ is the *individualist–collectivist* orientation. Western culture, and that of the United States especially, holds that individuals should strive to achieve the best they can for themselves. Collectivist cultures, on the other hand, value those who work for the collective good. Within a nation, of course, there may be different subcultures, especially nations built on migrant communities such as the United States. The argument is that collectivist cultures are less conducive to rape than individualist cultures. Unfortunately for Hall and Barongan, superficially their idea does not fit the available statistical evidence well. For example, despite the fact that African-American communities may be regarded as relatively more collectivist in orientation, African-American men tend to be over-represented in the rape statistics. Hall and Barongan suggest that this may be illusory – a function of socio-economic status differentials between black and white Americans. Low socio-economic status is a risk factor in committing rape and also more characteristic of black rather than white Americans.

International crime statistic comparisons are problematic since one is unsure whether like is being compared with like. For example, rape might be defined differently, women less likely to report rape, police less likely to seek prosecutions for rape and so forth. There is some evidence when American and collectivist Hong Kong Chinese college students are compared that the American men were rather more likely to report using coercion sexually such as when touching a woman's genitals against her will. Among the reasons why collectivist cultures will show lower levels of sexual violence are:

- interpersonal conflict (including violence) tends to be minimal in collectivist cultures partly because of the sharing of group goals;
- individual needs are subordinated to the well-being of the group in collectivist cultures;
- a personal sense of shame at letting down the community is a major deterrent against crime.

Similarly, socio-cultural values are intimately related to rates of rape in different parts of the United States (Baron and Straus, 1989). Their research design was statistically complex but essentially simple. They took the 50 American states and compared them in terms of rates of rape based on publicly available statistics. Of course, such statistics are gathered from official sources and are subject to a degree of error since they are dependent upon reporting by the victim, recording by the police and other factors that may lead to a degree of inaccuracy. While accepting that there is inaccuracy, Baron and Straus argue that in relative terms such indexes are satisfactory for their purposes. Some states such as Alaska and Florida tended to have high rates of rape given the size of their population and other states such as Maine and North Dakota tended to have substantially lower rates of rape compared to their population size. The crime figures were rape reports in the Uniform Crime Report statistics from the early 1980s.

The researchers also collected a number of other indexes of significant differences among the 50 states based on sociological theory. These included the following, which essentially constitute three different theories about why rape rates vary across different communities:

- *Gender inequality*: this was an index of the economic, legal and political status of women compared to men. The measures included the proportion of the state's senate that was women and the average income of employed women compared with that of employed men.
- *Cultural spillover*: this was measured in terms of the *Legitimate Violence Index* which involved state-approved violence such as the acceptance of corporal punishment in schools and capital punishment rates for murder.
- *Social disorganisation*: this was based on indicators of social instability due to weakening forces of social regulation. Factors such as geographical mobility, divorce, the proportion of lone-parent families and a lack of religious affiliation were included in these.

Box 9.2

Key concept: sexual fantasy and sex offending

It is commonly accepted that sexual fantasy, especially violent sexual fantasy, has some role to play in the most serious sexual crimes including sexual murders. The work of MacCulloch *et al.* (1983) was particularly influential in this regard. Clinicians believe that there is a process by which somewhat obsessive sexual fantasies escalate in frequency and extremity. Eventually these may lead to violent and sexual criminal acts. Following this there may be satiation. This sort of escalating cycle of fantasy is described in the writings of clinicians dealing with paedophiles (e.g. Wyre, 1990, 1992). Fantasy-reduction and fantasy control is an important theme in the therapy employed with sex offenders. Some therapists employ the term *directed masturbation* in which the offender is encouraged to masturbate to sexual imagery which is appropriate (e.g. consensual sex with two adult women) in an attempt to recondition appropriate sexual preference (Cooper, 2005). It is also useful to note that research seems to have established that child molesters tend to have more fantasies about children when they are in a negative mood state (feeling depressed or miserable, for example) than at other times (Looman, 1999).

Others, dealing with non-offender populations, have taken a rather different view about the role of fantasy in sexual relationships (e.g. Cramer and Howitt, 1998). It would seem clear that in sexual relationships, there may be a big difference between the contents of fantasy and expectations about sexual relations. Sexual thoughts that lead to sexual arousal are commonplace for both men and women (Jones and Barlow, 1990). Sexual fantasy within the relationships of ordinary couples may be at variance with principles such as monogamy, tenderness and sharing. This is as true of women as it is of men. Sexual fantasy in sexual intercourse and masturbation occurs at very high rates (Knafo and Jaffe, 1984). In other words, sexual fantasy may be construed as normal and it is common to find somewhat unacceptable themes in fantasy. For example, Kirkendall and McBride (1990) established that more than a third of men and a quarter of women fantasised of being forced into sexual relations.

A number of possible links between sexual fantasy and offending may be hypothesised (Howitt, 2000, 2004). One crucial piece of information would be to assess whether the reduction of sexual fantasy through therapeutic intervention actually reduces offending. There is little direct evidence on this. Hall *et al.* (1995) describe a meta-analysis of studies of the effects of sex offender treatment programmes on recidivism. There was a negative effect of behavioural therapies directed mainly towards fantasy reduction: that is, more recidivism where sexual fantasy had been reduced. Also of significance is Daleiden *et al.*'s (1998) finding that the difference between offenders and non-offenders is not in terms of having 'deviant' sexual fantasies but that offenders have fewer normal fantasies! The lack of normal fantasy is what is dangerous. Interestingly, a small study involving largely homosexual paedophiles found that those engaging in deviant fantasy were less likely to use coercion and more likely to engage in 'friendship formation' in the process of offending (Looman, 1999).

Where do fantasies come from? They seem to emerge developmentally at a quite early stage. More than 80% of offenders reported having deviant sexual fantasies by the age of 15 years (Bates, 1996). Such fantasy might have its origins in childhood sexual abuse since some claim that there is a close link between early fantasy and features of their abuse (Howitt, 1995a, 1998a). Others find no such link (Waterhouse *et al.*, 1994). Fantasy, in this formulation, is regarded as rising out of experience. If this is the case, then it becomes feasible that offenders engage in offending not because they are driven by their fantasies but in order to provide fantasy imagery. Sex offences are quite frequently non-consumatory in that intercourse and orgasm do not take place (Howitt, 1995a). An offender, for example, might limit his sexual contact to touching a child through its clothes. One explanation of such behaviour may be that it is to provide the fantasy rather than to act out the fantasy.

In an attempt to see whether preventing masturbation could reduce sexual fantasy, Brown *et al.* (1996) had outpatient paedophiles randomly assigned to a masturbation-allowed or masturbation-not-allowed condition. Self-report measures were used to assess the effectiveness of masturbation prevention. Only about a fifth of the paedophiles were able to abstain from masturbation for the required four-week period. There seemed to be no differences between the two groups in terms of intensity of sexual urges, urges to masturbate, urges for sex with adults and urges for sex with children. The low compliance of the offenders with the therapist's request not to masturbate should be assessed against the finding that paedophiles masturbated about four times each week. The authors regard what they see as a low sexual interest in this group as reason not to employ masturbation prohibition.

There was support for the *gender inequality* and *social disorganisation* explanations of rape. *Cultural spillover theory* was rejected on the basis of the data. In other words, the findings suggest that the greater gender inequality in favour of males and the greater social disorganisation then the greater the amount of rape.

More on the theory of rape

There has been one systematic attempt to compare the different theoretical explanations of rape that should be considered. Ellis (1989) identified three major theories of rape:

- Feminist theory;
- Social learning theory;
- Evolutionary theory.

In many ways influenced by the socio-biological approach to crime (see Chapter 8), Ellis suggests that it is possible to generate testable hypotheses from each of these theories.

Feminist theory

This essentially argues that rape is built into the gender structure of society. A dense network of different ways of controlling women buttresses male power. As such, one would expect this control to be manifest in many aspects of society. It has been manifest in the law (e.g. the denial of women's property rights, considering it reasonable that a man should be allowed to beat his wife and so forth) as well as domestic relations between men and women. Basic tenets of feminist theory, according to Ellis, are:

- Rape should be associated with sex disparities in social status and power. (p. 20)
- Rape is primarily motivated by a desire for power and dominance rather than a desire for sex. (p. 21)

From these basic ideas of feminist theory, Ellis derives what he considers to be formal hypotheses that can be tested against empirical data concerning rape:

- Societal trends toward sexual egalitarianism should be associated with a lessening of rape victimisation. (p. 28)

The evidence does support the idea that gender equality in society is associated with fewer rapes, as we have already seen.

- Rapists should hold less egalitarian and more pro-rape attitudes toward women than non-rapists. (p. 29)

This hypothesis is not clearly supported by the studies that find that rapists are no different from other offenders in terms of their cognitions about rape and women, as we saw above.

Social learning theory

This basically suggests that rapists learn to be rapists by learning pro-rape beliefs and attitudes from their social milieu. For various reasons, rapists tend to learn the pro-rape cognitions more effectively than non-rapists do. Ellis mentions the following hypotheses based on social learning theory, among others. Notice that the hypotheses derived from social learning theory are not necessarily very different from those proposed by feminist theory:

- Rapists should hold attitudes that are more favourable towards rape, and towards violence in general, than other men. (p. 33)

We have seen that this hypothesis is not clearly supported.

- Exposure to violent pornography should increase male propensities to commit rape, and otherwise to behave violently toward women. (p. 35)

This is one of the pornography-related hypotheses listed by Ellis who regards pornography as an almost essential learning course for rape. This is a somewhat controversial area and Ellis's views reflect just one side of the controversy (Box 10.1).

Evolutionary theory

Socio-biological theory is largely about one's adaptiveness for the transmission of one's genetic material to the next generation. Rape, according to a socio-biological perspective, should reflect this basic principle of behaviour. In other words, the hypotheses for evolutionary theory should emphasise the functionality of rape for the transmission of genetic material to the next generation. The following hypotheses are feasible:

- Tendencies to rape must be under some degree of genetic influence. (p. 43)
- Forced copulations should impregnate victims, at least enough to offset whatever risks rapists have of being punished for their offences. (p. 47)
- Rape victims should be primarily of reproductive age. (p. 50)
- Rape should be vigorously resisted by victims, especially when the offender is someone to whom the females are not sexually attracted. (p. 50)
- Rapists (especially those who assault strangers) should be less likely than other males to attract voluntary sex partners. (p. 52)

To the extent that these hypotheses are clear, there is generally some evidence to support them. Ellis's (1989) position is that basically each of the different theories has some commendable features and that a synthesis of various elements is essential to understanding rape. Unlike some recent writers, Ellis is an advocate of the view that rape is partially a sexual rather than a violent crime.

More recently, another theory about rape claiming to be based on evolutionary psychology has received a great deal of publicity especially in the United States. Thornhill and Palmer (2000) are not psychologists despite this. Their argument is that subject to conditions all men are capable of rape. Rape, they argue, has to be considered to be motivated by sex. Men who are essentially disenfranchised from society, lacking status in the sexual order, still are driven to procreate. Cognitions may play a part in that men are calculating beings capable of evaluating the benefits and costs of rape.

In the theory, women are regarded as contributing to their victimisation by rapists by failing to avoid dangerous situations conducive to rape attack. The trauma that follows rape is regarded as a beneficial matter since the women would be less inclined to put themselves in any of the situations which are conducive to rape in future. Many of their ideas have placed Thornhill and Palmer at the centre of significant criticism from academics and others.

Others have recently outlined their own theoretical relationships between evolutionary concepts and crime. A good example of this is Quinsey (2002) who relates evolutionary theory to sexual crimes as well as other types of crime. Evolutionary theory, he suggests, is environmental and selectionist in nature because the environments of our ancestors have helped select particular characteristics of individuals which are genetically transmitted over generations. Those characteristics that tend to be emphasised as a consequence of natural selection are termed *adaptations*. They are related to successful reproduction strategies since if they were not then the adaptations would die out. Quinsey gives a simple example. He suggests that a man in the 'ancestral environment' who had a genetically produced sexual proclivity for trees would have little reproductive success with females and so would not sire future offspring. So males would demonstrate features that lead to reproductive success with females which may not be the same as those that lead to reproductive success in females themselves. Males and females, in the evolutionary view, do not share reproductive interests entirely. Quinsey argues that sexual coercion illustrates this divergence between males and females. While, according to the environmental psychologists, it is in the interest of women to seek a male who provides the greatest advantage in terms of protection and care and genetic potential, sexual coercion essentially prevents women exercising choice in this respect. So one argument from the evolutionary perspective is that in circumstances where the costs of disregarding the mating preferences of females are insignificant then coercive sexual behaviour is more common. Circumstances in which this would happen include the situation of soldiers in an occupying country or when the man expresses sexually callous attitudes towards women anyway. The problem is, of course, that without the crucial evidence that links sexual coercion to genetic make-up in some way, many other explanations of sexual coercion are equally viable. For example, Quinsey points out that psychopathy and sexual deviation as measured by plethysmography together predict new sex offences. Unfortunately, for this explanation, psychopaths commit many types of crime more frequently than others and not just sexually coercive crime.

Rape is a complex matter and we need to research it from a range of different perspectives. An example of alternative ways of studying the topic can be found in the work of Dale *et al.* (1997). They investigated the conversations between rapists with their victims during the offence. It might be possible to analyse the discourse used at the time of the rape with the type of the rape and the psychological nature of the offender. Rape, they argue, is a constrained activity in which what the victim can say is limited by the situation as much as what the attacker may say. Information was obtained concerning over 250 offences by 55 rapists. Examples are provided by Dale *et al.* of different types of speech act that have been used by rapists. One strategy they mention is described as scripting. This 'essentially' is telling the victim just what to say and what to do:

> 'Kiss me: cuddle me: pretend I'm your boyfriend. Say something . . . Say "Hello Robert" . . . Louder.'

(pp. 663–4)

Or acts of justification may be used to close the offence:

'You'll look back on this in a couple of weeks and think you enjoyed it.'

(p. 665)

Or the victim might be told:

'I wouldn't have done it if you were a virgin.'

(p. 665)

The co-occurrence of different discourse strategies and their relative occurrence in particular types of crime may hold valuable information for the eventual identification of offenders.

Main points

- The legal definition of rape often now includes non-consensual anal and oral penetration with a penis as well as that of a vagina. In the last two decades or so conceptions of the nature of rape have changed especially under the influence of feminist thinking which construes rape not simply as a sexual crime but as another aspect of male control of women. Rape, defined legally, has happened to one in twenty women at some time in their lives although the annual rate is much lower. This is according to victim studies. Rape is a relatively under-reported crime and is much more commonly carried out by men that the woman knows rather than strangers. It is a crime more commonly carried out by younger offenders and shows much the same characteristics in terms of offender characteristics as other crimes of violence.

- Anger is a component of some rapes but not all. The commonest type of rape is described as the power-assurance rape. The offender is insecure in his masculinity which he tries to assert through his use of power. As a consequence, he does not actually get the reassurance that he needs from his actions and is likely to reoffend after a short period of time. Other researchers find that other patterns can be identified in the characteristics of the rape itself without reference to psychological motives. One pattern is involvement in which the offender tries to reassure the victim throughout the act in some way or he may indicate that he knows her or try to intrude into her home – so he may compliment her. It is commonly accepted that rape myth's are conducive to rape offenders. Rape myths are exemplified by such ideas as if a woman wears sexy clothes, she is to blame if she is raped. However, there is no evidence that such ideas distinguish rapists from other men. Evolutionary explanations of rape also tend to emphasise traditional gender stereotypical ideas and seem, in many ways, the antithesis of feminist ideas about rape.

- In the forensic setting, there are a number of issues that are especially pertinent. One is the use of phallometry/plethysmography, which is basically a technique for assessing a man's sexual responsiveness to different types of sexual imagery. It involves using a tube or cuff around a penis. Changes in the volume or circumference of the man's penis can be recorded from this apparatus and are held to be indicative of sexual arousal. In this way, a man's responsiveness to rape imagery can be assessed, for example. Sexual fantasy, although commonly accepted as a driving force in sexual offences, is poorly understood and inadequately dealt with in forensic and criminal psychology. The common view is that sexual fantasies will be acted upon and, sometimes, this will be in criminal ways in the form of sex offences. This contrasts with what we know about sexual fantasy in non-offender groups, which indicates that fantasy does not always need to be acted out in order to have erotic effects.

Chapter 10

Sexual offenders 2: paedophiles and child molestation

Overview

- The public show considerable levels of animosity towards sex offenders against children and seem to want a mixture of punishment and therapeutic treatment for convicted offenders although they do not want treatment centres in their own neighbourhood. Although psychologists seem less hostile towards paedophiles than some professional groups (e.g. police officers), there is a danger that forensic and criminal psychologists are affected in their professional work by this antagonism.

- The link between pornography and sex offending is a matter of some controversy. On balance, studies of actual sex crime rates and the availability of pornography reveal no causal influence of pornography on sexual offences.

- It has proven a somewhat fruitless endeavour to seek personality characteristics based on conventional measures that differentiate sexual offenders against children from other men or other offenders. It is more adequate to suggest that sex offenders against children do not stand out in the crowd. Nevertheless, paedophilia is a diagnostic category in the American Psychiatric Association's *Diagnostic and Statistical Manual*. This may make it a mental abnormality but it does not mean that paedophiles are suffering a psychotic illness. Many sex offences are committed by young people including ones against children.

- Child molesters are often classified as fixated or regressed. Fixated paedophiles are halted in their psychosexual development so that they retain a sexual interest in children. Regressed offenders have matured sexually but have returned to an earlier stage of psychosexual development. The regressed offender is much more likely to be an intrafamilial (incestuous) offender. These categories are problematic in that it has been shown that many incestuous offenders also offend against children outside their family.

- It is difficult to assess the true rate of paedophile orientation in the general population. One study found that a quarter of men in the sample showed greater sexual response (as measured by phallometry) to erotic stimuli involving children than to those involving women. About 4% claimed to have engaged in paedophile activity.

- Only a minority of paedophile acts involve penile penetration and many involve non-contact offences such as flashing and peeping. Bribery rather than other more violent forms of coercion is typical of paedophile contact with children.

- Recidivism in sex offenders against children seems to be comparatively low. Reconviction (as well as previous convictions) tends to be for non-sexual offences.

- There are a number of important theoretical models which attempt to explain sexual offences against children: 1) *The preconditions model* suggests that the paedophile needs emotional congruence with children, sexual arousal by children, blockages against social contact with other adults, and the removal of inhibitions against sex with children; 2) *The psychotherapeutic/cognitive model* is built on the idea that offenders have distorted beliefs about the sexuality of children and engage in various types of denial to minimise the psychological impact of offending on themselves; 3) *The sexualisation model* assumes that certain forms of early abusive experiences and sexual contacts with other children lead to paedophile interests and a paedophile lifestyle; and 4) *The pathways model* suggests that there are several routes to paedophile offending which include intimacy and social skills deficits, sexual scripts learnt in childhood are distorted due to early sexual experiences in some individuals, and emotional dysregulation when offenders avoid guilt when offending against children or when they fail to learn the coping skills to help them deal with stress development.

- Internet paedophile offenders can commit a number of offences but ones associated with child pornography are the commonest. Few seem to have had previous convictions for contact offences against children. They are theoretically of great importance since they seem to be difficult to differentiate from other paedophiles other than by their lack of contact offenders. Consequently, they appear to be desisters from acting out their sexual interest in children by contact offending, thus making the link between paedophile orientation and paedophile offending less clear-cut than is often suggested.

Paedophiles and other sexual offenders against children are regarded with a special hostility by the general public. This should be of particular concern to forensic and criminal psychologists for three major reasons:

- It is possible that their professional judgement will be affected by these general anti-paedophile feelings.
- That assessment of the risk of recidivism (reoffending) by paedophiles sometimes has to be made under the pressure of public opinion in particularly notorious cases.
- Treatment for sex offenders, and paedophiles in particular, may be put in jeopardy because of the public's reluctance to have treatment facilities in their communities.

From time to time, there have been public protests about the location of treatment facilities. For example, in the 1990s the UK's Gracewell Clinic's new premises were apparently subject to an arson attack. Similarly, units have been forced to close down or not allowed to start their work in other countries such as the United States. More formal evidence of the public's hostility towards paedophiles can be found in the findings of a postal survey conducted in the United Kingdom (Brown, 1999). This research investigated stereotypes about sex offenders and attitudes towards their treatment. Mostly, the public felt that the treatment of sex offenders was desirable though they nevertheless wished offenders to be punished. The basic division of opinion on the treatment of sex offenders was that:

- 51% of the public felt treatment of sex offenders was a good idea;
- 35% were undecided;
- 13% said that sex offenders should never be given therapy.

Of those who were favourable towards the idea of treatment, a small majority (51%) believed that treatment facilities should be available in both prison and the community. Nearly as many (45%) thought that treatment should *only* occur in the prison sentence. Virtually no one thought that treatment should be confined to community settings. Generally, a mixture of custodial sentence together with treatment was seen as acceptable. The vast majority (88%) believed that treatment without a prison sentence was unacceptable.

This may sound fine and positive, especially to those involved in treating offenders. Unfortunately, the strength of feeling in favour of remedial work with sex offenders was not so strong as that in favour of punishment-based approaches. The participants in the survey were all living in the same community and were asked their views about a treatment centre to be located there. The findings on this contrast somewhat with attitudes to treatment in the abstract:

- Only 36% were in favour of a treatment centre to be located in their community.
- As many as 44% said that they would not be prepared to move house into an area in which there was a treatment centre for sex offenders.
- Those who were against a treatment centre in their community expressed willingness to take action in support of their views. Twenty-six per cent would start a campaign against it and 33% said that they would join an existing campaign against it; 80% would sign a petition against it.
- Those in favour of a treatment centre in their community were much less willing to take action in support of their belief. Only 9% of them were prepared to start a campaign in favour and just 7% said that they would join a pre-existing campaign; 50% said that they would sign a petition in support of the treatment centre.

There are other reasons to believe that the community is increasingly intolerant of sex offenders. La Fond (1999) suggests that, in the United States, this intolerance has resulted in extensive legislation aimed at controlling (rather than just punishing) sex offenders against children. Similar trends have been noted in the United Kingdom (Howitt, 2005). The American legislation includes sex offender registers, notification of the community about sex offenders in that community and laws encouraging chemical castration. More recently still, laws have been introduced allowing the commitment of sexual predators. The latter, known as *sexually violent predator (SVP) laws*, can result in sex offenders being detained after their prison sentence has finished. The legal requirement is that it has to be shown that the individual both is dangerous and presents a high risk of reoffending. Furthermore, the individual in question must have either a 'personality disorder' or 'mental abnormality' which may lead to the reoffending. The process involves a trial at which the offender is legally represented. Furthermore, the offender may have an expert of his own choice to conduct an evaluation separate from that carried out for the state. Offenders who are committed to further incarceration must be given therapy and the question of their release periodically reviewed.

Not merely are the attitudes of the general public important. The views of staff working in the criminal justice system have an even more direct impact on how offenders are treated in the system. Radley (2001) used the *Attitude Toward Sex Offenders Questionnaire* with samples of police officers, prison officers, and probation workers and psychologists. The sorts of items involved include (p. 6):

- sex offenders are different from most people;
- sex offenders never change;
- I think I would like a lot of sex offenders.

Although attitudes varied, it was clear that police officers were more hostile than probation workers and psychologists. There was also evidence of similar differences between prison officers and probation workers/psychologists. Female staff members were more favourably disposed to sex offenders. There was also, possibly, evidence that attitudes towards sex offenders have become less hostile in recent years.

Box 10.1

Controversy: pornography and sex offending

Ted Bundy, the notorious US serial killer, claimed to have been influenced to his violent sexual crimes by pornography. The role of pornography in creating sexual attitudes has been part of the feminist debate for two decades at least. Here, we are concerned only with the evidence that pornography might lead to sex offending. Analyses of the content of pornography indicate that at least some of it contains anti-woman themes such as rape, violence and degradation. The extent differs according to the study. For example, Thompson (1994) found little to support the view that pornography was full of such imagery whereas others (Itzin, 1992) find the reverse. This is partly a matter of how a particular image is interpreted and codified.

The range of studies is wide and stretches from laboratory experiments to case studies. Here are some of the more important studies:

- *The Danish Experiment*: Kutchinsky (1970, 1973) carried out research into the social consequences of liberalising the law in Denmark in the 1960s. Pornography became increasingly available. The crime statistics over this period tended to decline. The crimes affected were those such as indecent exposure, peeping, indecent language and so forth. These are the relatively trivial crimes which might be most affected by changes of public attitude towards sex such that they are less inclined to report trivial crimes to the police. There was no such change in the reporting of rape. In later studies, Kutchinsky has claimed to find that the liberalisation of pornography laws has not brought about increases in the rates of sex crimes: things have either held more or less steady or rape rates have declined. These researches were carried out in Denmark, Germany and the United States (Kutchinsky, 1991).

- *Court's propositions*: Court (1977, 1984) put forward several hypotheses about the effects of pornography on sex crimes. For example, he has suggested that in parallel to the availability of increasingly violent pornography, the amount of violence in rapes will have increased over time. Although Court has evidence for this proposition, it should be pointed out that he is a little selective in that he does not examine every country where crime statistics are available. For example, Howitt (1998b) showed that there is evidence that over a fairly lengthy period,

▶

rape in the United Kingdom shows trends upwards, which cannot be explained by changes in legislation (which became more controlling). Since the contents of pornography have tended to remain relatively free of violence, the steady rise in rape cannot be explained by that either (Thompson, 1994).

- *Developmental studies*: a number of researchers have studied the aetiology of interest and use of pornography in the life cycle of sex offenders. There is some evidence that masturbation comes early in the adolescent lives of sex offenders and earlier than use of pornography (Condron and Nutter, 1988; Howitt and Cumberbatch, 1990). Their deviancy seems to precede their use of pornography in general. This sequence of events suggests that pornography is not a cause of this deviancy although their interest in it may be a consequence of their deviancy.

- *Area studies*: Baron and Straus (1984, 1989) and others (Gentry, 1991; Scott and Schwalm, 1988) looked at the relationship between the amount of pornography circulating in different states of the United States and rape rates in those states. Although they found a relationship between the two, since this was strongest for the circulation of pornography aimed at women, it seems unlikely that this sort of pornography actually caused the rapes according to Baron and Straus.

- *Paedophile preferences*: in terms of paedophiles, the few available studies have concentrated on the use made of pornography by paedophiles. Marshall (1988) found, for example, that sex offenders show little preference for and arousal to pornography redolent of their offending. They tend to use a variety of pornographic stimuli. Similarly, Howitt (1995b) describes how paedophiles will use a variety of imagery in their fantasy including Walt Disney films featuring children, television advertisements for baby products and adult heterosexual pornography. This material is used to generate personal paedophile fantasy.

It would appear that, like many non-offenders, sex offenders use pornography and other imagery. It is difficult to argue that this material causes their offending.

Mental illness and sexual predators

According to Howitt (1995a), there is no reason to think that paedophiles share particular personality characteristics. Apart from their offending behaviour, they are fairly typical of men in general. Paedophiles, in general, simply do not stand out in the crowd – which is part of the reason that their offending goes undetected (La Fontaine, 1990). If the US sexually violent predator laws are to be applied to an offender, the matter of the personality disorder or mental abnormality that led to the offending has to be considered. Neither of these concepts is an easy one for psychiatry or psychology. They seem more readily defined by the law. A mental abnormality legally is 'a congenital or acquired condition affecting the emotional or volitional capacity which predisposes the person to the commission of criminal sexual acts in a degree constituting such person a menace to the health and safety of others'. There is no requirement that the condition is amenable to treatment for the sexual predator laws to apply. So what is the problem for psychology and psychiatry?

No generally accepted definition or meaning for the term mental abnormality exists in psychiatry (or psychology for that matter). In the *Diagnostic and Statistical*

Manual of the American Psychiatric Association (see Box 18.1) there is an entry for paedophilia. Some psychiatrists and psychologists claim that men who offend against children can be regarded as suffering from a mental abnormality on the basis of this. Without treatment, the abnormality may well lead to reoffending, they suggest. Legal concepts and psychological concepts do not always equate, as we saw in Chapter 1. Legal concepts may sometimes be extremely difficult to translate effectively into ideas acceptable to psychologists. Nevertheless, for psychologists to function effectively in court it is essential to bridge the differences between the disciplines of psychology and law. Consequently, forensic psychologists have to develop their own understanding of legal terms.

All of this may seem a reasonable approach. Nevertheless, according to La Fond (1999), there is no equivalent of paedophilia for rapists in the DSM. The idea of a personality disorder does not occur in DSM IV – the nearest thing being anti-social personality disorder (ASPD). The difficulty is that a very substantial minority of incarcerated offenders of all sorts fit this classification – the figure might be almost as high as 50%. All types of offenders may fit this classification including, but not exclusively, sex offenders. In other words, ASPD is so common that it is not really predictive of sexual reoffending. (Psychological risk assessment is discussed in Chapter 23.) In other words, although the concept of personality disorder may be 'extended' to fit dangerous sex offenders, this is at the expense of psychological rigour.

Classifications of child molesters

One of the commonest taxonomies of child molesters is the dichotomy between fixated and regressed offenders (Groth and Birnbaum, 1978):

- *Fixated offenders*: these are said to be developmentally fixated on a permanent or a temporary basis such that their sexual interest is in children rather than adults. Although they may have had sexual contact with adults, this contact is more coincidental than intentional since peer relationships are not psychologically an integral part of their sexuality.
- *Regressed offenders*: these are men who matured in their sexuality but demonstrated a return to an earlier level of psychosexual development. Their psychosexual history would show primary interest in peer age or adult individuals rather than younger ones. Interest in the latter seems to reflect almost a reversal to a more childlike sexuality.

Important differences are found between the two types especially in terms of their relationship history. This is perhaps not surprising given the above descriptions, but fixated offenders rarely are or have been married (something like one in eight have been married) whereas about three-quarters of regressed offenders have been married. Perhaps, even more significantly, the fixated offenders offend most commonly against strangers or acquaintances whereas the regressed type offend commonly within the network of friends or relatives. This is the very sort of victim which feminist writers on child sexual abuse have regarded as incestuous in its broadest terms (Howitt, 1992).

While it may seem commonsensical to suggest that adult men who have sexual relationships with women have 'regressed' when they offend sexually against children, this is actually somewhat naïve. Some offenders target women with children for the primary purpose of gaining access to the children. While they may engage in sex with the mother, in some cases they describe this as being accompanied by paedophile sexual fantasy (Howitt, 1995a). There are other reasons to be cautious about the taxonomy:

- Despite claims to the contrary, incestuous fathers have frequently also offended against children outside the family or raped women (Abel *et al.*, 1983). In other words, offending against children is a sexual preference, not the product of family circumstances such as stress or sexual privation. This does not mean that the groups are not to some extent different. For example, Miner and Dwyer (1997) found that incestuous offenders were more able to develop trusting interpersonal relationships than exhibitionists and child molesters.

- Incestuous offenders seem to show patterns of sexual arousal to 'erotic' depictions of children (Howitt, 1995a) despite the argument that they are 'forced' by circumstances to regress to sex with children. That is to say, explanations of family factors leading to offending against children by offenders possibly serve merely as excuses. Studer *et al.* (2002) used phallometry (see Box 9.1) in order to assess child molesters' responses to slides of different ages, genders and body shapes. The molesters could be grouped into incestuous and non-incestuous offenders against children. It was not possible to differentiate the two groups effectively on the basis of their responses to the slides. Just over 40% of each group showed their strongest erotic response to the slides that featured pubescent children. More of the incestuous offenders showed their major response to slides of adults (37%) compared to 19% of the non-incestuous group. More of the non-incestuous group (30%) showed their primary erotic response to pre-pubescent children compared to 13% of the incestuous group. So, clearly, there are some differences but equally clearly there are sizeable numbers of incestuous offenders who show exactly the same sort of erotic attraction towards under-age persons that non-incestuous offenders do. In terms of their self-reported offending, over 40% of incestuous offenders had committed sexual offences against children outside the family.

- Groth and Birnbaum (1978) argue that homosexual men are never regressed offenders. By homosexual we mean men whose adult sexual orientation is towards men. (This is in order to differentiate them from heterosexual paedophiles and homosexual paedophiles who are defined in terms of the sex of their child victim, not their sexual history with adults.) This is a remarkable claim in some ways and difficult to accept. The implication is that sexual privation and stress do not affect gay men in the same way as they do heterosexual men. This clearly needs support, if it is true, which has never been provided.

Interestingly, there are sentencing differentials between heterosexual and homosexual child molesters. Walsh (1994) studied a sample of serious sex offenders in Ohio including rape as well as sexual offenders against children. His interest was in those who offended against boys compared with those who offended against girls. The former were nearly seven times more likely to be put in prison for their offence than the latter. According to Walsh, this is only accountable in terms of homophobic attitudes and beliefs. None of his other predictor variables (e.g. previous sexual offences, victim cooperation and so forth) seemed to account for this sentencing differential.

How common is paedophilia?

There is plenty of evidence that sexual abuse of youngsters below the age of consent is common. The research surveys on child sexual abuse provide a range of different answers to the question of how common such abuse is. Depending on the definition of abuse used – e.g. self-definition by the victim or legal definition – various estimates will be obtained. Furthermore, relatively unintrusive sexual acts such as passing suggestive remarks may be very common but nevertheless experienced as abuse (Kelly, 1988, 1989) whereas penetrative sex is relatively rare in this abuse (Nash and West, 1985). Once again, studies of offenders provide alternative perspectives from studies of victims. The difficulties of under-reporting of sexual offences are particularly strong in this area. Conviction data are poor indicators of the extent of victimisation.

One theoretically important question concerns the extent to which paedophilic sexual arousal can occur in 'normal' men. Is sexual arousal to imagery of children confined to offenders? Research on this is sparse. Hall *et al.* (1995) recruited a sample of American men through a newspaper advertisement. Each man was assessed in several different ways including plethysmography (see Box 9.1) in which changes in the size of a man's penis is regarded as an indicator of sexual arousal. A number of slides of nude pre-pubescent girls, nude women and clothed pre-pubescent girls were shown in random order to each participant. Generally, there were fairly high relations between the effects of the different pictures – that is, there was a tendency for the men who were aroused by one type of stimulus to be aroused by others.

Most importantly, about a quarter of the ordinary men showed more arousal to child stimuli than to those of women. About a fifth of the total sample reported that they had 'paedophile' interests. Only about 4% of the sample reported that they had actually engaged in paedophile behaviour. This is a low figure compared with the figures for physiological arousal to paedophile stimuli and interest in children sexually. Nevertheless, one should be cautious when generalising from the findings of any single study:

- It is important to note that the men who were aroused by the paedophile stimuli were also aroused by other sexual imagery. This actually might indicate that they were not paedophile in their sexual orientation because they found all imagery, including that of adults, arousing. The men most easily aroused by the explicit pictures of adult women often could be aroused by the paedophile stimuli too.
- The men in the study were encouraged to allow themselves to be aroused. While this is not uncommon in studies using plethysmography, it may be a limitation in that it may result in more men showing signs of sexual arousal. The researchers have no way of knowing what was actually causing the arousal – what was in the experimental stimuli or personal fantasies created by the participant in order to become aroused? (See Boxes 9.1 and 9.2.)

Despite these criticisms, this is of theoretical importance since it may mean that paedophile orientation does not necessarily have to be acted out in the form of sexual abuse – that is, it is possible to desist from sexual crime against children.

The nature of paedophile offences

The general public learn about sex offending through the media. The media, of course, have their own agenda (Los and Chamard, 1997) in which the sensational and extreme acts are presented as the image of sex offenders and what they do. Paedophiles are mainly seen as murderous child abductors. Some are. However, in the United Kingdom, for example, convictions for child abduction averaged 44 annually in the 1990s. Of these abductions, 60% were motivated by sexual factors (Erikson and Friendship, 2002). Research suggests that as a group, molesters carry out a wide range of different types of activity. Some, such as frottage and peeping behaviour, may not be recognised by the victim as such.

Like most crime issues, the picture of paedophile offending varies according to one's source of information. The context in which data are collected is also important. Studies of victims of child sexual abuse illustrate this. In a Los Angeles study, Wyatt (1985) found non-contact incidents such as flashing, improper comments and the like formed 40% of the abusive experiences. Intercourse/attempted intercourse made up about a quarter of the incidents. A study of the perpetrators of child sexual abuse coming before the court in an area of south-east London over a period of two years also reveals something of the varied nature of such offending (Craissati and McClurg, 1997). The offences with which they were charged were overwhelmingly indecent assault (68%). Gross indecency (11%), buggery, i.e. anal intercourse, (9%) and rape (7%) were much less common. Under a third (29%) of the men were convicted of penetrative offences. Nearly three-quarters (71%) were convicted of offences against just one child (at that hearing) and 14% were involved with offences involving a total of three or more victims. Male victims tended to be abused outside the home whereas female victims were relatively more likely to be victimised by relatives at home. The methods of grooming were: 40% used bribery to gain the participation of the victim, 24% used verbal threats and 16% used physical threats. One of the subgroups, and the one most at risk of recidivism, tended to show the following characteristic pattern:

- to have been sexually abused as a child;
- to offend against boys;
- to have more victims;
- to have victims outside their family;
- to exhibit cognitive distortions;
- to have previous convictions for sexual offences.

Whatever the overall pattern, individual offenders may have very distinctive patterns of offending. For example, Robert Black, a lorry driver who killed girls and left their bodies in locations in various parts of the United Kingdom, had a pattern of penetrating the child's vagina with his finger and then killing her (Wyre and Tate, 1995): in other words, extreme violence but less extreme sexual acts.

Box 10.2

Controversy: sex offenders: minor or major recidivists?

A number of initiatives have been introduced in recent years against sex offending in a number of countries. The measures include sex offender registers that require that offenders, meeting the minimum requirements for registration, report their addresses to local police. Megan's Law-type initiatives require that the locations of sex offenders be revealed to the community. These initiatives seem to presume that sex offenders are repetitive and persistent in their offending and are persistently dangerous. There are two totally opposite points of view on this matter:

- *Little reoffending.* The clearest statement of this sort of position would include West's (1987) finding that most sex offenders convicted in British courts only appear once in court.
- *Major reoffenders.* A study by Abel *et al.* (1987) is frequently quoted as support for the view that sex offenders are chronic offenders. Taking 561 sex offenders attending a private clinic for sex offenders, the total offences that these men reported was approximately 250,000. In other words, the numerical average is 446 offences per man! This gives the very clear impression that sex offending is habitual and virtually without respite. These figures disguise the actual trends. For example, if the rapists alone are considered, the mean number of rapes admitted per rapist was 7. The median number of rapes is 1. The median is the number of rapes committed by the rapist who is at the top of the bottom 50% of rapes but at the bottom of the remaining 50% of rapes (that is, exactly in the middle of the frequency distribution). Most rapists actually admitted to just one rape. In other words, the vast proportion of rapes is committed by a small number of rapists.

This sort of analysis is complicated by a number of factors:

- The influence of the methodology employed. For example, men attending a private clinic may be inclined to admit to more offences simply because they feel that the therapist will see them as being cooperative and *not* in a state of denial of their offending behaviour. Indeed, there may be a motive for exaggerating the number of offences since the more cooperative an offender appears, the more likely he is seen as suitable for treatment and eventual release.
- Studies using reconviction rates severely underestimate the amount of reoffending. It is known that many rapes go unreported by the victim. Thus reconvictions may only identify a small proportion of reoffenders.

Fisher and Thornton (1993) argue that neither extreme captures the truth. There are some offenders who reoffend at a high rate and others who offend on a single occasion. Thus it is impossible to predict future offending simply on the basis of 'once a sex offender always a sex offender'. It is not true to say that all sex offenders are by definition high-risk and certain to reoffend if allowed to go free.

There is a question of whether sex offenders are 'trapped' in an escalating spiral of increasingly serious and frequent offences. Mair (1995) argues that some of the views about sex offenders described in the writings of professionals essentially distort the reality of such offences. She suggests that a number of the claims made about sex offenders do not adequately reflect the available research evidence. The reason why we target sex offenders is not to do with their likelihood of reoffending – that is low compared with other types of crime – but because we find their offences disgusting and we are concerned about their victims. There are some sex offenders who are extremely dangerous, but this does not reflect the typical sex offender in this context. Mair is critical about some of the 'classic' studies such as Abel *et al.* (1987) described above. This is a much-quoted study that claimed very high levels of sexual recidivism. She points out that the sample used was very unrepresentative of sex offenders:

- they were not currently being prosecuted for sexual offences;
- they were offered treatment in exchange for confessions that would not be reported to others;
- they were likely to be the most deviant and troubled sex offenders simply because they had sought help independent of arrest.

However, the broad findings of the study have been endlessly reported as factually true of all offenders.

Similarly, Laws (1994) argued that up to one half of rapists of adult women are at risk of being sexually violent to children. What does this mean? That studies have shown that half of rapists also sexually attack children? No: it means that he is referring to phallometric studies (see Box 9.1) which showed that a minority of rapists also show sexual arousal to child images.

The Grampian sex offenders study (Mair, 1995), much like other studies (see Box 23.3), demonstrated that after a follow-up period of, for almost all, over 10 years, about a half of the men were reconvicted – but for non-sexual offences. Those convicted of a hands-on offence (i.e. a sexual offence involving touching the victim) were *less* likely to sexually reoffend than those with hands-off offences (e.g. indecent exposure). Such reconviction trends are reflected in the most recent figures. The UK Home Office (2004) has published figures which show that 19% of sex offenders are reconvicted within two years of leaving prison. However, the reconviction rate for all adult prisoners is 52% in the same period. Recidivism, in this case, is recidivism for any type of offence. Some would argue that sex offences are hard to detect and largely go unreported. However, it is difficult to explain why sex offenders should be better than other types of offender at avoiding arrest for crime in general and not just sex crime.

Recidivism rates are different for different types of sex offence. Hood *et al.* (2002) investigated sex offenders in the UK who had received prison sentences of four or more years. Most (59%) had been convicted for penetrative or attempted penetrative sexual intercourse. The period studied in which the men were at risk of recidivsm was up to six years following release from prison. Incestuous offenders (intrafamilial offenders) had very low reconviction rates. In fact, none of them in this study was reconvicted for a sexual offence and sent to prison. Only 2% were re-imprisoned for any type of offence. Extrafamilial offenders were rather more likely to reoffend sexually – up to 26% of them did so. Only 11% of the incest group was reconvicted for any type of offence whereas 47% of the extrafamilial offender group were. The evidence suggested that those convicted of the most serious extrafamilial offences were the most likely to reoffend.

Youthful offenders

Despite the public image of sex offenders as being dirty old men, there is considerable evidence that young offenders are responsible for significant proportions of sex offences. For example, it has been estimated in the United States that up to half of child sexual abuse is carried out by persons under the age of 21 (Graves *et al.*, 1996). This is important for several reasons:

- These are a substantial proportion of sexual offences so need to be considered in any account of sex offending.
- They support the view that frequently sex offending emerges in childhood and adolescence and continues, almost career-wise, into adulthood (Howitt, 1995a).

Graves *et al.* (1996) carried out a meta-analytic review of studies of youthful sex offenders by studying empirical research studies from 1973 to 1993. Meta-analysis is the study of trends across different studies of similar phenomena (Howitt and Cramer, 2005) (see Box 5.1). The study concentrated on the demographic and parental characteristics of youthful offenders. The authors believed that the youthful offenders could be classified into three different, exclusive categories:

- Paedophilic – generally their first offence was committed between 6 and 12 years of age. They consistently molest younger children and prefer female victims.
- Sexual assault – these are youthful offenders whose first reported offence is between 13 and 15 years but their victims may vary substantially and include both older victims than themselves and younger victims.
- Mixed offence – these are youngsters who commit a variety of offences such as sexual assault, molesting younger children, exhibitionism, voyeurism, frotteurism, etc.

Overall, youthful sex offenders in general tended to have the following characteristics:

- lower socio-economic class origins;
- pathological family structures and interaction style;
- their fathers were physically neglected as a child;
- their mothers were physically abused as a child;
- substance abuse was common among the fathers.

There were considerable differences between the three different types of youngster as shown in Table 10.1. Care has to be exercised since despite the rather pathological picture painted of the families of youthful sexual offenders, these are only trends in the data. A substantial proportion of youthful sex offenders came from homes identified as healthy.

Table 10.1 The family and social characteristics of different types of youthful male sexual offenders obtained from meta-analysis

Characteristic	Paedophilic	Sexual assault	Mixed offence
Low to middle social class	✓	✓	✗
Low social class	✗	✗	✓
Lives in foster care	✓	✗	✗
Lives in lone-parent family	✗	✓	✗
Mother physically abused as child	✓	✗	✗
Mother neglected as child	✗	✗	✓
Mother abuses drugs	✗	✗	✓
Father abuses alcohol	✗	✓	✗
Father abuses drugs	✓	✗	✗
Maladaptive, dysfunctional family	✓	✗	✓
Rigid family	✗	✓	✗
Maternal neglect	✗	✗	✓
Protestant religion	✗	✗	✓

A ✓ indicates that this characteristic is especially common in that group of youthful offenders.

Theories of paedophilia

There have been a number of attempts to explain paedophilia. None of them is completely satisfactory in itself, although most have at least some virtues. The ones that we will consider in some detail are:

- the preconditions model;
- the psychotherapeutic/cognitive model;
- the sexualisation model;
- the pathways model.

The preconditions model

Araji and Finkelhor (1985) proposed the preconditions model of abusive behaviour. It is illustrated in Figure 10.1. As can be seen, several different types of factor are listed, which are seen as partial preconditions for sexual abuse. These broad types of factor include emotional congruence, sexual arousal, blockage and disinhibition. The following points should be made:

- This model is relatively old and was developed at a time when empirical research on sex offenders was very limited in its scope.
- It is based on a number of almost common-sense assumptions, not all of which have or had been supported and some have not even been adequately tested.
- It assumes that child molestation is multiply caused and does not assume that any of the preconditions are necessarily involved in any given case.
- It has the advantage of linking the theory with therapy that has tended to assume the multi-causality of abusive behaviour and, consequently, the need for complex therapeutic methods.
- Unfortunately, as was acknowledged by Arajii and Finkelhor, very few of the preconditions have been shown in empirical research to be associated with abusive behaviour.

1. Emotional congruence with children Offenders lack self-esteem Offenders are psychosocially immature Offenders may have a need to dominate	**2. Social arousal by children** Sexually socialised by child pornography Hormonal abnormalities/imbalances
3. Blockages preventing adult contact Lack of effective social skills Problems in relating to adult females Experienced repressive sexual socialisation in childhood	**4. Disinhibition of norms against adult/child sex** Offenders may be senile Alcohol may decrease inhibitions Possibly in an incest-tolerant subculture

Figure 10.1 The preconditions model of molestation

Furthermore, it is descriptive in the sense of merely describing the characteristics of abusers rather than trying to identify the root cause of the abusive behaviour, say, in their own childhood.

The preconditions model was the first attempt at a comprehensive theory of sexual offending against children and amongst its achievements was its help in clarifying the goals of treating such offenders. In particular, according to Ward and Hudson (2001), the model encouraged the following: concentration on deviant sexual arousal, working with problems of intimacy, showing offenders how to effectively identify and manage situations in which they are at high risk of offending, and the incorporation of socio-cultural factors such as the possible role of pornography. However, it could be argued that the theory has merely encouraged a highly unspecific multi-faceted approach to the treatment of offenders which, consequently, has not helped develop our understanding of the process of becoming an offender.

The psychotherapeutic/cognitive model

This model is rarely systematically described in total although elements of it are very common in the literature (e.g. Salter, 1988; Wyre, 1987, 1992). The main emphasis of this model is on the cognitive and behavioural steps involved in offending behaviour. Broadly speaking, the model suggests that there are four steps in the process:

- Cognitive distortions or distorted thinking of the sort effectively captured by the Abel Rape Index Scale (Abel *et al.*, 1977). Such distorted beliefs include 'Having sex with a child is a good way for an adult to teach a child about sex', and include other beliefs about the sexual nature of children, how their behaviour signals sexual interest and so forth.
- Grooming – these are the methods by which offenders contact children and gain their trust and confidence. Violence or threats of violence may be part of this, but probably more typical are bribes of sweets, money, trips out and the like.
- Planning through fantasy: this is the idea that the offender plans in fantasy the likely scenarios of events in, for example, finally trying to seduce the child. What will they do, say, if a child says they are going home?
- Denial is the mental process by which offenders appear to be denying the consequences of their actions and perhaps blaming someone else. For example, they would tend to agree with the following statements from the Abel scale (Abel *et al.*, 1977). 'Sex between an adult and a 13-year-old (or younger) child causes the child no emotional problems' and 'A man (or woman) is justified in having sex with his (her) children or step-children, if his wife (husband) doesn't like sex'. Denial can take a wide range of forms according to Salter (1988) and others:
  - the denial that abuse actually took place;
  - minimisation of the abuse by claiming few victims, for example;
  - denying seriousness – by admitting fondling but not anal sex, for example;
  - denying that there is anything wrong with them – they have found God so do not need therapy;
  - denial of responsibility – blaming the child for seducing the offender.

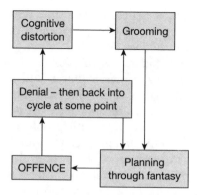

Figure 10.2 The clinical/cognitive model

While it is fairly well established that there is cognitive distortion or distorted think-ing in paedophiles and other sex offenders, this idea is often mixed together with that of paedophiles being adroitly manipulative people. They are keen to manipulate others, including psychologists and others working with them. Hence, whatever they think will be to their advantage they will try to convince the other person of. Thus it becomes a little unclear whether or not they really do think in particular ways or whether they are simply trying to manipulate their therapists, researchers and any other individuals who become involved. The writing on this is not particularly coherent in the sense that concepts are somewhat inconsistently used. Sometimes similar words are used to describe very different processes, so one finds the terms minimisation and denial used somewhat interchangeably. Figure 10.2 presents aspects of this model as a diagram.

Studies of cognitive distortions in paedophiles and other sex offenders are rather rare compared to the numerous mentions of them in the professional literature. Nevertheless, research does seem to suggest the importance of cognitive distortions. Barbaree (1998) found that substantial numbers of paedophiles and rapists denied carrying out the offences they were charged with. This Barbaree refers to as denial. Some adopted strategies that essentially minimised the offence in some way. Approximately 30–40% of the offenders sought to minimise the seriousness of the offence or the extent of their culpability by strategies such as:

- blaming the victim;
- suggesting that the amount of force used was smaller than it actually was;
- holding personal factors such as stress or unemployment responsible.

Interestingly, the effects of psychological therapy on the men who initially denied the offence were quite impressive. About two thirds changed from denying to admitting their offence. Denial of the offence was replaced by minimisation of the seriousness or their culpability for the offence. The excuses were largely about their use of force and just how sexually intrusive the sexual acts involved were. Of those in the study who initially admitted involvement in the offence but minimised other activities, the tendency was overwhelmingly for them to continue to minimise but at reduced levels. Hence, Barbaree argues that these cognitive strategies are amenable to change through therapy and recommends that they are tackled early in therapy. At the same time, it should be noted how strongly offenders persist with minimisation despite admitting the offence itself in general terms.

Of course, there is nothing unusual about the denial of an offence since it occurs among all sorts of offenders. Any court of law will demonstrate this on a daily basis.

It has been argued that the use of denial is exceptionally common among sex offenders (e.g. Abel *et al.*, 1987). According to Nugent and Kroner (1996), clinical experience suggests that child molesters are more likely to admit to their offences than rapists, though this appears not to be supported by Barbaree's study described above. There are claims that, for example, sex offenders who admit the offence may differ from those who do not in terms of the self-justification strategies they employ. Men who are offence *deniers* tend to attribute responsibility to the victim (Scully and Marolla, 1984) whereas the *admitters* attribute the cause to their emotional problems or substance abuse, in particular. This is a further indication that the style of cognitive distortion differs although such distortion is common.

Nugent and Kroner's Canadian study concerned offenders prior to treatment. The different groups of offenders involved were rapists, intrafamilial and extrafamilial offenders. Two measures in particular are of interest. These assess the tendency of offenders to characteristically seek to present themselves in a favourable light. So the balanced *Inventory of Desirable Responding* was given as well as the defensive response style part of the *Basic Personality Inventory*. Men whose victims were under 14 years were considered molesters. They divided the offenders into four categories (although in general the type of offence affected the findings more than the style of response):

- non-admitters who claimed no illegal interaction with the victim;
- partial-admitters who admitted that they had sexual contact but believed no offence had taken place;
- partial-admitters who again admitted a sexual act such as fondling but not penetrative sexual intercourse;
- admitters who admitted the offence as on the official record.

One way of conceptualising this research is in terms of the ways in which offenders represent themselves to those in authority. The findings indicate that the child molesters were trying to manage the impression they created more actively than rapists. Interestingly, in this study, more child molesters admitted their offences than rapists (i.e. 43% versus 27%).

The sexualisation model

Howitt (1995a) regards paedophilic orientation as developing out of the characteristics of early sexual experiences. In particular, he suggests that experience of sexual abuse in childhood is the start of a process that ends in paedophile activity. Not all abuse is equally likely to lead to sex offending of this sort but penetrative sex, abuse by females and similar uncharacteristic abusive acts are more likely to have this effect. Furthermore, it is possible that sexual experiences in childhood with other, probably older, children may also be influential. In this approach, paedophilia is seen more as a developmental process beginning from early sexual experiences but often continuing through adolescence into adulthood. One possible consequence of this early experience is the way in which the paedophile regards sexual activity between adult

Box 10.3

Key concept: cycles of abuse

It is a fairly uncontroversial matter to suggest that a sizeable proportion of sex offenders had been victims of sexual abuse as a child. What is controversial is the issue of whether this abuse is a causal influence on sex offenders. Imagine, for example, that there is evidence that 100% of sex offenders had been sexually abused as children. These are some of the comments that might be made:

- Many youngsters who are sexually abused as children do not grow up to be abusers themselves.
- Girls are the commonest victims of sexual abuse but women are much less likely to be abusers than men are.
- This merely provides offenders with excuses and inappropriate justification for their offending.

The first two points, although correct in themselves, do not mean that the sexual abuse had no effect on later offending. They may merely imply that one needs to explore factors that insulate some children from growing up to be offenders or that there may be further characteristics of their victimisation which lead to some becoming victimisers themselves and others not.

On the other hand, what if 10% of sex offenders claimed to have been sexually abused as children? What might be argued in these circumstances?

- This does not seem to be a very high percentage and is in line with low estimates of abuse in the general population. Hence abuse cannot be causal.
- Offenders might be reluctant to admit their abuse or may not even see their childhood experiences as sexually abusive. Hence the data are inadequate. Men, in general, known to have been abused sexually tend not to regard their experiences as sexual abuse in a ratio of 6 to 1 (Widom and Morris, 1997).

These are really the extremes. Certainly, there are a number of authorities who deny the strength of the cycles of abuse argument (Finkelhor, 1984; Hanson and Slater, 1988) for the reasons given above and others. Equally, there are a number of studies which suggest that the incidence of abuse in the childhoods of sex offenders is low. For example, Waterhouse *et al.* (1994) suggest that offenders are little different from non-offenders.

Unfortunately, these studies are based on survey methods that tend to ask quite direct questions such as 'Were you sexually abused as a child?' This is a sensitive issue that may well elicit denial from any person abused in their childhood. It may be a matter with which they have not come to terms. Hence it is not surprising that studies that examine the question but in groups of offenders post-treatment find that the admission rates of sexual abuse in childhood increase dramatically from 22% to about 50% (Worling, 1995). Howitt (1998b) provides evidence that, using a similar style of questioning, the experience of abuse was admitted by 80% of young sex offenders compared with 25% of non-offenders.

The importance of this issue lies in the argument that sexual crime may be a re-enactment in some form of childhood experiences of being abused (Burgess *et al.*, 1988).

and child. He will see adult–child sexual contact as normal since it is the normal thing in his experience. The following should also be considered:

- This account also partly explains the apparent relationship between the characteristic abuse experienced by the paedophile-to-be and the characteristics of his offending against children in the future. Others have noted similar tendencies in abused children. Haapasalo *et al.* (1999) describe the concept of *isomorphic behaviour*. They point out 'Physically abused children tend to commit physically violent crimes whereas sexually abused children are prone, in adulthood, to sexual violence, including pedophilia, child molestation, and rape' (p. 98). Groth and Burgess (1978) mention that there are age and type of act similarities between offender and victim and Howitt (1995a) gives other examples. One reason for the isomorphism of sexual offending may be that it involves repetition of strategies for achieving basic feelings of safety and security. It could equally be simply a further instance of the importance of childhood experiences in determining adult behaviour.

- One potential difficulty with the explanation lies in the mixed support for cycles of sexual abuse in the literature. Box 10.3 suggests that the evidence is stronger than some researchers have indicated. Furthermore, not all acts of sexual abuse are as damaging as others.

- Another potentially crucial problem is that not all children who are abused become abusers themselves. The sexualisation model, since it assumes that the more extreme/repetitive forms of abuse have greatest effect, actually has an explanation of why some abused youngsters become abusers. Howitt (1998a), for example, points out that sexual abuse of boys by women seems to be particularly associated with later sexual offending by the victim.

There has been a growing recognition that sex offending in childhood is a matter that should not be neglected and that it is actually rather extensive in scope. Coleman (1997), for example, has mentioned the following 'explanations' of adolescent offending – that the offender is experimenting or curious, that sexual aggression is common in adolescence, or boys will be boys. She sees the denial of juvenile sex offending as a problem as part of the means by which such offending is cultivated. If it is not a problem then nothing needs to be done about it and adolescent offenders proceed to adult offending. Of course, increasingly juvenile sex offending is being recognised as a significant problem. This model is illustrated in Figure 10.3.

The treatment of sex offenders is dealt with in Chapter 22.

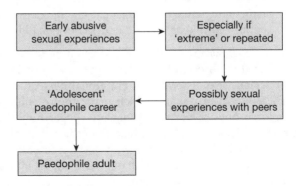

Figure 10.3 The sexualisation model

The pathways model

Ward and Siegert (2002) integrated the best features of several important multi-factorial theories of child sexual abuse into a single, comprehensive model. This they call the pathways model. The term multi-factorial means that for a particular form of behaviour, there are many determinants of that behaviour that the theoretical model needs to take into account. These determinants should be considered individually or in combination in order to understand sex offending against children. Virtually all of the theories of paedophilia discussed in this chapter accept that child sexual abuse is multi-determined in this way. They differ in important ways. Finkelhor's approach tends to imply that offenders are diverted from the path of a normal sexual interest in adults by a variety of factors which push the offender towards children or remove inhibitions against sex with children. The psychotherapeutic/cognitive model makes very similar assumptions in that it assumes that the way to stop the sexual abuse of children is to change a wide range of cognitions and behaviours which are conducive to child sexual abuse. Howitt's sexualisation model is different in a key respect. Sex offending in this model is regarded as a part of a lifestyle starting in childhood in which sexual orientation to children begins early and remains into adulthood. This does not mean that sexual abusers of children never involve themselves in sexual relationships with adults: they do. However, the model does imply that the task of the researcher is to understand the origins of the offender's sexual interest in childhood rather than regard it as a substitute of sexual activity with adults. In other words, sexual interest in children should be regarded as more akin to a sexual orientation.

Theories operate at three different levels according to Ward and Siegert. Level I is the multi-factorial level; level II is a theory which postulates a single factor though in many respects these amount to little more than a hypothesis about the relationship of a variable to the sex offending against children; and level III is the micro-level or offence process level, which is little more than descriptions of the behavioural sequence leading to offending or possibly relapsing into offending behaviour.

A distinction is made by Ward and Siegert between *distal* and *proximal* factors in relation to the offending behaviour:

- *Distal factors*: these are causal factors which lie in the predispositions of the offender. They may have a number of origins. They may be in the genetic make-up of the offender or in his childhood development and beyond. They are long-term psychological mechanisms which may lead to offending when the environmental situation encourages offending.
- *Proximal factors*: these are the factors in the environment that change the distal factors into actual offending. They, in other words, trigger the predispositions into action. Possible proximal factors could include negative mood states or stress.

Ward and Siegert (2002) propose four psychological mechanisms which may be involved in an offender's offending behaviour: 1) intimacy and social skill deficits; 2) deviant sexual scripts; 3) emotional dysregulation, and 4) cognitive distortions. These are distal factors which make the offender vulnerable to offending against children but are not the immediate trigger for offending. The four pathways constitute different etiological factors in the sexual abuse of children though offenders will exhibit the other three with varying intensities. So there is a central pathway which may be associated with other less important pathways for a particular offender. The four pathways are then:

- *Intimacy and social skill deficits*: as a consequence of abuse and/or neglect in childhood, the way in which a child understands relationships and 'the emotional availability' (p. 331) of important others are adversely effected. They may have difficulties in emotional disclosure to others. Furthermore, other people may not be valued as people as a consequence of these adverse early experiences. The attachment style corresponding to this is best described as insecure since the offender may fail to develop the appropriate trust of others and see the social world as a dangerous place. So they lack socially and emotionally intimate contacts and avoid such contact. According to Ward and Siegert, insecure attachment can result in lasting difficulties in managing mood and problem solving.

    This sort of offender is hypothesised by Ward and Siegert to only offend at specific times such as when their normal adult sexual partner is unavailable. The child in the abuse is effectively an 'adult substitute'. The intimacy deficits are the result of insecure attachment and abuse is directly consequent on the offender failing to achieve satisfactory relationships with adults. Other pathways such as cognitive distortions will be involved. In particular, the offender may believe that he has a right to sex with whosoever he pleases. According to Ward and Siegert, this sort of offending is likely to have its origins in adulthood. When faced with rejection or emotional loneliness, the offender diverts his attentions towards children.

- *Sexual scripts*: 'A sexual script spells out when sex is to take place, with whom, what to do, and how to interpret the cues or signals associated with different phases in a sexual encounter. These cues can be internal to the individual, interpersonal, or broadly cultural in nature.' (p. 332.) Sexual scripts are learnt during psychological development and represent the broad framework of understanding how complex social behaviours play out. As a consequence, the scripts in part guide social behaviour. It is argued that sexual experiences before the child is capable of cognitively and emotionally handling them lead to distortions in the script in comparison to those devloped by others. The distorted script might involve inappropriate sexual partners (e.g. age discrepancy), inappropriate behaviours (deviant practices), or inappropriate contexts (e.g. sex devoid of interpersonal feelings).

    Sexual abuse in childhood may be the basis of their offending. These offenders seek emotional reassurance through sexual activity and sexual behaviour is equated with intimacy. Sexual cues are not differentiated from or confused with the cues to affection and closeness. They also fear rejection in intimate relationships. They choose children sometimes because of opportunity or because of intensified sexualised emotional needs. Sexual abuse of children is likely to emerge in adulthood in this group.

- *Emotional dysregulation*: we need to regulate our own behaviour in order to function effectively. This self-regulation allows an individual to achieve their goals. For example, we might be afraid of flying but wish to travel abroad for holidays. To achieve that goal we will have to adopt behaviours that allow us to succeed in that goal. That is, we have to control our anxieties about flying. Part of self-regulation is the regulation of emotions. Sometimes we may seek to elevate our emotional state (such as listening to particularly evocative music or watching an emotional film) but equally we may need to reduce emotions in some way. The offender may exhibit emotional dysregulation when, for example, avoiding guilt and other emotional feelings while offending against children or when they fail for whatever reason to use coping skills to deal with stress leaving them at greater risk of offending against children.

This group develops essentially normal sexual scripts. However, their emotional regulation system has substantial problems. For example, they may have difficulty in using social support effectively in times of distress or some may have difficulty in identifying particular emotional states in themselves accurately. They may have problems in dealing with anger and resort to the sexual abuse of children as part of an attempt to punish a partner who has angered them. Sexual fantasies help ameliorate negative feeling states and, consequently, increase the risk of offending. Such offenders are unlikely to attempt to develop emotional intimacy with their victim but have profound sexual arousal when they are strongly emotionally aroused.

* *Cognitive distortions*: these have already been discussed but Ward has suggested that cognitive distortions are generated by a much smaller number of schemata or implicit theories held by the offender. Ward's view is that many varied expressions of distorted thoughts which are manifested by offenders actually reflect a small number of implicit theories which the offender holds. We all have such theories or schema about the world but the offender's are maladaptive because they can lead to offending behaviour. Five important implicit theories are listed by Ward:

  - Children as sexual objects: Just as the offender regards adults as sexual, children are equally regarded as able to enjoy and desiring sexual relationships with adults.
  - Entitlement: Offenders regard themselves as being entitled to have their sexual needs met because they are more important than other people.
  - Dangerous world: Children are not seen as being the threat that other adults are and their reliability and trusting nature gives the offender comfort against the danger.
  - Uncontrollable: The offender is not in control of his actions but is driven by external factors such as those resulting in stress or the effects of drugs or alcohol.
  - Nature of harm: Not all sexual activity with a child is harmful and children can benefit in a variety of ways from sexual activity with adults.

These offenders tend to be antisocial generally and demonstrate strongly criminal attitudes. These offenders are patriarchal in their attitudes towards children and believe in their own superiority. Their sexual offences against children do not reflect a sexual preference but more their general antisocial behaviour pattern.

There is a fifth group which Ward and Siegert suggest may represent the 'pure paedophile' in the sense that they have critical deficits in all four of the above pathways, not just a preponderance of just one sort of deficit. They idealise the relationship between an adult and a child in their sexual scripts.

Internet paedophile offenders

The Internet has provided the legal impetus for a range of new offences in countries throughout the world. According to Robbins and Darlington (2003), 27,000 people throughout the world go on to Internet child pornography sites each day and over 1 million images of child sexual abuse are in circulation. While child pornography involves the sexual abuse of children, Internet offences may be committed by those who have not made physical sexual contact with children themselves. So offences related to the possession of child pornography downloaded from the Internet may or not be related to contact sexual offences against children. There are other modern offences, such as using Internet chat rooms to groom children for sex, which are not in themselves contact offences though the intent may be to eventually meet the child for sex. Internet offences are important in that they raise the possibility that some adults may be sexually interested in children but never contact children sexually. This is theoretically important in that it suggests that there are some paedophiles who desist from sexual activity with children despite their sexual interest in children (c.f. Howitt, 1995). Understanding more about how paedophiles may desist from contact offending against children might help us to understand better how to help paedophiles cease offending despite their sexual leanings (Howitt, 2005). There is evidence that 97% of UK Internet paedophiles have no previous convictions and have not previously come to the police's attention (Brookes, 2003).

Internet pornography offences have come to court in increasing numbers in recent years, mirroring the rapid growth in the spread of the Internet. In jurisdictions such as Britain and the United States, Internet pornography offenders risk lengthy prison sentences. Child pornography is a graphic representation of the sexual abuse of children and, it is argued, downloading the material contributes tangibly to the sexual abuse of children by encouraging further production of such material. However, the suggestion that Internet child pornography users will then go on to offend against children is based more on speculation than evidence. Sullivan and Beech (2003) are among the psychologists who believe that fantasing to imagery of child abuse encourages men to act out their fantasies through the direct sexual abuse of children.

Can we be confident that non-contact offenders of this sort are actually paedophiles? The essential characteristic of paedophiles is they have a sexual interest in young children under the age of consent to sexual intercourse. Just like there are people with heterosexual interests who remain virgins all their life, there is no reason why a paedophile has to act out their sexual interest. Anecdotal evidence suggests that many Internet pornography offenders collect substantial quantities of the material and that a good proportion of these will masturbate while at their computers to such imagery.

As yet, psychological research on Internet offenders is sparse. So we cannot say with confidence the ways in which contact offenders and Internet offenders differ and are similar. One promising line of research involves the cognitive distortions of these offenders – the ideas and beliefs which facilitate the offender. There is evidence that Internet offenders are cognitively similar to contact offenders in terms of the broad pattern of their cognitive distortions. For example, it has been claimed that Internet offenders who view pictures of children involved in sexual intercourse tend to interpret a child's smiles just as contact offenders do (Drake *et al.*, 2001). That is, the children's smiles are seen as indicting that children are sexual beings and are enjoying their abuse (Taylor and Quayle, 2003).

Using a conceptualisation developed by Ward (Ward, 2000; Ward and Keenan, 1999), the patterns of cognitive distortions in contact and Internet offenders have been explored by Sheldon (2004). Sheldon interviewed both Internet only and contact offenders about many different aspects of their lives and analysed the interview transcriptions for evidence of the above, Ward's five 'implicit theories'. She found similarities throughout in terms of the use of these theories by both types of offender. For example, take the first implicit theory – children as sexual objects. One of her interviewees who had Internet as well as contact offences said of his victim:

> She was a bit of a tart dressed in a provocative manner the way she put herself to you verbally and physically . . . the way she walked, the clothes she wore you pick it up straight away . . . probably even blokes think she's a puller (MH: Mixed).

(p. 27)

This clearly demonstrates how that offender regarded a child as a sexual being – much of the language is more commonly used to describe adult women and would not be used of a child by many people. Sheldon found evidence of similar beliefs in Internet only offenders. For example:

> My favourite [fantasy] would be consensual sex with a child . . . the most arousing thing would be to give the child pleasure.
>
> *(GA: Internet)*

Notice that this ideal sex is described as consensual and that the child in the fantasy has an orgasm. If it were applied to an adult woman, such a fantasy would not be regarded as deviant in anyway. Because of their similarities in the use of cognitive distortions, we should hesitate in assuming that the two groups are essentially distinct.

Main points

- Sex offenders against children, in general, are difficult to differentiate from the rest of the population in general. Various attempts have been made to categorise different types and one of the most common is that of fixated versus regressed offenders. Despite being common, there are problems with this especially when regressed offending is regarded as typical of intra-familial offending. Some data suggests that paedophile response to erotic images of children is quite common though self-reported paedophile acts are relatively uncommon. In order to understand sex offending against children, it is important to recognise that adolescent sex offending is quite a high percentage of all sexual offending.

- An important issue is the extent to which sex offenders, and sex offenders against children, are frequent recidivists. The evidence is that sexual reoffending is relatively uncommon after conviction even several years after release (see also Chapter 23). Recidivism for other types of crime is more frequent. Similarly, the previous criminal histories of sex offenders against children are more likely to involve non-sexual crimes. Despite this, it is common to read that paedophiles have large numbers of victims. This may be so for some offenders but the majority seem to have committed a very small number of offences. It should also be noted that modern policy on sex offenders includes considerable activity monitoring the lives of offenders when in the community (see also Chapter 23).

- There are a number of theories to account for sexual offending against children. The pre-conditions model is of historical importance for the most part and very few of its principles have been established empirically. The psychotherapeutic/clinical model stresses cognitive aspects of the offending cycle such as fantasy and cognitive distortions. There is more support for this model and it has a degree of validity in terms of describing the abuse process though it does not address the issue of the aetiology (development) of offending behaviour. There is reasonable evidence to suggest that offenders' early abusive and other sexual experiences are associated with sexually offending against children. However, it is clearly untrue to suggest that all sexually abused children will grow up to abuse others. Nevertheless, there are some indications that certain types of sexual abuse and repeated abuse in childhood are more conducive to the development of sexually abusive behaviour towards children. This supports the basic idea of sexualisation theory. One question is whether a single factor cause of offending is adequate. The pathways model suggests that there may be a number of different developmental routes to offending though it accepts much of what is central to the other models of sexually abusive offending.

Chapter 11

Police psychology

Overview

- Within the criminal justice system, the organisation most highly regarded by the general public tends to be the police. Since they are work organisations, their operation can be regarded as part of the remit of organisational psychology such that recruitment and selection of police officers, their working group dynamics, occupational stress, and many other factors such as these are aspects of the psychology of policing. Other chapters pertinent to policing include Chapters 12 to 17.

- The police have a distinctive organisational culture that emphasises heterosexual, white male attitudes. It also stresses the importance of confessions obtained through interview. As a consequence, researchers have studied police interviewing techniques in some depth. Many bad practices have been identified over the years though good practice is also to be found. *Intimidation* by maximising the seriousness of the event, *robust challenges* such as accusing the interviewee of lying, and *manipulation* in which the officer suggests that the interviewee was not totally responsible for the offence or that the offence was not so serious are among the most common tactics identified in police interviews. So there is considerable doubt that police interviewing and evidence are as good as forensic training could ensure. There is a considerable body of evidence to suggest that the cognitive interview can improve the interviewing of cooperative witnesses better than other techniques such as forensic hypnosis.

- Language inconsistencies in statements taken by the police can reveal fabricated evidence.

- The *cognitive interview* consists of techniques designed to improve the quantity and quality of eyewitness evidence based on principles developed from the psychological study of memory. Some of the recommended strategies are reporting everything that they possibly can from the events that they witnessed no matter how trivial or seemingly irrelevant, trying to relive the context of the eyewitnessed events such as their own personal feelings, and trying different methods of retrieving information from memory. *The enhanced cognitive interview* adds elements from good interview techniques in general such as establishing rapport and asking questions effectively. There is evidence from a range of studies that cognitive interviewing is effective at eliciting greater quantities of good quality information although there is an attendant risk of more inaccurate information.

- Forensic hypnosis is not held in great regard by forensic and criminal psychologists who generally prefer the cognitive interview. Although forensic hypnosis tends to increase the numbers of both accurate and inaccurate memories, this problem can be offset by limiting the number of memories elicited.

- The broad consensus, until recently, was that police officers, in general, are no better as eyewitnesses than other people. However, there is emerging evidence that where the events witnessed were stressful that the police tended to be at an advantage and produced better eyewitness testimony possibly as a result of their experience and training.

- Being witness to the consequences of offending has a stressful and traumatic effect on a proportion of the officers involved. Dealing with the aftermath of a suicide is a particularly traumatic experience. The stress of working in a bureaucratic organisation also takes a toll on officers.

- Among other issues that psychologists have raised in relation to the work of the police is the clarity of the police caution. There is evidence that police cautions are poorly understood by many of those who receive one. Furthermore, there should be concern when arrestees waive their rights in law since they may be unaware of the impact of this decision.

Of all agencies in the criminal justice system, the police are the most highly regarded by the public (Howitt, 1998b) irrespective of objective evidence about performance (Christensen *et al.*, 1982). In the British Crime Survey of 2000 (Mirrlees-Black, 2001), 53% of the British public said that the police were doing a good or excellent job. In comparison, all of the other agencies in the criminal justice system did badly. Prisons got 31% saying good or excellent, magistrates 26%, the probation service 23%, the Crown Prosecution Service 23%, judges 21% and youth courts 12%. Such relative approval of the police has been found in other countries. American research suggests much the same general appreciation of the police (Graber, 1980; Skogan, 1996). On the other hand, the police tend to receive quite some criticism in the research findings of forensic and criminal psychologists.

Police forces are work organisations. Thus, potentially, there is a strong role for psychology with the police as with any other organisation. In other words, police psychology could be construed as merely a subfield of organisational psychology. According to Ainsworth (2000b), psychologists working with the police fulfil much the same role as organisational psychologists in any organisation. As such, they tend to work directly with police management on matters such as assessment and selection procedures. Other types of psychologist, such as offender profilers, are not typical of psychologists working with the police. In some countries, profilers would only be brought in on an *ad hoc* basis as the need arises. Elsewhere, in the United States for example, profilers are found fairly commonly in regular, permanent employment with the police. Of course, it is extremely difficult to identify a distinct police psychology that does not encompass issues from other chapters in this book (e.g. lie detection – Chapter 16, effective interviewing with children – Chapter 17, false allegations – Chapter 14, confessions – Chapter 15, and crime analysis – Chapter 13). In this chapter we will concentrate on some of the issues which are central to police work.

A distinction has to be made between psychology as used by the police and the psychology of the police. This chapter reflects both of these.

Recruitment and selection

The question of how to recruit and select effective police personnel seems deceptively easy. There is not space to review the major issues in the general recruitment and selection process as covered in organisational psychology. Nevertheless, it is possible to make a number of points specifically about police recruitment following the account given by Ainsworth (1995). It is important to note that the costs to the police of poor selection of recruits may be quite large. It is expensive to train police officers so inadequacies of selection have a direct financial cost, but there are also fewer tangible costs in terms of public relations and public appreciation that poor recruits bring to the police. Psychological tests have long been used in personnel selection. Nevertheless, the development of appropriate tests for police selection has not proven to be the easiest of tasks (Ainsworth, 1996).

- Testing could serve either or both of two functions: (a) screening out unsuitable applicants to avoid spending substantial amounts of money on intensive selection processes which may, for example, involve fairly senior police personnel, or (b) concentrating on selecting the very best applicants out of the field.
- Police work involves a multiplicity of different tasks – traffic patrolling and delivering bad news to relatives being just two examples. It is not easy to imagine a relatively simple approach to finding suitable recruits that could select the best personnel for such a variety of tasks. Conversely, it is difficult to imagine the sort of array of measures that would be needed to recruit for specific types of task.
- Detailed studies of what sorts of recruit are ideal for the police force seem not to have been carried out in all police forces. When asked, serving police officers suggest that recruits should possess 'common sense' or 'a sense of humour'. Concepts such as these are difficult to translate into known or potential psychometric tests.

The notion of a 'police personality', to the extent that it has any validity at all, is probably at least as much to do with the requirements of police work as it is to do with any pre-existing personality predispositions or any selection characteristics (Bull, 1984). Stress seems endemic and indicators such as divorce and suicide show elevated levels in police officers. Another characteristic of police work is the common requirement that all officers graduate through the ranks to achieve promotion. This not only brings about problems of reorientation towards one's previous peer group but may well be the prime way in which the police occupational culture is transmitted.

Police culture

Skolnick (1966) was the first to suggest that the culture of the police influences the work of the police force. It is fairly easy to recognise the different cultures typical of different organisations. Since culture is little more than the sum of the shared knowledge, behaviours and practices of members of that culture, then it should be possible to identify the particular characteristics of different organisations. The organisational culture of a hospital is obviously different from that of a school. Similarly, there are typical characteristics of the organisational cultures of police forces that are not found in the same measure or the same combination in the cultures of other organisations. While there are occupations for which relatively minimal amounts of training will prepare incumbents for the major eventualities, as we have seen, multiplicity and diversity of tasks are characteristic of police work.

Ainsworth (1995) suggests that no two days of police work are ever the same. He lists among the diverse situations with which police officers have to deal the following: attending road traffic accidents, going in pursuit of a teenage vandal, taking drunks to the police station, attending domestic disputes, helping to police a riot and working through backlogs of paperwork. At the same time, the police officer is required to have a good working knowledge of the law and to act lawfully. Finally, the officer is expected to promote a positive image of the police force. This is a range of tasks with which, say, the average supermarket checkout assistant or psychologist does not need to cope. The training of police officers is, consequently, a compromise between what is practical to put in training and what would be ideal. While earlier generations of police officers received little training except that provided by on-the-job experience, increasingly policy is towards fairly extensive training. Ainsworth (1995) indicates that police training in the past encouraged rote learning of legislation and the powers available to police. Nowadays, it increasingly concerns how to deal with the wide variety of incidents that come under the rubric of police work.

Part of the training of new recruits is through contact or on-the-job training with more seasoned or experienced officers. At one level this can be regarded as teaching the recruits the job at a practical level. On the other hand, seasoned officers may employ practices that are less than ideal or even unacceptable to their managers. Consequently, the novice police officer may merely learn bad practice from his or her colleagues. This is particularly important when we consider the transmission of the occupational subculture or *police culture*. Police culture refers to the characteristic patterns of belief, behaviour, thinking and interaction that police officers tend to share in common. They are essentially *normative* as they are the accepted and prescribed standards of police personnel. This does not mean that they are fixed and unchanging. Although personnel may be recruited because they seem to reflect the characteristics of a 'good' police officer, they learn police culture by interacting with other police officers. The occupational culture may be in some ways at odds with what new officers have learnt at police college. There may be a painful reality shock when they try to put their college knowledge into practice. They may find that their new ways of doing things clash with what is acceptable to the transmitters of police culture – the old school of officers.

Canteen/cop culture

While police culture is a generic description of the cultural characteristics of the police, there is also evidence of the prevalence of certain sorts of attitude that characterise the general thinking of ordinary police officers. We may call this canteen or cop culture in order to differentiate it from the more general police culture. There may actually be a clash between the management subcultures and the subculture of the rank-and-file officers. Wootton and Brown (2000) summarise canteen culture as involving and valuing:

- action;
- cynicism;
- conservatism;

- mission;
- pessimism;
- pragmatism;
- solidarity;
- suspicion;
- racial prejudice.

The list might be extended further since, in addition to racism, sexism, homophobia and heterosexism are characteristic of the culture. Essentially, cop culture determines the rules abided by police officers that allow them to be seen as being effective in their work. This means that the standards of the dominant group within the police and their styles of interaction determine what is regarded as effective policing and the effective police officer. Gay and lesbian officers, for example, can then be seen as subordinate to the dominant group – their values disregarded. The nature of the canteen culture is such that homosexual officers do not 'come out'. This choice can do nothing to challenge the homophobia and, in a sense, reinforces it.

After joining the police, the processes of occupational socialisation may create a situation in which the individual's police identity is not psychologically compatible with other aspects of the individual's identity (e.g. their sexuality). In-group identification refers to the sense of a common identity shared by members of the force. This sexist, heterosexist and homophobic culture would readily identify gays and lesbians as out-groups. This may encourage hostility and discrimination by the majority group towards the out-group. Women, ethnic minorities, lesbians and gays are not readily tolerated because they are 'other' or different from the accepted norm. The problem for officers with these characteristics (e.g. they are women or homosexual) is that the dual identities of police officer and being homosexual, for example, can be extremely difficult to reconcile and handle.

Wootton and Brown (2000) studied police officers. One group consisted of officers who belonged to one minority (e.g. the officer was female). The other group had two minority positions (e.g. they were black women or they were homosexual black men). The officers were interviewed and what they had to say was coded in terms of the presence or absence of a number of themes. A grid was then created in which the different officers were listed against the different themes emerging in the interviews. This was then analysed using a complex statistical technique (multi-dimensional scalogram analysis). This essentially plots people into a chart indicating their similarity/dissimilarity across the themes. There seemed to be a cluster of heterosexual officers who shared similar experiences. Lesbians and gays were not among them. Furthermore, officers with just one minority characteristic (e.g. being black or being homosexual) tended to group together as similar in terms of their experiences. Individuals with two minority characteristics (e.g. black homosexuals) tended to be at the periphery – separate from the dominant heterosexual group and the minority group. Wootton and Brown recommend that it is members of the heterosexual core, those demonstrating the discriminatory attitudes, who should be seen as having the problem – not their victims.

There are other aspects of police culture that warrant attention. In particular, there is some evidence that the police have systematically different beliefs about the criminality of men and women. Horn and Hollin (1997) took a sample of police officers and a broadly similar comparison group who were *not* police. A lengthy questionnaire was used to extract, in particular, ideas about women and men offenders. Factor analysis, a complex statistical technique, revealed three dimensions underlying ideas about criminals:

- *Deviance* which includes beliefs such as 'Trying to rehabilitate offenders is a waste of time and money' and 'In general, offenders are just plain immoral'.
- *Normality* as reflected by agreeing with statements like 'There are some offenders I would trust with my life' and 'I would like associating with some offenders'.
- *Trust* which is measured by such matters as 'I would never want one of my children dating an offender' and 'You have to be constantly on your guard with offenders'.

There were two versions of the questionnaire – one with female offenders as the subject, the other with male offenders as the subject. Women offenders were seen as less fundamentally bad (deviant) than men who offend. This was true irrespective of the sex of the police officer. Compared with the non-police group, police officers saw offenders as fundamentally deviant or bad. The police viewed offenders as less normal than the general public (factor 2), though they tended to see offending women as more normal and like the general public than they saw male offenders. They also regarded offenders as less trustworthy than did the general public and male offenders were seen as less trustworthy than female offenders.

It should be remembered that rapid changes occur within police organisations as a consequence of the pressures on police management coming from political sources as well as legal judgements and reviews of particular policing episodes. These will differ from country to country and force to force but nevertheless they put established practices continually under review.

Confession culture

Not all people detained by the police are formally interviewed. Robertson *et al.* (1996) found that only about 30% were interviewed in London (many minor offences do not require one) and interviews are largely conducted by junior officers. Nevertheless, the interview was common for other and, particularly, serious offences. Despite the belief among psychologists that coercive interviewing by police runs the risk of false confession (Chapter 15), observers of the police suggest that the interview is regarded as a crucial stage in a criminal investigation and may encourage all sorts of tactics. The interview situation is different from a normal conversation because one person, the police officer, is the prime controller of the content, structure and direction of the exchanges. Suspects are discouraged from interrupting, initiating conversation or challenging the officer's authority at any level. In the United Kingdom, concerns about miscarriages of justice have led to legal changes. The *Police and Criminal Evidence Act* of 1984 changed the underlying ideology of interviewing to discourage practices which courts of law in the United Kingdom have found unacceptable (Sear and Williamson, 1999). This has resulted in substantial differences between the United Kingdom and the United States:

- *United Kingdom*: a number of principles underlie modern UK training in investigative interviewing. These are:
  - The function of interviewing is the search for the truth rather than justification for a prosecution.
  - The interview should be approached with an open mind.

- The interviewing officers should behave fairly and recognise, for example, the special difficulties of the groups who may be most at risk of making false confessions – such as those with very low intelligence.

- *United States*: in contrast, in the United States very different legal decisions have meant that trickery and deception are acceptable in substantial parts of police investigative work. The training of officers involves training in these techniques as well as others. Training is frequently by outside agencies.

Part of the American approach is to present the suspect with an acceptable justification for their offending. These are appealing psychologically whether or not they have any basis in law. The self-respect of the offender is ostensibly redeemed by these 'excuses'. Examples include justifying theft by suggesting that the company is rich or that the offender was stealing to help support their family. Another example is feigning support for the offender with comments such as 'Her mother dresses her in those little tiny pants, deliberately turning you on . . .' (Sear and Williamson, 1999, p. 76). A further strategy is to minimise the crime such as suggesting that this was the first crime or that there are far worse crimes.

While it seems beyond doubt that the systems of interviewing are different, care needs to be taken not to idealise the British police in this respect. There is reason to believe that more junior officers, if not others, continue the tradition in the police of viewing confessions as very important if not central to their interviewing work. Cherryman *et al.* (2000) suggest that there are a number of substantial reasons for this despite the growth of evidence of the risk of false confessions in interviews:

- Confessions are seen as very convincing evidence even though courts in some jurisdictions may require further corroborative evidence over and above the confession.

- Many suspects confess during an interview and so confessions may be regarded as routine and expected within the interrogation contexts. The lack of other evidence makes confession important.

- Pressures within the police organisation to meet crime clear-up targets may put a premium on any evidence including confession evidence.

- There is a curiously twisted logic that supports the use of any technique to obtain a confession: that is, if for any reason the police officer is convinced of the guilt of the suspect, then any pressure to obtain a confession is defensible.

- Confessions gained using forceful questioning were ruled inadmissible in only a third of British cases (Pearse and Gudjonsson, 1999). So, in a sense, this validates the use of forceful questioning.

In order to demonstrate the influence of confession on police officers' evaluations of interviews, officers listened to various real-life, audiotaped interviews. These varied in competence levels (as judged by researchers) and in terms of whether or not a confession was obtained. The police participants rated the interviews on a large range of factors that experts regard differentiate good from bad interviews. The following are among the characteristics of a good interview:

- all information released at the beginning of the interview;
- appropriate use of pauses or silences;
- appropriate use of pressure;
- communication skills;
- conversation management;
- development and continued rapport;

- empathy/compassion;
- information released appropriately;
- interview has structure;
- keeps interview to relevant matters;
- knowledge of the law;
- open-mindedness;
- planning and preparation;
- purpose of interview explained;
- responds to what interviewee says;
- summarises appropriately;

whereas the following are characteristics of a bad interview:

- apparent use of tactics;
- closed questions;
- closure;
- creation of apprehension;
- inappropriate interruptions;
- leading questions;
- over-talking;
- questions too complex or long;
- undue use of pressure.

The officers making the ratings tended to see the interviews as better when they resulted in a confession or admission compared to when no confession or admission was obtained.

According to the research of Pearse and Gudjonsson (1999), police tactics in interviews with suspects of serious crimes may be classified empirically into six main categories:

- Intimidation: in this the seriousness of the event and the anxiety felt by the suspect are maximised. Long silences, attempts to manipulate the self-esteem of the suspect and the use of more than one officer to ask questions while not giving the suspect time to answer are additional features of this.
- Robust challenge: this involves direct challenges such as suggesting the suspect is lying. This is often repeated at different stages.
- Manipulation: minimising the seriousness of the offence, minimising the suspect's responsibility, suggesting themes to explain events and so forth.
- Questioning style: leading questions used, echoing the answer and asking more than one question in a single sentence.
- Appeals: this might be appeals to tell the truth, appealing to the suspect's good character, and suggesting that it is in the suspect's interest to confess.
- Soft challenge: soft, friendlier tone, challenges with questions such as the possibility that the witness is lying, and attempts to reduce shame of the acts especially in child sexual abuse cases.

It was found that the greater use that was made of the first three tactics above (the authors call these the overbearing tactics) the greater the likelihood that the court would dismiss the evidence as inadmissible.

Box 11.1

Forensic psychology in action: forensic linguistics and the veracity of witness statements

There have been numerous examples of dubious convictions in recent years. Many of the most famous have been British and associated with terrorism. Obviously, dishonesty by police officers is a possibility, especially in high-profile cases in which political and organisational pressure on police officers to find the offenders is strong. Although it is not possible to quantify the dishonesty of police officers definitively given that it may not always be easy to detect, it is clear that at least on occasion there is falsification of evidence. Just how is it possible to challenge a confession putatively taken down by a police officer? Obviously, the tape or video recording of the statement would reduce the possibility substantially but although this may occur in some countries, in many parts of the world it is not the practice. Even where it is the practice, disputed evidence may pre-date the use of recordings. Forensic linguistics involves a set of procedures that have been used on occasion in this sort of circumstance. An excellent example is Coulthard's (1994) analysis of the 'confession' of William Power, a member of the Birmingham Six who were accused of the IRA bombing of two public houses in Birmingham in 1974. Power claimed that his confession as produced by the police was manufactured. Coulthard examined this and related documents for evidence to confirm or reject this claim. The Birmingham Six were released in 1991 because their conviction was unsafe. We will concentrate on the confession of Derek Bentley which Coulthard also analysed. Some of the aspects of the confessions which can be analysed using forensic linguistics include the following (Coulthard, 1999).

Differences between spoken and written English

Spoken and written languages are not the same. If we take the following sentences from a confession, we can see that they may differ markedly in certain features:

> I drove down to the flats and I saw him up on the roof and I shouted to him and he said that he would be down in a couple of minutes.

> I wish to make a further statement explaining my complete involvement in the hijacking of the Ford Escort van from John Smith on Monday 28 May 1987 on behalf of the A.B.C. which was later used in the murder of three person (sic) in Newtown that night.
>
> *(Coulthard, 1999, p. 112)*

Linguists have recognised for a number of years that written English, the language of education, varies markedly from the language of speech (Halverson, 1991; Olson, 1977). Even without this knowledge, probably most of us would correctly identify the first statement as being spoken language. (a) It has low lexical density – that is, there are a lot of words such as to, the, and, on and so forth which largely serve a grammatical function and are not altogether essential to making the sentence meaningful. If they are blanked out then the sentence remains fairly readily decipherable. (b) The clauses in the first sentence are relatively short, e.g. the first clause is 'I drove down to the flats' and the other clauses are of a similar length.

The second sentence seems to show the features of written language which, apart from lexical density and the length of the clauses, include: (a) many examples of nominalisation which is turning verbs into nouns (i.e. statement, involvement, hijacking and murder) and (b) the extensive use of repeated subordinate clauses. The second sentence was part of a disputed confession – the

▶

police officer in question admitted that the statement might not be quite the order in which the suspect spoke the words.

Register

The context in which we are speaking or writing has an effect on the language that we use. We use different language in different contexts. Professions differ in terms of the way that language is used. Thus there is a risk that if a police officer attempts to fabricate a statement, elements of that officer's professional language may infiltrate the fabricated statements. Coulthard (1999) provides the famous example of the Derek Bentley case in which Bentley and the teenager Chris Craig were attempting to break into a warehouse. Bentley was arrested but his partner resisted arrest and killed a policeman. Despite being under arrest at the time of the shooting, Bentley was hung for murder whereas Craig, being young, served a prison term. The famous phrase 'Let him have it Chris' uttered by Bentley was translated by the police as 'Shoot him Chris' rather than 'Give him the gun Chris'.

Derek Bentley was virtually illiterate so his statement was taken down by a police officer. The version appearing as evidence in court was claimed to have been a mixture of what he had said but also a partial fabrication by the police. Coulthard argues that significant in the disputed statement was the frequent appearance of the word 'then' which appears ten times in nearly six hundred words. There would seem to be little odd about this except when it is revealed that the statements of other witnesses in the case contained the word 'then' once in nearly a thousand words. On the other hand, the statements of police officers show that the word 'then' is used as frequently as once in about eighty words. In other words, the police's professional need to be precise in reporting may have spilled into the fabricated statement. Derek Bentley, posthumously, received a pardon in 1998.

Improving police work

Police psychology consists largely of attempts by psychologists to try to enhance or facilitate good police practice. Research tends to be centred on the competence of the police at their routine tasks, such as interviewing and providing testimony, and approaches to improving this competence. While many of us have obtained our knowledge of police work from the many media portrayals of police activity (Sacco and Fair, 1988), this does not necessarily reflect the reality of police work properly. Motorists may be very familiar with the role of police in road traffic matters, but what about their role in relation to crime? We have been encouraged by the media portrayals of famous fictional detectives to assume that the police operate largely through detection and theorising about the motives of offenders or unknown offenders. So it is worthwhile noting that a study by Farrington and Lambert (1997) found a more routine picture of crime detection. They explored the factors associated with arrest of suspects for different types of crime. Apprehension for burglary involved the following factors:

- Offender caught in the act by the police – 15%.
- Information supplied by an informant – 13%.
- Offender caught near the scene of the crime – 12%.

- Articles left somewhere or disposed of by the offender – 11%.
- The offender arrested when seen acting suspiciously in the crime area – 8%.
- The offender arrested for another crime – 7%.
- Eyewitness descriptions of the offender – 6%.

For arrests for violent offences, the pattern was a little different:

- Offender detained at the scene – 16%.
- Victim description of the offender – 15%.
- Witness description of the offender – 13%.
- Caught in the act of violence – 11%.
- Vehicle description – 11%.
- Number plate – 11%.

In other words, Sherlock Holmes, Maigret and Miss Marple would have rather wasted skills in the police force.

The cognitive interview

The cognitive interview attempts to enhance recall by witnesses using techniques deriving from psychological research into memory retrieval. Recall does not just happen, it is dependent on the types of probe used to retrieve the memory. If one type of probe does not work, then another may (Tulving, 1974). Cognitive interviewing is a practical reality, at least up to a point, since it has been adopted in police work. For example, since 1992 it has been part of the standard interview package used to train officers in England and Wales. It takes just a few hours for a police officer, for example, to obtain improvements in the information obtained from witnesses (Memon *et al.*, 1994). The cognitive interview is not recommended for use with suspects or witnesses who are uncooperative or resistant to the interview. In this case, the recommended best practice is to use conversation management approach (Shepherd and Milne, 1999). This involves building of trust and confidence in the interviewer. It is known as GEMAC (greeting, explanation, mutual activity, close). Thus the initial greeting signals equality. The interviewer discusses the reason for the interview, the agenda of activities, routines employed such as the taking of notes or the recording of the events and the expectations of the interviewer, e.g. that the interviewer regards silence as positive and interruptions to these will be avoided. Mutual activities include monitoring activities such as active listening. Finally, the close of the interview can be an opportunity to summarise what has been said in order to check on the detail.

The original cognitive interview adopted two basic principles (Geiselman *et al.* (1984)):

- Recall in an environment that successfully reproduces features of the original encoding context is likely to be superior (Tulving, 1974).
- Memory is a complex thing and there is no whole representation of events stored in the brain. Instead there is a complex array of events and happenings which may not be stored in a coherent manner but will require a variety of strategies to tap in their entirety.

The cognitive interview then consists of four 'strategies' for improving the process of retrieving memory. In it, witnesses should be encouraged to do the following:

- Report everything that they can think of about the witnessed events, even including trivial or incomplete fragments that they might feel to be irrelevant.
- Mentally reinstate the circumstances of the witnessing. This includes their feelings at the time (e.g. they felt scared) or external factors that they recall (e.g. the noise of the building work in the background). So it should be explained at the start of the interview that they should mentally recreate the external physical environment and their internal state including affective (emotional), physiological and cognitive states at the time of witnessing the events (Fisher, Brennan and McCauley, 2002).
- Vary retrieval methods. For example, the interviewer should encourage the witness to report events in a number of different sequences and not just in chronological order. So recall could be obtained from the point that the police arrived or perhaps by recalling in reverse order. The underlying idea is based on research evidence that different components of a complex event may be recalled when different cues are present to aid retrieval from memory. Fisher, Brennan and McCauley (2002) stress that these methods need care, otherwise the interviewer may be dissatisfied with the evidence presented.
- Report events from alternative perspectives such as that of another witness, the offender or from another physical location.

Additional considerations have been added as interest in the cognitive interview has grown. For example, witnesses should be encouraged to concentrate on their senses. Although we memorise in terms of concepts, we also memorise in terms of events sensory features. So one simple technique for improving retrieval is to have the witness close their eyes and visualise the events.

Eventually, a number of problems became apparent that are not to do with memory directly. For example, the witness may be nervous and anxious, inarticulate and very unsure of what is expected of them in the context of the interview. For that reason, Fisher and Geiselman (1992) introduced what is known as the *enhanced cognitive interview*. This can be seen as the cognitive interview combined with techniques from communications psychology to help alleviate communication problems. For example, an interview can be ineffective because it fails to take into account the fact that people have limited mental resources to cope with the information flow. The interviewer may have a too complex task if they have to frame the questions, pay attention to the interviewee and make notes at the same time. As a consequence, they may fail to hear all of the information being provided perhaps because they are distracted by the need to frame their next question. Similarly, if the interviewee is faced with a barrage of questions they may be so overloaded cognitively that they can only search their memory superficially (Fisher, Brennan and McCauley, 2002).

The enhanced cognitive interview hands control of the interview to the witness by making it clear that they have as much time as they require to respond to questions. Instead of the police officer determining, say, when as much has been recalled as could be recalled, this among other things becomes the prerogative of the witness. Other changes included training in the following:

- The process of building rapport or easy dialogue between the officer and the witness.
- How to use appropriate body language in the interview to reduce the feeling of intimidation experienced by some witnesses being interviewed, for example.

- How to ask effective questions – that is, for example, questions asked in a way that facilitates both understanding and a clear reply.
- How to use pauses effectively – for example, allowing the witness time to think and reply rather than rushing from one question to the next.

So the basic principles of the cognitive interview seem to be effectively based on detailed and well-founded research on effective memory retrieval. Nevertheless, simply knowing the basics of the cognitive interview is insufficient to effectively conduct one. Fisher, Brennan and McCauley (2002) explain that the cognitive interview should be structured into five different sequential components:

- Introduction: this is a crucial stage in that it provides the witness with an appropriate psychological and social setting for the cognitive interview to work. So it is at this stage that the interviewer must develop rapport with the interviewee, explain the need for as much information in as great a detail as possible, and encourage the interviewee to engage actively in the interview and freely offer information without waiting for a direct question pertinent to that information.
- Open-ended narration: by allowing the interviewee an opportunity to freely indicate what they remember of the witnessed events, the interviewer is provided with the basic material needed to plan what aspects should be probed using the techniques of the cognitive interview. During the course of the witness's narration, the interviewer notes what appear to be the mental images of important aspects of the events. For example, what images does the witness have of the perpetrator and significant objects such as weapons.
- Probing: because the interviewer has established the general features of the interviewee's recollections, the aspects of memory which might be the best sources of information are focused on. So the interviewer 'guides' the interviewee to these aspects and provides the cognitive interview techniques which help maximise the information gathered. The interviewer might suggest that the witness closes their eyes and thinks about the best view that the witness had of the offender (Fisher, Brennan, and McCauley, 2002). This best view is then described in as much detail as possible. Of course, the interviewer may ask additional questions (probes) in order to get more information.
- Review: the interviewer takes the interviewee through the evidence that the interviewee has provided in order to find any inaccuracies in what has been recorded. Naturally, in the course of this the witness may recall more things.
- Close: this may include fulfilling the official requirements in respect to interview such as signing any required forms and the like. The witness may be encouraged to get back in touch with the officer when new things occur to the witness which were not recalled in the interview.

Doubtlessly, the cognitive interview works. Quite how it achieves its objectives and how well is not so clear. For example, there is the question of what to compare the cognitive interview with. The standard police interviewing techniques can be extremely poor and based on little or no appropriate training. So is it reasonable to compare this sort of interview with the outcomes of special training in the cognitive interview? Officers trained in the cognitive interview may be motivated by their training to interview better without the cognitive interview itself having much effect on witnesses' recall (Kohnken et al., 1999). For that reason, researchers have chosen to use what is described as the structured interview as a control procedure to the cognitive interview. These interviews are similar to the cognitive interview in terms of the good and positive characteristics they possess but the mnemonic memory techniques of the cognitive interview are missing (Kohnken *et al.*, 1994).

There is some evidence that cognitive interview techniques are well received by police officers. Kebbell *et al.* (1998) surveyed police officers about the cognitive interview. Officers trained in the method showed evidence of using some of the techniques more often, in particular the mental reinstatement of context, changing the order of events and describing the events from another perspective. Features of cognitive interviewing such as reporting everything, establishing rapport and transferring control did not seem to differ between trained and untrained officers. In terms of the usefulness of different components of cognitive interviewing, establishing rapport was rated as the most useful. Some of the cognitive interview techniques such as changing perspective, trying different orders and transferring control were seen as much less useful even though these are key aspects of cognitive interviewing.

Memon *et al.* (1994) trained police officers in cognitive interviewing and examined their performance with witnesses to a simulated robbery. The police had some difficulties. For example, they tended to continue with the faults of conventional police interviewing such as rapid fire questions with little opportunity for the witness to respond and questions about specific matters. They incorporated, most commonly, the cognitive interview strategies of context reinstatement, perspective changing, reporting everything and focused retrieval. On the other hand, officers trained in structured interviewing techniques (see above) also commonly used context reinstatement and reporting everything. After cognitive interview training, context reinstatement, perspective changing and focused retrieval were used more. Overall, it would appear that despite its successes, there are problems in implementing the cognitive interview entirely.

The evidence from studies of the impact of the cognitive interview on memory quality is also broadly positive. There are numerous studies and too many to consider here individually. The technique of meta-analysis (see Box 5.1) allows trends over a range of studies to be assessed. Kohnken *et al.* (1999) put into such an analysis studies that involved recall (rather than recognition) as the measure of memory. Their main selection requirements for including a study were that a full cognitive interview strategy was employed and that the outcome was compared with some form of standard interview (non-cognitive interview). Over 40 studies were found meeting these criteria:

- The cognitive interview compared to the standard interview produced more correct details. Translated into a correlation coefficient, the type of interview correlated 0.4 with the amount of correct details recalled.
- Factors that led to poorer outcomes in the cognitive interview included the length of delay between the witnessing of the event and the interview, how little the interviewees were involved in the events they witnessed and the research laboratory where the study took place. It was the research carried out in the laboratory of the originators of the technique that had the best effects on recall.
- There were no identifiable differences between the effectiveness of the original cognitive interview and that of the enhanced cognitive interview.
- The cognitive interview tended to increase the number of errors (incorrect recollections) made.
- The type of cognitive interview made a difference. The enhanced cognitive interview was especially error-prone. Again, the research conducted in the laboratory of the originators of the technique tended to get the highest error rates. To clarify

matters a little, while increases in errors may be undesirable, an increase in the correct detail is more important as this aids detection. If one calculates the proportion of correct details remembered to the total number of details, the cognitive interview produces a 40% increase in the relative numbers of correct details. It has been recommended for work with children (Milne and Bull, 1994). Milne *et al.* (1995) showed children to be resistant to leading/suggestive questioning after the cognitive interview (also Hayes and Delamothe, 1997, and Milne and Bull, 1996, for children with mild learning difficulty).

As far as can be ascertained, it would appear that the use of cognitive interviewing has not been a contentious issue in courts of law. For example, Fisher, Brennan, and McCauley (2002), experts in the field, indicate that they are aware of only two court cases in which the use of the cognitive interview was raised as a point of contention. One of these is American and the other British. Both occurred over ten years ago which is significant in itself.

Forensic hypnosis

Hypnotic suggestion as a defence against criminal charges has occurred from time to time. There is evidence that the public regard 'automatism' due to hypnosis as the basis for seeing the defendant as less responsible for the offence than a similar crime carried out under duress (Roberts and Wagstaff, 1996). Potential jurors with experience of hypnotism tend to be less believing that hypnotism had affected individuals' behaviour (Wagstaff *et al.*, 1997). Another aspect of hypnosis in forensic contexts is the investigation of crime. This seems to be regarded favourably by the media (McConkey *et al.*, 1989). Many psychologists who are experts in the field are less than enthusiastic about forensic hypnosis compared to, say, the cognitive interview (e.g. Wagstaff, 1996). It also needs to be said that hypnosis has had a somewhat checkered history in courts of law. This is documented for the United States by Lynn *et al.* (2002). The use of forensic hypnosis only became popular in the 1960s. Even then it attracted controversy and legal ambivalence about where and when hypnosis is appropriate in testimony. The Hurd rules (or Orne rules after the famous psychologist Martin Orne) may be used as procedural guidelines and safeguards. Briefly they include, according to Lynn *et al.* (2002):

1. Qualified expert: the psychiatrist/psychologist conducting the hypnotic session needs to be experienced in the use of hypnosis.
2. Independence: the hypnotist should be independent of the major parties in the case (prosecution, investigation and defence) and should not be in the regular employment of any of these parties.
3. Recording of information: the information received from any of the major parties should be recorded in writing (or another acceptable form).
4. Pre-hypnosis gathering of facts: a full account of the events should be obtained from the witness prior to any hypnotic session. The hypnotist should not influence the description by their interview technique or add details in error to the description.
5. All contact between the hypnotist and the 'witness' must be recorded.
6. No other persons should be present during the hypnotic suggestion phase – including any pre-hypnotic testing and any interview after hypnosis.

Despite all of this, the American judiciary have tended to accept hypnotically obtained evidence rather than reject it.

While it would appear a reasonable question to ask 'what is hypnosis?' a clear and consensual answer is not forthcoming (Wagstaff, 1997). To suggest that it is a different or altered mental state compared to normal conscious behaviour is to ignore a lot of evidence. This would imply that people who have not been hypnotised will carry out much the same behaviours and at similar rates as those who have characteristically been seen as showing hypnotic behaviour. The latter viewpoint is the non-state view. Its proponents see hypnotic behaviours as the result of less extra-ordinary psychological mechanisms such as conformity, compliance and expectations. According to Wagstaff, one of the reasons why hypnosis remains a point of conten-tion is that simply because a non-hypnotised person will do things like a hypnotised person will (e.g. handle snakes), this does not mean that hypnosis is not a distinct state of consciousness. Any given behaviour may have a number of different deter-minants, of course.

Not surprisingly, there is an extensive academic research base evaluating hypnot-ically induced testimony. While hypnotic practitioners may have a different view, the academic consensus tends to doubt the value of hypnosis compared to other methods of improving witness recall (Kebbell and Wagstaff, 1998):

- Inaccurate recall sometimes results from hypnosis, thus decreasing the overall accuracy rate. According to Lynn *et al.* (2002), meta-analyses (Box 5.1) of large numbers of studies have pointed to the conclusion that although hypnosis increases the amount of material remembered, this is at the cost of also increas-ing the amount of false recollections. This is much the same criticism as for the enhanced cognitive interview. The reason for this appears to be that hypnotised witnesses simply report more of both inaccurate and accurate recollections. When witnesses are required to recall a fixed number of memories, there was no difference between hypnotised and non-hypnotised individuals in terms of their accuracy.

- Confidence in hypnotised witnesses may increase without commensurate improvements in accuracy. Indeed, they may well have more confidence in what they inaccurately remember under hypnosis than the accurate information (Lynn *et al.*, 2002). This is of particular concern in the legal context given the importance of witness confidence in persuading courts of the value of a witness's testimony. Some witnesses appear to be more suggestible to the effects of leading questions and misleading information. Nevertheless, Lynn *et al.* (2002) state that 'vulnerability to suggestive information' may be commoner among those who are high or medium on hypnotisability who tend to report false memories (pseudomemories) much more commonly than those low on hypnotisability. As high and medium hypnotisability is characteristic of most of the population, then Lynn *et al.* puts the figure of those susceptible to suggestive memory recovery techniques as high as 60%. Even those low on hypnotisability sometimes report false memories.

- It should be considered that the hypnotic interview may be technically better executed than the typical police interview. So memory performance may actually be better but not because of hypnosis.

It should be stressed that most of the findings are based on generalisations from laboratory situations. Consequently, there may be some reason for caution before hypnotism is rejected entirely by forensic psychologists.

While there are advantages in using hypnotism, it has been suggested that the cognitive interview out-performs it. It is a particular concern to some that hypnotism may have a distorting effect on memory. That does not mean that it invariably does so. Wagstaff (1996) argues that without detailed knowledge of the process of hypnosis involved in a particular case and other details, it is not possible to draw firm conclusions about the degree of adverse influence of hypnosis on the witness. Others (Berry *et al.*, 1999) suggest that hypnosis, irrespective of its effectiveness, may have a variety of drawbacks for practitioners. These include the number of lengthy hypnotic sessions necessary and the possible need for aftercare in cases where the memories emerging in hypnosis are particularly distressing.

Police as eyewitnesses: how accurate are they?

Common sense suggests that the police, because of their training and experience, should be accurate witnesses. They are, after all, experienced professionals. Whether or not police officers make especially accurate witnesses is probably not the most important issue. Crucial is whether those responsible for making legal decisions believe in the superiority of police eyewitness evidence. A majority of the general public believed that officers were more accurate than people in general (Clifford, 1976). Not only that, but there is evidence that the majority of legal professionals such as judges, lawyers and police officers also believe in the superiority of police evidence. To the extent to which this leads to greater acceptance of the evidence of the police, then this is a significant social fact.

Forensic and criminal psychologists have argued differently. Police officers and others were asked to identify crimes that had occurred at a street corner depicted in a video. They seemed to be no more skilful than civilians (Ainsworth, 1981). Actually, there were differences in the sense that the police officers were more suspicious that a crime was taking place when, in fact, it was not. Clifford and Richards (1977) found that police officers could give better descriptions than could civilians of a person who stopped them to ask for directions. Briefer encounters than this produced no differences.

In Sweden, Christianson *et al.* (1998) studied students, teachers, trainee police and police officers. These groups were shown a series of somewhat gory photographic slides of a violent incident – a man's gloved hand holding a bloody knife, a woman with slashed throat and copious bleeding, a distant shot of a woman lying bleeding. They were then shown photos of the perpetrator making his escape. The next stage was a filler stage in which participants were shown photographs of faces. The findings were somewhat different from those of earlier studies. In terms of the proportions able to recall information related to the crime slides correctly, service police officers were clearly superior to the other groups – especially school teachers. Specifically, the police tended especially to recall more about the perpetrator. In a line-up/identity parade situation, 'hits' (correct identifications) were highest for police officers. False alarms (the wrong person selected) were little different between any of the groups. Incorrect rejects were the least for the police officers. That is to say, the police officers less often failed to identify the culprit when he was actually in the line-up. Length of service more than age or any other factor tended to be associated with better recall. While memory in general was not superior in police officers, it may be that the emotive nature of the task here worked to the advantage of police participants.

Lindholm *et al.* (1997) wondered whether experience in policing brings with it a knowledge of crime events which facilitates the way in which officers remember events. This would follow from early research indicating that familiarity with a particular domain of memory tends to facilitate recollection of events relevant to that domain. This is possibly because previous experience provides a structure for the organisation of memories. Swedish police recruits, police officers in service and students were shown to be similar on all measures. The memory material consisted of one or other version of a video of a robbery of a grocery store. It takes the viewpoint of an eyewitness who picks up items like lettuce and spaghetti before arriving at the checkout. At this point, a man runs through the store threatening the people queuing. He then robs the cashier, slashing his face with a knife. There were two versions of the robbery which differed in terms of the robber's ethnicity – in one case he had a Scandinavian blonde appearance whereas in the other he had a dark, more southern European appearance. After a short filler task, participants were asked to write down as much detail as they could remember. They were also given a multiple-choice questionnaire concerning: (a) people in the video (such as their clothing) and (b) the sequence of events in the film. A photo line-up and a line-up of the knife from the video and others were also employed. The findings were:

- Police officers were better at identifying the actual knife.
- Police officers were better at identifying relevant crime information.

One possible reason for the superior performance of the serving police officers may be that the stress of the events in the video was less for them because they were used to dealing with violent events in their work. Their lower emotional responses to the video may have provided them with more freedom to form an accurate opinion rather than rely on stereotypes. In the light of the earlier comments, it is worth noting that the police officers seemed less affected by the ethnicity of the offender than the others.

Whether or not features of the training of police officers in Scandinavia contribute to their superior performance over the public is not known. Comparative data collected in similar circumstances from police officers in other parts of the world are simply not yet available.

Box 11.2

Forensic psychology in action: dealing with hostage taking

Just how to conceptualise people who do extreme things has long been a difficulty for psychologists. For example, are the terrorists mad who hijack aircraft, force them to another country and then hold passengers as hostages? There is a temptation to label out-of-the-ordinary actions as insane since this seems to justify the behaviour. One of the contributions of social psychology to understanding extreme behaviours has been to point out the rationality rather than irrationality of the participants. The classic studies of Milgram (1974) on obedience demonstrate how ordinary citizens can be encouraged to obey dangerous commands that might harm others. So, the atrocities of Nazi Germany may be the consequence, in part, of normal social processes. In a review of the mentality of terrorists, Maghan (1998) suggests that terrorists range through all character types from the self-doubting wretch to those haunted by indescribable demons. But, in general, the issue of madness simply is not an important consideration.

Wilson and Smith (2000) argue that behaviour during hostage-taking situations is bound by two sets of rules: (1) rules about the 'normal' behaviour that should be followed in hostage-taking situations and (2) rules about everyday behaviour which act as a fallback if the specific rules cannot be applied. They propose the importance of the following:

- *Motivation*: although it may be a complex task to understand the motives of the hostage takers, there may be clues to motive in the actions of their behaviour in the situation. They may give information to newspapers and television about the reasons for their action. If the demand is solely for money, according to Wilson and Smith, then this suggests a personally motivated crime rather than a politically motivated one. If the hostage takers demand the release of fellow terrorists then the hijacking may be a strategic attempt to fill a gap in the organisation. On the other hand, if the demand is to release prisoners in general, then this may be a simple expression of ideological beliefs about injustice as it applies widely.

- *Planning and resources*: the amount of planning that goes into a terrorist situation may indicate various things. For example, it may indicate the determination of the terrorists to fulfil the mission. Their behaviour should be more predictable than in circumstances in which the incident occurred spontaneously. Resources and the lack of them may give other insights into the planning of the operation.

In negotiations with hostage takers, the underlying 'rules' include the following:

- Both parties should demonstrate a willingness to negotiate.
- The parties should show willingness to demonstrate 'negotiability' by, for example, being willing to extend deadlines.

The hostages are the 'currency' of exchange with which the terrorists may bargain and negotiate. The release of all hostages is a bad strategy because only things such as the aircraft remain with which to bargain. At the same time, not releasing some prisoners may be regarded also as a bad strategy. The reasons include the good publicity accruing to the terrorists if some prisoners are released, especially women, children and the sick. Wilson and Smith suggest that breaking the rules of hostage taking may lead to a direct response by the authorities. They give the example of 'bluffing' about the situation, such as the terrorists claiming to have hostages whom they do not. Negotiations may break down in these circumstances.

The *Hostage Identification Syndrome* (or the Stockholm syndrome) refers to the tendency in hostage-type situations for hostages to develop a psychological affinity with their captors. This can involve the emergence of antipathies towards the authorities trying to rescue them. This may work both ways between terrorists and hostages such that the safety of the hostages is improved by this positive social feeling.

Use of lethal force

According to Blau (1994), in the United States something of the order of 100 police officers die each year at the hands of civilians. Nevertheless, the police are more likely to kill than to be killed. Nearly 300 civilians are legally killed by police officers each year. The officers were not killed by deranged individuals. The killers were not 'mad psychopaths' but, generally, criminals attempting to escape a crime scene. Blau suggests, based on this, that one of the strongest cues to danger for a police officer should be when the offender is attempting to escape arrest. It is difficult to judge danger but the following may be particularly dangerous:

- suspects who have a history of dangerousness;
- suspects who associate with people with a history of dangerousness;
- suspects who live or work in situations or settings where violent and dangerous events are likely to occur.

There is a buffer zone which when breached greatly increases the likelihood that the suspect will react violently (Blau, 1994). A dangerous stimulus moving from four feet (1.2 m) to closer is especially likely to produce a dangerous response in the officer. In the United States, 50% of police officers are frequently required to carry guns on duty and the remaining 50% of officers are permitted and encouraged to do so. Research for the 1980s discovered about 800 felonious killings of on-duty police officers:

- 40% were killed while attempting to make an arrest;
- over 90% were killed with firearms;
- 15% were killed by their own weapons taken from them physically by their killers.

The costs of being involved in armed violence as a victim are not merely personal. In the United States, four-fifths of police officers involved in shooting incidents left their police department consequently.

Of course, very different patterns may exist in other countries. This is especially so for countries with lower levels of violence in the community in general, or those where the police are not normally armed. Surprisingly, figures on the use of force in police work such as when making an arrest are not always available. For example, Rappert (2002) explains that such figures were unavailable for the United Kingdom and had to rely on the data collection initiative of a particular United Kingdom police force to provide any systematic data. (The United Kingdom has no national police force.) In one area, force was used in 6% of arrests. This contrasts with a figure of less than 20% for arrests in the United States. In the British data, evidence was found that the arresting officers sustained injuries in about 16% of these instances. In other words, in roughly 1% of arrests police officers sustain an injury. Rappert puts the situation this way: 'As the police patrol the boundaries of respectability in society, the resort to the use of force is always a possibility' (p. 690). In the United Kingdom, *Armed Response Vehicle* personnel are likely to be called in when there is a critical incident that appears to be sufficiently dangerous. Such officers are likely to drive or be driven at high speeds to the incident. Barton *et al.* (2000a, b) argued that this sort of situation might have potential for encouraging violent responses based on the *excitation transfer theory* of aggression (Zillman, 1979, 1982). Basically, this proposes that:

- emotional events are physiologically arousing;
- we become aware of physiological arousal from cues such as heart rate, breathing getting heavier and sweatiness;
- this internal state is generally labelled by us according to the environmental stimuli available at the time;
- failure to recognise the true cause of the emotional arousal will result in other factors being identified as the cause of the emotion.

This is relevant to the work of the *Armed Response Unit* since their rapid travel to the scene of the incident is physiologically arousing. If the officer attributes his or her physiological arousal to the suspect at the incident, this may well result in their acts being labelled differently.

Previous research has shown the efficiency of 'incident' simulators to research in this area. Generally, officers are very accurate in their marksmanship when they appropriately evaluate the situation as being a risk to themselves or others. When they *inappropriately* decide to shoot then their accuracy is relatively poor (Doerner and Ho, 1994). In their study, Barton *et al.* (2000a, b) had officers drive either at normal patrol speeds or at a high 'emergency' speed. Normal driving should produce less physiological arousal than high-speed driving. Based on the theory, it might be predicted that high-speed driving may produce physiological responses that may or may not be identified correctly as being the consequence of the high speed of driving. The officers were then exposed to one of two simulated incidents. In one case they would be justified to shoot under British law. In the other case shooting would not be justified:

- Shooting justified: they enter a shopping centre and see the suspect kneeling by cash machines picking up money. Following a warning of 'armed police' the suspect fires a handgun at the officer.
- The unjustified situation: the suspect pulls a small child to his body as protection, then releases the child, lifts a firearm and places it on the table and surrenders.

The findings were:

- The speed of travel affected the officers' self-rated willingness to shoot.
- Another variable known as *field dependence* (Witkin and Goodenough, 1981) (this is, essentially, the perceptual dependency of the individual on the environment around them) affected outcomes where the shooting was justified. Field-dependent officers rated themselves as more likely to shoot the suspect.

The impact of offending on the police

Practices will vary in different police organisations, but one British police force is currently experimenting with a system of requiring members of its staff and officers to attend a 'counselling' session with an independent counsellor on a twice-yearly basis. This is recognition that stress is an important adverse factor on police performance. Karlsson and Christianson (1999) asked Swedish police officers to describe the most stressful and traumatic event that had happened to them. Commonest among the stressful/traumatic policing episodes were:

- being threatened with a weapon;
- traffic accidents, especially being the first to arrive at deaths and bad injuries;
- homicides and suicides;
- notifying next of kin about deaths;
- complex investigations requiring them to deal with relatives of the victim and handle the press, and being under pressure to find the perpetrator;
- taking children into custody.

Armed threats and traffic accidents accounted equally for a total of about half the events reported. Their memory for the events was highest for suicide but each of the other categories of events was not much different. The commonest consequences of the event were 22% who felt depressed, 19% who felt fear when reminded of the event and 15% who mentioned feelings of guilt. Tension, sleeping problems, nightmares and overreacting were also included.

Police work is built around working teams that are to a degree mutually inter-dependent. Consequently, it is wrong to regard police officers solely as individuals acting in isolation. Considered as part of a team then the problems of a stressed-out or underperforming colleague are actually shared by the team. The team has to cover for the inadequacies of their colleague, which will extend stress far beyond the individual officer.

Generally, the officers felt a lack of support from superiors and a lack of pre-paration for what they were going to experience. It was brushed aside with a joke, one should be able to deal with that sort of thing. Significantly, a half mentioned fellow workers; a half mentioned close family members; a quarter mentioned neigh-bours, friends and relatives; and about a sixth mentioned other persons at the event as those who helped with the effects of the stressful events. Doctors, psychologists and priests were mentioned by about 1 in 20. A tenth reported that nobody had helped them.

A further study compared ratings of the impact of a particular event ten months and four-and-a-half years after the event. The event was a mass shooting incident. Things remained fairly stable in terms of emotional impact – if anything getting worse or more negative with time (Karlsson and Christianson, 1999).

This brings us to the question of the impact of traumatic incidents on the officers involved. It is obvious that some of the situations faced by the police during their work are horrific. Equally, a great deal of police work involves following largely bureaucratic procedures. According to Rallings (2002), there is little direct informa-tion about the impact of the offences they come across on the police. The way in which the media tend to cover police work encourages the impression that their work is dangerous, morbid and gruesome. As a consequence, the idea is encouraged that police officers are resilient and immune to any psychological consequences that their work may have on them. Some describe this as the impervious perspective or the John Wayne syndrome. However, there is another, more realistic, view which construes police officers as hidden victims suffering from much the same adverse consequences that members of the public would suffer in similar circumstances but their problems go unrecognised. Post-traumatic stress disorder, an extreme and debilitating response to severe trauma, is to be found within the police at a prevalence rate of about 7%. See Chapter 4 for a detailed discussion of PTSD. This is probably a fraction of the figure that would be achieved if exposure to traumatic events invariably led to post-traumatic stress disorder. There are far higher rates of exposure than cases in which particular events lead to post-traumatic stress disorder, which implies that other, mediating, factors may be at work. Among these factors would be good social support at home and at work.

Shooting incidents produce quite profound emotional reactions in the majority of officers. The typical reports are of crying, depression, anger, elation, nightmares, flashbacks of the incidents, bodily and emotional disturbances, loss of interest in work. Some officers had problems with adjusting back to work on the streets after the shooting incident. The sort of incidents that seem to be most associated with psychological symptoms are those in which the officer is subjected to violence, a colleague dies, children are dead, sudden deaths and mutilated bodies or decomposed ones. In this sort of study, the officers nominate the most traumatic work-related event that they have experienced. These can then be compared with the symptoms of trauma experienced by the officers.

Two recommendations made by Rallings are particularly important:

- It may be possible to focus resources on affected officers rather than all officers following a traumatic policing episode. By examining the immediate effects on physiology, emotion and mental dissociative responses then the at-risk personnel may be identified.
- Work-place characteristics have an impact on whether or not a traumatic event will lead to psychological trauma. So workplaces should be perceived by officers as supportive, morale should be good, and communications in the workplace should be improved.

The police caution

The police caution is the 'warning' that a police officer is required to give when arresting a suspect for an offence. The current police caution in much of the UK is: 'You do not have to say anything. But it may harm your defence if you do not mention when questioned something which you later rely on in court. Anything you do say may be given in evidence.' In other words, it is a warning that silence after arrest may carry a message to the court. Police cautions to suspects vary from legal system to legal system. In the United States, the police caution reminds the suspect of their right to remain silent so as not to incriminate themselves. This, along with the right to a lawyer, forms the basis of informing the suspect of what are known as his or her Miranda rights. Thus British and US systems are now quite different. Previously, in the UK, citizens had the right to remain silent and exercise of this right could not be considered by the court. One key issue, despite the variation between nations and over time, is the extent to which statements of rights are actually understood by the public.

A survey of the modern police caution in Britain (Shepherd et al., 1995) found that relatively few members of the public could explain the components of the caution (Police and Criminal Evidence Act of 1995):

- 'You do not have to say anything.' This was understood by 27%.
- 'But it may harm your defence if you do not mention when questioned something which you later rely on in court.' This was understood by 14%.
- 'Anything you do say may be given in evidence.' This was understood by 34%.

Scotland has a different tradition of caution that does not depend on quite such a precisely prescribed position although the officer should explain it. The basic common law caution is that a suspect is not obliged to say anything but anything she or he does say will be noted and may be used in evidence. (Common law is that established by custom and the decisions of judges. It is law that is not contained as such in statutes or legislation.) Young offenders are known from previous international research to have particular difficulties with the standard cautions. In other words, suspects do not understand their basic rights. Cook and Philip (1998) studied the comprehensibility of the Scottish caution in a number of ways. One of the things they did was to ask the young offenders to decide whether phrases actually meant the same as the phrase in the caution:

- 'You are not bound to answer' was seen by 59% as equivalent to 'You do not have to say anything until the police ask you questions' though its legal implications are quite different from this.
- The phrase in the caution 'Your answer may be used in evidence' was interpreted by 90% as meaning the same as 'As long as you are polite to the police, whatever you say will not be used against you in court'.

Whether or not psychologists could develop phraseology that would improve matters is a moot point if the legal implications of the caution are to remain unchanged. Nevertheless, it seems clear that offenders in the normal intelligence range are having difficulty understanding their legal rights.

Other studies find similar findings. For example, the UK Police and Criminal Evidence codes of practice are available at police stations. They supplement the statutory verbal and written material. Various matters are covered. These include the rules governing detention. Very few arrestees actually ask to see the code of practice. When they do, based on the observations of Joyce (1993), they read a passage or two and then discard the booklet. Readability of text can be analysed. For example, the average sentence length is a useful index. One example of this approach is the Flesch Index. This is the average sentence length adjusted by the average number of syllables in a word. Joyce took 40 passages from the code. Overwhelmingly, they fell in the fairly difficult to very difficult range. An IQ in the range above average to above 126 is needed in order to comprehend material of this level of difficulty. What is the readability of the paragraph you are reading? It is in the fairly difficult range. Irrespective of this, it is easier to read than nearly all of the samples of text in Joyce's study.

Of course, the decision-making process when waiving the right to remain silent under the United States constitution needs to be understood. Kassin and Norwick (2004) report an intriguing laboratory study in which groups of 'suspects' were subjected to different styles of interviewing by a 'detective' including sympathetic and hostile styles. The 'detective' was trying to get the 'suspect' to forego their Miranda rights so that more evidence could be obtained which would be legitimate in court. The style of interview actually made no difference of note to the decision to waive one's Miranda rights. However, the researchers had included a guilty-innocent dimension into the study. Some participants 'stole' money from a nearby teaching laboratory, others did not. Actually, they had received instructions about what to do from the experimenters. Nevertheless, some were 'guilty' because they had taken the money on instruction and others were 'innocent' because they had not taken the money. When put under some pressure by the 'detective' it was found that the 'innocent' group were more likely to waive their Miranda rights than the 'guilty' group. Kassin and Norwick (2004) argue that Miranda warnings may not protect the most vulnerable from the actions of the police. False confession is not uncommon and we need to understand the process that includes waiving Miranda rights. One important case involved an 18-year-old who confessed to the murder of his mother and was imprisoned until independent evidence showed that he could not have possibly committed the crime. When asked why he did not remain silent during the interview he said: 'I hadn't done anything wrong and I felt that only a criminal really needed an attorney, and this was all going to come out in the wash' (reported in Kassin and Norwick, 2004, p. 218). Thus the innocent may be put at risk more than the guilty.

Main points

- Psychologists from a wide variety of backgrounds can and have contributed to our understanding of the police and their work. It is particularly important to note that the police as orgnisational cultures tend to have particular attitudes and values, some of which may make the problems of a psychologist working in this context more difficult. It is commonly held that the police have a somewhat macho culture which may make helping them deal with stress or certain groups difficult.

- A major area where psychological research and theory has contributed to our understanding of the work of the police is in terms of interviewing techniques. Of particular note in this context is the enhanced cognitive interview, which is part of the training of some police officers. The enhanced cognitive interview takes concepts and techniques from laboratory studies of memory and communications psychology in an attempt to improve interviewing with eyewitnesses. The research evidence tends to point to the superiority of the enhanced cognitive interview in extracting good quality accurate memories of the eyewitnessed events despite an increased risk of generating inaccurate memories. There is generally little support for the use of forensic hypnosis as it is felt that there are no respects in which it is superior to the enhanced cognitive interview.

- Stress affects police work in a number of ways. As any other work organisation, aspects of the bureaucratic structure may add to felt stress levels. Stress is relevant to police work in ways that are not characteristic of other organisations. In particular, police work involves being involved in highly stressful situations such as the aftermath of crimes or suicides, for example. The requirement sometimes to use lethal force and the risk of being victims of lethal force are also characteristics of police organisations not shared by other organisations. Features of the organisation may make dealing with the stress more difficult to deal with such as the machoness of police culture and attitudes towards the working team. However, the police may be better able to perform under stress than others since there is some evidence that they make better eyewitnesses of stressful events than the general public.

Chapter 12

Eyewitness testimony

Overview

- DNA evidence has proven beyond doubt the innocence of some people wrongfully convicted of a crime. Two-thirds of these wrongful convictions in the most recent US study involved incorrect eyewitness evidence. Despite this, surveys of police officers show that they value eyewitness evidence and believed that eyewitnesses are usually correct. It should be remembered that in some jurisdictions convictions based solely on eyewitness evidence are not acceptable.

- Eyewitness evidence can be accurate or inaccurate. There is evidence that for certain features such as gender and eye shape there are high levels of accuracy whereas for beards and moustaches accuracy is low. It is possible that offenders change some of their characteristics as disguise.

- There is a considerable literature into the characteristics of eyewitness memory. Of importance is the evidence that events following the incident (e.g. interviews) may affect what is remembered as well as the type of questioning. This is of importance, for example, when examining issues such as allegations of sexual abuse that occurred many years before.

- The confidence of eyewitnesses in their testimony and their accuracy are quite distinct things. At best, there is a weak relationship between the two. One implication is that witnesses who seem less than confident would probably provide as accurate identifications as any other witness. Certainly, one should be careful about legal suggestions that confidence is a sign of a good witness.

- The line-up or identity parade needs to be planned and executed following a number of rules to minimise errors. It has been suggested that some of the care that goes into designing laboratory experiments in psychology could benefit line-ups. For example, the person conducting the line-up should be unaware of the identity of the suspect in order to avoid the risk of biasing the situation. Experimental studies tend to suggest that eyewitnesses who make their decisions quickly tend to be the most accurate.

- Relative judgement theory suggests that an eyewitness tends to choose someone similar to the culprit if the culprit is not in the identification parade. Eyewitnesses, therefore, do not apply absolute criteria for matching their memories with the members of the line-up. The use of procedures which indicate that the culprit may not be present in the line-up may reduce the relative judgement effect.

- Some police tools such as CCTV and the use of facial composites have been under critical scrutiny. CCTV footage does not readily lead to the identification of individuals unknown to the person viewing the tape. Facial composites are not particularly recognisable even for well-known individuals.

- Despite a great deal of empirical research, it is not possible to evaluate with any precision a particular witness's evidence. Even well-researched topics such as the effects of length of exposure to the offender on the accuracy of eyewitness evidence is difficult to translate from the psychological laboratory to real life.

Few would doubt that human memory is fallible. An intriguing demonstration of this was a study of memory concerning the crash of an El Al Boeing 747 jet onto a residential area of Amsterdam (Crombag *et al.*, 1996). The crash had only been verbally reported on news bulletins as no film or video of the plane crashing exists. Apart from eyewitnesses, no one could have seen the events. Nevertheless, participants in the research were misled into thinking that they may have seen such images on television by asking them about their recollections of the news coverage. Substantial numbers of participants in the study readily provided visual details of the crash as if they had seen it on film. One can only presume that they gleaned this information from film of crashes that had been broadcast. The key finding of the research is the failure of participants to recognise the falsity of their claims. That is to say, they did not realise that they were manufacturing memories.

The implications of this for forensic and criminal psychology are obvious. Imagine the following circumstances. Police officers show a photograph to a woman who had witnessed a crime. They ask her whether the man in the photograph is the offender. She decides that it is the man who committed the crime. Just what degree of confidence should one have in a conviction based solely on this identification? There are many reasons why the witness identified the photograph as being that of the offender. She might feel that:

- the police must have strong reasons to suspect this particular man;
- the man in the photograph may have a passing resemblance to the offender;
- she may feel that she has seen the man in the photograph somewhere before;
- she may feel that she would appear foolish if she says that she cannot remember whether or not this is the man.

Clearly this is a very unsatisfactory procedure for identifying the offender. Nevertheless, this was common practice until the Supreme Court of the United States recognised the risk of a miscarriage of justice brought by such procedures (*Simmons vs. United States*, 1968). Any procedure used to obtain identification evidence needs to be much less risky than this.

Nevertheless, there is evidence that police officers have great faith in eyewitness evidence. A survey of British police officers found that, generally speaking, they valued witness evidence positively. The majority believed that witnesses are usually

Box 12.1

Forensic psychology in action: CCTV video evidence

There has been a vast increase in the use of closed-circuit television (CCTV) video cameras in public areas such as town and city centres. One of their prime purposes is to act as deterrents to crime. They can also be considered as evidence collection systems. We are all familiar with footage of crimes observed in this way. Despite this, cameras do not provide irrefutable evidence of a crime and offenders in practice. This is partly the consequence of the very poor images produced due, for example, to the amount of enlargement of the image required. Image enhancement techniques are available but they do this at the expense of the movement in the image. The current psychological research suggests that the problems are substantial with current technology:

- There is evidence that CCTV systems do reduce crime in the *short term* in locations where they are installed although there is a return to previous levels in the longer term (Brown, 1995). The growing awareness that the system is not altogether effective in ensuring arrest leaves some people willing to take the risk.

- Familiarity with the person in a low-quality video makes it far easier to recognise them compared with strangers. Nevertheless, there is not a proportionate increase in the recognition of strangers as the video quality increases (Burton *et al.*, 1999). Henderson *et al.* (2000a) investigated the effects of allowing participants to become modestly familiar with individuals by showing them a short video clip of a face they would later be asked to identify. The consequence was no improvement in recognition of faces in a photo line-up of similar faces compared with circumstances in which no opportunity for familiarisation was given. There is an important exception to the general rule that CCTV images are problematic for identification (Davies, 2003). Davies cites the court case involving a soldier who was assaulted in a nightclub surveyed by a poor quality CCTV system. The video did not show the features of the assailants clearly. The assault had been carried out by members of a different regiment. Nevertheless, officers from the regiment in question were able to identify the culprits independently of each other. They all agreed on the assailants! However, if familiarity with the person in the video is associated with very accurate identification then the question is what degree of familiarity is required before acceptable accuracy in identification is achieved.

- With strangers, it is very difficult with even high-quality videos to determine whether two different images are of the same person (Kemp *et al.*, 1997). For example, Davies and Thasen (2000) found that only 65% of viewers of a CCTV video of a woman in an 'incident' in a car park in which she was seen in close-up actually picked out another 'innocent' person from a line-up. Only 29% correctly identified the woman, the remainder made no choice.

- When they compared various measures of the recognition of CCTV-simulated video and stills taken from the video, Kemp *et al.* (2000) found evidence of the superiority of the video clip. Participants made more correct identifications and were less likely to make false recognitions from the (moving) video. This involved recognition of familiar faces, *not* strangers.

Henderson *et al.* (2000b) recommend that great caution is needed in assessing evidence from CCTV from people who are not very familiar with the person(s) in the video. Part of the solution lies in the improvement of CCTV images which are poor in comparison to broadcast television or domestic camcorders with which many of us are more familiar. They see CCTV as more important in assessing what happened at a crime scene.

correct and three-quarters thought that they were never or rarely incorrect. On the other hand, about half felt that witnesses did not remember as much as the officer wanted (Kebbell and Milne, 1998). In other words, witness evidence may have an important role in police investigations irrespective of its validity.

Of course, risky identification evidence is an issue in only a minority of crimes. Criminal statistics, as we have seen, show quite clearly that many victims already know their victimisers socially. Thus the risk of innocent misidentification in these circumstances is minimal. In other words, identification evidence is unproblematic in the vast majority of these cases. It is in circumstances in which the witness and the offender are strangers that difficulties arise.

Eyewitness testimony as a central issue in forensic and criminal psychology

As we saw in Chapter 1, as long ago as 1896 the German psychologist Albert Von Schrenk-Nortzing testified at the Munich trial of a triple murder. Basing his argument on the then emerging academic research into the nature of suggestibility and memory, Von Schrenk-Nortzing unsuccessfully argued that witnesses confuse real-life events with events they read about in the press. He used the phrase 'retroactive memory falsification'. Just a few years later, Munsterberg, who may be seen as the founder of the field of applied psychology, returned to this field. He argued that there was probably no relationship between the accuracy of an eyewitness and the eyewitness's confidence in the accuracy of his or her testimony. This conclusion still, more or less, accurately reflects available research findings.

The topic remains important in terms of justice. This is graphically illustrated by work on wrongful convictions (Wells *et al.*, 1998, which extended an earlier review by Connors *et al.*, 1996). This is an account of the false convictions established in American courts on the basis of genetic fingerprint (DNA) testing. Forty trials that led to wrongful conviction were available for review. In each of these the testing of genetic material with new techniques established the unjust conviction beyond any doubt. These were serious miscarriages of justice. All of the men who were convicted served prison sentences. Five of them spent time on death row awaiting execution. The testimony of at least one eyewitness was in 90% of these proven miscarriages of justice. In one instance, as many as five eyewitnesses were involved. The case of Ronald Cotton is typical. Cotton spent 10 years in prison for a rape actually committed by another man, Bobby Poole. There was remarkably little evidence against Ronald Cotton. One victim had identified him from a photographic line-up (a selection of photographs possibly including the offender). In a line-up/identity parade, just one witness identified him as the rapist. Eventually, the DNA evidence from semen left by the actual rapist resulted in Cotton's release. Remarkably, the real rapist, Bobby Poole, had already confessed to the crimes and this confession had been rejected by a court as reason to release Cotton. More recently (Weber, Brewer and Wells, 2004b), the Innocence Project found that two-thirds of 138 cases of DNA exonerated convicted offenders involved wrongful eyewitness identifications. The Innocence Project deals with cases in which a conviction might be challenged on the basis of DNA evidence. Partly this study involved some of the same cases that were included in the earlier DNA study.

Box 12.2

Forensic psychology in action: facial composites and identification

One investigative technique familiar to the general public is the police's uses of facial composites. That is, images of the 'suspect' based on the reports of victims and other witnesses. These have changed with changes in technology. Originally, an artist would sketch a picture of the face based on the information supplied by the witness, then in the 1970s Identikit (based on 'sketched' material) and Photofit (based on photographs) approaches were used. These used 'kits' of facial features from which, say, a nose with the appropriate shape was selected from a range of noses in the kit. The different elements of the face were then built into the total image. More recently still, technological advances have enabled the use of computer techniques to produce the images. These allow the size, for example, of the feature to be adjusted quickly so increasing the flexibility of the approach. Such computerised facial composite approaches include E-FIT and PROfit which are used by some police forces. Research into earlier methods of creating facial composites before computerisation generally found that the quality of the composites was not good. So are the newer methods more satisfactory?

Frowd *et al.* (2004) had the 'witness' work with a facial composite operator to produce an image of a target person (popular personalities but ones identified as not being known to the 'witness'). The image of the target was shown for about one minute and there was a delay of three to four hours before the next stage of the research. The operator did not know the identity of the 'target' and worked solely on the basis of the descriptions given by the 'witness' and the normal interactions between the witness and the operator. These facial composites could then be shown to people who were asked to identify who the celebrity was. Accuracy was not outstanding. E-FIT and PRO-fit produced 20% of recognition from the composite, artist's sketches resulted in 10% recognition, and Photofit yielded 5% recognition. The results were essentially replicated when participants were asked to match the facial composite to an array of photographs including that of the target. In other words, the composites were not very good matches to the original photographs. One other feature of the design should be mentioned – the 'witnesses' underwent a cognitive interview before engaging in the facial composite construction task. However, the delay of three or four hours between exposure to the target and reconstruction was relatively short compared to most forensic situations.

A study by Frowd *et al.* (2004) followed many of the above procedures but extended the delay between exposure and facial reconstruction. The witnesses were showed pictures of celebrities (in this case, actors and pop music performers) until they came across one which the witness did not recognise. They looked at this for one minute. Two days later the facial composite recognition task was carried out. This again involved a cognitive interview (see Chapter 11) and witnesses were asked to think of the time that the target photo was seen and the context of this. This is the reinstatement of context procedure from the cognitive interview. Then, once a clear picture had been formed, the witness described the face taking as much time as they needed. This was then followed by cued recall where the descriptions of each feature were read to the witness who then added anything further that came to mind. The precise procedures used for creating the 'likeness' varied but were similar to the standard practice employed with each particular method.

A separate group took part in the 'identification' process based on the composites. Overall, only a small percentage of composites were correctly named (2.8%). This is partly a function of the composite method employed. Actual sketches were the most frequently recognised. Of course, this could be a consequence of the target individual not being recognisable from the original photograph. However, this group of participants were asked a number of questions about the person in the photograph. The recognition figures for the composites were adjusted on this basis so that how recognisable the composites were adjusted for the recognisability of the personality. This resulted in a modest increase in naming to 3.3% over all the composites. Once again, sketches were the best named (8.1%) with E-FIT and PRO-fit only being recognised by less than 2%.

The accuracy of witness evidence

Eyewitnesses, of course, can be very accurate in their descriptions despite failing to identify offenders precisely. Very little research is available that compares the characteristics of offenders with those descriptions given to the police. What evidence there is suggests that witnesses can be accurate in terms of describing individual characteristics but not always so. One of the best studies in this field was carried out in the Netherlands (Van Koppen and Lochun, 1997). Data were obtained from official court records in store at the offices of prosecutors. The researchers targeted offences involving robberies of commercial buildings and dwellings. Street robberies (muggings) were not included. In the Netherlands, witnesses are rarely questioned in court. Instead, the prosecution depends on statements obtained by the police from witnesses. In the cases studied, there was very little delay between the offence and the collection of witness statements:

- 80% had been collected within two days – about two-thirds in one day;
- over 400 different robberies were studied;
- 1,300 witnesses were involved;
- 2,300 offender descriptions were obtained;
- only 1,650 descriptions could be used since not all could be verified against the robber's true appearance;
- mostly the witness had seen the robbery (over four-fifths);
- the remaining witnesses had seen the escape or preparations being made for the robbery.

Other information was available from various sources on the characteristics of the witness and the circumstances of their evidence:

- witness characteristics such as their sex and age;
- the amount of delay before they gave their statements;
- the quality of the lighting conditions at the robbery;
- whether the witness's view was obstructed;
- the estimated distance between the witness and the robbery.

The actual offender characteristics were assessed using the police's own descriptions of the arrestee, which were available from official forms designed for that purpose. The correspondence between the witness description and the police description of the suspect varied according to the physical feature under consideration. The greatest correspondence was found for:

- sex (100% agreement);
- eye shape (100%);
- hair colour (73%);
- face shape (69%);
- race (60%);
- height (52%);
- ears protruding (50%).

While the correspondence for some of the above is generally impressive, some features were rarely mentioned in the witness descriptions. Sex and height were the most commonly mentioned features. Overall, the witness descriptions were relatively sparse. So, out of the maximum of 43 different characteristics that could be mentioned, on average each witness mentioned only eight features.

Of course, offenders have an interest in altering their physical appearance either specifically for the offence or after the offence. So it is of some interest to note that the characteristics that are the most easily altered tend to be those with the lowest agreement:

- beards (1%);
- moustaches (3%);
- accents and dialects (32%).

Some variables predicted the accuracy of the eyewitness description. For example, the longer the statement, the greater the eyewitness accuracy. Given the large sample size involved, the relationships between predictors and accuracy were not strong despite being statistically significant. Generally speaking, the relationships were much as would be expected. Factors such as the distance between the offender and the witness, the duration of the crime, the physical position of the witness in relation to the offender and the feelings of threat experienced by the witness all had predictable relationships with witness accuracy. Surprisingly, the longer the delay between the crime and the statement by the witness, the better was the accuracy of the witness's description.

The overall impression, nevertheless, is of rather vague descriptions that are dominated by very general characteristics such as the offender's gender, race, height and age. The witnesses are accurate in their description of these characteristics. However, these are the very characteristics that are poor at distinguishing offenders from others who are suspects. For example, knowing that the offender is male is not very much use in identifying the particular person in question.

This is about accuracy in describing characteristics of offenders; who gets picked out in line-ups is a different issue.

Later intrusions into eyewitness memory

The early studies of human memory in the first part of the twentieth century largely consisted of the memorising of nonsense syllables following the work of Ebbinghaus (1913). Hardly a situation conducive to the study of eyewitness testimony. Things gradually changed from the late 1960s onwards in ways that encouraged psychologists to investigate eyewitness psychology. Increasingly, the importance of studying real-life memory was recognised, e.g. Neisser (1982) and Neisser and Winograd (1988) published seminal work on human memory in real-life contexts. Consequently, from the 1970s onwards, academic memory researchers carried out numerous studies of eyewitness memory. Nevertheless, coming, as they did, largely from the laboratory tradition of psychology, their emphasis was on theoretical rather than practical matters.

Some of the most important theory in this area emerged from the work of Elizabeth Loftus. Her interests eventually extended into practical matters such as recovered memories (see Chapter 14). Perhaps the most famous of her studies were demonstrations that subsequent events influenced testimony about incidents. Witnesses to a robbery or accident may be exposed later to new information – perhaps during a police interview, for example. In some circumstances, that new information can influence recollections of the incident. Furthermore, information in one modality may affect memory for events held in a different modality. Thus verbal information may affect visual recall. The most familiar study is that of Loftus and Palmer (1974). Participants witnessed film of a car accident and were later asked a series of questions in which key information was embedded. There were alternative versions of the key question:

- 'About how fast were the cars going when they *hit* each other?'
- 'About how fast were the cars going when they *smashed* into each other?'

Other variants on this theme had the cars colliding, contacting each other, bumping and so forth. Estimates of speed were affected by the word used in the questioning. The estimates were of speeds about a third faster when the word smashed was used than when the word contacted was used. It might be objected – and it was – that, in itself, this does not mean that what was stored in the brain changed. Subtly leading questions may have simply encouraged faster estimates without affecting the 'memory trace'. It is not possible to get into the mind of the witness to measure the speed the cars are travelling in the brain trace. Perhaps this is a theoretical issue rather than being of practical importance. Nevertheless, researchers, including Loftus herself, pursued this issue with some vigour.

In this series of studies, a visual recognition procedure replaced the problematic verbal statement (Loftus *et al.*, 1978). Participants in the research were shown a series of colour slides of the stages of a car–pedestrian accident. The car in question was a red Datsun that was seen driving towards a road intersection where there was either a stop sign or a yield sign (give way sign), depending on the experimental condition. Later a series of questions was asked in which was embedded one of two variants of the key question:

- Did another car pass the red Datsun while it was stopped at the stop sign?
- Did another car pass the red Datsun while it was stopped at the yield sign?

After a short diversionary activity, a yes/no recognition test was administered immediately or a week later. The crucial recognition slides were the stop and the yield slides. Essentially, then, the experimental design was as follows:

- Some participants saw a stop sign and were asked about a stop sign.
- Some participants saw a stop sign but were asked about a yield sign.
- Some participants saw a yield sign and were asked about a yield sign.
- Some participants saw a yield sign but were asked about a stop sign.

In other words, some participants were asked questions *consistent* with what they had seen and others were asked questions *inconsistent* with what they had seen. Some of the findings were:

- Questioning consistent with the contents of the original experience enhanced correct visual identification for the crucial slide immediately after exposure.
- Questioning inconsistent with the original experience depressed correct identification initially.
- Generally speaking, these effects tended to reduce after a week such that the initial differences disappeared.

Given the great numbers of laboratory studies of eyewitness testimony, it is not possible to review all of the findings. We can, nevertheless, turn to some major forensic issues that illustrate the implications of research findings for court decisions.

Eyewitness evidence in court

Witness confidence

The issue of eyewitness confidence markedly divides the legal and the psychological views. In the United States, the Supreme Court decided in 1972 that witness confidence was an indicator of witness accuracy. Thus witness confidence can be regarded as 'markers' (Weber *et al.*, 2004a) or assessment variables (Sporer, 1993) which might help when assessing the value of any witness's testimony. Equally, confidence should also be taken into account when assessing the risk of misidentification. Furthermore, it is known from other research that lawyers in general accept the validity of this link and jurors tend to subscribe to this view too. In contrast, research has demonstrated that confidence is a rather poor predictor of accuracy. Cutler and Penrod (1989) studied a wide range of investigations of confidence expressed prior to identity parades/line-ups and correct identification of the offender. The overall correlation for the studies was 0.20 or less. While this is evidence of a relationship, it is nevertheless a rather weak relationship statistically speaking. Consequently, Cutler and Penrod suggest that the poor relationship is a good reason not to ignore the evidence of witnesses who express a lack of confidence. Confident witnesses are not much better, in general, than non-confident ones in their identifications.

As might be expected, witnesses after the line-up (identity parade) demonstrate a slightly better association between confidence as measured after the line-up and accuracy. Nevertheless, this remains a small correlation of 0.25 (Bothwell *et al.*, 1987).

Kebbell *et al.* (1996) were among those to question such a counterintuitive finding. They pointed out that researchers have avoided memory tasks that are either very easy or very hard. So, for example, witnesses may be asked the culprit's gender or their eye colour. Sex is a relatively easy thing to identify but in the circumstances of the witnessed events, the witness may have no opportunity to register the offender's eye colour. In their study, student eyewitnesses watched a short video showing the implied murder of a man by a woman. Following a filler or distracting task, they were asked to complete a 33-item questionnaire about the film. The questions were open-ended and varied in terms of difficulty. Confidence was fairly closely related to item difficulty – that is, easy questions produced a high correlation between accuracy and confidence. Difficult questions produced a low correlation between accuracy and confidence. Interestingly, virtually every time that a participant rated themselves as being absolutely certain about the accuracy of their answer to a question they were correct – that is, their accuracy was 97% in these circumstances.

The 10–12 second 'rule'

Another possible 'marker' or criterion for distinguishing between the good eyewitness testimony and the poor eyewitness testimony lies in the '10–12 second rule' (Dunning and Perretta, 2002). This is an idea derived from a great deal of evidence from experimental research on eyewitness psychology which has tended to find that that eyewitnesses who identify someone from a line-up quickly tend to be more accurate than an eyewitness who takes rather more time. In other words, there is a negative

Box 12.3

Controversy: critique of research on eyewitness testimony

Ebbesen and Konecni (1997, also Konecni *et al.*, 2000) wrote a fierce critique of eyewitness testimony research. Apart from its implications for forensic psychology, this critique contains food-for-thought for any psychologist working in any applied field of psychology. The critique makes the serious charge that psychologists acting as expert witnesses have systematically misled courts of law about the validity, consistency and generalisability of research findings on eyewitness testimony. This is primarily the result of researchers' overconfidence in their expertise. They argue that there is no generally accepted theory of eyewitness testimony. This is despite a number of sophisticated models of memory available to psychologists. So it is not valid for predictions to be made about the accuracy of eyewitnesses in particular cases in which eyewitness evidence may be vital.

Part of the difficulty is the vast difference between the circumstances of real eyewitness testimony and those of research studies – especially the psychology laboratory and other factors that limit their usefulness in court according to Ebbesen and Konecni (1997):

- Studies of eyewitness testimony show many inconsistencies in their outcomes.

- The vast majority of eyewitness testimony research involves the use of only college students (Yuille and Cutshall, 1986).

- The lengths of exposure to the criminal events vary substantially between real life and research. The median duration in real life lies somewhere between five and ten minutes. Remarkably, in research studies the typical length of exposure to the criminal is six seconds, give or take a little. In other words, research studies involve exposure times of a fiftieth to a hundredth of exposure in real crimes (Moore *et al.*, 1994).

- Researchers are not in a position to translate such key variables as length of exposure to the crime into the likelihood that the witness is wrong. Although it is correct to suggest in broad terms that greater exposure leads to greater accuracy, the precise risks of error cannot be calculated. So it is not possible to say that after two minutes of exposure the rates of being correct are 60% or any other figure.

- Research generally shows that increasing exposure time is associated with increased accuracy in offender identification (Shapiro and Penrod, 1986). A precise mathematical function describing the relationship between these two factors is not known. Even if it were, things are not simple. Increasing exposure time for the witness to the crime is also associated with an increased risk of identifying the wrong person as the criminal (Ebbesen and Konecni, 1997).

- An analysis of transcripts of trials involving expert testimony on eyewitness accuracy shows overwhelmingly that these problems in interpreting the implications of longer exposure to the crime are not mentioned.

Ebbesen and Konecni (1997) argue:

> Because the evidence is either inconsistent or insufficient in almost every area in which eyewitness experts testify and because there is no research that provides the experts, much less the jurors, with rules to use when translating the evidence to particular decisions in particular cases, we believe that eyewitness expert testimony is more prejudicial than probative and should not be allowed in courts.

(p. 24)

relationship between response latency and identification accuracy. One possible explanation of this is that the eyewitness who correctly identifies the offender needs to match the characteristics of each member of the line-up against the characteristics of the offender held in memory. This takes time but is relatively speedy because the major characteristics can be identified quickly – where the offender is not in the line-up the process takes longer since each line-up member has to be checked against the remembered characteristics. Similarly, if the memory of the characteristics of the offender is weak, then it takes a longer time to check these weak memories against the actual characteristics of people in the line-up. However, eyewitnesses who correctly fail to find a target in an identification parade (line-up) do not do this quicker than those who incorrectly decide that their target is not in the line-up. This makes sense in terms of the matching process just described since in both cases all of the checking process has to be gone through.

Weber *et al.* (2004b) studied the applicability of the 10–12 second rule using a number of data sets involving adults and children. A major finding is that the optimum delay differentiating accurate from inaccurate identifications was not constant and varied somewhat from the 10 seconds according to the age groups involved, for example. At best, they found a figure of 80% accuracy using the optimally differentiating time for any of their studies. They say that this makes the rule problematic for application in forensic settings. Indeed, they specifically suggest that the 10–12 second rule is an inadequate indicator of the accuracy of identification evidence (Weber *et al.*, 2004a). Nevertheless, the evidence did support the idea that decision speed was a good indicator of witness accuracy. The problem is that quite what decision speed is indicative of decision accuracy is tantalisingly variable and, as yet, not clearly identified with any particular aspects of research design. However, when a witness's confidence as well as their speed are both used in the assessment of accuracy, it became clear that accuracy of identification neared 90% for the confident witness who answered within the optimum time limit for accuracy.

Improving the validity of the line-up

Practices concerning line-ups or identification parades vary from country to country. The United Kingdom is particularly advanced in its thinking on these largely because of a record of wrongful convictions on the basis of identification evidence. In the 1970s, critical reviews of identification evidence were published including the influential *Devlin Report*. Other countries do not have quite the same procedural protection for suspects as the United Kingdom. Penrod (2003) argued on the basis of data from US line-ups that even cases where the guilty party is identified by the witness, that maybe as many of 20% of these are lucky guesses and not actual identifications as such. Furthermore, he estimates that as many as 50% of witnesses who made a choice were guessing. It is therefore important to note that Wells *et al.* (1998) proposed four general principles to protect the suspect. They are intended to guide the procedures used in line-ups/identification parades as well as photospreads. All of these seek to identify the offender. An analogy is drawn between a good line-up and a good psychological experiment:

- A properly designed experiment should be a fair test of the research hypothesis.
- A good experiment should be, as far is possible, free from biases.

Wells *et al.* suggest that two broad issues need to be taken into account:

- Structural properties, e.g. the appearance of the line-up in terms of how similar to and different from each other its members are.
- Procedural properties, e.g. the instructions given to the witnesses, the numbers in the line-up and so forth.

Consider some of the ideal characteristics of a study of human memory. The participants in the research listen to a list of words. They are then shown a sequence of words that may or may not have been in the original list. If the researcher testing their memory knows which words are in the original list then he or she may subtly and non-consciously give clues as to what these words were. For example, the researcher might pause fractionally longer over the critical words. There are indications that researchers are able inadvertently to bias an experimental outcome such that it favours the favoured hypothesis (Jung, 1971; Rosenthal, 1966). One way of reducing this influence is to keep the actual researcher in the dark about the hypothesis or leave them blind as to other aspects of the procedure (such as the list of words to be remembered). The rule for line-ups and photospreads is:

> Rule 1: The person who conducts the line-up or photospread should not be aware of which member of the line-up or photospread is the suspect.
>
> *(p. 17)*

Even where the experimenter does not have knowledge about the list of words to be remembered, the participants may think that they do. Thus participants might inadvertently and wrongly read into the experimenter's behaviours what they believe to be cues about the correct words. For example, the experimenter might find certain words amusing and respond differently to these. Explaining to participants that the experimenter is unaware of what words are correct may reduce the effect.

> Rule 2: The eyewitness should be told explicitly that the person administering the line-up does not know which person is the suspect in the case.
>
> *(p. 19)*

The participant in the memory research might be inclined to pick out certain words simply because they are more interesting, more dramatic or in some way different. They may be inclined to pick these words as the correct ones as a consequence:

> Rule 3: The suspect should not stand out in the line-up or photospread as being different from the distracters based on the eyewitness's previous description of the culprit or based on other factors that would draw extra attention to the suspect.
>
> *(p. 19)*

In the light of what we know about eyewitness confidence (see above), the recommendations also include the following:

> Rule 4: A clear statement should be taken from the eyewitness at the time of the identification and prior to any feedback as to his or her confidence that the identified person is the actual culprit.
>
> *(p. 23)*

Kassin (1998) feels that there is an omission from these recommendations. He recommends that the identification parade/line-up and witness identification should be videotaped. This is because records of the line-up are often not carefully kept such that the police and eyewitnesses differ markedly in terms of their recollections of events at the line-up. He points out that police procedures in relation to evidence of various sorts have been subject to a variety of criticisms. For example, in the United Kingdom, the Police and Criminal Evidence Act of 1986 requires that all custodial interviews with crime suspects are taped. This, of course, is primarily to protect individuals against police malpractice.

Relative judgement theory answers the question of how eyewitnesses choose the culprit from a line-up/identity parade. In the absence of the culprit, the theory suggests that the line-up members most similar to the culprit will be picked out. In other words, the eyewitness acts as if the culprit is present and forms a judgement on the best of what they recall of the culprit. No mechanism exists for deciding that the offender is not in the line-up (Wells, 1984). If participants were responding using absolute judgements, then each line-up member would be compared with the memory of the culprit. Then unless the line-up member meets the criteria they will be rejected. Evidence demonstrating the validity of relative judgement theory comes from studies such as that of Wells (1993). In this, some witnesses were shown the line-up including the culprit and others were shown exactly the same line-up with the culprit absent. Despite being told that the culprit may not be present, 54% of those who identified the culprit when the culprit was present would have identified someone else in the culprit's absence! When the offender was present, 21% failed to make a choice but this increased to only 32% when the culprit was actually absent. In other words, mostly when the offender is absent other, innocent, line-up members are chosen.

Obviously a major factor in this is that explicit warnings that the culprit may not necessarily be present substantially reduce wrongful identifications (Malpass and Devine, 1981). They do not affect rightful identifications when the culprit is present.

A number of studies have shown some of the factors that affect relative judgements in real cases. For example, Doob and Kirkenbaum (1973) reported on a Canadian robbery at a department store. The accused was said to be one of two men who had committed the crime. The cashier who witnessed the events recalled that the offenders were neatly dressed, good looking and could be brothers. Despite this somewhat sketchy recollection, she picked out the accused from a line-up. One of Doob and Kirshenbaum's studies had 20 women pick 'a rather good looking man' out of 12 parade participants from the original line-up. The women chose the accused extremely frequently despite not having witnessed the crime. This would appear to be evidence of the unfairness of the system employed.

Similarly, in Poland, Wojcikiewicz *et al.* (2000) were involved in a pertinent court case. The suspect was actually a man of 29 years of age. They were asked by the defence to assess how likely it was that a particular man, from the viewpoint of a 12-year-old rape victim, could be described as being a 40–50-year-old man with a rat-like face. Adult participants in the research did see him as the 29-year-old that he was. However, about a fifth of the children saw the accused as being in the 40–45-year-old age group. Adults described him as having a rat-like face although children did not have a significant tendency to do so. In view of this evidence, it remained possible that the accused was indeed the perpetrator. Nevertheless, the research evidence is indicative of a possible problem and was used in court by the defence.

One way of assessing the likelihood that a person will be susceptible to relative similarity effects when choosing is their performance in the *dual line-up*. This involves an initial (or blank) line-up containing only people known to be innocent followed by a second line-up containing the suspect. Wells (1984) showed that:

- if a witness resists choosing from the blank line-up, it is more likely that they choose accurately in a proper line-up later;

- witnesses who did not go through the blank line-up first were more likely to make mistakes in the second line-up.

Sequential procedures also seem to work better than conventional line-ups. In these, the group of people selected to be in the line-up is shown in sequential fashion – one individual at a time. This makes it much more difficult simply to use a process of elimination in choosing the guilty party (it cannot be a, b or d so it must be c). It is less likely that relative similarity will operate in the sequential line-up (Dunning and Stern, 1994). Another identification method, very common in parts of the United States, is the show-up. This is a single individual which the eyewitness has to identify as the culprit or not. In one sense, this should be better in that a relative judgement cannot be made since there is only one person to decide about. On the other hand, the fact that the police have picked out this individual for the show-up may be strongly suggestive that they regard this individual as the prime suspect.

Steblay *et al.* (2003) carried out a meta-analysis (Box 5.1) of studies which compared the single-person line-up (the show-up) with six person line-ups (these included both sequential and simultaneous versions). Furthermore, both single-person show-ups and six person line-ups included conditions in which the target suspect was present in the majority of the studies. Interestingly, the line-up was much more likely to result in a choice by the eyewitness than the show-up. If the target were present, on average 71% out of 10 line-ups resulted in a choice whereas the figure was only 46% for the show-up. Where the target was absent, 43% of line-ups resulted in a choice as opposed to 15% of show-ups. Correct identification where the target was actually present did not differ between line-ups and show-ups. Around 46% correctly identified the suspect when the suspect was present in either type of identification procedure. Furthermore, when the target is absent, the false identification rate is approximately the same at about 16% for both show-ups and line-ups. What is happening when the eyewitness makes a wrong identification in a target absent line-up is that the errors are spread across all of the foils. This results in a situation in which if one classified all of these latter errors into a non-identification category with other non-identification outcomes, then line-ups show no difference from show-ups in terms of outcomes. It is important to note that those studies in which the foil is more similar to the target resulted in a worse performance in show-ups than in line-ups. False identifications of an innocent foil is more common in show-ups than in line-ups.

The procedures actually employed by police officers when they plan identification line-ups have been investigated by Wogalter, Malpass and McQuiston (in press). Over 200 police jurisdictions in the United States were surveyed about their practices. There were examples of good and bad practice as verified by laboratory studies. Some of the common good practices included:

- Officers tended to choose line-up foils on the basis of upper facial features such as race/ethnic group, facial hair characteristics, colour of hair, and overall shape of face. Whatever the reason why the officers chose to do this, it is important to note that there is a substantial amount of research evidence which suggests that people recall such upper facial features more readily than lower facial features (e.g. shape of the chin).
- Substantial numbers of officers report that they gave witnesses the option of not choosing anyone from the identification line-up though this is known to reduce errors as we saw above. However, very few warned eyewitnesses that facial features may change or that photographs may be of poor or insufficient quality. These factors may affect eyewitness accuracy according to research.

Examples of bad practice included:

- Most respondents (83%) claimed to base their choice of foils in the line-up on their similarity to the suspect. In contrast, only a small number (9%) based their choices of foil on the verbal descriptions provided by eyewitnesses. Research evidence has suggested that there may be problems with the use of similarity to the suspect as a criterion for choosing foils. This may seem to be a strange assertion given it would seem common sense to use identification line-ups of similar looking people. The problem is not in the theory but the practice. What actually happens is that the foils are chosen because of their similarity to the suspect rather than to each other. As a consequence, the suspect stands out because they have characteristics in common with many of the foils but the foils do not look too much like each other. In other words, there is a powerful clue in the situation which encourages the selection of the suspect.

- Generally, assessments about the fairness of the procedures being used by an officer are made by that officer (94%). They also might ask the advice of another officer (77%) or a prosecution lawyer (51%). However, these are not completely independent judgements as they are all on the side of prosecuting the suspect. Asking the advice of the defence lawyer was fairly uncommon (only 15%) although this sort of advice might be regarded as a much more acid test of fairness.

- The use of video line-ups that do not require the direct recruitment of foils was relatively uncommon. But this is the sort of line-up that enables things like the editing out of any biasing behaviours on the part of members of the line-up.

Main points

- Eyewitness testimony is a proven source of wrongful convictions in jurisdictions in which conviction is possible on the basis of such eyewitness evidence alone. Police officers place a great deal of reliance on it. It should not be assumed that eyewitness evidence is without worth. Research has shown that for some types of physical features, eyewitness descriptions can be quite accurate. However, little credence can be placed on the idea that confident eyewitnesses are also accurate eyewitnesses.

- Memory can be influenced by a range of factors and there is evidence to show that memory can be affected by later events and questioning style. Much of the pertinent research tends to come from laboratory studies, which can be problematic to apply to real-life situations with precision. For example, it is difficult to generalise the effects of time of exposure to the witnessed event from the laboratory to real-life settings for very mundane reasons such as exposure times in laboratory studies are a fraction of the time that a real-life eyewitness observes the offender for.

- The planning of the line-up or identification parade should proceed with care as there are many pitfalls. There is evidence that police line-ups may sometimes reflect good practice but sometimes bad practices prevail – for example, it is much more common to choose the foils (stooges) in a line-up on the basis of their similarity to the suspect whereas good practice holds that they should be like the eyewitness's description of the offender. In line-ups, eyewitnesses tend to identify someone who is like their memory of the offender even when the offender is not present in the line-up. This is in accordance with the theory of relative judgement. Factors that may improve eyewitness performance in line-ups include informing the eyewitness that the person administering the line-up does not know who the suspect is and making sure that that person indeed does not know who the suspect is.

Chapter 13

Profile analysis

Overview

- Offender profiling dates back to the nineteenth-century case of Jack the Ripper though its modern origins are in the work of the Behavioural Science Unit of the FBI located in Virginia in the 1970s. This form of profiling is based on clinical intuition whereas more recent approaches have been more research-based and statistical in nature.

- Offending profiling of all sorts is based on the work of the police in gathering information especially from the scene of the crime. Most homicides are seen by police officers as 'self-solvers' in that the witness evidence points to the culprit or the culprit reports their crime to the police, for example. Obviously, offender profiling would only help where the police have problems identifying suspects and organising the information collected.

- FBI style offender profiling is based on information recorded by the police. This is used to classify the crime scene into organised (where there is evidence that the crime has been carefully planned) or disorganised (where the crime scene looks chaotic and there is little sign of preparation for the crime). It is held that organised and disorganised crime scenes indicate some broad characteristics of the offender. An organised crime scene suggests, for example, a sexually competent, charming person who lives with a partner. The disorganised crime scene is indicative of an offender with low intelligence, unskilled occupation and who lives alone.

- The actuarial or statistical approach to offender profiling is most closely associated with the work of David Canter. His approach is set within the broader framework of investigative psychology. Increasingly, offender profiling has been applied to a wide variety of crimes beyond the initial FBI focus (serial sexual homicides and rape) such as arson and property crimes. Nevertheless, the statistical approach to offender profiling is built on the assumption that patterns in crime scenes may be linked to characteristics of the offender. However, the patterns in the crime scenes are sought using empirical evidence of what crime scene characteristics tend to co-occur together.

- Statistical profiling uses statistical techniques such as smallest space analysis in order to plot the relationships between crime scene characteristics on a diagram or plot. The crime scene characteristics that tend to co-occur most frequently are physically close together on the plot. Characteristics that are common in crime scenes are at the centre of the plot, those that are relatively uncommon in crime scenes are at the periphery of the plot. The researcher then identifies the major segments of the plot and identifies their linking characteristics.

- Generally, there has been little success using standard psychological measures of personality when assessing the relationship between the crime scene and offender characteristics. This is a different issue from whether or not there is a criminal personality which is different from normal personality.

- Currently, considerable research attention is devoted to the statistical profiling of crime. There seems to be less interest in evaluating profiling in the context of actual police work. The evidence of the effectiveness of profiling is varied. It would seem that the police like it and value it although it seldom is the basis for an arrest. What seems to be important is what the profiler contributes to dealing with the mass of information available to the police and in providing the police with advice that facilitates other aspects of the policing process.

Offender profiling uses information gleaned from the crime scene in order to identify the characteristics of the offender. Controversy surrounds offender profiling for several reasons:

- Its nature – is it and should it be art or science?
- The paucity of evidence that profiling is effective.
- The role of profiling in police work.
- Its high profile in the public imagination through media attention.

In profiling work there is a marked disparity of opinion between two extremes. One extreme holds profiling is akin to clinical research – informed by research but inevitably a subjective matter dependent on the insight and skill of the profiler. The other extreme regards that profiling must be led by research and aspire to objectivity.

Crime fiction is littered with numerous insightful, subjective profilers who make amazing interpretations of evidence. Remarkable deductions lead inexorably to the culprit. Fictional detectives have incredible insight into the psychological motives behind crime. It might be mentioned that the great fictional detective Sherlock Holmes was inclined to make statements redolent of the ideas of offender profiles. A good example is that a criminal returns to the scene of the crime – which is echoed in the writings of modern profilers (Canter, 2004). Modern movies and television are replete with psychological detectives adroit in the psychology of the criminal mind. Much of this media coverage has produced somewhat hostile responses from psychologists concerned about what they see to be extremely weak psychology (e.g. Williams, 1994).

According to Canter (2004), offender profiling probably has its origins in 1888 when Dr Thomas Bond provided what might be regarded as a profile of Jack the Ripper. Bond was of the opinion that

[t]he murderer must have been a man of physical strength and great coolness and daring. There is no evidence he had an accomplice. He must in my opinion be a man subject to periodic attacks of homicidal and erotic mania . . . The murderer in external appearance is quite likely to be a quiet inoffensively looking man probably middle-aged and neatly and respectably dressed. Assuming the murderer

be such a person as I have just described, he would be solitary and eccentric in his habits, also he is likely to be a man without regular occupation, but with some small income or pension.

(cited in Canter, 2004, p. 2)

Canter suggests that the profile of The Ripper provided by Dr Bond is remarkably similar to profiles of sexual murderers in recent times.

The modern origins of offender profiling in psychology are usually traced back to 1956 and the work of the psychiatrist James A. Brussel into the New York Bomber crimes of that time. Brussel, basing his theorising on psychoanalysis, studied the crime scene. Based on his assessment of this, Brussel gave a description of the bomber containing the following features:

- heavy;
- middle-aged;
- male;
- single;
- living with a sibling.

This is held by some to be a convincingly accurate picture of George Metesky who was eventually convicted of the crime. He was actually living with two siblings but this is held to be of little consequence. Brussel, at first sight, had demonstrated the power of psychological approaches to detective work. Accounts vary but some reports claim that Metesky was arrested in connection with another crime and the profile was not used by the police. Nevertheless, the case demonstrates another feature of offender profiling – the seemingly mysterious nature of the profile. Just how can this information be gleaned simply on the basis of the characteristics of the crime scene?

The more direct origins of offender profiling lie in seminal work at the US Federal Bureau of Investigation's Academy, Quantico, Virginia. This housed, in a nuclear bunker, the Behavioral Science Unit that, to this day, provides research, consultation and training in the application of psychology and the other social sciences to crime and detective work. During the 1970s, the unit began to research the personality, behaviours, crimes and motivations of serial killers showing sexual aspects in their crimes. This formed much of the research base for their method of profiling (Douglas *et al.*, 1992). The term 'serial killer' is held to be an innovation of members of the Unit. It should be stressed that there may well be serial killers who do not show sexual elements in their crime. For example, a bank robber may kill on several different raids yet it would be difficult to identify this as being in any way sexually motivated. The FBI investigators defined serial homicide as 'three or more separate events in three or more separate locations with an emotional cooling off period in between homicides (Douglas *et al.*, 1992, p. 21).' Ferguson *et al.* (2003) argue that there is a lack of an agreed definition of serial murder that makes progress in the field difficult. He rejects the idea put forward by Douglas *et al.* (1992) that serial killers seek to express their need for power since it could be argued that every crime is an expression of power. Instead, Ferguson *et al.* suggest the following three elements are crucial to the definition of serial (sexual) murder:

- Three or more victims killed during multiple and discrete events.
- Causing death to the victim, at the time of the killing, was considered to be pleasurable, stress relieving, or otherwise consistent with the perpetrator's internal set of values. The attacks themselves did not fulfill only functional purposes.

- The murders did not occur under the discretion or blessing of any political or criminal organisation. (p. 4)

Notice that this definition does not necessarily define the crime as sexual. However, it is questionable whether it achieves a great deal other than excluding the serial killings that occur for reasons of gain, for example.

In strict social scientific terms, the methodology employed by the FBI team in order to develop their ideas about serial killing was not the most rigorous. However, it not only involved the collation of research findings but also drew on the Unit's collective experience in developing offender profiling. Indeed, one of the most remarkable things is the extent to which so much developed out of a study of just 36 offenders.

This form of profiling is still practised today – crime scene profiling. Several popular accounts of the work of ex-FBI profilers have been published (e.g. Douglas and Olshaker, 1995, 1997; Ressler and Shachtman, 1997). The FBI style of profiling is presented more as a 'special art' (Canter, 2004) rather than a scientific endeavour. FBI profiling's main features are as follows:

- A willingness to encompass experience and intuition as a component of profiling.
- A relatively weak empirical database which is small in comparison to the extent to which the method is used.
- A concentration on the more serious, bizarre and extreme crimes such as serial sexual murder.
- It tends to involve an extensive contact with the investigating team of police officers at all levels of the investigation rather than simply providing a profile. For example, the profiler may make recommendations on how to respond to letters and similar communications from what appears to be the offender.

The next major step in the development of offender profiling is much more European in location. This approach could be termed statistical or actuarial offender profiling. This approach is associated with Professor David Canter (e.g. Canter and Alison, 1999) who downplays the need for an intuitive or subjective input into profiling. The main features of the statistical approach are as follows:

- A greater emphasis on the need for a research base for profiling.
- A statistical approach to the relationship between crime scene evidence and offender characteristics.
- A rejection of clinical intuition as an important aspect of profiling.
- A willingness to encompass a greater range of crimes in profiling than the FBI profilers had.

Much of Canter's work in this area is classifiable as offender profiling. Aspects of his work are more accurately described as investigative psychology, which includes

the effective utilisation of police information, through interviews and from police records, as well (as) the study of police investigations and decision support systems.

(Canter, 2004, p. 7)

Canter, and Youngs (2004), describe investigative psychology as the systematic, scientific study of: (a) investigative information, its retrieval, evaluation and utilisation; (b) police actions and decisions, their improvement and support; and (c) the inferences that can be made about criminal activity. Its development, differentiation

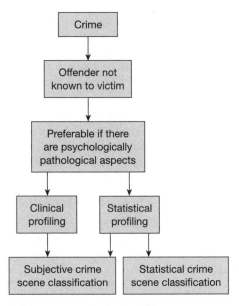

Figure 13.1 Features of FBI versus statistical profiling

and prediction. The objective is to improve criminal and civil investigations (p. 177). Thus investigative psychology includes profiling but has a wider scope.

Figure 13.1 provides a schematic overview of offender profiling. Some profilers would dispute certain points. What sorts of crime should be profiled? This may be decided on a number of bases:

- There is little point profiling trivial crimes since they are unlikely to be actively investigated because of their relatively trivial nature. Similarly, there is little point in profiling a crime that shows few distinguishing characteristics at the crime scene.
- Are the investigating officers unaware of a likely offender? Frequently, offenders are friends or family members of the victim. Thus there is an obvious pool of possible suspects without even considering strangers.
- Profile analysis is especially appropriate if the crime scene indicates pathological psychological features. For instance, objects may be found inserted in the victim's genitals or even body parts taken as 'trophies'. Nevertheless, some psychologists consider that crimes lacking such bizarre features may also be suitable for profiling. Increasingly, profiling is carried out for crimes that traditionally would not be regarded as particularly suitable of profiling (e.g. fraud).

The process of police investigation

Profiling is seen as an adjunct to the police investigation process. Innes (2002) carried out a qualitative study of how the police in an English police force investigated homicides. The national clear-up rate for homicide is very high with approximately 90% of cases being 'solved'. This is less than surprising since most homicides are committed by associates of the victim. Nevertheless, there may be problems in solving some crimes that often lie in the complex set of events involving a number of people which culminates in the murder. This can make it difficult to know precisely who did what and the reasons for this. The police make an informal distinction between cases which are 'self-solvers' and those that might be termed 'whodunnits'. Different processes of investigation would be involved in the case of the self-solvers from that of the 'whodunnit'. Something like 70% of cases of homicide could be classified as self-solvers. A suspect emerges very early because there are witnesses, or the offender goes to the police, or the physical forensic evidence points to a particular individual. However, these are not always easy cases – they can be highly emotive – and deconstructing the events to provide a 'coherent, explanatory account' (p. 672) taxing. Often self-solving cases are investigated using a three stage approach:

- The collection and analysis of information from the crime scene.
- Pursuing lines of enquiry relevant to the suspect. Such as a formal interview with the suspect, tracing and interviewing witnesses who may have seen the suspect with the victim earlier, inquiries from neighbours, and inquiries into the family background.
- Case construction: selecting and organising the material into an account of the events which is appropriate to the needs of the legal system and presented in appropriate legal language. For example, it can be important to carefully define the events as murder or manslaughter in the UK.

The 'whodunnit' investigation is somewhat more complex and involves five stages:

- The initial response: the primary task is to deal with the evidence available at the crime scene. Witnesses are interviewed and the area of the crime scene subjected to a systematic search for forensic evidence.
- Information burst: the police quickly generate substantial amounts of information. There may be a variety of sources which includes interviews with the immediate relatives of the victim and ex-partners, business associates, and local house-to-house inquiries. Other sources include criminal intelligence resources to identify the victim's criminal connections. A number of suspects might be arrested and released without charge on the basis of having committed similar crimes in the past.
- Suspect development: the police proceed to elicit more detail about possible suspects. Some suspects may be dropped at this stage and others may come under suspicion as the evidence becomes clearer. A prime suspect is being sought even on the basis of hunches.
- Suspect targeting: once other suspects have been eliminated or a prime suspect has been identified, the police will change their approach and start targeting this particular individual in terms of their information gathering.
- Case construction: this is the stage at which the police attempt to formulate an account of the events of the homicide in a way that is in keeping with legal considerations.

FBI profiling

There are several stages in a Federal Bureau of Investigation profile.

Box 13.1

Key concepts: defining terms

Profile analysis: 'Behaviour is exhibited at a crime, or a series of similar crimes, and studying this behaviour allows inferences to be made about the likely offender' (Jackson and Bekerian, 1997, p. 2). Jackson and Bekerian suggest that profile analysis includes offender profiling, psychological profiling, criminal profiling and criminal personality profiling.

According to Homant and Kennedy (1998), the following three types of profiling should be carefully distinguished among others:

- Crime scene profiling: uses information from the scene of the crime (physical and other evidence) to generate a full picture of the unknown offender.
- Psychological profiling: the use of standard personality tests together with interviewing in order to assess the extent to which the individual fits the known personality template of a certain type of offender such as child sex abusers.
- Offender profiling: the collection of empirical data in order to collate a picture of the characteristics of those involved in a certain type of crime.

Terminology is not always rigorously applied in this field and other terms are used to refer to much the same type. For example:

- Specific profile analysis: '. . . constructing a hypothetical picture of a perpetrator of a crime on the basis of data from the scene of the crime, witness statements and other available information' (Davies, 1997, p. 191).

Stage 1: Data assimilation stage

The earliest stage of FBI profiling involves the collection of a variety of information as seen in Figure 13.2. A crime usually has a variety of associated documentary materials: for example, the pathologist's report about the medical circumstances that led to death, photographs taken at the crime scene, witness statements and police reports and so forth. This information may not appear at first sight to be of any value at all. Nevertheless, there is always the potential for unpromising materials to be

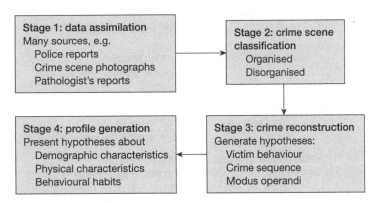

Figure 13.2 Major stages of FBI crime scene profiling

crucial in terms of the ultimate profile. The time of death, for example, may have an important implication for the psychology of the offender. Basically, the process is one of seeking to identify the psychological signature of the offender. This psychological signature is different from the modus operandi – the latter broadly refers to the style of committing the crime. It is the characteristic way in which that particular criminal works. The psychological signature concerns what can be gleaned from the crime scene about the personality of the offender. This is most likely to include the fantasies of the offender.

Stage 2: Crime scene classification

Remember that serial sexual murders are the most important crimes profiled by the FBI psychologists. Profilers developed a dichotomy to describe two characteristic crime scenes – the *organised* and the *disorganised* crime scenes.

- Organised = evidence of planning.
- Disorganised = chaotic.

The organised/disorganised crime scene classification was based on offenders' reports of their crimes in the early study by profilers (Douglas *et al.*, 1992). The two types of crime scene reveal different aspects of the psychology of the offender. Table 13.1 gives examples of the relationships based on Holmes and Holmes (1996). Notice that they extend into matters such as interview techniques. Gierowski *et al.* (1998, 2000) studied 120 murderers classified by their crime scenes as planned or not planned. This appears to be very similar to the FBI profilers' dichotomy of the organised versus disorganised. The factors associated with a planned crime include the choice of weapon and how death was inflicted, the location and time at which the crime occurred, and other aspects intended to hide the identity of the culprit. Disordered socialisation factors (e.g. inconsistent upbringing methods and running away from home) were associated with the organised crime scene. Organised crime scene offenders had frequent changes of sexual partners, were low on alcoholism and showed evidence of psychopathy. They also tended to have higher regard for their personal appearance.

Table 13.1 The relationship between crime scene type and aspects of investigation

	Organised non-social offender	Disorganised asocial offender
Personal characteristics	Sexually competent Lives with partner Has charm	Low intelligence Unskilled Lives alone Poor personal hygiene
Post-offence behaviour	May move body Police 'groupie'/follower	May turn religious May change job
Recommended interview technique	Use direct strategy Be accurate about details	Show empathy Interview at night

(Source: Holmes and Holmes, 1996)

Stage 3: Crime scene reconstruction

The crime scene is not a simple fixed event. Instead, it is the result of a complex set of circumstances. Consequently, there are aspects of the crime scene that cannot be understood unless attempts are made to understand the events as a dynamic process involving a minimum of two people – offender and victim. There may be witnesses, actual or potential, to consider. The information collected in *Stage 1* is essential to the reconstruction. Inference and deduction are involved. Reconstruction does not have to involve playing out the events as in a television reconstruction. The purpose of the reconstruction may be to clarify the offender's modus operandi. Knowing this may help tie the crime to other crimes. The sequence of events (for example, where there are signs that the victim was stalked) would be considered. Also, could the victim's response have affected the offender (for example, if she fought and struggled then this may have affected the offender's ability to act out his fantasies)?

Stage 4: Profile generation

Hypotheses about the profile of the offender are drawn together. These hypotheses are not necessarily psychological in nature and may include, for example, demographic features (social class, type of work, employment/unemployment), lifestyle (such as living alone, being in a relationship), behavioural habits (e.g. poor at mixing socially, solitary hobbies) and personality dynamics (e.g. offending linked to depression).

In FBI offender profiling, there are a number of possible functions of the profile. Obviously, helping police improve the efficiency of information processing by suggesting features of the offender which would narrow the search is a major one. Another function of profiling is to help answer questions of links between a series of crimes and the possible number of different offenders involved. Linking crimes to offenders in this way means that information and resources can be pooled by different police teams investigating seemingly unconnected crimes.

An example of FBI profiling

Characteristically, it is quite difficult to explain exactly how a profile emerges out of the different inputs available. FBI profilers have rarely, if ever, made totally clear the inferential processes involved and there is plainly a degree of subjectivity inherent in the method. Some insight into profiling can be obtained by comparing the inputs with the actual profile. The following case is reported in detail in Ressler *et al.* (1988):

- A nude female's body was found at 3.00 p.m. on the roof of the apartment block where she lived.
- She had left home for work at 6.30 in the morning.
- She was 26 years of age, 90 pounds in weight, her spine was deformed and she was not dating men.
- Both of her nipples had been removed and placed upon her body.
- Her face was severely beaten.
- She had been throttled with the strap of her bag.

- A blunt instrument had caused many face fractures.
- Virtually all items used came from the victim's bag.
- The phrase 'You can't stop me' was written in ink on her inner thigh and 'Fuck you' on her torso.
- The pendant that she usually wore was missing.
- The victim's underwear had been taken down and pulled over her face.
- Her stockings were tied around her ankles and wrists but very loosely.
- A pen and an umbrella were inserted into her vagina.
- A comb was stuck in her pubic hair.
- There was no semen in the victim's vagina. The offender had ejaculated over her body from a standing position.
- There were bite marks on her thighs and various bruises/lacerations all over.
- Faeces from the murderer were very close by. They were covered with the victim's clothes.
- There was no evidence of similar crimes being carried out in the area.

This is obviously an incomplete account of the information available. Nevertheless, there is enough, perhaps, to form an impression of the murderer.

The psychological profile developed included the following major features:

- A white man.
- Aged between 25 and 35 years – similar in age to the victim.
- Sexual fantasies have been harboured by the offender for a long time and he possibly uses and collects sadistic pornography.
- He would fit into the context well – might reside in apartment or could be employed there.
- Average intelligence but dropped out of education.
- No military background.
- Possibly unemployed.
- Unskilled or skilled occupation.
- Alcohol and drugs were not material factors in the crime.
- Difficulties in personal relationships with women.
- Any dates would be younger so that they could be more easily controlled and dominated.
- Sexually inexperienced and inadequate.
- Never married.
- Disorganised offender – confused and perhaps mental difficulties in the past.

So what is it about the information we saw earlier about the crime scene and the associated information that leads to the profile above? The answer is that at least some of the profile can be understood in the light of the following considerations:

- Killers tend to be similar in terms of age and race to their victim.
- Fantasy tends to be embedded at the core of such extreme cases. The crime may be the result of the offender using the fantasy as a plan or blueprint for offending. Extreme cases such as this are substantially founded on fantasy, which serves as a guide for the crime. Thus the contents of the fantasy may be seen in the characteristics of the offence. Hence the sadistic nature of this crime is indicative

of the contents of the offender's sadistic fantasy. Keeping a pendant as a 'trophy' indicates that the offender has a need to fantasise in the future.

- There is little evidence that this crime was prepared for – except in fantasy. The crime scene was disorganised. The offender used whatever was to hand in the course of the crime: things were taken from the victim's bag.
- Although the crime was clearly sexual in nature, the offender used substitutes for sexual penetration. This suggests that he had sexual inadequacies. Consequently, the likelihood is that he lacked sexual experience and had never married.
- The offence has elements of control and domination, thus explaining his choice of victim.
- That the offender defecated near the crime scene indicates that the offence took place over a lengthy time period. Remember, though, that the murderer was in an exposed location and there was a great risk that he might be seen. One explanation linking these features together is that the killer is very familiar with that locality. Perhaps he is an employee or resident in that area.

Once this profile was available to the police, they studied their investigation records. They found a prime suspect – a man whose father lived in the apartments. Although they had been led to believe that the man was in mental hospital, it was discovered that security there was not perfect. He was convicted on the evidence of the bite marks on the body which matched his dental pattern.

Studies that have investigated the nature of profiles reveal a number of problems. In a nutshell, the profiles lack justification for the claims and assertions made about the offender based on the profiler's analysis. In the United Kingdom, the Association of Chief Police Officers have required that the profiler must explain the thinking behind their claims in the profile. Alison *et al.* (2003a,b) obtained a selection of real offender profiles largely from the United Kingdom and the United States. Using a systematic coding scheme, they analysed the 3,090 statements found in these profiles. The vast majority of the statements were merely reiterations of facts that were already known to the police, statements about the profiler's professional competence, or statements about the limitations of the use of the profile. This left only 28% which were profiles of the offender. Mostly these were unsubstantiated claims (82% of the 28%). About 16% provided some justification for the statement being made. A further 1% were simply illogical.

Statistical/actuarial profiling

The statistical or actuarial approach to offender profiling operates differently. In some ways it is a simpler approach. The statistical model is illustrated in Figure 13.3, which is based on the data of House (1997). Once again, the assumption is that features of the crime scene contain evidence of salient behaviours. These then reveal the distinguishing features or characteristics of the offender. In this way, it is similar

Figure 13.3 The statistical approach to profiling

to FBI profiling. The essential difference between statistical profiling and FBI profiling is that the former concentrates on establishing the relationships empirically using special statistical techniques. In a sense, this is a stripped-down version of the FBI approach but there is more to it than that. Statistical profiling is based on its own distinct ethos despite the overlaps between the two. It is much more empirical without the intuitive or clinical insight components.

There are a number of issues that manifest themselves much more clearly in statistical profiling than the FBI approach:

- How best can the crime scene be classified? This really refers to two distinct things: (a) the information that is collected about the crime scene and (b) whether there are features of certain crime scenes which warrant them being classified as being of a particular type, grouping or cluster.
- Do these types, groupings or clusters of crime scenes reveal psychological and other features of the offender?
- What degree of stability is there in the crime scenes of individual offenders? Will an offender leave similar patterns behind at a crime? To what extent do these patterns remain stable and consistent over time?

There is no full and definitive answer to these questions.

In the statistical approach, the classification of crime scenes is empirically based, using statistical methods such as smallest space analysis. This is a method of identifying just how likely features of crime scenes are to exist and coexist with another feature at a particular crime scene. Take the following features of rapes:

Apologises
Binding limbs
Clothing removed
Disguise
Element of surprise
Fellatio of the offender
Gratuitous violence
Humiliation
Inquisitive
Kisses
Multiple violence
Offender confident
Reassures victim
Sex language – victim
Sodomy
Takes time
Theft of money
Theft of personal belongings
Torture
Use of blindfold
Vaginal penetration
Verbal aggression

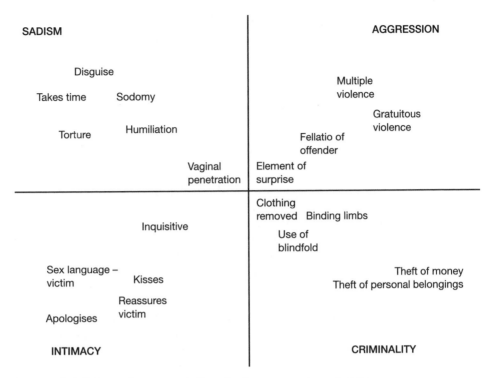

Figure 13.4 Schematic representation of crime scene characteristics

Some of these features are very common in rape (e.g. vaginal penetration is practically universal in rapes of women) whereas others are quite rare (e.g. cunnilingus). Some of the behaviours frequently occur together if they occur in a rape; other behaviours are rarely found together. House (1997) analysed the co-occurrence and frequency of these behaviours in rapes. The statistical analysis produced a pattern shown stylistically in Figure 13.4. This gives a visual representation of a smallest space analysis of data on the above and other characteristics of rape crime scenes. Vaginal penetration, the element of surprise and clothing removed are central in the diagram – this indicates that they are very common features of rape. As such they are not very useful for differentiating between different types of rape crime scene:

- Characteristics at the extremities of the diagram such as the rapist apologises are relatively rare in rapes.
- Characteristics that are close together occur together relatively often, such as theft of the victim's money and theft of the victim's personal property. Theft of the victim's money and sodomy rarely occur together. This is shown by the distance between them.

Also notice that labels have been given to the characteristics in the four different quarters of the diagram – sadism, aggression, intimacy and criminality – which seem to reflect the major integrative themes underlying the pattern of associations among characteristics. This is as if there are several major themes in rape – a variety of scripts for carrying out rape.

One practical implication of House's work is his finding that the type of rape is associated with the offender's past criminal history:

- The sadistic group were less likely to have an arrest and conviction history; the criminality group were the most likely to have been imprisoned (they are committing other types of crime alongside the rape, after all, as can be seen from Figure 13.4).
- The sadism and intimacy groups tended to be low on convictions for property crime; the sadistic group were the least likely to have convictions for violence.
- The sadism and intimacy groups were the most likely to have convictions for deception.

One potential application of this is that it might help prioritise searches of offender databases in the hunt for possible suspects for a rape attack. If rapists commonly have a criminal record and these records contain good quality information, then there may be something to be gained from searching the criminal records. This would merely help manage routine police work of interviewing, record keeping and so forth more effectively. It could never in itself prove that a particular individual is the rapist – unless, of course, there is a record of his DNA that matches the new crime scene sample.

While this is interesting and does point to some characteristics of the offender, it is desirable to extend this sort of analysis to include indications of the relationship between the major crime scene 'scripts' and the psychological and other character-istics of the offender. Salfati and Canter (1998) examined the relationship between murder crime scenes and the murderer's characteristics. They used methods much like those described by House (1997). A major hypothesis was that the murderers would show similar modes of interaction during the homicide as in much of the rest of their lives.

A sample of 82 British homicides in which a single offender attacked a stranger was studied. These were murders in which the police did not know the assailant at the time of the discovery of the crime. Although these are described as stranger murders, this is something of a misnomer. Seventy-four per cent of the offenders knew the victim at least slightly. Information about the crimes was drawn from police records. Some 48 variables were extracted from these records. Broadly speaking, they fell into the following categories:

- Things or actions done by the offender to the victim.
- Traces of behaviours left at the crime scene.
- Information reflected characteristics of the offender.
- Characteristics of the victim.

There were a number of informative features of the crimes:

- The victims averaged 45 years of age with a range of 1 to 70 years.
- Offenders were much younger with an average age of 27 years and a range of 15 to 49 years.
- Mostly the offenders were male (72%) and the victims female (55%).
- Mostly the victims were left at the place of death (76%).
- Mostly the homicide had taken place in the evening (66%).
- Nearly half of victims were found in their own home (44%).
- Few (12%) involved sexual elements.

- The majority of offenders (79%) were local or familiar with the area in which the crime occurred.
- Unemployment was common in offenders (41%).
- About half of offenders were married or cohabiting (48%).
- A further 23% had previously been married.
- 12% of offenders had served in the armed forces.
- Imprisonment was common in the histories of offenders (40%) with the commonest previous offences being theft (22%), burglary (18%) and violence against people (15%).

Box 13.2

Key concepts: facet theory and smallest space analysis

Shye and Elizur (1994) and Borg and Shye (1995) provide excellent and detailed summaries of facet theory and Canter (1983) describes its role in psychology. Canter (1983) explains how the use of facet theory requires the researcher to abandon many of the ideas which are held dear by psychologists. In particular, it involves the exploration of the area being researched thoroughly rather than quickly and developing a simple hypothesis which can be tested using simple tests of statistical significance. Those who can act on the findings of research (policy makers of all sorts) are usually only concerned about things under their control. Isolating factors in a situation (variables) one from another may be part of psychologists' training, but policy makers may be much more concerned with the total situation. Furthermore, Canter believes that facet theory allows the researcher to explore the definition of concepts at a theoretical level so eschewing the tendency of researchers to define concepts operationally by reference to the measurement procedure and other similar measures of similar concepts. He stresses that facet theory is a broad method for research – it should not be regarded as a narrow measurement technique or way of analysing data.

Consequently, there are a number of ideas that need to be understood a little before one can begin to appreciate the role of facet theory in crime scene analysis which tries to assess the psychological characteristics of the offender from characteristics of the crime scene. Facet theory can be used to relate crime scenes with offender characteristics:

- What is a facet? In facet theory, any domain of interest is a complex system. Research can only partially sample this system. Variables are seen as continuous throughout the system in facet theory. Each variable has other variables that differ only slightly from that variable and other variables. This is just like the faces or facets of a diamond, which are just one view of that thing that is the diamond. The same diamond can be cut in many ways and each facet is merely one of many minutely different ones that might have been cut.
- In crime scene analysis, the presence of multiple stabbing of the victim, for example, in itself fails to capture the fullness of the crime scene. Bloodiness, depth of penetration, the multiplicity of weapons used and other variables would be needed to capture crime scene ferocity more completely.
- Shye and Elizur (1994) describe a facet as 'A set playing the role of a component set of a Cartesian set' (p. 179). Cartesian means that facets can be represented in terms of a physical space. Usually, it implies the use of axes at right angles to each other. Put this way, a scattergram or scattergraph

▶

would represent the position of individuals in a two-dimensional physical space defined by the horizontal and vertical axes. In terms of crime scene analysis, the two axes might be:

- Amount of effort by offender to hide own identity (rated on a scale from very high to high to fairly high to fairly low to low to very low).
- Amount of effort by offender to hide the identity of victim (rated on a scale from very high to high to fairly high to fairly low to low to very low).

Crime scenes could be rated on these facets and each crime scene represented on a scattergram by a single point. This would roughly correspond to the Cartesian approach. The analogy is with a map and facet theorists speak of mapping.

- The matrix below takes a simple case of three murders A, B and C and four different characteristics of the crimes such as whether they took place at night.

	Murder A	Murder B	Murder C
Multiple weapons	1	1	2
Sexual humiliation	1	1	2
Night-time	2	1	2
Victim left naked	1	1	2
1 = yes, 2 = no			

It is obvious that there are patterns in this matrix – Murders A and B are similar in terms of the presence of three of the four characteristics, whereas Murder C is rather different. One step onwards is to produce a matrix of the correspondence of the four facets across the three murders in order to see what sorts of thing tend to occur together. So, if we consider Multiple weapons and Sexual humiliation, the three different murders show complete agreement as to whether these things co-occurred or not. There is a match for these variables on the three murders so there is a score of 3 entered into the table.

	Multiple weapons	Sexual humiliation	Night-time	Victim left naked
Multiple weapons				
Sexual humiliation	3			
Night-time	2	2		
Victim left naked	3	3	2	

Night-time and Multiple weapons match twice over the three murders so 2 is entered as the amount of match or similarity between Night-time and Multiple weapons in the table.

Each of these numerical values (similarity scores if you like) can be represented in space. The Cartesian basis of the approach comes into play here. It is not quite like drawing a scattergram since we do not know where the axes should be. Nevertheless, the information in the above table can be represented in physical space. All that we know is how close or distant the points representing the table would be. Three of the four facets (Multiple weapons, Sexual humiliation and Victim left naked) are at the identical point in space. The remaining facet (Night-time) is 1 away from a complete match with the other three facets (according to the data in the table). We can arbitrarily place any of the facets and plot all of the other facets in relation to it. This plotting would look something like this:

In this simple example, Multiple weapons, Sexual humiliation and Victim left naked all lie at the same point in space – there is no difference between them and they match perfectly. Only Night-time fails to match completely with the other three. The maximum match for this and the other three variables is 2 so it is different by just 1.

It may take several dimensions in order to reproduce the case. Take for purposes of illustration this little puzzle: Greater Aston, Middle Aston and Little Aston are three different villages. Each of them is four miles by foot as the crow flies from each other. You can probably work out that the three villages would look like they were at the points of an equilateral triangle on a map. The sides of the triangle are four miles long each. There is another village – Great Spires – that is three miles exactly from each of the other three villages. How can that be? Well the answer has to be that either Great Spires is on the top of a hill in the middle of the other three villages, or that it is in a valley with the other three on the ridge above. In other words, the first three villages can be represented by a two-dimensional map (a triangle is two-dimensional) but the four villages require an extra dimension to represent their relative distances from each other.

Statistical techniques, in an analogous way, can plot a multitude of distances or differences into Cartesian space. We need not know precisely how it is done and it is best left to computer programs. There are numerous techniques available. They are all built on indexes of similarity or closeness or correlation between the variables. In the case of crime scene analysis, they are based on whether Variable A and Variable B tend to occur *together* at different crime scenes. This is then extended to include the relationships between *all* possible pairs of crime scene variables. This can be expressed as a matrix of similarity or a matrix of correlation. Smallest space analysis (often just referred to as SSA in research publications) is one of the statistical techniques available that will represent matrices of similarity or correlation matrices in multi-dimensional space. As mentioned earlier, this process is known as mapping. One important question is that of how many dimensions? 1, 2, 3, more? (Yes it is possible to have more.) The computer programs doing smallest space analysis will produce the best outcome they can for the number of dimensions specified by the researcher. If the researcher wants a two-dimensional plot then that is what they should request from the computer. The computer gives something called the coefficient of alienation. This is simply an index of how well, say, the two-dimensional plot fits the data. If the coefficient is zero then this means that the data fit the two-dimensional plot perfectly. The poorer the fit, the greater the need for more dimensions. There is something of a trade-off between the adequacy of the plot and how useful it is for most analysts.

What emerges is a two-dimensional map. On this map are placed the attributes of a crime scene. The closer two attributes are to each other then the more likely they are to coexist at the crime scene. Attributes that are common to crime scenes tend to be at the centre of the map. The more central, the more crime scenes they are found at. The figure illustrates this using a few facets of a crime scene.

▶

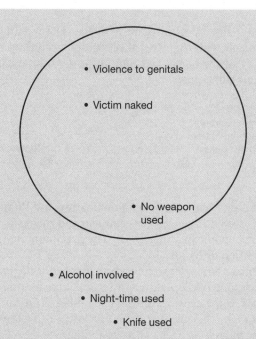

             • Alcohol involved

               • Night-time used

                • Knife used

This (imaginary) plot tells us the following:

- Where a knife is used it is likely to be night-time and that alcohol is involved since these three things tend to be close together on the plot.
- That typically no weapons are used in the murders (since No weapon used is close to the centre of the plot).
- Where the victim is naked and there are signs of violence to the genitals, then it is unlikely to find a knife used.

The researcher is also likely to segregate or partition the plot into sectors, largely subjectively, in order to identify the broad types of crime scene. This is somewhat difficult with the simple example above but one obvious sector consists of the murder crime scenes with a sexual component. That is, lines would be drawn (usually from the centre) to enclose the aspects of crime scenes that are sexual in nature (i.e. a naked victim, violence to the genitals). Examination of real analyses will demonstrate the value of this better.

Using smallest space analysis (Box 13.2), the researchers found three major groups of crime. These were classified as instrumental opportunistic, instrumental cognitive and expressive impulsive. Two thirds of the homicides could be classified fairly readily into one of the three categories. Very approximately, a third of the classifiable crimes fell into each of the three. Each of the themes had different typical offender characteristics. Table 13.2 gives the major crime scene characteristics and the associated offender characteristics. This is impressive but with one caveat – just how well can offender characteristics be predicted from the crime scene? Just how useful is the analysis in police work? What does it tell the police about where to search for the offender? How effective will this search be?

Table 13.2 The relationship between crime scene theme and offender characteristics

Crime theme	Crime scene characteristics	Corresponding offender characteristics
Instrumental opportunistic	Face hidden Sexual Partially undressed Manual attack Neck attacked Female victims Old victims Multiple wounds in one area Premises of the victim	Previous offences for theft Previous offences for burglary Previous vehicle theft offences Having previously come to police notice Unemployed Familiar with the area of the crime Knew victim
Instrumental cognitive	Body transported Body hidden Body carefully placed Blunt instrument Face up	Served in the armed services Served a prison sentence
Expressive impulsive	Slash/cut Single wound Weapon taken to scene and also removed Limbs attacked Torso attacked Multiple wounds all over body	Previous violent offences Previous offences for public disorder Previous offences for damage to property Previous sexual offences Previous traffic offences Previous drugs offences Married at the time of the offence Previous marriage Female offender

Mostly these questions cannot be answered at the present time. Most statistical profiling remains research-based with no direct input into the conduct of police investigations. So, in that sense, it is not known if such profiling could enhance police work. The potential is there. Actual success may be an issue for the future. Statistical profiling does recognise better than FBI profiling that relationships are only probabilities and not certainties. Thus an instrumental cognitive crime scene merely indicates that the offender has an enhanced probability of having served in the armed forces.

Box 13.3

Forensic psychology in action: profiling past crimes

Davies (1997) studied a sample of rapists from the British National Crime Identification Bureau records. Their average age was 27 years and three-quarters were under 33 years of age although they ranged from 14 to 59 years. Most significantly, 84% of them had criminal records. Bear in mind, though, that sexual offences were the *least* common previous offences. Burglary and violence offences were the most common previous offences. Perhaps the fact that the vast majority of rapists had previous convictions is the crucial thing. It means that there should be police records existing on the offender in most cases.

▶

Davies concentrated on available information from the rape scenes that she describes as non-sexual aspects of rape. These are types of behaviour relatively easily identified, especially with the help of the victim. The important thing is that these different types of behaviour have different associations with past criminal behaviours on record. In other words, the type of behaviour at the crime scene can suggest what sort of past offences to search for. This is illustrated in the table.

Relationship between crime scene behaviours and criminal record

Type of behaviour	Previous record
Fingerprint precautions: 15% of offenders had worn gloves, or wiped off fingerprints, or some similar activity	4 times more likely to have burglary convictions if used 3 times more likely to be one-off rapist if *not* used
Semen destruction: 5% of offenders had made efforts to make sure that no useful forensic evidence was left by their semen	4 times more likely to have a conviction record
Reference to the police: 13% made some comment about the police	4 times more likely to have been in custody 5.5 times more likely to a have a conviction 2.5 times more likely to have a conviction for violence
Theft from victim: 20% stole money or property from the victim	4 times more likely to have prior convictions for property crime
Forced entry: 25% of the rapes were accompanied by a forced entry to the property where the rape took place	5 times more likely to have burglary convictions
Extreme violence – striking the victim twice or more – was used in 20% of cases	3 times more likely to have prior convictions for violent offences

Davies went on to show through logistic regression analysis that combining features of the crime scene could make good predictions:

- A previous record for burglary could be predicted with almost complete certainty on the basis of fingerprint precautions being taken, theft from the victim, a forced entry to the premises and the presence of alcohol at the scene or immediately before the crime.
- Previous convictions for violent offences are predicted by the use of extreme violence, comments about the police and deliberately lying to mislead about the offender's identity.
- A lack of previous convictions for sexual offences is predicted by a lack of fingerprint precautions, a lack of precautions about departure from the crime scene to ensure that they are not arrested, the presence of alcohol at the scene or immediately prior, and either a forced entry or a confidence (trickster type) approach although both of these cannot be possible at the same time.

Some caution is needed over what would otherwise seem to be a valuable approach to profiling. In particular, the idea that only one in seven rapists has no previous criminal record needs care. There may well be an interaction between an offender having a previous criminal record and the willingness of the police to prosecute. Only small proportions of rapes and rape allegations ever reach court and end in conviction. The criminality of rapists may be an artefact of police practices rather than a feature of all rapes. In this connection, date-rape might be mentioned since it has only recently been generally recognised as a major aspect of rape and a matter for police prosecution. On the other hand, victims know date-rapists so their identification is easy.

Profiling and personality

Anyone examining the research on profiling will find relatively little which relates criminal activity to conventional personality theory. There is, of course, some research which tries to make the link between criminality and personality such as Eysenck's biosocial theory (see Chapter 5). The profiling literature does make reference to personality characteristics but these are rarely based on theoretically advanced understanding of human personality. According to Youngs (2004), little research is available into the relationship between *styles of offending* and personality as opposed, for example, to studies of the personality of, say, violent offenders. Perhaps not surprisingly, most of the measures of personality used in these studies are ones created for clinical purposes. Their value, then, is limited to the extent to which clinical (abnormal) factors are responsible for criminal style. The alternative is to use non-clinical measures of personality. The upshot of these studies is less than clear. Some studies claim a relationship whereas others suggest that there is no relationship. According to Youngs (2004), 'it remains unclear, then, whether personlity is differentially related to offending style and, if so, which aspects of personality will relate to which aspects of offending style.' (p. 101) Youngs argues that the circumstances in which there will be a differentiating relationship between personality and style of offending are as follows:

a) The offending styles must be empirically defensible and defined.

b) The conceptions of personality employed must be appropriate to criminal behaviour.

c) The empirical research must be informed by an understanding of the way that behaviour is shaped by personality.

In other words, the researcher needs a sophisticated understanding of both personality and criminal behaviour.

It can be argued that criminal behaviour is an interpersonal activity. The extent to which crimes differ in this regard is enormous and in some cases, the relationship is extremely remote. For crimes like rape and murder there has to be some sort of direct relationship whereas for other crimes, such as burglary, the relationship is not direct but 'implicit'. So, for example, a burglar is affected by the behaviour of a victim even if this is merely in terms of when the victim is away from home. This is a very indirect level of interpersonal activity. It might be noted also that many of the concepts used to explain the characteristics of offenders really describe interpersonal relationships – controlling, dominant, and hostile are examples.

Youngs (2004) identifies Fundamental Interperson Relations Orientation theory (FIRO) as potentially a means of assessing interpersonal interaction characteristics which might have a bearing on criminal style (Shutz, 1994). A person's interpersonal style will be reflected in the characteristic behaviours they receive from others. The core personality characteristics of control, inclusion and openness may be defined as follows:

- Control: this consists of two components that are not strongly related to each other. Expressed control is essentially the exertion of control over others whereas received control is the individual's willingness to submit to the control attempts of others. Someone who attempts to control others may be willing to be controlled or resistant to control.

- Inclusion: expressed inclusion is basically the manifestation of the desire to receive attention, interact and to belong to others. High received inclusion refers to those persons who tend to receive the attentions of others.

- Openness: expressed openness refers to those who relate to others with affection and closeness. So they are not private and withdrawn in their relationships. Received openness refers to those who tend to receive the affection and closeness of others.

The offending behaviours of young men in the age range of 14–28 years (the median age was 19 years) were studied using a lengthy questionnaire. This included behaviours such as cheated at school in tests, being drunk regularly under the age of 16, trying to pass a cheque by signing someone else's name. A statistical analysis found two major modes or styles of offending behaviour. Expressive behaviours included things like breaking into empty buildings to cause damage, arson and sex in public. They are expressive since these acts are the aim of the behaviours. Instrumental behaviours included forging a cheque, shoplifting and burglary. Another dimension of the offence concerned the seriousness of the behaviours.

Among the findings was that the expressed control group tended to target their offending against others – commonly through the use of violence. Offences involving the use of a weapon and the carrying and use of a gun were especially common in this group. In terms of the received control dimension, higher scorers tended to be more involved in property offences with the highest levels being for vandalism. These, taken with other findings, are suggestive support of Youngs's assertions about the circumstances in which offence style might relate to personality.

Does profiling work?

There is a substantial quantity of research into profiling as a means of exploring, especially, the relationship between crime scene characteristics and offender characteristics. Long term, such research might contribute to more effective profiling, short term the problem is that the issue of the effectiveness of profiling in terms of policing has been much neglected. Equally noteworthy is the neglect of empirical evaluations of the theoretical adequacy of profiling – especially FBI type profiling which is criticised by some psychologists for its lack of scientific rigor. The glaringly minimal research base in support of FBI profiling is not rectified simply by repeatedly reiterating this criticism. Research is needed to extend the research base of FBI profiling appropriately. Of course, it could be argued that any research on profiling extends the database. However, by focusing on FBI profiling concepts, researchers would more rapidly make progress in understanding just what there is of value in that approach. Unfortunately, little work has been done in this spirit.

One notable exception is Canter and Wentink's (2004) attempt to test Holmes and Holmes' serial murder classification scheme (Holmes and Holmes, 1998). Five types of serial murder were proposed based on case material from serial killings. These are visionary, mission, lust, thrill, power/control. Canter and Wentink used archival data of public domain accounts of serial killings. All of the cases were from the United States. In order to give Holmes and Holmes' typology the maximum possible chance of success, the researchers coded each of the serial cases in terms of the presence or absence of characteristics relevant to the typology. There were 37 such characteristics. The researchers then identified which of these variables are pertinent to each serial killing type. The following is indicative of the type and the sorts of variables that Canter and Wentink identified as being especially relevant to each category.

- Visionary killers: this type of killer is largely acting on voices or visions from God, angels, devils and the like which tell him that he should kill a particular person or type of person (e.g. prostitutes). Thus, for example, the visionary killer is claimed by Holmes and Holmes to leave behind a chaotic crime scene – the typical disorganised pattern. Variables such as scattering of belongings, clothing spread around, weapon left in victim, ransacking and bludgeoning should help identify this type.

- Mission killers: this type of killer has decided that a certain group or type of person is unacceptable or valueless and that the world should be free of them. The crime scene characteristics that should identify this type in Canter and Wentink's data include murder weapon missing, firearm use, bludgeoning, throat cutting.

- Lust killers: this type is a subcategory of hedonistic killers. Lust killers kill as part of the process of fulfilling their sexual lusts. Sex is the point of the process. As a consequence, typical crime scene characteristics would include multiple sexual acts, penetration with object, vaginal rape, abdominal mutilation, torture, and violence to genitals.

- Thrill killers: this is another subcategory of hedonistic killers. The thrill killer basically enjoys the process of killing in the sense that they get pleasure and excitement from killing. The death may deliberately be extended to take a long time and may involve torture. Characteristics of thrill killing can be similar to those of lust killing (e.g. torture, vaginal rape and penetration with objects) but others are different (e.g. bite marks, manual or ligature strangulation, body covered after death and concealed perhaps in an isolated spot, and burns on body of victim).

- Power/control killers: the gratification in the killing is that the killer has control over the victim. Dominance over another person is the motive. Enjoyment of the killing is maximised by extending the process over time as a consequence. Typical crime scene characteristics include the use of restraints, torture and gagging, body parts missing, evidence tampered with, decapitation. Some of the characteristics it shares with thrill killing such as vaginal rape, ligature strangulation and the body concealed.

Canter and Wentink (2004) claim that their data offered some rather limited support for the typology. Nevertheless, simple, direct support for the typology categories did not emerge. The following summarises some of the more important findings:

- Power/control killing characteristics were actually very typical of the entire sample of cases and did not form a distinct group. Things like bludgeoning, attacks on the face, strangulation and violence to the genitals, then, are a feature of the other types of serial killing.

- There did appear to be a group of thrill killing variables which tend to go together though these seem to be best considered largely in terms of the restraint pattern that the killer used. For example, gagging, ligature use, and covering the dead body seem to form a cluster. However, other characteristics which seem to imply an inferred thrill according to Canter and Wentink were not so clearly identified with this particular pattern. So things like the weapon being missing and the victim being alive during the sexual attack were likely to be part of other patterns.

- There did appear to be some support for the idea of visionary killers. Characteristics such as bludgeoning to death the victim and leaving a trail of clothing around tended to co-occur frequently in crime scenes. On the other hand, some of the key characteristics of visionary killers according to Holmes and Holmes were not particularly close to this core of variables – e.g. leaving the weapon in the victim. The researchers add that facial disfigurement, which is characteristic of lust killing according to Holmes and Holmes, seems to be more associated with the core of visionary killer variables.

This is, of course, progress in academic terms. That it may make Holmes and Holmes' ideas more difficult to use by profilers is not the point. Canter and Wentink's findings indicate that the simple typology lacks sufficient clarity and empirical justification to be used without further modification.

Nevertheless, perhaps the most important aspect of profiling at least in the minds of the general public, is its contribution to the work of the police. There are a number of points to be made about the seemingly straightforward issue of the adequacy of profiling for police work: it is a deceptively simple question to ask whether profiling is effective. Try to imagine a research study to definitively answer the question of whether profiling is worthwhile. How would such a study be done? What crimes would be studied? Would a profiler be randomly assigned to some cases and not others? What is the criterion of success – arrests, reduction in time to arrests, the satisfaction of the senior investigating officers with the profiler, or what?

- Purely in terms of psychological research methods, the issue might be thought of as a simple technical exercise in evaluation research. As soon as we plan this research in detail, the practical and conceptual difficulties grow. A researcher might select, say, crimes and assign a profiler at random to half the crimes and no profiler to the other half. The outcome of this might be evaluated in terms of the proportion of crimes that were solved with and without a profiler. Even if the profiler condition seemed more successful, this in itself would not be definitive evidence that profiling itself worked. Profilers are usually very familiar with police methods and their apparent success might be the result of their good advice on how to conduct and prioritise the investigative operation. The profile itself may well be poor. Profiling has traditionally been applied to extreme crimes. Serial rapes and serial sexual murders may result in pressure on the police for an arrest. At the same time, the investigating police officers may have little experience of such rare crimes. Expert profilers may simply bring wider experience of such crimes. Their profiling skills, as such, may not be very helpful.
- The involvement of a profiler may be diverting resources away from other lines of enquiry. If other options are ignored simply because of the profile then this might reduce the success.
- Claims about the importance of profiling in a particular high-profile crime may appear impressive because an arrest is achieved. What does this tell us about crimes in which profiling was used but no arrest achieved or about the improvement in the chances of arrest due to profiling? It is a bit like a heart surgeon parading their living patients as evidence of the success of their techniques while ignoring the vast majority who ended in the graveyard.
- It is generally believed that only certain crimes are suitable for profiling or potentially helped by profiling. People with certain characteristics, for example, may commit car break-ins, but it is unlikely that resources will be found to mount an investigation of the vast majority of these crimes. So profiling could not make a contribution.
- Is detection of a particular crime the main objective of profiling? There are circumstances in which the role of the profiler is rather different: for example, when trying to assess whether crimes are linked to a particular offender or whether they are the work of several different offenders. Sometimes in high-profile cases there is the need to assess the likely validity of letters of confession which may be hoaxes. The hoax potentially could waste much police time. Just what strategy should the interviewing officers take when interviewing suspects? All of these seem worthwhile profiling endeavours but may impinge little on the question of whether the offender is arrested.

- The information provided by profiling research may be operationally useful in general without it having a discernible impact on individual cases. Potentially, ideas of what sorts of rapist are associated with particular crime scenes may generally inform police work without the direct input of a profiler, for example.

- Profiling potentially can inform the sorts of information collected at the crime scene and lead to improvements in the collection and recording of information. There is potentially a symbiotic relationship between profiling and crime scene information collection. The better the crime scene information, the better profiling research can be, and the better profiling research becomes, the more we will know about what crime scene information is useful.

- There have been studies of user satisfaction with profiling. By user satisfaction we mean in this case the senior officers managing a particular crime. It is notable in these that relatively few offenders are arrested as a result of the profile. Gudjonsson and Copson (1997) found that 3% of detections were attributed to the profiler's work. Do not forget that these figures are based on what the senior officers say and it may be that they are not keen to give credit to the profiler. It is interesting to note, nevertheless, that most senior officers express positive attitudes to profilers for other reasons.

- Of course, a profile may be good but the offender arrested without its help. In these circumstances, comparing the fit of the profile to that offender might better assess the validity of the profile. The difficulty is the lack of a clear standard for doing this. For example, is a count or tally of the similarities between the profile and the offender sufficiently sound for evaluating profiling? For example, if the profile of a killer was young, male, of average education, lived near the crime scene and has at least one previous arrest, most of us would not be impressed with the profile even if all of the listed characteristics proved to be true. On the other hand, if the killer was predicted to be a hotel worker, supporting his arthritic mother, living within two minutes of a railway station, with a history of exhibitionism and trans-vestism and it all turned out to be correct, we would be more impressed.

- Despite allegations of its less than scientific status, FBI crime scene profiling has been subject to more validity assessment than the statistical or actuarial approach. By validity assessment we mean its validity in relation to police work rather than its psychological methodological validity. Few, if any, studies have been conducted of the operational value of statistical profiling.

One of the perplexing findings on offender profiling is the claims made by the police that the profiles were useful but did not lead to the arrest. Alison, Smith and Morgan (2003) carried out a study in which they took a genuine FBI profile and asked police officers to evaluate the accuracy of the profile against the known facts about the criminal finally convicted. In this particular case, the offender was 19 years of age, a stranger to the victim, was unemployed in his work as an actor, had attempted suicide and suffered depression, had no previous conviction, had no relationships in his life, had no sibling, denied the offence, and had not suffered abuse within the family. Among the statements that the profile contained were the following:

- The offender will be a white male between 25 and 35, or the same general age as the victim and of average appearance.

- He will be of average intelligence and will be a secondary school (high school) or university (college) drop-out.

- He will not have a military history and may be unemployed.

- He will have a pornography collection.
- The subject will have sadistic tendencies.
- The sexual acts show controlled aggression, but rage or hatred of women was obviously present.
- He did not want the woman screaming for help.
- He probably will be a very confused person, possibly with previous mental problems.

The police officers overwhelmingly claimed that the profile was useful for crime investigation. Another group of forensic professionals tended to be less enthusiastic.

However, the study went further than this and for another similar group of officers the procedure was varied and a fabricated picture of the offender was provided. For example, in this condition he was 37, he knew the victim, he worked for the water board but had just been made redundant, he was an alcoholic, had several previous convictions for assault and burglary, had lived with a girlfriend and had had several relationships with women but each one was violent, he has two sisters, admitted the offence, and suffered an abusive family background. Despite the fact the the two descriptions of the offender were virtual opposites, the officers were just as likely to see the profile as being as useful for the bogus description as the real description. In other words, accuracy had no impact on how useful the officers regarded the profile!

Main points

- Offender profiling seeks to use information from the scene of a crime to assess characteristics of the sort of offender likely to have committed the crime. It ranges from somewhat intuitional approaches to those based on the careful analysis of aggregate statistical data. The latter is becoming increasingly characteristic of research in the field. All forms of profiling assume that there is some sort of homologous relationship between the crime scene and the offender in question. It is unclear whether the simple distinction between organised and disorganised crime scenes stands up to empirical scrutiny despite its impact on the work of FBI profilers.

- There is considerable evidence that the police regard offender profiling favourably. There is evidence that police officers find profiles equally useful even when they are given virtually opposite profiles for the same crime! There is evidence that FBI profiling is less accurate than statistical profiling in circumstances in which it is possible to assess the validity of elements of the profile. Some research indicates that some profiles may contain very high proportions of information which is little more than the facts already collected by the police themselves. Only a small proportion of statements in profiles include some justification for what was being claimed. There are clear signs that offender profiling is regarded as useful though it is just one of many sources of support that supervising officers find very useful without it necessarily leading to an arrest.

- Profiling has had a high public profile in recent years thanks to the various media depictions of profilers. Furthermore, profiling is intimately associated with the concept of serial killing. Given this, one would expect that public interest in the topic will continue to be disproportionate to the tangible achievements of profilers. One of the achievements of profiling is that it has moved research into serious crime away from the search for psychological abnormalities to the manifestation of individual characteristics in the behaviours of criminals when committing crimes.

Chapter 14

False allegations

Overview

- Miscarriage of justice is a legal rather than psychological concept and may involve procedural rather than factual matters. Psychologists have tended to focus on more limited issues such as false allegations and false confessions (see Chapter 15). False allegations may be made for a number of reasons – they are not simply motivated by malice in every case.

- Bad interviewing practices can lead to false information. There is clear evidence that at least in some circumstances, persistent leading questioning can result in individuals being falsely implicated in crime. Some children, especially, seem vulnerable to the implantation of false memories of events that are resistant to challenge in some cases.

- The recovered memory/false memory debate reflects opposite ways of understanding some allegations of sexual abuse dating back to childhood experiences. Recovered memory implies that the abuse happened and was lost to memory for a while whereas false memory implies that the memories are of events which did not take place. The debate centres around radically different perspectives on memory. A rather sceptical view on recovered memory comes from those experimental psychologists who have been inclined to use laboratory style experimentation in developing theories of memory. The more accepting approach comes from those who regard memory as being affected by repression especially following trauma. Some individuals retract claims to have had memories of childhood recovered in adult life.

- There are a number of graphic experimental demonstrations that children can be encouraged to make false claims about happenings which might be interpreted as sexually abusive. The *Mr Science* studies involved a classroom visit and later stories told to the children by their parents about that visit which contained inaccurate information. Some children claimed to remember events that happened in real life which were only to be found in the stories. 'Experts' in interviewing were not able to distinguish between the children's accounts of the real and fictional events.

- Professionals may make false allegations because they fail to understand the limited value of certain signs in diagnosing child sexual abuse, for example. The risk of false positives and false negatives should be part of any such assessment. However, there is a secondary problem in that when it becomes commonly believed that children are suggestible and easily influenced by interviewers, confusion may be caused by professionals about the adequacy of their interviewing technique.

Miscarriages of justice are identified when an appeal court overturns a conviction (Naughton, 2005). Consequently, the processes and procedures of the court of appeal determine what becomes classified as a miscarriage of justice. The concept of miscarriage of justice has tended to be used for those cases which failed on the first occasion that they went to an appeal court but were overthrown at a later appeal hearing. Such cases tend to be high-profile cases which receive considerable media publicity. Nevertheless, these are extremely infrequent since they amount to less that 0.001% of the annual number of criminal convictions in the United Kingdom. Unfortunately, this disguises the fact that Courts of Appeal regularly quash many thousands of convictions each year. Furthermore, in law, overturning a decision does not mean that the Appeal Court has decided that the convicted person is, in fact, innocent. The requirement for a conviction (in England and Wales) is that the legal standard of proof has been met – there is sufficient evidence that establishes beyond reasonable doubt the guilt or otherwise of the accused. So miscarriages of justice do not exclusively concern wrongful convictions of individuals who did not commit a crime but are also about the procedures that led to a conviction (and sometimes acquittal). Many aspects of miscarriage of justice have been ignored in forensic and criminal psychology. So most of the research in forensic and criminal psychology pertinent to miscarriages of justice has concentrated on false accusations and false confessions. The latter are dealt with in Chapter 15. Neither of these, necessarily, leads to a miscarriage of justice. For example, the accusation may not be believed or the confession may be retracted and this retraction accepted in court or by the police.

The true rate of false allegations is somewhat difficult to estimate for the reason that one's definition of false allegations partly determines that estimate. For example, it would be highly problematic to define false allegations in terms of the proportion of trials that end in not guilty verdicts. A not guilty verdict may or may not mean innocence and there is an obvious distinction to be made between false allegations and false convictions. Probably researchers have studied false allegations in relation to child sexual abuse more than in any other topic. The main areas of concern have been as follows:

- *False allegations of child physical and sexual abuse* made by professionals against parents. Perhaps the most noteworthy of these are the events in Cleveland, England, in the late 1980s (Bell, 1988; Howitt, 1992) when doctors and social workers made charges of child sexual abuse – largely sodomy – against a number of families in northern England. These allegations appear to be based on a faulty medical test of sexual abuse. The test, supposed to measure anal penetration, was eventually found to lead to a high proportion of misdiagnoses. This led to a public inquiry, as did a number of subsequent cases such as those involving satanic abuse.
- *Allegations of sexual abuse made against the conflicting parent in divorce cases* – especially cases in which the custody of children is in dispute.
- *The so-called false-memory syndrome* in which adults undergoing therapy come to 'recall' sexually abusive experiences in their childhood (see Box 14.1).

Of course, these are not the only circumstances in which false allegations may be made. They just happen to be the circumstances that have attracted the interest of researchers. Poole and Lindsay (1998) suggest that false allegation rates might vary from 5% to 8% for child sexual abuse – if we take into account only *intentional* false allegations. Such malicious motives exclude a great number where the police and social workers among others raise suspicions of abuse against families. When false suspicions of this sort are included, the false allegation rate increases markedly to between 23% and 35% according to the study in question (Howitt, 1992). Underlying these figures may be a reality of trauma, stress and distress for the child and its family. Risks include children being removed from their homes, fathers being forced to live away from home and imprisonment. Even if they do not lead to criminal convictions, well-intentioned false allegations may still take their toll on family life (Howitt, 1992). So, in this way, they cannot be regarded as trivial.

The reasons why false allegations seem to be common in allegations of sexual abuse include the following:

- In many cases, no physical evidence of sexual abuse can be detected. While penetrative sexual intercourse might damage the sexual organs of a physically immature child or its anus, sexual abuse takes many other and less invasive forms. Almost certainly, oral sex will leave no physical signs.
- What evidence there is often comes from an interview with relatively young children.
- Professionals and the public in general are sensitive about the dangers of abuse and feel it is important to protect children wherever possible.

There is a great deal more to be found in Chapter 15 on the problems of interviewing children and getting the best quality testimony from them.

Child sexual abuse

It is hard for the inexperienced to believe how, in some cases, bad interviewing technique can create false evidence. The psychiatrist Bernet (1997) described a case in which an allegation was made against a parent through repeated suggestive questions (i.e. leading questions). A babysitter developed suspicions about the family for whom she worked. She, as a precaution, taped an interview she conducted with their child, known as Betsy, then 5 years of age. As a consequence, the parents were reported to Child Protection Services and Betsy was removed from the family home for nearly two years. Generally speaking, repeated sessions of suggestive interviewing are not necessary to produce such effects. Notice how in the following extract the child very quickly begins saying untrue things. The babysitter had formed the opinion (or developed a theory) that Betsy was afraid of sweeping brushes or brooms because her parents played a game they called 'sweep the bootie' with her. There were several hundreds of questions on the tape. The following is representative of some of the things that can be heard on the tape:

> Joyce [the babysitter]: Okay. So Daddy plays sweeping the bootie with his hand. How does he use his hand? What does he do with his hand?
>
> Betsy: Touches.
>
> Joyce: He touches you. Did he touch your pee-pee where you go number one or did he touch where you go number two?
>
> Betsy: Number two.
>
> Joyce: Okay. You're saying he touched you where you go do-do at or where you go pee-pee at?
>
> Betsy: Do-do.

> *(Bernet, 1997, p. 968)*

Box 14.1

Controversy: the recovered memory/false memory debate

One of the most perplexing but familiar issues in forensic and criminal psychology is that of recovered memories/false memory. Legally this is a complex issue in some jurisdictions because conventional time limitations on prosecutions have to be set aside in order to try the accused. A very significant factor in the origins of the debate was the allegations made by an American professor of psychology, Jennifer Freyd (1996), against her parents, John and Pamela Freyd, concerning sexual abuse (Calof, 1993). These claims led to the False Memory Syndrome Foundation being set up. In adulthood, she had undergone therapy and her recollections of the events emerged following this. The basic issue is whether such memories are simply the product of suggestions made during psychotherapy (false memories) or reflect the uncovering of true childhood memories of repressed, stressful events (recovered memories). The language used to describe the 'phenomenon' is potentially value-ridden and evaluative. The so-called false memory syndrome is a severe psychopathology involving pseudomemories relating to beliefs about early sexual abuse. It is identified in terms of a belief in their memories concerning their abuse, the patterns in their current interpersonal relationships, symptoms of trauma in their life history and characteristics of their therapeutic experience (Hovdestad and Kristiansen, 1996a). Only a small proportion (less than about one in eight) of women with claims of recovered memories actually meet the diagnostic criteria.

Central to the debate is the idea that therapy instils the belief in some clients that the repression of sexual abuse is common and is the cause of the client's problems. In a sense, the issue is one of diagnosticity of signs, since some therapists believe that a wide range of emotional and psychological problems result from untreated child sexual abuse. One client has expressed this in the following terms:

> He [therapist] kept pressuring me by telling me that if I wanted to recover from my depression at that point and become a better mother, then I better look at these memories and do some work with them. He also thought if I left my children with their grandparents, they might be in danger. He kept insisting that I had all of the symptoms and I might as well admit it. He acted like he could see right through me and that he knew my story better than I did.
>
> *(Ost et al., 2002, p. 4)*

The recovered memory issue became important in legal settings. The fairly acrimonious debate within psychology was rehearsed in front of judges in many courtrooms. MacMartin and Yarmey (1998) regard the debate as being a dispute over who possesses the expertise on the matter. The battle involved confrontations between academic psychology (experimentalists for the most part) and clinician/practitioners (including clinical psychologists and psychiatrists):

- Support for the idea that recovered memories are reliable evidence of childhood sexual abuse comes largely from practitioners – the people who counsel the victims of abuse. They believe that through repression and dissociation, early memories of real events become unavailable to memory. The writings and evidence of this category of expert suggest that repression and dissociation help the traumatised victim of sexual abuse defend themselves psychologically against the resulting psychological pain. Broadly speaking, repression is regarded as the burial of memories of abuse deep in the mind whereas dissociation is a sort of laying to one side, or setting aside from memories normally available within our conscious experience. There are a variety of positions within the clinical perspective. The primary evidence for this idea is, of course, the case studies of recovered memories. There is also a long tradition in clinical theorising (starting with Freud and Janet) which adopts such a perspective. In addition, there are some examples from the research tradition of experimental laboratory studies that can be or have been used in support of this. While these do not directly study trauma for obvious reasons, these include studies in which forgetting is directed under hypnosis and could be seen as evidence of similar processes. Sheehan (1997) suggests that the cases in which a woman has forgotten her abuse but the offender validates that she was abused are persuasive evidence of repression.

- Academic psychologists are more likely to be dismissive of the value of recovered memories as evidence of childhood abuse. Some of them, according to MacMartin and Yarmey (1998), claim that clinicians work with what could be described as 'robust repression'. They are suggesting that repression in the clinical formulation screens off what is an accurate memory trace of the traumatic events of the sexual abuse. The difficulty with the notion of robust repression is that it relates poorly to the beliefs of experimentalists researching memory. Experimentalists tend to view memory as a reconstruction that blends fact and fiction. Experimentalists may be rather more accepting of the notion of dissociation. Doubters of the veracity of recovered memories sometimes point out that a person in a dissociative state is usually aware that there is something missing from their memory. This does not seem to apply to the cases of recovered memories. These sceptics generally believe that there is no definitive evidence favouring repression and dissociation as applied to multiple repeated experiences of sexual abuse.

While not feeling able to prefer one side of the debate over the other, Memon and Young (1997) stress the importance of exploring the possible mechanisms of recovered memories. Their conclusions echo those of others:

- They describe the 'grand' idea of repression to be of dubious validity if by repression we mean something other than the gradual forgetting of events.
- Repression in the sense of cognitive/emotional processes which essentially 'keep the lid' on events and memories that we would otherwise remember lacks laboratory evidence convincingly mimicking the process.
- There is evidence in favour of the ideas that memories may be suppressed, the dissociation of memories (as in multiple personality disorder) and inhibition.

It can be added that although repression is regarded as a consequence of the emotion surrounding the acts of abuse, there are a number of studies that indicate that highly emotional events can be remembered with high levels of accuracy as in flashbulb memory (Brown and Kulik, 1977).

Of course, the task of sceptics includes explaining the processes involved in false memories. These include the mechanism by which these 'memories' are recovered. This may be through a retrieval process of the sort that has frequently been described in the research literature. An especially graphic example of this is a study by Loftus and Pickrell (1995). Their study involved stories apparently recalled by older relatives about the early childhood of each participant. Three of the stories were in fact true recollections by the relatives but the fourth one was untrue. The participants remembered 68% of the true stories. Many fewer claimed to remember the fictitious events but, nevertheless, a quarter of them indicated that they at least partially remembered the fictitious events. The table on p. 246 provides a summary of some of the possible mechanisms of repressed memory.

One difficulty with the debate on the false/recovered memory debate is that memory as studied by most experimentalists is factual, conscious and reflective. This is termed explicit memory. Hovdestad and Kristiansen (1996b) argue that there is another form of memory – implicit memory – that is different in many respects. For example, it involves conditioned emotional responses, it is unconscious, it is not reflective, it appears from birth rather than infancy and it appears to be associated with the more primitive brain structures. This suggests that the traumatic experience of child sexual abuse may be processed totally differently from the way that experimentalists suggest.

▶

Kassin (1997a) suggests that there is a strong resemblance between false memories of victim- isation and some false confessions of offending where memories are confabulated and turned against oneself.

Not only are claims of recovered memories made, they are also sometimes retracted. De Riviera (1997) suggested that retraction of claims of abuse may be the result of a set of circumstances in the creation of these memories:

- an authority figure used techniques of emotional, information, behavioural and thought control to control their thoughts;
- the client creates a narrative that helps put their lives into a meaningful systematic structure aided by a few suggestions from the therapist.

Possible mechanisms of repressed memories

	Model 1: Classical repression	Model 2: Emotionally charged memory processes	Model 3: Retrieval processes from memory
Origins	Later writings of Sigmund Freud regarded repression as an unconscious response to distressing memories.	Studies of the accuracy of eyewitness testimony about stressful situations. Emotion adversely affects memory of abuse.	Encoding specificity theory concentrates on the role of memory retrieval cues.
Experimental support	Many studies have failed to show unconscious repression.	Generally the evidence is complex. Eyewitness studies support the opposite view – emotionally charged events are better remembered. However, even when clear, they are subject to distortions of memory.	There is a multiplicity of studies demonstrating that memory is a reconstruction rather than a pure trace of an event.
Clinical support	Repression is a central concept in psychoanalysis and clinical psychology.	This is not really a clinical issue distinct from the concept of repression.	Many psychodynamic approaches are designed to help uncover repressed memories. Psychotherapy is held to be the cause of false memories by some.
Status of recovered memories	Reflect true events hidden by the memory.	May reflect either true events or distortions.	Provides evidence of how entirely spurious memories can be created though it could not distinguish false from true recovered memories.
Other comment	There appears to be more evidence that some individuals consciously suppress memories than that unconscious factors at play.	Source monitoring theory suggests that emotion reduces concentration on peripheral information, such as the source of the memory, that makes recollection difficult.	Establishes the plausibility but not the actuality of claims that memories are false memories.

Ost *et al.* (2002) also studied retractors. Almost by definition, their evidence might be suspect given their lack of consistency (the change from not remembering the events, then recovering memories of the events and finally denying their recovered memories). Only a few retractors had any indication of memory of abuse before they recovered memories of abuse. Mostly the recovered memories were their first memories of abuse. The overwhelming majority claimed that there had been *no* pressure on them to retract the false memories. This contrasts with their claim that they were under pressure when they recovered their memories of abuse. Generally, they were not confident in the veracity of their recovered memories even at the time of making their allegations. Virtually all were firmly confident in their retraction of the recovered memories. The more pressure they had felt to remember abuse, the more likely they were to be confident in their retraction of those memories.

One fascinating piece of evidence puts the recovered memory/false memory debate into perspective. Quite clearly it is an issue that has attracted the interest of the public and is not confined solely to an acrimonious debate between squabbling professions. It is also a socio-political issue. Kristiansen (1996) has shown that for two different Canadian samples, participants who believed in the false memory syndrome (i.e. the invalidity of some abuse allegations) tended to have more anti-women ideas such as 'women who stay in abusive relationships obviously like to be beaten', or 'many women are unsuitable for top management positions because, for a few days each month, they simply can't function at their best' (p. 26). Similarly, Griffith *et al.* (1998) found that women jurors were less likely to believe the defendant than male jurors in a simulated repressed memory trial.

Taub (1996) provides a useful account of the US legal experience of 'recovered memories' especially in relation to the statute of limitations (i.e. time elapsed before reporting crime). There is good reason to accept Kristiansen *et al.*'s (1996) caution that beliefs about recovered/false memories are '[more] closely tied to autocratic misogynism and self-interest than they are to social values or science' (p. 56). It is an area where 'facts' can be readily supplied for any position that one wishes to defend.

Notice the way the babysitter gives forced-choice alternatives that gradually shape in the mind of the child the idea that the parents had molested the child's genitals and anus. The net effect of all of the questioning is that the parents appear to be being accused by the child of molesting her genitals and anus with a sweeping brush.

False claims of abuse and young children

It would seem relatively easy to demonstrate how false claims of abuse can be obtained from pre-school children (e.g. Bruck *et al.*, 1995; Ceci *et al.*, 1994). Essentially, the researchers had children interviewed about events that had happened to the child and also what were actually fictions (according to the child's parents). The studies involved, for example, a fictitious episode in which the child was supposed to have caught his or her finger in a mousetrap. As a consequence, a hospital visit was necessary to deal with the injury. For all (or the vast majority) of children in the studies these events had not happened.

How resistant were pre-school children to the pressure of the interview? During the course of the interview, the child was read a list of things that might have happened to them. They were required to think hard about each of them and to try to remember if the event really happened. About a third of children accepted fictitious events as real. This percentage remained much the same when they were interviewed on several occasions. There was some inconsistency since a number of the children switched one way or the other at each stage, balancing the changes in each direction. If the children were told by the interviewer that the fictitious events really did happen to the child, there were increases in the percentage of the children accepting the fictitious experiences as real (Ceci *et al.*, 1994). The extent of 'false memory induction' depended somewhat on the age of the child. Children who accepted the fictitious event as real would sometimes provide additional detail about the events. The event would be elaborated and they would describe the emotional feelings associated with it.

Of course, such evidence as this is only suggestive of the extent to which, in interview conditions, young children confuse fiction with fact. Limitations include the following:

- This age group is not representative of those involved in sexual abuse allegations and false memory induction may not apply to these older children.
- The questioning by the interviewers in these studies went way beyond what would be expected in a police interview or social work interview of a child involved in possible sexual abuse.

That is to say, the findings of the studies might not generalise to real-life situations. In order to disregard the suggestion in the question, the child must be able to do the following, according to Poole and Lindsay (1998):

- Understand that the interviewer actually wants them to report only their individual, personal experiences.
- Know what the sources of their knowledge actually are (i.e. they require source monitoring ability).

An important experiment in this context is Poole and Lindsay's *Mr Science* study. In essence, this can be summarised as follows:

- At school, a group of 3- and 4-year-olds experienced vivid science lessons given by Mr Science.
- Closely afterwards, they were interviewed and requested to tell the interviewer everything about the science lesson. Their reports were extremely accurate and very few of them made false claims.
- Three months later, the parents of the children were sent a storybook to read to their child. It contained descriptions of the Mr Science lessons that had actually happened, but also descriptions of lessons that had not happened. The fictitious material, for example, describes how the child was touched by Mr Science who then put a 'yucky' object in their mouth. The stories were told to the child three times.
- This was followed by another interview session in which open-ended and then leading questions were put to the child about whether or not the events were real or just from one of the stories.

The major findings from the study were as follows:

- Two out of every five children mentioned as if real events that originated only in the stories.
- Leading questions increased the rates of false reporting. Over half of all children answered yes to a question about whether Mr Science had put something 'yucky'

into their mouths. When requested by the interviewer, the majority of these children went on to describe details of the fictional event.

- The interview also included quite severe challenges to the children about the truth of what they said. Nevertheless, the majority of the children when challenged in this way continued to maintain that Mr Science had truly put a yucky thing into their mouth.
- Increasing the age range from 3 to 8 years of age did not result in a decline in false reports. These remained stable in free recall conditions.
- Challenges about the truth of their claims meant declines in false claims for the older children but not the younger ones.
- There was a fairly high degree of stability in the false claims. Follow-up of those who had made false claims a month later revealed that two-thirds were still making the same false claims.

There is another important study which reinforces the view that even young children are somewhat resistant to suggestive or leading questioning. It also shows that as children get older then even the simplest of challenges to their false claims rapidly produces recantation. Leichtman and Ceci (1995) had children aged 3–6 years watch as a stranger named Sam Stone visited their pre-school, walked about and left. They were interviewed four times about Sam Stone's visit. There was no leading or suggestive questioning up to this point. Then the children were asked about two fictitious events: did Sam Stone do anything to a book or a teddy bear? A high level of accuracy was produced. Only 10% said that he did do something and this figure reduced to 5% when they were asked if they actually saw him do it. When they were gently challenged about their false claims – you didn't really see him do anything to the book/teddy bear, did you? – this figure declined further to 2.5%. For the older children, this sort of challenge was especially effective.

Another group of pre-schoolers was exposed to repeated conversations about Sam's clumsiness and proneness to breaking things. They were subsequently interviewed with suggestive questions such as 'Remember the time Sam Stone visited our classroom and spilled chocolate on that white teddy bear? Did he do it on purpose or was it an accident?' In the final interview:

- 72% of the youngest pre-schoolers reported that Sam did something to the book or teddy;
- 44% said they actually saw him do these things;
- 21% maintained their false stories when gently challenged;
- 5–6-year-olds were less malleable since only 11% said they actually saw the misdeeds and less than 10% maintained the story when challenged.

Forensically, the issue is more complex than this. Children in sexual abuse cases are in the hands of professionals such as the police, social workers, psychologists and psychiatrists, all of whom must form judgements and make decisions. So one question must concern us: just how good are professionals at detecting false information? Poole and Lindsay (1998) argue that the ability of professionals is relatively poor. For instance:

- When clinical and research psychologists specialising in interviewing children were shown videos of children in the mousetrap experiments described above, they were unable to differentiate between fictional and real experiences at better than the chance level (Ceci *et al.*, 1994).

- Horner *et al.* (1993) showed workers in the mental health field a two-hour case study containing interviews with the parents, interviews with the child and child–parent interaction, and they could request additional information. In addition, groups of the workers discussed the case together for over an hour. The researchers found no relationship between whether or not the health worker believed that child abuse had taken place and recommendations about future contact of the child with its father – they all recommended that the child–father contact should be supervised irrespective of their judgements about abuse!

Bruck and Ceci (1997) construe the above research and others as evidence of the creation of suggestive interviews based on interviewer bias. Such biases are seen as involving a failure to challenge what children say when it supports the interviewer's preconceptions, and events inconsistent with the interviewer's preconceptions are not touched upon.

The concept of suggestibility has a long history in psychology but, perhaps more importantly, it is a notion familiar to professionals working in the criminal justice system and child protection. Over 100 years ago, William Stern (1904) regarded the predisposition to succumb to suggestion as suggestibility. Nevertheless, it was important to differentiate two different types of suggestion:

- Active suggestion: the activity of suggesting something to another person.
- Passive suggestion: the state of a person who is currently under the influence of suggestion.

These can be totally unrelated processes since 1) a suggestion may be made but it is NOT responded to but 2) a suggestion which has NOT been made may be responded to. In other words, one cannot simply find suggestion's influence in circumstances in which a suggestion has been made. According to Ceci and Bruck (1993), suggestibility refers to the extent to which all aspects of a child's memory for events are influenced by a variety of social and psychological factors. Suggestibility may influence the ways in which events are encoded into memory, the processes of retrieving the memory, and just what is reported to others in interviews and elsewhere. Thus it is a mistake to assume that suggestibility is exclusively the consequence of a particular interview or interview style.

Motzkau (2004) argues that 'suggestibility is itself suggestive' (p. 7) meaning that the widespread knowledge of the concept of suggestibility itself has an effect within the criminal justice system over and above what could be warranted by our current research-base knowledge. Some psychological concepts spread into common knowledge among other professions and the general public. The public finds out about psychological ideas in part through the media. Of course, the concept as understood by the public may be quite a simplistic one and involve rather overstated accounts of the findings of research (Motzkau, 2004). So, for example, the general public may be led to believe that children are extremely suggestible and easily influenced by parents and misguided professionals into making allegations that are simply untrue. The danger in this is that because of high profile cases in which children have made unfounded allegations of abuse, others will be reluctant to report the abuse simply because it is felt that no one will believe their story. As a consequence, there will be a decline in the number of reported child abuse cases. In Germany, argues Motzkau, people became concerned that the criminal justice system could be undergoing an 'epidemic' of false allegations of child sexual abuse especially in relation to child custody disputes since there had been a great deal of scientific, media and public interest in the issue of suggestibility. Objectively, this was totally unfounded as there were virtually no cases in which false allegations of sexual abuse were an issue. The issue focused on the disputed child custody cases in which allegations of abuse could result in unfair child custody decisions.

The important practical consequence of this can be illustrated by one of Motzkau's interviews with a police officer. The police had been called in by staff at a care home. A 12-year-old girl with learning disability had apparently reported to one member of staff another staff member for behaving inappropriately sexually towards her. The alleged perpetrator denied this. The police officer was concerned about his role as an interviewer fearing that he might not have interviewed the girl correctly since she disclosed nothing about her apparent abuse. The officer was also apprehensive about interviewing the girl again since this repeated interviewing might devalue the evidence in the eyes of others. It finally emerged in a chance comment from a different child that the alleged perpetrator had actually accidentally hurt the putative victim of abuse with a food trolley. With this information, it was possible to clarify with the 'vicitim' that this was the incident that had resulted in the allegation. Furthermore, the staff member who had reported the matter to the police initially had decided not to discuss the matter with the girl because she feared the suspicion that she had suggested the allegation to the girl in some way!

Box 14.2

Forensic psychology in action: testing for suggestibility

While it is extremely important to understand just how questioning styles, age and other factors influence responsiveness to suggestibility, there is another fundamental issue – do certain individuals tend to be more suggestible than other people in more situations? That is, is it reasonable to regard suggestibility as a characteristic of the individual rather than the situation? Gudjonsson (2003) explored this route by developing a scale, the Gudjonsson Suggestibility Scale (Gudjonsson, 1984), which attempts to establish the general suggestibility level of an individual. Quite clearly, if suggestibility is a characteristic of individuals then a test that measures it would have potential in the context of the work of forensic psychologists. The Gudjonsson Suggestibility Scale is more than a questionnaire – it is a procedure in which the practitioner gives the individual material to learn and then examines the way in which that individual responds to leading questions and other pressures. The point is, however, that the procedures are reasonably standardised. The steps in the process are as follows:

- Material presentation: a tape-recording of a short piece of narrative is played to the person being assessed.
- Immediate recall: the person being assessed is requested to remember as much of the narrative as possible in as much detail as possible.
- First asking of list of leading questions: the assessor asks a standard list of 20 questions about the narrative. Fifteen of these questions are actually leading questions that imply an answer which is actually inaccurate. A score is computed known as 'Yield 1' which is simply the number of the leading (inaccurate) questions that the person being assessed agrees with.
- Negative feedback: once the questions have all been answered, then the assessor says things like 'You have made a number of errors. It is therefore necessary to go through the questions once more, and this time try to be more accurate.' This is an attempt to influence the individual being assessed further.

▶

- Second asking of list of leading questions: the assessor reads out the same list of leading questions again. After this stage, two additional different scores are calculated: 'Shift' is simply the number of questions that the person being assessed actually gives a different answer to from the first time. It does not matter if the question is a leading question or one of the five other questions. 'Yield 2' is the number of leading questions which the person being assessed agrees with after the negative feedback. It indicates the direction of any change from the first leading question stage to the second.
- There is another measure – total suggestibility – which is simply the sum of 'Yield 1 + Shift'.

Research suggests that 'Yield 1' and 'Shift' are two quite distinct aspects of suggestibility. They are independent dimensions. Of course, this is a quite complex assessment and it is perhaps not surprising to find that procedural differences may have some but not necessarily a crucial influence on the outcome. For example, the negative feedback can be expressed in a more or a less hostile fashion (Boon and Baxter, 2004). It is also valuable to know that it is difficult to fake suggestibility on Gudjonsson's test (Baxter and Bain, 2002) since of course it would be in some offenders' interests to be able to appear suggestible when they are not. Some participants in a study were requested to pretend to act like a suggestible person on the test. The researchers found that it was possible to fake suggestibility well on the 'Yield 1' measure but, having done this, then their 'Shift' scores did not correspond to the pattern of a suggestible person. So, quite clearly, the participants knew some of the things that they needed to do in order to appear suggestible but they could not anticipate all of what was needed to put on an entirely convincing display.

Does the scale work with children? Scullin *et al.* (2002) studied an adaptation of the Gudjonsson measure which is known as the Visual Suggestibility Scale for Children. This is very similar except that the material is presented visually as well as auditorily and a number of other modifications made to ensure that the measure was suitable for this younger age range. What they did was to set up an independent field study in which the children were repeatedly interviewed about an event that occurred at school and things that did not actually happen. The question was, then, whether being influenced in these interviews actually was predictable on the basis of scores on the Visual Suggestibility Scale for Children. The 'Yield' and 'Shift' measures both independently predicted aspects of suggestibility in the field interviews.

Great care needs to be exercised over the question of the level of young children's suggestibility. As we saw above, there is evidence that they can be influenced to make accusations that emerge to be simply not true. However, just because they may be influenced, say, by leading questioning does not mean that they are always influenced or that they are more susceptible to suggestion than older children or even adults. Similarly, just because young children may be susceptible to influence on some matters does not mean that they are equally susceptible on all matters. A good example of this is Eisen *et al.*'s (1998) research. They studied a group of children who had been hospitalised for several days for assessment of abuse. This involved a medical examination which included an analysis of their genitals and anus as well as an interview concerning their possible abuse or neglect. Before they left hospital, they were subject to an interview which included misleading questions about the genital and anal examination and about other much more mundane matters. There were clearly signs that younger children were more susceptible to suggestion than older children. When asked suggestive questions about mundane matters, pre-school children were led to give untruthful responses nearly one third of the time whereas the figures for older children were half this and for teenagers a fifth of this. But when faced with leading questions on the topic of abuse such as 'The doctor did not have any clothes on, did he/she?' then pre-school children succumbed one fifth of the time, older children rarely and teenagers never. That is to say, that the youngsters were not so suggestible about the crucial issue of abuse.

There is little consistency across studies in terms of the percentages of children who succumb to suggestive questions. Poole and Lindsay (2002) describe the proportions across different studies which are affected by suggestive questioning as showing 'vast variability' (p. 369). Consequently, it is difficult and perhaps impossible to assess the likelihood that suggestion plays a role in real-life cases involving children. One remarkable suggestion they make is that there is a case for the use of leading questions in some circumstances. They urge professionals such as social workers not to use leading questions when working areas where the baseline rates of abuse are low. Children disclose about abuse without interviewers using leading questions, which risk increasing the risk of false claims by the child. On the other hand, professionals working in areas where sexual abuse is common may be justified in using leading questioning as their 'hit' rate is likely to be high. They can reduce the risk of false information by the use of instructions or procedures which clarify to the child what is expected. For example, they can be told that they can give answers such as 'I don't understand' or 'I don't know'.

The problem with this is that it is difficult to make a judgement about just what proportion of false allegations are tolerable. If one seeks to minimise the number of false allegations then what Poole and Lindsay have to say is unacceptable. On the other hand, if the objective is to maximise the number of correct identifications of child sexual abuse then what they have to say is appropriate. These are not matters for psychology but issues such as fairness, justice and ethics.

The diagnosticity of signs of abuse

Forensic and criminal psychologists and other clinicians usually spend their time forming judgements about a limited range of individuals. For example, they may work almost exclusively with sexually abused individuals. It is not surprising, therefore, to find that their expertise is largely limited to this group. They may take characteristics of such clients as indicators that there is a problem in people in general. For example, many of their sexually abused clients may report bed-wetting or enuresis in childhood and assume that this indicates a relationship between sexual abuse and bed-wetting. In other words, the psychologist may come to believe that bed-wetting is symptomatic of child sexual abuse. The trouble is that this is an illusory correlation since no comparisons are being made with non-abused children. If the psychologist dealt with non-abused individuals then he or she might well find that bed-wetting is just as common in this group. Hence bed-wetting has no power to differentiate between the abused and the non-abused.

So clinical experience may result in practitioners having false beliefs that certain indicators are signs of abuse. Denials by a child that they have been abused do not always seem to carry the evidentiary weight that might have been expected had the denial been made, say, by an adult. It is widely assumed that children are reluctant to disclose abuse for many reasons. A study, in Texas, took children in the age range of pre-school to 18 years on the files of the local child protection service (Bradley and Wood, 1996). Nearly three-quarters of them had already disclosed to someone that they had been abused. Only later did most of them come to the attention of the police or the child protection service. Denial of abuse by the children was rare at 6% of the cases. The recantation by the child of their claim to have been abused was also rather rare at 4% of the cases. One simple lesson to be drawn from these statistics is that children who deny abuse are probably not hiding the fact that they have been abused. It is more likely that abuse simply did not happen.

Berliner and Conte (1993) argue for caution when implementing the conclusions of studies that find a greater prevalence, say, of behavioural disorders in clinical samples of sexually abused individuals than in community controls. Most behavioural correlates of abuse are non-specific to abused children. That is to say, there are few, if any, factors that manifest themselves only in the behaviours of sexually abused children. Furthermore, the behavioural differences between abused and non-abused children are rather stronger when the behaviour is assessed through parents' ratings than when they are assessed through the children's ratings. It is possible, then, that the parents are aware of the possibility of abuse and consequently their ratings are affected by that knowledge. In this context, some of the indicators that have been claimed to be characteristic of sexually abused children do *not* emerge in the self-reports of those children. These are depression, anxiety and low self-esteem.

A key concept in understanding false allegations is that of diagnosticity. Broadly speaking, this is the extent to which certain features of a child's behaviour indicate that he or she has been sexually or physically abused (but see below). Howitt (1992) listed some of the many factors that have been suggested as indicating abuse. Text-books for teachers about abuse, for example, sometimes suggest that regularly being late for school is a sign of abuse. Medics in Cleveland, location of the first major sexual abuse scandal (Butler-Sloss, 1988), similarly accepted that the response of a child's anus to being touched by a doctor was a sign that that child had actually been abused (Hanks *et al.*, 1988). These are examples of the indicators approach to the identification of sexual abuse.

Their use may be flawed in practice, but it is encouraged by research findings. For example, Slusser (1995) reviewing six studies concluded that overt sexual behaviour that is inappropriate for a child of that age is an indicator of sexual abuse. Never-theless, any practitioner working with children should be aware that the baseline rates of childhood sexual activities are sometimes high. Gordon *et al.* (1990a, b) obtained parental reports on 2- to 7-year-olds:

- 29% of the families claimed that their child had been exposed to sexually explicit materials;
- half of the children were known to have masturbated;
- 30% of the children had been involved in exploratory sex-play.

The value of any indicator of sexual abuse is dependent on a number of factors:

- The frequency of this possible indicator of sexual abuse in the group in question.
- The frequency of the indicator in similar but non-abused children.

It is particularly important for an indicator to be common among abused children but rare or non-existent among non-abused children. Very often, the relative frequency of the indicator in the population is unknown. Diagnosticity of a sign of sexual abuse depends on how common the sign is in abused children compared with its frequency in non-abused children. If the sign is equally common in both groups of children then it is useless in the diagnosis of sexual abuse. Munchaussen's syndrome by proxy is a condition in which the offender fabricates symptoms and may deliberately injure a child

Table 14.1 The outcomes of using an indicator (or sign) to predict abuse

	Child abused in reality	Child not abused in reality
Indicator of abuse present	True positive	False positive
Indicator of abuse absent	False negative	True negative

in order to obtain repeated medical attention (Plassman, 1994). Some of the suggested indicators of the syndrome are actually diametric opposites (Howitt, 1992). So, for example, it has variously been suggested that evidence of the syndrome is demonstrated by confession to the crime but also by denial of the crime, or by over-concern about the child's health by the parent as well as unconcern about the child's health!

A study of paediatric psychologists (Finlayson and Koocher, 1991) suggests that their interpretation of the extent to which an indicator may be indicative of abuse varies enormously. The psychologists were, for example, given a short description of a child whose school performance declined fast, who wet its bed, who was saying things about a bad man and who became anxious at the prospect of separation from its parents. On the basis of this evidence, 9% believed that the likelihood of abuse was above 75% certain, and 35% suggested that the probability of abuse was less than 25% certain. According to Slusser (1995), certain indicators such as bed-wetting may be the result of a multiplicity of different aetiologies. Consequently, especially because they are common among children (i.e. high base rate of occurrence), these indicators are of little diagnostic value at all. Why is this?

The diagnosticity issue is illustrated in Table 14.1. This shows the possible outcomes of using an indicator to predict whether abuse has occurred. For an indicator to be useful, true positives and true negatives should be maximised but false positives and false negatives should be kept to the minimum. Otherwise the guilty will escape detection and the innocent will be falsely accused.

The lack of knowledge of how common an indicator is in the non-abused population affects the confidence that one can have in its diagnosticity. So, for example, it is fairly widely held that precocious sexual behaviour is an indicator of sexual abuse. Just how common is it in the non-abused population of children? Research is the only sure way to answer the question. Friedrich *et al.* (1992) have carried out extensive investigations into parents' reports of sexual behaviours in abused and non-abused children. Certain sorts of behaviour seem to occur at similar rates in groups of abused and non-abused children. So, for example, touching the breasts of a woman is equally common in both sexually abused girls and non-abused girls. Thus any psychologist who took such touching as an indicator of sexual abuse would be profoundly wrong. There are dangers in inadvertently choosing a variable as an indicator of abuse which, actually, does not discriminate between abused and non-abused children.

Even if we take an indicator such as masturbation that does differentiate between the two, there remain dangers despite the fact that this is commoner in abused children. Data collected by Friedrich (undated) demonstrated that in the 2–5 years of age female group, 28% of the sexually abused children masturbated whereas 16% of non-abused children did. In conventional psychological research terms this suggests that there is clearly an association between masturbation and sexual abuse. In terms of diagnosticity of indicators, things are not this simple. Take, for example, a class of 30 children. It is difficult to state precisely just how many of this class will have been sexually abused on average. Given the age group and the results of a variety of surveys, it is not unreasonable to suppose that 10% of the class will have been abused whereas the remaining 90% will not have been abused. Taking Friedrich's figures on rates of masturbation, we would expect the following outcome:

- *True positives* – one child correctly identified by the indicator as sexually abused.
- *False negatives* – two children who were abused are not correctly identified as such by the indicator (because they do not masturbate).
- *False positives* – four children wrongly identified as abused (because they are in the non-abused sample but masturbate).
- *True negatives* – 23 children correctly identified as not being abused.

Thus using this test, only a third of abused children are identified as being abused. For every abused child the test picks out, a further four are identified incorrectly as being abused. This is an unimpressive outcome especially given the distress that follows from false accusations.

Thus the requirements of the indicator approach are much more demanding than would appear initially (Wood, 1996). It has been suggested that an indicator that is three times commoner among abused children than non-abused children nevertheless is only very weak evidence of abuse. An indicator that is 14 times more common in abused than non-abused children might be described as a moderate to strong indicator. It is far from being perfect proof (Poole and Lindsay, 1998). The interpretation of ratios such as this may be difficult for practitioners and other professionals to appreciate and apply. It may be helpful to point out that Friedrich *et al.* (1992) found that imitation of intercourse occurred in precisely this ratio. Imitation occurred in 14% of abused children but only 1% of non-abused children. Another reason for caution about such indicators is that sexual interest in sexually abused children may be heightened by the child sexual abuse investigation itself: that is, that part of the apparent effect of child sexual abuse is actually a consequence of the interest in sexual matters among the professionals and parents involved.

Of course, it might seem sensible to seek two indicators rather than a single indicator of abuse. But the consideration of two indicators may not be much of an advance given the weak predictive strength of most predictors of abuse. Furthermore, the indicators may almost always occur together, which would do very little to improve the diagnosticity of the indicators.

Assessing the accuracy of young children's reports

Berliner and Conte (1993) suggested that there are two main strategies for improving professional judgement in child abuse cases:

- *Indicators approach*: this involves the search for evidence that distinguishes the true from the false report. As we have seen, one difficulty with this is the weakness of some of the indicators in use by practitioners.
- *Standards approach*: this specifies rules of conduct for those who carry out assessments. It seeks to minimise contamination of the child's reports through the use of best-practice procedures when dealing with children.

In this chapter we have largely examined the bad practice aspects of these approaches. Forensic and criminal psychology has made a more positive contribution. Chapter 17 discusses methods of assessing the value of a child's evidence and provides more information about how interviews can be better constructed to prevent the influence of suggestive and leading questions.

Main points

- The problem of false allegations is only one component of miscarriages of justice. It has proven particularly problematic in relation to allegations of child sexual abuse given the young age of many victims and the difficulty in interviewing them adequately. There is considerable evidence that some false memories for events may be created in children. Persistent leading questions can have an effect. One can overstate the fallibility of children's memories since there is plenty of evidence that they can be very accurate at recalling events. Nevertheless, some children in some circumstances will be affected by suggestion and make incorrect reports. However, a proportion of these will be retracted by the child when the interviewer questions their answer.

- There are a number of mechanisms that lead to repressed memories according to the theoretical approach in question. Freudian/Classical repression refers to an unconscious process by which the person is protected from distressing memories. An alternative are those studies that investigate the accuracy of eyewitness memory for emotionally charged events although the evidence seems to suggest that these tend to be well remembered. The repressed memory/false memory debate in psychology has attracted a great deal of public attention. Fundamentally, it sets different theories of memory in opposition to each other. It seems likely some recovered memories are indeed false memories because they are retracted.

- The issue of the diagnosticity of signs ought to be understood better by professional groups working with children. There are frequent claims in the professional literature of various professional groups that certain things are predictive of, say, sexual abuse. These include, for example, precocious sexual behaviour. Thus, say, a teacher who sees such behaviour exhibited by one of their students should be alerted to the risk that the child is being sexually abused. While it may be true that sexually abused children do demonstrate this more often, precocious sexual behaviour may not be a good indicator that a child has been sexually abused. The balance between the correctly identified abused and non-abused is important. A seemingly good indicator may result in many more false positive identifications of abuse than correct ones. The number of errors depends on the base rates of sexual abuse in the population and the frequency with which a sign occurs in the population in question.

Chapter 15

False confessions

Overview

- There is plenty of advice available to police officers about how best to elicit a confession. The environment for the interview should isolate the suspect and leave the officer in total command. The suspect may be intimidated by overstating the crime's seriousness or the strength of the evidence against them. Alternatively, a more sympathetic approach can be used in which excuses for the crime are provided.

- It is argued that the decision to confess is a rational process and false confessions follow similar rational processes. However, there are a number of different processes leading to false confession. Stress-compliant false confession is where the suspect confesses falsely merely to escape the stress of the police interview. Coerced-compliant false confessions may be induced by threats or offers of leniency subject to a confession being made. Persuaded false confession involves the suspect becoming persuaded that they may have committed the crime perhaps because they were drunk at the time and cannot remember it.

- False confession seems to be commoner among those with previous convictions in real life. Nevertheless, laboratory studies have shown how remarkably easy it is to induce someone to confess falsely and sometimes the confessor comes to believe their confession.

- There are very serious consequences that follow from confessions and this is true for false confessions. The evidence in the United States shows as many as half of the confessions which eventually were established to be false nevertheless led to criminal convictions. Furthermore, there is evidence that a jury knowing that certain confession evidence has been obtained by illegal means nevertheless may be affected by that evidence even when warned by a judge of the inadmissibility of such evidence.

It is claimed that false confessions are much the same as any other confession. American police investigation manuals (Inbau *et al.*, 1986) contain a great deal of advice on how to encourage a suspect to confess. While the tape recording of interviews might discourage unacceptable tactics elsewhere, it is not required in the United States. Inbau *et al.*'s advice includes suggestions about the arrangement and style of the room in which the interview is conducted. For example, it should be a small bare room and controls of things such as lighting should be inaccessible to the suspect. Invasion of the suspect's physical space by the officer is recommended. If possible, the room should be fitted with a one-way mirror so that another officer can secretly view the suspect for signs that he or she may be becoming distressed or tired, times when the suspect may be especially vulnerable to pressure to make a confession.

Generally speaking, such an environment will make the suspect feel socially isolated, and experience sensory deprivation. They will feel not in control of the situation. Figure 15.1 gives a résumé of the steps in obtaining a confession as put forward in the police manual. Advice is also given on how to differentiate guilty and innocent suspects. The manual suggests that there are verbal and non-verbal cues to lying. Innocent people give concise answers, sit upright but show little rigidity of posture and they make direct eye-to-eye contact (see Chapter 16 for a discussion of the characteristics of lying).

Two processes are involved in the interview:

- *Maximisation*: this consists of 'scare' tactics employed with the intention of intimidating the suspect. The officers overstate how serious the crime was and also the charges involved. Sometimes false or exaggerated claims are put forward about the evidence or its nature.

- *Minimisation*: this consists of the soft-sell techniques designed to encourage a sense of security. The techniques include offering sympathy, tolerance, giving face-saving excuses and moral justification by, for example, blaming the victim for the crime. The seriousness and extent of the charges may be minimised also.

Kassin and McNall (1991) found evidence that these strategies were effective in communicating high and low sentence expectations respectively, as might be expected. While these practitioner-oriented guidelines are of interest, there is more systematic information available about the process of confession. Ofshe and Leo (1997) regard false confessions as being the result of much the same type of factors that result in any other type of confession. Confession is largely the result of a *rational decision-making process*

Figure 15.1 Inbau's recommended technique for obtaining a confession

in which people optimise any situation for themselves in the light of the alternatives. Just as the police manual suggests, the police obtain confessions by leading the suspect to believe that the evidence against them is insurmountable. For example, it is certain that they will be convicted irrespective of any additional confessional evidence. By confessing, the suspect may gain some advantage such as a sentence reduction or a lesser charge. Following the confession, it remains possible that the suspect may be found to be innocent. For example, their confession may contain inaccurate information – they may describe using a weapon different from the one the police believe it to be. Leo (1996) likens the process to a confidence game in which the suspect exchanges trust and confidence in the police for the confession or other evidence. Only in this way, he argues, does the irrationality of not remaining silent (the suspect's right under the US Miranda rules that govern police interviews) become understandable.

There are various types of false confession, according to Ofshe and Leo (1997), which can be identified by the activities of the police who obtain the confession:

- *Stress-compliant false confession*: being accused of a crime is a stressful situation that may be compounded by insistent and seemingly endless questioning by the police. The suspect may have no answer to what they say. In an attempt to escape such a punishing situation, the suspect may confess.

- *Coerced-compliant false confessions*: threats of harm or promises of leniency may coerce the suspect into confession. For example, the detectives may appear to agree that the offence is an accident rather than a crime. Nevertheless, they insist on a confession in order to confirm this.

- *Persuaded false confession*: the suspect becomes convinced that the chances are that they actually committed the crime although they have no recollection of doing so. For example, the suspect may be persuaded that drugs or alcohol have induced a blackout, thus explaining the lack of memory of the event.

One false confessor describes his interaction with the interviewing police officer as follows. It clearly shows some of these techniques in action:

> He goes, 'If you'd just say it was an accident,' he said 'you all were having rough sex,' you know, 'and just got carried away and you accidentally killed her, they won't charge you with first degree. They will charge you with second-degree murder and then,' you know, 'your future looks so much brighter,' you know, he goes, 'because you're a clean-cut, respectable man from what I see. Your bosses think highly of you, and so do all the people I've talked to.' He goes, 'Now why would you throw your life away for some drunken coke whore who is nothing but a piece of white trash,' you know. And he goes, 'Well, if you say it was an accident I think I can possibly talk these guys into letting you go home.'
>
> *(Ofshe and Leo, 1997, pp. 1103–4)*

Another approach dependent on the analysis of conversation (as an interview may be regarded) starts with the linguistics notion of speech acts – that is, the way that language is used to achieve ends or get things done. Shuy (1998) argues that:

- confessions are constructed through dialogue;
- the suspect and the interrogator each contribute to the dialogue;
- the dialogue will contain uncertainties and lead to questions about what was actually confessed and what is admitted, i.e. things may be admitted ('I did have sex with the woman') but these may not be seen as a confession to the crime ('She readily agreed to having sex').

The interrogator may make rather different inferences about what is admitted. This interpretation forms the central thrust of subsequent legal action.

Shuy (1998) provides an analysis of a number of transcripts of police interrogations. The transcripts of the interrogation were analysed linguistically by Shuy for inconsistency. In the example to follow, he points out that the police may have misunderstood the language of the suspect. The verb 'to know' has a series of dictionary meanings but, in addition, it has a number of non-dictionary meanings. The verb may be used in the following contexts to mean rather different things such as in the sentences 'I know that Jones is going to win the election' and 'I know it's going to rain tomorrow when we have our picnic'. A strict dictionary definition of these words actually makes these sentences unintelligible.

In the case in question, Jerue is one of the suspects for a crime. The investigator asks him a question that uses this verb 'to know'. Jerue's reply is:

No

Yea, but I didn't know he was gonna shoot him though

We didn't plan to kill him when we were goin' over there.

This can be interpreted as a statement by Jerue that there was no intent to murder. That is the implication of saying that he did not know that the other man was going to shoot the victim.

This theme of intent occurs at other stages in the dialogue. The police, in their attempts to obtain an admission of the intent to kill the man, employed other words. Read through the following exchanges – it may be useful to read the passage first of all as the police seeking an admission of intent would and then in terms of the perspective of the accused who was essentially trying to deny intent:

You guys intended to go over there and rob him and kill him, didn't you?

No, we didn't plan to kill him at all.

But it was an understanding and a plan between the two of you for him to do it, right?

Yeah.

You both planned to do it – before – up to two hours before you and Lavon actually shot him, you both planned on shootin' him, right?

Right.

OK, that's what we thought, and you just had to kill him to rip his stuff off.

No, we were just gonna hold him at gunpoint, that's what I thought.

But about two hours before he actually shot him is when he changed your mind and decided to shoot him, right?

Right.

Then, if I understand you right, you guys changed your mind from robbin' him to shootin' him about two hours before he actually shot him, right?

Yeah, about that, yah.

That's when both of you changed your mind, you both agreed on it at that point, right?

Right.

(Shuy, 1998, pp. 35–6)

Early on, the suspect seems to be admitting intent but the interpretation depends on how the word 'it' is to be understood in the officer's second question. Does 'it' refer to killing the man or to going to his house with an intent to steal? Similarly, how is one to understand the penultimate sentence just before the suspect's comment 'Right'? It might appear to indicate that the suspect had finally capitulated and admitted the intent to kill. This may be an erroneous interpretation. Notice the structure of the final questions from the police officer. They are somewhat complex and it is not definite exactly what the suspect is agreeing to. It could be planning to kill but it may be that he was a little confused by the structure of the question and thought he was agreeing that the decision to rob was made two hours before.

The suspect was convicted of aiding a planned homicide.

Box 15.1

Forensic psychology in action: who confesses falsely?

False confessions are the result of the interaction between the police and the suspect: that is, they are a consequence of the situation. A different approach is to study the sorts of person most likely to falsely confess (Gudjonsson, 1992). The Birmingham Six were the group of men convicted of the Irish Republican Army's bombing of a Birmingham pub, killing several people. Flawed forensic evidence suggested that they had been involved with explosives. There was a serious degree of ill treatment of the men by the police. Four of the six had made confessions. Eventually, they were acquitted of the crime after many years in prison. Gudjonsson had collected psychological data from the men in 1987. His data on compliance and suggestibility indicated that the two men who were the most resistant to the pressure of the police to confess were the two men who scored lowest on these measures.

Another study examined 56 prison inmates in Iceland who had claimed to have made a false confession to the police and compared them with over 400 other prisoners (Sigurdsson and Gudjonsson, 1997). The researchers suggest that there are two types of explanation of false confession:

- Inexperience of police methods and procedures makes some suspects especially susceptible to police manipulation and attempts at coercion. It is known from previous research that those who score highly on interrogative suggestibility as measured by Gudjonsson's Susceptibility Scale had fewer previous convictions.
- False confession is part of the criminal lifestyle of some offenders. It is known from previous research that false confessors tended to be illicit drug users and to have a history of drug dependency.

The findings of the research included the following:

- The false confession concerned only their current sentence in 5% of cases.
- False confessors had previously served prison sentences more often than the control group (65% versus 38%).
- False confessors were younger than people who did not falsely confess when first convicted.
- False confessors were younger when they first went to prison.
- False confessors had more previous prison sentences.
- False confessors had spent more time in prison prior to their current offence.
- Nearly all had a criminal record before the false confession (88%).
- The commonest offence associated with false confession was property crime (59%). The second category was serious traffic violations. Violent offences amounted to 7%.

Pearse *et al.* (1998) carried out forensic clinical interviews with suspects at a police station in order to assess their psychological vulnerability. Measures included anxiety, intelligence and reading as well as suggestibility. There was no evidence to suggest that such clinical assessments of vulnerability related to confession. Indeed, the best predictor of confession was whether the suspect had taken illegal drugs in the previous 24 hours. The reasons for this are not yet clear – it could be merely that they confessed so as to get out of the police station into an environment where they could obtain drugs. They tended to confess less if a solicitor was present.

Types of false confession

Kassin and Kiechel (1996) classify three different types of false confession:

- *Voluntary false confession*, which is personally motivated and which occurs in the absence of external pressure from others.
- *Coerced-compliant false confession* in which the suspect confesses in order to escape an aversive interrogation, secure a promised benefit or avoid a threatened harm.
- *Coerced-internalised false confession* in which the suspect comes to believe in their own guilt of committing the crime.

It is difficult to believe that individuals come to believe in their own guilt over something that they have not done. Perhaps it is more understandable that people may confess when they find themselves in a no-win situation and are offered a way of making things easier for themselves. In an intriguing experiment, Kassin and Kiechel (1996) simulated aspects of false confession in a laboratory experiment. Remarkably, participants could be encouraged to make up details of an offence that they simply had not committed.

American university students were assigned to one of four different groups by Kassin and Kiechel. These were defined by the independent variable high versus low vulnerability and by a second independent variable, which was the presence versus absence of a false incriminating witness:

- Participants worked on an individual basis with a female 'plant' or confederate of the experimenter.
- Both the participant and the plant worked together on a reaction time study.
- A list of letters of the alphabet was read aloud by one of them and typed on the computer keyboard by the other.
- Initially, the confederate did the typing but after three minutes the roles were reversed.
- They were warned not to press the ALT key because a software fault would crash the computer and so the data would be lost.
- Some of the participants had to type fast and others could type slowly because of the speed of reading out the letters. This is known as the vulnerability manipulation – the speedier one works then the less opportunity one has to self-monitor what one is doing.
- Typing errors were greatest for the high rate, confirming the validity of the procedure in this regard.

- After 60 seconds the computer crashed as had been planned by the experimenter.
- The experimenter accused the participant of pressing the forbidden key – all denied this.
- At this stage, false incriminating evidence was introduced for some participants. The confederate admitted that she had seen the participant hit the ALT key on the computer. In the control condition, the no witness condition, the same confederate said that she had not seen what had occurred.

So, the experimental situation had resulted in the participant being accused of doing something that they had not. In some cases, there was also a witness claiming to have seen the participant doing that thing. These are much the same circumstances in which false confessions in real life have been obtained. The different aspects of false confession could be identified according to the participant's behaviours:

- *Compliance*: the experimenter wrote a 'confession' for the participant ('I hit the ALT key and caused the program to crash') which counted as compliance if the participant then agreed to it.
- *Internalisation*: a second confederate asked the participant later what had happened. If the participant said they had hit the wrong key without qualification (i.e. without saying something like 'I think') then this counted as internalisation.
- *Confabulation*: the experimenter reappeared and asked whether the subject could recall specific details to fit the allegation.

The outcome of the research suggested that the fast or pressurised version of the study tended to increase all three forms of influence. Each of these was increased by the presence of the witness who claimed she had seen the participant hit the wrong key. Confabulation was common where there was a witness and a fast pace but not otherwise.

One criticism of this research is that falsely confessing to something one had not done had no adverse consequences. Falsely confessing in a police interview may lead to punishment in the form, say, of a prison sentence. Horselenberg, *et al.* (2003) essentially replicated the Kassin and Kiechel (1996) study but added a punishment in that the false confessions led to a financial loss by the confessor. That is, they lost part of their fee for participating in the study by accepting that they caused the computer to crash. Despite this, the findings of the new study were much the same as those of Kassin and Keichel's. That is to say, the majority of participants falsely confessed. However, despite the evidence that there are personality factors that might lead to false confession (see Box 15.1 for details), falsely confessing in this study was not associated with Gudjonsson's Compliance Scale and a measure of compliance tendencies. In circumstances in which over 80% of people will falsely confess, would one expect that personality factors would be a factor? The situation is enough to create the confession so this will be little affected by some people being more prone to confess falsely than others.

Consequences of a false confession

Confession is common. It has been estimated that in the United Kingdom something like 60% of all police detainees actually confess (Pearse *et al.*, 1998). Just how many of these are likely to be false confessions is anyone's guess. Not all false confessors are victims of police interviewing methods. Some false confessions are nuisances and in no way solicited by the police. There is such a phenomenon as voluntary false confession. For example, 200 people confessed to the kidnap of the US aviator Charles Lindbergh's baby in the 1920s. At one extreme is the anonymous false confession which, if followed up by the police, may take up a lot of time. The classic example of this in Britain was the Yorkshire Ripper case of the 1970s. The police investigating this case were hampered severely by a number of highly publicised tape recordings purporting to be from the Yorkshire Ripper himself. He appeared to be taunting the officers. Senior officers mistakenly regarded them as genuine. This diverted police resources along a false trail. It, possibly, may have delayed arrest and allowed further murders. McCann (1998) mentions another example of false confession that is not the result of police pressure. Young members of gangs may be pushed into confessing by other members of the same gang in the belief that the court will deal leniently with young people.

Leo and Ofshe (1998) argue that there are numerous documented cases of police-induced false confession. These researchers systematically studied such cases. They systematically searched media, case files and secondary sources for examples of false confession. All cases selected for inclusion in the study satisfied the following criteria:

- no physical or other credible evidence indicated the suspect's guilt;
- the state's case consisted of little other than the suspect's confession;
- the suspect's factual innocence was supported by evidence.

In this way, they found 34 proven cases of false confession: for example, the murder victim actually turned up alive after the trial, or the true offender was eventually found guilty, or scientific evidence proved the innocence of the false confessor. In addition, there were another 18 cases that seemed highly likely to be false confessions. Eight cases were classified as probably false confessions – since the majority of the evidence indicated the innocence of the accused.

Whatever the reason for false confession, the consequences of doing so in the United States are often great as these US data show:

- 8% were fortunate and suffered only arrest and detention by the police;
- 43% were prosecuted but the case was eventually dismissed;
- 48% of the cases ended up with a criminal conviction.

This final figure included:

- 17% who were sentenced to more than 10 years;
- 5% who were given death sentences;
- 2% who were actually executed.

Nearly three-quarters of all of the false confessors were found guilty if they went to trial. Considering the certain false confessors alone showed that 55% were released prior to going to trial. Of this group who were eventually established as not guilty by further evidence, 3% were acquitted by the court, 29% were convicted despite their not guilty plea, and 15% actually plead guilty in court despite their eventual proven innocence.

Can confession evidence be disregarded?

There is evidence from experimental studies that confession evidence is especially potent. Studies by Kassin and Neumann (1997) found it to produce higher conviction rates than character testimony and eyewitness identification. Confession evidence is subject to rules. In the United States, confession evidence is not normally admissible in court if it was elicited by any of the following (Kassin, 1997b; Kassin and Sukel, 1997):

- brute force;
- prolonged isolation;
- deprivation of food or sleep;
- threats of harm or punishment;
- promises of immunity or leniency;
- without notifying the suspect of his/her constitutional rights except in exceptional circumstances.

Of course, this confession evidence may be given in court before its admissibility is challenged. This begs the question of whether in these circumstances the jury members can completely disregard the confession evidence as is required in accordance with legal principles. The alternative, of course, is that the confession evidence, despite its inadmissibility, sways the jury.

Kassin and Sukel (1997) set out to test, experimentally, this hypothesis. In one study, introductory psychology students in the United States were randomly assigned to one of four confession groups. The groups were those produced by the following variables:

- high-pressure versus low-pressure interrogation;
- admissible versus inadmissible confessions as ruled upon by the judge during the 'trial'.

Each 'mock' juror studied a trial transcript that took 20 to 25 minutes to read. They then completed questionnaires without jury deliberations.

The transcript was of the trial of a man charged with murdering his estranged wife and a male neighbour. The district attorney charged that the man, Wilson, killed the pair after coming across them together. The defendant, on the other hand, claimed that he merely found the bodies when he went back to his former abode to collect financial papers. With the exception of the confession, the evidence against Wilson was entirely circumstantial (the killer was 6 feet tall and left-handed), incomplete (there was no murder weapon) and ambiguous (before calling the police he fled the scene and phoned his attorney). The transcripts consisted of opening statements, closing arguments, the examinations of five witnesses and a brief judge's instruction on the charge of first-degree murder and the requirements of proof: presumption of innocence, burden of proof and reasonable doubt.

Other participants rated interrogation situations based on Inbau *et al.*'s (1986) manual for police officers:

- The high-pressure condition: 'They drove me back to the police station, where Officer Heffling handcuffed me, took out his gun and started asking me questions about the murders. My arm really hurt from the handcuffs, but he wouldn't remove them . . . I told him that my right arm had just come out of a cast and was very sore.' When asked 'were they trying to pressure you to confess?', the defendant replied that 'yes he was angry and yelling'. The police officer also testified but rejected the suggestion that Wilson was under so much stress that he would confess to a crime he did not commit.

- In the low-pressure condition, the defendant was said to have confessed immediately upon questioning. He was not handcuffed, verbally abused or threatened with a weapon.
- In the no-confession control group, the defendant and police officer both testified that Wilson denied murdering his wife and neighbour during his interrogation.

The remaining condition to be manipulated was the admissibility or not of the confession:

- Admissible condition: the defence lawyer raised an objection to the police officer mentioning the confession material. The judge overruled the objection. The prosecuting lawyer mentioned the confession in the closing argument.
- Inadmissible condition: the judge supported the defence's objection to the police evidence about the confession. The confession was deemed inadmissible and struck off the transcript of the trial though, of course, the jury was aware of it. The jury was then instructed by the judge to disregard the police officer's remarks about the confession.

The evidence showed that the inadmissible evidence affected the mock jurors' perceptions of the guilt of the accused. They gave more guilty verdicts when they knew of this evidence. This was the case even in circumstances where they believed that the confession was a coerced one and they knew that information about that confession was inadmissible in court. A second study that contained more evidence in support of the prosecution produced similar findings. The US Supreme Court's view is to describe the admission of coerced confession as a harmless error. Kassin's findings are clearly at variance with this.

Main points

- False confessions may be motivated by a range of factors. Particularly serious are those that are the consequence of police interrogation methods which are designed to encourage confession by the guilty but may encourage confession by the innocent. Although in some cases, false confessions may be made simply to obtain relief from the interview situation with the police, sometimes the decision to confess falsely is the result of a rational decision faced with apparently strong evidence.
- There are some remarkable demonstrations of false confessions based on laboratory experiments. These are important since they suggest that virtually anyone, given appropriate circumstances, can be put into a situation where they confess to doing something that they have not done. What is more remarkable, is that some false confessors do not simply acquiesce under certain circumstances but that they seem to believe that they did what they confess to.
- The consequence of falsely confessing may be as serious as those for a true confession. People who are eventually proven to have falsely confessed stand a high risk of retractions not being accepted and a high risk of being convicted by a court of the crime they did not commit. Perhaps even more disturbing is the evidence that juries can be influenced by inadmissible confession evidence that a judge has warned them to disregard.

Chapter 16

Lies, lie detecting and credibility: polygraphy and statement validity analysis

Overview

- The assessment of the accuracy of testimony is a complex process. Few experts suggest that there are simple, infallible indicators of untruthful testimony such as characteristic body language. Lying might be defined as the intention to deceive without making the other person aware of this intent. Most forms of lie detection do not detect lies at all but the emotion that may go alongside lying and the fear of its detection.

- Most professional groups – police officers and psychologists, for example – are no better than chance at detecting lies without specialised training. Experience may lead to confidence in one's abilities to detect lies though it is not associated with better ability in practice at detecting lies. There are problems in detecting liars due to our mistaken ideas about cues to deception and the sheer complexity of interview situations which may make it difficult for the interviewer to concentrate on key things. Professionals also may have false beliefs about how to detect lies. For example, police officers may believe that making a lot of body movements is a good indicator of lying but liars actually make fewer body movements. The lack of feedback on whether one has successfully identified a liar or not is one reason why professionals cannot improve their lie detecting ability.

- Good keys to false emotion are asymmetrical facial expressions and the overly quick facial expression of emotion.

- The polygraph test is a controversial technique depending on the physiological response to the fear of being caught lying. While it has some success, it also risks relatively high rates of wrongful accusations against innocent individuals. The threat of the polygraph or its findings can be effective in inducing a confession. Although the use of the polygraph may be unacceptable in court in a number of jurisdictions, there is a trend to using it as part of the supervision of sex offenders.

- The polygraph is more than simply a physiological instrument since the administration of polygraphy is more complex than that implies. In particular, it should be noted that the polygraph examiner knows a great deal about the case generally and is not unaware of the strength of the other evidence against the suspect.

- The validity of the normal police polygraph test is good for the guilty but rather poorer for the innocent.

- European psychologists have developed statement validity analysis as a way of assessing the competence of witnesses in giving evidence. This is a complex set of procedures that yield probabilistic statements about the evidential competence of the witness. It consists of criterion-based content analysis and the lesser-used validity checklist. Criterion-based content analysis is based on the working assumption that the way we present memories of real events is different from that for fictitious events. There are approximately 19 different criteria which may be used. For example, accounts of true events tend to contain indications that the person accepts that aspects of their account may be flawed. Generally, the evidence seems consistently to point to the value of statement validity analysis in the assessment of the value of some forensic evidence. There is evidence from both laboratory experiments and forensic settings that the methods are of value.

Not all of the problems of the criminal justice system would be solved if psychologists could identify liars accurately. But some of them would. This chapter examines some important approaches to understanding just what differentiates truthful from untruthful testimony:

- Ekman's psychological theory of lying which suggests that there are cues to deception that can be gleaned from aspects of the liar's language, demeanor and a number of other features.

- The polygraph test which can be used to assess the physiological arousal patterns manifested by a person anxious about the risk of identification as a liar.

- Statement validity analysis which takes a broad view of the differences between memories for real events and lies.

The psychology of lying

According to Ekman (1992, 1996) a lie has to include two components:

- the intention to mislead the victim of the lie;
- the victim is not informed about this intention.

It follows from this that not all forms of deception are lies – magicians, for example, are open about their intention to deceive. Keeping secrets is not a lie if the secret is known to be a secret – such as consistently refusing to reveal one's age. Giving false information with no intention to deceive is not lying. Not revealing information may be a lie if the intention was to deceive.

However, such a definition seeks to differentiate liars from truth tellers. It disregards the accuracy of statements made if there was no intention to deceive. That means that false memories of child abuse would not be considered a lie despite their extreme consequences for the accused. The accused is probably more concerned about the accuracy of the claims made against him or her in general than the motivation for the false allegation.

Assessing truthfulness is central to much professional work in psychology as well as forensic work in particular. Nevertheless, few psychologists are formally trained in any of the methods of detecting lies. There is good reason to be suspicious of rigid systems of lie detection. None of the techniques discussed *favourably* in this chapter are based on the detection of lies from signs or signals as such: that is, body language, language and physiological signs are often poor and misleading indicators of lying. Successful detection of lies requires the examination of the total context. Judgements are made on the basis of a broad variety of evidence.

Similarly, some of the researchers discussed in this chapter are reluctant to use the term *lie detecting*. There are a number of reasons for this. Some of the methods use the emotions that may be associated with the fear of being caught telling lies but stress that there is no particular emotional pattern associated with lying. Other researchers use methods more based on the psychology of memory to assess the validity of statements especially those made by child witnesses. Again, it cannot be said that lies are being assessed directly, merely the differences between memory for true events and 'false memories'.

Ekman's theory of lie detection

It is hardly surprising that lies are hard to detect – their function is to mislead. There is a general consensus that the detection of lies is a skilled and rare talent. Studies have shown that most professional groups who deal closely with people such as the police, psychologists, lawyers and the medical profession can detect lies only at the chance level in standard conditions (Ekman, 1992, 1996). Indeed, contact with liars seems to have little impact on improving the ability to differentiate them from truth tellers. Garrido and Masip (1999) reviewed studies from different parts of the world concerned with police officers' ability to identify lying and truth telling. Their conclusions were as follows:

- Experienced police officers and newly recruited ones do not differ in their lie- and truth-detecting ability.
- Police officers are no better than the general public at detecting lies.
- Usually police officers are no better than chance at identifying truth telling and lying.
- Confidence about their lie-detecting ability was unrelated to actual ability to detect lies.
- Experienced officers are over-confident about their lie-detecting ability.
- Police officers use worthless indicators that a person is lying (e.g. social anxiety and assertiveness).

One criticism of much of the research on the detection of lies is that often the lying studied is induced for the purposes of a laboratory study and there are no consequences for the liar on being detected. How well would, for example, real police officers succeed at spotting the lies of a murderer? One intriguing study by Vrij and

Mann (2001) used videos of press conferences in which a relative makes a televised appeal to help find a missing relative or the killer. There are a number of instances in which a relative making such appeals was actually the killer and eventually convicted of the crime. They were clearly lying at the press conference and the consequences of detection were high. So are such high-stake lies more readily detectable? Dutch police officers were shown a number of such press conferences as well as similar ones that did not involve such lies as 'filler'. The murders were all British ones hence the decision to carry out the research with Dutch police officers. They identified the liars at exactly chance level – 50% accuracy. As with other studies, amount of experience as a police officer and amount of experience interviewing suspects were unrelated to accuracy. An officer's confidence in their judgements was also unrelated to accuracy; although officers with more interviewing experience were more confident about their judgements. A number of types of reasons were given by the officers for their decisions about lying. For example, they frequently mentioned things like fake emotions, real emotions and gaze aversion. Nevertheless, there was no correlation between these reasons and accuracy with one exception. That is, those who mentioned real emotions were actually less accurate in detecting lies than those who did not.

While some individuals are better than others at lie detecting (Ekman *et al.*, 1999), there is no simple way of detecting lies with a single indicator – such as body posture – which will work with all people. Problems in detecting lies include the following (Ekman, 1992):

- The sheer complexity of the task of monitoring all aspects of what the possible liar is doing – their talk, their facial expression, their voice expression, their hand movements, their posture, their gestures and so forth. It is simply impossible to focus on all of these at the same time. Sometimes, as a consequence, we may concentrate on the verbal and facial aspects of their behaviour. Unfortunately, these aspects of lying are the ones that the liar him- or herself is most able to monitor and change. Thus they are concerned to disguise their lying through these modalities.

- There are considerable individual differences in all of these bodily processes. For example, there is some evidence that an increase in manipulators (touching, stroking and otherwise manipulating one's own body) is a cue to deceit. That is because negative emotions increase. There are many individuals who normally use few manipulators so they are judged honest when they are in fact lying. So it is important to have some knowledge of the individual's baseline behaviours when assessing for lying.

- Unless the truth is known, the detection of a lie takes convoluted pathways. The majority of clues to deceit are actually signs of strong emotion. The deceitful person may fear being caught telling a lie. As a result, they may show physiological signs of emotion at the point of telling a lie. The difficulty for the observer is that these same emotions may be raised because of factors other than lying. For example, many of us will become angry if we are accused of lying. Consequently, on their own, emotions can be misleading guides to deceit. A great deal of other information is required.

- The context of the lie may vary enormously. So, for example, it is easier to tell a lie if one can anticipate when it will be necessary to tell a lie. If one has to lie unexpectedly, then there is little time to formulate a convincing lie.

- The spillage of inappropriate emotion given the context and contents of the lie is the real clue to deceit. Emotion, itself, is an unreliable indicator.

Nevertheless, despite all of these difficulties, individuals may be trained to be better at detecting lies. Ekman (1992) writes of *leakages*. These are the clues to emotion that may (but not inevitably) reveal that someone is lying. Included among the clues that should be examined are:

- Pauses and speech errors – these suggest a lack of preparation of the 'story' or strong negative emotions, especially fear.
- Raised pitch of voice – associated with anger and/or fear.
- Louder speech – most likely anger.
- Frequent swallowing, faster/shallower breathing, sweating, increased blinking, pupil dilation – all of these are signs of emotion although it is not possible to say which sort of emotion.
- Whitening of the face – anger or fear.

Furthermore, there are clues that the facial expression of emotion is *not* real. These offer additional clues to deceit:

- Asymmetrical facial expressions are indicators of falsehood: that is, if both sides of the face do not reveal the same emotion.
- The onset of the emotion should not be too abrupt as this is a sign of falseness.
- The emotional expression should be at an appropriate place in the verbal account.
- *Negative* emotions that do not involve sweating, breathing change or increases in the use of manipulators are more likely to be false.
- Happiness should involve eye muscles otherwise it is false.
- Fear and sadness involve a characteristic forehead expression especially involving the eyebrows. If this is missing then the emotion is false.

Ekman developed a 38-item lying checklist (Ekman, 1992, pp. 335–40) which considers many questions about 'the lie' and the ease with which it can be detected. If the following questions and others are answered with a yes, then this indicates that there is an increased difficulty in detecting the lie:

- Does the lie involve concealment only, without any need to falsify?
- Is the situation one in which the target is likely to trust the liar, not suspecting that he or she may be misled?
- Is the lie authorised? Lies that are socially permitted are harder to detect because there is less guilt involved in telling such lies.
- Does the liar have a good memory?

It should be evident from this that the detection of lying is not easy but not impossible. Perhaps the most important lesson is the multi-faceted approach to lie detecting. The idea that there is a single indicator of a liar is patently absurd from this perspective.

From the point of view of forensic and criminal psychology, the fact that many 'experts' in the criminal justice system remain convinced of their ability to detect lies means that many important lessons from research are essentially being ignored. Stromwall and Granhag (2003) studied three separate groups of legal professionals in Sweden. These were judges, prosecutors and police officers. As we have seen, there are some fairly well-established cues concerning lying established in the literature. Stromwall and Granhag mention that cues like higher pitched voices when lying and fewer body movements of the leg, foot, hand and arm. Of course, these are not infallible signs of lying though they seem to be effectively used by professionals when evaluating the truthfulness of a witness. They do have beliefs about the signs of lying but many are worthless signs according to the research evidence and so mislead practitioners into focusing on the wrong cues or simply add confusion to the process of judgement. The evidence from a survey of these professional groups indicated some marked discrepancies between what research evidence seems to suggest and the beliefs of the professionals:

- Lack of detail: all three groups of professionals tended to believe that untruthful statements contain little detail. This is supported by the mass of relevant studies into the relationship between truthfulness and the amount of detail.
- Liars avoid eye contact (are more gaze aversive): most police officers subscribed to this belief. However, the prosecutors and judges tended to believe that there was no difference between liars and truth tellers in gaze aversion more often than any of the alternatives. The research evidence is that there is no relationship between lying and gaze aversion – some studies even suggest that liars make more eye contact.
- Untruthful statements are less consistent over time: all professional groups tended to believe this. There is some research evidence to suggest that untruthful statements may be more consistent over time than truthful ones.
- Body movements: police officers tended to believe that liars made more body movements whereas the prosecutors and judges believed that body movement could not be used as a sign of lying. The research evidence suggests that liars may actually make fewer body movements than truth tellers.
- Pitch of voice: this was not generally seen as an indicator of lying in any of the groups of professionals. The most common belief was that pitch of voice made no difference to whether or not a person was lying. The research evidence does, however, suggest that there is a relationship.
- It is easier to detect a liar in face-to-face situations: the professionals tended to believe that interrogators interacting with witnesses in face-to-face situations would be better at identifying lying. Observers would be worse at detecting lying. This view of the professionals reverses what research evidence suggests. That is, objectively, observers are better at detecting liars than interrogators.

One of the reasons put forward for the relatively poor performance of professional lie detectors when detecting lies is that they rarely have any feedback about their actual performance. Thus, they cannot improve. Granhag et al. (2004) carried out a study in Sweden which was founded on this idea that adequate feedback is required in order that skills at detecting deception may be improved. They reasoned that among the groups of people who actually get feedback about the best cues to deceptions would be criminals who gain from telling lies successfully but are punished if, for example, the police do not believe them. So the researchers compared three groups – prisoners, prison personnel and students – in terms of their replies to a questionnaire concerning beliefs about what the characteristics of lying are. The questionnaire included a number of questions that had several responses from which to choose. For example:

Liars include fewer details than truth tellers.
Liars include more details than truth tellers.
There is no difference in the amount of details given by liars.
Don't know.

(p. 108)

The answers to the various questions could be assessed against the findings of research. So, for the above question, the correct answer according to research was the first alternative – liars include fewer details than truth tellers. Other research-based correct answers would include that liars move less than truth tellers and that planning of deceptive things to say increases the impression of honesty. The findings of the study tended to indicate that the prisoners did have different beliefs about the cues to deception from prison staff and students. They tended to have fewer stereotypes about cues to deception than the other two groups. Relatively, prisoners had the greatest insight into deception psychology – evidence in favour of the feedback hypothesis.

There have been suggestions about how a professional lie detector could improve their 'hit' rate about the derisory levels that research indicates are typical. One is that the actual interview techniques employed could be varied in order to improve lie detection. For example, the interviewee could be asked to go through something that they had just said or elaborate it in much greater detail (Vrij, 2004). In other words, increase the cognitive load on the inteviewee in order to increase the chances that they will reveal the signs of deception.

The polygraph process

It is frequently suggested that the polygraph or lie detector works because of the fear of offenders of being found to be lying. The Federal Bureau of Investigation in the United States maintained a website where it claimed that the polygraph or lie detector has a variety of uses (now unavailable):

- It can identify guilty people.
- It can eliminate suspects.
- It can establish the truth of statements made by witnesses or informants.
- It can save money by shortening investigations.
- It can increase conviction rates by encouraging confession by those who have lied prior to the polygraph examination.

This would seem to be a remarkable achievement for a device that does little more than measure some autonomic responses of a person's body when answering questions. The polygraph is a surprisingly elderly piece of equipment. Its foundations were in attempts around 1914 to assess lying using the pneumograph – a device that measured breathing patterns. The work of Larson (1922) and Keeler (1934) resulted in the polygraph machine which is more or less the same as used today. Sensors are attached to various parts of the body to detect various responses:

- Blood pressure variations reflecting cardiovascular (heart and veins) changes. These are measured using a version of the blood pressure cuff, which is placed around the arm when a nurse or doctor measures our blood pressure.
- Respiration rates and amplitude are measured by changes in pressure on inflated tubes placed strategically around the individual's torso.
- Sweating in the palms of the hand. This is part of the galvanic skin response.

The word polygraph merely means many drawings – several 'pens' draw lines on a moving paper chart in the technique. These pens move under electrical control

Figure 16.1 The phases of the FBI polygraph process

determined by a variety of physiological responses of the body. Physiological changes produce wave patterns that may become more frequent (e.g. the suspect breathes more rapidly) or increase in amplitude (e.g. the suspect breathes more deeply). Nowadays the apparatus is small enough to be stored in an attaché case. Furthermore, advancing technology has meant that computers may be connected to the polygraph. In this way, complex waves may be broken down into their component parts for easier interpretation. Increases in the physiological responses to a question, as measured by the polygraph, are held to be indicators of lie telling.

Figure 16.1 gives the phases in the FBI interview using the polygraph. Note the following things:

- The test itself, Phase 2, is just one component of the procedure using the polygraph or lie detector test.
- The examiner develops the list of questions to be used in a particular application in a pre-phase, partly in collaboration with the investigating officers.
- The process involves rapport building with the suspect that is different from the element of surprise we might expect from movies and video. In particular, the questions to be asked are not entirely unknown to the suspect before the polygraph test. It is the threatening nature of certain questions that is mainly the focus since these are the ones that make the suspect fear that they will be caught lying by the machine.
- Most importantly of all, the polygraph examiner does not merely make an assessment of the truth-telling of the suspect: the examiner (or the police officers involved) may confront the suspect with evidence that they were lying on the test. At this stage they are encouraged to tell the truth in various ways.
- Suspects who are deemed to be innocent by the test are unlikely to receive any further questioning.

Thus rather than speaking of 'the polygraph test' it is more appropriate to describe it as 'the polygraph process'. Not only does this give a better idea of the context but also it relates to the major criticisms of the technique. Few would argue that the polygraph is anything but controversial. In parts of the world polygraph evidence is not acceptable in court; elsewhere it is. The polygraph is a notable feature of the legal system in the United States despite there having been legislation which restricts of use of polygraph testing in terms of the selection of employees. So, although many thousands of polygraph tests are still given each year, in the United States the *Employee Polygraph Protection Act of 1988* essentially reduced pre-employment polygraphy to a trickle of 15% of the previous numbers. There are at least 70 countries in the world where the polygraph test is used extensively (Grubin and Madsen, 2005).

It is also important to note that the use of the polygraph may be increasing even in countries that shun the use of the polygraph as evidence of the guilt or innocence of an accused person. In the United Kingdom, for example, the government has initiated trials of the use of the polygraph in the supervision and management of convicted paedophiles when back in the community. This is the post-conviction use of the polygraph though much more limited in scope than, say, in the United States where it is used in a majority of states as a condition of probation and parole. Many sex offender treatment programmes also use polygraphy. The use of post-conviction polygraphy is not new and dates back to the 1970s in the United States (Grubin and Madsen, 2005). The polygraph is used, for example, to assess the truthfulness of what paedophiles say to probation workers about their day-to-day activities. So denials by paedophiles that they are targeting playgrounds in parks may be assessed using polygraph techniques. It is claimed that this has prevented the sexual abuse of a number of children and led to the re-imprisonment of some offenders (BBC News, 2005). The validity of the polygraph in these settings has not been extensively researched. Researchers in the United Kingdom have used polygraphy with sex offenders who were in the community and under the supervision of a probation officer (Grubin *et al.*, 2004, Madsen *et al.*, 2004). One of the problems in dealing with sex offenders is that of denial and avoidance in many aspects of their lives (see Chapter 10). Can polygraphy be used to ensure more reliable information from offenders about their activities and can polygraphy motivate offenders to avoid high risk situations that might lead to reoffending against children (or other targets)? For example, if an offender carries on masturbating to sexual fantasies about children, the belief is that he is much more likely to carry out that fantasy in real life, or if an offender gravitates towards children's play areas then this also would put him at greater risk of reoffending. Some participants in the study were told that they would retake a polygraph test after three months whereas the other offenders were not told this. At the polygraph reassessment they were asked questions like 'Have you done anything over the last three months that would concern your probation officer?' Out of the men who took the second polygraph test, the vast majority (97%) admitted engaging in this sort of high risk of reoffending behaviour. This meant that only one man did not admit any high risk behaviours – and he actually failed the test. One way of looking at all of this is that where the offender wishes to reduce their risk of reoffending, the polygraph can be helpful in helping them maintain a risk-of-reoffending-reduced lifestyle. There was evidence of a great deal of resistance to taking part in the polygraph testing on the part of some offenders and significant numbers of failures to turn up for the second polygraph test. The researchers suggest that these are individuals with little or no motivation to change their offending behaviour. In contrast, those motivated to change seem to have found it helpful in avoiding risky situations and reoffending.

Nevertheless, before concluding the polygraph is a good thing, a number of issues concerning polygraphy should be concerned.

Problems with the polygraph

There is little doubt that those who use the polygraph are convinced of its value. There is quite clearly a value in the technique even though it might be incapable of distinguishing between lies and the truth. People, in general, believe that it can detect lies and, more to the point, so do some offenders. Consequently, to tell a suspect that he or she has failed the lie detector test may induce confession in the guilty and false confession in the innocent. Because failing the polygraph test may induce such confessions, the examiners who use the polygraph may regard this as clear evidence of its validity – they decide that someone is showing signs of lying and that person subsequently confesses. In this sense, it is not surprising that police officers used to polygraphy see value in its use. Nevertheless, this may be merely an example of confirmation bias – the disproportionate emphasis we put on evidence that supports our point of view and the relative underplaying of evidence that contradicts our view. Probably more important, and systematically excluded from the FBI-style process, are the individuals who are 'cleared' by the polygraph process. Does this group consist solely of the innocent? If not, just what proportion of this group is in fact telling lies? What is known as the 'ground truth' (objective reality) cannot ever be known, of course. Without examining the evidence of the shortcomings of polygraph evidence, we may confuse ground truth with what the operator decides is the case.

The basic polygraph equation is given in Figure 16.2 together with some of the issues raised by the equation. The most serious of the problems are (partly based on Iacono and Lykken, 1997; Iacono and Patrick, 1997) as follows:

- In the normal polygraph process, the adequacy of the control questions is vital and it may be difficult to get them right. So, for example, the question 'Have you ever thought of taking revenge against someone who has done you a wrong?' is intended to encourage a lie in everyone, including the innocent. Most of us have done this although we do not care to admit it. On the other hand, some may answer 'no' to this question not because they are wilfully lying but because they had forgotten the occasions when they had.

- To be accused during the course of polygraphy of, say, murdering one's wife may be emotive for both the guilty and innocent. In these circumstances, there is reason to believe that the polygraph may fail to differentiate between lying and 'honest denial' (Iacono and Patrick, 1997).

- The control questions may disturb the guilty more than the innocent. For example, if asked in the context of a homicide, 'Have you ever stolen anything in your life?' the guilty might remember a series of armed robberies they had committed.

Increases in physiological rates and intensities	=	Evidence of lying if in response to relevant questions
• Can be caused by factors other than the fear of being caught lying • Can be faked to increase response to neutral questions • Increases comparative with control questions which may be poor controls		• Interpretation partly up to the discretion of examiner • Examiner knows some of evidence against offender and that he/she is a suspect, i.e. not totally blind procedure

Figure 16.2 The basic polygraph equation

Thus they show the same emotional signs to the control questions as they did to the relevant questions since, for them, the control question is also a relevant question.

- Faking and countermeasures are possible in response to a polygraph test. Indeed, some experts advertise such claims as that they can teach their clients to deceive the lie detector in half an hour on the Internet. The essential theory of this is simple: manifest the same physiological response to the control questions as the relevant questions. Thus practical advice might be to press down hard with one's toes to the control questions or to engage in a complex task such as mental arithmetic, which might produce a similar physiological response. Another simple technique is to bite one's tongue in response to the control questions.

- In its practical application, the polygraph test is not subjected to 'fair test' procedures. The operator normally does not operate 'blind' to other information about the suspect coming from interview and from police sources. Furthermore, it is known that the suspect is a suspect so it is likely that there is other evidence against him/her. In normal practice, the polygraph is not tested out against groups of known innocent people.

- Even the basic theory of the polygraph may be challenged since it has not been established that the only way that the body responds to fear of detection in lying is increases in the physiological measures utilised by the polygraph.

In the defence of polygraphy, the following points are worth considering:

- The polygraph questionnaire normally consists of several sets of questions. Inadequacies in any question may be compensated for by the other questions.

- There is a distinction to be drawn between the practical utility of the polygraph and its scientific adequacy. If polygraphy encouraged more guilty individuals to tell the truth then this could be seen as an advantage. But this has nothing to do with the validity of the polygraph to detect the fear its advocates claim is the basis of its success. Actually, to play the devil's advocate, it could be argued that it would be more useful if all suspects were adjudged liars by the polygraph. Then all suspects could be confronted with the evidence of their guilt and encouraged to confess. Provided that one is prepared to accept the consequences in terms of increased numbers of false confessions – and it is anyone's guess how many this would be – then one would maximise police success.

- The criticisms of present practice do not mean that the concept of polygraphy is worthless – there are other approaches to polygraphy such as the *guilty knowledge test* that have yet to be generally adopted.

Studies of the validity of polygraphy

Several surveys of psychologists exist about the validity of polygraphy. Members of a society devoted to psychological physiological research fairly consistently rejected its sole use in the absence of other information, but it was considered as a useful diagnostic tool when used in conjunction with other information. In the 1980s and 1990s as many as 60% of the psychologists surveyed considered it useful in those circumstances. Virtually no one considered it totally worthless (Iacono and Lykken, 1997). A more recent survey specifically mentioned the different types of polygraph test. The common *control question technique* (relevant versus control questions) was seen by only about a third of two separate groups of psychologists to be based on sound psychological principles. Only about a quarter were in favour of the use of the polygraph in courts of law. On average, the psychologists thought that the control question technique was 63% accurate with innocent suspects and 60% accurate with guilty suspects. These figures would indicate a high proportion of errors.

There are a number of laboratory studies that have investigated the validity of the polygraph using the control question technique. Essentially, the procedure is to inculpate some participants in the research, for example in a 'mock crime', and not others, the control group. The polygraph examination is then used to assess which group each participant was in. This seems a reasonable procedure though there are a number of problems:

- In real life, failing the polygraph test may have very serious consequences. Failing the laboratory set-up's polygraph test simply does not carry the same implications about punishment. There is no obvious strong motivation to pass the test. Indeed, the motivation may be to fail the test if you are in the guilty group as it is fairly obvious that the researchers are interested in the validity of the test.

- Because there is no cost of failing the test, it is possible that the control questions are relatively more intrusive and anxiety provoking. For example, as the experiment is possibly seen as play-acting, the participant may be more concerned about questions that bring into question their integrity and morality. So a question such as 'Have you ever told a lie?' might produce a more physiological response than 'Did you take part in the (mock) crime?'

- Iacono and Patrick (1997) are critical of the so-called friendly polygraph test organised by the defence. Failure on the test would not be publicised whereas passing the test would be lauded as evidence of innocence. Furthermore, in the friendly test the examinee has nothing to fear from detection. Remember that it is the fear of detection that is crucial to the success of the polygraph.

One obvious major advantage of the laboratory experiment is that the 'ground truth' (whether the suspect was actually involved in the crime) is easily established – indeed it is imposed by the researchers. Field studies of real-life polygraph examinations have severe problems in establishing ground truth. The normal criterion of confession is hardly adequate for reasons already mentioned. Primarily, the confession is a response to the outcome of the polygraph test so it could hardly fail to support the validity of the polygraph test. The failure to examine the 'cleared' suspects any further is a less obvious problem but nevertheless crucial. If we look at Table 16.1, only the true positives and the false positives are encouraged to confess. The false negatives and true negatives are essentially ignored. All of this contributes to a spurious enhancement of the apparent validity of the polygraph.

Table 16.1 Possible outcomes of the polygraph test

	Guilty according to polygraph examiner	Innocent according to polygraph examiner
Actually guilty	True positive	False negative
Actually innocent	False positive	True negative

It would obviously be very useful to examine the guilt and innocence of those excluded by the polygraph test – those whom we have classified as true negatives and false negatives. Ideally, then, field studies of the validity of polygraphy should do the following:

- Explore the group of individuals who passed the test as innocent for later evidence of guilt or innocence, e.g. later confession to the crime.
- The polygraph charts should be independently re-scored blind to the original examiner's conclusions and other information that might have influenced the examiner to decide that the suspect was guilty.

Few studies have met these requirements. Patrick and Iacono's (1991) study did and found the following:

- There was a 98% success rate of the re-scoring of the polygraph tests in correctly identifying the guilty. In other words, the polygraph test is extremely good at detecting the guilty.
- The polygraph had correctly classified individuals as innocent in only 55% of cases.

In other words, the bias was against the innocent, not with the guilty. These findings are similar in some ways to earlier studies. These do not involve the search for later, non-polygraph influenced confessions. The best of these studies showed 76% (Kleinmuntz and Szucko, 1984) and 77% (Horvath, 1977) of the guilty were correctly classified while 63% (Kleinmuntz and Szucko, 1984) and 51% (Horvath, 1977) of the innocent were correctly classified. These trends are true of studies involving the control question test which is the typical situation in forensic settings. But this is not the only form of polygraphy. Table 16.2 gives some information on the different types of polygraph test which are based on different questioning techniques. A British Psychological Society report (British Psychological Society Working Party, 2004) gives a detailed comparison of these techniques together with the directed lie test (Raskin and Honts, 2002) in which the suspect liar is told to answer no to questions which everyone should say yes to. There are other questions that are more pertinent to the 'crime' in question. The idea is that innocent people should be more concerned about the first sort of question than those questions about the 'crime'. Unfortunately, as the control question technique is almost exclusively the one used in forensic settings, the research on the other techniques is of lesser forensic interest.

Research on the accuracy of the guilty knowledge test tends to demonstrate exactly the reverse trend. Elaad (1990) and Elaad *et al.* (1992) found that the guilty knowledge test was extremely accurate in identifying the innocent – over 90% were correctly classified. The guilty, on the other hand, were correctly identified in only 42% of cases in the first study and in 76% of cases in the second.

Statement validity analysis: criterion-based content analysis and the validity checklist

Since lying is a verbal process then the use of physiological techniques would appear to be indirect compared to examining language itself for lies. The difficulty, though, should be obvious by now – most of us are fairly bad at recognising lies. In continental Europe, research interest has focused on a group of techniques known as *statement validity analysis*. This derives largely from the pioneering work of

Table 16.2 The different types of polygraph test question

	Guilty knowledge test	Relevant/irrelevant question technique	Directed lie test	Control question technique
Type of questions used	'If you killed your wife, then you will know the sort of weapon. Was it a craft knife . . . a kitchen knife . . . a chisel . . . a Bowie knife . . . a hatchet?'	Irrelevant question: 'Is today Friday?' Relevant question: 'Did you kill your wife?'	Control questions such as 'Before age 27, did you ever break even one rule or regulation?' Instructed to answer 'No'. Other questions relevant to crime.	Control question (emotive question for most people): 'Have you ever plotted revenge on an enemy?' Relevant question: 'Did you kill your wife?'
Evidence of its validity		None		
Basis of interpretation	Does not detect lying as much as being aware of information which is only available to the offender and the police normally.	Truth is indicated by similar physiological response to relevant and irrelevant questions. The examiner questions the suspect in order to ascertain whether the suspect has an appropriate demeanour and explanation.	Innocent persons will be more concerned about lying in response to the control questions than to questions relevant to the crime.	Guilty will show more response to the relevant question, innocent will show more response to the control question.
Limitations	Needs careful knowledge of the crime scene to write questions. Not all crimes are amenable to the construction of guilty knowledge questions.	Confounds lying and emotive questions – many people would feel troubled by being asked if they had murdered their wife.		
Popularity	Rare.			Common in forensic applications.

German psychologists, especially Undeutsch (1992). Indeed, researchers speak of the Undeutsch hypothesis as being fundamental to the method. The hypothesis essentially states that witnesses' descriptions of experienced and fictitious events are different in a number of ways. Truthful narratives are not the same in form and structure as untruthful ones. These differences are potential indicators differentiating truthful accounts from falsehoods.

Statement validity analysis is important in sexual abuse assessment because rarely can sexual abuse be determined on the basis of physical evidence. Despite popular beliefs about the nature of sexual abuse of children, much of it leaves few or no physical signs. Thus touching and stroking, for example, leave no independent evidence such as semen for DNA testing or damage to the anus or genitals. In the absence of physical evidence, it is necessary to depend on the victim's testimony. This may be contaminated in a number of ways. Adults may suggest events that never occurred to the child or sometimes there may be a deliberate lie by the child who is, say, angry with an adult for some reason. These matters were discussed in Chapter 15 in more detail.

Figure 16.3 The components of statement validity analysis

Statement validity analysis consists of the two major components shown in Figure 16.3:

- *Criterion-based content analysis* involves an analysis of the content of a statement about the crime to see which of about 19 different criteria of 'truthfulness' are present.
- The *validity checklist* is much more of an in-depth psychological assessment of the possible victim for motivations for giving false statement. It may incorporate wider knowledge from other sources about the crime.

Of the two major components of statement validity analysis, research has concentrated on criterion-based content analysis with the validity checklist largely ignored.

Statement validity analysis should not be evaluated in terms of traditional North American assessment techniques. It does not provide a numerical score that can be judged against normative data of statement validity. Thus it is not possible to say that if a witness statement has 14 of the characteristics of a truly experienced account then they are telling the truth. It is impossible to use the method to differentiate truth from fiction in a simplistic way. Instead, the psychologist must gather information about the child's general competence in narrating memories of events to compare with the specific statement that is forensically of interest (Greuel *et al.*, 1999). There are several stages in statement validity analysis which help assess whether a witness is probably credible. To concentrate on individual components of statement validity analysis such as criterion-based content analysis is to misunderstand the method's intent and fundamental strategy. A child can be judged as a competent witness only by reference to a number of features. The concept of credibility refers to a cluster of three essential components: (1) the individual's competence to testify in court; (2) the quality of the witness's statement; and (3) the reliability of the statement. The process of assessing credibility is illustrated by the flowchart in Figure 16.4.

What differentiates credible from fictitious testimony? These differentiating characteristics are usually classified into general characteristics, specific contents, peculiarities of content, motivation-related content and offence-specific elements (e.g. Bekerian and Dennett, 1992). The major features of narratives based on experience are presented diagrammatically in Figure 16.5. Generally speaking, truthful accounts are ones that:

- contain evidence that the witness regards their account as possibly flawed because of poor/incomplete memory for events;
- contain a greater amount of detail of context, conversations and interactions relevant to the narrative;
- contain a greater amount of irrelevant detail to describing the events that occurred;
- describe logically feasible events in a somewhat unstructured or disorganised fashion.

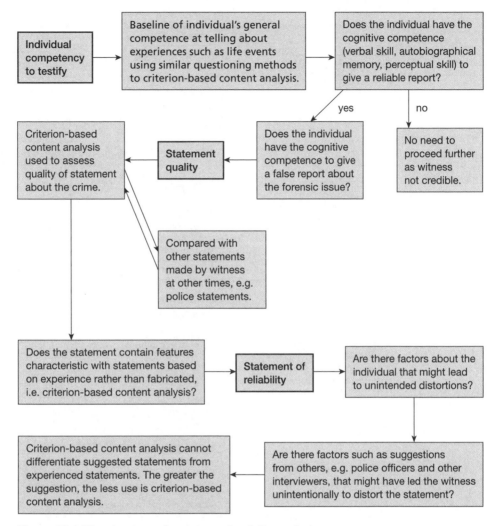

Figure 16.4 The structure of a statement validity analysis

Criterion-based content analysis uses these features, in conjunction with other evidence, in order to assess the likelihood that the witness's account is credible as an account of experienced events. Most of these criteria seem to be reasonably valid since many of them are based on empirical evidence from cognitive psychology. Psychologists using the method tend not to write of lies and truth but to refer to credibility instead. A child influenced by an adult into making allegations of abuse is not lying by the criterion of a deliberate intention to deceive. On the other hand, that child is not giving an accurate account of events that they actually experienced.

Comparison with *other* people is not a feature of statement validity analysis as it would be in a typical psychological test. In statement validity analysis comparisons are made but it is with other data collected about the child in question. There are numerous reasons why it is necessary to compare individuals with themselves rather than others. For example, some credible witnesses will be extremely good at telling narratives about their experiences whereas other credible witnesses will be less good at telling narratives about their experiences. Some witnesses will have good memory

Figure 16.5 Criterion-based content analysis: some aspects of truthful narratives

for detail, for example, whereas others will have poor memory for detail. As you can see in Figure 16.5, some of the criteria of credible statements are partly dependent on good memory. Thus you would expect a credible witness statement about a crime coming from an individual with a good memory to have high memory content whereas a credible witness statement about a crime from a witness with a relatively poor memory will start at a lower baseline. The three major stages in a statement validity analysis are as follows:

- *Stage 1: witness competence to testify*. Returning to Figure 16.4, you will see that the initial stage of statement validity analysis is to assess the competence of a witness to testify. There is little point proceeding any further with a non-competent witness. There are a number of reasons for non-competence. A witness who shows poor ability at giving narrative accounts of recent events in their lives may have a brain disease, for example, which makes their statements suspect. Another witness may give the impression of being unable to tell the truth about anything. On the other hand, yet other witnesses may give the impression of being unable to give a false account about anything. In addition to this sort of assessment, this initial stage provides the opportunity to obtain baseline indications of the ability of the witness to give good narrative accounts of their experiences as well as gathering an impression of the characteristics of their narratives.

- *Stage 2: statement quality*. This involves the assessment of statement quality. This is essentially criterion-based content analysis. This is done in two ways: (1) internally to the statement collected from the witness (known as the immanent view) or (2) comparatively between that statement and ones obtained in other circumstances such as in court or during the police interview. This means, first, that it is possible to assess the extent to which the statement contains criteria indicative of experience-based statements relative to one's expectations of the individual in question. Secondly, it is also possible to assess whether these criteria are stable in all accounts of the events provided by the witness.

- *Stage 3: statement reliability*. Witnesses may unintentionally provide testimony that departs materially from the credible. This may be the result of the witnesses' personal characteristics. Distinctive styles of attribution, perceptual styles or motivations may be involved. Childhood victims of sexual abuse, for example, sometimes have distorted perceptions of who was responsible for initiating the abuse and blame themselves rather than the adult who perpetrated the crime. Other victims may consistently embellish or dramatise the truth. The major part of assessing statement reliability involves the issue of suggestibility. This might be the tendency of the witness to be influenced by distortions due to leading or suggestive questioning by other people such as police officers, social workers or others. However, more important is whether or not the previous interviews and interrogations involved suggestion. So, for example, is there evidence of a suggestive interviewing style in the transcripts of previous interviews? Does the narrative provided by the witness change markedly following an earlier interview? The answers to these questions have an important bearing on how the criterion-based content analysis from the previous stage is to be interpreted. There may be no evidence at all of suggestion being involved in the statement. For example, there may have been no previous interrogations and so no opportunity for suggestion to have an influence. In these circumstances, criterion-based content analysis can be directly interpreted according to what criteria it contains together with the psychologically based expectations of that individual developed in Stage 1 – competence assessment. If there is evidence of suggestion then caution is necessary. Criterion-based content analysis cannot distinguish suggestion-based narratives from experientially based ones. The greater the suggestion, the less can be said on the basis of the content analysis.

The forensic use of statement validity analysis has largely been confined to Continental Europe and Germany in particular, although research on it has been much more international.

However, there has been an intriguing analysis of eyewitness evidence surrounding the claims that a UFO (unidentified flying object) crashed near Roswell, New Mexico, USA (Houran and Porter, 2005). An investigation by military claimed that the fragments found were those of a weather balloon, not a flying saucer. Jim Ragsdale provided a deathbed 'eyewitness' account of the crash and the contents of this flying saucer. He was with a woman who was later killed in a car crash. Ragsdale provided two accounts – one of 600 words and the other an affidavit of 1,000 words – which were published in 1996 by Jim Ragsdale. The delay between 'witnessing' the events and his description was 48 years. This is the sort of material that might be assessed using statement validity analysis for its veracity as a product of human memory. Part of Ragsdale's testimony was as follows:

> Since it was the Fourth of July weekend, I had several days off work. I was work-ing driving a truck, tranporting heavy equipment for a gas line. My girlfriend was from Las Cruces, and I lived in Carlsbad. We decided to go to the perfect place near Boy Scout Mountain in a campsite where we could have some solitude. We went up Pine Lodge Road and turned onto a gravel road heading toward the campsite. We went where there is a picnic ground and we had access to water. I parked my pickup behind a clump of trees, got the quilts out and put them in the back of my pickup, and we started drinking and making-out. We were lying in the back of my pickup truck, buck naked, drinking beer, and having a good ole time when about 11:30 the night of July 4, 1947, all hell broke loose. From the northwest, there was a big flash, an intense, bright explosion, and then, shortly thereafter, with a noise like thunder, this thing came plowing through the trees, sheering off the tops, and then stopped between two huge rocks. It was propped up against one rock. It was about twenty feet around. As it was approaching, huge streams like fire were coming out from behind. After the impact, silence. There was a hole in one side about four feet wide and two feet high. There was junk scattered around the disc, and we picked some of it up. I looked inside the hole, and inside, there was a chair that looked like a throne. It looked like it was made of rubies and diamonds. There were other little chairs – four or five and a lot of instruments on a panel. There were also the little people, four of them. They looked like midgets, about four feet long. Their skin, if it was skin, was sort of gray and when I touched one of them, it felt like a wet snake.
>
> *(pp. 68–9)*

Houran and Porter (2005) suggest that the following were missing among other features of truthful accounts though the accounts were, for example, coherent and also showed a degree of contextual embedding such as the detail of the couple's activities in the back of the truck:

- Description of interaction: although the events prior to the explosion do contain detail of the interaction between the couple, the description following these events contains nothing of contact or interaction that the couple may have had.
- Reproduction of conversation: no conversation between the couple is described in Ragsdale's account.
- Spontaneous corrections: Ragsdale corrected his memories on no occasion during the two reports.
- Admitting lack of memory: Ragsdale did not question his ability to recall the events in any way during his account.

Other criteria of truthful accounts were also missing as can be seen. Thus the analyst concluded that the accounts were not characteristic of memories of real events since very few indicators of truthful accounts according to statement validity analysis were present.

The validity of statement validity analysis

Forensic validity

The origins of statement validity analysis were in practical forensic applications of psychological research, especially in child sexual abuse cases. As such, the forensic rather than the laboratory validity of the approach is important. Undeutsch made great claims about the effectiveness of the methods as he employed them within the German court system. For example, he suggested that of the cases assessed by him in order to provide evidence of the guilt of the suspect, no instances have emerged to indicate that statement validity analysis was wrong. Acquittals on appeal after new evidence has emerged of the innocence of the accused would indicate that statement validity analysis was leading to false convictions. As Undeutsch was involved in thousands of cases, this appears to be strong evidence of the validity of the method. However, Undeutsch's, and similar assertions, have not been extensively or adequately documented (Bekerian and Dennett, 1992). Basically, the claim is that statement validity analysis is effective and leads to no false convictions but there are a number of considerations that reduce the impact of the claim:

- The evidence is that false allegations of child abuse possibly amount to no more than about 10% of allegations (Howitt, 1992). Thus an allegation is a good sign of guilt and reversals of a conviction are only likely in this small percentage of cases.
- It is unclear what aspects of statement validity analysis led Undeutsch to his conclusions. Statement validity analysis can draw evidence from a wide variety of sources, as we have seen. Could it be that Undeutsch was more influenced by other forensic evidence than, say, criterion-based content analysis?
- It is not known what numbers of false negatives the method produces. If Undeutsch decided that the allegation was not very credible, this might result in a decision not to prosecute despite there being other evidence of guilt – leaving a guilty individual unpunished. The potentially more risky prosecutions are thereby excluded from trial, which obviously minimises the potential for appeals.
- It could be that the decision to obtain a statement validity analysis from Undeutsch was only made if the evidence was strong enough to make a conviction likely, Undeutsch's support being requested merely to strengthen an already strong case. In these circumstances, later reversals of the conviction would be unlikely.

These are conjectures that merely serve to reinforce the view that statement validity analysis needs more evaluation in its practical application. For example, Lamers-Winkelman and Buffing (1996) provide evidence from the Netherlands that certain of the components of statement validity analysis show age trends so that if the child's age is not taken into account, the validity of the method is reduced.

Laboratory validity

The ideal study of the validity of statement validity analysis is impossible. It would probably involve psychologists, well experienced in the method, making judgements of the credibility of witnesses to apparently the same event – one witness telling the truth, the other lying. Using statement validity analysis, the psychologists would decide which was the credible witness. Of course, this sort of situation does not normally occur. Furthermore, unless the 'witnesses' were randomly allocated to truth telling or lie telling conditions even this would not be fully capable of providing evidence of the value of statement validity analysis. Perhaps naturally honest people would choose to tell the truth and dishonest people would choose to lie. In these circumstances, it may be that the psychologists pick the truthful account from the angelic faces of the honest people and the fictitious account from the scowling demeanour of the naturally dishonest person. Clearly, certain issues can be resolved only by using random allocation in controlled experiments. Unfortunately, this does not work very well in other respects. One of the major difficulties is that laboratory experiments cannot involve the serious crimes perpetrated against the witnesses. Another difficulty is the desire of the researchers to simplify the procedures as much as possible by concentrating on the criterion-based content analysis and ignoring the validity checklist. As we have seen, this is to do an injustice to the assumptions of statement validity analysis. Consequently, the laboratory studies can often be criticised as failing to reach the full potential of statement validity analysis. In other words, we should not be surprised that statement validity analysis appears only moderately effective if we rely on research that does fundamental disservice to the approach. Others have noted that the quality of forensic interviews with children may be so poor as to mask the worth of the method to a degree (Lamb *et al.*, 1997).

Nevertheless, it is unlikely that the North American tradition of psychological testing will readily yield to the requirements of this European approach. For example, Lamb *et al.* (1997) argue that trained assessors using criterion-based content analysis fail to show satisfactory levels of inter-rater reliability on many of the dimensions of the technique (see Figure 16.5). Some should be dropped as of no value and others need to be more carefully defined. Criterion-based content analysis dimensions that were not useful in differentiating truthful from false accounts included logical structure, complications, superfluous details, misunderstood details, external references, subjective feelings, perpetrator feelings and spontaneous corrections.

However, the following criterion-based content analysis dimensions were helpful in differentiating between allegations believed to be true according to independent judgements and the false allegations:

- unstructured production;
- quantity of details;
- contextual embedding;
- interactions;
- conversations;
- unusual details.

All of these were more common in the plausible accounts.

In this context, some American research findings may be even more positive than it at first appears. Porter and Yuille (1996) studied a range of verbal indicators of deception in interrogations. The verbal indicators were partly taken from criterion-based content analysis or one of three other approaches to differentiating truth from lies (such as reality monitoring, and a training programme in detecting lying). The participants in the research were required to give accounts of events that were either truthful or deceptive. Of a substantial list of verbal indicators of lying, only those of quantity of details, coherence (that is, what others call logical structure) and admission of lack of memory were effective. These are all from criterion-based content analysis. The other three methods failed to distinguish truthful from false accounts.

Evidence of the validity of the validity checklist is rare. Lamers-Winkelman (1997) is one of the very few researchers to have studied this aspect of statement validity analysis. His Dutch team studied over 100 possible sexual abuse victims in the 2- to 12-year-old-age range. While we might assume that the vast majority of these allegations are truthful, a small percentage are likely to be false allegations, the researcher suggests. Because the normal medical practice in the Netherlands is not to physically examine child victims of sexual abuse, no independent evidence of abuse exists. Of course, physical signs of abuse are not common. By the usual criteria of psychological assessment, there was good agreement between different raters both in terms of criterion-based content analysis and the validity checklist. Both of these had inter-rater reliabilities of over 0.8, indicating good consistency between raters. It should be stressed that the interviewers were trained by the leading experts in the method (Undeutsch and Max Steller). We might expect that this led to greater reliability. A number of validity checklist items were explored in these interviews:

- *Age appropriateness of language in general*: a child who uses language more advanced than his or her chronological age may be reporting under the influence of older people. Generally speaking, in this sample there was no evidence of age inappropriate language.

- *Age appropriateness of sexual knowledge*: sexual knowledge too advanced for the child's chronological age and level of development might be an indication that sexual abuse had taken place. Age inappropriateness was common among all of the age range. Thus, the minimum at any age level was 50% but with younger children the figures went much higher: for example, 95% of the 4- to 5-year-olds had knowledge too advanced for their age and level of development. These high figures might be expected in a group of sexually abused children; it is difficult to judge without the benefit of interviews with a group of non-abused children. There was a further problem. The interviewers found it difficult to decide what was sexually appropriate knowledge for the older age groups. Boys in the 9- to 11-year-old age group are mentioned as a particularly difficult group. Be cautious about these figures. Remember that in Chapter 15, it is pointed out that some sexual behaviours such as public masturbation do not differentiate sexually abused children from other children very effectively.

- *Resistance to suggestive questioning*: as part of the validity analysis, the children are examined to see whether they are susceptible to the interviewer 'planting' ideas in their mind. A child who is susceptible to leading or suggestive questioning may be a child who has previously been led by another adult to make the allegations of abuse falsely. From quite an early age – 4 years – the children demonstrated high levels of resistance to suggestive questions. Younger children than these were more influenced by such questions: 29% of children under 4 years failed to resist suggestive questions.

- *Appropriateness of affect*: the emotional signs accompanying descriptions of abuse should be appropriate to the abuse and general signs of emotionality may be present. In the study, about half of the children supported their descriptions of abusive events with gestures signalling emotion.

The performance of children when assessed using criterion-based content analysis varies according to the age of the child. The characteristics of the testimony of 2-year-olds and 14-year-olds are different. Criterion-based content analysis has no specific way of dealing with age trends of this sort. Buck *et al.* (2002) obtained transcripts of real-life child sexual abuse interviews and had them rated using criterion-based content analysis. The reliability between different raters was modest. Use of most of the criteria of criterion-based content analysis correlated with age. So older children, for example, demonstrated greater logical structure, quantity of details and contextual embedding. Only criteria such as the amount of unusual detail, references to the offender's mental state, doubting own testimony, self-deprecation and pardoning perpetrator showed no overall correlation with age. So, in general, indicators of truthfulness were commoner in the older age groups. Some of the criteria of truthfulness simply did not appear for some ages of children. For example, comments doubting their own testimony did not appear until the 12- to 14-years-of-age group and pardoning perpetrator only appeared in 9- to 11-year-olds. This, of course, raises the question of precisely how to deal with age when assessing children's accounts. The temptation might be to assume that older children are simply more honest in their reports but there is no evidence on this one way or another. They may simply have a different style of reporting events which corresponds better with the criteria of truthfulness. (This is a complex issue – see Chapters 14 and 17 for more on children's age and testimony). One should also be aware that the interviews subjected to analysis in this study were not the sort that criterion-based content analysis usually employs – they were standard child sexual abuse interviews instead. Thus the comments actually only apply to standard child sexual abuse interviews.

Finally, it should be mentioned that some researchers have used statement validity analysis and criterion-based content analysis in attempts to detect deception in adults. One particularly important study made use of London police interviews with rape victims. Some of these interviews contained demonstrably false claims since, for example, the 'victim' freely acknowledged that their allegations were false, there was evidence of the falsity of the claims from eyewitnesses or medical evidence and so forth. The interviews were studied using relatively structured scoring sheets. Correct identifications of true rape victim statements were high based on criterion-based content analysis (88% correct) and the validity checklist (100% correct). The figures for interviews correctly identifying false statements as being false were 92% for criterion-based content analysis and 58% for the validity checklist. Combining criterion-based content analysis with the validity checklist led to a 100% correct identification for true statements and a 92% correct identification for false statements. False statements tended to be much more organised in style whereas true statements tended to present a mixed range of emotions and unstructured delivery of the account. There is a lack of confusion in a false account. The validity criteria which differentiated the two types of interview included 'inconsistencies within physical evidence', incongruous affect during interview, and 'inconsistent statements'. The researchers also had experienced detectives evaluate the interviews. They concluded that the police officers demonstrated 'little consistency' (p. 249) in their decisions about the truth or otherwise of the statements. Statement validity analysis did better at identifying false statements than any of the individual officers or the group of officers as a whole.

Main points

- There is no simple way of detecting a liar. There is considerable evidence to suggest that for the most part, such groups as the police and psychologists do little better than chance when assessing the truthfulness of those they interview. Nevertheless, given appropriate circumstances, it is possible to improve on this. Most methods of detecting lies actually rely on detecting the emotions that may go along with lying. By concentrating on this, rather than relying on unproven ideas of the signs of lying, a better hit-rate may be achieved. There is reason to think that observers at an interview do better than the interviewer at detecting lies – presumably because they are faced with a simpler task and can concentrate more on the hard-to-detect indicators of lying.

- The polygraph test may become a more common feature in jurisdictions that do not allow it in court. There is increasing interest in its use in the monitoring of sex and other offenders while out in the community. There are several different ways of asking questions in the polygraph examination and they do not necessarily generate the same outcomes. Not all of the methods are used in practice by professional polygraph operators. The polygraph is more than a piece of physiological apparatus and is better seen as a process in practice. The operator usually has rather more information about the case and the suspect than a totally 'blind' procedure would require. The polygraph can be effective at generating a confession irrespective of the validity of the technique. The major problem with the polygraph is its error rate, which in polygraph assessment tends to produce more false positives in that a proportion of innocent individuals are judged guilty by the polygraph operator.

- Statement validity analysis is a set of techniques which attempt to establish the credibility of witness evidence and is especially pertinent to the evidence of children in sexual abuse cases. It consists of a mixture of various matters to consider in relation to the testimony. Central to the approach is the idea that memory for events that were truly experienced is different than for imaginary events. In addition to features of the situation such as the child's apparent resistance to suggestive questioning and the appropriateness of the language used to the child's age group since inappropriate language may indicate adult influence on the child. There is evidence of the effectiveness of the approach and there are examples of its use with adult victims of rape in which statement validity analysis seemed able to distinguish 'known' false witness statements from true ones.

Chapter 17

Children as witnesses

Overview

- Social and legal perceptions of children as witnesses have changed markedly in the last century or so. They were once regarded as dangerously unreliable witnesses whereas the modern view is that, given appropriate interviewing and support, they can supply good quality evidence. Countries differ markedly in their presumptions of the competence of children as witnesses.

- Bad professional practices in interviews with abused children can create problems in terms of the value of the evidence produced. It is the case that children present characteristic problems as witnesses but it is equally true to suggest that the interviewer may also create problems by not using an appropriate questioning style.

- Anatomically correct dolls can have a place in forensic interviews with children for a number of reasons to do with the enhancement of communications. They allow discussion of topics. Sexual play with such dolls is not a risk indicator of child sexual abuse and it is not appropriate to use the dolls to make such assessments.

- It is possible to suggest improvements to all aspects of professional work with children that improve the quality of the information provided. Generally speaking, open-ended questioning tends to produce the best quality information for child witnesses. However, the extent to which a question is leading is only partially determined by the structure of the question. Some would argue that leading questions have a role to play.

- There is evidence that lawyers in the courtroom do not modify their questioning appropriately for the age of the child witness. Typical problems include overly complex language, the use of legal terms that the child may not know or fully understand, and dwelling on concepts of time and distance which are not fully developed in early childhood.

- Further material pertinent to this chapter may be found in Chapter 16 (statement validity analysis) and Chapter 14 (false allegations).

The last hundred years have seen remarkable changes in the way that children's evidence has been viewed. In the nineteenth century children were seen as dangerous witnesses in the sense that they could not be relied on, or worse (Baartman, 1992; Myers *et al.*, 1999). This view has changed substantially, so much so that towards the end of twentieth century it became fashionable among some professions to claim that children never lie (Silas, 1985; Driver, 1989). Children have increasingly been regarded as young people with rights during the last century (e.g. Kitzinger, 1988). It should not be forgotten that, in some jurisdictions, quite young children are tried for criminal acts sometimes in adult courts. Consequently, there may be issues, in some cases, of the competence of that young person to stand trial (see Chapter 17). Some aspects of this, such as whether juvenile competence is different from adult competence, are discussed in Heilbrun *et al.* (1996).

Courtrooms have traditionally been very adult environments. Generally speaking, they have lacked orientation to the needs of children. This is hardly surprising given that the evidence of children was regarded with such suspicion. In some states of America jurors would be instructed by the judge to consider the evidence of children especially carefully. Public disquiet about child abuse and child sexual abuse in the 1970s and 1980s respectively inevitably meant that the needs of child witnesses in the courtroom became a prime focus for research and innovation. Without the evidence of children, a lot of sexual abuse of children could not be prosecuted. Much the same process applied to the treatment of victims of rape in the criminal justice system. Numerous changes have been made in recent years as far as the evidence of children is concerned in a lot of countries. Myers (1996) reviewed many of these changes.

Myers argues that a distinction has to be made between legal systems based on common law (United States, United Kingdom, Australia, Canada, New Zealand, South Africa, Republic of Ireland) and those based on civil law (Germany and France). The common law systems have adversarial court systems in which the prosecution is pitted against the defence in front of judge and jury. The civil law system gives courts an inquisitorial role and the responsibility of uncovering what has happened. This is quite different from the role of a court being to decide which is the more convincing of two opposing arguments. In the inquisitorial system the judge would normally be the leading figure in questioning the witnesses, rather than the lawyers. Adversarial systems have more difficulty in coping with the needs of the child witness. For example, examination and cross-examination by lawyers is not constructed to be much other than a battle. In the United States, for one example, the right to have witnesses cross-examined is incorporated into the constitution.

Children may not have the ability to cope with what may be fairly oppressive cross-examination. Special arrangements may have to be applied to child witnesses. In some jurisdictions are to be found one or more of the following:

- *Preparation for court*: youngsters can be given professional help to understand court procedures, to deal with stress and anxiety about court as well as their abuse and to testify competently in court. They may also be provided with an official advocate who works on their behalf with agencies. Sattar and Bull (1996) surveyed professionals working with children in a legal context in the United Kingdom. They were well aware of the problems for child witnesses such as the fears and anxieties. The provision of support for children in this context included special child witness preparation provided by agencies. Facilities after the hearing were not so good.

- *Children's hearsay statements*: usually hearsay (essentially second-hand evidence) is disallowed in adversarial systems except in exceptional circumstances. Some states of the United States, England and Wales and Scotland now allow hearsay in proceedings for the protection of children.

Competence to testify and give the oath is a key issue with child witnesses. A child witness is required to meet standards of cognitive and moral ability if they are to testify. Three different arrangements seem to apply:

- Some jurisdictions impose a presumptive incompetent criterion. This means that under a certain age (say 10 years but it does depend on location), the child has to be examined on competence to testify. If they meet these criteria, they can give evidence.
- In other jurisdictions, everyone is accepted as competent irrespective of their age. Should an individual's competence become an issue, then it can be evaluated.
- Still other jurisdictions judge all victims of abuse as competent although they may not be assumed competent in other circumstances. In some jurisdictions (e.g. Canada, United Kingdom, France and Germany), the child does not have to be sworn before they can provide evidence.

Another set of changes involves methods of altering the court physically and in other ways to be rid of the intimidating over-powerful aura of traditional courtrooms. For example, expecting lawyers to remain seated when examining child witnesses may make a less daunting arrangement. The court may allow the use of leading questions with young children. The court may sit in a simpler, more comfortable environment for the child. Other changes may include the following:

- Closing the court to the public/press.
- Video testimony: interviews with the police or social workers as part of the investigation process may be shown through video. In England and Wales, interviews with police or social workers may be used as a substitute for the child's in-court evidence. This has been adopted by, for example, some American states; video may be used to present either live or pre-recorded testimony from the child. Many countries allow closed-circuit television to help the giving of evidence by children. This was first developed in the United States in 1983 but Britain, New Zealand and Australia, among others, followed suit. Not only is there evidence that children are happier using the video links, but the quality of their evidence seems better (Davies and Noon, 1993).

What is difficult about forensic interviews with children?

This chapter is about the voice of children in courts of law. So it may be apposite to examine the problem from the point of view of the child who has been abused and then has to face the criminal justice system. Westcott (1995) studied a small group of children and young people, each of whom had experience of sexual abuse investigation interviews. For the most part, these children had disclosed their abuse. The comments the children made give some indications of what is good practice and extend our understanding beyond what researchers and practitioners have suggested:

- *Language and questioning styles*: complex words and sentences were mentioned as well as the interviewer talking extensively and interrupting the child.

- *Cognitive issues*: sometimes the children and young people had problems with the amount of detail they were being asked about their abuse. This may well have involved them recalling events that had happened a few years before. One of the sample mentioned being asked about the frequencies and dates of their abuse.
- *Personal issues*: discussing the detail of what happened in the abuse may be embarrassing to some children and young people. They were also scared of giving information for fear that their abuser would take revenge on them for disclosing the abuse.
- *Motivational issues*: who was present at the interview could influence the victim's willingness to talk. For example, not all children wanted their parents present. Neglect of the child's feelings by the interviewer who might appear to be mainly interested in the punishment of the abuser was perceived by some of the children.
- *Social characteristics*: some interviewers were disliked for reasons such as: made it feel unimportant, disbelieving, bored, treated me younger than I am.

From the researcher's and practitioner's point of view some of these comments may be a little uncomfortable since they appear to put the onus onto them for some of the problems of interviewing child witnesses. Many of the points made by the children would require an interviewer sensitive to the needs of children and accepting of their personal responsibilities for the inadequacies of their interviews. So with this in mind, we can turn to some ideas about the nature of children's testimonies. Lamb *et al.* (1999) suggest that the following factors may have an influence on the quality of children's evidence:

- *Fantasy*: some believe that children are especially prone to fantasise events and report them as fact. The research evidence, though, is that certainly by the age of 6 years, children are probably little different from adults in terms of their ability to differentiate reality from fantasy (Woolley, 1997). If an interviewer asks a child to imagine or pretend, they will respond appropriately by being imaginative and pretending. Similarly, the presence of dolls and toys encourages fantasy behaviour, it is argued (see Box 17.1). Forensic interviews should be planned to exclude the possibilities. Lamb *et al.* (1999) indicate that the children who have a tendency to fantasise are no more likely to make false reports or fabrications when giving evidence.
- *Language*: children's accounts of events tend to be short and lacking in much detail. Their speech can be difficult to follow because of their inconsistencies in enunciation and they sometimes use words of which they have little understanding. These can be quite simple words such as 'yesterday' or 'before', which are readily understood by adults.
- *Interviewers*: it is too easy for adults to pose questions in ways that are difficult for even adolescents to understand. The consequences are obvious. Children do not always correct an adult who has failed to understand what the child is saying. So, with support from the research literature, it can be recommended that children should not be expected to:
  - reverse negative statements by adults (Is it not true that you stole the apples?);
  - understand passive wording (Was the apple taken by her?) as opposed to active wording (Did she take the apple?);
  - have a complete mastery of adult vocabulary; or confirm complex summaries of the information that the child has provided.

There is evidence (e.g. Brennan and Brennan, 1988) that about one-third of questions asked by lawyers in court were not understood by 6- to 15-year-old children.

- *Memory*: the brevity of young children's accounts does not mean that their memories are bad. In fact, their memory is quite good. There is a distinction to be made between memory performance and memory capacity. Thus a young child may appear not to have a good memory capacity simply because they provide only a brief account of events. This may really be an issue of memory performance – they have poorer vocabularies, they lack motivation to provide the account, and they are less capable of using analogy to elaborate their descriptions.

- *Suggestibility*: in some settings even 3- and 4-year-olds are very resistant to leading questions that were irrelevant to the actual events. Questions such as 'Did he kiss you?' and 'Did he keep his clothes on?' failed to lead the children.

- *Interviewer characteristics*: the characteristics of the interviewer such as their friendliness or accusativeness do not appear consistently over studies to influence the suggestibility of the children they interview.

Box 17.1

Controversy: anatomical dolls and the diagnosis of abuse

It is an obvious idea to use toys as an aid when interviewing children. Anatomical dolls have been used extensively in child sexual abuse assessment. Quite simply, they are dolls with 'extra' anatomical details – genitals, anuses, mouths. According to the *American Professional Society on the Abuse of Children* Practice Guidelines (APSAC, 1996), research shows that the use of such dolls does not increase sexualised behaviour in non-abused children and they do not seem to encourage suggestibility and error in recall. The doll is almost invariably clothed but for exceptional circumstances in which the child has previously said that sexual abuse had taken place with naked individuals.

Anatomical dolls should only be used by skilled interviewers. 'Sexual' play with dolls such as inserting another doll's penis into a doll's mouth, anus or vagina is *not* diagnostic of sexual abuse. While such behaviour may be more common among sexually abused children, the risk of misdiagnosis is too great to interpret it as such (see Chapter 14 on diagnosticity of signs). Four-year-old boys from low social class families are the group most likely to display such behaviour. Exploration of a doll's genitals or anus with the finger is not infrequent among young children. However, the interviewer should be sensitive to other possible indications of abuse. In short, it would be a bad mistake to attempt to diagnose sexual abuse on the basis of play with anatomical dolls in the absence of other supportive evidence.

The use of the dolls should not be presented as pretend or play. Instead, the interviewer should encourage the child to talk about 'things that really happened'. Putting pairs of dolls in sexual positions and asking whether this had ever happened to the child is tantamount to a leading question and should not be done. On the other hand, anatomical dolls help communication and promote better recall of events though drawings or ordinary non-anatomical dolls may be equally effective:

- The dolls can be used as an *icebreaker*, allowing the child to talk on sexual issues that might be taboo to the child normally.
- The dolls can be used as an *anatomical model* to find out the names used by the child for the different parts of the body and what they know about their functions.
- The interviewer might also use the dolls to make clear just what it is the child has said about the acts of abuse (i.e. as a *demonstration aid*).

- The doll may also be used in a non-threatening setting to gain insight into the child's sexual interest and knowledge (i.e. as a *screening tool*). After a period of free play, the interviewer may add questions to elaborate on what had been observed. The guidelines suggest that spontaneous 'suspicious' comments by the child should be followed up. For example, 'Daddy's pee-pee gets big sometimes'.

According to Everson and Boat (2002), anatomical dolls may also be used as a *memory stimulus*. Seeing the doll's sexual characteristics (genitals and breasts) may help the child remember sexual episodes in which they were involved – for example, as victims of sexual abuse.

The Guidelines suggest that other matters of good practice when using anatomical dolls need to be considered, including the following:

- The interviewer should recognise that children of less than 4 years may be unable to re-enact scenes well.
- Interviewers using anatomical dolls should be trained in their use and regularly updated on new research findings relevant to the use of the dolls.
- Videotaping interviews using anatomical dolls is a wise precaution as it is with other aspects of forensic investigation.

There is a substantial body of research on the usefulness of anatomical dolls and similar props (such as drawings) in sexual abuse interviews with young children. Everson and Boat (2002) address two critical issues concerning anatomical dolls which research has raised. The first is that anatomical dolls are so suggestive that sexual fantasy and sexual play will be encouraged by the dolls in a way that some interviewers will interpret as sexual abuse in children who have not been abused. The second is that the evidence that the use of the dolls facilitates disclosure of abuse is missing or non-existent:

- *Suggestibility of dolls for non-abused children*: Everson and Boat (2002) mention 11 studies concerning the behaviour of non-sexually abused children (2- to 8-year-olds) when playing with anatomical dolls. Some interest in the doll's genitals was fairly common, explicit play involving sexual intercourse with the doll or oral sex was fairly rare. Only 4% of children in all of the studies combined demonstrated such heavily sexualised behaviours. Furthermore, there may be other sources of sexual knowledge even where the child displayed sexualised behaviours of this sort. These sources would include pornography or observing sexual activity at home, for example. This could account for the majority of instances of such sexual knowledge in non-sexually abused children.
- *Efficacy of the use of anatomical dolls*: the better research relevant to this tends to use real medical examinations/procedures which would necessitate the medic to touch the child's genitals or anus, for example. In other words, a situation which is realistic and pertinent in that it involves what in other circumstances would constitute sexually abusive acts. Children can be interviewed some time after the medical procedure in order to see whether they reveal the genital or anal touching. Whether interviews using anatomical dolls are more successful at identifying the touching can be assessed. Steward and Steward (1996) carried out a study along these lines. About a quarter of the children revealed the touching without the anatomical dolls. This figure more than doubled to three-fifths of children in interviews using anatomical dolls. It increased to nearly three-quarters when the children were interviewed with the anatomical dolls and the interviewer asked direct and suggestive questions. False reports were not very common. No false reports were made in the simple verbal interview. This increased to 3% in the anatomical doll interview and 5% where the anatomical doll interview included the direct and suggestive questions.

Improving forensic interviews with children

According to researchers, open-ended questions produce the most accurate answers from children. This is partly because open-ended questions encourage children to give as much detail as they can in their replies. They act as recall probes. In contrast, focused or closed questions, directive questions or leading questions involve the child in a recognition task that can be answered completely with merely a yes or no. That is, leading and similar questions act as recognition probes about the things on which the interviewer wishes to focus. As such, they may pressure the child into a response even though the child does not know what that response should be. Table 17.1 illustrates the differences between the two different forms of questioning.

Most lawyers and psychologists are familiar with the concept of leading questions. These are questions that encourage a particular reply. Myers *et al.* (1996) argue that there is a continuum of suggestiveness in questioning:

open-ended → focused → specific → leading

This is very important since there is a tendency to concentrate on the two questions – open-ended and leading. This, to a degree, misrepresents the situation in interviews. By considering more types of question then we begin to appreciate how structuring can take a number of different forms. The underlying order is from the least to most suggestive questioning style:

- An open-ended question is a fairly general question which is little other than a request for the interviewee to speak as in 'Did anything happen?' or 'Tell me about that'.
- A focused question brings a child's attention to a particular issue such as a location or a person. So a question such as 'Shall we talk about school?' brings a child around to the topic of school without suggesting anything about the sorts of information that the interviewer wants. Questions such as 'where' or 'who' and 'when' are other examples. There is no rigid dividing line between focused and the next level of specific questioning.

Table 17.1 Open-ended versus focused/closed questions as they might appear in a child sexual abuse interview

Open-ended
Tell me everything that happened.
Closed-ended
Does he do things you don't like?
Open-ended
And then what happened?
Closed-ended
Did he touch you with his private parts?
Open-ended
What else can you remember about that day?
Closed-ended
Was anybody else there?

Source: Based on Lamb, M.E., Sternberg, K.J. and Orbach, Y. (1999) Forensic interviews of children. In A. Memon and R. Bull (eds) *Handbook of the Psychology of Interviewing.* © 1999 John Wiley & Sons, Ltd

- Specific questioning may be similar though generally specific questions call for a greater level of detail. Questions in this category include 'What is her name?' or 'What colour dress did she have on?'
- A leading question is one that implies that the interviewer is expecting a particular answer. Leading questions are often statements of fact to which the interviewee is expected to agree. So 'You felt very angry, didn't you?' makes it very clear what answer is expected. This is a continuum of suggestiveness since each level has increasing likelihood to suggest answers to the child. Even the open-ended question, according to circumstances, may be suggestive. For example, a parent who asks a child what happened in school yesterday might be suggesting the sort of reply if, for example, the child had been caught cheating in an exam. See Table 17.1 for examples.

It is overly simplistic, some argue, to regard open questions as good and closed questions as bad. Professionals who carry out sexual abuse interviews are presented with a serious dilemma: that is, only using open-ended questions may well fail to obtain the necessary information from a child who has been abused (Myers *et al.*, 1996). Unfortunately, there may be a trade-off between the poorer disclosure coming from open-ended questioning and the contamination of evidence emerging out of leading questions. The issue, then, is somewhat intangible. Is it better to have some false allegations in order to maximise the detection of actual abuse, or is it better to have no false allegations but fail to maximise the detection of abuse? The answer depends, in part, on one's perspective. Is it more important to have abuse disclosed or is it more important to be successfully able to prosecute abusers in court? This dilemma cannot be addressed by research evidence on different questioning styles. It is a moral, ethical and political issue.

Of course, there is always a great need for research into the way practitioners work. The following study generally supports the conclusion that open-ended questioning tends to produce superior evidence from children. However, more importantly, it reveals some of the problems in encouraging practitioners to use this form of questioning. The research took place in Israel and the United States and involved coding recordings of real-life interviews with children (Sternberg *et al.*, 1997). The interviewers' utterances were classified into a number of categories:

- Invitations to open-ended responses.
- Facilitators such as okay, feedback of the child's previous statement, and general encouraging comments.
- Directive utterances – directing the child towards certain aspects of the events already mentioned by the child.
- Leading utterances – directing the child towards things *not* already mentioned by the child.
- Suggestive utterances which could indicate strongly to the child what reply is expected by the interviewer or include references to details that have not previously been mentioned by the child.

The children's answers were coded in terms of the number of new details supplied by the child. These details would include such matters as identifying and describing individuals, objects, events and actions relevant to the incident under investigation. Irrespective of the age of the child being interviewed, the findings showed that open-ended questions encouraged the child to give longer replies (that is, up to four times longer), containing about three times the amount of new detail.

Despite the superiority of open-ended styles of questioning, experienced interviewers generally used the least productive, closed interview techniques. The majority (over four-fifths) of the interviewers' dialogue consisted of focused or closed prompts. Only 6% were invitational (open) questions and statements. The researchers attempted to improve interviewing technique during intensive interviewing workshops over the period of a week. These explained children's memory capacities, discussed what factors might encourage suggestibility and stressed in various ways the advantages of open-ended questioning. Unfortunately, this made little or no difference as the interviewers carried on using their focused questioning style!

In an attempt to find a solution to what was seemingly an intangible problem, Sternberg *et al.* (1997) provided introductory scripts to the interviewers. Some of the scripts were open-ended whereas the others were closed-ended. This led, irrespective of the questioning style adopted by the interviewer later in the interview, to lengthier narratives from the children in the open-ended condition. In other words, once the children had begun to respond to questions in detail, then they continued to do so irrespective of the nature of the later questioning. When the introductory script was used, the children on average provided 91 details compared to the five or six details obtained when the script was not used.

Questioning styles are not the only way in which interviews can affect adversely the information obtained. Poole and Lindsay (2002) explain that sometimes an interviewer can produce ambiguity in ways that are very different from leading the child. Young children drift readily off topic and fail to appreciate what is actually being discussed, they can be difficult to interview. Poole and Lindsay (p. 358) highlight the following excerpt of transcript of an interview with a child originally reported by Warren *et al.* (2002):

Interviewer: Is it good or bad to tell a lie?
Child: G.A. touched me.
Interviewer: Jesus loves me? Is that what you said?
Child: Yeah.

This is clearly a situation in which the difficulty of interviewing the child led the interviewer to offer the child an interpretation which amounted to a suggestion. However, there was no intent to produce that outcome. In this case, what appears to be a claim of abuse was essentially turned into something very different.

The trade-off of accuracy against completeness

There is an obvious but extremely important distinction to be made between:

* the amount of accurate information collected in an interview;
* the amount of inaccurate information collected in an interview.

Unfortunately, in real life, it is often not easy to know what is accurate information and what is inaccurate information. Nevertheless, the distinction means that there is an important choice between the risk of incorrect information and the risk of incomplete information. There seems to be little doubt that general, non-directive questions yield from children testimony that is accurate and low on inaccuracy. Unfortunately, this is at the expense of answers that are complete. The question is which is to be accepted – inaccuracy or incompleteness? Both reflect adversely on the quality of the evidence of child witnesses. Hutcheson *et al.* (1995) accept that there is such a dilemma when questioning young children. They found that the age of the child makes a considerable difference to the effect of questioning. The researchers found that interviewers who tended to ask a high proportion of focused or specific questions obtained success according to the age of the child:

- Focused and specific questions addressed to 5- and 6-year-olds produced more inaccurate answers. There was no benefit of increasing the completeness of the answers.
- Interviewers who asked 8- and 9-year-olds a high proportion of focused questions obtained more complete answers. In this case accuracy was not affected.

Box 17.2

Controversy: communicative competence in the courtroom

Adult language can be complex especially when sophisticated users of language such as lawyers and forensic psychologists are involved. There is good reason to believe that the language of the courtroom is inappropriate for many children. Some of the following issues have been raised in connection with other forms of interviewing, but they bear repetition because they are drawn from courtroom experience:

- *Linguistic complexity*: the following question in a court transcript: 'On the evening of January third, you did, didn't you, visit your grandmother's sister's house and didn't you see the defendant leave the house at 7:30, after which you stayed the night?' (Myers *et al.*, 1996). The child expected to answer this was 4 years of age!
- *Children may not understand legal terms*: Myers *et al.* (1996) point out that quite young children of 5 or 6 years do understand some terms, so they know words such as lie, police and promise. This does not mean that they have full understanding of the terms. So a child may have an idea of what the police do but will certainly not know the full ramifications of the job. Other words are beyond the understanding of even teenagers in the forensic setting. There is a potential for misunderstanding legal terms such as court (which is a place where tennis is played), charges (which are to do with money), hearing (which is listening), party (which is a social gathering), and swear (which is to say a rude word).
- *Time, date and distance*: these are concepts built up gradually in the school years. It is pointless, for example, to ask a 7-year-old child the time that something happened because they do not have sufficient knowledge of the concept.
- *Comprehension*: monitoring is being able to assess how well we understand things that are said to us. Children are not particularly good at this and they may believe that they understand questions which, in fact, they do not. Furthermore, children rarely ask for clarification about the meaning of a question.

Lawyers' use of language in their dealings with victims in child abuse cases may be seen as oppressive and abusive from some perspectives. Brennan (1994) lists 13 different verbal tactics that are difficult or impossible for young witnesses to deal with effectively because they stretch their linguistic competence. For example, the following is an example of a multi-faceted question: 'And did your mother ever say to you that if somebody asks you the questions I am asking you, you should say that we didn't say what was going to be said?' (p. 213). It should be stressed that this is a question addressed in court to a 10-year-old. A good illustration of the problem is reported in Carter, Bottom and Levine, 1996). Children were asked two versions of a question. One version was in legalese: 'To the best of your knowledge, X, in fact, kissed you, didn't she?' and the other version was simpler: 'X kissed you didn't she?'. The version in legalese was much more likely to produce inaccurate replies in 5- to 7-year-olds than the simpler wording. Actually, even this version of questioning introduces a feature that may be problematic – the tag – as in a question like 'Amy touched your bottom, didn't she?' as opposed to the direct version which is 'Did Amy touch your bottom?'. With questions such as these, the child's answer is vital in that a case of abuse could rest on it. Krackow and Lynn (2003) investigated this very tag question and others in a sample of 48- to 70-month-old children. They set up a situation (actually an innocuous game) that included either innocuous bodily touch or no such touch. All that happened actually was that half of the children were touched on their hands, arms, calves or feet by an assistant whereas the others were not touched at all. A week later the children were interviewed about the events using tag and direct questioning techniques. 'Did Amy touch your bottom?' produced fewer erroneous yes answers than the corresponding tag-question version 'Amy touched your bottom, didn't she?'. It did not matter whether there had been any touch at all during the play session with Amy. In fact, the children who answered the direct question were almost always accurate in their answer, those answering the tag question seemed responding almost at random since nearly 50% falsely agreed that their bottom had been touched when none of the children's bottoms had actually been touched.

How to interview child witnesses

Saywitz (1994) has a number of practical guidelines for interviewing very young children under the age of 7 years although there are lessons for interviewing older children contained with them.

- Avoid using personal pronouns (him, her, they, she) in favour of proper names such as Darren or Sue. Personal pronouns can cause confusion about what they actually indicate during speech.
- Use short sentences. Break down compound or overloaded questions into several simple questions.
- Use short words rather than longer ones (e.g. 'mend' rather than 'repair').
- Use simple verb constructions. Avoid complex verb structures (e.g. 'Do you think it possibly could have been?').
- Jargon words should not be used (e.g. legalese such as 'sentence' and 'charge' which also have more obvious meanings).
- Avoid complex grammatical constructions such as double negatives (e.g. 'You're not saying you didn't steal the apple, are you?').
- Make it absolutely clear to what you are referring (e.g. 'When did your mother go to work?' is better than 'When did that happen?').
- The passive voice should be avoided (e.g. the active voice 'Did Adam steal the money?' is clearer than the passive voice 'Was the money stolen by Adam?').
- Concrete terms are better than abstract ones (e.g. 'gun' is better than 'weapon').

- Avoid questions requiring counting ability if the child is too young to be able to count. Similarly, time, linear measurements and similar concepts may be beyond the child's cognitive ability.
- With younger children, concrete, imaginable and observable things are better than abstract things.
- Children may appear to be uncooperative and uninformative because of their emotional and psychiatric states. Social withdrawal, as a consequence of abuse, should not be confused with uncooperativeness, for example.

Warren *et al.* (1996) investigated the adherence of interviewers to such good practice guidelines. They obtained transcripts of child protection workers' videotaped interviews with children. Typically, the interviews were conducted by a single interviewer but in some cases more than one additional person was present at the interview. Some of the more important findings were:

- Establishing rapport in order to relax the child and make them feel comfortable: most (71%) of the interviews studied included an attempt to establish rapport. However, rather than encouraging the child to talk, the interviewer did something like three times the amount of talking during the rapport stage. Equally important is the fact that in nearly one-third of interviews no attempt was made at all to build rapport with the child.
- Establishing interview ground rules: only a minority of the interviewers (29%) made any reference to the sort of ground rules that establish in the mind of the child just what is expected by the interviewer. Children erroneously assume that they have to give an answer to every question, that there is a right and wrong answer to every question, that the interviewer knows exactly what happened and so the child defers to the 'superior' knowledge of the interviewer where the interviewer seems to differ from the child, and that it is inappropriate to ask for clarification or say that they do not know in response to a question. In various ways, the interviewer can indicate that such assumptions may be wrong. But they rarely did. In only 29% of the interviews were the children told to tell the truth, in 14% of interviews was it explained to the child that it was appropriate to say 'Don't know' in answer to a question, and in only 7% of cases was the child told to tell the interviewer that they didn't understand a question. Other ground rules were never or rarely mentioned.

Some care needs to be taken not to assume that simply because the child is given instructions not to lie, for example, that this will be completely effective. Huffman *et al.* (2001) carried out research into the effectiveness of such warnings with young children. They point out the difficulty in trying to do this with the youngest children. They report the following exchange between an interviewer (I) and a child (C):

I: Now, B., do you know the difference between the truth and a lie?

C: [Nods]

I: If I told you that – that you were standing on your head right now, what would I be telling you?

C: Old McDonald said that at the police station.

I: Uh-huh. At the police station?

C: You've got to take his shirt off. [Referring to small boy doll]

(p. 10)

Problems similar to these can even emerge when trying to establish interview ground rules with older children.

The researchers obtained a substantial sample of transcripts of interviews with children, largely of pre-school age. A small majority (56%) of these interviews actually contained a discussion between the interviewer and child about the difference between the truth and a lie. Not only this, but this analysis provided information about the standard procedures used by interviewers in this context. Consequently, a further study actually investigated the effectiveness of the discussion about lies on the quality of the information supplied by the child. Two procedures were employed:

- The standard protocol: this was based mainly on the transcripts which contained a discussion with the child about truth and lies. So one question was included which asked the child if they understood what is different between lies and truths. Then they would have to answer a real example such as 'If I said that you were a boy, would that be a truth or a lie?' Finally, the interviewer would ask the child only to give truthful answers.

- The elaborated protocol: this was much more open-ended in terms of questioning and focused on the concept of a lie by the use of examples of lies and definitions of lies. The researchers believe that the concept of truth is too abstract to communicate. The children were given three different scenarios involving possible lies and they had to judge them. The following is an example:

  One day Jane/Jim and his/her mother were at home and the phone rang. Jim/Jane's mother did not want to talk on the phone and asked Jim/Jane to answer the phone but say she was not at home. When Jim/Jane answered the phone and the person asked for Jim/Jane's mother, Jim/Jane said, 'My mother is not at home.' Did Jim/Jane tell the truth, a lie, or something else? Why is that a ____? Was it okay for Jim/Jane to say his/her mother was not at home? Why/Why not?

It was found that the value of the children's evidence was enhanced by the elaborated protocol. There was little difference between using the standard approach and not having any discussion of the difference between truth and lies.

Interviewer features

It is too easy to assume that the only difficulties in interviewing children are to do with the characteristics of children and the way in which questions are posed. This is a too focused view of the interview situation. Children are interviewed for particular purposes and the interviewer often will need to report the contents of the interview to others – perhaps in a court of law. Evidence based on what the child says in interview when discussed in court is 'hearsay' since it is passed on by a third party and not the child's direct evidence. So a crucial question is that of how accurate are professionals carrying out interviews with children? Warren and Woodhall (1999) studied this question by asking a group of mainly child protection workers with between 4 and 21 years of experience to conduct interviews with 3- to 5-year-olds. The children were to be questioned about a magic show (which involved a disappearing book and lights pulled out of the magician's ears among other things) and a silly doctor session in which the child played with Dr Tracy who took their blood pressure, checked their ears, tested their knee jerk response, and measured the child's muscle among other things. The interviews took place a month after these experiences. The interview started with a cue question such as 'Tell me about the time you went with Tracy to play silly doctor.' (p. 360). The task for the interviewer was to find out as much as possible about the events that the child had experienced. The interviews were recorded. The interviewers were asked to give a written account from their memory of the interview, its contents and sequence as accurately as they could. They were to use as accurate wording as possible.

Each interview was transcribed and broken down into 'units' which was the number of aspect of the events that the child recounted in the interview. So, for example, mentioning the lights being pulled out of the magician's ear would be one unit. Each unit was broken down into more specific subunits and involved greater detail of things that happened when the magician pulled the lights out of their ear. The interviewer's recollections of what had been said were good. They recalled 83% of the major units of the events and 65% of the detail. They also recalled 60% of the errors made by children when they recalled the events such as claims that the magician had a magic wand which he did not have. So, according to Warren and Woodhall, there is some degradation of the child's testimony such that some of the important detail is omitted in the 'hearsay' evidence supplied by the interviewer.

It is worthwhile mentioning the suggestive evidence from a 'laboratory' study which compared how mock student jurors evaluated evidence presented as if it were that of a child with the same evidence but presented as hearsay evidence from an expert interviewer of children (Warren *et al.*, 2002). Although the evidence was not perfectly consistent, there was some evidence that the jurors tended to regard the evidence of the interviewer as more believable – but largely in a condition where they only presented the gist of the child's evidence rather than the detail. In other words, interviewer testimony may be effective, so care must be needed over the degradation of that testimony compared with that of the child's original interview.

Main points

- In order for child victims to gain justice under the law it is necessary for them to provide evidence that is credible in a specific case. There are a number of procedures that have been adopted which may reduce some of the stress of appearing in court – a very adult environment normally. In some jurisdictions, video links of either the children giving testimony live or pre-recorded links may reduce the stress, as does making the court less formal by allowing lawyers to be seated when they examine the child.

- Experienced interviewers of children may employ closed questions a lot despite the research evidence which suggests that this tends to generate a much smaller amount of material from the children involved. It may be advantageous to use scripted introductions to interviews, which use open-ended questioning, as once children are freely answering they tend to carry on in the same way no matter the type of questioning style used. It should not be forgotten that children at different stages of childhood may have very different communication skills. Some types of question – tag questions for example – may cause inaccurate testimony.

- Many of the problems in interviewing children are not ones of the child's competence and accuracy but matters to do with the interviewer. For example, there is evidence that lawyers in court have difficulty in consistently phrasing questions in a manner appropriate to the child's developmental stage. Furthermore, when interviewers were asked to recall the detail of interviews with children they are less than perfectly accurate despite the importance of being able to do so. The way in which the interviewer raises issues of truth and lying can have an influence on the accuracy of the child's testimony.

Chapter 18

Mental illness and crime

Overview

- In popular culture, the link between mental illness and crime has consistently been made. This is true of fictional and news media. The media, through selectivity, exaggerate the violence and extreme nature of crimes perpetrated by the mentally ill. Individual dramatic news events increase public antagonism towards the mentally ill. However, the evidence of major mental illness in a substantial minority of killers is quite strong.

- The relationship between mental illness and crime is complex and there are a number of confounding factors which can cloud the evidence: (1) the mentally ill tend to drop in social economic status, which means that they may live in more violent communities; (2) psychiatric categories of mental illness tend to involve violence in their definition. Consequently, the mentally ill are violent because they are required to be if they are so categorised, and (3) the public may be more alarmed by a given level of violent behaviour if that person shows signs of mental illness. As a consequence, the violence of the mentally ill may more readily be reported to the police.

- Surveys involving general population samples and objective measures of psychiatric illness are the ideal to avoid the biasing effects of using clinical/hospital/prison samples. Mental illness does increase the risk of violent crime in these studies but other factors such as substance abuse have much greater influence.

- Late starters in criminal behaviour tend to be identified in the criminal justice system as mentally ill. Certain sorts of psychotic symptoms are also more likely to be associated with violence – such as delusions and command hallucinations. It should not be overlooked that the mentally ill people are themselves more likely to be victims of violence. Nevertheless, reoffending by those with a criminal history which led them to be confined in high security special hospitals is quite frequent after release from the hospital. A quarter of those discharged are reconvicted for serious (largely violent) offences.

- Other pertinent material may also be found in Chapter 19 on mental problems in court and Chapter 23 on risk and dangerousness.

The professions of law and psychology share little in terms of how they conceptualise their subject matter – people. The causes and motivations of behaviour are central to both, nevertheless the two professions are essentially split by the way they construe human nature. This sometimes causes great confusion. Even a concept such as 'mental illness' means different things in the law compared to in psychology. Thus a definition of mental illness, for example, from clinical psychology or psychiatric textbooks tells one little about the legal meaning of the term. Under English law, for example, mental illness is not a technical phrase. It means what it means in ordinary language to ordinary people. It is for the jury or court to decide whether the term applies to a particular defendant (Pilgrim, 2000).

Belief in an association between mental illness and violent crime has a long history (Howitt, 1998b). As long ago as 1857, a Dr John Gray suggested that serious mental illness is associated with attempted or actual homicide. This theme became common in the mass media. As early as 1909 *The Maniac Cook* movie had the mentally ill as homicidal maniacs. Modern cinema continues exactly the same themes in *Psycho*, *Silence of the Lambs* and many others. Dangerousness and unpredictability have been shown to be the dominant characteristics of the mentally ill in the media (Day and Page, 1986; Wahl and Roth, 1982). Furthermore, public opinion surveys indicate that mentally ill people (especially schizophrenics) are perceived as violent and dangerous. In other words, the idea that the mentally ill are dangerous is well supported in Western cultures.

Not surprisingly then, research indicates that the media may shape the public's beliefs about the dangerousness of the mentally ill. A German study concentrated on the way in which daily newspapers portray the mentally ill (Angermeyer and Schulze, 2001). A German tabloid newspaper (*BILD-Zeitung*) with daily sales of 11 million copies was analysed in terms of its coverage of mental illness in relation to crime. The largest proportions of stories about the mentally ill concerned murder, multiple murder, physical injury/grievous bodily harm, attempted murder, rape/sexual abuse, multiple infanticide, and infanticide. This amounted to a total of 68% of all of the reported crimes being in this category, which is essentially the more extreme forms of violence. Indeed, 49% involved some form of homicide. The researchers also showed that individual news events in which public figures were violently attacked by mentally ill people seemed to affect the public's attitudes to mentally ill people in general. The public's attitudes to the mentally ill became more negative after highly publicised violent incidents involving the mentally ill such as the knife attack on court against the tennis star Monica Seles in 1993.

The criminal justice system (the police, courts, prison, probation services) is only one aspect of a complex structure dealing with mental illness. Medical services such as hospitals clearly have a part to play, as do voluntary services, say, dealing with mental health issues or homelessness. Furthermore, we should not forget that the community and family also have a central role and that some individuals with mental disturbances never seek or receive psychiatric or psychological help. The relationship between different parts of the system is dynamic and changing and there is an interplay between the medical system and the criminal justice system: that is, problematic individuals will be diverted into one or other system according to what capacity there is in the medical system. It has been shown, for example, that British mental hospital admissions correlate negatively with rates of prison imprisonment (Weller and Weller, 1988). The prisons were apparently receiving cases who previously would have entered psychiatric institutions. In this context, one should note the findings of Robertson *et al.* (1996) concerning people detained at London police stations. About 1% of detainees were acutely ill. They tended to get diverted to other services and not to go through the criminal justice system. Violence, at the time of arrest, tended to lead to processing through the criminal justice system.

To get matters into proportion, it is useful to quote a few statistical findings. Based on data from 500 homicide cases in England and Wales in 1996–7 for whom psychiatric reports could be obtained, the levels of mental disorder were (Shaw *et al.*, 1999):

- 44% had a record of mental disorder at some time in their life;
- 14% had symptoms of mental illness at the time of the offence;
- 8% had had contact with mental health services in the year before the offence.

Only in a small proportion of homicides did the offender show signs of mental illness at the time of the offence. According to Hodgins and Cote (1993), studies using 'unbiased' samples of killers find rates of major mental illness among them from about a fifth to over a half. One should bear in mind that mental disorder is very common in the general population when assessing these trends. Relatively frequent problems include depression.

One intriguing possible explanation of the link between mental illness and violent crime emerges out of the observation that the mentally ill are actually more likely to be victims of crime than other people. Hiday *et al.* (2001) interviewed severely mentally ill patients (e.g. schizophrenic or another psychotic disorder) who had been involuntarily admitted to a psychiatric unit. Some of them had substance abuse histories. Demographically, the patients in this sample reflected national trends. In the four months prior to the interview, over a quarter (27%) had been the victim of any sort of crime, 8% had been a victim of a violent crime, and 22% had been a victim of a non-violent crime. However, half of the sample was known to have acted violently in the same time period. Thus it cannot be said that these violent acts were simply fights involving a mentally ill person rather than attacks on a mentally ill person, for example. Compared to the general population, the rates of non-violent victimisation of the mentally ill were average. On the other hand, they were rather more likely to be victims of violent crime than a member of the general population. This was still the case when demographic variables were controlled in the analysis. Consequently, it seems unlikely that the relationship between mental illness and being a victim of violent crime is a spurious one. However, since this was a cross-sectional study, one should be cautious about inferring exactly what the causal relationship is. Nevertheless, the findings of this study are consistent with the view that a mentally ill person may be violent because of their earlier violent victimisation.

The problem of evidence

The question 'What is the relationship between mental illness and crime?' is relatively simple to answer compared with the methodological and conceptual difficulties inherent in the question 'Does mental illness cause violent crime?' (Arboleda-Florez *et al.*, 1996) There are a number of other difficulties that need to be resolved.

Controlling for confounding factors

No matter what the statistical association between mental illness and violent crime (positive, negative or none), there remains the possibility that the apparent relationship is an artefact of the influence of third variables or confounding factors. So, to give a somewhat unlikely example, it is possible that the mentally ill appear to be more violent because they respond to taunts about their behaviour. Without these taunts, there might be no violent response. There are other possibilities:

- Some variables cannot be considered to be alternative causal variables. Mental illness cannot cause a person's age or sex, for example. This is not to say that mental illness does not correlate with age or sex. Schizophrenia was originally called *dementia praecox* because it was seen as an illness of young people. It is a common observation that, for whatever reason, women appear more frequently than men among the statistics on rates of mental illness. Such variables as gender can be appropriately partialled-out or controlled using common statistical techniques.

- Other factors that initially appear to be appropriately dealt with by statistical methods may actually be somewhat problematic. What is considered to be a confounding factor is a complex matter. Social class is a case in point. It is known that there is downward social drift among the seriously mentally ill (Monahan, 1993). A company director who becomes mentally ill may be launched into a downward spiral because of being unable to keep a job, say, because they no longer cope with the stresses of a managerial career. Their consequent income drop may cause them to lose their homes and any work they obtain will be poorly paid. Once their socio-economic status has dropped markedly, they may find themselves in contact with violent subcultures (e.g. from living on the streets if they become homeless). The net effect of the downward spiral is that the mentally ill will tend to be disproportionately of lower socio-economic status. In this sense, mental illness can cause their social class. Removing socio-economic status from the association between mental illness and violent crime statistically would distort the findings in this case.

- Things can be even more complicated than this implies since such downward drift does not always happen and may be caused by factors other than mental illness anyway. For example, what if mental illness is sometimes the consequence of stress caused by bad housing or financial difficulties? In these circumstances, there is potentially a need to control for socio-economic status since it is part of the chain of factors causing mental illness.

- Neither of the preceding points of view is wrong. Nevertheless, they lead to very different approaches to statistical control in the data. Of course, if both approaches lead to the same broad conclusion, then interpretation is easy.

Confounding by overlapping definitions

Mental illnesses are largely defined in terms of a number of diagnostic categories. Imagine that among those diagnostic features is violence itself. One possible consequence is that there will be an association between mental illness and violent crime. People who are violent then have a greater chance of also being defined as mentally ill since they show one of the symptoms of mental of illness – violence. For many of the psychiatric disorders described and defined in the *Diagnostic and Statistical Manual of the American Psychiatric Association*, the 'bible' of psychiatric classification, violence is listed as a key diagnostic feature. Illnesses such as *antisocial personality disorder* and *borderline personality disorder* are partly defined in terms of violence. For other disorders, such as schizophrenia, violence is mentioned as an associated feature although not a diagnostic characteristic (see Box 18.1 and Chapter 19):

- A study of DSM-I (published 1952) showed that only 2% of the listed disorders characteristically involved violence. In DSM-II (published 1968), this percentage increased slightly to just 13% of disorders. Things changed markedly with the issue of DSM-III in 1980. This time, 47% of the psychiatric categories listed violence as a characteristic (Harry, 1985).
- These changes in definition coincided with changes in research findings. Prior to this time, research studies tended to show *no* relationship between mental illness and violent crime. After that time a relationship was more often shown (Link *et al.*, 1992).

The confounding effects of medication

Psychiatric drugs are often prescribed to the mentally ill to control the symptoms of their illness. These drugs may have side effects leading to violent behaviour. For example, it is known that certain tranquillising drugs with neuroleptic effects can make users more aggressive. In other words, the drugs that the mentally ill take to alleviate undesirable symptoms are the actual cause of their aggressiveness, not the mental illness as such. Thus aggression in this case is not a direct effect of mental illness.

The clinical sample problem

Imagine that there is no relationship between mental illness and violence. It would still be possible to produce an association by selecting one's sample of mentally ill people in such a way that the mentally ill who are also violent have a better chance of being sampled. One way in which this might happen is to draw one's samples from mental hospitals. These people may be in hospital because they drew attention to themselves in the community – perhaps they were violent and so were arrested. In reality, violence may be no more common in the mentally ill than the general population. Any selection method that favours the violent mentally ill may be responsible for a spurious association.

Misclassification of the mentally ill and violent

The use of hospital and crime records to classify people as mentally ill and violent may depend on a flawed classification system. For example, the general public may be more likely to report violence or threats of violence by people who show signs of mental illness. This is because their psychiatric symptoms make their violence more disturbing. As a consequence, the relationship between mental illness and violent crime would strengthen.

Effects of general social trends

It is possible that the apparent relationship between mental illness and violent crime will vary with major changes in social policy. Since the early 1980s there has been a policy of retaining fewer of the mentally ill in mental institutions in favour of supporting them within the community (Bachrach, 1984, 1989; Shadish, 1984). This is known as deinstitutionalisation. This, in itself, places the public at greater risk. Intriguingly, opinions have changed about violence carried out by the mentally ill. Prior to the 1980s, researchers tended to conclude that the mentally ill were, if anything, less violent than people were in general. This could have been an artifact of the likelihood that the violent mentally ill were kept institutionalised and not allowed to return to the community. Since then, the view has been that mental illness has a slight tendency to be associated with violence.

Box 18.1

Controversy: psychiatric diagnosis

Forensic and criminal psychologists associate professionally with a variety of other professions – the law, social work, policing, prison administrators, prison officers and psychiatrists. This means, inevitably, that forensic and criminal psychologists should be able to communicate effectively across professional boundaries. This poses special problems in relation to psychiatry. Psychiatry overlaps with psychology in seeking to understand and explain human behaviour including criminal activity while at the same time the two disciplines are very different in their practical and theoretical base. One particularly problematic area is that of psychiatric diagnosis in which individuals are classified as manifesting the characteristics of a particular mental illnesses, for example, or not. This is much the same as diagnosing physical diseases such as typhoid, carcinoma and the like.

Psychiatrists have mainly worked with diagnostic schemes based on the work of Emil Kraepelin in nineteenth-century Germany. For Kraepelin, each psychiatric disorder should demonstrate a cluster of symptoms that tend to occur together invariably. The prognoses of people classified as having the same 'mental disease' should be similar since the same pathological root is shared by all of them. Kraepelin believed that there were three major types of psychosis:

- dementia praecox or schizophrenia – hallucinations and delusions;
- manic depression – extremes of mood including depression and mania;
- paranoia – delusions of a persecutory or grandiose nature.

Given the origins and rationale of this psychiatric classification, it is hardly surprising that many psychologists regard it as the epitome of the medical model of *mental illness*. According to Eastman (2000), any conception of mental illness in terms of diseases such as lesions or disturbances of the function of a part of personality are indicative of the underlying acceptance of the medical approach. His term for this is the psychiatric phenomenological approach. Control of symptoms is an important part of the 'treatment' of such conditions and one may seek a 'cure'. In contrast, what he terms as the psycho-understanding approach sees psychological content as valid and enlightening (rather than the outcome of a fault in the system as it is in the medical model).

Currently, there are two standard diagnostic systems. The most famous is the *Diagnostic and Statistical Manual of the American Psychiatric Association* (DSM-I to DSM-IV have been issued) and the *International Classification of Diseases*.

▶

DSM-IV uses a system of classification involving five broad aspects of psychiatric diagnoses which are labelled from Axis I to Axis V:

- Axis I includes clinical disorders (such as major depression, substance dependence and schizophrenia).
- Axis II includes personality disorder and mental retardation.
- Axis III includes general medical conditions.
- Axis IV includes psychosocial and environmental problems.
- Axis V includes global functioning.

The various categories of mental illness are defined by various characteristics. So, for example, *schizophrenia* would be defined by the demonstration of the following things:

- Two or more symptoms from the following shown over a month:
  - delusions;
  - hallucinations;
  - disorganised speech;
  - grossly disorganised or catatonic behaviour;
  - negative symptoms such as flattened emotions.
- Social and/or occupational dysfunctions.

The problems for a psychologist using these diagnostic manuals include the following (Pilgrim, 2000):

- Diagnostic categories are created by psychiatrists and others. Consequently, they may change, get abandoned, subdivided and so forth based largely on expert opinion rather than scientific utility.
- Unlike many diagnoses of physical illness, even for major psychiatric classifications of illness such as schizophrenia, the utilitarian value of the diagnosis is unclear. For example, the bodily causes of schizophrenia have not been clearly identified despite years of research. This is quite different from the situation with physical illnesses such as typhoid and carcinoma for which the physical mechanisms are known.
- There are major difficulties when the user tries to differentiate one diagnostic category from another. Different diagnosticians may put the same patient in very different categories. Similarly, simply diagnosing people as normal or abnormal is far from an objective process with different clinicians reaching different conclusions.
- Some would argue that these diagnostic systems have nothing extra to offer than does ordinary language. So to suggest people are mad, bad, sad or afraid may be to effectively offer the equivalent of diagnoses such as schizophrenia, antisocial personality disorder, depression or phobia. Pilgrim (2000) suggests that the psychiatric diagnoses tend to stigmatise people more than ordinary language does. The descriptions of ordinary language tend to be associated with relatively subtle explanations of why a person is a particular way and often a variety of notions about what can be done to help the person with the problem.
- The diagnoses may merely present technical terms that fulfil no other function than to enhance the technical reputation of diagnosticians. The ordinary person in the street understands the violent, often repetitive and antisocial nature of rape, so what extra is gained by diagnosing such a person as a psychopath?
- There is circularity in the definition of mental illness. A person is classified as mentally ill on the basis of their behaviour, then this diagnosis is used to explain their behaviour. This circularity

is illustrated below. Notice that things are different in medical diagnosis since although the disease is often defined by its symptoms, frequently there is an independent test to determine the correctness of the diagnosis. Interestingly, Pickel (1998) found evidence that simulated jurors tended to make judgements about the insanity of defendants accused of homicide if there were unusual features about how the crime was committed, e.g. that the body was covered with strange designs done with yellow mustard.

Mental illness and violent crime in community samples

Two important studies have been carried out involving substantial samples from the community (as opposed to, say, prisons or mental hospitals). This design removes some potential artefacts (McNeil, 1997) and may be regarded as the ideal type of study to answer the question of whether mental illness is linked to crime:

- Link *et al.* (1992) studied representative samples of 500 never-treated community residents in New York City together with a mental patient sample. As might be expected, mental patients had the highest levels of a variety of official and self-report measures of violent and illegal behaviour. Statistical control for socio-demographic and community context variables still left the mental patient group more violent and more criminal. The researchers employed the *Psychiatric Epidemiology Research Interview* with both samples. This assesses the extent of mental illness symptoms independently of the mental health system. There was a relationship between having psychotic symptoms and violence. Despite this, the presence of psychotic symptoms was a weaker predictor of violence than other variables such as age, education level and gender.

- Swanson *et al.*'s (1990) study was similar in that psychiatric symptoms were assessed using the *Diagnostic Interview Schedule*. They obtained a sample from the communities of Baltimore, Raleigh-Durham and Los Angeles in the United States. Socio-demographic variables including age and sex were statistically controlled. Following this, it was clear that schizophrenia and major affective disorders were associated with an approximately fourfold increase in the likelihood of violence in the year following assessment. These findings need to be set against the 14-fold increase in the likelihood of violence associated with substance abuse. The presence of mental disorder and substance abuse together increased the likelihood of violence to 17-fold. Mental disorders differ in their relationship with violence. Psychotic illness (i.e. schizophrenia and similar) resulted in higher levels of violence than affective or anxiety disorders. Nevertheless, serious mental illness is rare compared to, for example, substance abuse. Consequently, the relative risk is far greater from substance abusers than the mentally ill.

Clinical aspects of violence

There are other factors in mental illness that affect the likelihood of violence (McNeil, 1997). Mental illnesses, as we have seen, are not all associated with violence and in the same way. Furthermore, mental illness is not an invariant feature of a person's life. It changes in intensity and form over time. Consequently, studies of patients in the acute phase of a mental illness may find higher levels of violence. Studies of patients in remission (the non-acute phase) may find lower levels of violence. In particular, schizophrenics in stages of frequent and intense symptoms (i.e. during acute exacerbation) are more violent than groups of patients with a different psychiatric classification. In the case of mania (manic depression/bipolar disorder), the manic phase may show the highest levels of violence.

Mental disorders can be the consequence of traumatic injuries or physical disease. Head injuries tend to elevate the risk of violence – in particular, damage to the temporal or frontal lobes may encourage aggressive behaviours.

Other factors need to be taken into account. *Command hallucinations* (the hearing of voices instructing the patient to commit violence or other harm against a third party) seem to heighten the risk of violence. The famous case of the Yorkshire Ripper who, in the 1970s, murdered at least 13 women, generally prostitutes, featured such hallucinations. It was claimed at Peter Sutcliffe's trial that he was instructed by the voice of God to carry out the murders. This may have been a failed attempt to be pronounced mentally ill by the court (Ainsworth, 2000a). However, a study of schizophrenic men detained under the UK Mental Health Act of 1983 for serious sexual offences against women considered by the courts to be a special risk to the public, found a poor relationship between their delusions and their sexual offending. Ninety-four per cent had some sort of delusions and hallucinations at the time of the offence but did the contents of these have any relationship to the offence? For 51% of these offenders the delusions were just coincidental and had no bearing on the attack. Another 25% had delusions that were of a sexual or persecutory nature but which did not reflect the characteristics of the sexual assault. Eighteen per cent had delusions that appeared to be directly related to the sexual attack (Smith and Taylor, 1999). O'Kane and Bentall (2000) concentrate on severe psychotic disorders, which they see as characteristically involving hallucinations, delusions and apparent loss of contact with reality. They discuss the symptom approach to violence in the mentally ill in which the search is for the symptoms associated with violence (as opposed to the diagnosis approach, which concentrates on the psychiatric diagnoses associated with violence). The sorts of symptoms they implicate in violence are already partly familiar:

- Delusions and passivity delusions with paranormal influences.
- Psychotic individuals with organised delusions are especially likely to commit either lethal or near-lethal acts.
- Paranoid symptoms are associated with violent behaviour.
- Command hallucinations often involve aggression and self-punishment. They have also been implicated in sexual offences.

McNeil (1997) believes that the following should be considered when trying to understand the violence of individuals with psychiatric difficulties:

- A previous history of violence is the best single predictor of future violence in both clinical and non-clinical populations.
- Gender is a poor predictor of violence. Violence by male psychiatric patients may be perceived as more fear provoking because they are more likely to threaten and damage property. Nevertheless, women psychiatric patients would appear to commit more assaults. Studies of people *living in the community* who attend psychiatric emergency facilities generally suggest that the genders are comparable in violence levels.
- Being victimised by child abuse or observing adults being violent to each other at home increases the risk of acting violently.
- Race, ethnicity and culture are inconsistent and so worthless predictors of violence in the mentally ill. This is the case after social class and similar variables have been taken into account.
- Care-givers and nurses are at the greatest risk of violence from the mentally ill.
- Poor social networks are associated with violence.
- Some environments are actually threatening, which may encourage violence.
- Among the mentally ill, homelessness is associated with violent behaviour.
- The availability of weapons increases risk.

While some forms of mental illness carry an increased risk of violence to others, caution is needed about the issue. The rates of serious mental illness are small compared to people manifesting other risk factors for violence (e.g. substance abuse, youth). In other words, the likelihood of an individual being assaulted by someone with a serious mental illness is less than that of being assaulted by someone with a different risk factor.

So what are the characteristics of the offending associated with different types of mental illness? One area of particular interest is homicide. In Finland, Hakkanen and Laajasal (in press) obtained samples of forensic psychiatric statements for four different DSM-III-R diagnostic groups – schizophrenics, abusers of alcohol or drugs, offenders with personality disorder, and offenders with no diagnosis or a relatively minor disorder. There were some characteristics particularly associated with these different groups:

- Schizophrenics: sharp and blunt weapons are used more often than guns perhaps because their crimes are more impulsive; they injured their victim's face more frequently than the other groups of mentally ill offenders possibly because the face is symbolically the essence of a person or because they find facial expressions threatening; their attacks were less likely to follow arguments; mostly they suffered from hallucinations/delusions at the time of the attack; their victims were frequently relatives.
- Personality disorder: guns and blunt and sharp weapons were associated with this group as was kicking and hitting; there were few other characteristics that may reflect the tenuous nature of this classification.
- Drug addicts: these stole more frequently from their victims and they killed in the context of another crime more frequently; surprisingly, they showed some of the pattern of schizophrenics since their choice of weapons was very similar and

the killings of both of these groups seem not to be the consequence of external events such as quarrels.

- Alcoholics: they were all drunk when committing the homicide; they were the group most likely to use a weapon present at the crime scene; they were most likely to kill following an argument; they were the most likely to give themselves up; they were very unlikely to use a handgun.

Who among the mentally ill is violent?

The origins of criminals with major mental disorders (schizophrenia, major depression, bipolar disorder, other non-toxic psychoses) are not uniform. There are two clearly definable groups (Hodgins, 1997; Hodgins et al., 1998):

- *Early starters* have a stable history of antisocial behaviour from childhood and throughout their lives. Interestingly, within the criminal justice system, they are not usually identified as mentally disordered. When they are in the acute stages of mental illness, they show no pattern of antisocial behaviour so they are not seen by the psychiatric services as criminal or antisocial.
- *Late starters* do not have the early history of criminal and antisocial behaviour. Such behaviours only emerge at about the same time as symptoms of the mental disorder appear. The late starters are more likely to be positively helped by treatment of the mental disorder.

Laahasalo and Hakkanen (2004) studied the schizophrenics in their sample by sub-dividing them into those whose criminal convictions started by the age of 18 years (early starters) and those whose criminal convictions began after that age (late starters). Early start offenders, compared to the late start offenders, were more likely to have killed following an argument, were less likely to kill an acquaintance, and were more likely to kill their victims by strangulation using some object. Overall, however, despite these differences, the use of crime scene characteristics was only modestly successful in predicting the age of onset of their criminal career

It is possible that at least some of the violence of the mentally ill has not been included in the analysis of the relationship between violence and mental illness. If we concentrate our attention on the sort of violence that is measured by criminal convictions and recidivism, we probably underestimate the violence of the mentally ill. The violence of the mentally ill when inpatients in clinics and hospitals is unlikely to lead to prosecution and conviction. It probably leads to prosecution only when it is very extreme. Inpatient violence ranges from 3% for hospitalised patients to 45% for outpatients to 62% for committed individuals (Dernevik et al., 2000). Obviously, this is a clearer issue in relationship to violence in an institution or prison than out in the community. For instance, Dernevik et al. (2000) found some evidence of the effectiveness of risk management on violent incidents. High-risk management was the amount of time spent on a high-security ward with no community access. Medium-risk management was an amount of time spent living in the hospital but with some access to occupational and recreational activities in the community. Low-risk management was time spent in a less secure living arrangement and having access to the community while still being regularly monitored. While a standard risk assessment measure predicted violence in the final two risk situations well, it was a poor predictor within the high-security arrangement.

Mental illness and crime in general

While the threat of violence by the mentally ill has been a major aspect of this area of study, there is a more general question of the general criminality of those suffering a major mental illness. According to Hodgins (1997), three different types of evidence support the association between major mental illness and criminality:

- Major long-term studies of people born in a particular time period which show that those who develop a major mental illness also tend to have higher levels of criminality.
- Studies that compare the criminality of those suffering a major mental disorder on release into the community with members of that same community with no mental disorder.
- Studies showing the higher levels of mental illness in convicted offenders.

A good example of the relevant research is a study of the 15,000 people born in Stockholm during 1953 (Hodgins, 1992). This was an unselected sample except in so far as people no longer living in Stockholm ten years later were excluded. The figures varied somewhat by sex, but there was an association between the development of a major mental disorder and having committed a criminal offence by the age of 30. For men, 32% with no mental disorder (or mental retardation) became criminal but 50% of those with a major mental disorder were criminal. For women, 6% of the non-mentally ill compared with 19% of the mentally ill became criminal. The risks were somewhat greater for violent than non-violent crime. This and other research (Hodgins et al., 1996) suggests that many of the mentally ill commit their initial crime at the age of 30 plus. About a third of the mentally ill men and two-thirds of the mentally ill women demonstrated this pattern.

Why should there be greater criminality among the mentally ill?

The question of why criminality should be commoner among those with a major mental disorder needs to be addressed. There are a number of explanations (Hodgins, 1997):

- The police easily detect mentally ill offenders because they tend to offend in public, do not flee the crime scene too readily and are more likely to confess their crimes. Research evidence on this is equivocal.
- The co-morbidity of major mental disorders with alcoholism and drug abuse. In other words, alcoholism and drug abuse can lead to criminality. These conditions seem to exist in high proportions among offenders with a major mental disorder.
- Treatment delivery is more problematic with deinstitutionalisation. This may be made worse by the greater rights of patients to refuse treatment.

Reconviction and mental illness

Of particular public concern are those groups of offenders who commit serious offences but are found to have a major mental disorder. There have been a number of high profile cases in which it would appear that offenders seek to use provisions for dealing with offenders with such problems to avoid prison. In England, many such offenders would be detained in high security special hospitals such as Broadmoor and Rampton. Among the criteria for such admissions would be that the offender has one of the major psychiatric classifications according to DSM-IV (see Box 18.1) and is an immediate danger to the public. The majority in such hospitals have a psychotic illness, a smaller proportion have personality disorders (e.g. borderline personality disorder, antisocial personality disorder, schizoid and paranoid), and the very small proportion have general learning disability. Jamieson and Taylor (2004) studied a complete cohort of patients discharged from special hospitals in a single year (1984). A twelve-year follow-up period was possible and the releases were after the implementation of important legislation in the Mental Health Act of 1983. Some would have been discharged to another type of hospital, some would be returned to a prison following hospitalisation in the special hospital because of a major crisis in their behaviour in prison or returned to court for sentencing, and others would be discharged into the community.

Reconviction data was obtained from a variety of sources including the offenders index and the police national computer. A quarter of patients were reconvicted of a serious offence (e.g. homicide, violence and sexual, though the commonest by far were grievous bodily harm/actual bodily harm, robbery and assault) after discharge from the special hospital. Overwhelmingly, they were in the community at the time of the reconviction (86%) though, of course, others were reconvicted for offences which took place when they had moved on to another type of institution. Predictors of reconviction included having a psychopathic disorder, number of previous court appearances, younger age on discharge and amount of time spent in the community. Those with a psychopathic disorder were seven times more likely to commit a serious offence on discharge than those with a mental illness. Those with mental impairment and those with a psychopathic disorder were equally likely to be reconvicted.

In the United States, Gagliardi et al. (2004) studied recidivism in a sample of mentally ill offenders who had been released from Washington prisons in 1996–7. These prisoners were defined as mentally ill on the basis of having at least two of the following: 1) a diagnosis of a major mental illness recorded; 2) had a prescription for indicative psychotropic medications, and 3) had spent over 30 days on a residential mental health treatment programme while in prison. Quite clearly, this is a different sort of mentally ill sample from the one used in the special hospitals study just described. Presumably the members of the US sample were regarded as less dangerous. Also, the follow-up period in the US study was only 27–55 months. Nevertheless, after release the mentally ill offenders demonstrated high levels of arrest or charge for crime. Over three-quarters (77%) came to the attention of the police in this way. Forty-one per cent of the entire sample were found guilty of a new crime, which is much the same as the 38% of a similar sample of offenders who were not mentally ill. The figures for violent crimes are particularly relevant – 10% of the mentally ill committed a violent felony offence, exactly the same percentage of the comparison sample of non-mentally ill offenders. Felonies are grave – that is, serious – offences.

Main points

- There seems to be little doubt that some forms of mental illness and certain patterns of symptoms elevate the likelihood of violent crime and crime in general. A major difficulty is in identifying exactly what the pattern of risk is and who among the mentally ill is the most likely to be violent and criminal. It is also difficult to form a clear impression of the risk posed by the mentally ill. Other factors such as drug or alcohol abuse seem to have much greater effects relative to mental illness simply because there are proportionately fewer mentally ill people compared to those who drink excessively. So, the relationship between mental illness and crime is relatively small and, in general, the public is at greater risk from, for example, young men and substance abusers than from schizophrenics. The latter are relatively rare in the population.

- Exactly why mental illness is associated with violence is equally difficult to explain. It is a little too simplistic to suggest that mental illness is a cause of violence. There are many reasons for this. For example, some of the drugs used to treat mental illness are known to cause aggression. Furthermore, the extent of the relationship between mental illness and violence can change with changes in social policy dealing with the mentally ill. With the use of care in the community, the risk to the public may increase.

- The risk factors that predict the likelihood that a mentally ill person will commit a violent offence are increasingly understood. Factors which affect the pattern, apart from type of diagnosis, include whether antisocial behaviour began in childhood or much later and hallucinations and delusions. The mentally ill may have an elevated risk of being victims of violence though whether this is the consequence of their aggressive behaviour is not known.

Chapter 19

Mental, personality and intellectual problems in court

Overview

- Courts make decisions partly on the basis of certain legal requirements related to certain psychiatric and intellectual states. The nature of the issues varies according to the matter in question. Competency to stand trial refers to mental state at the time of trial whereas, for example, the psychological state of the defendant at the time of the crime may be mitigating circumstances relevant to sentencing (e.g. diminished responsibility/capacity and insanity pleas).

- Defendants have to be competent at the time of their trial. The definition of this depends on the legal jurisdiction in question and the differences are often quite subtle. Typically, a fundamental requirement is that defendants should be able to partake in their defence (with the aid of a lawyer) and understand the court procedure. There is evidence that substantial minorities of juvenile offenders seem to fail the competency requirement when assessed by a standardised test of competency.

- The most familiar competence assessment test is the MacArthur Competence Assessment Tool for Criminal Adjudication which deals with the American standard of competence. Nevertheless, it is more likely that competence will be assessed by judgements of clinicians such as psychiatrists and psychologists. There is evidence that a psychotic illness diagnosis, non-psychotic diagnosis and being unemployed are predictive of an incompetence assessment by the clinician. Other research suggests that, generally, psychiatrists are unaffected by legally irrelevant factors when coming to their decisions. For example, having had a spell of time in a psychiatric hospital is not relevant to current competency to stand trial but sometimes can affect decisions.

- Individuals with learning disability are often vulnerable and may be subject to various forms of sexual abuse, for example. As such, their testimony may be essential for justice to be done. There is evidence that they can supply good quality evidence and can make legally competent witnesses. However, the style of questioning adopted should be open ended as closed or leading questioning can lead to poor quality evidence. In court, too, little appropriate questioning seems to be employed and judges seem reluctant to intervene to support these witnesses when they are giving testimony.

- Psychopaths do not always manifest the criminality which is frequently used to characterise them. As such, since the condition may be adaptive, it is difficult to equate it with the idea of a dysfunctional mental disease. The McNaughten rule suggests that a person is not criminally responsible if at the time of the crime they did not know the nature and quality of the act they did. Despite this, some experts believe that psychopathy should be regarded as a reason for more punishment not less. Others argue that psychopaths do not pass through crucial stages of moral development which leads them to be incapable of knowing right from wrong and punishment is inappropriate since they cannot learn from it. This does not mean that they should go free but should be treated appropriately to their condition.

There are a number of circumstances in which a defendant's psychological state may be taken into account in court. These do not necessarily apply at the same stages of a trial. For example, competence to stand trial needs to be considered prior to the start of the trial as this decision determines what happens next. The reasons for judging a person incompetent to stand trial may be to do with poor cognitive functioning or mental illness. Competence to stand trial has nothing to do with the reason why an individual committed a criminal act, it refers solely to a person's situation at the time of their trial. If someone is judged incompetent to stand trial, it does not mean that they will go free but merely that they will be processed differently – for example, they might be sent to a psychiatric facility.

Sentencing decisions may be influenced by psychological factors which were present at the time of the offence. That is, there are some psychological factors which might work in mitigation of the sentence. Of course, simply because an individual has a psychological condition is not necessarily a reason not to punish or punish more leniently. Courts of law are not psychologists' consulting rooms; arguments appropriate in court are not necessarily ones that would be appropriate in a psychology lecture. Consequently, there are controversies, as we shall see, about the standing of diagnoses such as psychopathy as a mitigating factor. Indeed, some argue that psychopathy is an aggravating factor and may warrant greater punishment.

Competence/capacity to stand trial

Many different criminal justice systems require that defendants should be able to contribute effectively to their own defence (Hollin and Swaffer, 1995). Such a precaution is necessary in adversarial systems of justice. In these, winning in court is the key objective of the court appearance. As such, the opposing sides of prosecution and defence line up against each other, much as in a battle. Should the defendant be a hapless individual incapable of understanding and coping with this affray, then is it possible for him or her to have a fair trial? It is clearly important for the public credibility of the legal system that their trials are fair, that the legal process is dignified and demonstrates integrity, and that the defendant understands the reason why they are being punished (Zapf and Roesch, 2001). A 'reasonable and legitimate' justice process would be severely compromised without the requirement of competence to stand trial. In contrast, the inquisitorial systems employed in many parts of Continental Europe and elsewhere involve much more of a guided search for the 'truth' by the inquiring judge. So, in the inquisitorial court system, the issue of fitness is not so important as it is in the adversarial system. It is noteworthy, then, that the inquisitorial legal systems of Austria and Denmark, for example, have no fitness to stand trial criteria. As might be expected, psychiatric reports may be called for if there appear to be any problems with the mental state of the accused that may help inform the judgement of the court.

The issue of competence is more frequently raised in some jurisdictions than in others. Competence is a commoner issue in the United States than in the United Kingdom, for example (Hollin and Swaffer, 1995). In England and Wales, the annual numbers of defendants judged unfit to stand trial is very small – around 20 cases per year. This is not because there are few offenders with poor capacities, but because many would be taken out of the justice system at an earlier stage under mental health legislation. In other countries, such as the United States, the competence to stand trial decision is much more common. For example, Bonnie and Grisso (2000) estimate that there are about 60,000 competency evaluations in the United States annually. Sometimes competence to stand trial is referred to as the capacity to stand trial.

The following case from the United States demonstrates graphically some of the problems associated with the issue of competence:

> Andy was just 11 when he started hanging around with the teenage gang members in his neighborhood. They used him as a lookout when they sold drugs . . . until one drug deal turned violent and two people were shot. That's how Andy ended up facing a charge of murder. The prosecutor offered a deal: Andy could admit he was there, testify against the others, and face a few years in juvenile detention. Otherwise he would be transferred to adult court and, if found guilty, spend a much longer time in detention and prison. Andy had just a few minutes to make a decision that would determine the rest of his life. He chose to take the risk: he would go to trial.
>
> *(Steinberg, 2003)*

The psychologist who assessed Andy's competence to stand trial asked him whether he understood what would happen if he was found guilty of the crime. 'I'll go to prison for a long, long time,' was his reply. He was assessed a few weeks later by another person and asked the identical question. Andy gave much the same reply but he was then asked to explain what he had said. His reply was that 'It's like when you do something bad and your mother sends you to your room for the whole weekend.' Andy seems not to understand the nature of the process of which he was part, since his conception of imprisonment is inadequate. This is not an exceptional circumstance. Steinberg (2003) reports the findings of a study of the competence of young Americans to stand trial using a standardised competence assessment procedure. Thirty per cent of 11- to 13-year-olds were not competent to stand trial, as were 19% of 14 and 15 year olds and 12% of later adolescents and young adults. This is of major importance in a country like the United States where increasingly young people have been tried in adult rather than juvenile courts.

There is a concept in English law that dates back to the fourteenth century and is also found in Australian law, for example. *Doli incapax* refers to the assumption that children below a certain age are incapable of being evil, which may be equated with an incapability of committing a crime because they do not know the difference between right and wrong. *Doli incapax* is a presumption and it does not mean that children cannot be tried for crimes but it has to be established that they did know what they were doing when they committed the offence. Without using the *doli incapax* phrase, other countries may have ages below which children may not be tried in an adult court. This varies substantially from legislature to legislature.

The United Kingdom

The court, prior to the commencement of the trial proper, assesses competence. The criteria vary according to jurisdiction. Taking the United Kingdom first, the criteria determining whether a defendant is fit to stand trial include (Grubin, 1996a):

- sufficient ability to enable the defendant to follow court proceedings;
- the ability to understand that jurors may be challenged (objected to);
- the ability to comprehend the details of the evidence;
- an ability to understand the meaning and implications of the charges;
- the ability to instruct lawyers effectively.

A number of matters are important (Grubin, 1996a):

- Competence is judged by the jury in Britain (elsewhere it may be an issue for the judge solely).
- The consequences of being found unfit to stand trial are drastic. In the United Kingdom, the defendant may be compulsorily detained in some sort of hospital for indeterminate periods of time. Given this serious outcome, the issue of fitness to stand trial or competence is far more frequent for trials of extremely serious offences.

In Britain, modern legislation requires the following. After the decision that the defendant is not competent to stand trial, a hearing is held to determine whether it is likely that the defendant committed the offence. If unlikely or disproved, then the accused will be discharged. This ensures that the judgement of incompetence for the innocent is not followed by extremely serious consequences.

- Poor mental functioning is not the main reason for classifying an offender as unfit to stand trial. British evidence (Grubin, 1996b) indicates that the majority are classified as schizophrenics.

The United States and Canada

Recent court rulings in Canada and the United States which establish that decisions to waive counsel, decisions to confess and decisions to plead guilty all require a certain and invariant level of competency which is unaffected by particular circumstances (Coles, 2004). In some parts of the United States, expert witnesses can only advise the court about an individual's abilities relevant to their competency – not on the matter of their competency to stand trial directly. In the United States, competence to stand trial is whether (the defendant) has sufficient present ability to consult with his lawyer with a reasonable degree of rational understanding – and whether he has a rational as well as factual understanding of the proceedings against him. This standard was established in the Supreme Court ruling *Dusky vs. United States (1960)* (Heilbrun *et al.*, 1996). In practical terms, competence to stand trial requires that the accused can comprehend the charges against them and understand what the judge, jury and lawyers do. However, in Canada, there is a different competency that does not include the criterion of rationality. Zapf and Roesch (2001) suggest that the Canadian standard only requires the defendant to be able to communicate with and understand their lawyer.

Assessing competence is a specialist skill and there is a risk that different practitioners would not agree on an individual's competence to stand trial. There are, of course, guidelines to help establish common standards in the United States (e.g. Baker *et al.*, 1998). However, one important development in the United States is the *MacArthur Competence Assessment Tool for Criminal Adjudication*. This is a standardised instrument to assess fitness to participate in legal proceedings within the US legal system (Otto *et al.*, 1998). There are other MacArthur competence measures (e.g. for competence to agree to medical treatment). The MacArthur charity funded the *MacArthur Research Network on Mental Health and the Law* which developed this competence measure. The assessor using the competence assessment tool presents a short description of a crime and consequent events. The administrator then asks a series of questions concerning court procedures, the roles of various people (e.g. the jury), and the reasoning processes underlying the decisions made in court.

Strictly speaking, the *MacArthur Competence Assessment Tool for Criminal Adjudication* is only applicable to the United States. It may assess people incompetent to stand trial who would be competent in other jurisdictions. Zapf and Roesch (2001) compared the *Fitness Interview Test (FIT)* with the *MacArthur Competence Assessment Tool*. The FIT test measures competence in terms of Canadian legal definitions whereas the MacArthur tool measures competence in American terms. Both measures were given to a sample of males remanded in a forensic psychiatry institute. Although the two measures correlated moderately well, it was clear that the MacArthur measure was more likely to classify individuals as unfit to plead than the measure based on the Canadian standard of competence. This confirms that the American criteria for competence are stricter than the Canadian. This is a reminder, if a further one is needed, that forensic and criminal psychologists must be aware of the legal codes and practices of the jurisdiction in which they operate.

Since there is clearly a degree of discretion in any clinical assessments and in assessments of competency to stand trial in particular, is the process of decision-making a biased one? It is important to note that clinical assessments of competence to stand trial and court decisions concerning competency concur highly. Of course, such a high degree of overlap may simply reflect that clinicians and courts share the same biases. Cooper and Zapf (2003) looked at the question of how competency decisions are made by clinicians by using a variety of demographic, clinical and criminological measures extracted from files on over 400 individuals assessed for competency. Only about a fifth of those assessed had been previously classified as unfit to stand trial. Those with a psychotic disorder (e.g. schizophrenia) or with a major non-psychotic disorder were much more likely to be classified as unfit to stand trial. However, those who had an alcohol or a drug related disorder were less likely to be deemed 'unfit to stand trial'. Four variables were strong predictors of the classification as incompetent when the researchers tried to develop a statistical model of the decisions. These were psychotic diagnosis, non-psychotic major diagnosis and non-psychotic minor illness diagnosis – all clinical dimensions – together with unemployment. Based on this model, it was possible to predict the actual classification of 89% of the competent cases and 47% of the incompetent cases. Thus prediction was substantially superior for the competent cases. The authors argue that because the clinical variables are so important in the decision-making model, there is no evidence of bias in the judgements. This, however, assumes that there are no biases in these clinical assessments in the first place. Furthermore, there are a lot of instances where these seemingly rational judgements fail to apply – for example, 53% of the incompetent cases could not be predicted on the basis of the clinical variables plus unemployment.

Some research provides a more reserved interpretation. Plotnick *et al.* (1998) used an experimental design. Psychiatrists rated a number of vignettes relevant to fitness evaluations. In some conditions, the vignettes actually contained legally irrelevant information which should not be considered as part of the evaluation of fitness to plead. These potentially biasing but legally irrelevant variables were a previous psychiatric hospitalisation (or not), the nature of the current crime (violent versus petty larceny) and prior legal involvement (six prior arrests versus no prior arrests). In addition, there were several conditions that were legally pertinent to fitness evaluations. For example, the unfit condition involved the defendant having psychotic symptoms in abundance and being incapable of communicating with their lawyer. The research findings suggested that overwhelmingly the fit and unfit categories were correctly used. Over 70% of both the fit and unfit vignettes were correctly classified. Nevertheless, for the legally fit vignettes, sometimes legally irrelevant factors affected the psychiatrists' judgements. The psychiatrists tended to misclassify legally fit individuals if they had been charged with a violent crime and had a lot of previous psychiatric admissions to hospital but no previous arrests. In other words, classification as fit or unfit to plead could be affected by legally irrelevant information but, nevertheless, the psychiatrists tended to make correct classifications in general.

Box 19.1

Forensic psychology in action: mental illness in court

Mental illness is common among non-convicted and convicted prisoners. Indeed, there may be more persons with serious mental illnesses in prisons than in mental hospitals (Blaauw *et al.*, 2000). Furthermore, current prevalence rates for any psychiatric disorder for those in European prison systems has been estimated as anywhere between 37–89% according to the study in question. Not surprisingly, then, mental states may be significant in relation to certain trials. Issues related to mental illness and limited cognitive functioning may influence the course of a trial. This can be both in terms of the requirements of proof and mitigation of punishment. Two Latin phrases cover the requirements of proof in a criminal trial: (1) *actus reus* and (2) *mens rea* under British law. These are not universal to all legal systems, of course, but they are important concepts in their own right:

- *Actus reus*: this is the requirement in some jurisdictions that a prosecution needs to show that a crime has indeed been committed and, further, that the accused was the person who committed that crime. This may be a matter for psychologists since forensic practitioners may be asked, for example, to evaluate the confession evidence that implicated the accused. The self-confession may have been obtained unfairly or from a person incapable of understanding the police caution, for example.

▶

- *Mens rea*: this is the legal requirement in some jurisdictions that the accused actually understood that what they did was wrong or that they had behaved recklessly. Intentionality or recklessness is the important factor. Actually, this requirement does not apply to all crimes. Some offences are *strict liability* to which matters of recklessness or intentionality are inapplicable. Road traffic offences are often strict liability offences (see Ward, 1997). Lack of criminal intent can be used in strict liability cases, but only in mitigation.

Diminished responsibility (diminished capacity in the United States) is an excuse offered by the defence that although the defendant broke the law they are not criminally liable since their mental functioning was impaired in some way. An obvious situation in which diminished responsibility might apply is where the defendant is intellectually very challenged. There are other defences such as insanity that may be very similar. However, the choice between diminished responsibility and insanity defences may depend on the jurisdiction in question. Beck (1995) points out that in the United Kingdom, the defence of *insanity* had hardly been used. This was because disposal after a decision of not guilty by reason of insanity meant indefinite diversion into a mental hospital until the new legislation in 1991. Legislation has changed things to allow commitment to a mental hospital for a limited time or, even, release back to the community given certain provisions. *Diminished responsibility* is used as a defence only in murder trials since, if accepted, murder becomes the less serious crime of manslaughter. The only sentence for murder is a mandatory life sentence. There is a variety of options for manslaughter – probation, prison or hospital. In the United States, the use of the insanity defence is also rare and where used is rarely successful. So less than 1% of felony charges would meet with an insanity defence and aquittals on the grounds of insanity occurred in about one in four hundred felony cases (Lymburner and Roesch, 1999).

Defences of insanity and diminished responsibility/capacity (among others) may be supported by psychiatric or psychological evidence of mental disorder in the accused. This is true also of the crime of infanticide, which is a lesser form of homicide. The distinction between insanity and diminished responsibility, according to a survey of psychiatrists (Mitchell, 1997) is not something that causes difficulties for the majority of practitioners. It is also worthwhile noting that there is some question as to whether psychiatric assessment that an individual demonstrated diminished responsibility actually is acted on by courts when sentencing. Ribeaud and Manzoni (2004) suggest that taking into account the legal seriousness of the crime, psychiatric assessment of diminished responsibility slightly *increases* the likely sentence in the Swiss cases they studied. This is clearly an issue about which more research is needed.

In Britain (as in other countries such as the United States), an offender may be placed on probation subject to the condition that they undergo psychiatric treatment. Treatment is voluntary and those who refuse it will be disposed of otherwise by the criminal justice system. In different countries, different standards apply about the involuntary treatment of the mentally ill. The British allow the mentally ill (and mental illness is not defined by law or regulation) to be identified solely by psychiatric opinion. Forced medication for up to three months is also allowed. This is different from the United States where substantial legislation surrounds any attempt by the authorities to deny citizens their liberty (Beck, 1995).

In the United Kingdom, recent legal provisions limit the 'right to silence' which means that a jury may interpret the silence of a witness in whatever way it wishes (Criminal Justice and Public Order Act, 1994). If it appears that the mental or physical condition of the accused means that they do not give evidence, then the court may not make such an inference (Grubin, 1996a). This is clearly an area in which forensic experts may be expected to provide evidence on the mental condition of the accused.

Temporary psychiatric states are particularly problematic in court. For example, dissociation is the term for the experience in which the individual ceases to be fully aware of their self, time or the external environment. Dissociation may be a fairly normal everyday experience such as when the indvidual becomes lost in a television programme so that the sense of the passage of time is lost and with it a sense of the surroundings. Dissociation may be a feature of post-traumatic stress disorder, for example (see Chapter 4). Bert Stone murdered his wife in Canada in 1993. Part of his account of the murder is as follows:

> I sat there with my head down while she's still yelling at me that I'm nothing but a piece of shit and that when she had talked to the police, that she had told them lies, that I was abusing her, and that they were getting all the paperwork ready to have me arrested, and that all she had to do was phone them, and once they had me arrested, that she was going to get a court order so that I wouldn't be allowed back onto our property and that I would have to go and live with my mother and run my business from there, that she was going to quit working and she was just going to stay in the house with her children and that I would have to pay her alimony and child support . . . Well, she just continued on and she just said that she couldn't stand to listen to me whistle, that every time I touched her, she felt sick, that I was a lousy fuck and that I had a little penis and that she's never going to fuck me again, and I'm just sitting there with my head down; and by this time, she's kneeling on the seat and she's yelling this in my face.
>
> *(McSherry, 2004, p. 447)*

His wife was killed by 47 stab wounds to her body. Stone was unaware of the moments during which he stabbed his wife repeatedly. Bert Stone describes how his wife's voice faded away and a 'whooshing' sensation enveloped him. The defence argued that under extreme provocation, Stone demonstrated a degree of loss of self-control 'and the dissociation which resulted in automatism was the result of extreme levels of external stress.' The jury decided that Stone was provoked, which led to a partial loss of self-control though they did not accept that he was experiencing dissociation, which would have made his actions involuntary.

Psychopaths and mental illness

Criminal jurisdictions commonly employ rules in order to protect some offenders suffering from insanity. The M'Naghten or McNaughten case of 1843 led to a rule to protect such individuals in the United Kingdom. The McNaughten rule indicates that a person is not criminally responsible if:

> at the time of the committing of the act, the party accused was labouring under such a defect of reason from disease of the mind, as not to know the nature and quality of the act he was doing; or if he did know it, he did not know he was doing what was wrong.

This is a difficult rule for psychologists because it promulgates a nineteenth-century view of mental illness as a disease and a defect. Not all, perhaps not many, psychologists subscribe to this medical view of mental illness. The American Law Institute proposed a different rule to accommodate the mentally ill offender in the 1960s:

> a person is not responsible for criminal conduct if at the time of such conduct as a result of mental disease or defect he lacks substantial capacity to appreciate the criminality of his conduct or to conform his conduct to the requirements of law.

This 'rule' also causes problems since it promotes the idea that the bad can be excused as mad. To offset this, the American Psychiatric Association offered the Bonnie rule in 1983 which identifies a person as mentally ill if:

> as a result of mental disease or defect he was unable to appreciate the wrongfulness of his conduct at the time of the offence.

This seems to hark back to the original McNaughten rule.

The question of 'mad or bad?' is particularly difficult in relation to the concept of psychopathy. Just what is a psychopath? The answer to this question has changed constantly over the years. Hodgins (1997) suggests that there are a number of reliable research findings concerning psychopaths. In particular, there is physiological evidence to suggest that when threatened with a noxious/unpleasant stimulus, the psychopath shows few or no physiological signs. Thus the indicators of emotional arousal (e.g. skin conductivity or heart rate) hardly or do not change. Psychopaths generally fail to anticipate emotional noxious events. So they might learn to avoid touching a hot stove through experience of touching one; they do not learn to avoid criminal activity through anticipating the aversive consequences of being arrested and imprisoned.

One important debate concerns the following:

- Is psychopathy a dimension of personality along which people can be placed in terms of degrees of psychopathy?
- Is psychopathology a discrete unit or class when applied to a person? The term 'taxon' is proposed for such a discrete class.

Some have proposed that psychopathy is not a mental disorder but a cheating lifestyle that has evolved over history (Rice, 1997). The characteristics of psychopaths suggest that they should make excellent cheaters – things such as glibness and charm, pathological lying and so forth. The idea is that psychopathy is adaptive and facilitative in many environments. So some highly successful business people are psychopaths and not involved in the violence of the typical psychopath. Perhaps a violent and hostile upbringing leads some psychopaths down the violent route.

It has been argued by Hare (1998) that psychopathy is the most important clinical psychological concept relevant to the criminal justice system. He also claims to be able to assess it with a high degree of certainty. Hence the ironic quote from one prisoner talking to Hare: 'So what if 80% of criminals with a high score on your psycho test, or whatever the hell it's called, get nabbed for a violent crime when they get out. What about the other 20% who don't screw up? You're flushing *our* lives down the drain' (p. 101). Hare's conception of the term psychopath is relatively exact and so his measure cannot be used to assess psychopathy in terms of anyone else's conception of what psychopathy is (Hare, 1998). This is very important in connection with any forensic use of the scale. For example, in one case, a forensic psychiatrist claimed a very high score on Hare's Psychopathy Checklist Revised (PCL-R score) for an offender using his own personal understanding of the term. A proper examination by trained personnel found the man to have a very much lower score. The judge directed the dismissal of the psychiatrist's evidence in this case. According to Hare (1998):

- Psychopaths readily engage in predatory, dispassionate and instrumental violence (p. 104).
- The violence of psychopaths is remorseless, frequently motivated by vengeance, greed, anger, money and retribution.

- Psychopaths tend to attack strangers.
- Psychopaths are responsible for half of the deaths of police personnel who die on duty.
- Probably 1% of the general population is a psychopath.
- Psychopaths are much commoner than this in prison populations.
- Antisocial personality disorder and psychopathy are sometimes confused even in professional writings. According to Fine and Kennett (2004), antisocial personality disorder is very common in prison populations at somewhere between 50% to 80% of prisoners. In contrast, psychopathy is present in 30% of the forensic population. The antisocial lifestyle is only part of the diagnosis of psychopathy but it is the defining feature of antisocial personality disorder. Furthermore, neither is Hare's concept of psychopathy the same as *antisocial personality disorder* as discussed in the *Diagnostic and Statistical Manuals* of the American Psychiatric Association (1987; 2000). Hare's ideas about the nature of psychopathy are discussed more extensively in Chapter 23. A few people classified as manifesting antisocial personality disorder can also be classified as psychopaths. The vast majority of the research on psychopaths has been carried out on offender populations (as opposed to clinical populations, for example) so it is not surprising to find that the concept of psychopath is regarded as associated with antisocial behaviours. The *Diagnostic and Statistical Manual of the American Psychiatric Association IV* (DSM-IV) published in 1987 deals with antisocial behaviours in terms of the diagnostic category antisocial personality disorder.

Blackburn (1995a) suggests that the question of whether psychopaths are bad or mad is nonsensical. Psychopaths can be both mad and bad, or just mad or just bad. Mad and bad are not opposites, they are different. Reduced to its elements, the real question for the forensic psychologist is whether the presence of a personality disorder should affect the eventual disposal of the offender. The essential problem, for forensic and criminal psychology, is that the concept of psychopath brings together a personality concept with deviant and criminal activities. This fails to differentiate between the following two distinct things:

- the medical/psychiatric state of psychopathy;
- the behaviour which amounts to its symptoms.

Despite the concept of *antisocial personality disorder* being listed in the DSM-IV, is it only possible to recognise the disorder by the antisocial and criminal behaviours that its victims possess? If so, then how can one differentiate between the different causes of those behaviours: ASPD, unemployment, poor parenting and so forth?

According to Blackburn (1995a), the English Mental Health Act category of psychopathic disorder is similar. The only way in which psychopathic disorder can be defined is using the symptoms of serious antisocial conduct that are also the consequence of having psychopathic disorder. Blackburn, in his research, noted that legally defined psychopaths are a varied (heterogeneous) selection of individuals. This observation strengthens the view that the antisocial behaviour of legally defined psychopaths is not dependent on any single psychological state. Furthermore, there appears to be a great difference between:

- legally defined psychopaths confined to special hospitals;
- psychopaths defined psychologically by the Hare Psychopathy Checklist.

The latter includes characteristics such as superficial charm, unreliability, lack of remorse and egocentricity. Blackburn suggests that no more than a quarter of the psychopaths studied by him would be also defined as psychopaths using Hare's Psychopathy Checklist.

For Blackburn, the ultimate question appears to be whether or not a disorder of personality, such as psychopathy, as seen to be in terms of modern psychological research, can also be regarded as a mental disorder. The *Diagnostic and Statistical Manual of the American Psychiatric Association* (DSM III-R) defines a mental disorder as a syndrome:

> that is associated with present distress or disability or with significantly increased risk of suffering death, pain, disability, or an important loss of freedom.

Thus many have taken the view that psychopathy should not be a mitigating factor in court but, instead, should be treated as an aggravating factor perhaps deserving of greater levels of punishment. This is a view expressed by Robert Hare, the leading researcher in the field of psychopathy, too, given that psychopaths show callousness, indifference to the rights of others and lack remorse for what they do. In this way, the diagnosis seems to lack of redeeming features (Fine and Kennett, 2004). However, Fine and Kennett take the view that there is considerable evidence that psychopaths do not pass through crucial stages in normal moral development and perhaps can be considered as not criminally responsible in the sense that they have not got a proper understanding that what they do is wrong or immoral. This does not mean that they go free, it merely means that to punish them is wrong as they cannot respond to punishment. Nevertheless, detaining psychopaths proven to have committed serious crimes serves as self-defence for society.

Box 19.2

Forensic psychology in action: victims and learning disability

The level of intellectual functioning of those with learning disability can be extremely low. Three-quarters of learning disability individuals in Texas replied 'yes' when they were asked 'Does it snow here in summer?' Despite the fact that none of them was Chinese, 44% said that they were Chinese when asked 'Are you Chinese?' (Siegelman *et al.*, 1981).

Individuals who suffer mental retardation amount to 1% of Western populations. Competence to stand trial may be separated conceptually from competence in terms of giving evidence. Some countries allow evidence from people with limited intellectual ability without requiring them to swear an oath (Kebbell and Hatton, 1999). Nevertheless, the full picture suggests that there is a serious risk that people with limited intellectual powers will be served extremely poorly by the criminal justice system:

- They may be unable to report offences against them to the police.
- In the absence of other evidence, the evidence of victims of crime who are mentally impaired may be regarded as too unreliable to present in court.
- Those who live in institutions may be at a disadvantage because the managers looking after them may not have appropriate procedures for contacting the police about crimes reported by residents. Alternatively, they may actively discourage staff from reporting such matters to the police because the victim would make a poor witness in their eyes.

Possibly people with an intellectual impairment have a greater than average chance of witnessing a crime. The practice of deinstitutionalisation, which ensures that many of them live in poor neighbourhoods, puts them at increased risk of being victimised by others in the community. Sexual assaults on people with a mental impairment can often only be prosecuted if they can provide evidence in court or in interview (Kebbell and Hatton, 1999). The quality of witness evidence from people with mental impairment varies but nevertheless may be valuable. Gudjonsson *et al.* (2000) assessed approximately 50 men and women residents at two private residential homes. These were clients incapable of surviving independently. There were allegations of ill treatment by members of the staff. These allegations were eventually proven in court. As part of the assessment the following were administered:

- the Wechsler Adult Intelligence Scale;
- the Gudjonsson Suggestibility Scale, which measures memory, suggestibility and confabulation;
- a measure of acquiescence specially developed for the purpose.

Pairs of incompatible statements were given and the resident replied whether each was true or false. For example:

- I am happy most of the time.
- I am sad most of the time.

A yes to both statements was scored as acquiescence. Acquiescence is the tendency to agree irrespective of the content of the statement.

Under British case law, a witness is classed as competent if the judge is satisfied on two main issues for which the advice of psychologists and psychiatrists may be sought. They are:

- Does the witness understand the oath and its implied sanction, i.e. I swear by Almighty God, that the evidence I shall give will be the truth, the whole truth, and nothing but the truth?
- Is the witness capable of giving an accurate account of what they have seen?

The potential witnesses among the residents were assessed. The highest IQ for 'mental retardation' is 70. Many of the residents assessed could not complete the IQ test because they lacked the verbal ability to do so. More than a third of them were right at the bottom of the IQ scale since they did not achieve any score on the items or subtests of the intelligence scale. Similarly, they generally showed poor ability to recall either immediately or on a delayed basis a story read to them by the assessing psychologists. For example, over a quarter were unable to remember any of the story in an immediate recall test. Delay before being asked to recall the story resulted in nearly a half of the residents being unable to remember anything from the story.

The residents were asked to say what the standard oath, as given above, meant. Some were capable of doing this and said things like:

> You swear on the Bible to tell the truth. You must tell the truth. The whole truth means you give a complete picture of what happened.
>
> A lie is when you are not telling the truth.

About a fifth could explain the oath to the satisfaction of the psychologists' standards. Almost without exception these had an IQ score of 60 or over. Of course, some of the clients had difficulty answering the question so they were presented with alternative questions:

- If I said your name was (the client's actual name given) would that be true or a lie?
- If I said your name was Fred (or the female equivalent) Bloggs would that be true or a lie?

▶

A resident who could answer these questions was considered to have some understanding of the concepts of lies and truth. This may be considered as part of understanding the oath entirely. Another fifth of the residents could answer at this level. Almost without exception, those who could explain a lie in this concrete situation had an IQ of 50 or more.

According to Kebbell and Hatton (1999), the style of questioning used with people with mental limitations may have an influence on the quality of the testimony elicited. The most accurate answers by witnesses with mental retardation are open-ended free recall ones: for example, 'What can you tell me about what you saw?' Accuracy may be regarded as the ratio of correct to incorrect information. As the question becomes increasingly specific, the answers become less accurate. So, for example, the question 'What was he wearing?' would produce better results than 'What colour jacket was he wearing?' Similar trends are found in the general population but the trends are a little more extreme for people with mental retardation. Another characteristic of people with mental impairment is their tendency to respond more to leading questions. This is only a minor trend since many people with limited intelligence can be accurate even with such leading questions. The reason for their greater suggestibility might lie in their poorer memory capacity. These individuals may only be suggestible on matters about which they are unsure. They also have less intellectual resources to cope with unfamiliar and stressful tasks such as those involved in providing eyewitness testimony.

People who are classified as 'mentally retarded' are often able to provide accurate enough testimony (Kebbell and Hatton, 1999). Lawyers' tactics as employed in examination and cross-examination interfere with the quality of the information obtained. The use of complex questions, such as those involving double negatives, is especially problematic. People in general tend to reply 'don't know' to such questions but will reply accurately to similar but simply expressed questions. The language used by the criminal justice system is complex for even intellectually able people:

- An IQ of 111 is needed to understand the rights notice used to inform detained suspects of their legal rights (such as the Miranda in the United States).
- People with mental disability only understood about a tenth of the sentences in some of the rights notices.
- The closed questions used in cross-examination are a strain for verbally fluent, well-educated and trained expert witnesses to deal with effectively.

Milne *et al.* (1999) describe research which suggests that the cognitive interview (see Chapter 11) may be helpful in obtaining information in adults with mild learning disabilities.

Of course, false confession under, say, police pressure, is a risk with such a vulnerable group. The law will vary under different jurisdictions: in the United Kingdom, three criteria were set out to help deal with this situation. In the case of confessions, the judge should consider the following:

- Does the prosecution case solely depend upon the confession?
- Does the defendant exhibit a significant degree of mental handicap?
- Is the confession unconvincing? Would a properly directed jury be unable to convict because of these inadequacies?

In these circumstances, the judge's responsibility is to withdraw the case from trial by the jury (Torpy, 1994).

This brings us to the question of how people with learning deficiencies are dealt with as witnesses in court. Are their needs accommodated by judges and lawyers? As we have seen, in appropriate circumstances, people with intellectual deficiencies give accurate information though this is highly dependent on the way in which they are interviewed or questioned. The accuracy of their testimony was best when they are asked open-ended 'free recall' questions such as 'What happened?'

Questions that are very specific ('tell me about the shirt the man was wearing') produce poorer quality information. They may produce more details with the latter form of question but the information is more likely to be inaccurate. Kebbell *et al.* (2004) located transcripts of British trials half of which contained evidence provided by a person with intellectual disability. These witnesses were matched as closely as possible with witnesses who were not intellectually impaired in terms of type of crime and the court. A high proportion were trials for rape and sexual assault but some were for assault. The researchers coded the types of questions asked of the witnesses including open questions ('What was Mr Jones wearing?'), closed questions ('And what was he wearing on top?'), yes/no questions ('And your keyworker does the shopping for you?'), either/or questions ('And when you lived at St Anne's, did you have your own bedroom or did you share a bedroom?'), leading questions ('I suggest that on this occasion Kate did not come into the flat at all, that you left before Kate had come home?'), negative questions ('Did you not think it might be important to tell somebody?'), double-negatives ('Now, did you say that you did not say that it was something that you did not like?'), multiple questions (two plus questions without allowing a chance for the reply to be given before the next question is asked), and repeated questions (when the same question is asked more than once). There was virtually nothing to differentiate the questions asked of witnesses with intellectual limitations and those asked of members of the general population. In other words, lawyers were making no adjustments in their questioning style in order to meet the special needs of those with low intellectual abilities. However, fewer leading questions were asked of people with intellectual limitations but they tended to have questions repeated more often. The most disturbing feature of Kebbell *et al.*'s findings was that those with intellectual limitations were the most likely to agree with the implied direction of the leading in response to leading questions and were less likely to provide additional information.

In a further analysis of the same data, O'Kelly *et al.* (2003) studied the judge's interventions in the court hearings by coding the transcripts of the hearings into three broad categories – interactions with witnesses, interactions with lawyers and interactions with the jury. The most frequent interventions with those with learning disabilities were clarifying issues with witnesses, calling breaks and asking additional questions about issues not raised by the lawyers. Overall, there were actually fewer such interventions with witnesses with learning disabilities though this was not statistically significant. The same is true of interventions directed towards the lawyers though, once again, this was not statistically significant. Probably most important among the findings was that the judge did not intervene more with people with learning difficulties to simplify the questions or to stop oppressive questioning.

Main points

- Legal concepts such as competency/capacity to stand trial and diminished responsibility are not simple to equate with psychological variables and are not exactly the same in different jurisdictions. In practice, such concepts will largely be assessed on the basis of clinical judgement although, gradually, more objective psychological measures are becoming available though clinical judgement is probably the main method. A person may be incompetent to stand trial for reasons of low intellectual functioning or as a consequence of suffering certain psychiatric conditions both of which make it difficult to be a party to one's own defence and to understand the procedures of the court. Only factors relevant to the individual's psychological state at the time of trial should be part of the assessment of competency.

▶

- The extent to which practitioners who assess competence are objective in their judgement is clearly an important question. Doubts have been cast on the validity of clinical assessment in other contexts. The evidence that practitioners use psychiatric variables in making their assessment rather than other information such as criminal background is indicative of the objectivity of these assessments. There are many decisions that are poorly predicted by these psychiatric variables so we do not know the basis of the decision. There is evidence that practitioners can be influenced by inappropriate factors from experimental studies but generally factors irrelevant to the assessment of competence are ignored.

- Psychological and intellectual problems can affect the likelihood of obtaining justice. Victims of crime who have limited intellectual resources may be victimised (e.g. sexually abused) in order to make a prosecution possible. As with many issues in forensic and criminal psychology, it is not possible to state absolutely that such individuals do or do not provide good evidence. If interviewed appropriately, especially using open-ended questioning, the quality of the evidence provided may be perfectly satisfactory. Nevertheless, there is emerging evidence that judges and lawyers in court do not always behave appropriately towards people with intellectual limitations. The questioning style of lawyers tends to be too complex and lacks adaptation to the needs of the witness, and judges tend not to intervene in these cases in support of the witness's needs.

Chapter 20

Judges and lawyers

Overview

- The public are reasonably satisfied with the criminal justice system. Yet a considerable minority believe that not all accused persons are treated fairly and have their rights respected by courts of law. Victims are seen as being poorly served by the system (Chapter 4) and a majority feel that the system does not bring criminals to justice. Substantial numbers of the public have attended court in some capacity – one in ten of the British public have been accused of committing a crime.

- The roles of judges and lawyers in the Anglo-American adversarial system are different from those of the inquisitorial systems where the prosecution and defence are not in battle. Nevertheless, even within the adversarial system, the styles of trial can be very different. For example, in the United Kingdom, lawyers' objections are not dealt with in the presence of the jury whereas in the United States they can be. The differences lead to differences in the relative strengths of the two systems and outcomes do not seem to be materially affected overall. Nevertheless, there is evidence that the mechanisms of persuasion may be different in the two contexts.

- There is evidence that outcomes of trials are only modestly predictable from a range of relevant variables. However, most of us will consult a lawyer in the hope that he or she will be able to accurately assess the outcome of a particular legal situation we face. Lawyers' assessments of likely outcomes follow the principles of the psychology of decision making under conditions of uncertainty. There is evidence that the way the issue is framed in terms of the numbers of factors to consider, for example, affects the probabilities of different outcomes as assessed by the lawyer.

- Considerable attention has been given to how evidence can be more effectively presented in court. There is advice that is based on general psychological developments in understanding effective communications, though their adequacy in the legal context needs to be assessed more thoroughly. For example, the use of powerful speech styles in which directness, assertiveness and rationality are characteristic tend to be perceived as delivering the more credible message.

- Many researchers have pointed to the importance of studying the effectiveness of narrative when trying to understand legal arguments. The effectiveness of evidence depends on the narrative context in which it is placed rather than its 'factual value' in order to achieve its impact. The better the narrative is based in common sense notions, the more positive the outcome. However, effective structures for the presentation of evidence can involve concentrating in part on the legal context in which the jury has to reach a decision.

- Legal judgements may be seen as ideological in nature. They often appear to reinforce dominant social ideologies. This is especially easily demonstrated by reference to the work of feminist analyses of courtroom interactions.

According to the British Crime Survey for 2000 (Home Office, 2001b), a third of British adults had been to court as a witness, spectator or juror at some time. Ten per cent of the population had been to court accused of a crime. About two-thirds of British people believe that the criminal justice system respects the rights of and treats fairly people accused of committing a crime. The figure is slightly lower for those who have been in trouble with the law but, nevertheless, even they remained as a group very satisfied with the criminal justice system. There was less belief that the criminal justice system brings people who commit crime to justice. Only about 40% agreed with this. There was only a low level of agreement (approximately one in five) with the statement that the criminal justice system meets the needs of victims.

There is an obvious need to understand better what happens in courts of law. However, one must be realistic about the direct impact of courts on much crime. In the majority of cases, questions of guilt have been already settled by the admission of the accused. Williams (1995) points out that in some jurisdictions something like 90% of cases are settled by a plea of guilty. Of course, in the United States, this may involve plea bargaining – that is, prosecution and defence agreeing a guilty plea to a less serious charge than the prosecution originally intended (Colvin, 1993). This encourages more guilty pleas.

Types of trial

The adversarial system is described by Dabbs *et al.* (1998) as 'lawyers arguing, judges refereeing, and juries deciding the outcome. Litigation is a form of combat, and good lawyers excel at combat' (p. 84). Trial lawyers have many similarities with the blue-collar worker of industry and commerce. They work in a place where concrete demands are made on their services rather than with abstract concepts involved in, for example, giving advice that does not demand delivery of results. They have to achieve and this requires knowledge and skills that are not taught in law school. Based on this analogy with the blue-collar worker, the researchers anticipated that trial lawyers will show characteristics that are similar to those that have been found in other studies. One possibility is that they will show higher levels of the hormone testosterone. This has been linked to heightened interpersonal dominance as well as sexual activity. Trial lawyers of both sexes were studied as well as other lawyers who had not been trial lawyers for a period of at least five years. Saliva samples were analysed for testosterone and it was found that in all the cases studied, irrespective of gender, the trial lawyers had higher testosterone levels than non-trial lawyers. In another study, they compared trial lawyers and appeal court lawyers with similar outcomes.

The institution of the jury has a history that goes back to Socrates but, more importantly, the Norman (French) law of trial by jury (Arce *et al.*, 1996). The jury is associated with British and US developments and other countries whose legal systems derive from these roots. History developed very differently in Continental Europe. There, legal experts working with lay people decided on matters such as guilt. (The mixed jury is different since in this lay people working as a group reach the verdict but the judge(s) also contribute in terms of deciding sentence.) The *escabinato* system first developed in Germany. Today, in Germany, the system deals mainly with rather minor offences. In France and Italy the development of escabinatos was associated with Fascism in the first half of the twentieth century.

Naturally, one of the questions is whether the legal professional has undue power over the other members in such a 'jury'. Arce *et al.* carried out research into the escabinato system using a real rape case that was video recorded and edited down to 75 minutes of tape. The escabinato juries were composed of five lay persons together with a judge. The results showed that the judge's initial verdict was usually very persuasive for the lay persons. No lay member changed to be against the judge. Given the two-thirds majority rule for the verdict applied in this study, the groups overall tended to adopt the judge's stance.

Chapter 21 is devoted to the Anglo-American type of jury.

British and American trial procedures are different despite both being based on the broad adversarial strategy (Collett and Kovera, 2003). There are many differences between the two. For example, in the British system, the lawyers are confined and are not free to roam around the courtroom while presenting their case; the opening statement from the defence is given after the other side has presented its case and not right at the beginning of the trial; objections from lawyers are not dealt with in the presence of the jury; British judges are more active in the general flow of evidence during the trial than American judges who may be described as being more reserved. All of this led Collett and Kovera to the view that these differences in the demeanor of both judges and lawyers in the two systems may have consequences for how the proceedings affect the jury.

One possibility is that the process of persuasion in the two systems is different. Modern theories of persuasion suggest that there are two methods by which information is processed. One is the central route in which people actively process all the information that is pertinent to their situation. Since this is a relatively cerebral and rational process, the quality of the arguments determine the level of persuasion. The peripheral route involves considerably less effort since it involves relatively simple decision-making rules or procedures when coming to a decision. This route also involves the use of peripheral cues. For example, in the peripheral to persuasion, things such as the status of the person making the argument affects acceptance of that argument. Distractive US courtroom environments would encourage the peripheral route to be more influential, say on the jury, than the more orderly British system which would favour the more central route to persuasion. On the other hand, the greater level of involvement of the British judges may mean that jurors are more influenced by their non-verbal cues concerning the case than would be a jury with an American judge.

In an experiment testing this possibility, Collett and Kovera (2003) set up mock trials some of which followed the British ways outlined above and others followed the American way. All other things were standard to all of the trials. The amount of non-verbal behaviour expressed by the judge was varied as well as the strength of the evidence in the trials. Those who were subject to the British-style trials could remember the evidence presented in the trial better than those who experienced the American style trial. However, there was no evidence that the British style trial allowed the jurors to be more influenced by the stronger evidence than did the American style trial. The non-verbal cues given by the judge were clearly drawn attention to by the British style procedures since participants rated the judge's non-verbal cues as more salient. There was also evidence that the British style trial resulted in the jury being more confident in their verdicts. However, the study failed to demonstrate that the two systems differentially affected the trial outcomes. The study does not show the superiority of one system over the other. The strengths of the British system in terms of allowing the jury to focus unfettered on the evidence are offset by the apparently greater risk that non-verbal signals from the judge will affect the jury.

Are trial outcomes predictable?

Fitzmaurice *et al.* (1996) studied how accurately sentencing could be predicted for a sample of 4,000 cases in England. The possible sentences included discharge, fine, probation order, community service order, fully suspended sentence, partially suspended sentence and custody. Over 30 variables were assessed for each case. Different combinations of predictor variables predicted different types of sentence most effectively. In general, the predictions were not particularly good. Thus the percentage of correctly predicted sentences (i.e. the sentence matched that predicted by the measures) could be as low as 20% and no higher than 60%. The correlation between the prediction and the actual sentence similarly could be lower than 0.2 and no higher than 0.5.

However, despite these relatively modest sentencing predictions, one of the most important functions that lawyers have in relation to courts of law is making predictions about the most likely outcome of taking a case to court or appealing a court decision. Clients go to lawyers partly for advice on what the law is, but also for an assessment of the consequences of legal processes. So, a client who wishes to sue another person for damages needs to know from their lawyer some sort of forecast of the likelihood of success. The advice offered by lawyers may be extremely influential on whether a case goes to court. So lawyers' advice needs to be understood. As yet, not a great deal is known about this. There is one exception, Fox and Rirke (2002) argued that the task facing a lawyer when making predictions about the outcome of a trial is analogous to any other decision-making process under conditions of uncertainty. Support theory is built on the research into such judgements. It assumes that probabilities are attached to descriptions of events (or hypotheses) rather than the events as such. Since descriptions of what constitutes a set of events are different from each other, the probabilities assigned to what is otherwise the same event will also differ.

Imagine the client wants to know whether seeking damages would be successful in court. The lawyer has to judge the probability of outcome A (damages awarded) versus the probability of outcome B (no damages awarded). The theory assumes that the lawyer's estimate of the probability of outcome A plus the probability of outcome B should equal 1, just as it would in statistical probability theory where the probability of a head or a tail when tossing a coin sums to 1. That is simple. However, the theory suggests that where the possible outcomes are more finely subdivided, the principle of sub-additivity should apply. For example, imagine the lawyer decides that the probability of winning the damages cases is .6 (that is, that the client would win in 6 out of every 10 cases like this). What would happen if the probability of winning damages were calculated for two subdivisions of damages? For example, where the damages are more than 10,000 euro and where the damages are less than 10,000 euro. What happens is that the sum of the two probabilities actually sum to more than the .6 that they should in theory. The lawyer might assess the probability of getting over

10,000 euro at .4 and the probability of getting under 10,000 at .5. Adding these together, this amounts to a probability of .9, which is bigger than the rational outcome of .6. The more subdivisions of a category, the more the sum of the probabilities of the individual categories would be. There is a further idea – that of implicit sub-additivity. This basically says that the more subdivisions of a category that are listed, the greater the probability that will be assigned. So, for example, if asked the probability that a case will end in a guilty verdict and the defendant put on probation, fined, or sent to prison then the probability given will be greater than for when a laywer is asked simply what the probability is of the case ending in a guilty verdict.

In one study, a group of lawyers were asked to give an estimate of the probability of one or other of a variety of trial outcomes. So one set of lawyers were asked to make some judgements about the outcome of an antitrust case involving Micosoft in the United States. Some estimated the probability that the case would go directly to the Supreme Court. The average judged probability for this was 0.33. However, when the other group were asked to assess the probability that the case would go directly to the high court and be affirmed, reversed or modified then the probability was judged to be .40. This difference supports the principle of implicit sub-additivity. Of course, there is a great deal more that needs to be known but even this one study points in the direction of improving decision making in relevant legal situations by compensating for the biases in lawyers' judgements. It might be useful here to point out that there is a variety of evidence about the impact of particular lawyers on trials. Williams (1995) reviewed the evidence on this matter and found that the lawyer did not matter much or at all in the majority of studies. His own research was on appeal level courts. Whether the lawyer was privately employed or a counsel supplied by the public defender made no difference overall. Private attorneys, then, were not more likely to win the appeal. One of the reasons for this may be that many criminal appeals (these were in Florida) are seen as hopeless, frivolous or routine, i.e. unlikely to be affected even by the most brilliant of courtroom performers.

The presentation of evidence in court

It is not possible to present just any evidence in court. Structural constraints are defined which essentially prescribe how, what, where and when evidence may be provided. The precise nature of these constraints varies according to jurisdiction, who and what is being tried. There are usually constraints on the *order* in which evidence may be presented in court (Bartlett and Memon, 1995). For example, the accepted structure may involve one-way questioning by lawyers and judges exclusively. The answer may also have an accepted form. Replies such as 'I would say so, wouldn't you?' violate such principles. There are other requirements:

- In adversarial systems, restrictions on the use of information about previous offences are common. Such evidence may be admissible only in circumstances where there are common features between the present charge and the past offences. Even in these circumstances there are constraints. The prejudicial effect of the information should not exceed the benefits of its provision.
- Furthermore, again commonly in adversarial systems, the accused may only be cross-examined about their past convictions if the character of prosecution witnesses is contested or if the defence concerns evidence of the good character of the defendant (McEwan, 1995).

The procedure is for the prosecution to give its case first which is then followed by the defence evidence. Many psychologists will be reminded of the research on the effectiveness of different orders of presenting opposing persuasive communications. It has been demonstrated that arguments presented first differ in their persuasive impact from arguments presented second. This is known as the primacy-recency effect. The findings of different studies reveal a complex picture and it is difficult to say that the first argument has greatest impact. Similarly, with court evidence, the research does not result in a simple formula such as the case presented first always has the advantage. The longer the trial, the greater the advantage to the more recent case; the shorter the trial, the greater the advantage of the case presented first (Lind and Ke, 1985).

Bartlett and Memon (1995) suggest a number of strategies that may help a lawyer to persuade jurors and judges of the strength of their case. The first few can be regarded as means of increasing persuasiveness in the argument:

- *Vivid language* enhances the impact of important testimony. Thus they regard 'He came towards me' as bland whereas 'He lunged at me with flashing eyes and a contorted grimace . . .' (p. 546) might have more effect on the listener.
- *Repetition* of particularly important pieces of information may be an effective strategy.
- *Loaded questions* such as 'Did you see the broken window?' (p. 546) contain an implication that the unwary might accept – that indeed the window was broken. The question 'Did you see the window in question?' contains no such implication.
- *Subtle shifts in wording* may profoundly influence what meaning is chosen for a sequence of events. For example, the phrases 'to sit with you' and 'to sit near you' can have rather different meanings. Nevertheless, despite this, an unwary witness might accept either.

The following strategies concern the manipulation of the credibility of the witness:

- *Powerful speech* styles are characterised by directness, assertiveness and rationality. In contrast, powerless speech contains a high density of 'intensifiers' such as 'so', 'well' and 'surely' together with many words dealing with hesitations such as 'you know' and 'well'. It is also characterised by polite words such as 'please' and 'thank you very much'. According to Bartlett and Memon (1995), the powerful typifies male speech and the powerless typifies female speech. Generally speaking, males using powerful speech were regarded as more credible and much the same was true for female speakers.
- *Making witnesses appear incompetent* by providing, say, expert testimony that casts serious doubt on whether they could possibly have seen what they claim to have seen. For example, it might be impossible to see a face at a given distance in the dim lighting at the time.

The major advances in understanding powerful legal arguments have come from trying to understand the narratives that underlie lawyers' cases. Decision making in a legal context is an example of a top-down process (Van Koppen, 1995). One can consider the hypothesis presented in court (the allegation of a crime) as preceding the fact-finding to support or reject that hypothesis. There is not a body of facts that is sifted through and then the most likely person to accuse selected on the basis of the facts. Quite the reverse: someone is thought to be responsible for a crime and then the facts sought that explain the accused's responsibility for the crime. The evidence verifies the charge rather than the charge verifying the evidence. The evidence, as such, though is not the key. The important thing is the story that links the evidence together. Take the following instance from legal writing that begins with the observation that in car accidents the facts are interpretable in more than one way:

> The fact that the driver did not see the pedestrian is at once an explanation of the collision in terms of accident rather than recklessness, and also a suggestion that he was not keeping a proper lookout.
>
> *(Abrahams, 1954, p. 28)*

Research evidence has demonstrated that the quality of the narrative is vital in making judgements. In a classic study, Bennett and Feldman (1981) adopted a very simple methodology. They simply asked students to tell a story to other students – half of them had to tell a true story and the other half were told to invent a story. As might be expected from what we know about lie detection (Chapter 16), listeners could not differentiate between the true story and the invented story at better than the chance level. But, of course, they believed some stories but not others. So here was an opportunity to study the features of stories that made them appear truthful. Stories that were believed contained what might be termed 'a readily identifiable central action'. This provides an easily believed context for the actions of the participants. Pennington and Hastie (1981, 1986) found that the following were crucial to a good narrative:

- physical conditions;
- psychological conditions;
- goals of the participants.

Bennett and Feldman (1981) give the example of a story that was seen as made up by persons listening to it. It was a story about a birthday party:

> Ummm – last night I was invited to a birthday party for a friend her name's Peggy Sweeney it was her twenty-fourth birthday. At the party we had this just super spaghetti dinner – you know – just great big hunks of meat and mushrooms and what not – a nice salad. And then for dessert we had a um cherry and blueberry um cheesecake. It was really good.
>
> *(p. 75)*

The researchers argued that this story can be broken down into a number of structural elements: the connections between them being ambiguous. The two elements – I was invited to a birthday party and last night – are joined together as a meaningful connection. Others are not:

> I was invited to a birthday party – At the party we had this just super spaghetti dinner

The significance of the phrase *At the party we had this just super spaghetti dinner* does not lie in the context of the birthday party. The spaghetti dinner is ambiguous in terms of its relevance to the birthday party story. Similarly, what is the relevance of the phrase 'her name's Peggy Sweeney' to the spaghetti meal? Why mention it? Unless the hearer knows who Peggy Sweeney is, her mention just complicates the picture. If the hearer thought that Peggy Sweeney was an expert in fine food then the ambiguity might be resolved.

> It is not clear what facts, logic, norms, or the like, would yield a clear inference about the relationship between these story elements.
>
> *(Bennet and Feldman, 1981, p. 78)*

Story ambiguities can be of three distinct types:

- If an obvious interpretative rule (fact, language category, norm, etc.) is not available to provide a meaningful link between two elements of the story.

- The listener can see many possible links between the two elements but the rest of the story fails to provide the information to support any of these plausible links.

- When the listener can make sensible, that is unambiguous, connection between the story elements but then realises that it is inconsistent with the most obvious connections among the other elements of the story.

Bennett and Feldman suggest that the number of ambiguous linkages of this sort (what they term 'structural ambiguities') partly determines and undermines the credibility or perceived truthfulness of the story. Indeed, they studied a number of predictors of story credibility. Of these, only structural ambiguity showed a substantial relationship with the credibility of the story. The length of the story, the number of actions performed in the story, the number of pauses in the story, and the length of the pauses each had no bearing on story credibility. The structural properties of the story far outweigh factors such as witness credibility, lawyer histrionics and so forth in perceptions of its truthfulness, claim Bennett and Feldman.

The birthday party story, by the way, was true despite being perceived otherwise.

Bennett and Feldman's argument then suggests that the following areas are employed by lawyers in the courtroom when constructing plausible accounts of reality:

- *Definitional tactics*: the language used by witnesses (elicited by lawyers) to define pieces of evidence. Bennett and Feldman give the example of a drunk driving case in which the prosecution lawyer tried to establish the number of beers the defendant had had prior to the offence. The defence tactic was to stress the extended period of time in which drinking had taken place:

  Prosecution: How much did you have to drink that evening prior to being stopped by these police officers?

  (Objection by the defense)

  Prosecution: Answer the question, Mr. H_____

  Defendant: Well, now, I was working (at) my locker the whole day on Fisherman's Wharf. I have a locker there.

  Prosecution: How much did you have to drink?

  Defense: May he be permitted to answer the question, be responsive. Your Honor? He started to . . .

  The Court: Go ahead. Let him explain.

  Defendant: Well, it will have to all come into this now, what I am going to say.

  Prosecution: Fine.

  Defendant: I left Fisherman's Wharf . . .

Notice how the defence lawyer shaped the defendant's testimony despite not actually asking the questions. Furthermore, the definition of the drinking behaviour was extended to provide a different picture from the negative impression that would have been created by a simple tally of the number of beers drunk.

- *Establishing and disrupting connections in stories*: inferential tactics. The structural location of a piece of evidence is made in relation to the remaining elements of the story. Bennett and Feldman give the example of the woman prosecuted for robbery. One of the salient facts was that the defendant gave her shoulder bag to a friend before committing the robbery so that she would be able to make a better robbery without this encumbrance. Under questioning, she explains that the bag kept slipping because of the leather coat she was wearing, the implication being that this was the reason for handing the bag over:

  > Q: You could ball the strap in your hand like a leash, couldn't you?
  > A: Yes.
  > Q: Isn't it true, Miss V_____, the reason you gave the purse to D_____ was because you wouldn't be burdened down with it when you ran?
  > > *(Bennett and Feldman, 1981, p. 126)*

  In other words, the lawyer made explicit the connection between handing over the bag and the crime.

- *Establishing the credibility of evidence*: validational tactics. Can (a) and (b) be validated by other information and explanations, or can they be invalidated by showing plausible alternative definitions and connections between the elements of the story? An example of this is the use of objections. These serve three purposes: one is to stop prejudicial evidence being presented, a second is to build up a catalogue of errors on which to base an appeal, and the third is really to address the jury:

  > Prosecution: Isn't it true that in February of 1964 you were convicted of manslaughter and sentenced to twenty years in the state penitentiary?
  > Defendant: Well, yeah.
  > Defense: We object to that for the record.
  > The Court: Overruled.

  The prosecution lawyer was acting properly in terms of the location of the court studied. By objecting 'for the record' the impression is deliberately created that such questioning is on the margins of acceptability and that, as such, it should not be given too much weight for fear of inadvertently prejudicing the case.

Anchored narratives are also based on narrative theory that emerges out of cognitive psychology. This argues that evidence is meaningless without being placed into a narrative context. The story is decided upon, not the evidence. The story may have gaps but these are filled automatically by the listener. Wagenaar *et al.* (1993) point to some of the gap-filling in the following:

> Margie was holding tightly to the string of her beautiful new balloon. Suddenly, a gust of wind caught it. The wind carried it into a tree. The balloon hit a branch and burst. Margie cried and cried.
> > *(p. 33)*

Now this you probably took to be the equivalent of the following:

> Margie, *a little girl*, was holding tightly to the string of her beautiful new balloon. *The wind was so strong that* suddenly a gust of wind caught it. The wind carried it into a tree. The balloon hit a branch and burst *on a sharp twig. The loss of her balloon made* Margie cry and cry.

But, equally, the story that fits the facts could have been:

> Margie, *a young mother*, was holding tightly to the string of her beautiful new balloon. *Forgetfully, she let go of the balloon.* Suddenly a gust of wind caught it. The wind carried it into a tree. The balloon hit a branch and burst *when a boy managed to hit it with a stone from a catapult.* Margie cried and cried *when the boy turned the catapult on her.*

The story context determines the meaning of the central factors of the story. As a consequence, it is possible to find two radically different stories in which to set the facts to different effects. This is, after all, what prosecution and defence lawyers do to try to achieve opposite ends.

Wagenaar *et al.* (1993), working within the context of earlier 'good story' theories of evidence, suggest that good stories are 'anchored' into a system of general rules which are most of the time valid. This knowledge of the world helps determine the truth-value of the evidence to the listener. Evidence, in itself, does not have this truth-value in the absence of these rules. For example, suppose that the evidence from DNA testing says that X's semen was found in the victim's vagina. This does not prove, in itself, that X murdered the woman. It does not even prove that the pair had intercourse, forcibly or not. The victim might have been a lesbian wanting a child who obtained the sperm from her friend X. She might have inserted the semen using a spatula as she could not bring herself to have sex with a man.

Among the common sense or legal rules that firmly anchor some stories as true are the following:

- Drug addicts are thieves.
- Once a thief always a thief.
- Police officers are the best witnesses.
- Witnesses rarely lie under oath in court.
- If a witness has a good sighting of the perpetrator then they will accurately identify the offender.
- Prosecutors usually do not take innocent individuals to trial.
- The associates of criminals are criminals themselves.

These rules need not have any factual basis at all.

There is another way of construing lawyers' activities. From a social psychological perspective they could be regarded as attempting to manipulate guilt attribution. So the job of the lawyer for the defence is to present his or her client's behaviour in a way that minimises guilt attribution. Schmid and Fiedler (1998) suggest that the social psychological notion of the peripheral route to persuasion (as opposed to the central route) is appropriate to lawyers' arguments. The central route presents the substantial arguments that are listened to and evaluated. The hearer would normally be critical in their evaluation of these arguments. In the case of the peripheral route, influence is achieved far less directly in a way that does not arouse this critical evaluation. Subtle cues of an evaluative nature, which suggest the response hoped for by the lawyer, become the basis for persuasion. Schmid and Fiedler argue that most listeners in court will be skilled language users who recognise the sorts of strategy for peripheral persuasion employed by the lawyers. If too positive, the risk is that the hearers will simply discount the argument the lawyer is making. The researchers videotaped the closing speeches of lawyers in training. Listeners (jurors had this been real life) responded to the arguments in terms of a composite of blame attributed to the defendant, the competence of the lawyers, the fairness of the lawyer and so forth. Severity of punishment for the offences was, predictably, dependent on how serious was the crime involved. But there was evidence that subtle language strategies also played a role:

- *Intentionality of negative behaviour*: this is defined in terms of the internal attribution of the negative behaviour to the offender. The focus of the cause of the offence is on the offender rather than the victim. This corresponds to different language characteristics. For example, more punishment was suggested when the lawyer used more negative interpretative action verbs (such as hurt as opposed to help) to the offender and less to the victim.
- *Dispositionality of negative behaviour*: language characteristics that brought about higher punishment recommendations included descriptive action verbs (such as push and shout).

Do not assume that good narrative accounts of the evidence which favour one side are the only requirements of a good legal case. Spiecker and Worthington (2003) studied the influence of what they call the lawyers organisational strategies on decisions made in simulated civil courts in the United States. The organisational strategies are the ways in which the lawyer chooses to organise the evidence. Two broad structures were identified – the narrative structure and the legal-expository structure. The narrative organisational structure emphasises things like describing the setting of events, describing the series of events in a meaningful and interrelated way, describing the important people in the narrative and organising the narrative in a meaningful temporal fashion. The legal-expository structure emphasises the legal requirements of the decision to be taken. These legal elements may include a description of the relevant law to the case, the nature of the burden of proof required for such cases, and the identification of the legal elements needed in order to establish the case. Both sides may take different views as to whether or not the case in question meets the requirements of proof. Of course, lawyers have more than one opportunity to make their argument. For example, they make opening statements and closing statements. So it is possible to mix the organisational strategies within a case – the opening statement could be narrative and the closing statement legal-expository. In the study in question, various possible combinations of strategies by both sides of the case were studied in terms of their effects on the jury. Broadly, it was found that both sides benefit from having the closing statement centred around a legal-expository format. That is, the lawyer should identify the legal aspects that should govern the case and offer an interpretation as to how well the evidence in a particular case meets these requirements. In terms of the overall strategy, this study showed that using a narrative opening and a legal-expository closing was more effective for the plaintiff's side than using the narrative approach for both. In contrast, the defence fared better with mixed strategy or a legal-expository approach throughout. In other words, the situation is not simply one of the narrative approach being best, it is one in which ignoring other strategies can lead to poor outcomes – strictly narrative approaches were not in the interest of the defence in this case.

Judgements

From the perspective of forensic and criminal psychology, the judges and courts are largely of interest in terms of consequences for the individuals who pass before them. This is a somewhat limited perspective. Feminist writers, on the other hand, note that the higher courts, especially, have great power to define the parameters of a range of important topics. For example, Williams (1991) describes the role of the US Supreme Court in relation to gender equality. She suggests that legal cases are a 'focal point' where the issue and meaning of equality may be argued.

Courts of law work through the rather formal language of legal experts including judges and lawyers. Inevitably, then, a primary focus of research into that work must concentrate on their language use. Considerable efforts have been made to understand the narrative structure of evidence as we have seen. Other aspects of language in court have received attention from socio-linguists, discourse analysts and feminist writers. Harris (1994) argues that the language of the law is basically and effectively highly ideological. So she regards concepts such as equality before the law and impartiality of judgement as the meat of ideological conflicts in courtroom exchanges. She suggests that the magistrates in the courts she studied use propositions that are inevitably ideological in that they are not verifiable for their truth. They reinforce power and domination relationships, and are effectively presented as common sense. However, this is expressed in complex ways. Clear examples of similar processes have been found in other legal texts as we will see.

Box 20.1

Key concept: the hypothesis testing model

According to Van Koppen (1995), it is inappropriate to regard judicial decision making as being based on a hypothesis testing model. Nevertheless, such a model has been put forward a number of times. The hypothesis testing process (that X committed the crime they are accused of) is evaluated firstly in terms of the prior odds that the hypothesis is true in advance of consideration of the evidence. The hypothesis is essentially the charge or indictment:

The prior odds

$$\text{Prior odds that charge is true} = \frac{\text{probability that charge is true}}{\text{probability that charge is false}}$$

Thus the prior odds have a theoretical numerical value. One difficulty is deciding what these probabilities are in any given set of circumstances. A total presumption of innocence until proven guilty would have values of 0 and 1 for the respective probabilities. In these circumstances, the prior odds are 0/1 or zero. An experienced judge may set the probabilities otherwise – that the probability of the charge being true = 0.9 and the probability that the charge is false = 0.1. Thus the prior odds that the charge is true are 0.9/0.1 = 9. The assessment of such prior odds is difficult and, given that most people probably do not express themselves well in terms of probabilities, it may be a fruitless task. The statistical procedures are based on Bayesian statistics.

Revised odds – posterior odds

The next stage is the introduction of evidence. Let us assume that it is a fact that the accused was picked out in a line-up/identification parade by a witness. This information will have a diagnostic value that indicates the probability that a person picked out at an identification parade is in fact accurately identified rather than wrongfully identified. Perhaps the judge has had a lot of experience of poor procedures for conducting the line-up being used and regards their accuracy as being relatively low. The judge believes that 7 in 10 identification parades accurately identify the individual in question. Thus the accuracy expressed as odds will be 7/3 (i.e. 7 correct identifications for each 3 incorrect ones), which equals 2.33. Thus it is 2.33 times more likely that the accused is the offender than without this evidence. This will increase the odds that the accused is guilty as charged.

Posterior odds = prior odds × certainty of the evidence = 9 × 2.33 = 21.0

The posterior odds are merely the odds after evidence has been introduced. Thus our prior odds (of 9) need to be multiplied by 2.33. Since this equals 21.0 then the probability that the accused is guilty increases.

Further evidence may be introduced, thus adjusting the odds. This is achieved merely by multiplying the existing odds at that stage (that is, the new prior odds which are, of course, the posterior odds calculated above) by the certainty of the further evidence. The new evidence may be the defence witness's claims to have seen the accused in a bar at the time of the offence. This should reduce confidence in the guilt of the accused. So the odds based on this information alone would suggest that the probability that the witness is mistaken should be relatively low. Turned into the ratio of the probability of being right over the probability of being wrong, the odds of the accused being guilty might be 0.5. We simply multiply the odds prior to the introduction of new evidence (i.e. 21.0) by the odds ratio for the new information. This gives us a new posterior odds value of 10.5: that is, it is substantially less likely that the accused is guilty.

The decision

In such a model, the decision is assumed to be guilty – that is, the hypothesis of guilt supported – if the posterior odds exceed a critical value. Below that value the decision will be not guilty.

Critique of the model

- The model seems not to resonate with our experiences of decision making – most of us are not skilled at expressing ideas in terms of statistical probabilities.
- As a purely statistical model (rather than a psychological model) it would only have value if it were possible to stipulate the odds ratios of various types of evidence sufficiently precisely for the model to be predictive of actual court outcomes.
- The probability of guilt assessed before the submission of evidence is conceptually difficult to define. A literal presumption of innocence until proven guilty would set the prior odds ratio at zero (0.0/1.0) since there is no chance of being guilty and a certainty (i.e. 1.0) of being innocent. The consequence of this is that no matter what the new evidence, no matter how indicative of guilt it is, the posterior odds will have to be zero. This is obviously ludicrous. It is more likely that we assume that there is a likelihood that the accused is guilty. Reading newspapers would suggest that a high percentage of prosecutions result in convictions. Should this be the figure we use? There seems to be no way of answering the question satisfactorily.
- The value of a piece of evidence is not normally easily translated into an odds ratio that can be taken as indicative of guilt. So what would we make of the testimony that the accused had been seen elsewhere at the time of the offence if the witness were the man's wife?
- The question of the odds that are high enough to convict demands a complex answer that cannot be provided by the model. Does it vary with offence type? What other factors might it vary with?

In short, the mathematical underpinnings of the model do not overcome its psychological inadequacy.

If judges do ideological work then just how is this achieved? The lack of a repertoire of discourse appropriate to certain crimes may result in them being interpreted through other inappropriate frameworks (Coates *et al.*, 1994). These authors mention a Canadian trial judgement concerning a man who went into a room and put his penis in the mouth of a sleeping woman. How one describes these events may vary according to perspective, but the trial judge described this as 'the act of offering his penis' (p. 189). Now this is a rather strange use of the verb 'to offer'. Had the woman been sexually attacked in the street it is inconceivable that a judge would use a phrase such as 'the accused offered the victim his penis' if he had put his penis in her mouth or told her to fellate him. That is, in terms of our usual discourse about stranger rape, the phrase 'to offer' has no meaning. It implies choice on the part of the woman. The language might be more appropriate if the events are interpreted using the discourse repertoire of erotic/affectionate relationships. In the context of a long-standing relationship, it is just about possible to understand the use of the verb 'to offer'. That is, it was a direct and forthright sexual invitation in a relationship in which the partners had previously established a mutually acceptable robust approach to sex and the man was 'offering' sexual intercourse. The authors surveyed a number of relevant judgements and suggested five 'anomalous' themes in similar trials:

- *Erotic/affectionate characterisation*: judges who described sexual crimes in terms of a man carrying out an offence against women or children as for the man's sexual gratification. This is to minimise or deny that the crime is an assault and also to suggest that it is sexual in nature rather than violent. Similarly, the language used to describe the attacks carries very different implications from what had actually happened. For example, forced oral contact was described as 'attempted unsuccessfully to kiss'. Forced oral/genital contacts were described as 'acts of oral sex'. Forced vaginal penetration was described as a 'bout of intercourse' (p. 192).

- *Sexual assault distinct from violence*: especially from a feminist viewpoint, to describe a sexual assault as non-violent is to undermine the notion that sexual assault is a violent act: for example, 'there was no violence and no physical force . . .' (p. 194)

- *Appropriate resistance*: this is the idea that victims have certain obligations to prevent or resist the attack on them. Physical struggling is part of the appropriate actions of a victim, it would appear from the judges' comments. In one of the judgements, the victim is described as eventually acquiescing to her own rape once she ceased struggling: 'She testified that after the first bout of intercourse she stopped struggling and that she acquiesced in the second bout, although the intercourse was still without her consent' (p. 195). Ehrlich (1999), dealing with a university disciplinary hearing, describes related linguistic effects. One woman was questioned in the following way: 'You never make an attempt to put him on the floor or when he leaves the room, to close the door behind him or you know you have several occasions to lock the door. You only have to cross the room. Or move him to the floor, but these things are offensive to you?' (p. 244). Ehrlich suggests that this actually contains forceful illocutory assertions rather than questions. In other words, 'You should have put him on the floor; you should have closed the door; you should have locked the door' (p. 244).

- *Offender's character*: the judges often described the man's character in very positive terms. For example, a man who raped a woman on two occasions was described as being of 'impeccable character' (p. 196).

- *Avoidance of agency for assault*: the actions involved in the sexual violence were frequently ascribed to the events themselves rather than to the offender, in phrases such as 'the struggle got into the bedroom' and 'there was advantage taken of a situation which presented itself' (p. 196). The acts seem to be doing themselves rather than being done by the offender.

In a similar vein, Cederborg (1999) shows how in the context of child abuse trials, Swedish judges construct children's credibility as witnesses. Overwhelmingly, the judgements encouraged the view that the children were credible. Such children, according to Cederborg, were perceived as credible because they fitted the judge's common-sense theory of what behaviour is normal. For example, 'Nancy told her story calmly and clearly and with no contradictory details. Her stories at the main hearing agreed well with her previous statements' (p. 151). The material in the judgement relevant to Nancy's character included 'It must be regarded as out of the question that at the age of 11 Nancy would have been sexually interested in him and should have even suggested that they have intercourse' (p. 151). Nancy's case was one of the majority in which the accused was convicted. In cases in which there was not a conviction, the judgement almost always lacked any assessment of the character of the child. An instance of the sorts of terminology and style used by the judges in these cases is the following: '. . . despite the efforts of the interrogating officer, this questioning does not give any clear impression that Hilda F actually experienced the events about which she answered questions' (p. 153). The judge's assessment of the child cannot be validated by any existing test so the interpretation becomes a subjective reality.

Main points

- Courts of law provide procedurally-based settings in which evidence is presented and judgements made. The procedures in different jurisdictions will differ markedly but the two broad approaches are the adversarial system employed in the Anglo-American approach in which opposing sides do battle against each other and the inquisitorial system which is largely led by the judge/magistrate who may be involved at an early stage of police work. Nevertheless, even within a particular system, there are many procedural and other variations. All of this makes it very difficult to study the processes involved in courts of law.

- Despite there being a great deal known about persuasive communications from the psychology of communications and attitude change, for example, the modern emphasis when applying psychology to effective presentations of evidence has tended to emphasise the importance of narrative structures rather than, for example, peripheral factors such as the authority of the lawyers involved. A good narrative structure is one that unites the individual components of evidence into a coherent story which supports one's own side in the case. Anchored narrative theory goes one step further by suggesting that notions which are grounded in common-sense notions of what is true, for example, will tend to make for more effective communications.

- From a feminist perspective, judges seem to do a great deal of ideological work when faced with cases involving women victims. So commentaries made about particular events tend to present the evidence in terms favourable to the man's point of view. So, a man who had a history of raping women might be described as having an impeccable character. These tendencies can be contrasted with the idea that decision making in court follows a hypothesis testing model in which probabilities are calculated mentally about each stage of the evidence. There is no reason to believe that such a model applies in court.

Chapter 21

Juries and decision making

Overview

- Only a small percentage of criminal cases are heard before a jury. The jury system has been subject to criticisms in some notorious cases. Trials with juries reduce the importance of the judge on decisions of guilt or innocence. Evidence is presented orally in jury trials so there is less reliance on written documentation than in inquisitorial systems.

- Some problems for jurors can be alleviated by simple changes such as permitting note-taking by jurors and allowing them to ask questions in court.

- Jury decision making is governed by rules which can affect the permissible size of the jury as well as the size of the majority on which a guilty verdict can be reached. The larger the jury, the longer the decision time. Where a majority decision as to guilt is required, the more effort the jury makes to try to reach a verdict.

- Pre-trial publicity can influence potential jurors. However, in law, prejudice is not conceived in the same way as it would be in a psychological study. For example, in the United States this influence would need to be accompanied by a resistance to change of mind in the light of new information. Mass media are so pervasive that for some trials it is unlikely that a location for the trial could be found where media publicity has not had an effect. Researchers may help find a relatively unaffected venue for the trial.

- In the US legal system there is some scope for lawyers to influence the make-up of the jury by peremptory challenges of some jurors. There has been some research on improving the effectiveness of these challenges by using social scientific surveys to assess what sorts of juror are sympathetic to, say, the defence. This is known as scientific decision making. The evidence on this is not compelling though such services are often offered.

The role of the jury trial can be overstated. In England and Wales, only about 2% of criminal cases are put before a jury (Lloyd-Bostock, 1996) although the figures are higher elsewhere. We can all think of well-publicised instances of juries acquitting a defendant whom we felt was beyond doubt guilty: for example, acquittal of the white police officers in the United States who had been videotaped beating up Rodney King, a black person. Such cases have encouraged a lot of criticism of the jury system. At the same time, we probably appreciate the substantial pressures on members of the jury. This is especially so in complex trials with weeks if not months of evidence. Is there anything that can be done to aid jurors in these circumstances? Very simple procedural changes, such as allowing jurors to take notes or perhaps to ask questions, might be advantageous. Like many other forensic issues, there is considerable doubt about the worth of laboratory experiments for addressing research questions such as these. It matters little if psychologists are happy with such procedures if those responsible for policy will not accept their findings. The procedures are easily defined as artificial since real juries are not involved. Field studies, because they usually lack random allocation to experimental and control conditions, are similarly beset with problems in terms of interpretation.

The differences between the inquisitorial and adversarial systems of court proceedings have been mentioned elsewhere in this book. It is believed that the adversarial system of England was a response to the historical shortcomings of the European system. Torture was used sometimes in some secular judicial proceedings using the inquisitorial model (McEwan, 1995). The contrast between the Continental European inquisitorial legal system and those based on the British adversarial system is marked. The latter is common to other parts of the world including the United States and judicial systems emerging out of British colonialism. The adversarial system can be seen to have the following characteristics:

- The judge's role is minimised as far as deciding the question of guilt is involved.
- The lawyers or advocates are partisan and act for opposed parties.
- The jury is commonly employed although it is not strictly a requirement of the adversarial system.
- Evidence is presented orally rather than as written evidence or submissions.

The two systems are not quite so distinct as they might appear. Sometimes the two systems are employed within the same jurisdiction. For example, proceedings concerning the care of children are often closer to the inquisitorial model than the adversarial model. Coroner's courts, which deal with matters of the causes of death (and treasure trove) in England, employ something closer to the inquisitorial approach. Similarly, in France and other countries there is no pure inquisitorial system. A large proportion of cases do not go through the examination by the investigating magistrate. In the inquisitorial system, the police may be called on to investigate matters pertinent to the defence and not just the prosecution.

There are two broad types of jury:

- The lay person jury consisting only of lay persons. This often has 12 people but the number can vary. It is 15 in Scotland.
- The escabinato jury which has a mixture of lay persons and legal experts. For example, there may be one legal expert and two lay persons. This is the system used in Germany (Arce, 1998) (see Chapter 20).

There is plenty of advice for lawyers written by lawyers about juries and jurors (Fulero and Penrod, 1990). This advice includes 'theories' about what sorts of person make 'good' jurors. Take, for example, the advice given in a number of texts about female jurors:

- Women are sympathetic and extraordinarily conscientious jurors.
- Avoid women as they are unpredictable and influenced by their husbands.
- Women are not good for the defence of attractive females.
- Women's libbers may be antagonistic to male defendants.
- Old women wearing too much make-up are unstable and bad for state prosecutors.

It should be taken for granted that none of this advice is based on empirical research.

Advice and help about jurors and other aspects of trials is available through various commercial companies. It is worthwhile exploring the Internet for information about the sorts of services are offered. The following are just a few:

- Focus groups – which are recommended in order to identify themes for test cases.
- Mock trials – which are described as formal exercises that reliably find the likely outcome for a particular case.
- Community attitude surveys – which are used to develop jury profiles and accurately assess the quality of the lawyer's case.
- Prospective juror questionnaires – which will give the lawyer a strategic advantage when selecting a jury.
- Jury selection – a senior consultant will assist the lawyer when selecting a jury.

Simple improvements to aid jurors

Research into jury decision processes has been based almost exclusively on simulations of trials. These simulations are unrealistic to varying degrees. There is evidence of considerable inconsistency between the real jury verdict and that of shadow juries. Shadow juries sit in on the court proceedings at the request of the researcher, so they hear exactly the same evidence delivered in the same manner as the real jury, and then retire to reach a verdict. The difference is that they can be studied by researchers whereas normally researchers do not have access to real juries. Once in a while the courts in the United States have allowed research into the effects of various sorts of change to the system – for example, permitting jurors to take notes, which has not been permitted in the US system since the times of high illiteracy. With the complexity of modern legal evidence, one can imagine that note-taking is a tempting option. Penrod and Heuer (1997) review the evidence coming from field experiments involving a fairly large number of different judges, trials, lawyer and jurors. In one national study, judges gave the jurors permission to take notes as soon as was practicable in the trial. The majority of jurors took up the option although as many as a third chose not to in some instances. On average, taking into account the civil and criminal trials, just over half a page of notes were taken each hour of the trial. While studies do not show a spectacular effect of note-taking, some of Penrod and Heuer's conclusions are of particular interest:

- Note-taking does not interfere with a juror's ability to keep up with the proceedings.
- Note-taking seems to be neutral in regard to the prosecution and defence cases in terms of its effects.

- Note-takers do not concentrate more on the evidence in their notes than on the other evidence available.
- Note-taking jurors are not more satisfied with the trial, the judge or the verdict than those who do not take notes.
- The notes are at best a small assistance to remembering aspects of the evidence.
- The notes taken tend to be accurate records as far as they go.

Similarly, research into the effectiveness of allowing jurors to ask questions using similar methods led Penrod and Heuer to the following conclusions:

- Jurors do understand the facts and issues better if they ask questions.
- Allowing questions seems to make no difference to the jurors', judge's and lawyers' satisfaction with the trial and verdict.
- If a juror asks an inappropriate question, lawyers will object and the jury does not draw inappropriate conclusions from this. However, generally speaking, the jurors ask perfectly appropriate questions.

In other words, research of this sort tends to demonstrate little or no negative consequences of the potential innovations of note-taking and juror questions, and modest, at best, improvements.

The effect of jury decision rules

Interest in the influence of jury size on the verdict came partly as a result of *Williams vs. Florida* (1970). In this case, the US Supreme Court decided that six-person juries were as good as twelve-person juries. Factors considered included quality of deliberation, reliability of jury's fact finding, the verdict ratio, ability of dissenters to resist majority pressure and the capacity of the jury to involve a fair cross-section of the community.

A jury may vary in terms of its size but also in terms of the proportion of the jurors who must agree in order to decide the guilt of the accused. These rules may vary according to the jurisdiction involved but may also vary within a jurisdiction (Arce *et al.*, 1998):

- In the United Kingdom there is sometimes a combined decision rule. Unanimity may be required at first followed by a 10 out of 12 majority after a period of deliberation.
- In Spain, a qualified majority decision rule has been used. A not guilty verdict requires a simple majority of 5 out of 9 but a guilty verdict needs 7 out of 9.

Other jurisdications employ different rules. An important question is whether factors such as the size of the jury and the decision rule in force make a substantial difference to deliberations and outcomes.

Zeisel (1971) suggested the greater the size of the jury, the greater the risk of a hung jury. A hung jury is one in which a verdict is not possible. There is some evidence that a requirement of unanimity in the decision increases the likelihood that the jury will be hung. Similarly, it is possible that complex cases are more likely to result in failure to reach a decision. In research to test these ideas (Arce *et al.*, 1998), participants eligible for Spanish jury service were selected at random from the electoral register. Gender was equalised in the juries. Participants viewed the re-enactment of a real-life rape trial including the testimony of eyewitness and forensic experts, opening and closing defence and prosecution arguments, and the judge's definition of the legal terms involved and the decision rule. The participants were randomly assigned to one of a number of juries that were then studied through the use of questionnaires. Among the findings were the following:

- Hung juries deliberated longer.
- Hung jury members employed more assertions in their communications with each other.
- Hung juries tended to manifest more simultaneous interruptions.
- Hung juries report perceptions of intransigence, lack of dialogue and irrelevant deliberations.
- Hung juries tended to use less of the trial evidence.

It is impossible to summarise the studies into the effects of jury size on verdicts and other matters. Fortunately, there is available a meta-analysis (see Box 5.1) which summarises the findings of 17 studies (Saks and Marti, 1997). The following trends were found in the research studies:

- Deliberation time is longer for larger juries.
- Hung verdicts are commoner for larger juries. This is a finding that is really only true for studies that used a mock jury. In studies involving real juries, hung verdicts were rare – they occurred in only about 1% of instances.
- Guilty verdicts are not more common in large juries.
- For civil cases, smaller juries tend to award more to the injured party.

These trends were found for studies that have a unanimous decision rule (that is, all of the jurors must agree for a guilty verdict). There is evidence to suggest that such juries tend to be evidence driven. For example, they make more references to the evidence, establish more connections between the evidence and legal issues, examine the evidence in detail, and their deliberations are more exhaustive and detailed. Juries operating with a majority decision rule are more driven to reach a verdict. So majority verdict juries are more likely to begin their deliberations with a vote. For example, Arce *et al.* (1998) compared six- and twelve-person juries that used un-animous decision criteria. The smaller juries made rather fewer references to the evidence and seemed to make fewer pro-defendant arguments.

More on real jury deliberation

Generally, very little is known about the psychological processes that happen in real juries as opposed to the mock juries of the psychological experiment (McCabe and Purves, 1974). Myers (1979) chose a somewhat circuitous approach. She considered the cases of about a thousand defendants on felony charges in Indiana. Two-thirds of the cases involved trials by jury. Myers obtained qualitative data from a variety of sources:

- file folders of the assistant prosecutor;
- police arrest records;
- telephone interviews to obtain any necessary supplementary data.

She was on the prosecutor's staff at the time so was also able to conduct informal discussions with prosecutors and court personnel.

Box 21.1

Forensic psychology in action: pre-trial publicity

O.J. Simpson was tried for the murder of his wife and a male companion. Shortly after the murders, the sportsman/actor was seen on national television apparently speeding along American freeways trying to avoid arrest. Thus the issue of the effects of pre-trial prejudicial events communicated through the media on the outcome of a trial. Does pre-trial publicity prejudice the result of a trial?

- Different countries/jurisdictions have different practices about media coverage of crime. In the United States, the constitutional guarantee of freedom of speech effectively reduces controls over media coverage as also does courtroom TV. In other countries, restrictions are in place. So, for example, in the United Kingdom, media coverage is limited once a suspect has been charged. Offending media may be charged with contempt of court and the criminal trial of the suspect abandoned. Civil trials are not subject to pre-trial publicity restrictions.

- Factors limiting the influence of pre-trial publicity include: (a) that most suspects plead guilty at trial anyway and these cases cannot be influenced by prejudicial publicity and (b) very few trials receive any coverage in the national press. In the United States, the figure may be as low as 1% (Simon and Eimermann, 1971). There is five times the likelihood that the trial will be covered by the local press. A trial tried by jury has at least twice the baseline probability of being reported.

- Prejudice, in legal terms, should not be seen in social scientific terms which would suggest that prejudice leads to biasing the outcome of the trial (Howitt, 1998b). In the United States, the Supreme Court has ruled that prejudice involves both (1) a preconceived notion of the defendant's guilt and (2) this opinion being fixed and resistant to change (Moran and Cutler, 1991). In other words, what is prejudicial to a psychologist may not be prejudice in the eyes of a US judge.

Research into the effects of media on verdicts goes back to the origins of forensic psychology in nineteenth-century Germany. More intensive research began in the 1960s. Some of the research is problematic as it was based on 'mock' juries assembled solely for research purposes. Obviously this has the inevitable ecological validity problem – just how representative are the verdicts of mock juries of the verdicts of real juries? Some research involved exposing the participants to a fictitious news story and then obtaining their views about the guilt of the accused and so forth without even allowing jury discussion.

Studebaker and Penrod (1997) point out how complex the modern media environment is and how voracious the demand for news. This means that often there is nowhere the trial could be held where the jurors are unaware of the publicity given to the crime. However, some venues may be less prejudiced than others. One suggestion is that researchers could help by investigating factors in pre-trial publicity which may lead to prejudice in laboratory studies and then seeking evidence that this sort of publicity is especially common in the area where the case would normally be tried (Studebaker et al., 2000). They undertook research relevant to a hearing for a change of venue for the trial of those accused of the Oklahoma City bombing (Timothy McVeigh and Terry Nichols). Newspapers in the Oklahoma City area were analysed as were those for a number of possible alternative locations for the trial. The researchers coded the contents of these newspapers along a number of dimensions known to be relevant to pre-trial publicity effects from experiments. These aspects were: 1) measures of the general amount of publicity given to the crime; 2) negative characterisations of the defendants; 3) information about the emotional suffering of those involved as victims of the crime; 4) information about putative confessions; 5) suggestions about the defendants' motives for the crime and 6) information about eyewitness identifications.

▶

Compared to *The Denver Post*, newspapers in the Oklahoma City area had more negative pre-trial publicity about the defendants and the suffering of the victims.

The researchers then compared their content analysis findings with those of surveys of the general public carried out at the time. There were parallels between the content analysis and the findings of the survey. For example, respondents in Oklahoma were much more likely to believe in the guilt of one of the defendants, McVeigh. Respondents in Denver, away from the possible venues for the hearing in Oklahoma, were relatively unlikely to claim that they were absolutely confident of McVeigh's guilt – less than 20% did so. In contrast, about 50% of the Oklahoma respondents were absolutely confident of his guilt. They were also more likely to follow the news of the crime and trial carefully and they knew a great deal more about the events. The findings are indicative of the value of the content analysis approach to venue selection according to Studebaker *et al.* (2000).

However, researchers do not always have an easy time in court when they argue that, based on their data, the venue of the trial should or should not change. Posey and Dahl (2002) describe some of the problems including the likelihood that a judge will ask the researcher why questions were not included in the survey which asked respondents the extent to which they could be impartial. Research suggests little value in such questions although they are the sort of questions asked in court during a *voir dire* examination. There is no relationship between a potential juror's claims to be impartial and how much they know about the case and how strong they believe the evidence against the accused to be.

She found that the following factors influenced the jury's decision of guilt:

- a weapon was recovered;
- a large number of witnesses were specified;
- the defendant or an accomplice made a statement either concerning involvement in crime or lack of involvement in crime;
- the defendant had large numbers of previous convictions (admissible evidence there);
- the defendant was not employed;
- the victim was young;
- it was a less serious rather than more serious crime.

Juries were not dependent on the following in their decisions:

- eyewitness identification of the defendant;
- expert testimony;
- recovery of stolen property;
- victim's prior criminality and relationship with the defendant;
- past conduct of victim perhaps warranting the injury.

Scientific jury selection

The *voir dire* is the stage at the beginning of a trial at which judges (and lawyers according to the jurisdiction) seek to identify bias or prejudice among potential jurors. The phrase *voir dire* means to speak the truth in French. There is no systematic and

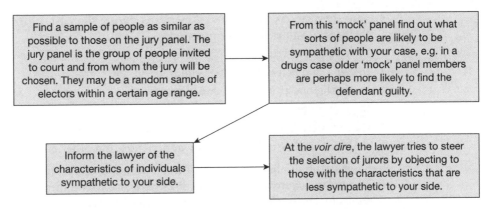

| Find a sample of people as similar as possible to those on the jury panel. The jury panel is the group of people invited to court and from whom the jury will be chosen. They may be a random sample of electors within a certain age range. | From this 'mock' panel find out what sorts of people are likely to be sympathetic with your case, e.g. in a drugs case older 'mock' panel members are perhaps more likely to find the defendant guilty. |

| Inform the lawyer of the characteristics of individuals sympathetic to your side. | At the *voir dire*, the lawyer tries to steer the selection of jurors by objecting to those with the characteristics that are less sympathetic to your side. |

Figure 21.1 Scientific jury selection. The *voir dire* is often described as a 'trial within a trial'. It is the stage at which judges and lawyers sort out legal matters between themselves, including who should be excluded from the jury

common way of assessing bias so different questions may be asked of each potential juror on the venire (the list from which the jury is selected). Lawyers are more concerned about prejudice that might adversely affect their side rather than a just outcome, no matter what it is. Scientific jury selection is built on the *voir dire* and the wish to gain advantage for a particular side. In parts of the US system, the lawyer makes a challenge for cause when it is felt that there is overt prejudice on the part of the potential juror or for some other reason. However, it is for the judge to decide whether the challenge is accepted and the judge may ask the potential juror if they can put their prejudice aside. Peremptory challenges require no stated reason and lead to the dismissal of the potential juror (Kovera *et al.*, 2002). Scientific jury selection uses research evidence on the sorts of juror who are likely to favour a particular side. Figure 21.1 illustrates the steps.

The first major account of scientific jury selection comes from the group of social scientists, in the United States, who helped the defence of the Harrisburg Seven for conspiracy. The accused included priests and ex-priests, nuns and ex-nuns! The trial took place in 1972 against the backdrop of America's war in Vietnam. Philip Berrigan and others were accused of various plots against the State – for example, they were accused of planning to bomb heating tunnels in Washington and to kidnap Henry Kissinger, Assistant to the President for National Security Affairs. The problem for the defence was that the trial was taking place in an area that was fundamentally conservative but the defendants were anti-war activists.

The researchers became involved because they were unhappy that informers and agents provocateurs were being used against the accused. They regarded the location of the trial in Harrisburg, Pennsylvania as favourable to the prosecution. A survey was carried out around Harrisburg using a sample matched to be similar to the panel from which the jury was to be selected (Schulman *et al.*, 1973). So factors such as age, occupation, education and race were taken into account. Over 1,200 individuals were obtained by random sampling from similar voters on the voting list.

The questionnaire was detailed and covered a range of issues – including the matter of the influence of the media. The participants' choice of media to use, their knowledge of the defendants, and their knowledge of their case were measured and the following covered:

- who they saw as the greatest Americans during the past 10 to 15 years so that their social values might be assessed;
- their degree of trust in government;
- the ages and activities of their children;
- their religious attitude and commitment;
- their spare-time activities;
- the organisations to which they belonged and so forth;
- the acceptability of certain anti-war activities and other political indicators.

Religious attitudes had a bearing on trial relevant predispositions. Religions bad for the defendants were Episcopalians, Presbyterians, Methodists and fundamentalists; religions better for the defence included Catholics. Other trends were as follows:

- Overwhelmingly, the public in Harrisburg agreed with the statement that the right to private property is sacred.
- Nearly two-thirds thought that a citizen should support his/her country even when it was wrong.
- Four-fifths believed that the police should use violence to maintain order.
- Although sex and political party were weak predictors of attitudes, Democrats and women were more liberal on certain questions. Education and contact with metropolitan newspapers in this area were associated with conservatism/republicanism.

The researchers considered that the ideal juror for the defence should have the following characteristics: female, Democrat, no religion, a white-collar job/skilled blue-collar job, sympathy with the defendants' views regarding the Vietnam war, tolerance of peaceful resistance to the government's policies, and would presume the defendants innocent until proven guilty. Based on this profile, the researchers and lawyers selected prospective jurors who were closest to these requirements although the choices were also partly informed by the responses made by potential jurors in court. Of the final jury of 12, seven could be rated as good prospects from the point of view of the defence. A typical example of these good jurors was:

> Pauline Protzline, a housewife in her late 40s or early 50s, whose son-in-law had been killed in Vietnam. Concerning the war, she had said: 'I wasn't too much at first, but the last few years I've been against it.' We considered this statement to be a good sign. She listed no church affiliation.

(p. 25)

The researchers re-interviewed a sample of the original survey chosen as being a match to the real 12-person jury. Of the three-quarters who were prepared to give further opinions, the following were found:

- Just over half presumed the defendants to be guilty. The others were classified as having only low to moderate presumptions of the guilt of the defendants.
- Age and political preference made little difference to presumptions of guilt.
- Only 37% of women thought the defendants guilty on all or most counts. For men, the figure was 57%.
- Of the respondents with high-school education and the preferred religious stance for the defence, only about a fifth had a strong presumption of guilt.

At the trial, the defence chose to offer no defence and the defendants, consequently, did not state their case. For the minor charges, the jury found the accused guilty of smuggling letters out of a federal prison. They could not agree a verdict on the conspiracy charge. Ten of the jury were against conviction. This is not particularly impressive evidence in every respect in favour of scientific jury selection. The surveys certainly picked up on the ambiguity of the jury's position.

Whether or not this is the best way in which lawyers can help their clients is also in some doubt. There is not a lot of research into the effectiveness of scientific jury selection which is surprising since it is claimed that trial consultation in the United States has over 700 practitioners and has a turnover of 400 million dollars (Strier, 1999). Lloyd-Bostock (1996) points out that research on over 2,000 cases in the United Kingdom found that the use of peremptory challenge did not lead to more acquittals. Horowitz (1980) is another important exception. The important details of the study are as follows:

- Evening class students were used as 'mock' jurors.
- Law students acted as lawyers at the 'trial'.
- These were specially trained in the use of scientific or normal methods of selecting the jury.
- Real lawyers reviewed the information about the case and predicted the sentencing decisions.

In terms of the two different methods of jury selection, the following were found:

- Scientific jury selection methods were most accurate (i.e. agreed with the real lawyers' view) for drug and courts martial crimes.
- These were the cases studied for which the survey produced the most accurate results.
- Conventional methods of jury selection were the most accurate for murder.
- The survey was of low accuracy for the murder case.

It would be risky to generalise too much from this one study. Other research suggests that experts are often poor at identifying biased potential jurors. One study had groups of potential jurors who had been challenged in court as biased for a trial and compared their verdicts with those of the actual jurors who had not been challenged (Zeisel and Diamond, 1978). Essentially, there was no difference between the verdicts of the actual and the 'biased' juries. So this is evidence that jury selection is ineffective. This may not be surprising given that lawyers use little more than stereotypes in making their challenges.

As ever, caution needs to be exercised to take due regard to the fact that jurisdictions differ. The peremptory challenge in which no reason is given for wishing to reject a potential juror is a feature of the US legal system. Peremptory challenges are not possible in some other jurisdictions. In England and Wales, the right to make peremptory challenges was abolished in 1988 (Lloyd-Bostock, 1996). This means that the US style of scientific jury selection is not possible for the defence. Commenting on the American situation, Van Wallendael and Cutler (2004) express some reservation about the general efficacy of scientific jury selection methods in the United States. One of the reasons for this is that very little is known about the activities of lawyers in *voir dire* situations. For example, it is not known whether lawyers actually assess case relevant attitudes effectively during the *voir dire*. Furthermore, there are many situations in which the lawyer has little influence on the process of jury selection: courts in some states do not allow lawyers to assess the attitudes of members of the venire panel.

Ethical issues

A number of ethical issues have been raised about the above intervention (scientific jury selection) by Saks (1987):

- The researchers did not explain to the respondents in the survey that the information they were providing might be helpful to the defence. They were merely told that the information was for research purposes.
- A further ethical issue concerns the fact that most defendants could not afford to employ researchers (the interviewers in the Harrisburg study were volunteers). Consequently, in the long run, the prosecution is normally much more likely to benefit from this sort of research. They are the side most capable of funding the research.

Furthermore, Lecci *et al.* (2004) argue that trial consultants are largely an unregulated group of practitioners who have not been required to establish the validity of their procedures. They should be required to employ standardised measures to assess juror bias.

Main points

- Research on the jury is considerably affected by legal constraints on studying real juries making real decisions. As a consequence, a great deal of research has simulated trial procedures in psychological laboratories as an alternative means of studying the jury. Sometimes the simulation involves individuals reacting in isolation rather than in interaction as in a real jury. There have been attempts to improve the validity of jury research by using shadow juries which sit and listen to the evidence in court and then 'sit' in parallel to the real jury. Quite clearly great care is needed when generalising from the findings of such 'laboratory' juries to real-life juries.

- Juries differ in many ways, which may have a detrimental effect on the quality of the decision making. For example, in some countries juries are larger and in others they are smaller. The research evidence, such as it is, finds relatively small differences between large and small juries in terms of decisions made but they do not operate identically. The rules that govern how the jury must reach a decision (e.g. is a majority verdict allowed) can affect how the jury operates.

- Psychologists have been involved in providing expert guidance to lawyers about how best to conduct a trial, which potential jurors to reject if possible, and arguments about the effect of pre-trial publicity. Virtually all of the research in this field has been conducted in the United States rather than in other jurisdictions which, for example, may not allow lawyers to challenge jurors in this way. Nevertheless, if there were better evidence on scientific jury selection available and other related activity, it would inform us about some aspects of jury decision making.

Chapter 22

Effective prison

Overview

- There are a number of ideologies concerning what prison is for. Retribution holds that prison is for punishment; utilitarianism suggests that prison should produce changes that reduce the risk of reoffending, and humanitarianism suggests that the role should be rehabilitation of casualties of social deprivation and victimisation. Various models of how prisoners should be treated are available according to what views one has on crime's origins. For example, if one believes that there are too many rewards for crime and too little punishment, then the appropriate treatment for prisoners may be harsh and severe in order to make the punishment a deterrent to reoffending and others.

- Prisoners are a population at risk. There is the risk of violence from other prisoners though homicides within the prison environment are relatively infrequent. Additionally, there is a risk of suicide, which is a matter of some considerable concern. There is some evidence that prison itself increases the risk of suicide and this has to be set against the fact that prisoners (largely young males) tend to be a high-risk group for suicide in the community anyway. The period spent in prison before trial is associated with a higher risk of suicide than other time in prison. Action to reduce such imprisonments or increased vigilance on the part of staff have been recommended.

- 'Nothing works' was a dominant view of prison until relatively recently. Increasingly, it is accepted that a lot of the work done within the prison service pays off in terms of reducing future reoffending. In recent years, there has been a more consistent attempt to offer effective treatment programmes to prisoners in an attempt to reduce recidivism. Cognitive behavioural therapies are commonly used by psychologists in prisons for the treatment of various sorts of offender especially sex offenders such as paedophiles and rapists. These are multi-faceted strategies based on groupwork to provide knowledge and insight into the offending process. There is evidence of their immediate effectiveness in terms of treatment goals but also in terms of reducing recidivism, though the latter is based on less extensive research.

- Manualisation is an attempt to improve the delivery of psychological treatment which is based on the empirical observation that the effectiveness of treatment varies in different settings. By ensuring that all therapists understand the rationale of the treatment and adopt appropriate therapeutic strategies, the consistency of the delivery of treatment is improved as well as the overall effectiveness of treatment.

- There is a good deal of evidence based on meta-analyses of numerous studies that prisons and other forms of sentence have some, if limited, effectiveness in terms of criteria such as the reduction of recidivism. Educational programmes for prisoners within prison seems to be the most effective aspect of the prison experience in this regard.

Well, we have finally got to prison. Although it may seem like the end of the process, it is actually the start of a new one. For some, prison will contribute something to their rehabilitation and, perhaps, change of lifestyle. For others, prison will be the end of the road – they may spend the rest of their lives there. Others will pass through and return again several times. There is no consensus about the purpose of prison. Hollin (2002), along with many others, regards imprisonment as the focus of a current moral debate which has long historical roots. The three major views about prison are retribution, utilitarian and the humanitarian. Retributionists regard the purpose of prison to deliver punishments; utilitarians see prison as part of a process of bringing about changes which reduce the probability of reoffending, and humanitarians see that prisoners often come from backgrounds of deprivation and victimisation so are deserving of rehabilitation. There is a complex debate that goes far beyond the work of psychologists in the prison service. It hardly needs pointing out that crime and punishment are at the forefront of the political agenda in many countries. Hollin points out that sex offenders are a good example where confusion can reign because 'moral beliefs, principles and utility, and effectiveness become fused and can lead to confusion in policies and procedures within the criminal justice system' (Hollin, 2002, pp. 1–2). The repugnance that many feel for sex offenders might encourage lengthy prison sentences in order to make the punishment proportionate to the heinousness of the crime. However, the utilitarian would argue that this in itself has little point unless it reduces the chances of others being victimised in the future and so more than imprisonment is required. The humanitarian might suggest that sex offenders in many instances have been victims of sexual assault themselves such that harsh punishment alone is inappropriate. Humane treatment is required in order to meet the needs of the offender and in order to stop the endless cycle of abuse in which victims become future offenders. The various 'ideologies' associated with imprisonment (retributionism, utilitarianism and humanism) tend to coexist in varying proportions within the criminal justice system. Pure retribution, for example, may be relatively uncommon.

There are many different types of punishment available within the criminal justice system apart from imprisonment. In some systems such as the United Kingdom, relatively minor offences committed by minor offenders might be dealt with by admonitions in the form of a police caution. Generally speaking, monetary fines are the commonest punishment. Sometimes one will find direct compensation of the victim or community associated with the crime. This may involve financial compensation or service to the community through a work programme. Suspended prison sentences are a step up in seriousness. Prison sentences are regarded as being suitable for the most serious offences and more committed or persistent offenders though it is far from certain that prison is reserved for the worst offenders. For example, those who default on fines may well receive prison sentences eventually.

The utilitarian approach requires that penalties of all sorts should increase the likelihood that the offender (and others seeing the possible outcome of the risk they are taking) will stop offending in the future. The effectiveness of the penal system in reducing crime may be evaluated in various ways. Recidivism in the form of further crimes is very common. There are many offenders who repeatedly offend despite being punished repeatedly. Depending on a large number of factors, about half of criminals reoffend after punishment. These could be regarded in two ways:

- as depressing statistics on the persistence of crime, or
- evidence of the large numbers who do not reoffend after punishment.

Punishment and rehabilitation are not the only ways in which justice can proceed. For example, there is the concept of restorative justice (*Contemporary Justice Review*, 1998) which is discussed in Chapter 4. A central theme in restorative justice is the righting of the wrong done to victims by helping them to return to their former self as a survivor. The process encourages the offender to reflect upon their harmful behaviours and to accept responsibility for their offending. Restorative justice utilises the methods of reconciliation and mediation in meeting its ends. Sometimes the process operates in parallel with the criminal justice system.

See Table 22.1 for further indications of the functions of prison.

Murder is rare in prison in the United Kingdom. For the 15 years between 1972 and 1987, the total of homicides in prison was just 16. Suicide is much more common.

Table 22.1 Treatment strategies associated with criminality

Model of criminogenesis	Treatment model
Insufficient deterrent to crime: the rewards for crime are greater than the costs of punishment.	Harsher prison regimes, 'boot camps' for offenders possibly in exchange for reductions in offending.
Emotional distress: deep-seated emotional problems are expressed in criminal behaviour. Crime is thus seen as a consequence of pathological aspects of the individual.	Psychodynamic treatments such as psychoanalysis. Client-centred counselling.
Educational deficit: failure to complete schooling leaves the individual with important skill deficits which exclude them from society's mainstream in many instances.	Education programmes such as reading, mathematics, etc. Training in practical job skills.
Learning of criminal behaviour: criminal conduct is learnt.	Institutions organised as token economies in which members are rewarded in tangible ways for improvements and changes in standards of conduct.
Social interaction skills: offenders have difficulty in interacting with others effectively in a social context.	Cognitive behavioural intervention in which the offender's deficits in cognitive and interaction skills are examined and regular group sessions are held involving such things as interpersonal cognitive problem solving and social skills training.
Social/institutional balance: possibly because of early experience of institutions such as children's homes, offenders do not learn a healthy and balanced approach to life and may resolve difficulties inappropriately through the use of violence.	Creating a healthy institutional environment by reducing rigid controls and sanctions, giving the task of controlling the inmates' behaviour to the whole of the community and having forums to discuss problems arising in the institutions.
Labelling individuals as deviant ensures that it is difficult for them to operate effectively in normal contexts, thus forcing them into deviant social systems and crime.	Divert individuals such as young offenders from the prison system into probation, mediation, reparation, community supervision, etc.

Source: Based on Redondo, S., Sanchez-Meca, J. and Garrido, V. (2002) *Offender Rehabilitation and Treatment: Effective Programmes and Policies to Reduce Re-offending.* © John Wiley & Sons, Ltd

There were 300 suicides during the same period. At special hospitals dealing with mentally ill offenders in the United Kingdom, the record is similarly low. Over a 30-year period, in the United Kingdom there were two homicides at Broadmoor, one at Rampton, and the murder of a nurse and a patient at Carstairs State Hospital. Elsewhere, the rate seems to be higher. The rate in the United States seems to be about ten times higher (Gordon *et al.*, 1997). The infamous serial killer Jeffrey Dahmer (Masters, 1993) was killed in prison.

As already mentioned, suicide is a much more significant factor in prisons. McHugh (1999) suggests that while not frequent, suicide is a significant issue in the prison context. This is not a surprise since the offenders entering prison have heightened risk because of their low socio-economic status, they come from dysfunctional families and have involvement with drugs (McHugh, 1998). The extra factors of prison build on these. In the United Kingdom, for instance, the average suicide rate is about two per week. The prison environment appears to encourage suicide which, in the United Kingdom, is something like four times as common in prison as it is in the community. There is also some evidence that suicide in prison in the United Kingdom is increasing (Towl, 1996). One of the more disturbing features of prison suicide is the fact that remand prisoners, people in prison awaiting trial and who have not been sentenced, have a high risk of committing suicide. Of the remand prisoners, a minority of about 40% will be sent to prison after their trial. The majority will be acquitted, given some non-custodial sentence, or will be deemed to have served the appropriate term while on remand. Thus the possibility of an innocent person killing himself or herself on remand is a realistic concern.

It may be tempting to explain prison suicides in terms that suggest that the overcrowding of prisoners, the population density, is responsible. There is plenty of evidence to show that human beings have preferred space requirements and that crowding, at least in some circumstances, is distressing. Nevertheless, one should not jump to conclusions. For example, in the United States it has been noted that about half of prison suicides occur during the first day of confinement. This cannot be explained in terms of the stress of population density. According to Cox *et al.* (1984), as prison populations increase there is a tendency for rates of death from all causes to increase disproportionately to population increase. Of particular relevance is the finding that single-occupied cells (where clearly crowding is less of an issue) produced very few deaths whereas death was much more common in multi-occupied cells (Ruback and Innes, 1988). Nevertheless, prison is a safe place and the overall risk of death in prison is less than in the outside world. Of course, the proper comparison between prison and the outside world needs to compare like with like. Prisoners tend to be younger and disproportionately from a racial minority compared with the general population. Adjusting for these trends, this leaves the following:

- Deaths due to illness and homicide were significantly *lower* in prison.
- Deaths due to suicide were significantly *higher* in prison.

One can overstate the dangers, since the rate of prison suicide in the United States was 29 per 100,000 of the prison population as opposed to 20 per 100,000 in similar non-prisoner populations.

The possibility of suicide is not an easy one for prison authorities and psychologists working in a prison context to manage effectively. One obvious strategy is to classify prisoners as either suicidal or not at risk. According to Towl, this has its own dangers. If a prisoner has been classified as non-suicidal then this may be a signal for prison officers to lessen their vigilance over them: that is, a great weight is placed on the classifying system, which may be rather less than perfect. There are a number of high-risk-of-suicide situations that may encourage greater vigilance. These include the period immediately after admission, significant clinical improvement and the achievement of some insight, and during periods of leave for offenders in medium secure units for psychiatric difficulties (James, 1996). Towl (1996) suggests a number of strategies that may be helpful in dealing with the potential problem of suicide:

- Reduce the numbers of remand prisoners and those with mental illness.
- Try to avoid the negative consequences for prisoners who report suicidal thoughts to staff. The consequences may be extremely unpleasant such as routine strip searches and the like which may deter reporting.
- Enable staff to identify and assist prisoners with suicidal feelings.

Death from other causes can be a significant factor in deaths in prison. For example, Kullgren *et al.* (1998) found that 7% of Swedish offenders who had been subject to a major forensic psychiatric examination died within a follow-up period of no more than eight years. Less than 3% of these were from suicide in general although it constituted 6% for those with personality disorders. This is a similar finding to that found in other mentally disordered offender populations.

Cognitive skills programmes

Currently, there is optimism that the work of psychologists within the prison system can contribute to crime reduction since treatment programmes are available that are known to reduce the risk of reoffending or produce changes in prisoners that are conducive to them not reoffending. This contrasts with the pessimism of 50 years before in which it was felt that 'nothing works'. Studies of the effectiveness of treatment suggest that overall treatments reduced reoffending by about 10% but that some forms of treatment worked better than this. As we will see, among the most effective programmes are those based on the principles of cognitive behaviour therapy. Such cognitive skills programmes are regarded by some as an effective means of reducing the recidivism by those taking part (Blud, 1999). The extent of this reduction is put in the order of 10–30%. Arguably, these treatment programmes are effective because they work to correct a number of cognitive deficits exhibited by offenders. These cognitive deficits are identified as follows:

- Self-control – to correct impulsiveness and action.
- Cognitive style – lack of empathy with abstract social concepts. Such matters as social harmony and justice may be involved here. Such offenders may be rigid and inflexible in their thinking. They may be poor at tolerating ambiguity, which results in what may be described as rather simplistic, dogmatic thought processes.
- Interpersonal problem solving – offenders are often socially handicapped without recognising the fact. They are sometimes unaware of the other courses of action available to them. They rarely examine the likely consequences of their actions.
- Social perspective taking – prisoners are often egocentric. They fail to understand why they should consider other people. They may lack the skill involved in seeing matters from the perspective of other people. They tend to interpret the actions of others in their own terms and interpret the actions of others wrongly as a consequence.

- Values – their moral reasoning skills are poor. They do not recognise the incongruity between their actions and their beliefs.
- Critical reasoning – their thinking is often irrational and illogical. Self-analysis is avoided. They justify what they do by blaming others and, consequently, do not see themselves as to blame.

In the United Kingdom, the prison service has an accreditation system for therapeutic programmes that demonstrates a commitment to research-based therapy. The criteria for evaluation may include:

- clear and research-based model of change;
- targeted on criminogenic factors;
- responsivity;
- effective methods;
- skills oriented;
- a range of targets addressed;
- sufficient 'dosage' or amounts of treatment;
- thorough care;
- ongoing monitoring;
- ongoing evaluation.

Of course, there are alternatives to cognitive therapy within the context of a conventional prison environment. One of these is the therapeutic institutional regime. This has the aim of providing offenders with an institutional environment that will encourage their development as members of an effective community, which may then lead to more effective participation in their community on release. A therapeutic regime has the following characteristics (Woodward, 1999):

- A structured living environment.
- An aim to change the behaviour of the residents.
- Control of behaviour by authorities is not the sole means of changing behaviour.
- Consenting participation in the programme expected from those involved.

There is some evidence that therapeutic regimes work in some regards. They also appear to reduce recidivism in the residents on release.

Sex offender therapy in prison

The effective treatment of sex offenders originated in the behavioural therapies that began to become common in the 1960s. The most significant previous contribution was Sigmund Freud's belief that sex offenders were untreatable using the psychodynamic therapies of the first half of the twentieth century. The treatment of sex offenders was not a priority in prison services until the last few years. For example, in Britain in the 1980s there was clear evidence that sex offenders were more likely to receive custodial sentences (Fisher and Beech, 1999) – a 50% increase in a decade. However, this did not correlate with an increase in determination to help prisoners to avoid reoffending after release. It has to be said that prison is just one of a number of contexts in which sex offenders may receive therapy:

- The probation service has devoted quite a lot of resources to group work with sex offenders in the United Kingdom. Of the 7,000 sex offenders being supervised by the probation service, half of them are supervised in the community and there was capacity to treat half of these men.
- In England and Wales, some sex offenders would receive psychological treatment from psychiatric services in regional secure units and special hospitals. Both of these cater for mentally disordered offenders as inpatients. Others may be treated as outpatients. Generally speaking, sex offenders constitute only a small proportion of the work of these units.

There are numerous accounts of the use of cognitive behavioural therapies in the treatment of sex offenders – both those in prison and those in the community (e.g. Craissati and McClurg, 1997). It is useful to concentrate on a concrete example of what may be typical within the prison service context. As ever, the precise details will differ somewhat from jurisdiction to jurisdiction. The case of the British prison service is well documented and, as it was far from the first of such programmes developed, it has adapted features from other programmes. As such, it should be of interest more widely. It is known as the STEP programme (Beech *et al.*, 1998).

Fundamental to a treatment programme is a set of decisions about how, when, where, to and by whom therapy is to be delivered. The basic decisions for the prison Sex Offender Treatment Programme included the following:

- *Where*: in a limited number of prison establishments which could be resourced appropriately to deliver the treatment.
- *Who*: priority is given to offenders at the greatest risk of reoffending according to a formal risk-assessment procedure. Some characteristics such as mental illness, lack of English, very low IQ, suicide risk and severe personality disorder effectively debar the individual from the programme.
- *When*: at an appropriate stage in a sentence of two or more years provided that time is available to complete the programme.
- *Whom*: the approach is multi-disciplinary. That is, all sorts of staff besides psychologists may be involved such as prison officers, teachers and chaplains. Of course, they are given appropriate training in terms of knowledge of cognitive behavioural treatments and relevant skills in working with others in groups.

The therapeutic situation is based on *structured group work*. A group consists of eight offenders and two tutors/therapists. The treatment manual contains a structured series of cognitive behavioural activities and exercises that are explained and described in detail. It concentrates on the thought processes involved in offending as well as attempting to place limits on the behaviour on the offender. The core programme is designed to work on the motivation of the offenders to avoid reoffending and to develop personal skills that enable this. These latter skills are collectively known as *relapse prevention*. According to Beech *et al.* (1999), the programme consists of 20 blocks (treatment sessions) that cover a number of areas. These for the purposes of this description may be classified as cognitive modification and relapse prevention. The methods employed in group treatment of this sort are a mixture of methods familiar to those who have engaged in any type of group work, and matters much more specific to sex offending. Some of the techniques involved include the following:

- *Brainstorming and group discussion*: topics discussed by the group are often written down as a list on a board or flip chart. An individual often responds to this collection of ideas in terms of his experiences.

- *Smaller or buzz groups*: some activities are carried out by a pair of offenders, perhaps three or four. This sort of activity helps the offender develop communicative skills with others, assertiveness and a degree of empathy. The experience with the small group can then be combined with that of other groups in a 'plenary' session.
- *Role-playing*: members of the group (and this may include the tutors or facilitators) may play out a situation. The rest of the group observe and respond to the role-play. The actual participants may also analyse their experiences.
- *Focus on the individual*: the work of one individual is subject to scrutiny and evaluation by the rest of the group.
- *Videos*: film is available which deals with various aspects of sex offending. In particular, there may be video available about the experiences of victims. Viewing this is then followed by individual response and group discussion.
- *Homework*: activities such as keeping a diary are carried out by members outside the group meeting itself. This is almost always written work.

The above are the main treatment methods employed. Substantial areas are covered using these methods including the following:

- *Describing the offence*: it is known that sex offenders tend to describe their offences in ways that are self-exculpatory. Often the offender will present himself almost as if he were the victim. Vagueness and being non-committal is characteristic of their responses. The following is a short extract from an interview (Howitt, 1995a, p. 95):

  > Interviewer: Did you kiss her on the breast?
  > Bennie: Maybe I did maybe I didn't . . . [when you are arrested] they try to use psychology on you, they make you say you did . . . so I am going to say I did.
  > Interviewer: . . . that's no use to me. . . . I don't want to know what they say, I want to know what it is.
  > Bennie: . . . maybe I probably did . . .

  At the end of the exchange, the reader may feel that they still do not know whether or not Bennie accepts that he kissed the girl's breasts sexually despite a clear challenge from the interviewer. Nevertheless, despite this, Bennie uses the phrase 'maybe I probably did . . .' which leaves him free psychologically to maintain his position that he said things because he, in fact, was the victim of pressure from other people. Therapists may describe this as a 'passive account' since it does not truly describe what the offender did. An active account would be much more direct. For example, in the above example, the offender might have said 'I encouraged the girl to roll about in front of the television with me. We were pretending to play at being animals. I pulled up her clothes and played at biting her stomach. Then I took it further and sucked her breast for a couple of minutes.' In order to encourage the active account, it is necessary for the offender to provide information about the following:
  - How the offender actually planned the offence – it did not just happen.
  - The offender's sexual or emotional preoccupation with the victim.
  - That the offender was responsible for initiating all of the aspects of the abuse.
  - That he took measures to try to prevent the victim from disclosing the abuse to others.

- *Challenging distorted thinking*: aspects of the distorted thinking that each offender has about his own offending will be familiar after a while to members of the group. This may be distorted thinking about children's sexual motivations and interest in adults or the adult rape victim's secret desire to be sexually violated, for example. The distorted thinking may be challenged by asking for evidence to support the offender's assumptions that may then be criticised by other members of the group. It has to be stressed that this may occur at any stage of the treatment and not simply during the sessions specifically devoted to distorted thinking.

- *Victim empathy work*: showing a video of victims of abuse talking about the consequences or having outside speakers come and describe these experiences. Given that many offenders will themselves have been victims (see Chapters 6 and 10), this may profoundly influence their response. Their own experiences of vulnerability and being unable to disclose their abuse at the time may contribute to the lessons learnt by the group. Eventually, the offenders will role-play the position of victim in their own offences.

- *Fantasy modification*: it is widely accepted that there is a relationship between sex offending and fantasy (see Chapter 11). Some believe that masturbation to sexual fantasy is the basis for its development. Irrespective of the actual role of fantasy in sex offending, there would seem to be a compelling case for attempting to reduce this fantasy as part of the treatment programme. This is not normally a direct part of group work except at the broad level of the role of fantasy in offending behaviour. This aspect of the treatment would normally be carried out using one of four or so main behaviour modification techniques on an individual basis with a psychologist:
  - *Aversive therapy* – the fantasy would be associated with some negative consequence.
  - *Masturbatory reconditioning* – new and socially more acceptable fantasies would be associated with masturbation. In other words, the offender masturbates and switches to the new fantasy at the point of orgasm. This is repeated until the new fantasy becomes sexually arousing.
  - *Satiation* – the offender repeatedly masturbates to the fantasy until the fantasy is incapable of causing sexual arousal.
  - *Covert sensitisation* – the fantasy is extended to the negative consequences. So a fantasy of raping a woman is associated with the negative consequences of arrest, trial and imprisonment, for example.

  Details of these techniques can be found in Howitt (1995a), for example.

- *Social skills, assertiveness and anger control*: while a lack of social skills is not a universal feature of sex offenders, by any means, the inability to form relationships with adults may be a contributing factor to the offending of some. Anger control problems have to be seen as an issue with rapists for whom issues of anger are common. Social skills including those of knowing how to deal with situations without aggression can contribute to a potentially more social prisoner at the time of release. Issues such as body language, the meaning of social cues and the range of behavioural alternatives available for dealing with situations may be dealt with through analysis and role-play, for example (see Box 22.1).

- *Relapse prevention*: relapse prevention (e.g. Marshall *et al.*, 1992; Pithers *et al.*, 1988) prepares the offender to deal with the feelings and experiences that he will have on release which are known to be progenitors of offending behaviour. These may be regarded as warning signs that must not go unheeded. It is known, for example, that sex offending patterns in some offenders are preceded by a negative mood state. Thus depression and anxiety might serve as danger signals for imminent offending. Similarly, the return of deviant fantasies may serve a similar function. There are other aspects of offending that a relapse prevention strategy would signal as dangerous: for example, moving into a job involving children, moving to a neighbourhood where there is a school nearby or just offering to babysit for a neighbour. For most people, these may be innocuous life-events; for the paedophile or child molester, they may be a precursor to the offending process.

Box 22.1

Forensic psychology in action: does treatment reduce recidivism?

The general finding of research appears to be that certain types of treatment reduce reoffending. Dutton *et al.* (1997) studied a group of wife-assaulters in Vancouver, Canada. The typical treatment was anger management. The men could be divided into several groups:

- men who did not show up for the assaultive husbands treatment programme;
- men who were assessed but deemed unsuitable for treatment;
- men who were assessed as suitable but did not complete the treatment programme;
- men who completed the treatment programme.

In terms of recidivism ratios (which are the total number of repeat assaults by the group divided by that group's sample size) there were differences. This measure is a better estimate of the amount of recidivism than is the incidence of recidivism:

- no-shows recidivism ratio = 9%;
- unsuitable for treatment = 20%;
- dropout = 11%;
- completers = 6%.

While these seem small differences, for 1,000 completers this would amount to a total of 320 crimes whereas those unsuitable for treatment would generate 810 (these are for all acts of violence). Non-completers would generate 550 and no-shows would generate 400. For violence against women, dropouts would commit 500, no-shows 230, rejects 290 and completers 230. Thus treatment is associated with fewer offences.

Research tends to demonstrate reductions in recidivism in treated offenders:

- Hanson *et al.* (2002) surveyed the findings of over 30 studies into sex offender reconviction in treated and untreated groups. On average, 17% of non-treated offenders recidivate sexually compared with only 12% of treated offenders. Much the same pattern applied to general recidivism in these two groups.
- Studer and Reddon (1998) in Alberta, Canada, found that treatment may affect the risk prediction for sex offenders. This study looked only at those who completed treatment versus those who failed to complete treatment. The treatment programme included educational components

on human sexuality and substance abuse amongst other things such as relapse therapy. The initial treatment period was up to 12 months followed by a further up to 8 months of out-patient treatment. They used as their predictor of recidivism prior sexual offences. For men who dropped out of the treatment programme the relationship between prior sexual offences and recidivism was statistically significant and positive. That is, previous sex offences predicted recidivism for those who did not complete their treatment. On the other hand, there was virtu-ally a zero correlation between previous offences and recidivism for the men who completed the full treatment. That is, the treatment broke the link between previous offence rates and recidivism. This was true despite the fact that prior recidivism in the two groups was at iden-tical levels. More generally, non-completion of treatment is a good predictor of reoffending (Hanson and Bussiere, 1998).

- Probably the best way of examining recidivism risk changes following sex offender therapy is the meta-analytic study of Hall (1995). (See Box 5.1 for an explanation of meta-analysis.) Hall reviewed 12 studies of recidivism involving a total of over 1,300 offenders. What is remarkable is the tremendous range of outcomes in the studies. For example, a few found no differences between the treated and untreated groups (or even slight negative relationships) whereas others showed a treatment versus comparison correlation (effect size) of 0.55. The latter, in one instance, corresponded to a recidivism rate of 15% for the treated group but 68% for the untreated comparison group. The overall recidivism was 19% for all of the treated groups versus 27% for all of the untreated groups. Treatment was not confined to cognitive behavioural methods – behavioural methods and hormonal treatments were also included. There was actually no statistical difference between the cognitive behavioural treatments and hormonal treatments. Behavioural modification seems to have a negative effect – that is, it makes matters worse if given alone than no treatment at all.

This demonstrates, as ever in forensic and criminal psychology, that it is unwise to generalise find-ings too much. One might glibly suggest that therapy can do no harm even if it does no good. We have already seen that this may not be the case. And there is other evidence that certain sorts of therapy can do harm (Rice, 1997; Rice *et al.*, 1992). The outcomes for men treated for two or more years (the mean was five years) in a Canadian therapeutic community were com-pared with those of a control group of men who had spent time in prison but had not received therapy. Most had been admitted to a psychiatric hospital for assessment following a violent offence. The offenders in the treatment and the prison groups were matched man to man in terms of age, type of offence and extent of criminal history. The outcome in terms of recidivism after ten years average at risk was unimpressive. Some recidivism was common assault but there were also cases of multiple homicides and sexual assaults. The men in the treatment programme fared little differently from those sent to prison.

The treatment programme had appeared to be especially suited to the needs of psychopaths (see Chapter 19). Consequently, the researchers studied the outcome of the treatment programme for psychopaths and non-psychopaths separately. The findings were opposite to those expected. For non-psychopaths (as assessed by the Hare Psychopathy Checklist) treatment was associated with much less recidivism. However, the psychopaths fared worse in treatment than in prison. This demonstrates, along with other research on psychopaths in therapeutic communities, that psychopaths may well be a totally different subgroup of offenders. Speculatively, it could be that treatment raised self-esteem in psychopaths, which resulted in a greater willingness to use aggres-sion. Alternatively, most prisoners may learn to be empathic with others in treatment whereas manipulatively the psychopath learns how to appear empathic and generally to manipulate the system.

There are many similarities between the contents of this programme and the activities in a medium security unit of the New Zealand prison system (Hudson *et al.*, 1995). Indeed, dissimilarities are few in number. For example:

- The men who volunteer for this treatment are required to undergo phallometric assessment (see Box 9.1) in order to gain information about any potentiality they may have to sexual arousal to deviant sexual stimuli.
- One therapist is used with a group of 10 offenders compared to the two tutors used in the UK prison service programme.
- The group meets four times a week – rather more frequently than in the United Kingdom – for about the same length of time (24 weeks in New Zealand).

Many of the components of this cognitive behavioural programme were much the same as those of any cognitive behavioural programme. Hughes *et al.* (1997) found evidence of improvements in personality disordered offenders in a high-security setting. They indicate that the cognitive programme in the context of a supportive ward environment (though not a therapeutic community) produced changes in a global measure of various aspects of change which included reduced impulsivity, reduced macho attitudes and better social problem solving.

Particularly pertinent to therapy given in prisons is the question of whether this reduces reoffending. Although evaluation research has been carried out into the cognitive behavioural programme described above, this could be criticised as stopping short of the question of recidivism. Instead, the evaluation concentrated on measures of things such as cognitive distortion, the reduction of which is only a step towards decreasing recidivism (Beech *et al.*, 1998). Box 22.1 contains more pertinent material.

Manualisation

As we have seen, there is sufficient evidence from a variety of sources to indicate that treatment programmes work. Consistency in terms of effectiveness, however, varies in ways which suggest that the quality of the programme's implementation is vital to its effectiveness. Different therapists do differ in terms of their effectiveness, of course, but there is more to it than that. McMurran and Duggan (2005) are among those forensic and criminal psychologists who suggest that effective treatment is 'driven' by theory and is based on research evidence. Adherence to the principles derived from these is termed 'treatment integrity'. A treatment programme that has a high degree of treatment integrity in practice will conform closely to the programme's underlying theory and design. Therapists in programmes demonstrating good treatment integrity will keep on the course determined by the principles of the treatment programme and will not drift away from these. Treatment integrity is dependent on a number of things of which the careful continuing training of personnel is an important component as is their continual monitoring.

Inexperienced therapists, especially, benefit from the use of highly structured materials that provide clear description of the techniques and processes to be used in therapy (Crits-Cristoph *et al.*, 1991). Of course, these highly structured materials are manuals for the treatment programme. Hence, there is a concept – manualisation – which simply means that the structure of the therapeutic programme is enshrined into a formal manual describing the practice of the therapy rather than leaving the programme to the whims of the therapists. Manuals vary in their style. Some are best described as prescriptive in the detail of how and what is to be done. Others stress the concepts underlying the treatment programme and leave more to the individual therapist by way of discretion in terms of how those principles are implemented. Manualisation is quite simply the process of turning the basic principles of the treatment programme into a detailed, systematic manual describing what must be done in practice.

Manualisation taken at face value may seem a simple, practical step in increasing the effectiveness of therapeutic programmes. However, it actually reverses many of the traditional principles that underlie psychological therapies. Hollin (2002) suggests that the following are among the major criticisms of manualisation although he does not share all of them:

- Negation of theoretical principles: rather than tailor cognitive behavioural treatments to the individual needs of offenders, manualisation encourages 'off the peg' treatment which is the same for all. This is particularly evident in the stress of cognitive behavioural programmes on working with groups of offenders rather than individuals. Rapists and child molesters go through identical treatment programmes.

- Lack of individual case formulation: the thorough assessment of the individual prior to treatment is a given in traditional cognitive behavioural treatment. So an individually tailored treatment plan would be integral to treatment. Assessment in cognitive behavioural programmes tends to be confined to excluding those unsuitable for cognitive behaviour therapy by virtue, say, of the low levels of intelligence.

- Lack of clinical artistry: things like the clinician's insights, personal qualities, skill in decision making, and judgements in relation to an individual client are seen by some as being integral to good therapy. Treatment is an unfolding process, the precise detail of which is dependent on the therapist's use of these skills. The use of a manual diminishes the opportunity for using such skills. However, it is these very processes in which the therapist makes continuing adjustments on the basis of their clinical skills that actually threaten the integrity of treatment programmes.

- Emphasis on single schools of therapy: a treatment manual will almost certainly feature a single theoretical approach to psychotherapeutic intervention. This, most commonly, will be the cognitive behavioural approach. Inevitably, then, this squeezes out eclectic approaches where features of different schools of therapy are used by the therapist depending on circumstances. One consequence of the monopoly of one school of therapy in a treatment programme is that it may stifle the development of new approaches to therapy as it prevents new things from being tried out.

The effectiveness of prison

This aim of rehabilitation is explicit to the penal systems of many countries. Examples include the Netherlands, Spain and Germany in Europe. This aim is not explicitly stated in some systems such as France and England and Wales. Nevertheless, rehabilitation may still be seen as an appropriate activity within the latter systems. There are many reasons why rehabilitation might not be a priority in some prison systems. Lack of the needed financial resources to pay for prison psychological, psychiatric, social and educational services might be exacerbated by rapidly expanding prison populations. The growth of offending might lead to a political climate that sees society as soft on crime. Consequently, tougher penalties are needed, not the easy option of training and therapy. Furthermore, only in recent years have effective treatments for, say, sex offenders been developed.

According to Redondo *et al.* (2002) criminology has demonstrated that punishment may not be effective on all offenders. Crime is not altogether dependent on rationality so sometimes will not be affected by punishment. There are many factors that contribute to crime. Redondo *et al.* list many of the factors already identified in earlier chapters of this book. These should include, among others, social factors such as school failure, ineffective child-rearing, unemployment, illegal drug trafficking, strains between social groups, criminal subcultures and individual psychological factors such as low educational level, aggressive tendencies, occupational incompetence, drug addiction, frustration, beliefs and criminal values, egocentrism, impulsiveness and lack of social perspective. Punishment, as such, is unlikely to have much influence on such criminogenic factors. However, they might be amenable to influence through educational programmes and psychotherapeutic programmes, either in the community or in prison. One would expect psychology to contribute effectively to these.

'Nothing works'

As you now know, 'nothing works' is the idea that interventions to prevent reoffending, especially those of a social or psychological nature, are ineffective. This idea has a long history. It largely developed out of concerns that psychodynamic therapies were ineffective. They simply did not change the behaviour of offenders in relevant ways (Martinson, 1974). Since that time, ideas about how psychological therapy should be conducted have substantially changed. This was a result of the introduction of behaviour therapies around the 1960s but, more importantly, the introduction of cognitive behavioural therapies in the last two decades of the twentieth century. There have been a number of influential analyses of the research into interventions aimed at preventing reoffending. These include, in North America, such reviews as those of Andrews *et al.* (1990). These, and many other similar reviews, employ meta-analysis (see Box 5.1). This involves statistically amalgamating the findings from as many as possible of the relevant studies. The analysis can be refined to examine the effects in subcategories of studies, e.g. those involving say sex offenders, or those involving a particular age group of offender, or those involving a particular type of cognitive behavioural treatment.

It has to be said that at first sight the effect sizes in such studies appear small. A correlation (effect size) of 0.1 or 0.2 between treatment and outcome seems unimpressive. This can be translated into the numbers of treated offenders who will not reoffend. A correlation (effect size) of 0.1 indicates a reduction in recidivism in the treated group of 10% of the rate of recidivism without treatment (i.e. the rate in the control group). Given that recidivism figures tend to be high without treatment, then this may well correspond to a reduction of as much as 5% in recidivism.

Redondo *et al.* (2002) carried out an important meta-analysis (Box 5.1) of a number of studies of the effectiveness of prison and community treatment programmes in Europe between 1980 and 1998. The same authors had previously published a related study in which they found a global effect size of 0.1, which equates to a reduction in recidivism of 10% (Redondo *et al.*, 1999). They confined their newer investigation to the prevalence of recidivism involving study designs that included a non-treated control group. Of the studies in their meta-analysis, about two-fifths were British, one-fifth were German and a sixth were Dutch. They found an effect size (correlation) of 0.2 between treatment and outcome. The differential in reoffending was 22% between the treated and untreated offenders. The best outcomes (largest effect sizes) were for educational programmes ($r = 0.49$) followed by cognitive behaviour therapy ($r = 0.3$). Therapeutic communities and diversion programmes were not so effective (effect size = 0.1). Programmes in the community had the greatest effects. Sex offending had bigger effect sizes than other crimes (such as drug trafficking).

The many dimensions of psychology in prison

The potential roles for forensic and criminal psychologists in prisons vary widely. By way of illustration of the variety, simply in terms of the work of psychologists with life prisoners in the United Kingdom, the following types of activity have been indicated (Willmot, 1999):

- *Risk assessment*: a prisoner's time in prison needs to be planned and targets set. For example, at what stage may the offender be moved to a less secure environment? When should home leave be permitted and when should the offender be released on licence?

- *Initial risk assessment*: this is dependent on the past history of the offender, including an assessment of the factors that led to their offending. Progress in dealing with these contributory factors needs to be assessed when making future decisions about particular offenders.

- *Individual clinical work*: this might include any of the following – anger and stress management, cognitive behavioural treatments for anxiety or depression and interpersonal skills.

- *Decisions to progress through the prison system possibly to final release*: this is a corporate task rather than for the psychologist alone, although the contribution of the psychologist to the decision may be substantial. Considerations would include attitudes to the offence, insight into offence-related behavioural problems, behaviour in prison and other factors indicating suitability for progression.

- *Discretionary life panels*: in the United Kingdom, once a lifer has completed their basic tariff, a parole board reviews the case every two years. This may include evidence or assessments from psychologists, who may be cross-examined by lawyers for the lifer.

These tasks clearly involve an estimate of the likely future behaviour of the offender. The next chapter considers some of the more objective ways of assessing the potential future risk of offenders.

Main points

- There is little or no role for psychology in the punishment of prisoners. On the other hand, the utilitarian and humanitarian functions of prison can utilise the skills of psychologists effectively in order to produce changes in prisoners that may reduce their likelihood of re-offending in many cases. Psychologists have a part to play in many aspects of prison life from the training of officers to decisions about the release of prisoners. Such activities are rarely carried out solely by psychologists working alone or as part of teams of psychologists only, it is much more likely that psychologists work with other professional groups as part of these activities.

- The range of psychological techniques employed with the prison service is wide. It stretches from assessment using psychological instruments such as intelligence tests to the delivery of therapy to individual prisoners or, more likely, groups of prisoners. Modern prison services are likely to have tailored cognitive behavioural programmes for the treatment of sex offenders and some violent offenders in particular. The important thing is that the demand that such programmes are evaluated for effectiveness has resulted in a number of studies which demonstrate beyond question that such programmes not only produce the changes they intend in some prisoners but that recidivism is also reduced as a consequence. One should not overestimate the effectiveness of such programmes but neither is pessimism appropriate. We have gone a long way from the time when 'nothing works' was the over-riding view to today when 'why does it work?' and 'how can we make it work better?' are the more common views. Manualisation refers to the standardisation of treatment such that therapy is effectively used in all locations irrespective of the experience and skills of the particular personnel involved.

- There is every reason to believe that prison, so long as appropriate services are provided, can have a limited but significant impact on crime. It is wrong to believe that this is the consequence of the work of psychologists alone since they are only part of the total package. Meta-analyses seem to suggest that educational services are the most important in terms of allowing prisoners to return to a crime-free life in society. Furthermore, we should not neglect the fact that what happens on release from prison may have an important bearing on an offender's ability not to reoffend. Such services include various forms of supervision as well as housing and employment. The key to all of this is not being too optimistic and not too pessimistic about the value of psychological work within prison.

Chapter 23

Assessment of risk, dangerousness and recidivism

Overview

- Psychological practitioners have an ethical responsibility and duty of care in relation to those who can be affected by the decisions they make. The decisions that are made by practitioners about the disposal (e.g. early release, to live in the community) of offenders may increase the chances of the public becoming victims. Risk and dangerousness assessments refer to a variety of methods developed to limit the levels of risk and danger to the public while at the same time providing less restrictive arrangements for offenders. The Tarasoff decision in the United States imposed legal requirements pertinent to this. Risk assessment is different from risk management. Risk management is the various techniques that minimise the risk to other people – keeping the potential offender in prison is a form of risk management.

- This is not a precise science though empirical studies have demonstrated that certain variables predict future behaviours reasonably well. These include historical factors such as a background of violent offending. Some psychological measures such as the Psychopathy Checklist are also effective.

- Social and welfare policy can rapidly change the situation in which all psychologists operate. A good example of this has been the process of deinstitutionalisation of the care of the mentally ill such that they participate much more freely in the community. The consequence of this is that decisions have to be made about the treatment of the mentally ill in the community which may, at some level, have an impact on how risk and dangerousness are assessed.

- The factors which need to be taken into account when assessing risk and dangerousness may be to some extent different for a sexual offender than for a violent offender. These in turn may be very different from the predictors of suicide by the offender. Different contexts will influence the risk posed by the offender. For example, a paedophile may not be generally dangerous to children except when he gets the opportunity to work in a setting such as a school when many potential victims are available. Different types of offence require different predictor variables. So the predictors of sexual reoffending are different from those of violent reoffending.

The predictors of suicide may also be different. Risk factors are those that predict recidivism, which are different from causal factors which caused the individual to be dangerous to others in the first place.

- Clinical judgement of risk is different from statistical assessment of risk which is based on empirically established relationships. There are many reasons why clinical judgement may fail including that rarely is the feedback available about whether a decision was the correct one. In recent years, structured clinical methods have been developed which still rely on the judgement of the clinician to some extent but provide a checklist of decisions to be made and means of reaching an assessment. The Psychopathy Checklist (PC-R) is a very successful example of this approach. One should not confuse sloppy and bad practices with the best clinical work can do. It should be stressed that some clinicians see things differently.

- The prediction of risk is a prediction of the statistical likelihood of, say, violence in the future. Prediction of dangerousness is different in that it refers to the likely level of, say, violence if it happens. Thus there is a high risk of any of us reacting, say, with a push if angered but the general level of dangerousness would be low – i.e. we could not be provoked to kill.

- Mistakes are inevitable in predictions. It is harder to predict rare events than common events. The numbers of false positives and false negatives are important. False negatives are the offenders who are declared safe but actually reoffend. False positives are those who are declared a risk but do not reoffend.

A British forensic psychiatrist once said 'I could let free half of my patients – if I knew which half' (Gretenkord, 1991). The German banker Josef Hermann Aba pointed out 'Prognoses are a difficult matter, especially when regarding future events' (Gretenkord, 1993). The assessment of the risks and dangers posed by offenders is a very serious matter, however. It is of concern to all in forensic work.

Duty to protect

There are a number of responsibilities inherent in decision making in forensic work. These include:

- protecting the general public from dangerous individuals;
- protecting staff of an institution from dangerous individuals;
- protecting other inmates of the institution from dangerous individuals;
- protecting individuals from dangers posed by themselves – including suicide.

These duties include an element of prediction. Individuals within the criminal justice system pass through a number of stages for which assessment of the consequences of particular decisions is required. For example, if a prisoner is to be transferred from a maximum security prison to one more open and free, then this decision implies that some consideration is given to their likely future behaviour: they should be unlikely to abscond from their new prison and constitute little or no danger to the general public, for example. A number of influential societal factors need to be taken into account in understanding assessment of risk and dangerousness.

The Tarasoff decision

This arose out of a Californian court case of the early 1970s. The outcome was basic-ally to impose a greater duty on psychologists to protect the general public from their clients. The basic facts are as follows:

- Tatiana Tarasoff was a young student at the University of California in the late 1960s and early 1970s.
- Another student, Prosenjit Poddar, told a student health therapist that he intended to kill Tatiana.
- These basic facts were reported to the medical authority at the campus and their response was to get Poddar checked out by the campus police. Apart from this no other action was taken.
- Shortly afterwards, Tatiana was killed by Poddar.
- Tatiana Tarasoff had not been informed about the threat to her life at any stage before her death.
- Her parents pursued the matter through the Californian legal system.
- In a watershed case, *Vitaly Tarasoff vs. the Regents of the University of California*, her father won in 1974 a legal ruling that therapists were legally obliged by duty to inform such potential victims of the threat to their safety made by clients of the therapist. This was a duty to inform.
- The judgement was reviewed in 1976 in the light of a number of practical diffi-culties raised by professional bodies. The 1976 judgement obliged therapists to use reasonable care in order to ensure the public's safety from the therapists' clients. The difficulties inherent in this led to a second judgement in 1976 which revised the obligation to that of using reasonable care to protect potential victims. This is a duty to protect. The new obligation on the therapist involved managing the dangerous individual better, say, with medication, institutionalisation or by whatever means.

One difficulty with the Tarasoff decision lies in the fact that the named potential victim may not be the actual victim: that is, the violence may be against individuals whom the client has not directly threatened. A client who threatens to harm members of his or her own family may actually end up violently assaulting staff supervising him in a psychiatric facility. The threat needs to be evaluated in terms of the potential for attack, which may involve many others apart from those mentioned directly in the threat (McNeil, 1997). Of course, a Californian legal judgement is not US law, let alone international law.

Bad welfare of the criminally insane

There were a number of lawsuits in the United States during the 1960s and 1970s con-cerning the civil rights of offenders diverted into institutions for the criminally insane:

- The question of who should be discharged from such institutions was brought before the US courts.
- In some cases, the court cases led to reviews of cases of large numbers of patients held in institutions for the medically insane. Of those reviewed under the direction of the court, a substantial majority were discharged back into the community.

- Many of these institutions manifested bad and unacceptable living conditions for people. This made it a civil rights issue.
- Furthermore, given that these individuals were being held in the institutions on the basis of decisions contributed to by psychiatrists, psychologists and other mental health professionals, this added to the view that such professionals could not predict dangerousness.
- The clients were also disadvantaged by a tendency to over-predict violence, thus acting to the detriment of inmates.

Social and welfare policy

Prior to 1960, the ideological climate favoured institutional care of the mentally ill in order to protect the public effectively.

- By the 1980s onwards, the ideology had changed to one in which the majority of the mentally ill should be cared for in the community. Institutional care was seen as a temporary respite for use only in acute circumstances when there was no realistic alternative.
- The present situation balances the right of individuals to their liberty with the inevitability that in some instances the general public and other third parties require protection (Glover, 1999).

Risk assessment

Risk assessment is a professional tool in its infancy despite having been part of forensic and criminal psychology for several decades. Traditionally, recidivism has been the crucial topic. This is the likelihood that an offender will reoffend after release or some other stage in the future. The study of this dates back to the early twentieth century when researchers used official records or files that held information about the demographic and criminal history of the offender. Conceptually, there is an obvious distinction to be made between the statistical risk of the occurrence of an event in the future and the dangerousness of that event. For example, the likelihood of an offender reoffending in the future by shoplifting may be very high. In terms of the consequences of this reoffending, it poses fairly small consequences for the individual victim (Clark, 1999).

The prediction of dangerousness seems to refer to two distinct professional activities (Hodgins, 1997):

- Deciding which patients or clients or offenders will behave violently or aggressively or criminally.
- Identifying the particular conditions in which a specific individual is likely to behave violently, aggressively or criminally.

These are very different activities although clearly interrelated. By knowing more about the conditions encouraging violence, say, in a particular individual, we may be in a position to make more accurate predictions of their dangerousness. If, for example, we know that a particular man is prone to violence only when under stress and challenged by a woman, we are likely to see him as of little danger to other male prisoners in a male-only prison environment. There are no universal predictors of future behaviours and the factors predicting different types of behaviour are different. For example, the predictors of rape are not the same as the predictors of non-violent criminality.

For criminal behaviour and other behaviours, a number of effective but simple predictor variables have been established. These are largely associated with the age of the offender (youthful offenders are more likely to reoffend) and criminal history (those with the most criminal offences are the most likely to reoffend). Such indicators are readily measured and are prime aspects in predicting future behaviour (Clark, 1999). One difficulty is the non-dynamic nature of these predictions. They would give a prisoner the same likelihood of reoffending at the start of a term of imprisonment as when it finishes. Thus if the prisoner has received therapy within the prison context, there perhaps should be some adjustment to the prediction (i.e. successful therapy might reduce reoffending) but much of the data available are not sophisticated enough to allow that to be done.

Care should be taken to distinguish between:

- those factors that predict dangerousness in an individual; and
- the factors that caused that particular individual to be a danger to others (Hodgins, 1997).

This distinction between predictors and causes is important. The predictors of dangerousness are often very simple things such as age and previous history of crime. The causes of crime are multiple and complexly interrelated. For example, assume that studies of twins have established that genetics plays a role in the aetiology of the violence of some offenders. This means that genetic characteristics caused the offending. Just because we know that the cause is genetic does not mean that we have the technology to identify precisely what genes are involved – thus we have no genetic test. Nevertheless, we may still be able to predict dangerousness though not through a genetic test. Research may show that a long history of crime is strongly correlated with future violence. This history of violent crime cannot be said to be the cause of future violent crime – genes are the cause in this example. In these circumstances, we can use history of crime as an indicator of likely future violence. Some predictors may turn out to be causes of violence.

Risk and dangerousness prediction is at the moment rather inexact and we are unlikely ever to have perfect predictors. In particular, currently we do not know how stable risk factors are across different forensic populations (types of offender, locations of offenders). This sort of uncertainty led Monahan (1993) to argue that *all* organisations dealing therapeutically or otherwise with potentially dangerous client populations (including all forensic settings) should adopt the following principles:

- Experts in assessing client dangerousness should be employed in all.
- *All* therapists should collect data on the risk demonstrated by their client pool as part of an effort to extend knowledge in the field.
- Data on risk and dangerousness are potentially of value to all practitioners. Consequently, it is incumbent on practitioners to communicate their findings to other practitioner/decision makers working with potentially dangerous client populations.

Box 23.1

Key concept: risk management

Risk management can be considered to be all of the actions that can be employed by professionals to prevent the risk that they assess to be present in an offender, client or situation materialising. Many of the techniques are not intended to have a lasting effect but merely an immediate one. According to Harris and Rice (1997) these include the following:

- *Static controls* include video monitoring, locked wards and so forth. Situational controls might include, for example, the exclusion of violent partners from the family home or reducing the availability of guns and access to them. Pharmacological controls are common. They involve the use of sedatives and other drugs to reduce aggressive behaviour, for example.

- *Interpersonal controls* include encouraging talking with others as a means of reducing or circumventing the arousal of emotions such as anger. There are procedures available for the use of counselling or therapy in increasing self-control, such as anger management programmes.

According to Monahan (1993), *risk management* involves the practices and procedures that minimise the risk of clients to others. It is not necessary to know the actual levels of risk posed by a particular individual before they are deployed:

- Hospitalisation or imprisonment may incapacitate (make less risky) potentially dangerous clients effectively compared with, say, releasing them on parole.

- Second opinions from experts in dangerousness are essential in all cases of potentially dangerous clients. A practitioner's sole opinion is insufficient.

- Non-compliance with treatment should not be simply regarded as a stumbling block to effective treatment. It is a major risk indicator for dangerousness and should be responded to in that light.

Some authors stress the positive aspects of risk assessment (e.g. Glover, 1999). If risk had only negative outcomes (such as the general public suffering violent assaults) then there would be no reason to take that risk. Just leave the offender behind bars which reduces the risk to the general public to the very minimum. It is because we want the positive benefits of taking the risk that we take that risk. For example, we may feel it more humane to release prisoners into the community wherever possible or we may seek the economic benefit of not having to pay the high financial costs of keeping an offender in prison.

Political context

Risk and dangerousness assessments are subject to political pressures of many sorts. Equally, the management of risk and dangerousness is not solely in the hands of the primary decision makers, including psychologists. In terms of the work of the British Parole Boards, McGeorge (1996) suggests that there is a relationship between the political climate regarding crime and decisions to allow parole. His index of political influence is the number of life sentence prisoners to whom the Home Secretary (the government minister responsible for law and order matters) refused parole out of those recommended by the Parole Board. As the number rejected increased so did the number recommended for release by the Parole Board decrease. This suggests that the parole recommendations were influenced by the toughness of the Home Secretary.

Clinical judgement versus statistical assessment

There is a common consensus that there are two types of risk and dangerousness assessment. The first, perhaps the traditional form, is based on *clinical judgement*. It is generally held not to be successful. The second type is *statistical or actuarial assessment* and is held to be more successful. The debate follows the pattern of Meehle's (1954) critique of the efficacy of purely clinical methods such as the interview. One needs to review the evidence with care before any final conclusions can be drawn on the best form of risk and dangerousness assessment. Figure 23.1 is a chart illustrating the complexity of risk and dangerousness assessment. Many factors need to be taken into account. The clear lesson is that the context and intentions of the assessment are a vital consideration in planning that assessment.

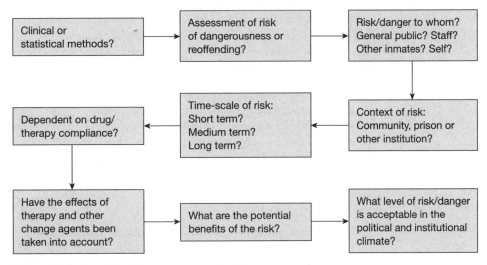

Figure 23.1 Aspects of the assessment of dangerousness

Clinical approaches in risk and dangerousness assessment

There are a number of distinct clinical approaches to the assessment of risk and dangerousness (Limbandari and Sheridan, 1995). They differ in their tactics and scope as much as anything. Some of these approaches are described as clinically based prediction models. This means that they rely on the experience and skilled judgement of the psychiatrist, psychologist or therapist involved rather than empirical evidence favouring the prediction:

- *Linear model*: this is the simplest sort of model. It is based on a limited number of decision choices that can be represented as a flow diagram or a decision tree. The simplicity means that relatively inexpert personnel may use it. An example of this comes from the work of Gross *et al.* (1987). In the event of a threat to the safety of other persons made by the client, the therapist or other decision maker should go through the steps of the decision tree to decide the appropriate action or whether action is appropriate. One route through the decision tree under consideration would be:
  - Is there a clear (as opposed to a vague) threat?
  - Is there serious danger (as opposed to marginal danger)?
  - Is there a specific victim (as opposed to a non-identifiable victim)?
  - Is there an imminent danger (as opposed to no imminent danger)?
  - Is the threat to a public official (as opposed to family member/acquaintances or other person)?
  - The therapist should contact the police (as opposed to, say, warning the person, warning the family, or going through involuntary hospitalisation procedures).

  Had the choices been different, then some clients might be recommended for family therapy.

- *Hypothetico-deductive model*: knowledge about the previous behaviour of the client allows a clinician to formulate hypotheses about the client's likely future behaviour. The hypotheses are integrated with, for example, theories of violence or other relevant theory. This inferential process becomes clearer when expressed with a concrete example:

  > While tightly clenching his fists, a young man tells his high school counselor that his grades plummeted because his girlfriend, whom he refers to in sexually derogatory terms, broke off their relationship. The counselor knows that this student has a history of frequent alcohol abuse and fighting on school grounds. The young man's father is in the Navy on an extended overseas assignment. The mother reports that her son refuses to accept her authority and that he has become difficult to manage in the absence of the father.
  >
  > *(Gross* et al., *1987, p. 7)*

  In this method, the clinician initially focuses on cues to the individual's behaviour to be found in the case history. Such possible clues include anger, rage, rejection and alcohol abuse. The combination of clinical theory and experience of similar clients might lead to the hypothesis that the client is depressed, full of feelings associated with being abandoned and out of control. Other important factors might include the observation that the location of the school is in an area noted for its high levels of violence. Say if this were confirmed by complaints by other students at the school, the indications are that there is a systematic problem with violence in the community which may lead to extra risk of the client acting violently. In this example, the counsellor recommended:
  - the therapeutic confrontation of the young man's anger;
  - that the boy is not to take the same lessons or classes as the individuals against which he had previously aggressed in order to minimise the risk of contact;
  - a counsellor–client contract in which the young man would agree to stay away from the girl and not to harm her in any way.

- *Risk assessment model*. This model (Gottfredson and Gottfredson, 1988) accepts the multi-dimensional nature of violence. Thus it is regarded not solely as a characteristic of the personality of an individual but also as the product of certain social and political climates. The following case study illustrates this approach:

> Convicted of felony assault on his former girlfriend, a 28-year-old male with a history of alcoholism is up for parole after serving half of a 12-month sentence. While in prison, he completed extensive alcohol treatment and anger management programs. On release from jail he intends to live with his mother. As the clinician, it would be imperative to know that his mother lives less than a block from the former girlfriend and that living in the mother's home are several alcoholic siblings.
>
> *(p. 8)*

In this case, to release the man to live in the home of his mother is tantamount to encouraging him back towards alcohol and its attendant risks. After all, several of his alcohol-dependent siblings still live at home. Equally, the former girlfriend's residence was close to that of his mother so enhancing the likelihood of future violence.

There is a general consensus in the literature that clinical inference based on case files and interviews is not a very powerful tool for assessing the probability of reoffending or the level of risk. Clark (1999) and Blackburn (1984) suggest on reviewing studies of this sort that clinical prediction is at best weak, at worst totally ineffective. Particularly important is the research that found that even experienced clinicians failed to predict future violence in cases which would have readily been predicted from simple indicators such as previous recidivism. Not all evidence against clinical methods constitutes a fair test. In particular, studies requiring clinicians to predict outside of their domain of expertise (i.e. clinical matters) are unfair. For example, we should not expect a clinician to be able to predict educational achievement accurately since this stretches beyond normal clinical experience.

Improvements using structured clinical methods

Clinical assessments are not necessarily confined to the sorts of subjective impression implied by the critics of the clinical method. Blackburn (2000) stresses that the provision of guidelines to focus the clinician on crucial aspects of prediction can serve to improve matters. Along these lines, Hollin and Palmer (1995; Palmer, 2001) point out that the research indicating the success of actuarial or statistical methods of prediction and the apparent failure of clinical prediction may mean several things. One possibility is that we need better clinical measures of clinical variables to equal the statistical approaches. If clinical variables do not matter then this suggests that there are no individual differences among offenders that might affect their likelihood of reoffending. This seems most unlikely. Furthermore, it is difficult to believe also that situational factors such as stress are not important in predicting violence in specific circumstances and these are not easily incorporated into future predictions. The distinction is between the role of clinical variables and clinical judgement.

Good clinical measures seem capable of predicting reoffending: for example, the Psychopathy Checklist (PCL and PCL-R) (Hare, 1980, 1991) consists of 20 items. These include a component that may be described as 'selfish, callous and remorseless use of others'. Items reflecting this tap aspects such as superficial charm or glibness, grandiose sense of self-worth, pathological lying, manipulativeness and failure to accept responsibility for one's actions. In many ways, this reflects the psychopath – a type of offender known to be highly involved in persistent offending and reoffending. The other dimension is of a 'chronically unstable and antisocial lifestyle' which includes a need for stimulation, a parasitic lifestyle, poor behavioural controls, early behaviour problems, impulsivity and juvenile delinquency. The Psychopathy Checklist is a good predictor of recidivistic tendencies. It may be as good as many purely actuarial measures of risk at predicting recidivism (Palmer 2001) which is not surprising given that the Checklist measures a wide range of criminogenic factors. There is a range of studies demonstrating that the Psychopathy Checklist is a robust indicator of recidivism. Sloore *et al.* (2004), for example, found that 36% of their sample of Belgian recidivists had a score on this measure, which defined them as psychopaths. It should also be stressed that the measure requires training before it can be used effectively by the clinician.

Predictors that are good for one sort of offence may be relatively poor at predicting recidivism for another sort of offence or using a different sort of prisoner group. Sjostedt and Langstrom (2000) carried out a study of *two* well-established measures associated with recidivism (the *Psychopathy Checklist Revised* and the *Violence Risk Appraisal Guide*). Their sample was a group of Swedish rapists diagnosed as having personality disorders. Follow-up was for an average of 92 months after release or discharge from prison or forensic treatment:

- The *Psychopathy Checklist Revised* (PCL-R), as we have seen, is highly regarded in predicting violent recidivism, and performed moderately well at predicting violent recidivism (of a non-sexual nature) in this sample. It predicted sexual recidivism badly. Similarly, the *Violence Risk Appraisal Guide* (VRAG) could predict violent recidivism (of a non-sexual nature). The VRAG includes additional assessment on a number of factors, such as:
  - maladjustment at elementary school;
  - separation from either parent under age 16 (except through death);
  - non-violent criminal offences before the index offence;
  - victim injury on a scale from no injury to death with mutilation;
  - previous failures of conditional release;
  - female victim of the index offence;
  - evidence on record at the time of the index offence of schizophrenia or personality disorder;
  - alcohol abuse history.
- On the other hand, the *Psychopathy Checklist Revised* and the *Violence Risk Appraisal Guide* measures (see Harris *et al.*, 1993; Rice and Harris, 1997) both totally failed to predict sexual reoffending.
- It was possible sexual reoffending was predictable from another measure – the *Rapid Risk Assessment for Sexual Offender Recidivism* (RRASOR). This consists of just four variables:
  - previous sexual offences;
  - offender is under 25 years old;
  - extrafamilial victim of a sex offence;
  - any male victim of a sex offence.

The more of these characteristics the offender possesses, the greater the risk of sexual reoffending. Despite being good at predicting sexual reoffending, this measure fared poorly at predicting violent recidivism of a sexual nature.

Statistical or actuarial prediction

The statistical prediction of dangerousness attempts to replace the subjectivity of clinical methods with empirically based prediction methods. The essential feature of this method is the availability of a database demonstrating the relationship between predictor variables and reoffending variables in a large group of offenders. These predictor characteristics would include demographic variables such as age, criminal history, personality and similar factors. Reoffending would involve appropriate measures of recidivism such as reconviction for a similar offence in a five-year period on release. The stronger the relationship between these predictor variables and recidivism, the more useful will be the characteristics in predicting recidivism in other similar offenders. The theory is fairly simple but, in practice, things are a little more complicated.

Box 23.2

Controversy: why is clinical judgement bad at risk assessment?

The first major critique of clinical judgement in the prediction of behaviour was Meehle's (1954) examination of clinical versus statistical prediction methods. Assuming for the moment that this is the case, just why are clinicians so poor? Dernevik *et al.* (2000) list some of the reasons:

- The diagnostic categories on which much clinical judgement is based (e.g. schizophrenia, affective disorder) are extremely broad. So allocating offenders to these categories does not say too much about their likely behaviour since, for example, schizophrenics are such a heterogeneous group.

- The ecological validity of the clinical judgement is important. One would not expect clinicians to make accurate judgement of violent behaviours on which their experience and training are not great. For example, they might be better at making predictions about the mentally ill (the usual location of psychiatry and clinical psychology) than the run of the mill offender with no particular or marked psychiatric characteristics.

- Human information processing, because of the limited capacity of short-term memory, means that we process information serially rather than in parallel. Thus very simple cues may be dwelt upon when we form our judgements.

- Biases: when making judgements we tend to stick with our initial assessments and do not make full use of new information. Furthermore, there is the issue of illusory correlation in which we assume that there is a correlation between two things if they appear to coexist. Thus, if we notice that children who are sexually abused turn up early for school, we may assume a relationship between the two which comparison with other children who have not been abused would show.

- The sheer amount of information available for clinicians to review when making their judgements may be counterproductive.

- Experience does not necessarily increase the validity of clinical predictions. For example, the true positives in risk prediction may never come to the attention of the clinician again. Their feedback is more likely from the false negatives who are released but reoffend. In other words, the feedback loop is poor with no certainty of useful information coming to the clinician's attention.

Table 23.1 Predicting recidivism

	Reoffends	**Does not reoffend**
Shows predictive characteristics	True positive	False positive
Does not show predictive characteristics	False negative	True negative

So basically, statistical prediction is founded on the assumption that a particular offender can be considered in the light of how other, similar offenders behaved. In this sense, the approach can deal only with the characteristics of recidivists that are common to a number of if not all offenders. At the same time, it does not take into account totally individual factors that might lead to recidivism in an individual case.

Table 23.1 gives a breakdown, which should help. It is similar to Table 14.1, the diagnosticity table. In predicting recidivism, particular signs are being used to identify the recidivists. So in terms of Table 23.1, the assessment of recidivism should maximise true positives (accurate predictions of recidivism) and minimise false positives (inaccurate predictions of recidivism). The best predictions of (say) recidivism occur when that behaviour is to be found in half (50%) of the group in question (Milner and Campbell, 1995).

This can be elaborated. Imagine that a researcher has developed a test of recidivism that is very accurate – say that it correctly classifies 90% of recidivists as recidivists and 90% of non-recidivists as non-recidivists. Imagine also that half of the sample of 400 offenders is recidivist:

- Then the recidivism test will correctly classify 90% of the 200 recidivists (i.e. it will find 180 recidivists).
- By the same token, it will also classify 10% of the non-recidivists as recidivists (i.e. 20 of the non-recidivists).
- In other words, 180 of the recidivists are correctly identified at the cost of 20 of the non-recidivists being wrongly identified as recidivists (see Table 23.2). This is an impressive 'hit' rate.

But what, say, if recidivism were much lower – 10% rather than 50%:

- The test remains 90% accurate but because there are only 40 reoffenders then it will classify 36 of them as reoffenders and 4 of them as non-recidivists.
- It is just as accurate with the non-recidivists. Out of the 360 non-recidivists the test will select 36 as recidivists and 324 as non-recidivists.
- In this case, the ratio of true positives to false positives is much poorer than in the previous example where the criterion of recidivism was to be found in half

Table 23.2 Theoretical accuracy in a sample of 200 recidivists and 200 non-recidivists using a 90% accurate test

	Reoffends N = 200	**Does not reoffend N = 200**
Shows predictive characteristics	True positive 180	False positive 20
Does not show predictive characteristics	False negative 20	True negative 180

Table 23.3 Theoretical accuracy in a sample of 40 recidivists and 360 non-recidivists using a 90% accurate test

	Reoffends N = 40	Does not reoffend N = 360
Shows predictive characteristics	True positive 36	False positive 36
Does not show predictive characteristics	False negative 4	True negative 324

of the participants. In fact, as many non-recidivists as recidivists are identified as recidivists in these circumstances (Table 23.3).

Thus, unless recidivism is common, even the best tests are likely to make many mistakes. The general principle is that it is easier to predict relatively frequent events than uncommon events. Thus one is more likely to be able to predict cases of domestic violence than murder simply because the rates of domestic violence are nearer the optimum 50% for accurate prediction.

Of course, one has to consider the costs involved. From the point of view of an offender, the possibility that he or she will not be put on parole is a major cost; from the point of view of the public, the issue may only be keeping in prison those likely to reoffend. If some prisoners are not given parole as a consequence then this is not a problem if this point of view is accepted.

Gretenkord (2000) demonstrates some of the advantages of preparing simple tables for assessing the likely rates of recidivism in a study of mentally disordered offenders. He carried out a study of men hospitalised in a forensic unit. Using complex statistical techniques (logistic regression) he was able to reduce his original list of predictors down to just four predictors of recidivism with a violent offence. These were:

- personality disorder (yes or no);
- violent pre-offence not included in the crime leading to present institutionalisation (yes or no);
- physical aggression during stay at the forensic hospital at least two times (yes or no);
- age at the time of discharge in years.

The worst prognosis by these criteria was for:

- the younger inmates – the group in their 20s;
- who also manifested a personality disorder;
- who had a violent previous offence in their records;
- who manifested physical aggression during the course of their treatment in the institution.

Sixty-five per cent of these reoffended violently after release. In contrast, the likelihood of a 60-year-old who did not have a personality disorder, did not have a violent pre-offence and did not show physical aggression during treatment, reoffending was only 1%. Gretenkord argues for simple contingency tables that allow the clinician access to data on probabilities. See Table 23.4. So, given the four contingencies known to predict violent reoffending, it is possible to predict the likelihood of this.

It should be noted that even Gretenkord's simple approach leaves a considerable margin for discretion (i.e. further decisions). It tells us only what groups are likely to reoffend, not which inmates should be released and which should not. That is a

Table 23.4 A simple prediction table based on Gretenkord's data

	Pattern of predictor variables							
	Has personality disorder				Does not have personality disorder			
	Violent pre-offence		No violent pre-offence		Violent pre-offence		No violent pre-offence	
	Aggression during treatment	No aggression during treatment	Aggression during treatment	No aggression during treatment	Aggression during treatment	No aggression during treatment	Aggression during treatment	No aggression during treatment
20 years	65%	36	39	16	37	15	17	6
30 years	52	25	27	10	25	9	11	4
40 years	38	16	18	6	16	6	6	2
50 years	27	19	11	4	10	3	4	1
60 years	17	6	7	2	6	2	2	1

further matter for our judgement. Very rarely do researchers actually stipulate scores on predictors that can be used as cut-off points for decisions of this sort.

Predictive factors

It is important to note that the more precise the question asked, the more likely is statistical prediction to be effective. Consider the following things:

- There may be better prediction if the type of offence is taken into account. For example, predictions of domestic violence against adults based on previous violence against adults may be better than predictions of domestic violence against children based on previous violence against adults.
- The time period of a prediction may affect its accuracy. For example, certain factors may predict the short-term or acute dangers posed by an individual but have little validity for predicting longer-term or chronic risks.

The predictive factors for any sort of criminal activity will vary according to the crime in question, the precise circumstances and numerous other factors.

The best predictors of a crime such as domestic violence have been broadly established. They tend to be relatively mundane for the most part (Milner and Campbell, 1995):

- Previous history: a person with a track record for domestic violence is more likely to act violently in the future.
- Mental illness is associated with domestic violence.
- Substance abuse (drugs and/or alcohol) is predictive.

It is too soon to form an overall picture in order to see if other types of offence can be predicted with similar sets of predictors. Furthermore, it is important to realise that even long-established predictors may only be moderately powerful. For example, Dowden and Brown (2002) surveyed 45 studies into the relationship between substance abuse and general recidivism – that is recidivism for any type of crime. Studies were included in their meta-analysis (see Box 5.1) if substance abuse was measured prior to the recidivism. This cuts down the risk that offenders will blame their recidivism on substance abuse as an easy excuse. In this study, general recidivism included things such as reconvictions, new charges, and violations, say, of suspended sentence such that the offender has to serve his or her sentence as a consequence. Studies focusing on violent recidivism separately were excluded from this meta-analysis. The analysis showed that various substance abuse indicators correlated (had an effect size of) between 0.1 and 0.2 in general. Alcohol abuse had the lowest effect size whereas a combined category which essentially assessed whether the offender had abused drugs or alcohol or both produced the largest effect size.

The use of a wider variety of predictors may increase the accuracy of predictions. Gresnigt *et al.* (2000) studied predictors of violent crime recidivism among Dutch prison inmates who were also drug users. The addiction severity index, cultural origin, level of education, duration of detention, diagnostic interval schedule and DSM-III classification were among the predictors. Classification as to the likelihood of future violent convictions was 82% accurate using cultural origin, history of violent offences and property offences. It increased very moderately to 85% when the diagnostic interview schedule was added. It reached 93% when all these factors plus the addiction severity index were added in.

Box 23.3

Forensic psychology in action: the prediction of child molestation and other sexual offences

Given the intense public interest in sexual offenders against children – paedophiles and others who molest under-age persons – the factors associated with their reoffending are important. Megan's Law (and similar initiatives outside the United States) is founded on the belief that sexual offenders are dangerous and highly likely to reoffend. Megan Kanka was a seven-year-old who was abducted and murdered in 1994 by a convicted sex offender who was living near her home in New Jersey. Megan's Law is US legislation concerning the provision of information to local communities about the presence of sex offenders in the community. For example, in the United States, sex offenders might have their home address, home telephone number, work address, vehicle description and licence plate number released to the community. Similarly, crimes such as rape may attract very significant sentences including life in some jurisdictions, implying that these men are in need of constant surveillance and review.

The research on reoffending in such groups makes fascinating reading and highlights many of the problems of prediction of dangerousness and recidivism. Good examples of this are to be found in the work of Firestone on Canadian sex offenders:

- Firestone *et al.* (1998a) carried out a study of convicted rapists who were followed up for up to 12 years and an average of 7.6 years.
- Because of the constraints of research, such varying lengths of follow-up are typical of studies since the researcher may be limited in the access to offenders and may be constrained to complete the research within a given amount of time.
- About half of these offenders had reoffended by the time they had been out of prison for five years.
- However, one needs to check the type of crime involved. In fact, only 16% reoffended with a sexual crime. Rather more reoffended with a violent crime (26%) though this included sexual crimes and over a half reoffended with any sort of crime (e.g. theft). This sort of figure is familiar elsewhere in the world for other sex offenders. In Germany, Egg (1999) carried out a 10-year study of recidivism in child molesters. About a half were reconvicted within that period but only about 20% for a sexual offence. In fact, in terms of their previous convictions, only about the same percentage had prior convictions for sexual offences.
- The more important question is whether or not the recidivists can be predicted. According to Firestone *et al.* prediction of recidivism for the sexual offence was not good. Sexual recidivists tended to have been removed from the family home under the age of 16 compared to non-recidivists. The use of the phallometer (see Box 9.1) was not effective in determining the recidivists.
- For a group of child molesters who committed their assaults outside the family, the reoffending figures were slightly lower but with a similar overall pattern.
- Furthermore, the prediction of sexual recidivism in this group was weak. Only men who rated themselves higher on alcohol abuse, men higher on guilt and men who were sexually aroused by assaultive rather than consenting sex stimuli involving children (i.e. the paedophile assault index) showed a greater likelihood of reoffending.
- Incestuous-only (family abuse) offenders showed a different pattern still. They reoffended in any category much less than extrafamily offenders or rapists. Only 6% had reoffended sexually at the end of the up-to-12-year period.
- Finally, Firestone *et al.* (1998b) attempted to differentiate homicidal (actual or attempted) child molesters from non-homicidal ones. Intrafamily offenders were excluded. In Canada, sexual murders constitute only 3% of killings and of these only 8% involve the deaths of children. In

other words, only about a quarter of 1% of murders involve the sexual killing of children. These are rare events not particularly conducive to prediction.

• Many factors did not differentiate between the homicidal and the non-homicidal offenders. Homicidal offenders tended to abuse complete strangers whereas non-homicidal ones rarely did. Homicidal offenders rated themselves as having a higher history of violence and having had contact with a forensic psychiatrist. They tended to have higher sexual arousal on the phallometric assault index. The murderers had more extreme sexual involvement with children than the kissing and fondling that was more typical of the non-homicidal offenders.

One of the common criticisms of recidivism statistics is that they deal with reconviction rather than reoffending. That is, offenders may commit crimes which are simply not reported to the criminal justice system hence the low recidivism. Falshaw *et al.* (2003) studied 173 offenders' records at a community based sex offender treatment programme in the United Kingdom. The period at risk of reoffending covered by the study was a minimum of nearly four years. Two different national information sources were examined for information about each of the offenders: the Offender Index had information about reconviction for only about a third of the men for which the Police National Computer had information. This implies that recidivism rates may appear low simply because of problems in recording information on the databases. However, the therapy records of the programme's clientele contained information about offending by clients which was collected in the course of the work of the programme itself. If this information is combined with the national information, then reoffending occurred in the at-risk period in 12% of the clientele. Additional information was available from the project's records about known instances of the sorts of behaviours known to encourage reoffending – for example, waiting around a school gate as children were leaving for home. If this information is added into the measure of recidivism, then 21% exhibited some form of recidivistic behaviour. This figure is between two and seven times higher than the information on the recidivism data on the national databases. Whether or not these figures would apply to offenders leaving prison cannot be assessed. In themselves, the figures still tend to confirm that recidivism in sex offenders is at relatively low levels.

With sex and violent offenders, especially, we should remember that there is provision for their monitoring in the community after leaving prison or even if there is suspicion about their behaviour. As a consequence, recidivism figures in recent years reflect a situation in which offenders' behaviour is controlled long after they are released from prison. In the United Kingdom, for example, there are two major pieces of legislation which concern the monitoring of sex offenders in the community. Britain does not have a 'Megan's Law' requiring the compulsory notification of communities of sex offenders in their midst. However, it does have a sexual offender register system which requires most sex offenders to keep the police informed about their current address and places severe limits on their foreign travel. Furthermore, there are multi-agency public protection arrangements (MAPPA) in which the police, prison, probation, social, and health services are required to work together in order to reduce the risk of reoffending. The evidence seems to suggest that these are effective since the UK figures indicate that 93% of offenders register their whereabouts (Expert Law, 2003). Rates of serious sexual or violent offences for offenders on a MAPPA programme seem low. In a year in which there were 25,000 offenders on the register, only 26 committed a serious sexual or violent offence (*Daily Telegraph*, 2004). In a rare study of offenders' response to community notification laws in the United States where community notification is common, it was found that over two-thirds of offenders believed that this was an incentive for them not to reoffend (Elbogen *et al.*, 2003).

So, in a sense, modern criminal justice system practices will change the meaning of recidivism statistics for the simple reason that sex offenders are not simply released back into the community with little by way of support. Instead, their situation is addressed by a variety of agencies and their activities monitored for signs of possible recidivism.

Issues in the assessment of risk and dangerousness

There are a number of issues associated with the assessment of risk and dangerousness that should be highlighted, some of which have already briefly been mentioned (Clark, 1999; Monahan and Steadman, 1994):

- The assessment of risk is different from the assessment of dangerousness. The assessment of risk (of occurrence) involves predicting how *likely* it is that the individual will in the future commit another crime. Dangerousness is more about the level of the danger or adverse consequences to the victim of such a crime. Thus an offender might be adjudged to be greatly at risk of reoffending but that offence is likely to be no more than getting involved in a modest brawl. On the other hand, a person may have a low risk of reoffending but, if they do, very serious consequences are expected for the victim.

- Along with the assessment of risk and dangerousness should go planning to safeguard others in the light of the level of risk and dangerousness. For example, if there is no option but to release an offender from prison, what is the point of a careful risk and dangerousness assessment? On the other hand, while the individual remains in prison, risk and dangerousness may be helped, say, by placing the offender on an anger management programme.

- Risk and dangerousness are not fixed parameters but will change with context and the passage of time and they should be regarded as such in any assessment.

- There is no single risk factor and consequent likelihood of risk. There are many possible risk factors that need to be understood. Information is also needed on the extent to which these can be found in different contexts of risk. So, for example, a prisoner may be much more at risk of offending violently in prison if sharing his cell with a violent fellow prisoner than if, on release, he goes to live with his mother in isolation.

- Different risk factors have different proven levels of influence on the future behaviour of an offender. Well-established risk factors such as previous recidivism should be given greater weight in decision making than a speculative factor such as that the man has taken up a new hobby or interest.

- There is no evidence at all that it is possible to predict serious criminal violence by individuals who have not already committed a violent act (Harris and Rice, 1994): in other words, the very group of individuals one needs predictions about the most.

- The criterion to be predicted needs careful consideration as many variants are possible. Gretenkord (2000) illustrates the importance of the criteria for deciding what is reoffending for the rates of reoffending. His was a sample of mentally disordered males in a forensic hospital who had largely committed violent physical or sexual crimes against other people. After discharge from this hospital for the average period of eight years, 44% had reappeared on the German crime register. This would include minor offences such as riding on a bus without paying the fare. Thirty per cent had to return to prison or a forensic hospital. Thirteen per cent committed a violent or sexual offence. Quite clearly, the rate of reoffending is substantially determined by the criteria employed.

It is notable that quite good predictions of reoffending can be obtained from relatively straightforward indicators. A good example of this is the British study that involved a 10-year follow-up of a representative sample of men convicted of sexual offences and sentenced to at least four years in prison (Clark, 1999). This classified higher-risk offenders as the men who had any of these characteristics: a current or previous conviction for a non-sexual violent assault, four-plus previous convictions for any offence, or a previous conviction for a sexual offence. Lower-risk men were those who showed none of these four features. The high-risk groups showed considerable recidivism in the 10 years after release. A quarter were reconvicted for a sexual offence (but only 1 in 20 of the low-risk group) and nearly a half for a sexual or violent offence (but only 1 in 8 of the low-risk group).

Types of predictor

There is a distinction between different types of predictor of reoffending (Palmer, 2001). Some of the predictors hardly change and are known as static variables: these would include family background, offence history and others. Another type of variable might in many cases change over time. These are known as dynamic variables and would include social and psychological factors. All variables may change in their correlates with risk but dynamic variables, because they change, are more likely to do so. A static variable such as sex may be a predictor of reoffending, but the association may become less as the individual ages. Dynamic factors such as situational and psychological factors may change. A paedophile who lives close to a school may be less at risk of offending if they move to a child-free location.

Blackburn (2000) offers another useful scheme for classifying risk factors into types:

- Historical factors – especially previous offending/violent patterns.
- Dispositional variables which include cognitive and emotional tendencies. For example, those who are deficient in social problem solving (e.g. for whom aggression is the only response in their repertoire to threat) are more likely to reoffend violently. Nevertheless, the sorts of dispositional variable measured by traditional personality tests (such as the MMPI) have not been shown to be useful in risk and dangerousness assessment.
- Clinical variables: mental disorders, such as schizophrenia, do increase the risk of violence. On the other hand, what they add to the prediction is very small.
- Personality disorder is problematic as criminal activities are both part of the definition of antisocial personality disorder and the effect of having the disorder (Chapter 18).

What stops recidivism?

There is very little research that asks what factors stop some high-risk violent criminals, i.e. men who have many of the signs of dangerousness, getting reconvicted. A Swedish study (Haggård, 2000; Haggård et al., 2001) found that the preventative factors included intense social isolation with the exception of a strong family orientation, physical disability and experience of shock such as those due to committing the crime, being arrested or incarcerated.

Risk of escape

Virtually totally missing from the research on the assessment of dangerousness and risk management is any attempt to understand the phenomenon of escape. Not only does escape from a forensic setting put more people at risk but also it questions the intimate relationship between dangerousness and risk management. There is regrettably little information on this. Gacono *et al.* (1997) studied patients who escaped from a Texan Maximum Security Forensic Hospital. Because of a pre-existing research programme, there was a great deal of diagnostic and other information available. They matched non-escapee prisoners with the escape group using variables such as age and ethnicity. Characteristically, the escapees who tended towards antisocial personality disorder did not seem to differentiate between the two but scores on the PCL-R were higher in the escapees who were glib and grandiose, liars and manipulators. Violent crimes against individuals were also more common in the escapees. The authors recommend that a score of 30 or more on the PCL-R should be seen as an indication that the detainee is a likely escapee.

Main points

- The assessment of risk and dangerousness had its impetus from US legislation requiring practitioners to deal with the risk to the public posed by their clients. In part this is achieved by managing the risk in various ways such as keeping the offender physically away from the public and others at risk. However, the decision about how likely a individual is to harm another (risk) and the assessment of how serious the risk is (dangerousness) is a complex one and is a characteristic of the situation as much as the offender in question.

- Risk assessment is an area of psychology to which clinical judgement and empirical research both have a role to play. There is reason to think that it is profitable to use the two methods together in ways that combine the advantages of the two. Empirical methods can demonstrate the broad relationship between risk factors and risk but cannot effectively deal with the individual instant which needs a careful evaluation within the parameters set by research. As a consequence, measures such as the Psychopathy Checklist Revised have shown themselves to be effective in identifying factors that are strongly predictive of recidivism.

- When we attempt to predict recidivism, we do so with less than perfect predictors, which means that there is always an amount of error. The amount of error that can be tolerated depends on the risk in question. One difficulty with predictions of this sort is that they tend to be the most accurate when the behaviour in question occurs in 50% of the population in question. So predictions of things like sex offences for which the recidivism rate is actually quite small are likely to be poor. Similarly, predicting which violent mentally ill offenders will kill in future is likely to be fraught with problems simply for statistical reasons.

References

A Abel, G.G., Barlow, D.H., Blanchard, E.B. and Guild, D. (1977). The components of rapists' sexual arousal. *Archives of General Psychiatry*, **34**, 895–903.

Abel, G.G., Becker, J.V., Mittelman, M.S., Cunningham-Rathner, J., Rouleau, J.L. and Murphy, W.D. (1987). Self-reported sex crimes on non-incarcerated paraphiliacs. *Journal of Interpersonal Violence*, **2**, 3–25.

Abel, G.G., Mittelman, M., Becker, J.V., Cunningham-Rathner, M.S. and Lucas, L. (1983). 'Characteristics of men who molest young children'. Paper presented at the World Congress of Behavior Therapy, Washington, DC.

Abrahams, G. (1954). *The Legal Mind: An Approach to the Dynamics of Advocacy*. London: H.F.L. Publishers.

Ainsworth, P.B. (1981). Incident perception by British police officers. *Law and Human Behavior*, **5**, 331–6.

Ainsworth, P.B. (1995). *Psychology and Policing in a Changing World*. Chichester: John Wiley.

Ainsworth, P.B. (1996). Psychological testing and police recruit selection: difficulties and dilemmas. In G. Davies, S. Lloyd-Bostock, M. McMurran and C. Wilson (Eds), *Psychology, Law, and Criminal Justice: International Developments in Research and Practice*. Berlin: Walter de Gruyter, pp. 579–84.

Ainsworth, P.B. (1998). *Psychology, Law and Eyewitness Testimony*. Chichester: Wiley.

Ainsworth, P.B. (2000a). *Psychology and Crime: Myths and Reality*. Harlow: Longman.

Ainsworth, P.B. (2000b). Psychology and police investigation. In J. McGuire, T. Mason and A. O'Kane (Eds), *Behaviour, Crime and Legal Processes*. Chichester: John Wiley, pp. 39–63.

Ainsworth, P.B. and Moss, K. (2000). 'Perceptions and misperceptions of crime amongst a sample of British students'. Paper presented at the conference of the European Association of Psychology and Law, Limosol, Cyprus.

Akers, R.L. (1999). *Criminological Theories: Introduction and Evaluation*. London: Fitzroy Dearborn.

Alison, L., Smith, M.D. and Morgan, K. (2003a). Interpreting the accuracy of offender profiles. *Psychology, Crime and Law*, **9** (2), 185–95.

Alison, L., Smith, M.D., Eastman, O. and Rainbow, L. (2003b). Toulmin's philosophy of argument and its relevance to offender profiling. *Psychology, Crime and Law*, **9** (2), 173–83.

Allen, J. (2004). Worry about crime. In S. Nicholas and A. Walker (Eds), *Crime in England and Wales 2002/2003: Supplementary Vol. 2: Crime, Disorder and the Criminal Justice System – Public Attitudes and Perceptions*. London: Home Office, pp. 41–54.
http://www.homeoffice.gov.uk/rds/pdfs2/hosb0204.pdf

Almond, L., Duggan, L., Shine, J. and Canter, D. (2005). Test of the arson action system model in an incarcerated population. *Psychology, Crime and Law*, **11** (1), 1–15.

American Psychiatric Association (1987). *Diagnostic and Statistical Manual of Mental Disorders*. Third Edition (revised). Washington, DC: APA.

American Psychiatric Association (2000). *Diagnostic and Statistical Manual of Mental Disorders*. Fourth Edition. Washington, DC: APA.

Andrews, D.A. and Bonta, J. (1995). *The Level of Service Inventory – Revised*. Toronto: Multi-Health Systems Inc.

Andrews, D.A., Zinger, I., Hoge, R.D., Bonta, J., Gendreau, P. and Cullen, F.T. (1990). Does correctional treatment work? A clinically relevant and psychologically informed meta-analysis. *Criminology*, **28**, 369–404.

Angermeyer, M.C. and Schulze, B. (2001). Reinforcing stereotypes: how the focus on forensic cases in news reporting may influence public attitudes towards the mentally ill. *International Journal of Law and Psychiatry*, **24**, 469–86.

APA (1987). *Diagnostic and Statistical Manual of Mental Disorders* (Third Edition – Revised). Washington, DC: American Psychiatric Association.

Appel, A.E. and Holden, G.W. (1998). The co-occurrence of spouse and physical child abuse: a review and appraisal. *Journal of Family Psychology*, **12** (4), 578–99.

APSAC (1996). Practice guidelines: use of anatomical dolls in child sexual abuse assessment. *Pacific Law Review*, **28** (1), 78–128.

Araji, S. and Finkelhor, D. (1985). Explanations of pedophilia: review of empirical research. *Bulletin of the American Academy of Psychiatry and the Law*, **13** (1), 17–37.

Arboleda-Florez, J., Holley, H.L. and Crisanti, A. (1996). *Mental Health and Violence: Proof or Stereotype?* Health Promotion and Programs Branch, Health Canada. http://hwcweb.hwc.ca/hppb/mentalhealth/pubs/mental_illness/index.htm

Arce, R. (1998). Empirical studies on jury size. *Expert Evidence*, **6**, 227–41.

Arce, R., Farina, F., Novo, M. and Seijo, D. (1998). In search of causes of hung juries. *Expert Evidence*, **6**, 1–18.

Arce, R., Farina, F., Vila, C. and Satiago, R. (1996). Empirical assessment of the escabinato jury system. *Psychology, Crime and Law*, **2**, 175–83.

Arce, R., Seijo, D., Farina, F. and Novo, M. (2004). Family interaction factor: analysing the effects on personal, social and school inadaptability and delinquent behaviour. Krakow, EAPL conference.

Arson Prevention Bureau (2005). Detecting and convicting the arsonist: lessons from the United States. Arson Prevention Bureau research paper. http://www.arsonpreventionbureau.org.uk/Publications/Files/Lessons%20from%20the%20United%20States.pdf

Artz, S. (1998). Where have all the school girls gone? Violent girls in the school yard. *Child and Youth Care Forum*, **27** (2), 77–109.

Attrill, G. (1999). Violent offender programmes. In Towl, G. and McDougal, C. (Eds), *Issues in Forensic Psychology 1: What do Forensic Psychologists do? Currrent and Future Directions in the Prison and Probation Services*. Leicester: British Psychological Society, pp. 58–61.

Avery-Clark, C.A. and Laws, D.R. (1984). Differential erection response patterns of sexual child abusers to stimuli describing activities with children. *Behavior Therapy*, **15**, 71–83.

B

Baartman, H.E.M. (1992). The credibility of children as witnesses and the social denial of the incestuous abuse of children. In F. Losel, D. Bender and T. Bliesner (Eds), *Psychology and Law: International Perspectives*. Berlin: Walter de Gruyter, pp. 345–51.

Bachrach, L.L. (1984). Deinstitutionalization and women: assessing the consequences of public policy. *American Psychologist*, **39** (10), 1187–92.

Bachrach, L.L. (1989). Deinstitutionalization: a semantic analysis. *Journal of Social Issues*, **45** (3), 161–72.

Baker, R.R., Lichtenberg, P.A. and Moye, J. (1998). A practice guideline for assessment of competence and capacity of the older adult. *Professional Psychology: Research and Practice*, **29** (2), 149–54.

Ballard, M.E. and Wiest, J.R. (1996). Mortal Kombat™: the effects of violent videogame play on males' hostility and cardiovascular responding. *Journal of Applied Social Psychology*, **26** (8), 717–30.

Bandura, A. (1973). *Aggression: A Social Learning Analysis*. Englewood Cliffs, NJ: Prentice Hall.

Bandura, A. (1977). *Social Learning Theory*. Englewood Cliffs, NJ: Prentice Hall.

Bandura, A. (1983). Psychological mechanisms of aggression. In R.G. Green and C.I. Donnerstein (Eds), *Aggression, Theoretical and Empirical Reviews Vol. 1: Theoretical and Methodological Issues*. New York: Academic Press, pp. 1–40.

Bandura, A. and Huston, A.C. (1961). Identification as a process of incidental learning. *Journal of Abnormal and Social Psychology*, **63**, 311–18.

Bandura, A., Ross, D. and Ross, S.A. (1963). Imitation of film-mediated aggressive models. *Journal of Abnormal and Social Psychology*, **66**, 3–11.

Barbaree, H.E. (1998). Denial and minimization among sex offenders: assessment and treatment outcome. *Sex Offender Programming*, **3** (4), 1–7.

Barclay, G., Tavares, C., Kenny, S., Siddique, A. and Wilby, E. (2003). *International Comparisons of Criminal Justice Statistics 2001*, Issue 12/03. London, England: Home Office Research, Development and Statistics Directorate.

Baron, L. and Straus, M. (1984). Sexual stratification, pornography and rape in the United States. In N.M. Malamuth and E. Donnerstein (Eds), *Pornography and Sexual Aggression*. New York: Academic Press, pp. 185–209.

Baron, L. and Straus, M. (1989). *Four Theories of Rape: A State Level Analysis*. New Haven, CT: Yale University Press.

Bartlett, D. and Memon, A. (1995). Advocacy. In R. Bull and D. Carson (Eds), *Handbook of Psychology in Legal Contexts*. Chichester: John Wiley, pp. 543–54.

Barton, J., Vrij, A. and Bull, R. (2000a). High speed driving: police use of lethal force during simulated incidents. *Legal and Criminological Psychology*, **5**, 107–21.

Barton, J., Vrij, A. and Bull, R. (2000b). The influence of field dependence on excitation transfer by police officers during armed confrontation. In A. Czerederecka, T. Jaskiewicz-Obdzinska and J. Wojcikiewicz (Eds), *Forensic Psychology and Law: Traditional Questions and New Ideas*. Krakow: Institute of Forensic Research Publishers, pp. 282–6.

Bates, A. (1996). The origins, development and effect on subsequent behaviour of deviant sexual fantasies in sexually violent adult men. Unpublished manuscript, Thames Valley Project, 17 Park Road, Didcot, OX11 8QL, UK.

Baxter, D.J., Barbaree, H.E. and Marshall, W.L. (1986). Sexual responses to consenting and forced sex in a large sample of rapists and non-rapists. *Behavioral Research and Therapy*, **24**, 513–20.

Baxter, D.J., Marshall, W.L., Barbaree, H.E., Davidson, P.R. and Malcolm, P.B. (1984). Deviant sexual behaviour. *Criminal Justice and Behavior*, **11**, 477–501.

Baxter, J.S. and Bain, S.A. (2002). Faking interrogative suggestibility: the truth machine. *Legal and Criminological Psychology*, **7** (2), 219–25.

Bazargan, M. (1994). The effects of health, environment, and sociopsychological variables on fear of crime and its consequences among urban black elderly individuals. *International Journal of Ageing and Human Development*, **38** (2), 99–115.

BBC News (2005). Sex offenders may face lie detector tests. http://news.bbc.co.uk/1/hi/uk/2208779.stm

Beck, J.C. (1995). Forensic psychiatry in Britain. *Bulletin of the American Academy of Psychiatry and the Law*, **23** (2), 249–60.

Beech, A., Fisher, D. and Beckett, R. (1998). *Step 3: An Evaluation of the Prison Sex Offender Treatment Programme*. London: Home Office.

Beech, A., Fisher, D. and Beckett, R. (1999). *STEP 3: An Evaluation of the Prison Sex Offender Treatment Programme*. A report for the Home Office by the STEP team November 1998. London: Home Office Information Publications Group, Research Development Statistics Directorate.

Bekerian, D. and Dennett, J.L. (1992). The truth in content analyses of a child's testimony. In F. Losel, D. Bender and T. Bliesner (Eds), *Psychology and Law: International Perspectives*. Berlin: Walter de Gruyter, pp. 335–44.

Bell, S. (1988). *When Salem Came to the Boro*. London: Pan.

Bender, D., Bliesener, T. and Losel, F. (1996). Deviance or resilience? A longitudinal study of adolescents in residential care. In G. Davies, S. Lloyd-Bostock, M. McMurran and

C. Wilson (Eds), *Psychology, Law and Criminal Justice: International Developments in Research and Practice*. Berlin: Walter de Gruyter, pp. 409–23.

Bennett, W.L. and Feldman, M.S. (1981). *Reconstructing Reality in the Courtroom*. London: Tavistock Publications.

Berkowitz, L. and Rawlings, E. (1963). Effects of film violence on inhibitions against subsequent aggression. *Journal of Abnormal and Social Psychology*, **66**, 405–12.

Berkowitz, L., Corwin, R. and Heironimus, M. (1963). Film violence and subsequent aggressive tendencies. *Public Opinion Quarterly*, **27**, 217–29.

Berliner, L. and Conte, J.R. (1993). Sexual abuse evaluations: conceptual and empirical obstacles. *Child Abuse and Neglect*, **17**, 111–25.

Bernet, W. (1997). Case study: allegations of abuse created in a single interview. *Journal of the American Academy of Child and Adolescent Psychiatry*, **36** (7), 966–70.

Berry, M.J., Robinson, C.A. and Bailey, J. (1999). 'The use of hypnosis to recover evidence from convicted offenders: issues and implications'. Poster presented at International Psychology and Law Conference, University College, Dublin, 6–9 July.

Biro, M., Vuckovic, N. and Duric, V. (1992). Towards a typology of homicides on the basis of personality. *British Journal of Criminology*, **32** (3), 361–71.

Bjorkqvist, K. (1994). Sex differences in physical, verbal, and indirect aggression: a review of recent research. *Sex Roles*, **30** (3/4), 177–88.

Bjorkqvist, K. (1997). Learning aggression from models: from a social learning toward a cognitive theory of modeling. In S. Feshbach and J. Zagodzka (Eds), *Aggression: Biological, Developmental, and Social Perspectives*. New York: Plenum, pp. 69–81.

Bjorkqvist, K. and Niemela, P. (1992). New trends in the study of female aggression. In K. Bjorkqvist and P. Niemela (Eds), *Of Mice and Women: Aspects of Female Aggression*. San Diego: Academic Press, pp. 3–17.

Bjorkqvist, K., Osterman, K. and Kaukiainen, A. (1992). The development of direct and indirect aggressive strategies in males and females. In K. Bjorkqvist and P. Niemela (Eds), *Of Mice and Women: Aspects of Female Aggression*. San Diego: Academic Press, pp. 51–64.

Blaauw, E., Roesch, R. and Kerkhof, A. (2000). Mental disorders in European prison systems. *International Journal of Law and Psychiatry*, **23** (5–6), 649–63.

Blackburn, R. (1971). Personality types among abnormal homicides. *British Journal of Criminology*, **11**, 14–31.

Blackburn, R. (1984). The person and dangerousness. In D.J. Muller, D.E. Blackman and A.J. Chapman (Eds), *Psychology and Law*. Chichester: Wiley, pp. 101–11.

Blackburn, R. (1993). *The Psychology of Criminal Conduct*. Chichester: John Wiley.

Blackburn, R. (1995a). Psychopaths: are they bad or mad? In N.K. Clark and G.M. Stephenson (Eds), *Issues in Criminological and Legal Psychology 22: Criminal Behaviour: Perceptions, Attributions, and Rationality*. Leicester: British Psychological Society, pp. 97–103.

Blackburn, R. (1995b). Violence. In R. Bull and D. Carson (Eds), *Handbook of Psychology in Legal Contexts*. Chichester: John Wiley, pp. 357–73.

Blackburn, R. (1996). What is forensic psychology? *Legal and Criminological Psychology*, **1** (1), 3–16.

Blackburn, R. (2000). Risk assessment and prediction. In J. McGuire, T. Mason and A. O'Kane (Eds), *Behaviour, Crime and Legal Processes: A Guide for Forensic Practitioners*. Chichester: John Wiley, pp. 177–204.

Blau, T.H. (1994). *Psychological Services for Law Enforcement*. New York: John Wiley.

Bliesener, T. and Losel, F. (1992). Resilience in juveniles with high risk of delinquency. In F. Losel, D. Bender and T. Bliesener (Eds), *Psychology and the Law: International Perspectives*. Berlin: Walter de Gruyter, pp. 62–75.

Blud, L. (1999). Cognitive skills programmes. *Issues in Forensic Psychology*, **1**, 49–52.

Bonnie, R.J. and Grisso, T. (2000). Adjudicative competence and youthful offenders. In R.G. Schwartz and T. Grisso (Eds), *Youth on Trial: A Developmental Perspective on Juvenile Justice*. Chicago, IL, US: University of Chicago Press, pp. 73–103.

Boon, J. and Baxter, J.S. (2004). Minimising extraneous interviewer based interrogative suggestibility. *Legal and Criminological Psychology*, **9** (2), 229–38.

Borg, I. and Shye, S. (1995). *Facet Theory: Form and Content*. Thousand Oaks, CA: Sage.

Bothwell, R.K., Deffenbacher, K.A. and Brigham, J.C. (1987). Correlation of eyewitness accuracy and confidence: optimality hypothesis revisited. *Journal of Applied Psychology*, **72**, 691–5.

Bowlby, J. (1944). Forty-four juvenile thieves: their characteristics and home-life. *International Journal of Psychoanalysis*, **25**, 19–53.

Bowlby, J. (1951). *Maternal Care and Mental Health*. Geneva: World Health Organization.

Bowlby, J. (1973). *Attachment and Loss: II. Separation Anxiety and Anger*. London: Hogarth Press.

Bowlby, J. (1980). *Attachment and Loss: III. Loss, Sadness and Depression*. New York: Basic Books.

Bradley, A.R. and Wood, J.N. (1996). How do children tell? The disclosure process in child sexual abuse. *Child Abuse and Neglect*, **9**, 881–91.

Brand, S. and Price, R. (2001). 'The social and economic cost of crime'. Home Office Research Study 217, http://www.homeoffice.gov.uk/rds/pdfs/hors217.pdf

Brennan, M. (1994). Cross-examining children in criminal courts: child welfare under attack. In J. Gibbons (Ed.), *Language and the Law*. London: Longman, pp. 199–216.

Brennan, M. and Brennan, R. (1988). *Stranger Language*. Wagga Wagga, New South Wales, Australia: Riverina Murry Institute of Higher Education.

Brewin, C.R. and Holmes, E.A. (2003). Psychological theories of post-traumatic stress disorder. *Clinical Psychology Review*, **23**, 339–76.

Brewin, C.R., Andrews, B. and Rose, S. (2000). Fear, helplessness and horror in post-traumatic stress disorder: investigating DSM-IV criterion A2 in victims of violent crime. *Journal of Traumatic Stress*, **13** (3), 499–509.

Brewin, C.R., Andrews, B. and Valentine, J.D. (2000). Meta-analysis of risk factors for post-traumatic stress disorder in trauma-exposed adults. *Journal of Consulting and Clinical Psychology*, **68** (5), 748–66.

Brewin, C.R., Dalgleish, T. and Joseph, S. (1996). A dual representation theory of post-traumatic stress disorder. *Psychological Review*, **103** (4), 670–86.

British Psychological Society (1998). *Psychologists as Expert Witnesses*. Leicester: British Psychological Society.

British Psychological Society Working Party (2004). A review of the current scientific status and fields of application of polygraphic deception detection: final report (6 October, 2004). Leicester: British Psychological Society.

Broken Spirits Network (2004). Post-traumatic stress disorder http://www.brokenspirits.com/information/ptsd.asp

Brookes, D. (2003). Investigating child abuse on-line: the interactive approach. In A. MacVean and P. Spindler (Eds), *Policing Paedophiles on the Internet*. Bristol: New Police Bookshop, pp. 49–60.

Brown, B. (1995). *CCTV in Town Centres: Three Case Studies*. Crime Detection and Prevention Series Paper 68. London: Home Office.

Brown, C.M., Traverso, G. and Fedoroff, J.P. (1996). Masturbation prohibition in sex offenders: a crossover study. *Archives of Sexual Behavior*, **25** (4), 397–408.

Brown, R. and Kulik, J. (1977). Flashbulb memories. *Cognition*, **5**, 73–99.

Brown, S. (1999). Public attitudes to the treatment of sex offenders. *Legal and Criminological Psychology*, **4** (2), 239–5.

Browne, D. (1999). 'From the frying pan to the fire: exploring the role of foster care in the development of criminal behaviour'. Paper presented to the Joint International Conference, Dublin.

Browne, D. (2000). Foster care and forensic psychology. *Forensic Update*, **61**, 11–14.

Browne, K. (1999). 'Violence in the media causes crime: myth or reality?' Unpublished inaugural lecture, University of Birmingham, 3 June 1999.

Browne, K.D. and Pennell, A.E. (1998). *The Effects of Video Violence on Young Offenders*. Home Office Research and Statistics Directorate, Research Findings No. 65. London: Home Office.

Bruck, M. and Ceci, S.J. (1997). The suggestibility of young children. *Current Directions in Psychological Science*, **6** (3), 75–9.

Bruck, M., Ceci, S. and Hembrooke, H. (1998). Reliability and credibility of young children's reports: from research to policy and practice. *American Psychologist*, **53** (2), 136–51.

Bruck, M., Ceci, S.K., Francoeur, E. and Barr, R. (1995). 'I hardly cried when I got shot!' Influencing children's reports about a visit to their pediatrician. *Child Development*, **66**, 193–208.

Buck, J.A., Warren, A.R., Betman, S.I. and Brigham, J.C. (2002). Age differences in criterion-based content analysis scores in typical child sexual abuse interview. *Applied Developmental Psychology*, **23**, 267–83.

Budd, T. and Sharp, C. (2005). Offending in England and Wales: first results from the 2003 Crime and Justice Survey. Findings 244, Home Office.

Budd, T., Sharp, C. and Mayhew, P. (2005). Offending in England and Wales: first results from the 2003 crime and justice survey. Home Office Research Study 275. http://www.homeoffice.gov.uk/rds/pdfs05/hors275.pdf

Budin, L.E. and Johnson, C.F. (1989). Sex abuse prevention programs: offenders' attitudes about their efficacy. *Child Abuse and Neglect*, **13**, 77–87.

Bull, R. (1984). Psychology's contribution to policing. In D.J. Muller, D.E. Blackman and A.J. Chapman (Eds), *Psychology and Law*. Chichester: Wiley, pp. 409–23.

Bureau of Justice (2001a). Criminal offender statistics. http://www.ojp.usdoj.gov/bjs/crimoff.htm#lifetime/

Bureau of Justice (2001b). Characteristics of crime. http://www.ojp.usdoj.gov/bjs/cvict_c.htm#findings/

Bureau of Justice (2001c). Drug and crime facts, 1994. http://www.ojp.usdoj.gov/bjs/abstract/dcfacts.htm

Bureau of Justice (2001d). Intimate homicide. http://www.ojp.usdoj.gov/bjs/homicide/intimates.htm

Bureau of Justice (2001e). The odds of being a crime victim. http://nsi.org/Tips/odds.htm

Bureau of Justice (2004). Homicide trends in the US: Long term trends. http://www.ojp.usdoj.gov/bjs/homicide/tables/totalstab.htm

Bureau of Justice Statistics (2004a). Criminal Offenders Statistics. http://www.ojp.usdoj.gov/bjs/crimoff.htm#lifetime

Burgess, A.W., Hazelwood, R.R., Rokous, F.E., Hartman, C.R. and Burgess, A.G. (1988). Serial rapists and their victims: reenactment and repetition. *Human Sexual Aggression: Current Perspectives*, **528**, August 12, 277–95.

Burt, M. (1980). Cultural myths and support for rape. *Journal of Personality and Social Psychology*, **38**, 217–30.

Burton, A.M., Wilson, S., Cowan, M. and Bruce, V. (1999). Face recognition in poor quality video: evidence from security surveillance. *Psychological Science*, **10**, 243–8.

Butler-Sloss, E. (1988). *Report of the Inquiry into Child Abuse in Cleveland 1987*. London: Her Majesty's Stationery Office, Cm 412.

C

Calof, D.L. (1993). A Conversation With Pamela Freyd, Ph.D. Co-Founder and Executive Director, False Memory Syndrome Foundation, Inc., Part I. In *Treating Abuse Today*, Vol. III, No. 3. Retrieved 12 July 2001 from the World Wide Web: http://idealist.com/facts/v3n3-pfreyd.shtml

Canter, D. (1983). The potential of facet theory for applied social psychology. *Quality and Quantity*, **17**, 35–67.

Canter, D. (1995). Psychology of offender profiling. In R. Bull and D. Carson (Eds), *Handbook of Psychology in Legal Contexts*. Chichester: Wiley, pp. 343–55.

Canter, D. (2004). Offender profiling and investigative psychology. *Journal of Investigative Psychology and Offender Profiling*, **1**, 1–15.

Canter, D. and Alison, L. (1999). *Profiling in Policy and Practice*. Aldershot: Ashgate.

Canter, D. and Wentink, N. (2004). An empirical test of Holmes and Holmes's serial murder typology. *Criminal Justice and Behavior*, **31** (4), 489–515.

Canter, D.V., Bennell, C., Alison, L.J. and Reddy, S. (2003). Differentiating sex offences: a behaviorally based thematic classification of stranger rapes. *Behavioural Sciences and the Law*, **21**, 157–74.

Carrado, R. and Dempster, R. (Eds), *Psychology in the Courts: International Advances in Knowledge*, 317–29.

Carter, C.A., Bottom, B.L. and Levine, M. (1996). Linguistic and socioemotional influences on the accuracy of children's reports. *Law and Human Behavior*, **20**, 335–58.

Ceci, S.J. and Bruck, M. (1993). Suggestibility and the child witness: a historical review and synthesis. *Psychological Bulletin*, **113** (3), 403–39.

Ceci, S.L., Loftus, E.W., Leichtman, M. and Bruck, M. (1994). The role of source misattributions in the creation of false beliefs among preschoolers. *International Journal of Clinical and Experimental Hypnosis*, **62**, 304–20.

Cederborg, A.-C. (1999). The construction of children's credibility in judgements of child sexual abuse. *Acta Sociologica*, **42**, 147–58.

Centerwall, B.S. (1989). Exposure to television as a cause of violence. *Public Communication and Behavior*, **2**, 1–58.

Centerwall, B.S. (1993). Television and violent crime. *Public Interest*, **111**, 56–71.

Chermak, S.M. (1995). *Victims in the News: Crime and the American News Media*. Boulder, CO: Westview.

Cherryman, J., Bull, R. and Vrij, A. (2000). 'How police officers view confessions: is there still a confession culture?' European Conference on Psychology and Law, Cyprus, March 2000.

Christensen, J., Schmidt, K. and Henderson, J. (1982). The selling of the police: media, ideology and crime control. *Contemporary Crises*, **6**, 227–39.

Christianson, S-A., Karlsson, I. and Persson, L.G.W. (1998). Police personnel as eyewitnesses to a violent crime. *Legal and Criminological Psychology*, **3**, 59–72.

Clark, D. (1999). Risk assessment in prisons and probation. *Forensic Update*, **1**, 15–18.

Clark, J. (2004). Crime, fears and phobias. *Psychiatry, Psychology and Law*, **11** (1), 87–95.

Clifford, B.R. (1995). Psychology's premises, methods and values. In R. Bull and D. Carson (Eds), *Handbook of Psychology in Legal Contexts*. Chichester: John Wiley, pp. 13–28.

Clifford, B.R. and Richards, V.J. (1977). Comparison of recall by policemen and civilians under conditions of long and short durations of exposure. *Perceptual and Motor Skills*, **45**, 503–12.

Clifford, S.R. (1976). Police as eyewitnesses. *New Society*, **22**, 176–7.

Cloninger C.R., Christiansen, K.O., Reich, T. and Gottesman, I.I. (1978). Implications of sex differences in the prevalence of antisocial personality, alcoholism and criminality for familial transmission. *Archives of General Psychiatry*, **35**, 941–51.

Coates, L., Bavelas, J.B. and Gibson, J. (1994). Anomalous language in sexual assault trial judgements. *Discourse and Society*, **5** (2), 189–206.

Cohen, L.E. and Felson, M. (1979). Social change and crime rate trends: a routine activity approach. *American Sociological Review*, **44**, 588–608.

Cohen, S. (1972). *Folk Devils and Moral Panics*. London: McGibbon and Kee.

Cohen, S. (1980). *Folk Devils and Moral Panics*. Oxford: Basil Blackwell.

Coleman, A.M. (1995). Testifying in court as an expert witness. In *Professional Psychology Handbook*. Leicester: British Psychological Society Books.

Coleman, C. and Norris, C. (2000). *Introducing Criminology*. Cullompton, Devon: Willan Publishing.

Coleman, H. (1997). Gaps and silences: the culture and adolescent sex offenders. *Journal of Child and Youth Care*, **11** (1), 1–13.

Coles, E.M. (2004). Psychological support for the concept of psycholegal competencies. *International Journal of Law and Psychiatry*, **27**, 223–32.

Coles, E.M. and Veiel, H.O.F. (2001). Expert testimony and pseudoscience: how mental health professionals are taking over the courtroom. *International Journal of Law and Psychiatry*, **24**, 607–25.

Collett, M.E. and Kovera, M.B. (2003). The effects of British and American trial procedures on the quality of juror decision-making. *Law and Human Behavior*, **27** (4), 403–22.

Collins, J.J. and Bailey, S.L. (1990). Traumatic stress disorder and violent behaviour. *Journal of Traumatic Stress*, **3** (2), 203–20.

Colvin, M. (1993). *Negotiated Justice: A Closer Look at the Implications of Plea Bargains*. London: Justice.

Condron, M.K. and Nutter, D.E. (1988). A preliminary examination of the pornography experience of sex offenders, paraphiliac sexual dysfunction and controls. *Journal of Sex and Marital Therapy*, **14** (4), 285–98.

Connors, E., Lundregan, T., Miller, N. and McEwen, T. (1996). *Convicted by Juries, Exonerated by Science: Case Studies in the Use of DNA Evidence to Establish Innocence after Trial*. Washington, DC: National Institute of Justice Research Study.

Contemporary Justice Review (1998). The phenomenon of restorative justice. *Contemporary Justice Review*, **1** (1), 1–166.

Cook, D.J. and Philip, L. (1998). Comprehending the Scottish caution: do offenders understand their right to remain silent? *Legal and Criminological Psychology*, **3**, 13–27.

Cooper, S. (2005). Modifying sexual fantasies using behaviour therapy: A case study. *Forensic Update*, **80**, 17–22.

Cooper, V.G. and Zapf, P.A. (2003). Predictor variables in competency to stand trial decisions. *Law and Human Behavior*, **27** (4), 423–36.

Cornish, D. and Clarke, R.V.G. (Eds) (1986). *The Reasoning Criminal*. New York: Springer-Verlag.

Coulthard, M. (1994). Powerful evidence for the defence: an exercise in forensic discourse analysis. In J. Gibbons (Ed.), *Language and the Law*. London: Longman, pp. 414–17.

Coulthard, M. (1999). Forensic application of linguistic analysis. In D. Canter and L. Alison (Eds), *Interviewing and Deception*. Aldershot: Ashgate, pp. 107–25.

Court, J.H. (1977). Pornography and sex-crimes: a re-evaluation in the light of recent trends around the world. *International Journal of Criminality and Penology*, **5**, 129–57.

Court, J.H. (1984). Sex and violence: a ripple effect. In N.M. Malamuth and E. Donnerstein (Eds), *Pornography and Sexual Aggression*. Orlando, FL: Academic Press, 143–72.

Cox, V.C., Paulus, P.B. and McCain, G. (1984). Prison crowding research. The relevance for prison housing standards and a general approach regarding crowding phenomena. *American Psychologist*, **39** (100), 1148–60.

Craissati, J. and McClurg, G. (1997). The Challenge Project: a treatment program evaluation for perpetrators of child sexual abuse. *Child Abuse and Neglect*, **21** (7), 637–48.

Cramer, D. and Howitt, D. (1998). Romantic love and the psychology of sexual behaviour: open and closed secrets. In V.C. de Munck (Ed.), *Romantic Love and Sexual Behaviour: Perspectives from the Social Sciences*. Westport, CT: Praeger, pp. 113–32.

Crick, N.R. (1997). Engagement in gender normative versus non-normative forms of aggression: links to social-psychological adjustment. *Developmental Psychology*, **33** (4), 610–17.

Crick, N.R. and Bigbee, M.A. (1998). Relational and overt forms of peer victimization: a multi-informant approach. *Journal of Consulting and Clinical Psychology*, **66** (2), 337–47.

Crick, N.R., Casas, J.F. and Mosher, M. (1997). Relational and overt aggression in preschool. *Developmental Psychology*, **33** (4), 579–88.

Crits-Cristoph, P., Carroll, K., Perry, K., Luborsky, L., McLellan, A.T., Woody, G.E., Thompson, L., Gallagher, D. and Zitrin, C. (1991). Meta-analysis of therapist effects in psychotherapy outcome studies. *Psychotherapy Research*, **1**, 81–91.

Croall, H. (1998). *Crime and Society in Britain*. Harlow: Longman.

Croll, P. (1974). 'The deviant image'. Paper presented at British Sociological Association Mass Communication Study Group.

Crombag, H.F.M., Wagenaar, W.A. and Van Kopen, P.J. (1996). Crashing memories and the problem of source monitoring. *Applied Cognitive Psychology*, **10**, 95–104.

Cullen, F.T., Gendreau, P., Jarjoura, G.R. and Wright, J.P. (1997). Crime and the bell curve: lessons from intelligent criminology. *Crime and Delinquency*, **3** (4), 387–411.

Cumberbatch, G. and Howitt, D. (1989). *A Measure of Uncertainty*. London: Broadcasting Standards Council/John Libbey.

Curtis, G.C. (1963). *American Journal of Psychiatry*, **120**, 386.

Cutler, B.L. and Penrod, S.D. (1989). Forensically relevant moderators of the relation between eyewitness identification accuracy and confidence. *Journal of Applied Psychology*, **74**, 650–3.

Czerederecka, A. and Jaskiewicz-Obydzinska, T. (1996). The factors neutralizing developmental disorders in children from broken families. In G. Davies, S. Lloyd-Bostock, M. McMurran and C. Wilson (Eds), *Psychology, Law and Criminal Justice: International Developments in Research and Practice*. Berlin: Walter de Gruyter, pp. 240–7.

D

Dabbs, J.M., Alford, E.C. and Fielden, J.A. (1998). Trial lawyers and testosterone: blue-collar talent in a white-collar world. *Journal of Applied Social Psychology*, **28** (1), 84–9.

Dahle, K.-P. (1999). 'Serious violent crime and offending trajectories in the course of life: an empirical lifespan development of criminal careers'. Paper presented at joint meeting of American Psychology-Law Society and European Association of Psychology and Law, Dublin.

Dale, A., Davies, A. and Wei, L. (1997). Developing a typology of rapists' speech. *Journal of Pragmatics*, **27**, 653–69.

Daleiden, E.L., Kaufman, K.L., Hilliker, D.R. and O'Neil, J.N. (1998). The sexual histories and fantasies of youthful males: a comparison of sexual offending, nonsexual offending, and nonoffending groups. *Sexual Abuse: Journal of Research and Treatment*, **10** (3), 19–209.

Daly, M. and Wilson, M. (1988). *Homicide*. New York: Aldine de Gruyter.

Davies, A. (1997). Specific profile analysis: a data-based approach to offender profiling. In J.L. Jackson and D.A. Bekerian (Eds), *Offender Profiling*. Chichester: Wiley, 191–207.

Davies, F.J. (1952). Crime news in Colorado newspapers. *American Journal of Sociology*, **57**, 325–30.

Davies, G. (2003). CCTV: identification in court and in the laboratory. *Forensic Update*, **72** (January), 7–10.

Davies, G. and Noon, E. (1993). Video links: their impact on child witness trials. In N.K. Clark and G.M. Stephenson (Eds), *Issues in Criminological and Legal Psychology 20: Children, Evidence and Procedure*. Leicester: Division of Criminological and Legal Psychology, British Psychological Society, pp. 22–6.

Davies, G. and Thasen, S. (2000). Closed-circuit television: how effective an identification aid? *British Journal of Psychology*, **91**, 411–26.

Day, D.M. and Page, S. (1986). Portrayal of mental illness in Canadian newspapers. *Canadian Journal of Psychiatry*, **31**, 813–16.

DCLP Training Committee (1994). The core knowledge and skills of the Chartered Forensic Psychologists. *Forensic Update*, **38**, 8–11.

De Riviera, J. (1997). The construction of false memory syndrome: the experience of retractors. *Psychological Inquiry*, **8**, 271–92.

Degenhardt, L., Conroy, E., Gilmour, S. and Collins, L. (2005). The effect of a reduction in heroin supply in Australia upon drug distribution and acquisitive crime. *British Journal of Criminology*, **45**, 2–24.

Dernevik, M., Johansson, S. and Grann, M. (2000). 'Prediction of violent behaviour in mentally disordered offenders in forensic psychiatric care'. Paper presented at European Association of Psychology and Law Conference, Cyprus.

Ditton, J., Chadee, D., Farrall, S., Gilchrist, E. and Bannister, J. (2004). From imitation to intimidation: a note on the curious and changing relationship between the media, crime and fear of crime. *British Journal of Criminology*, **44**, 595–610.

Dobash, R.P. and Dobash, R.E. (2004). Women's violence to men in intimate relationships: working on a puzzle. *British Journal of Criminology*, **44**, 324–49.

Docherty, D. (1990). *Violence in Television Fiction*. London: Libbey/Broadcasting Standards Council.

Doerner, W.G. and Ho, T.P. (1994). 'Shoot/Don't shoot': police use of deadly force under simulated field conditions. *Journal of Crime and Justice*, **17** (2), 49–68.

Doley, R. (2003). Pyromania: fact or fiction? *British Journal of Criminology*, **43**, 797–807.

Doob, A.N. and Kirkenbaum, H.M. (1973). Bias in police line-ups – partial remembering. *Journal of Police Science and Administration*, **1** (3), 287–93.

Douglas, J.E. and Olshaker, M. (1995). *Mind Hunter: Inside the FBI's Elite Serial Crime Unit*. New York: Pocket Books.

Douglas, J.E. and Olshaker, M. (1997). *Journey into Darkness*. New York: Pocket Star.

Douglas, J.E., Burgess, A.W., Burgess, A.G. and Ressler, R.K. (1992). *Crime Classification Manual*. New York: Lexington.

Douglas, K.S., Cox, D.N. and Webster, C.D. (1999). Violence risk assessment: science and practice. *Legal and Criminological Psychology*, **4**, 149–84.

Dowden, C. and Brown, S.L. (2002). The role of substance abuse factors in predicting recidivism: a meta-analysis. *Psychology, Crime and Law*, **8** (3), 243–64.

Drake, R.D., Ward, T., Nathan, P. and Lee, J.K.P. (2001). Challenging the cognitive distortions of child molesters: an implicit theory approach. *Journal of Sexual Aggression*, **7** (1), 25–40.

Driver, E. (1989). Introduction. In E. Driver and A. Droisen (Eds), *Child Sexual Abuse: Feminist Perspectives*. London: Macmillan.

Dunning, D. and Perretta, S. (2002). Automaticity and eyewitness accuracy: A 10- to 12-second rule for distinguishing accurate from inaccurate positive identifications. *Journal of Applied Psychology*, **87**, 951–62.

Dunning, D. and Stern, L.B. (1994). Distinguishing accurate from inaccurate eyewitness identifications via inquiries about decision processes. *Journal of Personality and Social Psychology*, **67**, 818–35.

Dutton, D.G., Bodnarchuk, M., Kropp, R. and Hart, S.D. (1997). Wife assault treatment and criminal recidivism: an 11-year follow-up. *International Journal of Offender Therapy and Comparative Criminology*, **4** (1), 9–23.

E

East, W.N. and Huber, W.H. de B. (1939). *Report on the Psychological Treatment of Crime*. London: HMSO.

Eastman, N. (2000). Psycho-legal studies as an interface discipline. In J. McGuire, T. Mason and A. O'Kane (Eds), *Behaviour, Crime and Legal Processes: A Guide for Forensic Practitioners*. Chichester: John Wiley, pp. 83–110.

Ebbesen, E.B. and Konecni, V.J. (1997). Eyewitness memory research: probative v. prejudicial value. *Expert Evidence*, **5** (Nos 1 and 2), 2–28.

Ebbinghaus, H. (1913). *Grundzuge der psychologie*. Leipzig: Von Veit.

Edwards, D.A. (1969). Early androgen stimulation and aggressive behavior in male and female mice. *Physiology and Behavior*, **4**, 333–8.

Edwards, D.A. and Herndon, J. (1970). Neonatal estrogen stimulation and aggressive behavior in female mice. *Physiology and Behavior*, **4**, 993–5.

Edwards, E. (2004). An ambiguous participant: the crime victim and criminal justice decision-making. *British Journal of Criminology*, **44**, 967–82.

Egg, R. (1999). 'Criminal careers of sex offenders'. Paper presented at Psychology and Law International Conference, Dublin, 7 July.

Ehrlich, S. (1999). Communities of practice, gender, and the representation of sexual assault. *Language in Society*, **28** (2), 239–56.

Eigen, J.P. (2004). Delusion's odyssey: charting the course of Victorian forensic psychiatry. *International Journal of Law and Psychiatry*, **27**, 395–412.

Eisen, M.L., Goodman, G.S., Qin, J. and Davis, S. (1998). Memory and suggestibility in maltreated children: new research relevant to evaluating allegations of abuse. In S.L. Lynn and K. McConkey (Eds), *Truth in Memory*. New York: Guilford, pp. 163–89.

Ekman, P. (1992). *Telling Lies: Clues to Deceit in the Marketplace, Politics, and Marriage*. New York: Norton.

Ekman, P. (1996). Why don't we catch liars? *Social Research*, **63** (3), 801–17.

Ekman, P., O'Sullivan, M. and Frank, M.G. (1999). A few can catch a liar. *Psychological Science*, **10** (3), 263–5.

Elaad, E. (1990). Detection of guilty knowledge in real-life criminal invesigations. *Journal of Applied Psychology*, **75** (5), 521–9.

Elaad, E., Ginton, A. and Jungman, N. (1992). Detection measures in real-life criminal guilty knowledge tests. *Journal of Applied Psychology*, **77** (5), 757–67.

Elbogen, E.B., Patry, M. and Scalora, M.J. (2003). The impact of community notification laws on sex offender treatment attitudes. *International Journal of Law and Psychiatry*, **26**, 207–19.

Ellingworth, D., Hope, T., Osborn, D.R., Trickett, A. and Pease, K. (1997). Prior victimisation and crime risk. *International Journal of Risk, Security and Crime Prevention*, **2** (3), 201–14.

Ellis, L. (1989). *Theories of Rape: Inquiries into the Causes of Sexual Aggresssion*. New York: Hemisphere.

Emerson, R.M., Ferris, K.O. and Gardner, C.B. (1998). On being stalked. *Social Problems*, **45** (3), 289–314.

Epps, K. (1995). Sexually abusive behaviour in an adolescent boy with the 48, XXYY syndrome: a case study. In N.K. Clark and G.M. Stephenson (Eds), *Investigative and Forensic Decision Making, Issues in Criminological and Legal Psychology No. 26*. Leicester: Division of Criminological and Legal Psychology, British Psychological Society, pp. 3–11.

Erickson, W.D., Walback, N.H. and Seely, R.K. (1988). Behavior patterns of child molesters. *Archives of Sexual Behavior*, **17** (1), 77–86.

Erikson, M. and Friendship, C. (2002). A typology of child abduction events. *Legal and Criminological Psychology*, **7**, 115–20.

Eron, L.D. (1963). Relationship of TV viewing habits and aggressive behavior in children. *Journal of Abnormal and Social Psychology*, **67**, 193–6.

Eron, L.D., Lefkowitz, M.M., Huesmann, L.R. and Walder, L.O. (1972). Does television violence cause aggresssion? *American Psychologist*, **27**, 253–63.

Evans, J.R. and Claycomb, S. (1998). 'Abnormal QEEG patterns associated with dissociation and violence'. Unpublished manuscript, University of South Carolina. Annual Meeting of the Society for the Study of Neuronal Regulation, Austin, Texas.

Everson, M.D. and Boat, B.W. (2002). The utility of anatomical dolls and drawings in child forensic interviews. In M.L. Eisen, J.A. Quas and G.S. Goodman (Eds), *Memory and Suggestibility in the Forensic Interview*. Mahwah, New Jersey: Lawrence Erlbaum, 383–408.

Eysenck, H.J. (1973). *The Inequality of Man*. London: Maurice Temple Smith.

Eysenck, H.J. (1980). *The Causes and Effects of Smoking*. London: Sage.

Eysenck, H.J. (1990). *Check Your Own IQ*. London: Penguin.

Eysenck, H.J. and Nias, D.K. (1978). *Sex, Violence and the Media*. London: Maurice Temple Smith.

F

Falshaw, L., Friendship, C. and Bates, A. (2003). Sexual offenders – measuring reconviction, reoffending and recidivism. Findings 183. Home Office, Research, Development and Statistics Directorate. London. http://www.homeoffice.gov.uk/rds/pdf

Farrall, S. and Gadd, D. (2004). The frequency of fear of crime. *British Journal of Criminology*, **44**, 127–32.

Farrington, D. (1998). Developmental crime prevention initiatives in 1997. *Forensic Update*, **54**, 19–25.

Farrington, D. (1999). 21 years of the DCLP. *Forensic Update*, **56**, 21–37.

Farrington, D. and Lambert, S. (1997). Predicting offender profiles from victim and witness descriptions. In J.L. Jackson and D.A. Bekerian (Eds), *Offender Profiling: Theory, Research and Practice*. Chichester: John Wiley, pp. 133–58.

Farrington, D.P. (1979). Experiments on deviance with special reference to dishonesty. In L. Berkowitz (Ed.), *Advances in Experimental Social Psychology, No. 12*. New York: Academic Press, pp. 207–53.

Farrington, D.P. (1987). Epidemiology. In H.C. Quay (Ed.), *Handbook of Juvenile Delinquency*. Chichester: Wiley, pp. 33–61.

Farrington, D.P. (1990). Age, period, cohort, and offending. In D.M. Gottfredson and R.V. Clarke (Eds), *Policy and Theory in Criminal Justice: Contributions in Honour of Leslie T. Wilkins*. Aldershot: Avebury, pp. 51–75.

Farrington, D.P. (1995). The psychology of crime: influences and constraints on offending. In R. Bull and D. Carson (Eds), *Handbook of Psychology in Legal Contexts*. Chichester: John Wiley, pp. 291–314.

Farrington, D.P. (1996). Psychosocial influences on the development of antisocial personality. In G. Davies, S. Lloyd-Bostock, M. McMurran and C. Wilson (Eds), *Psychology, Law and Criminal Justice: International Developments in Research and Practice*. Berlin: Walter de Gruyter, pp. 424–44.

Farrington, D.P. and Kidd, R.F. (1977). Is financial dishonesty a rational decision? *British Journal of Social and Clinical Psychology*, **16**, 139–46.

Farrington, D.P., Barnes, G.C. and Lambert, S. (1996). The concentration of offending in families. *Legal and Criminological Psychology*, **1** (1), 47–63.

Farrington, D.P., Langan, P.A. and Tonry, M. (Eds) (2004). *Cross-National Studies in Crime and Justice*. Washington: US Department of Justice.

FBI (2001) Uniform crime statistics. http://www.fbi.gov/ucr/Cius_99/99crime/99c2_04.pdf

Felson, R.B. (1996). Mass media effects on violent behavior. *Annual Review of Sociology*, **22**, 102–28.

Fenichel, O. (1933). Outline of clinical psychoanalysis. *Psychoanalytic Quarterly*, **2**, 562–91.

Ferguson, C.J., White, D.E., Stacey, C., Lorenz, M. and aBhimani, A. (2003). Defining and classifying serial murder in the context of perpetrator motivation. *Journal of Criminal Justice*, **31** (3), 287–92.

Fine, C. and Kennett, J. (2004). Mental impairment, moral understanding and criminal responsibility: psychopathy and the purposes of punishment. *International Journal of Law and Psychiatry*, **27**, 425–43.

Finkelhor, D. (1984). *Child Sexual Abuse: New Theory and Research*. New York: Free Press.

Finlayson, L.M. and Koocher, G.P. (1991). Professional judgement and child abuse reporting in sexual abuse cases. *Professional Psychology: Research and Practice*, **22**, 464–72.

Firestone, P., Bradford, J.M., McCoy, M., Greenberg, D.M., Curry, S. and Larose, M.R. (1998a). Recidivism in convicted rapists. *Journal of American Academy Psychiatry and Law*, **26** (2), 185–200.

Firestone, P., Bradford, J.M., Greenberg, D.M., Larose, M.R. and Curry, S. (1998b). Homicidal and nonhomicidal child molesters: psychological, phallometric and criminal features. *Sexual Abuse: A Journal of Research and Treatment*, **10** (4), 305–23.

Fisher, D. and Beech, A.R. (1999). Current practice in Britain with sexual offenders. *Journal of Interpersonal Violence*, **14** (3), 240–56.

Fisher, D. and Thornton, D. (1993). Assessing risk of re-offending in sexual offenders. *Journal of Mental Health*, **2**, 105–17.

Fisher, R.P. and Geiselman, R.W. (1992). *Memory Enhancing Techniques for Investigative Interviewing: The Cognitive Interview*. Springfield: Charles C. Thomas.

Fisher, R.P., Brennan, K.H. and McCauley, M.R. (2002). The cognitive interview method to enhance eyewitness recall. In M.L. Eisen, J.A. Quas and G.S. Goodman (Eds), *Memory and*

Suggestibility in the Forensic Interview. Lawrence Erlbaum Associates: Mahwah, New Jersey, pp. 265–86.

Fitzgerald, P. and Seeman, M.V. (2002). Erotomania in women. In J. Boon and L. Sheridan (Eds) *Stalking and Psychosexual Obsession: Psychological Perpsectives for Prevention, Policing and Treatment*. Chichester: John Wiley, pp. 165–80.

Fitzmaurice, C., Rogers, D. and Stanley, P. (1996). Predicting court sentences: a perilous exercise. In G. Davies, S. Lloyd-Bostock, M. McMurran and C. Wilson (Eds), *Psychology, Law and Criminal Justice: International Developments in Research and Practice*. Berlin: Walter de Gruyter.

Fowles, J. (1999). *The Case for Television Violence*. Thousand Oaks, CA: Sage.

Fox, C. and Rirke, R. (2002). Forecasting trial outcomes: lawyers assign higher probability to possibilities that are described in greater detail. *Law and Human Behavior*, 26 (2), 159–73.

Fox, J.A. and Zawitz, M.W. (2004). Homicide trends in the United States. US Bureau of Justice. http://www.ojp.usdoj.gov/bjs/homicide/homtrnd.htm

Freyd, J.J. (1996). *Betrayal Trauma: The Logic of Forgetting Childhood Abuse*. Cambridge, MA: Harvard University Press.

Friedrich, W.N. (undated). *Psychological Assessment Resources*. PO Box 998, Odessa, Florida FL33556.

Friedrich, W.N., Grambach, P., Damon, L., Hewitt, S.K., Koverola, C., Lang, R.A., Wolfe, V. and Broughton, D. (1992). Child sexual behavior inventory: normative and clinical comparisons. *Psychological Assessment*, 4 (3), 303–11.

Frowd, C.D., Carson, D., Ness, H., McQuiston-Surrett, D., Richardson, J., Baldwin, H. and Hancock, P. (2004). 'Contemporary composite techniques: the impact of forensically-relevant target delay'. Paper presented at XIV conference of the European European Association of Psychology and Law, Krakow, Poland.

Frowd, C.D., Carson, D., Ness, H., Richardson, J., Morrison, L., McLanaghan, S. and Hancock, P.J.B. (2005). A forensically valid comparison of facial composite systems. *Psychology, Crime and Law*, 11 (1), 35–52.

Fulero, S.M. and Penrod, S. (1990). The myths and realities of attorney jury selection and folklore and scientific jury selection: what works? *Ohio Northern University Law Review*, 17, 339–53.

Fullerton, R.A. and Punj, G.N. (2004). Shoplifting as moral insanity: historical perspectives on kleptomania. *Journal of Macromarketing*, 24 (1), 8–16.

G   Gacono, C.B., Meloy, J.R., Speth, E. and Roske, A. (1997). Above the law: escapees from a maximum security forensic hospital and psychopathy. *Journal of American Academy of Psychiatry and the Law*, 25 (4), 547–50.

Gagliardi, G.J., Lovell, D., Peterson, P.D. and Jemelka, R. (2004). Forecasting recidivism in mentally ill offenders released from prison. *Law and Human Behavior*, 28 (2), 133–55.

Galen, B.R. and Underwood, M.K. (1997). A developmental investigation of social aggression among children. *Developmental Psychology*, 33 (4), 589–600.

Garrido, E. and Masip, J. (1999). How good are police officers at spotting lies? *Forensic Update*, 58, 14–20.

Geiselman, R.E., Fisher, R.P., Firstenberg, I., Hutton, L.A., Sullivan, S., Avetissian, I. and Prosk, A. (1984). Enhancement of eyewitness memory: an empirical evaluation of the cognitive interview. *Journal of Police Science and Administration*, 121, 74–80.

Gelles, R.J. (1979). *Family Violence*. Beverly Hills, CA: Sage.

Gelles, R.J. and Cornell, C. (1985). *Intimate Violence in Families*. Beverly Hills, CA: Sage.

Gelles, R.J. and Straus, M.A. (1979). Determinants of violence: Towards a theoretical integration. In W. Burr, R. Hill, I. Nyer and I. Reiss (Eds), *Contemporary Theories About the Family*. New York: Free Press, pp. 549–81.

Gentry, C.S. (1991). Pornography and rape: an empirical analysis. *Deviant Behaviour*, 12 (3), 277–88.

Gerbner, G. (1972). Violence in television drama: trends and symbolic functions. In G.A. Comstock and E.A. Rubenstein (Eds), *Television and Social Behaviour, Vol. 1: Media Content and Control*. Washington, DC: US Government Printing Office, pp. 28–187.

Gerbner, G., Gross, L., Eley, M.E., Jackson Breek, M., Jeffries-Fox, S. and Signorielli, N. (1977). Television violence profile, No. 8. *Journal of Communication*, **27**, 171–80.

Ghubash, R. and El-Rufaie, O. (1997). Psychiatric morbidity among sentenced male prisoners in Dubai: transcultural perspectives. *Journal of Forensic Psychiatry*, **8** (2), 440–6.

Gierowski, J.F., Jaskiewicz-Obydzinska, T. and Slawik, M. (1998). 'The planning of a criminal act as a fundamental aspect of psychological profiling – its relation to the personality, motivation and modus operandi of a perpetrator'. 8th European Conference on Psychology and Law, Krakow, Institute of Forensic Research, Westerplatte 9, 31–033 Krakow, 2–5 September 1998.

Gierowski, J.F., Jaskiewicz-Obydzinska, T. and Slawik, M. (2000). The planning of a criminal act as a fundamental aspect of psychological profiling – its relation to the personality, motivation and modus operandi of a perpetrator. In A. Czerederecka, T. Jaskiewicz-Obdzinska and J. Wojcikiewicz (Eds), *Forensic Psychology and Law: Traditional Questions and New Ideas*. Krakow: Institute of Forensic Research Publishers, pp. 88–94.

Gilchrist, E., Bannister, J., Ditton, J. and Farrall, S. (1998). Women and the 'fear of crime'. *British Journal of Criminology*, **38** (2), 283–98.

Gilligan, C. (1982). *In a Different Voice: Psychological Theory and Women's Development*. Cambridge, MA: Harvard University Press.

Gina, R. and Sloore, H. (2004). Are recidivists psychopaths? Krakow, EAPL conference.

Glover, N. (1999). *Risk Assessment and Community Care in England and Wales*. Liverpool: Faculty of Law, University of Liverpool.

Glueck, S. and Glueck, E. (1962). *Family Environment and Delinquency*. London: Routledge and Kegan Paul.

Glueck, S. and Glueck, E. (1968). *Delinquents and Nondelinquents in Perspective*. Cambridge, MA: Harvard University Press.

Goncalves, R.A. (1998). Correctional treatment in Portugal. In J. Boros, I. Munnich and M. Szegedi (Eds), *Psychology and Criminal Justice: International Review of Theory and Practice*. Berlin: de Gruyter, pp. 327–31.

Gordon, B.N., Schroeder, C.S. and Abrams, J.M. (1990a). Age and social-class differences in children's knowledge of sexuality. *Journal of Clinical Child Psychology*, **19**, 33–43.

Gordon, B.N., Schroeder, C.S. and Abrams, J.M. (1990b). Children's knowledge of sexuality: a comparison of sexually abused and nonabused children. *American Journal of Orthopsychiatry*, **60**, 250–7.

Gordon, H., Oyebode, O. and Minne, C. (1997). Death by homicide in special hospitals. *Journal of Forensic Psychiatry*, **8** (3), 602–19.

Gossop, M., Marsden, J., Stewart, D. and Kidd, T. (2003). The National Treatment Outcome Research Study (NTORS): 4–5 year follow-up results. Addiction 98, 291–303.

Gottfredson, D.M. and Gottfredson, S.D. (1988). Stakes and risks in the prediction of violent criminal behavior. *Violence and Victims*, **3** (4), 247–62.

Graber, D.A. (1980). *Crime News and the Public*. New York: Praeger.

Granhag, P.A., Andersson, L.O., Stromwall, L.A. and Hartwig, M. (2004). Imprisoned knowledge: criminals beliefs about deception. *Legal and Criminological Psychology*, **9**, 103–19.

Graves, R.B., Openshaw, D.K., Ascione, F.R. and Ericksen, S.L. (1996). Demographic and parental characteristics of youthful sexual offenders. *International Journal of Offender Therapy and Comparative Criminology*, **40** (4), 300–17.

Green, D.P., Glaser, J. and Rich, A. (1998a). From lynching to gay bashing: the elusive connection between economic conditions and hate crime. *Journal of Personality and Social Psychology*, **75** (1), 82–92.

Green, D.P., Strolovitch, D.Z. and Wong, J.S. (1998b). Defended neighborhoods, integration and racially motivated crime. *American Journal of Sociology*, **104** (2), 372–403.

Greenberg, M.S. and Beach, S.R. (2001). The role of social influence in crime victim's decision to notify the police. In R. Roesch, R.R. Carrado, and R. Dempster (Eds), *Psychology in the Courts: International Advances in Knowledge*, pp. 305–16.

Greenberg, M.S. and Beach, S.R. (2004). Property crime victims' decision to notify the police: social, cognitive and affective determinants. *Law and Human Behavior*, 28 (2), 177–86.

Gregg, V., Gibbs, J.C. and Basinger, K.S. (1994). Patterns of developmental delay in moral judgement by male and female delinquents. *Merrill-Palmer Quarterly*, **40**, 538–53.

Gresnigt, J.A.M., Breteler, M.H.M., Schippers, G.M. and Van den Hurk, A.A. (2000). Predicting violent crime among drug-using inmates: the addiction severity index as a prediction instrument. *Legal and Criminological Psychology*, **5**, 85–95.

Gresswell, D.M. and Hollin, C.R. (1994). Multiple murder: a review. *British Journal of Criminology*, **34**, 1–14.

Gresswell, D.M. and Hollin, C.R. (1997). Addictions and multiple murder: a behavioural perspective. In J.E. Hodge, M. McMurran and C.R. Hollin (Eds), *Addicted to Crime?* Chichester: Wiley.

Gretenkord, L. (1991). *Prediction of Illegal Behaviour of Mentally Ill Offenders*. Proceedings of the 17th International Congress of the International Academy of Law and Mental Health, Leuven, Belgium, May.

Gretenkord, L. (1993). 'Actuarial versus clinical versus political prediction'. Paper presented at XIX Internal Congress of the International Academy of Law and Mental Health, Lisbon, Portugal, June.

Gretenkord, L. (2000). 'How to use empirical findings for the prognosis of mentally disordered offenders'. Paper presented at the 10th European Conference of Psychology and Law, Limassol, Cyprus.

Greuel, L., Brietzke, S. and Stadle, M.A. (1999). 'Credibility assessment: new research perspectives'. Joint International Conference on Psychology and Law, Dublin, 6–9 July.

Grey, N. (2002). The psychological impact of offending on a victim of physical assault: a case of chronic post-traumatic stress disorder. In L. Fanshaw (Ed.), *Issues in Forensic Psychology*. British Psychological Society: Leicester, pp. 9–19.

Griffith, J.D., Libkuman, T.M. and Poole, D.A. (1998). Repressed memories: the effects of expert testimony on mock jurors' decision making. *American Journal of Forensic Psychology*, **16** (1), 5–23.

Groscup, J., Penrod, S., Studebaker, C., Huss, M. and O'Neil, K. (2002). The effects of *Daubert v. Merrell Dow Pharmaceuticals* on the admissibility of expert testimony in state and federal criminal cases. *Psychology, Public Policy and Law*, 8, 339–72.

Gross, B.H., Southard, M.J., Lamb, R. and Weinberger, L.E. (1987). Assessing dangerousness and responding appropriately. *Journal of Clinical Psychiatry*, 48 (1), 9–12.

Groth, A.N. and Birnbaum, H.J. (1978). Adult sexual orientation and attraction to underage persons. *Archives of Sexual Behavior*, 7 (3), 175–81.

Groth, A.N. and Burgess, A.W. (1978). Rape: a pseudo-sexual act. *International Journal of Women's Studies*, **1** (2), 207–10.

Groth, A.N., Burgess, A.W. and Holmstrom, L.L. (1977). Rape, power, anger and sexuality. *American Journal of Psychiatry*, **134**, 1239–48.

Grover, C. and Soothill, K. (1999). British serial killing: towards a structural explanation. *British Criminology Conferences: Selected Proceedings*, Vol. 2. http://www.lboro.ac.uk/departments/ss/BSC.bccsp/vol02/08GROVE.HTM

Grubin, D. (1996a). *Fitness to Plead in England and Wales*. Hove: Psychology Press.

Grubin, D. (1996b). Silence in court: psychiatry and the Criminal Justice and Public Order Act 1994. *Journal of Forensic Psychiatry*, 7 (3), 647–52.

Grubin, D. and Madsen, L. (2005/In press). Lie detection and the polygraph: a historical review. *British Journal of Forensic Psychiatry and Psychology*.

Grubin, D., Madsen, L., Parsons, S., Sosnowki, D. and Warberg, B. (2004). A prospective study of the impact of polygraphy on high risk behaviors in adult sex offenders. *Sexual Abuse: A Journal of Research and Treatment*, 16, 209–22.

Gudjonsson, G.H. (1984). A new scale of interrogative suggestibility. *Personality and Individual Differences*, 5, 303–14.

Gudjonsson, G.H. (1992). *The Psychology of Interrogations, Confessions and Testimony.* Chichester: Wiley.

Gudjonsson, G.H. (1996). Forensic psychology in England: one practitioner's experience and viewpoint. *Legal and Criminological Psychology*, 1, 131–42.

Gudjonsson, G.H. (2003). *The Psychology of Interrogations and Confessions: A Handbook.* Chichester: Wiley.

Gudjonsson, G.H. and Copson, G. (1997). The role of the expert in criminal investigation. In J.L. Jackson and D.A. Bekerian (Eds), *Offender Profiling: Theory, Research and Practice.* Chichester: John Wiley, pp. 61–76.

Gudjonsson, G.H. and Haward, L.R.C. (1998). *Forensic Psychology: A Guide to Practice.* London: Routledge.

Gudjonsson, G.H., Murphy, G.H. and Clare, I.C.H. (2000). Assessing the capacity of people with intellectual disabilities to be witnesses in court. *Psychological Medicine*, 30 (2), 307–14.

Gunter, B. (1987). *Television and the Fear of Crime.* London: John Libbey.

Guthrie, R.V. (1998). *Even the Rat was White: A Historical View of Psychology*, 2nd edn. Boston: Allyn and Bacon.

H

Haapasalo, J. (1999). 'Sons in prison and their mothers: is there a relationship between childhood histories of physical abuse?' Dublin conference, Dublin, Ireland, 6–9 July.

Haapasalo, J. and Aaltonen, T. (1999). Child abuse potential: how persistent? *Journal of Interpersonal Violence*, 14 (6), 571–85.

Haapasalo, J. and Kankkonen, M. (1997). Self-reported childhood abuse among sex and violent offenders. *Archives of Sexual Behavior*, 26 (4), 421–31.

Haapasalo, J. and Pokela, E. (1999). Child-rearing and child abuse antecedents of criminality. *Aggression and Violent Behavior*, 4 (1), 107–27.

Haapasalo, J. and Tremblay, R.E. (1994). Physically aggressive boys from ages 6 to 12: family background, parenting behavior, and prediction of delinquency. *Journal of Consulting and Clinical Psychology*, 62 (5), 104–52.

Haapasalo, J., Puupponen, M. and Crittenden, P.M. (1999). Victim to victimizer: the psychology of isomorphism in the case of a recidivist pedophile in Finland. *Journal of Child Sexual Abuse*, 7 (3), 97–115.

Hagell, A. and Newburn, T. (1994). *Young Offenders and the Media: Viewing Habits and Preferences.* London: Policy Studies Institute.

Haggård, U. (2000). 'Against all odds – a qualitative follow-up study of high-risk violent criminals that were not reconvicted'. Paper presented at the European Association of Psychology and Law Conference, Limassol, Cyprus.

Haggård, U., Gumpert, H.C. and Grann, M. (2001). Against all odds – a qualitative follow-up study of high-risk violent offenders who were not reconvicted. *Journal of Interpersonal Violence*, 16, 1048–65.

Häkkänen, H. and Laajasal, T. (In press). Homicide crime scene actions in a Finnish sample of mentally ill offenders. Homicide Studies.

Häkkänen, H., Lindlof, P. and Santtila, P. (2004). Crime scene actions and offender characteristics in a sample of Finnish stranger rapes. *Journal of Investigative Psychology and Offender Profiling*, 1, 17–32.

Hall, G.C., Shondrick, D.D. and Hirschman, R. (1993). The role of sexual arousal in sexually aggressive behavior: a meta-analysis. *Journal of Consulting and Clinical Psychology*, 61 (6), 1091–5.

Hall, G.C.N. (1995). Sexual offender recidivism revisited: a meta-analysis of recent treatment studies. *Journal of Consulting and Clinical Psychology*, 63 (5), 802–9.

Hall, G.C.N. and Barongan, C. (1997). Prevention of sexual aggression: sociocultural risk and protective factors. *American Psychologist*, 52 (1), 5–14.

Hall, G.C.N. and Hirschman, R. (1991). Toward a theory of sexual aggression: a quadripartite model. *Journal of Consulting and Clinical Psychology*, **59**, 662–9.

Hall, G.C.N., Hirschman, R. and Oliver, L.L. (1995). Sexual arousal and arousability to pedophilic stimuli in a community sample of normal men. *Behavior Therapy*, **26**, 681–94.

Hall, S., Crilcher, C., Jefferson, T., Clarke, J. and Roberts, B. (1978). *Policing the Crisis: Mugging, the State and Law and Order*. London: Macmillan.

Haller, J.S. and Haller, R.N. (1974). *The Physician and Sexuality in Victorian America*. Urbana, IL: University of Illinois Press.

Halloran, J.D., Brown, R.L. and Chaney, D.C. (1970). *Television and Delinquency*. Leicester: Leicester University Press.

Halverson, K. (1991). Olson on literacy. *Language in Society*, **20**, 619–40.

Hanks, H., Hobbs, C. and Wynne, J. (1988). Early signs and recognition of sexual abuse in the pre-school child. In K. Browne, C. Davies and P. Stratton (Eds), *Early Prediction and Prevention of Child Abuse*. Chichester: Wiley.

Hanson, R. and Bussiere, M. (1998). Predicting relapse: a meta-analysis of sexual offender recidivism studies. *Journal of Consulting and Clinical Psychology*, **66**, 348–64.

Hanson, R.K. and Slater, S. (1988). Sexual victimization in the history of sexual abusers: a review. *Annals of Sex Research*, **1**, 485–99.

Hanson, R.K., Gordon, A., Harris, A.J.R., Marques, J.K., Murphy, W., Quinsey V.L. and Seto M.C. (2002). First report of the collaborative outcome data project on the effectiveness of psychological treatment for sex offenders. *Sexual Abuse: A Journal of Research and Treatment*, **14** (2), 169–94.

Hare, R.D. (1980). A research scale for the assessment of psychopathy in criminal populations. *Personality and Individual Differences*, **1**, 111–19.

Hare, R.D. (1991). *The Hare Psychopathy Checklist – Revised*. Toronto: Multi-Health Systems.

Hare, R.D. (1998). The Hare PCL-R: some issues concerning its use and misuse. *Legal and Criminological Psychology*, **3**, 99–119.

Harris, G.T. and Rice, M.E. (1994). The violent patient. In R.T. Ammerman and M. Hersen (Eds), *Handbook of Prescriptive Treatments for Adults*. New York: Plenum, pp. 463–86.

Harris, G.T. and Rice, M.E. (1997). Risk appraisal and management of violent behaviour. *Psychiatric Services*, **48** (9), 1168–76.

Harris, G.T., Rice, M.E. and Quinsey, V.L. (1993). Violent recidivism of mentally disordered offenders: the development of a statistical prediction instrument. *Criminal Justice and Behavior*, **20** (4), 315–35.

Harris, S. (1994). Ideological exchanges in a British magistrates court. In J. Gibbons (Ed.), *Language and the Law*. London: Longman, pp. 156–70.

Harrower, J. (1998). *Applying Psychology to Crime*. London: Hodder and Stoughton.

Harry, B. (1985). Violence and official diagnostic nomenclature. *Bulletin of the American Academy of Psychiatry and the Law*, **13**, 385–88.

Hartshorne, H. and May, M.A. (1928). *Studies in the Nature of Character*. New York: Macmillan.

Hayes, B.K. and Delamothe, K. (1997). Cognitive interviewing procedures and suggestibility in children's recall. *Journal of Applied Psychology*, **82** (4), 562–77.

Hazelwood, R.R. (1987). Analyzing the rape and profiling the offender. In R.R. Hazelwood and A.W. Burgess (Eds), *Practical Aspects of Rape Investigation: A Multidisciplinary Approach*. New York: Elsevier.

Hearold, S. (1986). A synthesis of 1,043 effects of television on social behaviour. In G. Comstock (Ed.), *Public Communications and Behavior*. New York: Academic Press.

Hebenton, B. and Pease, K. (1995). Weighing the pound of flesh: the psychology of punishment. In R. Bull and D. Carson (Eds), *Handbook of Psychology in Legal Contexts*. Chichester: Wiley, pp. 375–91.

Heilbrun, K., Hawk, G. and Tate, D.C. (1996). Juvenile competence to stand trial: research issues in practice. *Law and Human Behavior*, **20** (5), 573–8.

Heilbrun, K., Leheny, C., Thomas, L. and Huneycutt, D. (1997). A national survey of U.S. statutes on juvenile transfer: implications for policy and practice. *Behavioral Sciences and the Law*, **15**, 125–49.

Henderson, Z., Bruce, V. and Burton, M. (2000a). 'Effects of prior familiarity on video verification'. Paper presented at the European Association of Psychology and Law Conference, Limassol, Cyprus.

Henderson, Z., Bruce, V. and Burton, M. (2000b). 'Identification of faces from CCTV images'. Paper presented at the European Association of Psychology and Law Conference, Limassol, Cyprus.

Hennigan, K.M., Delrosario, M.L., Heath, L., Cook, T.D., Wharton, J.D. and Calder, B.J. (1982). Impact of the introduction of television crime in the United States. Empirical findings and theoretical implications. *Journal of Personality and Social Psychology*, **42** (3), 461–77.

Herrnstein, R.R. and Murray, C. (1994). *The Bell Curve: Intelligence and Class Structure in American Life*. New York: Free Press.

Hiday, V.A., Swanson, J.W., Swartz, M.S., Borum, R. and Wagner, H.R. (2001). Victimization: a link between mental illness and violence? *International Journal of Law and Psychiatry*, **24**, 559–72.

Hillbrand, M., Spitz, R.T., Foster, H.G., Krystal, J.H. and Young, J.L. (1998). Creatine kinase elevations and aggressive behavior in hospitalized forensic patients. *Psychiatric Quarterly*, **69** (1), 69–81.

Hodge, J.E., McMurran, M. and Hollin, C.R. (1997). *Addicted to Crime?* Chichester: Wiley.

Hodgins, S. (1992). Mental disorder, intellectual deficiency and crime: evidence from a birth cohort. *Archives of General Psychiatry*, **49**, 476–83.

Hodgins, S. (1997). An overview of research on the prediction of dangerousness. *Nordic Journal of Psychiatry*, **51**, Suppl. 39, 33–8.

Hodgins, S. and Cote, G. (1993). The criminality of mentally disordered offenders. *Criminal Justice and Behavior*, **20**, 115–29.

Hodgins, S., Cote, G. and Toupin, J. (1998). Major mental disorder and crime: an etiological hypothesis. In D.J. Cooke *et al.* (Eds), *Psychopathy: Theory, Research and Implications for Society* (NATO ASI Series. Series D, Behavioural and Social Sciences, No. 88.). Dordrecht: Kluwer, pp. 231–56.

Hodgins, S., Mednick, S., Brennan, P.A., Schulsinger, F. and Engberg, M. (1996). Mental disorder and crime: evidence from a Danish birth cohort. *Archives of General Psychiatry*, **53** (6), 489–96.

Hollin, C. (Ed.) (2001). *Handbook of Offender Assessment and Treatments*. Chichester: Wiley.

Hollin, C. and Palmer, E. (1995). *Assessing Prison Regimes: A Review to Inform the Development of Outcome Measures*. Commissioned report for the Planning Group, HM Prison Service.

Hollin, C. and Swaffer, T. (1995). Mental health: psychology's contribution to diagnosis, assessment and treatment. In R. Bull and D. Carson (Eds), *Handbook of Psychology in Legal Contexts*. Chichester: Wiley, pp. 129–44.

Hollin, C.R. (2002). An overview of offender rehabilitation: something old, something borrowed, something new. *Australian Psychologist*, **37** (3), 1–6.

Hollin, C.R. and Howells, K. (1991). *Clinical Approaches to Sex Offenders and their Victims*. Chichester: Wiley.

Holmes, R.M. and Holmes, S.T. (1996). *Profiling Violent Crimes: An Investigative Tool*. Thousand Oaks, CA: Sage.

Holmes, R.M. and Holmes, S.T. (1998). *Serial Murder* (2nd ed.). Thousand Oaks: CA: Sage.

Homant, R.J. and Kennedy, D.B. (1998). Psychological aspects of crime scene profiling. *Criminal Justice and Behavior*, **25** (3), 319–43.

Home Office (2001b). The British Crime Survey 2000. http://www.homeoffice.gov.uk/rds/bcs1.html

Home Office (2004), Reconvictions of prisoners discharged from prison in 1996. Prisons: research development statistics. http://www.homeoffice.gov.uk/rds/prischap9.html

Home Office (2005a). *Crime Reduction Toolkit: Arson.* http://www.crimereduction.gov.uk/toolkits/an020703.htm

Home Office (2005b). *Recorded Crime Statistics 1898–2002/03.* http://www.homeoffice.gov.uk/rds/pdfs/100years.xls

Hood, R., Shute, S., Feilzer, M. and Wilcox, A. (2002). Sex offenders emerging from long-term imprisonment. *British Journal of Criminology*, **42**, 371–94.

Hopkins, M. (2002). Crimes against business: the way forward for future research. *British Journal of Criminology*, **42**, 782–97.

Horn, R. and Hollin, C.R. (1997). Police beliefs about women who offend. *Legal and Criminological Psychology*, **2**, 193–204.

Horner, T.M., Guuyer, M.J. and Kalter, N.M. (1993). Clinical expertise and the assessment of child sexual abuse. *Journal of the American Academy of Child and Adolescent Psychiatry*, **32**, 925–31.

Horowitz, I.A. (1980). Juror selection: a comparison of two methods in several criminal cases. *Journal of Applied Social Psychology*, **10** (1), 86–99.

Horowitz, M.J. (1986). *Stress response syndromes* (2nd ed.). Northvale, NJ: Jason Aronson.

Horselenberg, R., Merckelbach, H. and Josephs, S. (2003). Individual differences and false confessions: a conceptual replication of Kassin and Kiechel (1996). *Psychology, Crime and Law*, **9** (1), 1–8.

Horvath, F. (1977). The effect of selected variables on interpretation of polygraph records. *Journal of Applied Psychology*, **62**, 127–36.

Houran, J. and Porter, S. (2005). Statement validity analysis of 'The Jim Ragsdale Story': implications for the Roswell incident. http://www.scientificexploration.org/jse/articles/pdf/12.1_houran_porter.pdf *Journal for Scientific Exploration*, **12** (1), Article 2.

House, J.C. (1997). Towards a practical application of offender profiling: the RNC's criminal suspect prioritization system. In J.L. Jackson and D.A. Bekerian (Eds), *Offender Profiling: Theory, Research and Practice*. Chichester: Wiley, pp. 177–90.

Hovdestad, W.E. and Kristiansen, C.M. (1996a). A field study of 'false memory syndrome': construct validity and incidence. *Journal of Psychiatry and Law*, **Summer**, 299–338.

Hovdestad, W.E. and Kristiansen, C.M. (1996b). Mind meets body: on the nature of recovered memories of trauma. *Women and Therapy*, **19** (1), 31–45.

Howells, K. and Hollin, C.R. (1989). *Clinical Approaches to Violence*. Chichester: Wiley.

Howells, K., Watt, B., Hall, G. and Baldwin, S. (1997). Developing programs for violent offenders. *Legal and Criminological Psychology*, **2** (1), 117–28.

Howitt, D. (1991a). Britain's 'substance abuse policy': realities and regulation in the United Kingdom. *International Journal of the Addictions*, **3**, 1087–111.

Howitt, D. (1991b). *Concerning Psychology*. Milton Keynes: Open University Press.

Howitt, D. (1992). *Child Abuse Errors*. Harlow: Harvester Wheatsheaf.

Howitt, D. (1995a). *Paedophiles and Sexual Offences Against Children*. Chichester: Wiley.

Howitt, D. (1995b). Pornography and the paedophile: is it criminogenic? *British Journal of Medical Psychology*, **68** (1), 15–27.

Howitt, D. (1998a). Are causal theories of paedophilia possible? A reconsideration of sexual abuse cycles. In J. Boros, I. Munnich and M. Szegedi (Eds), *Psychology and Criminal Justice: International Review of Theory and Practice*. Berlin: de Gruyter, pp. 248–53.

Howitt, D. (1998b). *Crime, the Media and the Law*. Chichester: Wiley.

Howitt, D. (1998c). 'Crime news'. Paper presented at the European Association of Psychology and Law, Krakow, Poland.

Howitt, D. (2000). 'Just what is the role of fantasy in sex offending?' Paper presented at the European Association for Psychology and the Law, Limmasol, Cyprus, April.

Howitt, D. (2002). Social exclusion – paedophile style. In R. Goodwin and D. Cramer (Eds), *Inappropriate Relations: The Unconventional, the Disapproved, and the Forbidden*. Mahwah, NJ.: Lawrence Erlbaum, p. 221–43.

Howitt, D. (2004). What is the role of fantasy in sex offending? *Criminal Behaviour and Mental Health*, **14** (3), 182–8.

Howitt, D. (2005/In press). Paedophilia prevention and the law. In M. Stevens and K. Moss (Eds), *Crime Prevention and the Law*. London: Routledge.

Howitt, D. and Cramer, D. (2000). *An Introduction to Statistics in Psychology: A Complete Guide to Students*. London: Prentice Hall.

Howitt, D. and Cramer, D. (2005). *Introduction to Statistics in Psychology*. Harlow: Pearson Education.

Howitt, D. and Cumberbatch, G. (1975). *Mass Media Violence and Society*. London: Elek Science.

Howitt, D. and Cumberbatch, G. (1990). *Pornography: Impacts and Influences*. London: Home Office Research and Planning Unit.

Howitt, D. and Owusu-Bempah, J. (1994). *The Racism of Psychology*. London: Harvester Wheatsheaf.

Hudson, S.M., Marshall, W.L., Ward, T., Johnston, P.W. and Jones, R.L. (1995). Kia Marama: a cognitive-behavioural program for incarcerated child molesters. *Behaviour Change*, **12** (2), 69–80.

Huesmann, L.R. and Eron, L.D. (Eds) (1986). *Television and the Aggressive Child: A Cross-national Comparison*. Hillsdale, NJ: Erlbaum.

Huesmann, L.R. and Malamuth, N.M. (Eds) (1986). Media violence and antisocial behavior. *Journal of Social Issues*, **42** (3).

Huffman, M.L., Warren, A.R. and Larson, S.M. (2001). Discussing truth and lies in interviews with children: whether, why, and how? In R. Bull (Ed.), *Children and the Law: The Essential Readings*. Malden, MA: Blackwell, 225–46.

Hughes, G., Hogue, T., Hollin, C. and Champion, H. (1997). First-stage evaluation of a treatment programme for personality disordered offenders. *Journal of Forensic Psychiatry*, **8** (3), 515–27.

Hutcheson, G.D., Baxter, J.S., Telfer, K. and Warden, D. (1995). Child witness statement quality. Question type and errors of omission. *Law and Human Behavior*, **19** (6), 631–48.

I

Iacono, W.G. and Lykken, D.T. (1997). The validity of the lie detector: two surveys of scientific opinion. *Journal of Applied Psychology*, **82** (3), 426–33.

Iacono, W.G. and Patrick, C.J. (1997). Polygraphy and integrity testing. In R. Rogers (Ed.), *Clinical Assessment of Malingering and Deception*. New York: Guilford, pp. 252–81.

Inbau, F.E., Reid, J.E. and Buckley, J.P. (1986). *Criminal Interrogation and Confession*. Baltimore: Williams and Wilkins.

Innes, M. (2002). The 'process structures' of police homicide investigations. *British Journal of Criminology*, **42** (4), 669–88.

International Crime Victimisation Survey (2001). http://ruljis.leidenuniv.nl/group/jfcr/www/icvs/Index.htm

Ireland, J.L. (1999). Pro-victim attitudes and empathy in relation to bullying behaviour among prisoners. *Legal and Criminological Psychology*, **4** (1), 51–66.

Itzin, C. (Ed.) (1992). *Pornography: Women, Violence and Civil Liberties*. Oxford: Oxford University Press.

J

Jackson, J.L. and Bekerian, D.A. (1997). Does offender profiling have a role to play? In J.L. Jackson and D.A. Bekerian (Eds), *Offender Profiling: Theory, Research and Practice*. Chichester: Wiley, pp. 1–7.

Jakob, R. (1992). On the development of psychologically oriented legal thinking in German speaking countries. In F. Losel, D. Bender and T. Bliesener (Eds), *Psychology and Law: International Perspectives*. Berlin: Walter de Gruyter, pp. 519–25.

James, A. (1996). Suicide reduction in medium security. *Journal of Forensic Psychiatry*, **7** (2), 406–12.

Jamieson, L. and Taylor, P.J. (2004). A reconviction study of special (high security) hospital patients. *British Journal of Criminology*, **44**, 783–802.

Jenkins. P. (1994). *Using Murder: The Social Construction of Serial Homicide*. New York: Aldine de Gruyter.

Johnson, J.G., Smailes, E., Cohen, P., Kasen, S. and Brook, J.S. (2004). Antisocial parental behaviour, problematic parenting and aggressive offspring behaviour during adulthood: a 25-year longitudinal investigation. *British Journal of Criminology*, **44**, 915–30.

Johnson, S.D. and Bowers, K.J. (2004). The stability of space-time clusters of burglary. *British Journal of Criminology*, **44**, 55–65.

Jones, J.C. and Barlow, D.H. (1990). Self-reported frequency of sexual urges: fantasies and masturbatory fantasies in heterosexual males and females. *Archives of Sexual Behavior*, **19**, 269–79.

Jones, S. (2000). *Understanding Violent Crime*. Milton Keynes: Open University.

Joyce, D. (1993). How comprehensible are the Pace Codes of Practice to the majority of persons who might wish to read them? In N.K. Clark and G.M. Stephenson (Eds), *Issues in Criminological and Legal Psychology 20: Children, Evidence and Procedure*. Leicester: Division of Criminological and Legal Psychology, British Psychological Society, pp. 70–4.

Jung, J. (1971). *The Experimenter's Dilemma*. New York: Harper and Row.

Junger, M. (1994). Accidents. In T. Hirschi and M.R. Gottfredson (Eds), *The Generality of Deviance*. New Brunswick: Transaction, pp. 81–112.

Junger, M. and Wiegersma, A. (1995). The relations between accidents, deviance and leisure time. *Criminal Behaviour and Mental Health*, **5**, 144–74.

Junger, M., Terlouw, G-J. and Van der Haijden, P.G.M. (1995). Crime, accidents and social control. *Criminal Behaviour and Mental Health*, **5** (4), 386–410.

K

Kamin, L.J. (1977). *The Science and Politics of IQ*. Harmondsworth: Penguin.

Karlsson, I. and Christianson, S.-A. (1999). 'Memory for traumatic events among police personnel'. Paper presented at the International Conference of Psychology and the Law, Dublin, 6–9 July.

Kassin, S.M. (1997a). False memories turned against the self. *Psychological Inquiry*, **8** (4), 300–2.

Kassin, S.M. (1997b). The psychology of confession evidence. *American Psychologist*, **52** (3), 221–33.

Kassin, S.M. (1998). Eyewitness identification procedures: the fifth rule. *Law and Human Behavior*, **22**, 649–53.

Kassin, S.M. and Kiechel, K.L. (1996). The social psychology of false confessions: compliance, internalization, and confabulation. *Psychological Science*, **7** (3), 125–8.

Kassin, S.M. and McNall, K. (1991). Police interrogations and confessions: communicating promises and threats by pragmatic implication. *Law and Human Behavior*, **15** (3), 233–51.

Kassin, S.M. and Neumann, K. (1997). On the power of confession evidence: an experimental test of the fundamental difference hypothesis. *Law and Human Behavior*, **21** (5), 469–84.

Kassin, S.M. and Norwick, R.J. (2004). Why people waive their Miranda rights: the power of innocence. *Law and Human Behavior*, **28** (2), 211–21.

Kassin, S.M. and Sukel, H. (1997). Coerced confessions and the jury: an experimental test of the 'harmless error' rule. *Law and Human Behavior*, **21** (1), 27–45.

Keane, T.M., Zimering, R.T. and Caddell, R.T. (1985). A behavioral formulation of PTSD in Vietnam veterans. *Behavior Therapist*, **8**, 9–12.

Kebbell, M.R. and Hatton, C. (1999). People with mental retardation as witnesses in court: a review. *Mental Retardation*, **37** (3), 179–87.

Kebbell, M.R. and Milne, R. (1998). Police officers' perceptions of eyewitness performance in forensic investigations. *Journal of Social Psychology*, **138** (3), 323–30.

Kebbell, M.R. and Wagstaff, G.F. (1998). Hypnotic interviewing: the best way to interview eyewitnesses? *Behavioral Sciences and the Law*, **16**, 115–29.

Kebbell, M.R., Hatton, C., and Johnson, S.D. (2004). Witnesses with intellectual disabilities in court: what questions are asked and what influences do they have? *Legal and Criminological Psychology*, **9**, 23–35.

Kebbell, M.R., Milne, R. and Wagstaff, G.F. (1998). The cognitive interview: a survey of its forensic effectiveness. *Psychology, Crime and Law*, **5**, 101–15.

Kebbell, M.R., Wagstaff, G.F. and Covey, J.A. (1996). The influence of item difficulty on the relationship between eyewitness confidence and accuracy. *British Journal of Psychology*, **87**, 653–62.

Keeler, L. (1934). Debunking the 'lie detector'. *Journal of Civil Law and Criminology*, **25**, 153–9.

Keen, J. (2000). A practitioner's perspective: anger management work with young offenders. *Forensic Update*, **60**, 20–5.

Kelly, L. (1988). *Surviving Sexual Violence*. Cambridge: Polity.

Kelly, L. (1989). What's in a name? Defining child sexual abuse. *Feminist Review*, **28**, 65–73.

Kemp, R., Pike, G., Brace, N. and Badal, P. (2000). 'Caught on camera: identification from CCTV footage'. Paper presented at the conference of the European Association of Psychology and Law, Limassol, Cyprus.

Kemp, R., Towell, N. and Pike, G. (1997). When seeing should not be believing: photographs, credit cards and fraud. *Applied Cognitive Psychology*, **11** (3), 211–22.

Kerby, J. and Rae, J. (1998). Moral identity in action: young offenders' reports of encounters with the police. *British Journal of Social Psychology*, **37**, 439–56.

Kilpatrick, R. (1997). Joy-riding: an addictive behaviour. In J.E. Hodge, M. McMurran and C.R. Hollin (Eds), *Addicted to Crime?* Chichester: Wiley, pp. 165–90.

King, M. (1984). Understanding the legal system: a job for psychologists? In D.J. Muller, D.E. Blackman and A.J. Chapman (Eds), *Psychology and Law*. Chichester: Wiley, pp. 67–82.

Kirkendall, L.A. and McBride, L.G. (1990). Pre-adolescent and adolescent imagery and sexual fantasies: beliefs and experiences. In M.E. Perry (Ed.), *Handbook of Sexology, Vol. 7: Childhood and Adolescent Sexology*. Amsterdam: Elsevier, pp. 263–87.

Kitzinger, J. (1988). Defending innocence: ideologies of childhood. *Feminist Review*, **28**, Spring, 77–87.

Kleinmuntz, B. and Szucko, J.J. (1984). A field study of the fallibility of polygraphic lie detection. *Nature*, **308**, 449–550.

Knafo, D. and Jaffe, Y. (1984). Sexual fantasizing in males and females. *Journal of Research in Personality*, **18**, 451–62.

Kohlberg, L. (1963). The development of children's orientations toward a moral order: 1. Sequence in the development of moral thought. *Human Development*, **6**, 11–33.

Kohlberg, L. (1984). *The Psychology of Moral Development: Essays on Moral Development*. (Vol. 2). New York: Harper and Row.

Kohnken, G., Milne, R., Memon, A. and Bull, R. (1999). The cognitive interview: a meta-analysis. *Psychology, Crime and Law*, **5**, 3–27.

Kohnken, G., Thurer, C. and Zoberbeier, D. (1994). The cognitive interview: are the interviewers' memories enhanced, too? *Applied Cognitive Psychology*, **8**, 13–24.

Konecni, V.J., Ebbesen, E.B. and Nehrer, E. (2000). Retrospective implications for the probative value of psychologists' testimony on eyewitness issues of exonerations by DNA evidence. In A. Czerederecka, T. Jaskiewicz-Obdzinska and J. Wojcikiewicz (Eds), *Forensic Psychology and Law: Traditional Questions and New Ideas*. Krakow: Institute of Forensic Research Publishers, pp. 41–8.

Kovera, M.B., Dickinson, J. and Cutler, B.L. (2002). *Voir dire* and jury selection: practical issues, research findings and directions for future research. In A.M. Goldstein (Ed.), *Comprehensive Handbook of Psychology, Vol. 11: Forensic Psychology*. New York: John Wiley & Sons.

Krackow, E. and Lynn, S.J. (2003). Is there touch in the game of twister? The effects of innocuous touch and suggestive questions on children's eyewitness memory. *Law and Human Behavior*, **27** (6), 589–604.

Kristiansen, C.M. (1996). 'Recovered memory research and the influence of social attitudes'. Unpublished manuscript, Ottawa, Ontario: Department of Psychology, Carleton University.

Kristiansen, C.M., Felton, K.A. and Hovdestad, W.E. (1996). Recovered memories of child abuse: fact, fantasy or fancy? *Women and Therapy*, **19** (1), 47–59.

Kruttschnitt, C., Heath, L. and Ward, D.A. (1986). Family violence, television viewing habits, and other adolescent experiences related to violent criminal behaviour. *Criminology*, **24** (2), 235–65.

Kullgren, G., Tengstrom, A. and Gran, M. (1998). Suicide among personality-disordered offenders: a follow-up study of 1,943 male criminal offenders. *Social Psychiatry and Psychiatric Epidemiology*, **33**, 102–6.

Kury, H. (1998). Legal psychology in Europe: results of a survey. In J. Boros, I. Munnich and M. Szegedi (Eds), *Psychology and Criminal Justice: International Review of Theory and Practice*. Berlin: Walter de Gruyter, pp. 428–35.

Kutchinsky, B. (1970). The effect of pornography: a pilot experiment on perception, behavior and attitudes. In *Technical Report of the Commission on Obscenity and Pornography*, Vol. VIII, *Erotica and Social Behavior*. Washington, DC: US Government Printing Office, pp. 133–70.

Kutchinsky, B. (1973). The effect of easy availability of pornography on the incidence of sex crimes: the Danish experience. *Journal of Social Issues*, **29** (3), 163–91.

Kutchinsky, B. (1991). Pornography and rape: theory and practice? *International Journal of Law and Psychiatry*, **14** (1/2), 145–51.

L

La Fond, J.Q. (1999). 'Clinical, legal and ethical issues in implementing a sexual predator law in the United States'. Paper presented to American Psychology-Law Society/European Association of Psychology and Law, Trinity College, Dublin, Ireland, 6–9 July.

La Fontaine, J. (1990). *Child Sexual Abuse*. Cambridge: Polity.

Laahasalo, T. and Häkkänen, H. (2004). Background characteristics of mentally ill homicide offenders: a comparison of five diagnostic groups. *Journal of Forensic Psychiatry and Psychology*, **15** (3), 451–74.

Lamb, M.E. and Sternberg, K.J. (1998). Conducting investigative interviews of alleged sexual abuse victims. *Child Abuse and Neglect*, **22** (8), 813–23.

Lamb, M.E., Sternberg, K.J. and Orbach, Y. (1999). Forensic interviews of children. In A. Memon and R. Bull (Eds), *Handbook of the Psychology of Interviewing*. Chichester: Wiley.

Lamb, M.E., Sternberg, K.J., Esplin, P.W., Hershkowitz, I. and Orbach, Y. (1997). Assessing the credibility of children's allegations of sexual abuse: a survey of recent research. *Learning and Individual Differences*, **9** (2), 175–94.

Lamers-Winkelman, F. (1997). 'The second part of statement validity analysis'. Paper presented at conference on Responding to Child Maltreatment, San Diego.

Lamers-Winkelman, F. and Buffing, F. (1996). Children's testimony in the Netherlands: a study of statement validity analysis. *Criminal Justice and Behavior*, **23** (2), 304–21.

Lande, R.G. (1993). The video violence debate. *Hospital and Community Psychiatry*, **44** (4), 347–51.

Langstrom, N. (1999). *Young Sex Offenders: Individual Characteristics, Agency Reactions and Criminal Recidivism*. Stockholm: Karolinka Instutet, Department of Public Health, Division of Psychosocial Factors and Health, Division of Forensic Psychiatry.

Larson, J.A. (1922). The cardio-pneumo psychogram and its use in the study of emotions, with practical applications. *Journal of Experimental Psychology*, **5**, 323–8.

Laws, D.R. (1994). How dangerous are rapists to children? *Journal of Sexual Aggression*, **1**, 1–14.

Laws, D.R. and Gress, C.L.Z. (2004). Seeing things differently: the viewing time alternative to penile plethysmography. *Legal and Criminological Psychology*, **9**, 183–96.

Lecci, L., Snowden, J. and Morris, D. (2004). Using social science research to inform and evaluate the contributions of trial consultants in the *voir dire*. *Journal of Forensic Psychology Practice*, **4**, 67–78.

Lees, S. (1995). Media reporting of rape: the 1993 British 'date rape' controversy. In D. Kidd-Hewitt and R. Osborne (Eds), *Crime and the Media: The Post-modern Spectacle*. London: Pluto, pp. 107–30.

Lefkowitz, M.M., Eron, L.D., Walder, L.O. and Huesmann, L.R. (1977). *Growing Up to be Violent: A Longitudinal Study of the Development of Aggression*. New York: Pergamon.

Leichtman, M.D. and Ceci, S.J. (1995). The effects of stereotypes and suggestions on pre-schoolers' reports. *Developmental Psychology*, **31**, 568–78.

Leo, R.A. (1996). Miranda's revenge: police interrogation as a confidence game. *Law and Society Review*, **30** (2), 259–88.

Leo, R.A. and Ofshe, R.J. (1998). The consequences of false confessions: deprivations of liberty and miscarriages of justice in the age of psychological interrogation. *Journal of Criminal Law and Criminology*, **88** (2), 429–96.

Lewis, N. and Yarnell, H. (1951). Pathological Firesetting (Pyromania). Nervous and Mental Disease Monographs, No. 82/437.

Leyton, E. (1986). *Hunting Humans: The Rise of the Modern Multiple Murderer*. Toronto: McClelland and Stewart.

Limbandari, B.J. and Sheridan, D.J. (1995). Prediction of intentional interpersonal violence: an introduction. In J.C. Campbell (Ed.), *Assessing Dangerousness*. Thousand Oaks, CA: Sage.

Lind, B., Chen, S., Weatherburn, D. and Mattick, R. (2005). The effectiveness of methadone maintenance treatment in controlling crime: an Australian aggregate-level analysis. *British Journal of Criminology*, **45**, 201–11.

Lind, J.E. and Ke, G.Y. (1985). Opening and closing statements. In S.M. Kassin and L.S. Wrightsman (Eds), *The Psychology of Evidence and Trial Procedure*. London: Sage.

Lindeman, M., Harakka, T. and Keltikangas-Jarvinen, L. (1997). Age and gender differences in adolescents' reactions to conflict situations: aggression, prosociality, and withdrawal. *Journal of Youth and Adolescence*, **26** (3), 339–51.

Lindholm, T., Christianson, S-A. and Karlsson, I. (1997). Police officers and civilians as witnesses: intergroup biases and memory performance. *Applied Cognitive Psychology*, **11**, 431–44.

Link, B.G., Andrews, H. and Cullen, F.T. (1992). The violent and illegal behaviour of mental patients reconsidered. *American Sociological Review*, **57**, 275–92.

Liska, A.E. and Baccaglini, W. (1990). Feeling safe by comparison: crime in the newspapers. *Social Problems*, **37** (3), 360–74.

Lloyd, C. and Walmsley, R. (1989). Changes in rape offences and sentencing. *Home Office Study No. 105*. London: HMSO.

Lloyd-Bostock, S. (1996). The jury in the United Kingdom: juries and jury research in context. In G. Davies, S. Lloyd-Bostock, M. McMurran and C. Wilson (Eds). *Psychology, Law and Criminal Justice: International Developments in Research and Practice*. Berlin: de Gruyter, pp. 349–59.

Loeber, R. and Farrington, D.P. (1998). *Serious and Violent Juvenile Offenders: Risk Factors and Successful Interventions*. London: Sage.

Loftus, E. and Palmer, J.C. (1974). Reconstructions of automobile destruction: an example of the interaction between language and memory. *Journal of Verbal Learning and Verbal Behavior*, **13**, 585–9.

Loftus, E. and Pickrell, J.E. (1995). The formation of false memories. *Psychiatric Annals*, **25**, 720–5.

Loftus, E.F., Miller, D.G. and Burns, H.J. (1978). Semantic integration of verbal information into a visual memory. *Journal of Experimental Psychology, Human Learning and Memory*, **4** (1), 19–31.

Lombroso, C. (1911). *Crime, Its Causes and Remedies*. Boston: Little, Brown.

Looman, J. (1999). 'Mood, conflict and deviant sexual fantasies'. Unpublished manuscript. Ontario: Regional Treatment Centre.

Los, M. (1990). Feminism and rape law reform. In L. Gelsthorpe and A. Morris (Eds), *Feminist Perspectives in Criminology*. Milton Keynes: Open University Press, pp. 164–72.

Los, M. and Chamard, S.E. (1997). Selling newspapers or educating the public? Sexual violence in the media. *Canadian Journal of Criminology*, **July**, 293–328.

Losel, F., Bender, D. and Bliesener, T. (1999). *Biosocial Risk and Protective Factors for Antisocial Behavior in Juveniles: Heart Rate and Family Characteristics*. Nuremberg: Department of Psychology, University of Erlangan-Nuremberg.

Lymburner, J.A. and Roesch, R. (1999). The insanity defence: five years of research (1993–97). *International Journal of Law and Psychiatry*, **22** (3–4), 213–40.

Lynn, S.J., Neuschatz, J. and Fite, R. (2002). Hypnosis and memory: implications for the courtroom and psychotherapy. In M.L. Eisen, J.A. Quas, and G.S. Goodman (Eds), *Memory and Suggestibility in the Forensic Interview*. Lawrence Erlbaum Associates: Mahwah, New Jersey, pp. 287–307.

M

MacCulloch, M.J., Snowden, P.R., Wood, P.J.W. and Mills, H.E. (1983). Sadistic fantasy, sadistic behaviours and offending. *British Journal of Psychiatry*, **143**, 20–9.

MacMartin, C. and Yarmey, A.D. (1998). Repression, dissociation and the recovered memory debate: constructing scientific evidence and expertise. *Expert Evidence*, **6**, 203–26.

Madsen, L., Parsons, S. and Grubin, D. (2004). A preliminary study of the contribution of periodic polygraph testing to the treatment and supervision of sex offenders. *British Journal of Forensic Psychiatry and Psychology*, **15**, 682–95.

Maghan, J. (1998). Terrorist mentality. In J. Boros, I. Munnich and M. Szegedi (Eds), *Psychology, Law and Criminal Justice: International Review of Theory and Practice*. Berlin: Walter de Gruyter, pp. 335–45.

Mair, K.J. (1995). Cognitive distortion in the prediction of sexual offending. In N.K. Clark and G.M. Stephenson (Eds), *Investigative and Forensic Decision Making, Issues in Criminological and Legal Psychology No. 26*. Leicester: Division of Criminological and Legal Psychology, British Psychological Society, pp. 12–17.

Malamuth, N.M. and Ceniti, J. (1986). Repeated exposure to violent and non-violent pornography: likelihood of raping ratings and laboratory aggression against women. *Aggressive Behavior*, **12**, 129–37.

Malpass, R. and Devine, P. (1981). Guided memory in eyewitness identification. *Journal of Applied Psychology*, **66** (3), 343–50.

Marsh, H.L. (1991). A comparative analysis of crime coverage in newspapers in the United States and other countries from 1960 to 1989: a review of the literature. *Journal of Criminal Justice*, **19**, 67–79.

Marshall, W.C. (1988). The use of sexually explicit stimuli by rapists, child molesters and non-offenders. *Journal of Sex Research*, **25** (2), 267–88.

Marshall, W.L., Hudson, S.M. and Ward, T. (1992). Sexual deviance. In P.H. Wilson (Ed.), *Principles and Practice of Relapse Prevention*. New York: Guilford Press, pp. 235–54.

Martinson, R. (1974). What works? Questions and answers about prison reform. *Public Interest*, **10**, 22–54.

Masters, B. (1993). *The Shrine of Jeffrey Dahmer*. London: Hodder and Stoughton.

McCabe, S. and Purves, R. (1974). *The Shadow Jury at Work*. Oxford: Blackwell.

McCann, J.T. (1998). Broadening the typology of false confessions. *American Psychologist*, **March**, 319–20.

McConaghy, N. (1991). Validity and ethics of penile circumference measures of sexual arousal: a critical review. *Archives of Sexual Behavior*, **19** (4), 357–69.

McConkey, K.M., Roche, S.M. and Sheehan, P.W. (1989). Reports of forensic hypnosis: a critical analysis. *Australian Psychologist*, **24** (2), 249–72.

McCord, J. (1979). Some child-rearing antecedents of criminal behavior in adult men. *Journal of Personality and Social Psychology*, **37** (9), 1477–86.

McEwan, J. (1995). Adversarial and inquisitorial proceedings. In R. Bull and D. Carson (Eds), *Handbook of Psychology in Legal Contexts*. Chichester: John Wiley, pp. 495–501.

McGeorge, N. (1996). Risk assessment and political decision making. *Forensic Update*, **45**, 21–2.

McGregor, G. and Howells, K. (1997). In J.E. Hodge, M. McMurran and C.R. Hollin (Eds), *Addicted to Crime?* Chichester: Wiley, pp. 107–37.

McGuire, J. (1997). 'Irrational' shoplifting and models of addiction. In J.E. Hodge, M. McMurran and C.R. Hollin (Eds), *Addicted to Crime?* Chichester: Wiley, pp. 207–31.

McGuire, J. (2000). Explanations of criminal behaviour. In J. McGuire, T. Mason and A. O'Kane (Eds), *Behaviour, Crime and Legal Processes: A Guide for Forensic Practitioners*. Chichester: Wiley, pp. 135–59.

McGuire, J. (2004). *Understanding Psychology and Crime. Perspectives on Theory and Action*. Open University Press: Maidenhead.

McHugh, M. (1998). 'Strategies for reducing suicides in prison'. Paper presented at Eighth European Conference on Psychology and Law, Krakow, September.

McHugh, M. (1999). Suicide and self injury. *Issues in Forensic Psychology*, **1**, 23–6.

McMurran, M., and Duggan, C. (2005/submitted). The manualisation of a treatment programme for personality disorder. *Criminal Behaviour and Mental Health*.

McMurran, M., Hodge, J.E. and Hollin, C.R. (1997). Introduction: current issues in the treatment of addictions and crime. In J.E. Hodge, M. McMurran and C.R. Hollin (Eds), *Addicted to Crime?* Chichester: Wiley, pp. 1–9.

McNeil, D.E. (1997). Correlates of violence in psychotic patients. *Psychiatric Annals*, **27** (10), 683–90.

McSherry, B. (2004). Criminal responsibility, fleeting states of mental impairment, and the power of self-control. *International Journal of Law and Psychiatry*, **27**, 445–57.

Mednick, S.A., Gabrielli, W.F. and Hutchings, B. (1994). Genetic influences in criminal convictions. *Science*, **224**, 841–94.

Meehle, P.E. (1954). *Clinical Versus Statistical Predictions*. Minneapolis: University of Minnesota Press.

Meloy, M.R. (2002). Stalking and violence. In J. Boon and L. Sheridan (Eds), *Stalking and Psychosexual Obsession: Psychological Perspectives for Prevention, Policing and Treatment*. Chichester: John Wiley, pp. 105–24.

Memon, A. and Young, M. (1997). Desperately seeking evidence: the recovered memory debate. *Legal and Criminological Psychology*, **2**, 131–54.

Memon, A., Holley, A., Milne, R., Koehnken, G. and Bull, R. (1994). Towards understanding the effects of interviewer training in evaluating the cognitive interview. *Applied Cognitive Psychology*, **8**, 641–59.

Memon, A., Vrij, A. and Bull, R. (1998). *Psychology and Law*. London: McGraw-Hill.

Messner, S.F. (1986). Television violence and violent crime: an aggregate analysis. *Social Problems*, **33** (3), 218–35.

Miethe, T.D. (1995). Fear and withdrawal from urban life. *Annals of the American Association of Political and Social Science*, **539**, 14–27.

Milavsky, J.R., Kessler, R.C., Stipp, H.H. and Rubins, W.S. (1982). *Television and Aggression: A Panel Study*. New York: Academic Press.

Milgram, S. (1974). *Obedience to Authority: An Experimental View*. New York: Harper and Row.

Miller, E. (1999a). The neuropsychology of offending. *Psychology, Crime and Law*, **5**, 515–36.

Miller, E. (1999b). Head injury and offending. *Journal of Forensic Psychiatry*, **10** (1), 157–66.

Miller, N.E. and Dollard, J. (1941). *Social Learning and Imitation*. Yale: Yale University.

Milne, R. (1999). Interviewing children with learning disabilities. In A. Memon and R. Bull (Eds), *Handbook of the Psychology of Interviewing*. Chichester: Wiley, pp. 165–80.

Milne, R. and Bull, R. (1994). Improving witness recall: the cognitive interview and the legal profession. *Journal of Child Law*, **6** (2), 82–4.

Milne, R. and Bull, R. (1996). Interviewing children with mild learning disability with the cognitive interview. In N.K. Clark and G.M. Stephenson (Eds), *Issues in Criminological and Legal Psychology 26: Investigative and Forensic Decision Making*. Leicester: Division of Criminological and Legal Psychology, British Psychological Society.

Milne, R. and Shaw, G. (1999). Obtaining witness statements: the psychology, best practice and proposals for innovation. *Medical Science and the Law*, 39 (2), 127–38.

Milne, R., Bull, R., Koehnken, G. and Memon, A. (1995). The cognitive interview and suggestibility. In N.K. Clark and G.M. Stephenson (Eds), *Issues in Criminological and Legal Psychology 22: Criminal Behaviour: Perceptions, Attributions and Rationality*. Leicester: Division of Criminological and Legal Psychology, British Psychological Society.

Milne, R., Clare, I.C.H. and Bull, R. (1999). Using the cognitive interview with adults with mild learning disabilities. *Psychology, Crime and Law*, 5, 81–99.

Milner, J.S. and Campbell, J.C. (1995). Prediction issues for practitioners. In J.C. Campbell (Ed.), *Assessing Dangerousness*. Thousand Oaks, CA: Sage.

Miner, M.H. and Dwyer, S.M. (1997). The psychological development of sex offenders: differences between exhibitionists, child molesters and incest offenders. *International Journal of Offender Therapy and Comparative Criminology*, 41 (1), 36–44.

Mirrlees-Black, C. (2001). Confidence in the criminal justice system. Home Office Research, Development and Statistics Directorate, Research Findings, 137. http://www.homeoffice.gov.uk/rds/pdfs/r137.pdf

Mitchell, B. (1997). Putting diminished responsibility law into practice: a forensic psychiatric perspective. *Journal of Forensic Psychiatry*, 8 (3), 620–34.

Monahan, J. (1993). Mental disorder and violence: another look. In S. Hodgins (Ed.), *Mental Disorder and Crime*. Newbury Park, CA: Sage, pp. 287–302.

Monahan, J. and Steadman, H. (1994). Toward the rejuvenation of risk research. In J. Monahan and H. Steadman (Eds), *Violence and Mental Disorder: Developments in Risk Assessment*. Chicago: University of Chicago Press, pp. 1–17.

Moore, P.J., Ebbesen, E.B. and Konecni, V.J. (1994). *What Does Real Eyewitness Testimony Look Like? An Archival Analysis of Witnesses to Adult Felony Crimes*. Technical Report. San Diego, CA: University of California San Diego, Law and Psychology Program.

Moran, G. and Cutler, B.L. (1991). The prejudicial impact of retrial publicity. *Journal of Applied Social Psychology*, 21 (5), 345–67.

Mosher, D.L. and Anderson, R.D. (1986). Macho personality, sexual aggression and reactions to guided imagery of realistic rape. *Journal of Research in Personality*, 20, 77–94.

Mossman, D. and Kapp, M.B. (1998). 'Courtroom whores'? – or why do attorneys call us? Findings from a survey on attorneys' use of mental health experts. *Journal of the American Academy of Psychiatry and Law*, 26 (1), 27–36.

Motzkau, J.F. (2004). 'Cross-examining suggestibility: memory, childhood, expertise: children's testimony between psychological research and juridical practice'. Paper presented at the 14th European Conference on Psychology and Law: Krakow: Poland.

Mowrer, O.H. (1960). *Learning Theory and Behaviour*. New York: Wiley.

Muir, G. and Macleod, M.D. (2003). The demographic and spatial patterns of recorded rape in a large UK metropolitan area. *Psychology, Crime and Law*, 9 (4), 345–55.

Muller, D.A. (2000). Criminal profiling: real science or just wishful thinking? *Homicide Studies*, 4 (3), 234–64.

Muncie, J. (1998). *Youth and Crime*. London: Sage.

Murphy, W.D., Haynes, M.R., Stalgaitis, S.J. and Flanagan, B. (1986). Differential sexual responding among four groups of sexual offenders against children. *Journal of Psychopathology and Behavioral Assessment*, 8 (4), 339–53.

Myers, J.E.B. (1996). A decade of international legal reform regarding child abuse investigation and litigation: steps toward a child witness code. *Pacific Law Journal*, 28 (1), 169–241.

Myers, J.E.B., Diedrich, S., Lee, D. and Fincher, K.M. (1999). Professional writing on child sexual abuse from 1900 to 1975: dominant themes and impact on prosecution. *Child Maltreatment*, 4 (3), 201–16.

Myers, J.E.B., Saywitz, K.J. and Goodman, G.S. (1996). Psychological research on children as witnesses: practical implications for forensic interviews and courtroom testimony. *Pacific Law Review*, **28** (1), 3–92.

Myers, M.A. (1979). Rule departures and making law: juries and their verdicts. *Law and Society Review*, **13**, 781–97.

Myhill, A. and Allen, J. (2004). Findings 157: Rape and Sexual Assault on Women: Findings from the British Crime Survey. The Home Office. http://www.homeoffice.gov.uk/rds/pdfs2/r159.pdf

N

Nash, C.L. and West, D. (1985). Sexual molestation of young girls: a retrospective survey. In D. West (Ed.), *Sexual Victimization: Two Recent Researches into Sex Problems and their Social Effects*. Aldershot: Gower.

Naughton, M. (2005). Redefining miscarriages of justice: a revived human rights approach to unearth subjugated discourses of wrongful criminal conviction. *British Journal of Criminology*, **45**, 165–82.

Nee, C. (2004). Research on burglary at the end of the millennium: a grounded approach to understanding crime. *Security Journal*, **16** (3), 37–44.

Nee, C. and Ellis, T. (2005). Treating offending children: what works? *Legal and Criminological Psychology*, **10** (1), 133–48.

Neisser, U. (1982). *Memory Observed: Remembering in Natural Contexts*. San Francisco: W.H. Freeman.

Neisser, U. and Winograd, E. (1988). *Remembering Reconsidered: Ecological and Traditional Approaches to the Study of Memory*. Cambridge: Cambridge University Press.

Nelson, J.R., Smith, D.J. and Dodd, J. (1990). The moral reasoning of juvenile delinquents: a meta-analysis. *Journal of Abnormal Child Psychology*, **18**, 231–9.

Newson, E. (1994a). Video violence and the protection of children. *The Psychologist*, **7** (6), 272–4.

Newson, E. (1994b). *Video Violence and the Protection of Children*. Report of the Home Affairs Committee. London: HMSO, pp. 45–9.

Nijboer, H. (1995). Expert evidence. In R. Bull and D. Carson (Eds), *Handbook of Psychology in Legal Contexts*. Chichester: Wiley, pp. 555–64.

Novaco, R.W. (1997). Remediating anger and aggression with violent offenders. *Legal and Criminological Psychology*, **2**, 77–88.

Nugent, P.M. and Kroner, D.G. (1996). Denial, response styles and admittance of offences among child molesters and rapists. *Journal of Interpersonal Violence*, **11** (4), 476–86.

O

O'Kane, A. and Bentall, R. (2000). Psychosis and offending. In J. McGuire, T. Mason and A. O'Kane (Eds), *Behaviour, Crime and Legal Processes: A Guide for Forensic Practitioners*. Chichester: John Wiley, pp. 161–76.

O'Kelly, C.M.E., Kebbell, M.R., Hatton, C. and Johnson, S.D. (2003). Judicial intervention in court cases involving witnesses with and without learning disabilities. *Legal and Criminological Psychology*, **8**, 229–40.

Ofshe, R.J. and Leo, R.A. (1997). The decision to confess falsely: rational choice and irrational action. *Denver University Law Review*, **74** (4), 979–1122.

Olson, D.R. (1977). Oral and written language and the cognitive processes of children. *Journal of Communication*, **27** (3), 10–26.

Ost, J., Costall, A. and Bull, R. (2002). A perfect symmetry? Retractors' experiences of recovering then retracting abuse memories. *Psychology, Crime and the Law*, **8** (2), 155–81.

Osterman, K., Bjorqvist, K. and Lagerspetz, K.M.J. (1998). Cross-cultural evidence of female indirect aggression. *Aggressive Behavior*, **24**, 1–8.

Otto, R.K., Poythress, N.G., Nicholson, R.A., Edens, J.F., Monahan, J., Bonnie, R.J., Hoge, S.K. and Eisenberg, M. (1998). Psychometric properties of the MacArthur Competence Assessment Tool – criminal adjudication. *Psychological Assessment*, **10** (4), 435–43.

Overholser, J.C. and Beck, S.J. (1988). The classification of rapists and child molesters. *Journal of Offender Counseling Services and Rehabilitation*, 13, 1715–25.

Owusu-Bempah, K. and Howitt, D. (2000). *Psychology Beyond Western Perspectives*. Leicester: British Psychological Society Books.

P

Paik, H. and Comstock, G. (1994). The effects of television violence on antisocial behavior: a meta-analysis. *Communication Research*, 21 (4), 516–46.

Palmer, E.J. (2001). Risk assessment: review of psychometric measures. In D.P. Farrington, C.R. Hollin and M. McMurran (Eds), *Sex and Violence: The Psychology of Crimes and Risk Assessment*. Reading: Harwood Academic Press, pp. 7–22.

Palmer, E.J. and Hollin, C.R. (1998). A comparison of patterns of moral development in young offenders and non-offenders. *Legal and Criminological Psychology*, 3, 225–35.

Parker, H. and Kirby, P. (1996). Methadone maintenance and crime reduction on Merseyside. Home Office Police Research Group. Crime Detection and Prevention Series Paper 72, Home Office Police Policy Directorate Police Research Group.

Passer, M.W. and Smith, R.E. (2001). *Psychology: Frontiers and Applications*. Boston, MA: McGraw-Hill.

Pathe, M. and Mullen, P. (2002). The victim of stalking. In J. Boon and L. Sheridan (Eds), *Stalking and Psychosexual Obsession: Psychological Perpsectives for Prevention, Policing and Treatment*. Chichester: John Wiley, pp. 1–22.

Patrick, C.J. and Iacono, W.G. (1991). A comparison of field and laboratory polygraphs in the detection of deception. *Psychophysiology*, 28, 632–8.

Pearse, J. and Gudjonsson, G.H. (1999). Measuring influential police interviewing tactics: a factor analytic approach. *Legal and Criminological Psychology*, 4, 221–38.

Pearse, J., Gudjonsson, G.H., Clare, I.C.H. and Rutters, S. (1998). Police interviewing and psychological vulnerabilities: predicting the likelihood of a confession. *Journal of Community and Applied Social Psychology*, 8, 1–21.

Pease, K. (2001) Rational choice theory. In E. McLaughlin and J. Muncie (Eds), *The Sage Dictionary of Criminology*. London: Sage, 233–4.

Pennebaker, J. (Ed.). *Emotion, Disclosure, and Health*. 1995. Washington, DC: American Psychological Association.

Pennell, A. and Browne, K. (1998a). Young offenders' susceptibility to violent media entertainment. *Prison Service Journal*, 120, 23–7.

Pennell, A.E. and Browne, K.D. (1998b). Film violence and young offenders. *Aggression and Violent Behavior*, 4 (1), 13–28.

Pennington, N. and Hastie, R. (1981). Juror decision making models: the generalization gap. *Psychological Bulletin*, 89, 246–87.

Pennington, N. and Hastie, R. (1986). Evidence evaluation in complex decision making. *Journal of Personality and Social Psychology*, 51, 242–58.

Penrod, S. (2003). Eyewitness identification evidence: how well are witnesses and police performing? *Criminal Justice Magazine*, **Spring**, 36–47, 54.

Penrod, S.D. and Heuer, L. (1997). Tweaking commonsense: assessing aids to jury decision making. *Psychology, Public Policy and Law*, 3 (2/3), 259–84.

Perry, C. (1997). Admissibility and per se exclusion of hypnotically elicited recall in American courts of law. *International Journal of Clinical and Experimental Hypnosis*, XLV (3), 266–79.

Philbrick, K. (2002). Imprisonment: the impact on children. In L. Falshaw (Ed.) *Issues in Forensic Psychology 3*. Leicester: British Psychological Society, pp. 72–81.

Piaget, J. (1970). Piaget's theory. In P.H. Mussen (Ed.), *Carmichael's Manual of Child Psychology* (Vol. 1). New York: Wiley.

Pickel, K. (1998). The effects of motive information and crime unusualness on jurors' judgments in insanity cases. *Law and Human Behavior*, 22 (5), 571–84.

Pilgrim, D. (2000). Psychiatric diagnosis: more questions than answers. *The Psychologist*, 19 (6), 303–5.

Pithers, W.D., Kashima, K.M., Cumming, G.F. and Beal, L.S. (1988). Relapse prevention: a method of enhancing maintenance of change in sex offenders. In A.C. Salter (Ed.), *Treating Child Sex Offenders and Victims: A Practical Guide*. Newbury Park, CA: Sage, pp. 131–70.

Plassmann, R. (1994). Munchhausen syndromes and factitious diseases. *Psychotherapy and Psychosomatic Medicine*, **62**, 7–26.

Plotnick, S., Porter, J. and Bagby, M. (1988). Is there bias in the evaluation of fitness to stand trial? *International Journal of Law and Psychiatry*, **21** (3), 291–304.

Pollock, P.H. (1999). When the killer suffers: post-traumatic stress reactions following homicide. *Legal and Criminological Psychology*, **4**, 185–202.

Poole, D.A. and Lindsay, D.S. (1998). Assessing the accuracy of young children's reports: lessons from the investigation of child sexual abuse. *Applied and Preventative Psychology*, **7**, 1–26.

Poole, D.A. and Lindsay, D.S. (2002). Children's suggestibility in the forensic context. In M.L. Eisen, J.A., Quas and G.S. Goodman (Eds), *Memory and Suggestibility in the Forensic Interview*. Mahwah, New Jersey: Lawrence Erlbaum, pp. 355–81.

Porter, S. and Yuille, J.C. (1996). The language of deceit: an investigation of the verbal clues to deception in the interrogation context. *Law and Human Behavior*, **20** (4), 443–58.

Posey, A.J. and Dahl, L.M. (2002). Beyond pre-trial publicity: legal and ethical issues associated with change of venue. *Law and Human Behaviour*, **26** (1), 107–25.

Pozgain, I., Mandic, N. and Barkic, J. (1998). Homicides in war and peace in Croatia. *Journal of Forensic Sciences*, **43** (6), 1124–6.

Prentky, R.A. and Burgess, A.W. (2000). *Forensic Management of Sex Offenders*. New York: Plenum.

Price, W.H., Strong, J.A., Whatmore, P.B. and McClemont, W.F. (1966). Criminal patients with XYY sex-chromosome complement. *The Lancet*, **1**, 565–6.

Q

Quinsey, V.L. (2002). Evolutionary theory and criminal behaviour. *Legal and Criminological Psychology*, **7** (1), 1–13.

Quinsey, V.L., Steinman, C.M., Bergersen, S.G. and Holmes, T.F. (1975). Penile circumference, skin conductance, and ranking responses of child molesters and 'normals' to sexual and nonsexual visual stimuli. *Behavior Therapy*, **6**, 213–19.

R

Radley, L. (2001). Attitudes towards sex offenders. *Forensic Update*, **66**, 5–9.

Rallings, M. (2002). The impact of offending on police officers. *Issues in Forensic Psychology* 3, pp. 20–40.

Rappert, B. (2002). Constructions of legitimate force: the case of CS sprays. *British Journal of Criminology*, **42**, 689–708.

Raskin, D.C. and Honts, C.R. (2002). The comparison question test. In M. Klener (Ed.), *Handbook of Polygraph Testing*. San Diego, CA: Academic Press, pp. 1–47.

Redondo, S., Luque, E. and Funes, J. (1996). Social beliefs about recidivism in crime. In G. Davies, S. Lloyd-Bostock, M. McMuran and C. Wilson (Eds), *Psychology, Law and Criminal Justice: International Developments in Research and Practice*. Berlin: Walter de Gruyter, pp. 394–400.

Redondo, S., Sanchez-Meca, J. and Garrido, V. (1999). The influence of treatment programmes on the recidivism of juvenile and adult offenders: a European meta-analytic review. *Psychology, Crime and Law*, **5**, 251–78.

Redondo, S., Sanchez-Meca, J. and Garrido, V. (2002). Crime treatment in Europe: a final view of the century and future perspectives. In J. McGuire (Ed.), *Offender Rehabilitation and Treatment: Effective Programmes and Policies to Reduce Re-offending*. Chichester: Wiley.

Ressler, R.K. and Shachtman, T. (1997). *I Have Lived in the Monster*. New York: St. Martin's Press.

Ressler, R.K., Burgess, A.W. and Douglas, J.E. (1988). *Sexual Homicide: Patterns and Motives*. Lexington, MA: Lexington.

Ribeaud, D. and Manzoni, P. (2004). The relationship between defendant's social attributes, psychiatric assessment and sentencing – a case study in Switzerland. *International Journal of Law and Psychiatry*, 27, 375–86.

Rice, M.E. (1997). Violent offender research and implications for the criminal justice system. *American Psychologist*, 52 (4), 414–23.

Rice, M.E. and Harris, G.T. (1997). Cross-validation and extension of the violence risk appraisal guide for child molesters and rapists. *Law and Human Behavior*, 21 (2), 231–41.

Rice, M.E., Harris, G.T. and Cormier, C.A. (1992). Evaluation of a maximum security therapeutic community for psychopaths and other mentally disordered offenders. *Law and Human Behavior*, 16, 399–412.

Robbins, P. and Darlington, R. (2003). The role of industry and the Internet Watch Foundation. In A. MacVean and P. Spindler (Eds), *Policing Paedophiles on the Internet*. Bristol: New Police Bookshop, pp. 79–87.

Roberts, K.P. and Blades, M. (1995). Do children confuse memories of events seen on television and events witnessed in real life? In N.K. Clark and G.M. Stephenson (Eds), *Investigative and Forensic Decision Making, Issues in Criminological and Legal Psychology No. 26*. Leicester: Division of Criminological and Legal Psychology, British Psychological Society, pp. 52–7.

Roberts, L. and Wagstaff, G.F. (1996). The effects of beliefs and information about hypnosis on the legal defence of automism through hypnosis. *Psychology, Crime and Law*, 2, 259–68.

Roberts, Y. (1995). Is this modern justice? *The Guardian*, 7 October, p. 6.

Robertson, G., Gibb, R. and Pearson, R. (1995). Drunkenness among police detainees. *Addiction*, 90, 793–803.

Robertson, G., Pearson, R. and Gibb, R. (1996). Police interviewing and the use of appropriate adults. *Journal of Forensic Psychiatry*, 7 (2), 297–309.

Roesch, R., Ogloff, J.R.P. and Golding, S.L. (1993). Competence to stand trial: legal and clinical issues. *Applied and Preventative Psychology*, 2, 45–51.

Rosenthal, R. (1966). *Experimenter Effects in Behavioral Research*. New York: Appleton-Century-Crofts.

Roshier, R.J. (1971). Crime and the Press. *New Society*, 468, 502–6.

Roshier, R.J. (1973). The selection of crime news by the press. In S. Cohen and J. Young (Eds), *The Manufacture of News*. London: Constable, pp. 28–39.

Royo, J.B. di (1996). Legal psychology in Spain: reflections on its short history. In G. Davies, S. Lloyd-Bostock, M. McMurran and C. Wilson (Eds), *Psychology, Law and Criminal Justice: International Developments in Research and Practice*. Berlin: Walter de Gruyter, pp. 598–601.

Ruback, R.B. and Innes, C.A. (1988). The relevance and irrelevance of psychological research. *American Psychologist*, 43 (9), 683–93.

Ruchkin, V.V., Eisemann, M. and Cloninger, C.R. (1998a). Behaviour/emotional problems in male juvenile delinquents and controls in Russia: the role of personality traits. *Acta Psychiatrica Scandinavica*, 98, 231–6.

Ruchkin, V.V., Eisemann, M. and Hagglof, B. (1998b). Aggression in delinquent adolescents versus controls: the role of parental rearing. *Children and Society*, 12, 275–82.

Ruchkin, V.V., Eisemann, M. and Hagglof, B. (1998c). Parental rearing and problem behaviours in male delinquent adolescents versus controls in Northern Russia. *Social Psychiatry and Psychiatric Epidemiology*, 33, 477–82.

Rudo, Z.H. and Powell, D.S. (1996). *Family Violence: A Review of the Literature*. Tampa, FL: Florida Mental Health Institute, University of South Florida.

Rushton, J.P. (1990). Race differences, r/K theory, and a reply to Flynn. *The Psychologist: Bulletin of the British Psychological Society*, 5, 195–8.

Russell, D.E.H. (1988). Pornography and rape: a causal model. *Journal of Political Psychology*, 9 (1), 41–73.

Russell, D.E.H. (1992). Pornography and rape: a causal model. In C. Itzin (Ed.), *Pornography: Women, Violence and Civil Liberties*. Oxford: Oxford University Press, pp. 310–49.

S

Sacco, V.F. and Fair, B.J. (1988). Images of legal control: crime news and the process of organizational legitimation. *Canadian Journal of Communication*, 3 (3–4), 114–23.

Saks, M. and Marti, M. (1997). A meta-analysis of the effect of jury size. *Law and Human Behavior*, **21**, 451–67.

Saks, M.J. (1987). Social scientists can't rig juries. In L.S. Wrightsman, S.M. Kassin and C.E. Willis (Eds), *In the Jury Box: Controversies in the Courtroom*. Thousand Oaks, CA: Sage, pp. 48–61.

Salfati, C.G. and Canter, D.V. (1998). Differentiating stranger murders: profiling offender characteristics from behavioral styles. *Behavioral Sciences and the Law*, **17** (3), 391–406.

Salter, A.C. (1988). *Treating Child Sex Offenders and Victims: A Practical Guide*. Newbury Park, CA: Sage.

Sarasalo, E., Bergman, B. and Toth, J. (1997). Kleptomania-like behaviour and psychosocial characteristics among shoplifters. *Legal and Criminological Psychology*, **2**, 1–10.

Sattar, G. and Bull, R. (1996). Pre-court preparation for child witnesses. In N.K. Clark and G.M. Stephenson (Eds), *Issues in Criminological and Legal Psychology 26, Child Witnesses*. Leicester: British Psychological Society, Division of Criminological and Legal Psychology, pp. 67–75.

Saywitz, K.J. (1994). Children in court: principles of child development for judicial application. In *A Judicial Primer on Child Sexual Abuse*. Chicago: American Bar Association Center on Children and the Law.

Schlesinger, P., Tumber, H. and Murdock, G. (1991). The media politics of crime and criminal justice. *British Journal of Sociology*, **42** (3), 397–420.

Schmid, J. and Fiedler, K. (1998). The backbone of closing speeches: the impact of prosecution versus defense language on judicial attributions. *Journal of Applied Social Psychology*, **28** (13), 1140–72.

Schneider, J.L. (2005). Stolen-goods markets: methods of disposal. *British Journal of Criminology*, **45**, 129–40.

Schulman, J., Shaver, P., Colman, R., Emrich, B. and Christie, R. (1973). Recipe for a jury. *Psychology Today*, **May**, 37–44, 77–84.

Scott, J.E. and Schwalm, L.A. (1988). Pornography and rape: an examination of adult theater rates and rape rates by state. In J.E. Scott and T. Hirschi (Eds), *Controversial Issues in Crime and Justice*. Beverly Hills: Sage, pp. 40–53.

Scullin, M.H., Kanaya, T. and Ceci, S.J. (2002). Measurements of individual differences in children's suggestibility across situations. *Journal of Experimental Psychology: Applied*, **8** (4), 233–46.

Scully, D. and Marolla, J. (1984). Convicted rapists' vocabulary of motives: excuses and justifications. *Social Problems*, **31** (5), 530–44.

Sear, L. and Williamson, T. (1999). British and American interrogation strategies. In D. Canter and L. Alison (Eds), *Interviewing and Deception*. Dartmouth: Ashgate, pp. 67–81.

Shadish, W.R. (1984). Policy research: lessons from the implementation of deinstitutionalization. *American Psychologist*, **39** (7), 725–38.

Shapiro, P.N. and Penrod, S. (1986). Meta-analysis of facial identification studies. *Psychological Bulletin*, **100**, 139–56.

Shaw, J., Appleby, L., Ames, T., McDonnell, R., Harris, C., McCann, K., Kiernan, K., Davies, S., Biddey, H. and Parsons, R. (1999). Mental disorder and clinical care in people convicted of homicide: national clinical survey. *British Medical Journal*, **318** (8 May), 1240–4.

Shaw, M. and Pease, K. (2002). Minor crimes, trivial incidents: the cumulative impact of offending. *Issues in Forensic Psychology*, **3**, 41–8.

Sheehan, P.W. (1997). 'Recovered memories: towards resolution of some issues across experimental and clinical domains'. Unpublished manuscript, University of Queensland, Australia. Plenary address, 14th International Congress of Hypnosis, San Diego, USA, June.

Sheldon, K. (2004). A new type of sex offender? Recent findings on Internet sex offenders: a pilot study. *Forensic Update*, **79**, 24–31.

Sheldon, W.H. (1940). *The Varieties of Human Physique: An Introduction to Constitutional Psychology*. New York: Harper.

Sheldon, W.H. (1942). *The Varieties of Temperament: A Psychology of Constitutional Differences*. New York: Harper.

Sheldon, W.H. (1949). *Varieties of Delinquent Youth: An Introduction to Constitutional Psychiatry*. New York: Harper.

Shepherd, E. and Milne, R. (1999). Full and faithful: ensuring quality practice and integrity of outcome in witness interviews. In A. Heaton-Armstrong, E. Shepherd, D. Wochover and Lord Bingham of Cornhill (Eds), *Analysing Eyewitness Testimony: Psychological, Investigative and Evidential Perspectives*. Blackstone Press: London.

Shepherd, E.W., Mortimer, A.K.O. and Mobaseri, R. (1995). The police caution: comprehension and perceptions in the general population. *Expert Evidence*, **4**, 60–7.

Sheridan, L. and Davies, G.M. (2001). What is stalking? The match between legislation and public perception. *Legal and Criminological Psychology*, **6**, 3–17.

Sheridan, L. and Davies, G.M. (2002). Stalking: the elusive crime. *Legal and Criminological Psychology*, **6**, 133–47.

Shoemaker, D. (1996). *Theories of Delinquency: An Examination of Explanations of Delinquent Behavior*. New York: Oxford University Press.

Shrum, L.J. (1996). Psychological processes underlying communication effects. *Human Communication Research*, **22** (4), 482–509.

Shutz, W. (1994). *The Human Element: Productivity, Self-esteem and the Bottom Line*. San Francisco, CA: Jossey-Bass.

Shuy, R.W. (1998). *The Language of Confession, Interrogation and Deception*. Thousand Oaks, CA: Sage.

Shye, S. and Elizur, D. (1994). *Introduction to Facet Theory: Content Design and Intrinsic Data Analysis in Behavioural Research*. Thousand Oaks, CA: Sage.

Siegelman, C.K., Budd, E.C., Spanhel, C.I. and Schoenrock, C.J. (1981). When in doubt say yes: acquiescence in interviews with mentally retarded persons. *Mental Retardation*, **19**, 53–8.

Signorielli, N. and Gerbner, G. (1988). *Violence and Terror in the Mass Media*. New York: Greenwood.

Sigurdsson, J. and Gudjonsson, G. (1997). The criminal history of 'false confessors' and other prison inmates. *Journal of Forensic Psychiatry*, **8** (2), 447–55.

Silas, F.A. (1985). Would a kid lie? *Journal of the American Bar Association*, **71**, 17.

Silvern, L., Karyl, J. and Landis, T. (1995). Individual psychotherapy for the traumatized children of abused women. In E. Peled, P. Jaffe and J. Edleson (Eds), *Ending the Cycle of Violence: Community Responses to Children of Battered Women*. Thousand Oaks, CA: Sage, pp. 43–76.

Simon, R.R. and Eimermann, T. (1971). The jury finds not guilty: another look at media influence on the jury. *Journalism Quarterly*, **48**, 343–4.

Sjogren, L.H. (2000). Problems and sources of errors when investigating alleged child sexual abuse. In A. Czerederecka, T. Jaskiewicz-Obdzinska and J. Wojcikiewicz (Eds), *Forensic Psychology and Law: Traditional Questions and New Ideas*. Krakow: Institute of Forensic Research Publishers, pp. 246–9.

Sjostedt, G. and Langstrom, N. (2000). 'Assessment of risk for criminal recidivism among rapists: a comparison of four different measures'. Unpublished manuscript, Karolinska Institutet, Stockholm, Sweden.

Skett, S. and Dalkin, A. (1999). Working with young offenders. *Issues in Forensic Psychology*, **1**, 31–5.

Skogan, W.G. (1996). The police and public opinion in Britain. *American Behavioral Scientist*, **39** (4), 421–32.

Skolnick, J.H. (1966). *Justice Without Trial: Law Enforcement in a Democratic Society*. New York: Wiley.

Sloore, H., Rossi, G. and Hauben, C. (2004). 'Are recidivists psychopaths?' Paper presented at the 14th European Conference of Psychology and Law, Krakow, Poland, July 2004.

Slusser, M.M. (1995). Manifestations of sexual abuse in pre-school-aged children. *Issues in Mental Health Nursing*, **16**, 481–91.

Smith and Allen (2004). Violent crime in England and Wales. Home Office Online Report 18/04. http://www.homeoffice.gov.uk/rds/pdfs04/rdsolr1804.pdf

Smith, A.D. and Taylor, P.J. (1999). Serious sex offending against women by men with schizophrenia. *British Journal of Psychiatry*, **174**, 233–7.

Spiecker, S.C. and Worthington, D.L. (2003). The influence of opening statement/closing argument organization strategy on juror verdict and damage awards. *Law and Human Behavior*, **27** (4), 437–56.

Spiegel, A.D. and Suskind, P.B. (1997). Chloroform-induced insanity defence confounds lawyer Lincoln. *History of Psychiatry*, **8**, 487–500.

Sporer, S.L. (1993), Eyewitness identification accuracy, confidence, and decision times in simultaneous and sequential lineups. *Journal of Applied Psychology*, **78**, 22–33.

Sprott, J.B. (1998). Understanding public opposition to a separate youth justice system. *Crime and Delinquency*, **44** (3), 399–411.

Stalans, L.J. (1996) Family harmony or individual protection? Public recommendation about how police can handle domestic violence situations. *American Behavioral Scientist*, **39**, 433–48.

Stalenheim, E.G. (1997). *Psychopathy and Biological Markers in a Forensic Psychiatric Population*. Uppsala: Acta Universitatis Upsaliensis.

Stanik, J.M. (1992). Psychology and law in Poland. In F. Losel, D. Bender and T. Bliesener (Eds), *Psychology and Law: International Perspectives*. Berlin: Walter de Gruyter, pp. 546–53.

Stanko, E.A. (1995). Women, crime, and fear. *Annals of the American Association for Political and Social Science*, **539**, 46–58.

Stark, E. (1993). The myth of black violence. *Social Work*, **38** (4), 485–90.

Steblay, N., Dysart, J., Fulero, S. and Lindsay, R.C.L. (2003). Eyewitness accuracy rates in police show-up and line-up presentations: a meta-analytic comparison. *Law and Human Behavior*, **27** (5), 523–40.

Steck, P. (1998). 'Deadly ending marital conflicts'. Paper presented at 8th European Conference on Psychology and Law, Krakow, 2–5 September.

Steinberg, L. (2003). Juveniles on trial: MacArthur Foundation study calls competency into question. *Criminal Justice Magazine*, **Fall 18** (3), http://www.abanet.org/crimjust/juvjus/cjmag/18-3ls.html

Steinmetz, S. (1977). The battered husband syndrome. *Victimology*, **2**, 499–509.

Stekel, W. (1911). The sexual root of kleptomania. *Journal of the American Institute of Criminal Law and Criminology*, **2** (2), 239–46.

Stephenson, G.M. (1992). *The Psychology of Criminal Justice*. Oxford: Blackwell.

Stermac, L.E. and Quinsey, V.L. (1986). Social competence among rapists. *Behavioral Assessment*, **8**, 171–81.

Sternberg, K.J., Lamb, M.E., Hershkowitz, L., Orbach, Y., Espli, P.W. and Hovav, M. (1997). Effects of introductory style on children's abilities to describe experiences of sexual abuse. *Child Abuse and Neglect*, **21** (11), 1133–46.

Steward, M. and Steward, D. (1996). Interviewing young children about body touch and handling. *Monograph Series for the Society for Research in Child Development*, **61** (4–5, Serial No. 248).

Stone, A.A., Smyth, J.M., Kaell, A. and Hurewitz, A. (2000). Structured writing about stressful events: exploring possible psychological mediators of positive health effects. *Health Psychology*, **19** (6), 619–24.

Straus, M. (1992). Sociological research and social policy: the case of family violence. *Sociological Forum*, **7** (2), 211–37.

Straus, M., Hamby, S.L., Boney-McCoy, S. and Sugarman, D.B. (1996). The Revised Conflict Tactics Scales (CTS2). *Journal of Family Issues*, **76** (3), 283–316.

Strier, F. (1999). Whither trial consulting? Issues and projections. *Law and Human Behavior*, **23**, 93–115.

Stromwall, L.A. and Granhag, P.A. (2003). How to detect deception? Arresting the beliefs of police officers, prosecutors and judges. *Psychology, Crime and Law*, **9**, 19–36.

Studebaker, C.A. and Penrod, S.D. (1997). Pre-trial publicity. *Psychology, Public Policy and Law*, **3** (2/3), 428–60.

Studebaker, C.A., Robbennolt, J.K., Pathak-Sharma, M.K. and Penrod S.D. (2000). Assessing pre-trial publicity effects: integrating content analytic results. *Law and Human Behavior*, **24**, 317–36.

Studer, L.H. and Reddon, J.R. (1998). Treatment may change risk prediction for sexual offenders. *Sexual Abuse: A Journal of Research and Treatment*, **10** (3), 175–81.

Studer, L.H., Aylwin, A.S., Clelland, S.R., Reddon, J.R. and Frenzel, R.R. (2002). Primary erotic preference in a group of child molesters. *International Journal of Law and Psychiatry*, **25**, 173–80.

Sullivan, J. and Beech, A. (2003). Are collectors of child abuse images a risk to children? In A. MacVean and P. Spindler (Eds), *Policing Paedophiles on the Internet*. Bristol: New Police Bookshop, pp. 11–20.

Swanson, J.W., Holzer, C.E., Ganju, V.K. and Jono, R.T. (1990). Violence and psychiatric disorder in the community: evidence from the epidemiologic catchment area surveys. *Hospital and Community Psychiatry*, **41**, 761–70.

Sweeney, J. (2004). The impact of individualism and collectivism on shoplifting attitudes and behaviour. The UCI Undergraduate Research Journal, 61–8. http://www.urop.uci.edu/journal/journal99/08_joanne/Joanne%20Sweeney.pdf

Szegedi, M. (1998). The development of Hungarian forensic psychology. In J. Boros, I. Munnich and M. Szegedi (Eds), *Psychology and Criminal Justice: International Review of Theory and Practice*. Berlin: Walter de Gruyter, pp. 441–56.

Szumski, J. (1993). Fear of crime, social rigorism and mass media in Poland. *International Review of Victimology*, **2**, 209–15.

T

Taub, S. (1996). The legal treatment of recovered memories of child sexual abuse. *Journal of Legal Medicine*, **17**, 183–214.

Taylor, M. and Quayle, E. (2003). *Child Pornography: An Internet Crime*. Hove: Brunner-Routledge.

Thompson, B. (1994). *Soft Core: Moral Crusades Against Pornography in Britain and America*. London: Cassell.

Thornhill, R. and Palmer, T. (2000). *A Natural History of Rape: Biological Bases of Sexual Coercion*. Cambridge, MA: MIT Press.

Tieger, T. (1981). Self-rated likelihood of raping and the social perception of rape. *Journal of Research in Personality*, **15**, 147–58.

Tjaden, P. and Thoennes, N. (1998). *Stalking in America: Findings from the National Violence against Women Survey*. Washington, DC: US Department of Justice.

Tjaden, P. and Thoennes, N. (2000). *Full Report of the Prevalence, Incidence, and Consequences of Violence Against Women: Findings from the National Violence Against Women Survey*. Research Report. Washington, D.C.: National Institute of Justice and the Centers for Disease Control and Prevention.

Torpy, D. (1994). You must confess. In N.K. Clark and G.M. Stephenson (Eds), *Rights and Risks: The Application of Forensic Psychology*. Leicester: British Psychological Society, pp. 21–3.

Towl, G. (1995). Anger management groupwork. In G.J. Towl (Ed.), *Groupwork in Prisons. Issues in Criminological and Legal Psychology*, No. 23. Leicester: British Psychological Society, pp. 31–5.

Towl, G. (1996). Homicide and suicide: assessing risk in prisons. *The Psychologist*, **9** (9), 398–400.

Towl, G., Snow, L. and McHugh, M. (2000). *Suicide in Prison*. Leicester: BPS Books.

Tracy, P.E., Wolgfang, M.E. and Figlio, R.M. (1990). *Delinquency Careers in Two Birth Cohorts*. New York: Plenum Press.

Travin, S., Bluestone, H., Coleman, E., Cullen, K. and Melella, M.S.W. (1985). Pedophile types and treatment perspectives. *Journal of Forensic Science*, **31** (2), 614–20.

Triandis, H.C. (1995). *Individualism and Collectivism*. Boulder, CO: Westview Press.

Trickett, A., Osborn, D.R. and Ellingworth, D. (1995). Property crime victimisation: the roles of individual and area influences. *International Review of Victimology*, **3**, 273–95.

Trickett, A., Osborn, D.R., Seymour, J. and Pease, K. (1992). What is different about high crime areas? *British Journal of Criminology*, **32** (1), 81–9.

Tseloni, A., Wittebrood, K., Farrell, G. and Pease, K. (2004). Burglary victimisation in England and Wales, the United States and the Netherlands: a cross-national comparative test of routine activities and lifestyle theories. *British Journal of Criminology*, **44**, 66–91.

Tulving, E. (1974). Cue-dependent forgetting. *American Scientist*, **62**, 74–8.

Undeutsch, U. (1992). Highlights of the history of forensic psychology in Germany. In F. Losel, D. Bender and T. Bliesener (Eds), *Psychology and Law: International Perspectives*. Berlin: Walter de Gruyter, pp. 509–18.

US Department of Commerce, Economics and Statistics Information (1996). *Statistical Abstract of the United States*. Washington, DC: US Government Printing Office.

Valier, C. (1998). *Psychoanalysis and Crime in Britain During the Inter-war Years*. The British Criminology Conferences: Selected Proceedings. Volume 1: Emerging Themes in Criminology, http://www.lboro.ac.uk/departments/ss/bccsp/vol101/

Van Koppen, P.J. (1995). Judges' decision-making. In R. Bull and D. Carson (Eds), *Handbook of Psychology in Legal Contexts*. Chichester: John Wiley, pp. 581–610.

Van Koppen, P.J. and Lochun, S.K. (1997). Portraying perpetrators: the validity of offender descriptions by witnesses. *Law and Human Behaviour*, **21** (6), 661–85.

Van Wallendael, L. and Cutler, B. (2004). Limitations to empirical approaches to jury selection. *Journal of Forensic Psychology Practice*, **4** (2), 79–86.

Viemero, V. (1996). Factors in childhood that predict later criminal behaviour. *Aggressive Behavior*, **22**, 87–97.

Vitelli, R. and Endler, N.S. (1993). Psychological determinants of fear of crime: a comparison of general and situational prediction models. *Personality and Individual Differences*, **145** (1), 77–85.

Voumvakis, S.E. and Ericson, R.V. (1982). *New Accounts of Attacks on Women. A Comparison of Three Toronto Newspapers*. Toronto: University of Toronto, Centre of Criminology.

Vrij, A. (2004). Why professionals fail to catch liars and how they can improve. *Legal and Criminological Psychology*, **9**, 159–81.

Vrij, A. and Mann, S. (2001). Who killed my relative? Police officers' ability to detect real-life high stake lies. *Psychology, Crime and Law*, **7**, 119–32.

Wagenaar, W.A., van Koppen, P.J. and Crombag, H.F.N. (1993). *Anchored Narratives: The Psychology of Criminal Evidence*. Hemel Hempstead: Harvester Wheatsheaf.

Wagstaff, G.F. (1996). Should 'hypnotized' witnesses be banned from testifying in court? Hypnosis and the M50 murder case. *Contemporary Hypnosis*, **13** (3), 186–90.

Wagstaff, G.F. (1997). What is hypnosis? *Interdisciplinary Science Reviews*, **22** (2), 155–63.

Wagstaff, G.F., Green, K. and Somers, E. (1997). The effects of the experience of hypnosis, and hypnotic depth, on jurors' decisions regarding the defence of hypnotic automatism. *Legal and Criminological Psychology*, **2**, 65–74.

Wahl, O.F. and Roth, R. (1982). Television images of mental illness: results of a metropolitan Washington media watch. *Journal of Broadcasting*, **26**, 599–605.

Walker, L.E. and Meloy, J.R. (1998). Stalking and domestic violence. In Meloy, J.R. (Ed.), *The Psychology of Stalking: Clinical and Forensic Perspectives*. San Diego: Academic Press, pp. 139–61.

Walmsley, R., Howard, L. and White, S. (1992). *The National Prison Survey 1991*. London: Her Majesty's Stationery Office.

Walsh, A. (1994). Homosexual and heterosexual child molestation: case characteristics and sentencing differentials. *International Journal of Offender Therapy and Comparative Criminology*, **38**, 339–53.

Walter, N. (1996). Dead women who suit the news agenda. *The Guardian*, 18 January, p. 15.

Ward, T. (1997). Insanity in summary trials. *Journal of Forensic Psychiatry*, **8** (3), 658–61.

Ward, T. (2000). Sexual offenders' cognitive distortions as implicit theories. *Aggression and Violent Behavior*, **5**, 491–507.

Ward, T. and Hudson, S.M. (2001). Finkelhor's precondition model of child sexual abuse: a critique. *Psychology, Crime and Law*, **7**, 291–307.

Ward, T. and Keenan, T. (1999). Child molesters' implicit theories. *Journal of Interpersonal Violence*, **14**, 821–38.

Ward, T. and Siegert, R.J. (2002). Towards a comprehensive theory of child sexual abuse: a theory knitting perspective. *Psychology, Crime and Law*, **8**, 319–51.

Warren, A.R. and Woodhall, C.E. (1999). The reliability of hearsay testimony: how well do interviewers recall their interviews with children? *Psychology, Public Policy and Law*, **5** (2), 355–71.

Warren, A.R., Nunez, N., Keeney, J.M., Buck, J.A. and Smith, B. (2002). The believability of children and their interviewers' hearsay testimony: when less is more. *Journal of Applied Psychology*, **87** (5), 846–57.

Warren, A.R., Woodhall, C.E., Hunt, J.S. and Perry, N.W. (1996). It sounds good in theory but . . . : do investigative interviewers follow guidelines based on memory research? *Child Maltreatment*, **1**, 231–45.

Waterhouse, L., Dobash, R.P. and Carnie, J. (1994). *Child Sexual Abusers*. Edinburgh: Central Research Unit.

Weber, N., Brewer, N., Wells, G., Semmler, C. and Keast, A. (2004a). Eyewitness identification accuracy and response latency: the unruly 10–12 second rule. *Journal of Experimental Psychology: Applied*, **10** (3), 139–47.

Weber, N., Brewer, N. and Wells, G.L. (2004b). 'Is there a "magical" decision latency that discriminates correct from incorrect eyewitness identifications?' Paper presented at 14th conference of the European European Association of Psychology and Law, Krakow, Poland.

Weller, M.P. and Weller, B.G. (1988). Crime and mental illness. *Medicine, Science, and the Law*, **28**, 38–45.

Wells, G.L. (1984). The psychology of line-up identifications. *Journal of Applied Social Psychology*, **14**, 89–103.

Wells, G.L. (1993). What do we know about eyewitness identification? *American Psychologist*, **48**, 553–71.

Wells, G.L., Small, M., Penrod, S., Malpass, R.S., Fulero, S.M. and Brimacombe, C.A.E. (1998). Eyewitness identification procedures: recommendations for line-ups and photospreads. *Law and Human Behavior*, **22**, 603–47.

West, D. (1987). *Sexual Crimes and Confrontations: A Study of Victims and Offenders*. Aldershot: Gower.

West, D.J. (1982). *Delinquency: Its Roots, Careers and Prospects*. London: Heinemann.

Westcott, H.L. (1995). Children's views on investigative interviews for suspected sexual abuse. *Issues in Criminological and Legal Psychology*, Leicester: Division of Criminological and Legal Psychology, British Psychological Society.

Widom, C.S. (1989). The cycle of violence. *Science*, **244**, 160–6.

Widom, C.S. and Morris, S. (1997). Accuracy of adult recollections of childhood victimization, part 2 Childhood sexual abuse. *Psychological Assessment*, **9** (1), 34–46.

Wiegman, O., Kuttschreuter, M. and Barda, B. (1992). A longitudinal study of television viewing on aggressive and prosocial behaviours. *British Journal of Social Psychology*, **31**, 147–64.

Williams, J.J. (1995). Type of counsel and the outcome of criminal appeals: a research note. *American Journal of Criminal Justice*, **9** (2), 275–85.

Williams, M. (1994). Murder in mind. *Division of Criminological and Legal Psychology Newsletter*, **36**, 9–11.

Williams, W.W. (1991). The equality crisis: some reflections on culture, courts and feminism. In K.T. Bartlett and R. Kennedy (Eds), *Feminist Legal Theory: Readings in Law and Gender*. Boulder, CO: Westview, pp. 15–34.

Willmot, P. (1999). Working with life sentence prisoners. *Issues in Forensic Psychology*, **1**, 36–8.

Wilson, H. (1980). Parental supervision: a neglected aspect of delinquency. *British Journal of Criminology*, **20** (3), 203–35.

Wilson, M. and Smith, A. (2000). Rules and roles in terrorist hostage taking. In D. Canter and L. Alison (Eds), *The Social Psychology of Crime: Groups, Teams and Networks*. Aldershot: Ashgate, pp. 129–51.

Winkel, F.W. (1998). Fear of crime and criminal victimisation. *British Journal of Criminology*, **38** (3), 473–84.

Winkel, F.W. and Blaauw, E. (2001). Structured trauma writing (STW) as a victim-supportive intervention: examining the efficacy of emotional ventilation and downward writing. In R. Rosesch, R.R. Young, N. (2003).

Winkel, F.W. and Vrij, A. (1998). Who is in need of victim support? The issue of accountable, empirically validated selection and victim referral. *Expert Evidence*, **6**, 23–41.

Witkin, H.A. and Goodenough, D.R. (1981). Cognitive styles: essences and origins, field dependence and field independence. *Psychological Issues Monograph No. 51*. New York: International Universities Press.

Witkin, H.A., Mednick, S.A. and Schulsinger, F. (1976). Criminality in XY and XYY men. *Science*, **193**, 547–55.

Wogalter, M.S., Malpass, R.S. and McQuiston, D.E. (2004). A national survey of US police on preparation and conduct of identification line-ups. *Psychology, Crime and Law*, **10** (1), 69–82.

Wojcikiewicz, J., Bialek, I., Desynski, K. and Dawidowicz, A.L. (2000). 'Mock witness paradigm in the casework of the institute of forensic research in Cracow'. Paper presented at the 10th European conference on Psychology and Law, Limassol, Cyprus.

Wood, J.M. (1996). Weighting evidence in sexual abuse evaluations: an introduction to Bayes' theorem. *Child Maltreatment*, **1**, 25–36.

Wood, W., Wong, F.Y. and Chachere, J.G. (1991). Effects of media violence on viewers' aggression in unconstrained social interaction. *Psychological Bulletin*, **109** (3), 371–83.

Woodward, R. (1999). Therapeutic regimes. *Issues in Forensic Psychology*, **1**, 39–43.

Woolley, J.D. (1997). Thinking about fantasy: are children fundamentally different thinkers and believers from adults? *Child Development*, **68**, 991–1011.

Wootton, I. and Brown, J. (2000). Balancing occupational and personal identities: the experience of lesbian and gay police officers. *Newsletter of the BPS Lesbian and Gay Psychology Section*, **4** (March), 6–13.

Worling, J.R. (1995). Sexual abuse histories of adolescent male sex offenders: differences on the basis of the age and gender of their victims. *Journal of Abnormal Psychology*, **104** (4), 610–13.

Wormith, J.A. (1986). Assessing deviant sexual arousal: physiological and cognitive aspects. *Advances in Behaviour Research and Therapy*, **8** (3), 101–37.

Wright, M. (2002). The court as last resort: victim-sensitive, community-based responses to crime. *British Journal of Criminology*, **42** (3), 657–67.

Wrightsman, L.S. (1999). *Judicial Decision Making*. New York: Plenum.

Wrightsman, L.S. (2001). *Forensic Psychology*. Stamford, CT: Wadsworth.

Wyatt, G.W. (1985). The sexual abuse of Afro-American and white American women in childhood. *Child Abuse and Neglect*, 9, 507–19.

Wyre, R. (1987). *Working with Sex Offenders*. Oxford: Perry.

Wyre, R. (1990). Why do men sexually abuse children? In T. Tate (Ed.), *Understanding the Paedophile*. London: ISTD/The Portman Clinic, pp. 17–23.

Wyre, R. (1992). Pornography and sexual violence: working with sex offenders. In C. Itzin (Ed.), *Pornography: Women, Violence and Civil Liberties*. Oxford: Oxford University Press, pp. 236–47.

Wyre, R. and Tate, T. (1995). *The Murder of Childhood*. Harmondsworth: Penguin.

Y

Yoshikawa, H. (1995). Long-term effects of early childhood programs on social outcomes and delinquency. *The Future of Children*, 5 (3), 51–75.

Youngs, D. (2004). Personality correlates of offence style. *Journal of Investigative Psychology and Offender Profiling*, 1, 99–119.

Yuille, J.C. and Cutshall, J.L. (1986). A case study of eyewitness memory of a crime. *Journal of Applied Psychology*, 71 (2), 291–301.

Z

Zapf, P.A. and Roesch, R. (2001). A comparison of American and Canadian conceptualizations of comptence to stand trial. In R. Roesch, R.R.Carrado and R. Dempster (Eds) *Psychology in the Courts: International Advances in Knowledge*. London: Routledge, pp. 121–32.

Zeisel, H. (1971). And then there was none: the diminution of federal jury. *University of Chicago Law Review*, 35, 228–41.

Zeisel, H. and Diamond, S.S. (1978). The effect of peremptory challenges on jury and verdict: an experiment in a federal district court. *Stanford Law Review*, 30, 491–531.

Zillmann, D. (1979). *Hostility and Aggression*. Hillsdale, NJ: Erlbaum.

Zillmann, D. (1982). Television viewing and arousal. In D. Pearl, L. Bouthilet and J. Law (Eds), *Television and Behavior. Ten Years of Scientific Progress and Implications for the Eighties*. Washington, DC: US Government Printing Office.

Name index

Subject index